Access™ 2
Power Programming

Chris St. Valentine

Access 2 Power Programming

Copyright© 1994 by Que® Corporation.

Library of Congress Catalog No.: 94-67364

ISBN: 1-56529-763-6

97 96 95 94   4 3 2

Interpretation of the printing code: the rightmost double-digit number is the year of the book's printing; the rightmost single-digit number, the number of the book's printing. For example, a printing code of 94-1 shows that the first printing of the book occurred in 1994.

Publisher: *David P. Ewing*

Associate Publisher: *Michael Miller*

Publishing Director: *Don Roche, Jr.*

Managing Editor: *Michael Cunningham*

Marketing Manager: *Greg Wiegand*

Credits

Publishing Manager
Don Roche, Jr.

Acquisitions Editor
Thomas F. Godfrey III

Product Directors
Ella Davis
Kathie-Jo Arnoff

Production Editor
Thomas F. Hayes

Copy Editors
Elsa Bell
Danielle Bird
Fran Blauw
Judy Brunetti
Patrick Kanouse
Jeanne Lemen
Lori A. Lyons
Diana R. Moore
Susan Ross Moore
Christine Prakel
Nicole Rodardello
Andy Saff
Linda Seifert
Heather Stith

Technical Editors
Brian Blackman
Claudia Mazzie-Ballheim
Margaret McGee

Book Designer
Paula Carroll

Cover Designer
Jay Corpus

Production Team
Stephen Adams
Jeff Baker
Stephen Carlin
Anne Dickerson
Karen Dodson
Brook Farling
Joelynn Gifford
Debbie Kincaid
Bob LaRoche
Elizabeth Lewis
Tim Montgomery
Nanci Sears Perry
Wendy Ott
Caroline Roop
Dennis Sheehan
Sue VandeWalle
Mary Beth Wakefield

Indexer
Charlotte Clapp

Composed in *ITC Century Light* and *MCPdigital* by Que Corporation.

About the Author

Chris St. Valentine

Chris St. Valentine has more than ten years of PC experience designing databases and vertical applications using GW-Basic, QuickBasic, Visual Basic, and Microsoft Access. He is an experienced Windows developer and has a background in technical training, on-line tutorials, and user education. As a member of the Access User Education team, he cowrote the *Microsoft Access Language Reference* and Help.

Chris also is an award-winning author and has written several books covering various aspects of Microsoft Access. He continues to provide consulting services and Access training at all levels.

You can reach Chris via CompuServe at 72702,724.

Dedication

This one is for my best friend.

Acknowledgments

To most people who have never written and published a book, it may come as a surprise to learn how many people it takes to take a book from concept to production. It's certainly true that writing the manuscript is the most difficult part, but that isn't meant to take away from the hard work of my technical reviewers, nor the editorial and production staff at Que.

I would like to thank all of the nameless people who never get any credit, never receive praise. They may have truly thankless jobs, but they should know I appreciate their individual contributions toward *Access 2 Power Programming*. This book is as good as it is because they made it so.

Trademark Acknowledgments

Contents at a Glance

Table of Contents

22 Implementing Security

Preface

I started out intending *Access 2 Power Programming* to be a step-by-step guide to building applications. My goal was to show you, in excruciating detail, exactly what to do, which keys to press, and which commands to choose. It didn't take long to realize that I was going to run out of room in an 800-page book if I was going to cover everything.

So, I started assuming a bit more about your current knowledge of Access, which is why some chapters in this book go into fine detail while other chapters seem to be written for a somewhat more advanced level of user. Also, consider that I didn't write all the chapters in sequence.

I wasn't able to include everything I started out to cover, but *Access 2 Power Programming* offers a little for everybody. If you are new to Access, the introductory material will benefit you more than if you are more experienced with Access. If you are a more experienced reader, you will probably find value in some of the new functions in Chapter 21. If you are somewhere in the middle, there's something in here for you, too.

From naming conventions to designing effective user interfaces, *Access 2 Power Programming* represents my vision of the way things ought to be. It is based on more than 15 years of experience developing systems and working with users in a wide variety of industries. Feel free to both agree and disagree with me, and implement what you find useful.

I hope you enjoy this book; please let me know what you think.

Introduction

Since its release in November of 1992, Microsoft Access has become the fastest-selling Windows database product of all time. Microsoft Access combines the best features of the standard Windows interface, a powerful relational database engine, and professional development features.

The ability to fully exploit the potential of Microsoft Access has been limited in part because Access is so powerful. With the release of Access 2.0, Microsoft has added even more features that further complicate the learning process. Of course, it is unrealistic to expect a new user to master Access in a single sitting. Still, experienced Windows users will find the basics of Access easy to learn and should be able to create useful, meaningful applications in a relatively short period of time.

Without a doubt, Microsoft Access is a sophisticated, somewhat complex software product. Although Access was originally designed to be an end-user application (that is, meant to be used by non-database experts), the product's rich feature set and fairly steep learning curve clearly define Access as a developer's tool. The degree to which Access can be used by typical end-users is defined by your programming and design skills and the degree to which you are willing to create professional, bulletproof applications.

Who Should Read This Book

Access 2 Power Programming was written with a number of readers in mind:

- New database developers

- Developers of other Windows or DOS database systems

- Current users and developers of Microsoft Access

New Database Developers

Access 2 Power Programming is a perfect companion if you are just starting out with database projects. The focus of this book is to show you ways to design and implement successful applications. Throughout this book you find details on how you can implement the many features and shortcuts available in Access.

A significant portion of this book describes how to navigate and use the Access environment to produce useful, efficient applications without complicating the process with unnecessary discussions or terminology. You will also find chapters on database fundamentals that provide the background material you need to confidently approach almost any Access database project.

Developers of Other Windows or DOS Database Systems

If you have tried to build applications with other systems and were not happy with the results, you will be surprised how easy it is to create these same applications with Microsoft Access. *Access 2 Power Programming* provides the background information you need to avoid some of the more common pitfalls. As you will see, designing applications in Access is accomplished with different techniques than you have seen in other products.

You may be unhappy with the features, capabilities, or performance of your current database system. You also might be thinking about future growth and the ability to access data from a variety of sources and file formats. If so, read *Access 2 Power Programming* for the information you need to implement a successful database application using Microsoft Access.

Current Users and Developers of Microsoft Access

Finally, *Access 2 Power Programming* was written for current Access users who already know how to create forms, queries, reports, and macros. You know how to build a database, but not necessarily how to pull all the pieces together into a seamless application. You have used Access over a period of time and you know there is a wide variety of features, but you may be unsure how these elements work together to create an application.

If you are a current user of a previous version of Access, you will want to browse *Access 2 Power Programming* to gain insight into the new features and techniques for using Access 2.0.

How This Book Is Different

Access 2 Power Programming is an ambitious book that explains not only how to use Microsoft Access but also why you should learn about the principles of good database design. This book will show you how to build a commercial-quality application from the ground up.

This book is far more than a simple tutorial on how to use the various features of Access. Indeed, *Access 2 Power Programming* shows you how to build a full-featured, commercial-quality application.

You see what needs to be done, in the order it needs to be done. You learn good development shortcuts and you avoid the pitfalls that come from trying to take the bad shortcuts that avoid good design strategies.

To make the design process flow smoothly, you do not find a separate chapter on how to create tables. This is because you do not create all your tables at one time. Instead, *Access 2 Power Programming* presents the necessary information as it is required. If you are in the middle of designing a form and discover that you need a new table to populate a list box, *Access 2 Power Programming* discusses creating the table and then goes back to discussing the form. This book approaches application development the same way you do in the real world.

How This Book Is Organized

Access 2 Power Programming is designed to serve two needs. First, it is a comprehensive tutorial you can use to learn and master basic and advanced database concepts to create your own applications. Second, this book is a reference guide to Microsoft Access you can use again and again to find answers to particular database design problems, or to just locate a useful function.

The book is divided into separate parts. Parts I, II, and III cover specific phases of the application development process and database or Access concepts and functions. At any time, you should feel free to skip over any portion that contains information you are already familiar with. If necessary, you can return to these parts later on.

In addition, Part IV contains material you may find useful as you continue to build your own applications.

Part I: Getting Started

Especially if you are a first-time database user, you will want to read the chapters in this part to learn about important database concepts and the principles of good database design. This part helps you learn to establish the objective of your application. Perhaps surprisingly, many developers start creating tables and forms and writing code without a clear understanding of where they are headed. Here, you learn that a good road map is essential.

- Chapter 1, "Database Fundamentals," provides the essential background, concepts, and terminology you need to fully understand the chapters that follow.

- Chapter 2, "Access as a Database Tool," introduces you to Microsoft Access and takes you on a quick tour.

- Chapter 3, "The Access Development Environment," describes each of the elements that make up Access. A thorough understanding of managing the environment is essential to your development efficiency and satisfaction.

- Chapter 4, "Customizing the Access Environment," explains the many available options for customizing the Access development environment and tailoring Access to more closely match your preferences.

- Chapter 5, "The HomeFinder Application," begins by explaining why performing a needs analysis is so important. Next, you see how a database schema and a clearly-defined program flow makes later development simpler.

- Chapter 6, "Building the HomeFinder Tables," explores the Table window and how to use the database schema to design the basic tables used by the sample application.

- Chapter 7, "Building the HomeFinder Queries," explores the Query window and how you can create queries to retrieve data from tables.

- Chapter 8, "Building the HomeFinder Forms," explores the Form window, the Toolbox, the property sheet, and the Palette. You see how to create the basic HomeFinder forms and how to "bind" the forms to the queries from the preceding chapter.

- Chapter 9, "Building the HomeFinder Macros," explores the Macro window and discusses ways you can automate simple actions in response to events on forms.

- Chapter 10, "Building the HomeFinder Reports," explores the Report window (remarkably similar to the Form window) and how you can create impressive, professional output from your applications.

Part II: Nuts and Bolts

Part II illustrates a wide variety of enhancements you can make to your functional application to ensure the application performs its goals without error, and without breaking.

- Chapter 11, "Enhancing Forms," shows how you can add the kinds of professional touches that users expect from commercial-quality applications. You see how to improve the "look and feel" of your forms.

- Chapter 12, "Migrating from Macros to Modules," discusses why you should avoid macros in favor of modules.

- Chapter 13, "Adding Data Validation," discusses a variety of techniques you can use to validate and restrict the data entered by end users. You learn how to prevent bad data as your first defense against an unreliable database.

Part III: Fit and Finish

This part illustrates the completed HomeFinder application, an example of the kind of applications you can create in Access with just a little extra effort.

- Chapter 14, "Adding Menu Bars," shows how you can add custom menu bars to make using your forms and reports easier to use and more flexible.

- Chapter 15, "Creating a Self-Configuring Application," highlights techniques for creating applications that self-configure for use at multiple client sites or in foreign countries.

- Chapter 16, "Adding Query-by-Form Capability," shows how you can add power and flexibility to your application by letting users define their own ad-hoc queries and output.

Part IV: Reference

The chapters in this part provide valuable information you can apply to all of your applications. Refer to Chapters 17 and 18 for guidelines on naming conventions and general application design. Other chapters cover libraries and security.

- Chapter 17, "Naming Conventions and Style Guidelines," covers strategies for naming and constructing each of the database objects (tables, forms, queries, reports, macros, and modules), plus conventions for Access Basic functions.

- Chapter 18, "Application Design Guidelines," discusses general design tips for creating clean, intuitive, and useful interfaces.

- Chapter 19, "Creating and Using Libraries," explains what libraries are, when you should consider using them, and how to create and install them.

- Chapter 20, "Macro Actions," lists and explains the more common macro actions you are likely to need in your own applications. Even though you should avoid macros, macro actions are among the more useful features of Access.

- Chapter 21, "Useful Functions," presents a collection of useful user-defined functions you can copy into your own applications.

- Chapter 22, "Implementing Security," explores ways you can protect your databases and its objects from unwanted user access and how you can administer users and workgroups.

- Chapter 23, "Data Compaction, Backups, and Data Recovery," describes techniques for compacting the database for improved efficiency, backing up the database for safekeeping, and restoring data in case the database becomes corrupt or the hardware fails.

Part V: Appendixes

Several appendixes round out the material presented in the preceding chapters of *Access 2 Power Programming*.

- Appendix A, "Windows API Declarations," lists the declarations you need in order to call common API functions.

- Appendix B, "Constants," lists the predefined Access constants, and the constants you need to call many of the functions listed in Appendix A.

- Appendix C, "Access Error Messages," contains all of the numbered error messages.

- Appendix D, "Converting Old Code," briefly discusses some of the issues related to using older and new coding techniques in Access 2.0.

Conventions Used in This Book

Throughout this book, certain conventions were used to help you distinguish the various elements of Windows, MS-DOS, their system files, and sample data. Before you look ahead, you should spend a moment examining these conventions:

- The names of keys on the keyboard appear like this:

    Ctrl

    Shift

    Del

    F1

- Key combinations appear like this:

    Key1+Key2

- Where appropriate, *shortcut keys* appear wherever they might help you complete a task more easily. Shortcut keys appear in small letters, just like the names of keys on the keyboard. For example, a discussion about pasting information from the Clipboard might list the Ctrl+V shortcut key sequence.

- The names of built-in functions, properties, and macro actions are in boldface. For example, the **Asc** function appears in **boldface** because it is a built-in function. Names of user-defined functions, such as `csvGotWindowText()`, do not appear in boldface.

- To help differentiate built-in functions from user-defined functions, names of user-defined functions appear with a pair of trailing parentheses and in a monospace font:

    `csvGetWindowText()`

- New terms appear in *italic*.

Special Text Used in This Book

Throughout this book, you will find examples of special text that explain or expand on a topic. These passages appear a bit differently than the other text so that you can instantly recognize their significance and so that you can easily find them for future reference.

Notes include extra information you will find useful or interesting, but which complements the discussion at hand instead of being a direct part of it. A note may describe special situations that can arise when you use Access under certain circumstances, and may tell you what steps to take when such situations arise.

Tips provide quick instructions for getting the most from Access as you follow the discussion in the main topic. A tip might show you how to conserve memory, how to speed up a procedure, or how to perform one of many time-saving and system-enhancing techniques. Tips may also tell you how to avoid problems with your software and hardware, or just how to perform a task faster with a shortcut.

STOP Warnings tell you about procedures and situations that could result in the loss of data. Warnings generally tell you how to avoid such losses, or describe the steps you can take to remedy them.

Case studies describe typical scenarios and database design problems, often preceding discussions that describe how the problem at hand might be resolved with Access. Try to imagine your own particular situation as you read the case studies to see how they apply to you and the problems you are trying to solve.

See Also references point you to additional sources of information about the current topic discussion. Most See Also references are to specific chapters in *Access 2 Power Programming*, but some are to topics in the Access Help file or in the retail documentation.

How To Use the Accompanying Disk

The bonus disk that accompanies *Access 2 Power Programming* includes the sample HomeFinder application.

The Files on the HomeFinder Disk

The HomeFinder disk includes the following files:

- The two MDB files included on the disk make up the complete HomeFinder database application, the basis for many of the examples throughout this book. These files create a code database and a data database. The code database, HOMECODE.MDB, contains the application's forms, reports, macros, and modules, but no data (tables). The data database, HOMEDATA.MDB, contains the application's tables.

- API.TXT contains all the declarations listed in Appendix A, "Windows API Declarations."

- CONSTANT.TXT contains all the constants listed in Appendix B, "Constants."

- ERRORS.TXT contains all the numbered Access error messages listed in Appendix C, "Access Error Messages."

- The IMAGES subdirectory contains a number of PCX graphic files that are used to enhance the HomeFinder application.

Uncompressing the Files

The HOMEFIND.EXE file on the accompanying HomeFinder disk has been compressed to conserve disk space. You must uncompress this file before you can use it. See the installation instructions on the last page of this book.

 Note: HomeFinder requires a little less than 2M of free disk space.

Reader Feedback

We at Que Corporation are committed to bringing you the very best in computer reference material. As part of this commitment to you, we invite your input and feedback. Please let us know if you enjoy this book, the areas you found most useful, any areas you may have had trouble with, comments about the examples presented, and how we might improve the next edition.

Please note, however, that we cannot serve as a technical resource for either Windows or Access-related questions, including hardware- or software-related problems. Instead, you should refer to the retail documentation that accompanies Windows or the Access product for help with specific problems.

If you have a question or comment about any Que book, however, please write to us at the following address. We will respond to as many readers as we can. Your name, address, and phone number will never become part of a mailing list, nor will it be used for any other purpose than to help us continue to bring you the best books possible.

Que Corporation
Attn: Managing Editor
201 W. 103rd St.
Indianapolis, IN 46290
USA

Or, you can send us a fax by dialing (317)581-4663. Finally, you can contact the author via CompuServe (ID 72702,724).

Part I
Getting Started

1

Database Fundamentals

You can use Microsoft Access to collect and report on all types of information. However, before you can build truly useful, efficient, and powerful database applications, you must have a solid understanding of database fundamentals. This does not mean you have to become a master of database theory, nor does it mean you have to become an expert in database design. It does mean, however, that you should at least be familiar with a few basic concepts.

This chapter covers the following:

- Examining Databases in the Real World
- Understanding Database Models
- Understanding the Structure of a Database
- Using Keys
- Ensuring Referential Integrity

Examining Databases in the Real World

Most applications developed for business today are database applications. These applications may not be written with a database language (such as dBASE) or product (such as Microsoft Access), but they nonetheless qualify as database applications because they store, manipulate, and report on data.

Making that data accessible is part of what makes the data valuable to a business. Business owners know that good data management and the ability to use and understand data often means the difference between profit and loss. As a database developer, your understanding of how to best implement a database application can go a long way toward fulfilling the promise of making the data useful.

For example, you might develop a database application for a small business to analyze its customers' needs and industry trends. The business could then target its marketing strategy for the following year and, if the data supports the decision, expand the company's operations. Without a database of reliable information, the business would simply be guessing at customer needs and industry trends and spending its resources ineffectively.

The Need for Databases

Every company has its own specific needs and uses for data, and the number of individual needs for databases is probably as great as the number of databases. These many specific needs can be grouped into three general needs; basically, businesses need to store, access, and integrate information.

The Need to Store Information

Before personal computers were invented, businesses maintained data in a variety of formats, including mainframes and midrange computer systems. Ledger sheets and even 3x5 cards have historically served as useful, if inefficient, databases. Almost any container can hold information, but as the volume of data grows, using that information quickly becomes difficult. You may be able to get by with a shoe box to store information about your personal CD collection, but a business cannot effectively store its information in this manner. Businesses need to store information so that the data can be used easily, regardless of the volume of the data.

The Need to Access Information

Libraries are great storage areas for books, but libraries have to provide a method for finding particular books. The card catalog, which is itself a kind of database, satisfies this requirement. It provides an easy way to locate a book according to its title, author, or subject. Rather than searching through thousands of books individually, you can use the card catalog to quickly locate specific books.

Because each book has three cards—one for the title, one for the author, and one for the subject—you can search for a book in a variety of ways. However, because two people cannot use the same card catalog file at the same time, libraries typically maintain several copies of the card catalog. A computerized card catalog system would provide a central location for the catalog itself and multiple computers or terminals for accessing the data.

Businesses have many of the same retrieval requirements as libraries. Employees need a way to access information quickly and concurrently with other users. Users all need to be able to use different search methods so that they can use the information in a number of ways.

The Need to Integrate Information

You might be supporting a small company that uses an accountant's ledger to keep track of orders, a card file to maintain a list of customers, and a filing cabinet to store sales records. Although each of these is a separate database, often all of them are used together for a common purpose. For example, to ship an order, the customer's address must be looked up in the card file and then typed on the invoice, credit information must be looked up in the ledger, and the completed order filed away (see fig. 1.1).

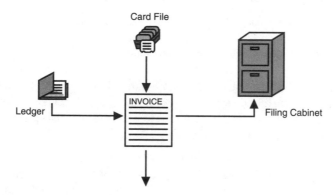

Figure 1.1. Databases come in many shapes and sizes.

In figure 1.1, each database was probably developed alone and is completely different in form from the others. You can integrate all of this data with a PC-based database and make order entry and other tasks easier to accomplish, even if the data is seemingly unrelated and comes from multiple sources.

Benefits of a PC-Based Database

This section describes some of the benefits of a PC-based database application developed with Microsoft Access. First, a properly designed Access system can make data useful, not burdensome, and make the data a corporate resource, not just an expense. Employees can be using the data, not spending all their time trying to maintain it. For example, keeping track of the records stored in dozens of filing cabinets can require a sizable staff to file the information, retrieve specific records on request, and maintain the security and integrity of the files. In contrast, you can design a PC-based database to perform these functions in a fraction of the time and at a far less cost.

An Access system provides almost-instant "information at your fingertips" to help users plan and make decisions. Access lets users retrieve and look at information in a variety of ways: they can view reports to spot statistical trends, create charts for presentations, and analyze multiple records simultaneously in a familiar row-and-column format.

Access database applications let users consolidate data into manageable collections. For example, instead of keeping written records in several filing cabinets, you can store data electronically in one or more integrated databases. However, databases you design with Access are far more than just static storage areas; Access applications are dynamic data management systems.

An Access-based application makes data entry and retrieval more efficient than manual record keeping systems alone. For example, a manual filing cabinet system involves preparing file folders, assigning each file a unique identifying number or name, finding the correct cabinet, and finally inserting the folders into the correct sequence. In contrast, you can insert records quickly in an Access database. Although the user must still enter the data as he would on a paper form, Access handles storing the record and finding the correct location in the database. If a folder is inserted in the wrong filing cabinet, someone has to go through each file drawer until he finds the misplaced folder. You can avoid this problem when you use Microsoft Access.

Retrieving data in an Access database is much more efficient than in a manual system. For example, retrieving data dealing with all 1992 orders for a specific customer means having to search through a file cabinet in which orders are stored by invoice number. Depending on how many orders there are, finding all the appropriate file folders could be an enormous task. Access can retrieve all of one customer's 1992 orders in far less time than it would take to find just one order in a manual filing cabinet system.

Finally, databases provide open access to data. Data is more powerful when it is shared with other users. Access provides multiple users with concurrent access to the data and lets many people view the same table or records at the same time. One person can even view a record while another person updates the same record. Suppose several people wanted to use the printed paper files you have on your desk. You would either have to fight over who got to use the files first, or the other people would have to look over your shoulder. Either way, such an arrangement is not efficient. When you install an Access database on a network, however, everyone has simultaneous, instant access to all the data in the database (subject to any restrictions you might design into the system). Instead of having to line up for access to a file cabinet, users can retrieve data from their desktops.

Understanding Database Models

Databases come in several different designs, or models, each with its own strength. The user's specific needs determine how and where you should store the data. Although you can use a spreadsheet for relatively simple data management needs, spreadsheets are not meant to replace a relational database management system. As always, choose the right tool for the right job.

This section looks at a few of the kinds of databases you can create with Microsoft Access—from a simple flat-file database to a more complex many-to-many relational database design.

Flat-File Database

The simplest database structure, called a *flat-file database*, consists of a single table that contains multiple rows and columns (see fig. 1.2). The term "flat-file" refers to the database being two-dimensional—no other tables are related to it. A spreadsheet is an example of a flat-file database.

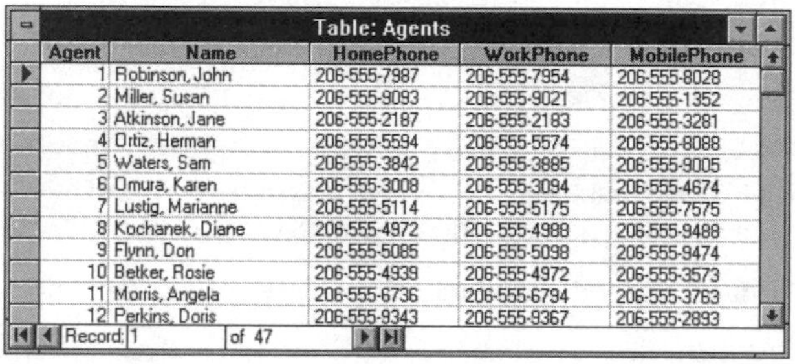

Agent	Name	HomePhone	WorkPhone	MobilePhone
1	Robinson, John	206-555-7987	206-555-7954	206-555-8028
2	Miller, Susan	206-555-9093	206-555-9021	206-555-1352
3	Atkinson, Jane	206-555-2187	206-555-2183	206-555-3281
4	Ortiz, Herman	206-555-5594	206-555-5574	206-555-8088
5	Waters, Sam	206-555-3842	206-555-3885	206-555-9005
6	Omura, Karen	206-555-3008	206-555-3094	206-555-4674
7	Lustig, Marianne	206-555-5114	206-555-5175	206-555-7575
8	Kochanek, Diane	206-555-4972	206-555-4988	206-555-9488
9	Flynn, Don	206-555-5085	206-555-5098	206-555-9474
10	Betker, Rosie	206-555-4939	206-555-4972	206-555-3573
11	Morris, Angela	206-555-6736	206-555-6794	206-555-3763
12	Perkins, Doris	206-555-9343	206-555-9367	206-555-2893

Record: 1 of 47

Figure 1.2.   A flat-file database model.

Flat-file databases are appropriate for simple, limited purposes. For example, you can create a flat-file recipe database with the appropriate fields: Food Name, Category, Recipe Book, Page, and Instructions. This type of information is easily stored in one table.

Relational Database

As you have seen, you can use a flat-file database to store customer addresses. However, you cannot use those same addresses in an order entry system. Because each table in a flat-file database is unrelated to any other table, you would have to reenter the customer and address information each time you added a new order. Not only would this result in duplicate data and extra data entry effort, when a customer's address changed, each instance of the address in the database would have to be located and changed.

A better way to handle this is to create two tables, Customers and Orders, and then join the tables, thereby creating a relational database. In a relational database, you store data in multiple tables and define relationships among the data in those tables. You join the individual tables on common fields in pairs of tables. Figure 1.3 shows a typical order entry relational database.

17

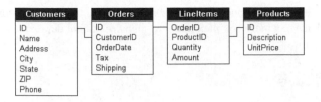

Figure 1.3. A typical order entry relational database model.

In this example, the invoices are related to the customers based on the values in the CustomerID and ID fields, the line items are related to the orders based on the OrderID and ID fields, and so on.

Nearly all database systems designed for the PC today, including Microsoft Access, are relational. Although academics may debate the definition of a "true" relational database, that is not the purpose of this book. What is most important is the "real world" meaning, the implications of using a relational database, and how you can use this type of database design to solve your data management problems.

Compared to a flat-file database model, a relational database design offers the following advantages:

- **Increased flexibility.** Individual tables in a relational database are typically small (that is, they usually contain relatively few fields) and store a specific kind of information. You can join, or link, tables as necessary. Changes to one table do not affect other tables in the database. In contrast, flat-file databases must store all categories of information in a single table. A relational database is far more flexible; you can add or modify fields in one table and not affect the entire database.

- **Decreased redundancy.** A relational database enables you to minimize data redundancy. For example, you might create an order entry system using the flat-file database model to store line items for each order. Because a given order can be for one item or dozens of items, storage of the item information is problematic. You could either enter a new record for each line item ordered (you have to duplicate the customer information for each record) or store each line item in a separate field in the order record (you have to anticipate how many line items an order can have, which results in wasted space for those orders with fewer than the maximum number.)

  If you use the relational database model, you can create two tables, Invoices and LineItems, and then link one invoice record to one or more line item records. This system lets you store as many line items as necessary for each order without establishing an arbitrary limit. Furthermore, you minimize redundant data because most of the order information (customer name, address, order date, and so on) is stored in the single invoice record, not in the individual line item records.

  The association between the invoices table and the line items table is called a one-to-many relationship, because each invoice can have many line items.

18

- *Increased organizational power.* A relational database lets you define relationships between data in different tables to present the data in various ways. In the flat-file database model, your view of the data is always two-dimensional; in the relational database model, you can present the same information different ways.

- *Increased manageability.* In many respects, a relational database is easier to handle than a single table that contains many fields. Tables in a relational database tend to contain fewer fields and are generally easier to manage and use.

In a relational database, you define relationships between tables through common fields. These relationships include one-to-one, one-to-many, and many-to-many. The following sections describe these relationships.

One-to-One Relationships

In a one-to-one relationship, each record in one of the tables corresponds to a record in the other table (see fig. 1.4). For example, you might store general employee information in a table named Employees. This table might contain information such as employee ID, name, address, and phone number. Because many departments in the company might need access to this table for daily tasks, you would not want to store sensitive information, such as salaries, in this table. You would create a second table, PersonalData, to store salary figures, evaluation results, and other personal information. Using a second table makes it easier for you to limit access to the classified information. Because each record in the Employees table has no more than one corresponding record in the PersonalData table, these tables have a one-to-one relationship.

Table: Employees						Table: PersonalData		
ID	LastName	FirstName	MI		EmployeeID	Salary	EvalResults
1	Newman	Jim	L.		1	$23,000.00	92
2	Anderson	Julie	A.		2	$58,000.00	95
3	Andrews	Stephen			3	$26,000.00	73
4	Younger	Regina	A.		4	$22,000.00	87
5	Johnson	Chad			5	$35,000.00	94
6	Godfrey	Tom	R.		6	$28,000.00	98
7	Taimsalu	Parn			7	$27,000.00	85
8	Raboy	James	D.		8	$18,000.00	98
9	Alexander	Cindy			9	$29,000.00	84
Record: 1	of 9				Record: 1	of 9	

Figure 1.4. An example of a one-to-one relationship: every employee has one record in both the Employees table and the PersonalData table.

The Employees table is joined with the PersonalData table through fields with common values. In the Employees table, the field is named ID; in the PersonalData table the field is named EmployeeID. One-to-one relationships are somewhat uncommon because the two tables could easily be combined into a single table. Even so, as in the Employees-PersonalData example, sometimes a one-to-one relationship serves a useful purpose.

Note: You may need to create a one-to-one relationship if the amount of data you want to store in a record exceeds Access' capacity for a single record (2K) or the number of fields exceeds the maximum number of fields for one record (255).

One-to-Many Relationships

A one-to-many relationship is the most commonly used association in a relational database. In a one-to-many relationship, each record in one table can have one or more associated records in another table, but each record in the second table has one (and only one) record in the first table. For example, in the HomeFinder database application (included on the disk that accompanies this book), the Agencies table, which contains information about the local real estate agencies, is the *one* table. The Agents table is used to maintain information about the individual real estate agents, including the agencies they work for. This table is the *many* table. These tables have a one-to-many relationship because each agent can have one and only one corresponding agency record, but each agency can have multiple agents. Figure 1.5 shows how these tables are joined on a common value, the agency ID.

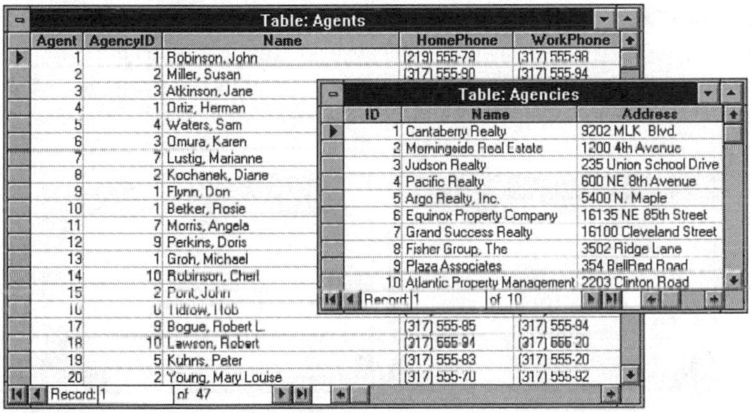

Figure 1.5. An example of a one-to-many relationship: the Cantaberry Realty Agency has at least five corresponding records in the Agents table.

Many-to-Many Relationships

A many-to-many relationship is one in which each record in one table can have one or more records in a second table, and each record in the second table can have one or more records in the first table. For example, you may want to keep track of the employees in each department of your company by using two tables, Employees and Departments (see fig. 1.6).

20

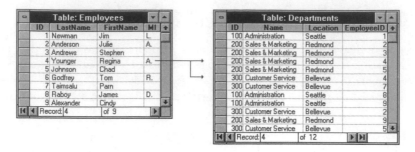

Figure 1.6. A many-to-many relationship.

In this example, Regina Younger works in both the Customer Service and the Sales & Marketing departments. The Employees and Departments tables have a many-to-many relationship: each record in the Employees table can have one or more corresponding records in the Departments table, and each record in the Departments table can have one or more corresponding records in the Employees table.

Although many-to-many relationships are common in real life, you must resolve them in the database structure with a linking table to reduce or eliminate unnecessary data redundancy and consumption of disk space. For example, department names and locations appear multiple times in the Departments table. In a properly designed database, you solve this design problem by creating a third table (the linking table) and forming two one-to-many relationships. Figure 1.7 shows how you can join the Employees and Departments tables with the EmpDept table.

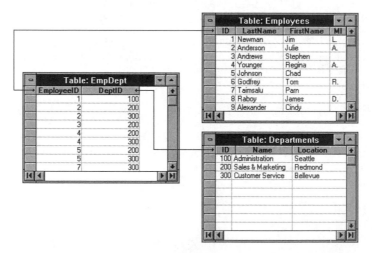

Figure 1.7. Breaking down a many-to-many relationship into two one-to-many relationships by adding another table decreases redundancy.

Understanding the Structure of a Database

A database is more than just a collection of random information. For this reason, the first step to defining a database is to make sure you have collected related information that serves a useful purpose. For example, the HomeFinder sample application included with this book lets you store and track residential real estate information. Most of the tables contain related information about houses (see fig. 1.8).

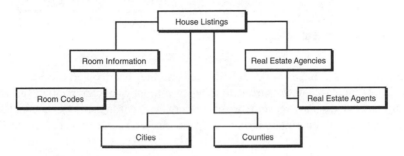

Figure 1.8. The database structure for the HomeFinder application.

Although a properly-designed database maintains related information, this does not mean the database can serve only a single purpose. Properly designed, a database can satisfy several needs, even though the underlying data is still related. For example, the HomeFinder database could be used as a source of data for a mailing list program that targets existing homeowners, even though HomeFinder's primary focus is on matching prospective buyers with available housing.

A good understanding of database design and composition is necessary before you begin working with databases. The following sections discuss the basic components of a database: tables, records, and fields.

Tables

A database contains one or more related tables. A *table* is a collection of related information, usually displayed as an arrangement of horizontal rows and vertical columns. In Access, you can view tables in Datasheet view.

Records

Each row in a table contains a variety of information related to a specific thing. The information in one row is called a *record*; each row collects pieces of related data to form a complete unit. For example, figure 1.9 shows 10 records; each record contains an ID number, name, street, city, state, zip code, and phone number.

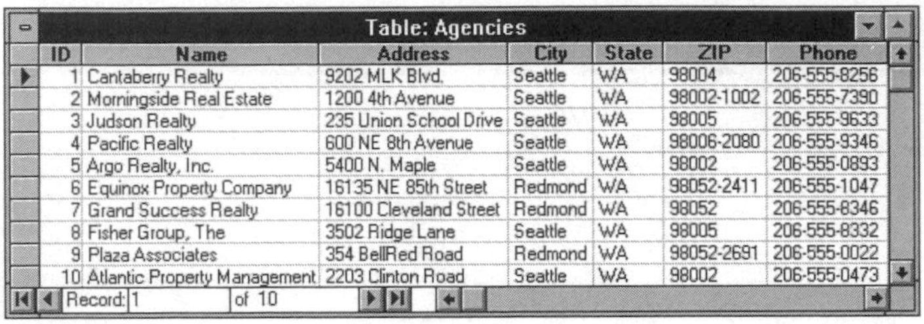

	ID	Name	Address	City	State	ZIP	Phone	
▶	1	Cantaberry Realty	9202 MLK Blvd.	Seattle	WA	98004	206-555-8256	
	2	Morningside Real Estate	1200 4th Avenue	Seattle	WA	98002-1002	206-555-7390	
	3	Judson Realty	235 Union School Drive	Seattle	WA	98005	206-555-9633	
	4	Pacific Realty	600 NE 8th Avenue	Seattle	WA	98006-2080	206-555-9346	
	5	Argo Realty, Inc.	5400 N. Maple	Seattle	WA	98002	206-555-0893	
	6	Equinox Property Company	16135 NE 85th Street	Redmond	WA	98052-2411	206-555-1047	
	7	Grand Success Realty	16100 Cleveland Street	Redmond	WA	98052	206-555-8346	
	8	Fisher Group, The	3502 Ridge Lane	Seattle	WA	98005	206-555-8332	
	9	Plaza Associates	354 BellRed Road	Redmond	WA	98052-2691	206-555-0022	
	10	Atlantic Property Management	2203 Clinton Road	Seattle	WA	98002	206-555-0473	

Table: Agencies

Record: 1 of 10

Figure 1.9. Each row in a table is a separate record.

Each record in the table is independent of every other record in the table. The information shown in fig. 1.9 includes records for many agencies. Although they are all part of one collection (all agencies), each record contains data unique to an agency.

In a spreadsheet, you determine the order of the records by inserting them in the correct sequence or by sorting the rows. In contrast, the physical order of the records in a database is not particularly important because you sort the records in the desired order whenever you view the data. Later sections of this chapter and other chapters in this book discuss different ways you can view and retrieve data.

Fields

Each column in a table stores a specific kind of information for each record. This category of data is called a *field*. For example, in a Customers table, the Name column is a field. In well-designed tables, each of the fields is related to the others for a specific purpose. For example, a customer record would have fields you can use to track information to help you maintain contacts with your customers.

Even so, you can add additional fields for other purposes. For example, you can add fields to keep track of which customers are members of a particular professional society. To do this, you can add a new field, ClubMember. Generally, however, you maintain this kind of additional information in a separate table and join it with other tables as necessary.

For more information about joining tables, see Chapter 6, "Building the HomeFinder Tables."

Each field contains data of a specific type, such as text or a number, date, or currency value. Defining field types ensures consistent, reliable data. Table 1.1 lists the Access field data types.

Table 1.1.   Access Field Data Types

Field Data Type	Example
Text	Smith
Memo	Mr. Smith is interested in a split-level, waterfront home. He works at home, so he also needs space for an office.
Number	890
Date/Time	08/16/94
Currency	$150,000.00
Counter	1, 2, 3...
Yes/No	Yes
OLE Object	(a bitmap image of a house)

 For more information about field data types, see Chapter 6, "Building the HomeFinder Tables."

In Access, the order in which you define the various fields is not particularly important. As you will see in subsequent chapters, you can view the fields in a variety of ways, no matter how you store the data physically in the tables.

Using Keys

One of the major benefits to using a relational database is the ease with which you can query the data to extract meaningful information and effective reports. Before you start sorting and querying a database, however, you must understand a concept fundamental to relational databases: *keys*.

Relational databases can use several types of keys; the most common being primary, composite, and foreign keys. In a relational database, you join two tables and form a relationship by first identifying common fields. For performance reasons, these fields are usually keys.

Primary and Composite Keys

As a rule, each table in a relational database has one or more fields that uniquely identify each record in the table. This unique identifier is called a *primary key* (or simply a key). For example, the ID field in the Agencies table is a primary key (see fig. 1.10).

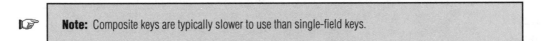

Primary Key

ID	Name	Address	City	State	ZIP	Phone
1	Cantaberry Realty	9202 MLK Blvd.	Seattle	WA	98004	206-555-8256
2	Morningside Real Estate	1200 4th Avenue	Seattle	WA	98002-1002	206-555-7390
3	Judson Realty	235 Union School Drive	Seattle	WA	98005	206-555-9633
4	Pacific Realty	600 NE 8th Avenue	Seattle	WA	98006-2080	206-555-9346
5	Argo Realty, Inc.	5400 N. Maple	Seattle	WA	98002	206-555-0893
6	Equinox Property Company	16135 NE 85th Street	Redmond	WA	98052-2411	206-555-1047
7	Grand Success Realty	16100 Cleveland Street	Redmond	WA	98052	206-555-8346
8	Fisher Group, The	3502 Ridge Lane	Seattle	WA	98005	206-555-8332
9	Plaza Associates	354 BellRed Road	Redmond	WA	98052-2691	206-555-0022
10	Atlantic Property Management	2203 Clinton Road	Seattle	WA	98002	206-555-0473

Record: 1   of 10

Figure 1.10.   The ID field is a primary key.

Sometimes a table will have more than one field that could function as the primary key. For example, the Agencies table contains two fields with unique information: ID and Name. As long as the Name field will never have duplicates, you can use either field for the primary key. Any field that can be used as a primary key in a table is called a *candidate key*.

You also can design a key that combines several fields that together make up a unique identifier for a record. This group of fields is called a *composite key*. A composite key allows duplicate values in one of its fields, but it does not allow duplicate values in all of the fields making up the composite key.

☞   **Note:** Composite keys are typically slower to use than single-field keys.

For example, the EmployeeID and DeptID fields form a composite key in the EmpDept table (see fig. 1.11). There can be multiple records with the same employee ID, and multiple records with the same department number, but only one record with a given combination of employee number plus department number.

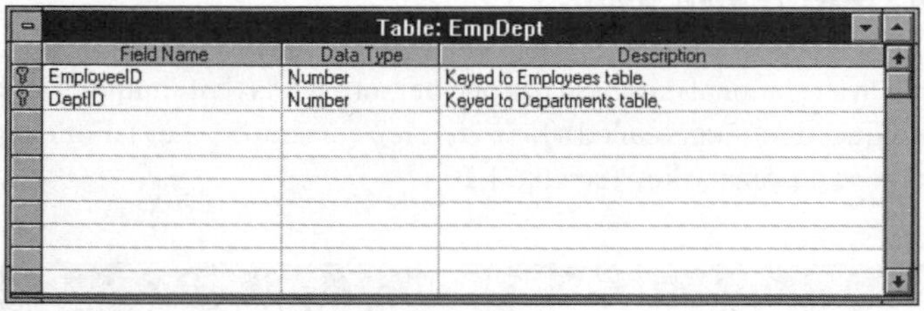

	Table: EmpDept		
	Field Name	Data Type	Description
▯	EmployeeID	Number	Keyed to Employees table.
▯	DeptID	Number	Keyed to Departments table.

Figure 1.11.   The EmployeeID and DeptID fields form a composite key.

One of your goals in creating an efficient design is to prevent duplicate data from being entered into the database. By using a primary or composite key, you eliminate the possibility of a table containing duplicate records because Access does not allow you to enter a duplicate value into a key field. For this reason, it may be a good idea for each table to have a primary or composite key.

When you select a field to be the key, you need to be certain that the field will never need to store duplicate values. Trying to add a second record with the same key value results in what is called a *key violation*. Thoughtful design of the database will minimize or eliminate the problem of key violations.

For example, the Agencies table (see fig. 1.12) contains a field for the name of the real estate agency. Using the Name field as the primary key is not a good design decision because of the future possibility of having two agencies with the same name. In this case, you would either have to replace the first agency's information, or enter the new agency record with a different name.

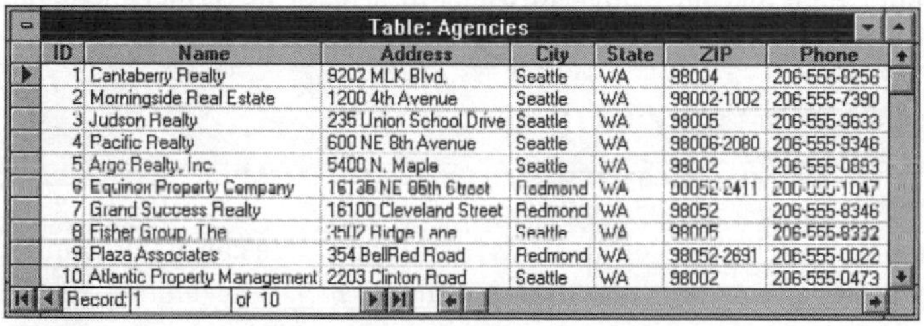

	ID	Name	Address	City	State	ZIP	Phone
▶	1	Cantaberry Realty	9202 MLK Blvd.	Seattle	WA	98004	206-555-0256
	2	Morningside Real Estate	1200 4th Avenue	Seattle	WA	98002-1002	206-555-7390
	3	Judson Realty	235 Union School Drive	Seattle	WA	98005	206-555-9633
	4	Pacific Realty	600 NE 8th Avenue	Seattle	WA	98006-2080	206-555-9346
	5	Argo Realty, Inc.	5400 N. Maple	Seattle	WA	98002	206-555-0893
	6	Equinox Property Company	16136 NE 85th Street	Redmond	WA	90052-0411	206-555-1047
	7	Grand Success Realty	16100 Cleveland Street	Redmond	WA	98052	206-555-8346
	8	Fisher Group, The	3517 Ridge Lane	Seattle	WA	98005	206-555-8332
	9	Plaza Associates	354 BellRed Road	Redmond	WA	98052-2691	206-555-0022
	10	Atlantic Property Management	2203 Clinton Road	Seattle	WA	98002	206-555-0473

Record: 1   of 10

Figure 1.12.   The Name field is a poor choice for primary key.

You might decide to create a composite key combining the values from two or more fields. Again, be sure the combination of all of the fields is not likely to ever result in a duplicate key.

Tip: An easy way to establish a primary key is to create a field that uses the Counter data type so that Access automatically assigns a unique identifier to each record. Then make that counter field the primary key.

Note: Access will not let you enter a record whose primary key field is empty.

 For more information about setting keys, see Chapter 6, "Building the HomeFinder Tables."

Foreign Keys

In a relational database, you join two tables and form a relationship by first identifying common fields. Figure 1.13 shows a relationship between the Rooms table and the RoomCodes table.

MLSNumber	RoomID	Width	Length	
113775	BR1	11	15	New carpeting
113775	BR2	11	11	
113775	DR	10	12	
113775	FR	11	18	
113775	KT	9	12	Refrigerator and ra
113775	LR	12	19	
149208	BR1	11	15	The master bedro
149208	BR2	12	12	
149208	BR3	11	11	
149208	BR4	11	10	
149208	DR	11	15	
149208	EXER	15	20	Previous owner w
149208	FR	14	12	
149208	KT	11	10	
149208	LR	11	18	
149208	RR	11	20	
158480	BR1	17	13	
158480	BR2	16	11	
158480	BR3	14	12	New carpeting.
158480	DR	14	14	

Table: Rooms

ID	Description
BPR	Back Porch
BR1	Bedroom 1
BR2	Bedroom 2
BR3	Bedroom 3
BR4	Bedroom 4
BR5	Bedroom 5
BR6	Bedroom 6
BR7	Bedroom 7
BR8	Bedroom 8
BR9	Bedroom 9
DR	Dining Room
EXER	Exercise Room
FPR	Front Porch
FR	Family Room
KT	Kitchen
LR	Living Room
MR	Mud Room
OFFIC	Office
REC	Recreation Room
RR	Recreation Room

Table: RoomCodes

Figure 1.13. RoomID in the Rooms table and ID in the RoomCodes table are the common fields between the two tables.

Each record in the Rooms table has a matching record in the RoomCodes table with the same field value. The RoomID field in the Rooms table is called a *foreign key*. A foreign key is a field in one table (RoomID) whose values match those of the primary key of another table (ID).

Although you can match a non-key field to another field in a second table, you will likely discover that critical interrelationships between tables are based on foreign keys.

Ensuring Referential Integrity

The integrity of a relational database depends on the assurance that the database does not include unmatched foreign key values; every foreign key value in a table requires a matching record in a linked table. This assurance is called *referential integrity*.

Referential integrity ensures that records in the RoomCodes table cannot be deleted if there are any matching records in the Rooms table. For example, deleting ID BR1 is not allowed because there are matching records in the Rooms table that contain the same BR1 value (see fig. 1.14).

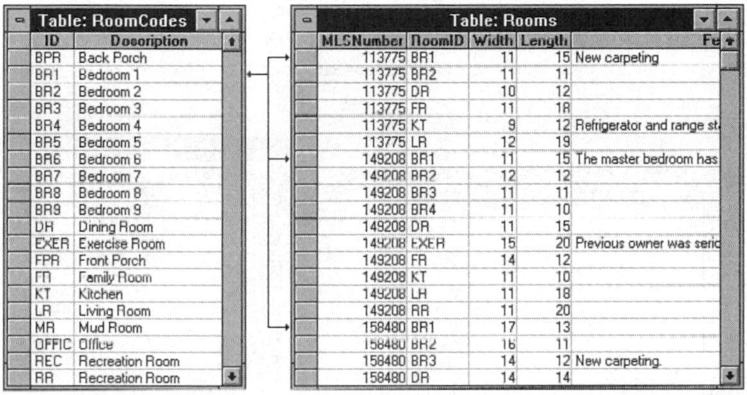

Figure 1.14. Referential integrity ensures that there are no orphan records.

An *orphan record* is a record in the second table whose matching "parent" in the first table has been deleted. Referential integrity prevents you from deleting ID BR1 from the RoomCodes table and creating orphan records in the Rooms table.

Enforcing referential integrity also prevents you from changing a primary key value that has a matching record in the linked table without also changing the foreign key values in the second table. For example, you cannot change the BR1 room code to MBR (master bedroom) because there are matching records in the Rooms table that contain BR1.

Summary

The need to store, manage, and use data is increasingly important to businesses, and your ability to implement an effective database management solution will likely play a vital role. Using the power of a relational database such as Microsoft Access will let you design efficient applications that let the user think of his data as a resource and not just an expense.

This chapter explained basic database concepts, such as one-to-many relationships, primary keys, and referential integrity, that you must understand to create effective Access applications.

2

Access as a Database Tool

Microsoft Access is a graphical tool you can use to develop relational databases and applications. Access includes all the tools you need in a Windows database application development environment. You can use Access to create a complete application with tables that contain data, user-friendly forms for data entry, and publication-quality reports.

This chapter covers the following:

- Developing with Access
- Using an Object-Oriented Database
- Introducing the QBE Grid
- Designing Forms
- Designing Reports

Developing with Access

Access implements a wide range of the standard Windows 3.1 API (Application Program Interface). Many functions emphasize the point-and-click and drag-and-drop capabilities that make Access easy to learn and use. In addition, Access shares many helpful features of other Windows-based products. If you are familiar with Microsoft Word for Windows, Excel, or Visual Basic, you probably will recognize the Access toolbars, the toolbox, and the Access Basic programming language (see fig. 2.1.).

Drag-and-drop capabilities simplify many operations by letting you design forms, reports, and queries graphically. For example, you can build a query by dragging field names from a field list down to the QBE grid (see fig. 2.2.).

Toolbar

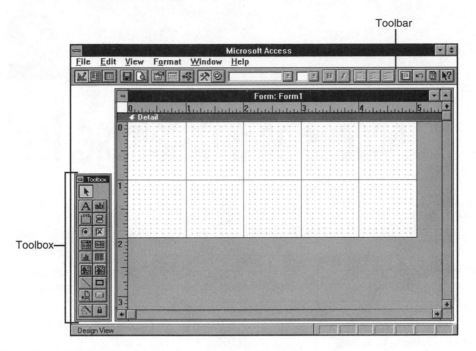

Toolbox

Figure 2.1. Use the toolbar and toolbox to quickly create forms and reports.

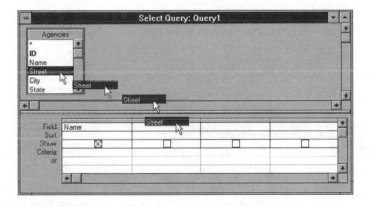

Figure 2.2. Building a query by dragging fields from a list down to the QBE grid.

 For more information about Query By Example (QBE), see Chapter 7, "Building the HomeFinder Queries."

Another example of the drag-and-drop method is the way you can establish a link between two tables. To create a link between two tables in the QBE grid, drag the linking field from one table to the matching field in the other table. Figure 2.3. shows a relationship between the Agencies table and the Agents table.

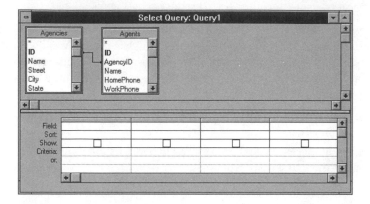

Figure 2.3. A solid line connects the linking fields.

Microsoft Access uses a multiple document interface (MDI) much like Excel or Microsoft Word for Windows (see fig. 2.4.).

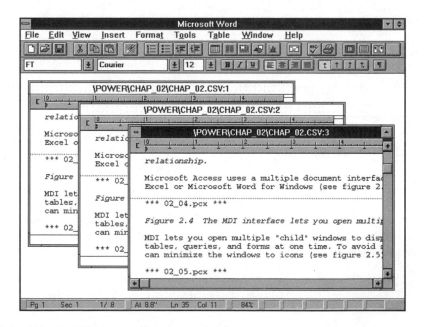

Figure 2.4. Using the MDI to open multiple document windows.

31

MDI lets you open multiple windows to display any number of tables, queries, and forms at one time. To avoid screen clutter, you can minimize the windows to icons.

You can create an entire database application using only the tools available in Access. Although many third-party add-ons are available, you do not need to supplement Access with report writers, form designers, or application generators in order to produce robust applications.

In addition, Access makes it easy to create enterprise-wide applications without abandoning your current databases. For example, you may want to work with data from an existing FoxPro, dBASE, or Paradox database so that some users can continue to use their current database-management systems. Or, you may need to work with mainframe data (by way of SQL). In all these cases, you can attach to external FoxPro, dBASE, Paradox, or SQL databases and then use Access as a front end.

You even can use Access to work with tables in different database formats at the same time. For example, you can create a single Access query that links tables from a mainframe SQL database, a dBASE database, and an Access table. Plus, you can import existing FoxPro, dBASE, or Paradox databases and convert them to the Access format.

Note: Importing data is not the same as attaching data. When you attach an external table, the table retains its existing format and properties (those established by the FoxPro, dBASE, or other database-management system). These other systems can continue to work with the table, oblivious to your having attached the table to Access. In contrast, when you import an external table, you create a new copy of the table in the Access format. The original table remains intact.

For example, when you attach a dBASE database to Access, the dBASE information remains in its original format. You can use the data as if it had been converted to the Access format. You can add, edit, or delete records, but you cannot change the dBASE file structure. As a rule, attach tables when non-Access users need to use the tables and import the tables when everyone uses Access.

For more information on attaching and importing external tables, see Chapter 6, "Building the HomeFinder Tables."

Most of the examples throughout this book come from the HomeFinder sample database application included on the disk that accompanies this book. HomeFinder contains a number of related tables and associated forms, queries, and reports. This chapter briefly examines some of these objects; more detailed information about how to create the tables, queries, and other database objects appears in later chapters.

You create the various database objects for your application inside the Database window (see fig. 2.5.).

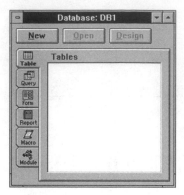

Figure 2.5. Using the Database window, which contains all the database objects.

Unlike DOS-based applications and most other Windows-based database management systems, Access is not limited by a DOS eight-character file-name rule. This means that you can assign truly meaningful names to your tables and queries (see fig. 2.6.).

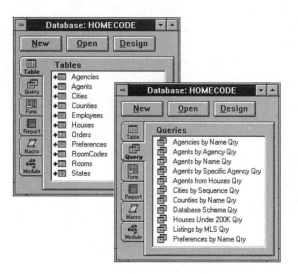

Figure 2.6. Using descriptive database object names.

Object names can include spaces, punctuation, and other characters that you cannot use for DOS file names. Some of the characters you can use include the dollar sign ($) and asterisk (*).

 For more information about naming conventions, see Chapter 17, "Naming Conventions and Design Guidelines."

33

> **Tip:** Although Access lets you include punctuation, you should consider avoiding them and limit object names to letters and numbers only. If you should someday port your application to a non-Access environment, you may discover that the other platform does not enable you to use the same special characters.

Using an Object-Oriented Database

Access is an object-oriented database; it deals with database objects that you can select and manipulate as a unit. Forms, reports, and queries are all objects. Each type of database object has its own set of properties, and because the properties are built into the object, you can use them immediately without programming.

Object orientation means that you do not need to memorize dozens (or perhaps hundreds) of cryptic commands to complete even the simplest operations. For example, to move to the preceding or next record in a table, you simply click one of the VCR-like buttons that appear along the bottom of a form.

Only six fundamental Access database objects exist: tables, queries, forms, reports, macros, and modules. To view an object of a particular type, click the corresponding button in the Database window (see fig. 2.7.).

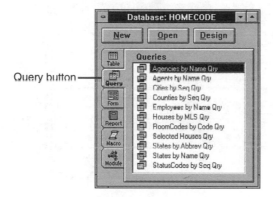

Figure 2.7.   Click the Query button to display a list of all query objects.

You can view a list of all the queries in the current database by clicking the Query button or by choosing the Queries command from the View menu (see fig. 2.8.).

You can click a button in the Database window to display a list of the corresponding objects for that type.

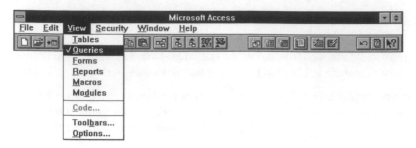

Figure 2.8. Choosing the appropriate command from the View menu to view specific objects.

In Microsoft Access, the text boxes, command buttons, combo boxes, list boxes, and other screen objects are called *controls* (see fig. 2.9.). Like the database objects, these controls have predefined properties or attributes that determine how the controls look and how Access responds when the user interacts with them. The behavior of these controls is predictable and consistent with most other Windows applications.

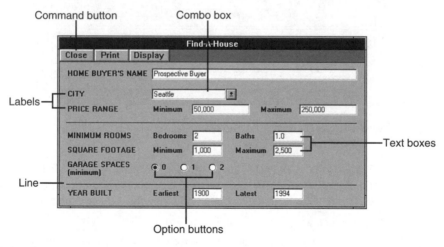

Figure 2.9. Some of the controls that Access supports.

The wide variety of controls saves design time and helps ensure a consistent appearance of forms and reports.

Introducing the QBE Grid

The Query By Example (QBE) grid lets you create queries—tools you can use to get answers to questions about your data—in an intuitive manner using drag-and-drop techniques. You use queries

to select a particular subset of data. For example, you can create a query that extracts information about listings for houses in Redmond.

You also can retrieve information from more than one table at a time. The Selected Houses Qry query in the HomeFinder database application uses three tables: Houses, Agencies, and Agents.

When you run a query, Access creates a *dynaset*, or dynamic data set, which you then can view, edit, save, use to create a new table, or use to provide the underlying data for a form or report. HomeFinder uses the Selected Houses Qry query to supply information to the Selected Houses report (see fig. 2.10.).

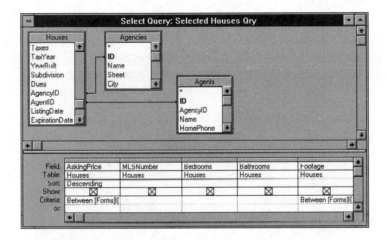

Figure 2.10. The Selected Houses Qry query using three related tables.

In this example, the Houses table is joined to the Agencies table by the AgencyID field; it is joined to the Agents table by the AgentID field. Although this particular query does not require it, you could link the Agencies and Agents tables by dragging the ID field from the Agencies table to the AgencyID field in the Agents table.

To create a link between tables, you drag one field from one table to the corresponding field in another table. The fields do not have to have the same names, and frequently will not. The fields, however, must contain matching data types (string versus string, integer versus integer, and so on). Similarly, you select fields for the query by dragging field names from the field lists to the grid.

Tip: If you create relationships between tables, you do not have to join tables when you create a query. Access adds the links automatically when a relationship exists.

To view the results of the query, click Run on the toolbar or choose Run from the Query menu (see figs. 2.11. and 2.12.).

For more information about relationships, see Chapter 6, "Building the HomeFinder Tables." For more information about queries, see Chapter 7, "Building the HomeFinder Queries."

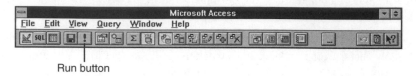

Run button

Figure 2.11.   Click the Run button to view the results of a query.

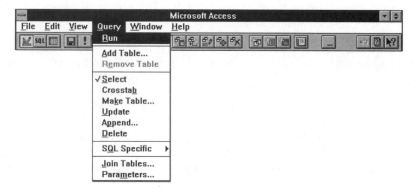

Figure 2.12.   Choose the Run command to run a query.

Figure 2.13. illustrates part of the results of the Selected Houses Qry query. The rest of the query output would be visible if you scrolled the window.

AskingPrice	MLSNumber	Bedrooms	Bathrooms	Sq Ft	City	Built
$399,000.00	281636	3	4.5	5288	2	1973
$259,000.00	271622	4	4.0	3350	2	1980
$194,500.00	281514	3	3.5	2596	4	1987
$163,900.00	271635	3	1.0	2310	1	1989
$162,900.00	256345	2	2.0	2100	3	1945
$159,500.00	281501	4	2.0	1900	1	1991
$149,000.00	655236	2	2.5	2400	1	1991
$136,000.00	281512	2	2.0	2100	5	1923
$125,000.00	531698	3	2.0	1800	4	1990
$124,900.00	224442	2	2.0	1900	1	1985
$114,400.00	253608	2	2.0	1950	4	1990
$113,900.00	149208	4	2.0	1875	1	1905
$112,900.00	555121	3	2.5	1600	7	1901
$112,500.00	281509	4	2.0	2020	6	1973
$111,500.00	335898	3	2.0	1800	1	1961
$110,000.00	291609	4	1.0	2020	3	1973
$105,900.00	113775	2	2.0	2590	1	1991
$100,000.00	654321	2	2.0	2190	1	1991
$95,500.00	291604	4	2.0	1736	4	1984
$95,000.00	281536	2	2.0	2105	7	1990
$32,900.00	251679	3	1.0	1450	2	1985

Select Query: Selected Houses Qry

Record: 1   of 30

Figure 2.13.   Viewing the results of a query.

Designing Forms

Access provides a workspace you can use to create attractive, user-friendly forms with text boxes, selection lists, drop-down combo boxes, and other controls. After you move out of the table-design phase of application development, most of your time spent in Access will be spent designing and enhancing forms.

Microsoft Access forms are similar to paper forms, except that you gain enhanced functionality. You can add drop-down lists, error checking, and validation to an Access form. You can add advanced design features simply by selecting a control from the toolbox and dragging it onto a form. You can enhance the functionality of each of the controls by attaching code. Access triggers this code in response to various events, such as clicking a command button.

Some other controls you can use on forms include text boxes (to enter or display data from a table), labels (to display static text you define at design time or run time), combo and list boxes (to select from a list of predefined entries), and check boxes (to represent a Yes or No condition).

You can add command buttons to execute procedures such as closing the current form or moving to a new record.

You can construct a form yourself, or you can use one of the built-in form wizards to quickly create any of several predefined form types—including single-column, tabular, graph, and main/subform. If a wizard-created form is not exactly what you want, you can modify the form and add your own special functionality or design touches. As you gain more experience, you may prefer to build the forms yourself and not use a wizard. In either case, Access controls greatly simplify the process of creating sophisticated forms.

You can display a form in three views:

- *Design View.* Use this view to create or modify the form design, but none of the form's underlying data (see fig. 2.14.).

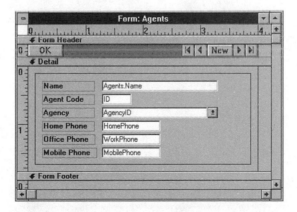

Figure 2.14.   The Agents form in Design View.

- *Form View.* This view typically shows a single record using the design you created in Design View (see fig. 2.15.). It is most useful for data entry and for examining a single record in its entirety. You also can create a continuous form, although this is less common. Continuous forms show multiple records at one time and are most useful when the amount of data in each record is rather limited.

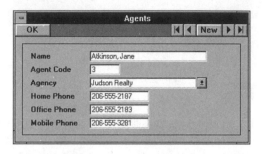

Figure 2.15.　The Agents form in Form View.

- *Datasheet View.* Use this view to present a spreadsheet-like view of a number of records (see fig. 2.16.). It is particularly useful for quickly scanning many records. You can see more records than in Form View, but unless the underlying tables of the form have only a few fields, you cannot see all the fields at one time. Requiring the user to scroll the window horizontally to see all the data is usually the result of a poor design choice.

Name	Agent Code	Agency	Home	Office	Mobile
Atkinson, Jane	3	Judson Realty	206-555-2187	206-555-2183	206-555-3281
Betker, Rosie	10	Cantaberry Realty	206-555-4939	206-555-4972	206-555-3573
Bogue, Robert L.	17	Plaza Associates	206-555-8554	206-555-8582	206-555-0662
Brockway, Jack	23	Plaza Associates	206-555-7256	206-555-7285	206-555-8107
Brooks, Randolph	22	Equinox Property Company	206-555-3175	206-555-3147	206-555-2721
Ewing, David	45	Plaza Associates	206-555-2542	206-555-2585	206-555-1243
Flynn, Don	9	Cantaberry Realty	206-555-5085	206-555-5098	206-555-9474
Groh, Michael	13	Cantaberry Realty	206-555-8888	206-555-8856	206-555-5205
Kochanek, Diane	8	Morningside Real Estate	206-555-4972	206-555-4988	206-555-9488
Kuhns, Peter	19	Argo Realty, Inc.	206-555-8334	206-555-8339	206-555-5232
Lamb, Davie	37	Atlantic Property Management	206-555-5174	206-555-5165	206-555-2272
Lankin, Diane	39	Argo Realty, Inc.	206-555-0353	206-555-0339	206-555-2573
Lawson, Robert	18	Atlantic Property Management	206-555-9498	206-555-9437	206-555-5281
Lindahl, Norma	40	Plaza Associates	206-555-7288	206-555-7213	206-555-0468
Lustig, Marianne	7	Grand Success Realty	206-555-5114	206-555-5175	206-555-7575
Machette, Robert	36	Pacific Realty	206-555-3782	206-555-3760	206-555-0159
Manley, Mary Lynn	26	Plaza Associates	206-555-3309	206-555-3367	206-555-8654
Mason, Gary	24	Judson Realty	206-555-7154	206-555-7168	206-555-7598

Record: 1　of 47

Figure 2.16.　The Agents form in Datasheet View.

To switch from one view to another, click the appropriate button on the toolbar or choose the appropriate command from the View menu (see fig. 2.17.).

39

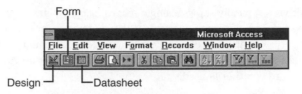

Figure 2.17.   Switch form views by clicking a button on the toolbar.

Designing Reports

Access comes complete with a built-in report designer. The report designer provides two shortcuts you can use to create publication-quality reports. Like the form wizards that help you quickly design forms, one of these shortcuts is the set of report wizards which guide you through the process of creating reports.

The various report wizards help you design reports in any of several predefined formats—including single-column, groups/totals, and mailing labels. As with forms you create with the form wizards, you can modify a report created by a report wizard to suit your exact needs.

The other shortcut is the capability to save a form as a report. This feature lets you take an existing form and create a report without having to go through much of the report-design process. To save a form as a report, open the form in Design View and choose Save As Report from the File menu.

After you choose the Save As Report command, Microsoft Access copies all the controls from the form to the new report (see fig. 2.18.). You may need to perform some fine-tuning on the report. For example, command buttons make sense on a form but not on a report, so you may want to delete them.

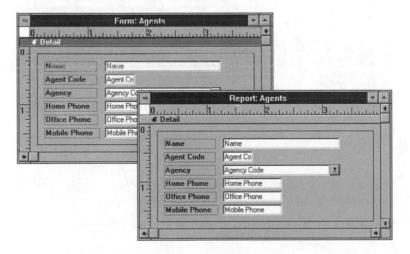

Figure 2.18.   A form saved as a report (note its resemblance to the original form).

Other changes you may want to make include changing some of the background colors to colors or shades that print better, and adding report or page headers and footers (see fig. 2.19.). Depending on the size of the report and the paper size you choose, multiple records may appear on one printed page (see fig. 2.20.).

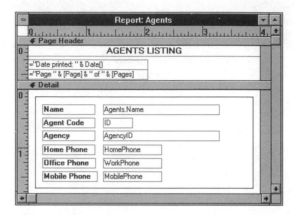

Figure 2.19. A modified version of the Agents Report, including a report header and footer.

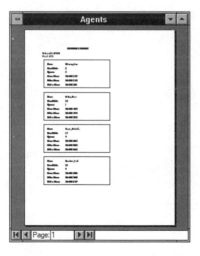

Figure 2.20. Viewing reports, which often include multiple records on each printed page.

 Note: The report shown in figure 2.20. is for illustration purposes only. You probably will want to make additional changes to the report's design to make it more compact and much more like a presentation-quality report. For more information, see Chapter 10, "Building the HomeFinder Reports."

Summary

This chapter briefly discussed the essential features of Microsoft Access, including the product's object orientation. Object orientation saves you development time and effort by building extensive functionality into the various database objects. The drag-and-drop capability you can use when working with objects makes it easy to create forms, reports, and queries.

In addition, this chapter described in more detail some of Access's powerful and easy-to-use design tools. Later chapters in this book describe each of the design features of Access in far greater detail and show you, step-by-step, how you can create your own queries, forms, and reports.

3

The Access Development Environment

The first two chapters of this book introduced you to the general concepts of relational databases and, in general terms, how you can use Microsoft Access to implement a relational database application. This chapter looks more closely at the development tools available in Access.

This chapter covers the following:

- Installing Access
- Starting and Exiting Access
- Exploring the Main Access Window
- Creating a database
- Exploring the Database Window
- Using Database Objects
- Getting Help

This chapter discusses each of these topics and explores how you can best use Access.

Installing Access

Part of the appeal of Microsoft Access is that it lets you work with a wide variety of data sources. Just as important is the fact that it lets you work in a variety of network environments.

If you already have installed Microsoft Access on your machine, you can skip ahead to the section "Starting and Exiting Access." Otherwise, this section can help you decide how you should install Access: as a stand-alone installation or as part of a network installation.

> Single-user applications you design in Access probably will work just as well in multiuser environment—usually without requiring you to make any design modifications. For more information about multiuser considerations, search Help for "multiuser access".

Choosing a Local versus Network Installation

If you are not connected to a network system, you can install Access only locally. If you are connected to a network, however, you can install Access locally or as part of a more global network installation. This section lists some of the advantages and disadvantages of each strategy.

Local Installation

In a local installation, you install a complete copy of Microsoft Access on each workstation and only a minimal number of files on the network server.

- **Advantage.** Applications load and start more quickly and generally perform better than if you install Access on the network server. Loading a form from even the slowest local hard disk probably will be much faster than loading the same form across the network.

- **Advantage.** Each user in a multiuser environment can customize the Access development environment according to his own preferences without having to worry about what other users are doing to their copies of the system.

- **Disadvantage.** Workstation hard disk space requirements are significantly higher than when you install Access on the network server. Depending on which options you install, each workstation requires between 5M and 23M of free disk space (see fig. 3.1).

- **Disadvantage.** Upgrades to Microsoft Access must be individually copied to or installed on each workstation. In a network environment involving many workstations, this can amount to significantly more time than it takes to update a single copy of Access located on the network server.

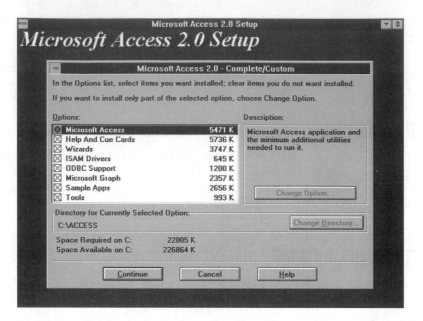

Figure 3.1. Selectively installing parts of the complete Access systems.

Network Installation

In a network installation, you install a complete copy of Microsoft Access on the network server only and only a minimal number of files on the individual workstations:

- **Advantage.** The individual workstations require only about 1M of free disk space because most of Access is located on the server.

- **Advantage.** You need to make updates to Microsoft Access to one copy only: the copy on the server. In a network environment involving many workstations, the time it takes to update a single network copy probably will be far less than the time it takes to update or install the revised copy of Access on each workstation's hard disk.

- **Disadvantage.** Performance is not as good as if you install Access on each workstation. For example, the time it takes to load forms across the network is more than if you load the same forms from a local hard disk.

- **Disadvantage.** The increased network traffic involved in loading Access code from the single copy of the system negatively affects other programs (other than Microsoft Access) that you run across the network. This traffic also slows down response times when you access data on the network server.

Note: No matter how you decide to configure your Access installation, you must run the Access Setup program on the network server and on each workstation.

Installing Access on a Network

The steps you follow to install Access on a network are not much different than the steps you take to install Access on one machine for single-user use. You run the Setup program once on the network server, and then once on each of the workstations, even if you plan to run Access from the network server.

Installing Access on a Network Server

The following procedure outlines the steps you follow to run the Setup program and install a complete copy of Access on the network server.

1. Make sure that you are connected to the desired network server; identify the logical drive on which you will install Access.

2. Start Microsoft Windows (or Microsoft Windows for Workgroups, if appropriate) and make sure that all applications, except the Program Manager or other program shell, are closed. You may want to check your Startup program group to see if any applications are loaded automatically after you start Windows.

3. Insert the first Microsoft Access disk containing the Setup program into drive A (or drive B, if appropriate).

4. From the Program Manager, choose Run from the File menu and type the following line in the Command Line box:

   a:\setup /a

5. Press Enter and follow the on-screen instructions. The Setup program prompts you to enter the path for the SYSTEM.MDA file (this is a directory on the drive you identified in step 1). Remember this path, because you need to type it again when you install Access on the individual workstations. For more information about the SYSTEM.MDA file, see Chapter 22, "Implementing Security."

6. Install Access on each workstation, following the instructions that appear in the following section.

> **Tip:** In a network environment, four kinds of Access files exist: The Access program files you just installed, the SYSTEM.MDA file (which contains user and security information), application databases, and data databases (tables). Each of these files should be in a separate directory; you should not place your application databases in the same directory as Access, and data should not go in the same directory as the application. This practice not only facilitates easier backups, but also lets you set specific directories on the network as read-only directories. You should make the directories containing the Access files and the application databases read-only. Leave only the SYSTEM.MDA and table directories as read/write.

Installing Access on a Workstation

You must run the Setup program on each workstation, even if you followed the instructions in the preceding section and intend to run Access from the network server. When you install Microsoft Access on the server, Setup installs only the necessary initialization files to each workstation.

The following procedure outlines the steps you can follow to install Access on the workstations (you do not need the Access disks for this procedure).

1. Connect to the network server on which you installed Access. (If necessary, refer to the preceding section, "Installing Access on a Network Server.")

2. Start Microsoft Windows and make sure that all applications except the Program Manager are closed. Be sure to check your Startup program group to see if any applications are loaded automatically after you start Windows.

3. In the Program Manager, choose Run from the File menu and type the complete path to the Setup program on the network server, followed by the /n command-line option (see fig. 3.2).

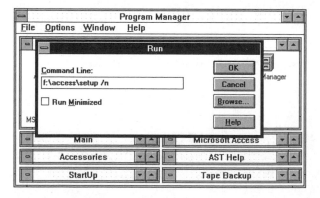

Figure 3.2. Running the Setup program from the network drive F.

4. Press Enter and follow the on-screen instructions. Setup prompts you to enter the path where the SYSTEM.MDA file is located. This is the location on the network server. If you want to join a workgroup, enter this path. If you do not want to join a workgroup, enter a different path (on the network server or on the local hard disk). See the following section, "Joining a Workgroup," and Chapter 22, "Implementing Security," for more information about workgroups.

 Note: If you configure a workstation to run Access from the network server, you must thereafter make sure that the workstation is connected to the network using the same drive letter. In the preceding example, Access was installed using drive F, so the workstation must be connected to the network server using drive F.

Joining a Workgroup

A *workgroup* is nothing more than a group of users who share data and a common SYSTEM.MDA file in a multiuser (network) environment. Microsoft Access stores information about users and their access rights in the SYSTEM.MDA file. To gain access to a secured database, you must join the appropriate workgroup.

 For more information about securing a database, see Chapter 22, "Implementing Security."

To join an existing workgroup when you run the Setup program, all you need to do is specify the path and file name for the SYSTEM.MDA file located on the network server.

You can create a workgroup on the network server in two ways:

- Install Access on a workstation, but do not join a workgroup. The Setup program creates a SYSTEM.MDA file on the local hard disk. Copy this file to the network server when the Setup program is finished.

- Run the Workgroup Administrator program, WRKGADM.EXE, to create and then join the new workgroup.

Starting and Exiting Access

At this point, you should have installed Microsoft Access on your computer. If necessary, refer to "Installing Access," earlier in this chapter.

The Setup program creates a Microsoft Access program group in the Program Manager (see fig. 3.3). You can add additional program items to the Access program group, or you can move the Access icon to another program group.

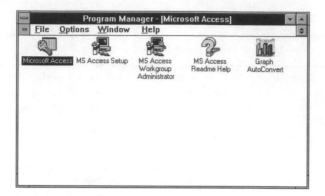

Figure 3.3. Launching Access from the Microsoft Access program group.

To start Microsoft Access, double-click the Access icon.

> **Tip:** You also can start Microsoft Access by choosing Run from the File menu and then specifying the path to the Access executable file, MSACCESS.EXE.

Launching Access with Command-Line Parameters

Most users start Access and accept the default startup behavior, but you may find it convenient or even necessary to start Access a bit differently. Table 3.1 lists the documented command-line options you can use to start Microsoft Access.

Table 3.1. Access Command-Line Options

Enter this...	*...to do this*
/Cmd	Specify that what follows on the command line is the value that will be returned by the Access Basic **Command** and **Command$** functions. When present, this option must be the last option on the command line. You can use a semicolon (;) as an alternative to /Cmd.
/Compact *<target>*	Compress the database specified before the /Compact option and then close Microsoft Access. To compress to a different name, specify a target database name.

continues

Table 3.1. Continued

Enter this...	...to do this
/Convert <target database>	Convert a version 1.x database to the 2.0 format with a new name and then close Microsoft Access. You must specify the source database before the /Convert command-line option.
<database>	Open the specified database. You probably need to include the complete path to the database.
/Excl	Open the specified database for exclusive access. In a multiuser environment, this command prevents other users from opening the same database. The default is to open the database for shared access.
/Ini <INI file>	Start Microsoft Access using the options in the specified initialization (.INI) file rather than the standard MSACC20.INI file located in your Windows directory. The specified .INI file generally must have the same entries as the standard MSACC20.INI file.
/Pwd <password>	Start Microsoft Access using the specified password; this bypasses the password screen. For more information about passwords, see Chapter 22, "Implementing Security."
/Repair	Repair the specified database and then close Microsoft Access.
/Ro	Open the specified database in read-only mode. You can view, but not change, the database.
/User <user name>	Start Microsoft Access using the specified user name.
/X <macro>	Start Microsoft Access and run the specified macro. You also can create an AutoExec macro that runs automatically whenever you open the database. For more information about AutoExec, see Chapter 9, "Building the HomeFinder Macros."

To use one or more of the command-line options, type them after the program name. The following command line starts Access, opens the HomeFinder sample application, and specifies the user name *Chris*:

```
C:\ACCESS\MSACCESS.EXE \HOMEFIND\HOMECODE.MDB /User Chris
```

When you launch Microsoft Access, it displays the opening Welcome screen (see fig. 3.4).

50

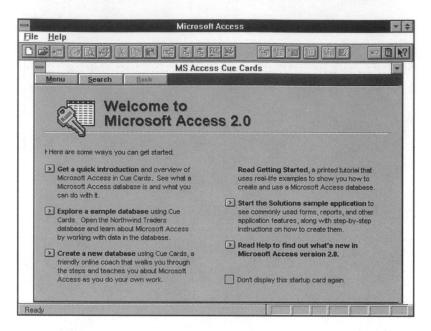

Figure 3.4. The Welcome screen.

The Welcome screen offers several options to help get you started with Access, including a quick introduction, exploring a sample database, and creating a new database.

Each of these options uses Cue Cards, a friendly on-line coach that guides you through the steps of the various Access procedures while using real databases—your own or the sample databases included with Access. To bypass the Welcome screen the next time you start Access, select the check box at the bottom of the screen.

> **Tip:** Notice that the Welcome screen is inactive after you start Microsoft Access (the title bar appears white or whatever color you chose for inactive windows). If you are accustomed to pressing Alt+F4 to close a window, you close Access—not the Welcome screen. You first must click somewhere on the Welcome screen to make it active and then press Alt+F4.

For now, close the Welcome screen to display the main Access window (see fig. 3.5).

Although the main Access Window starts out mostly empty, it fills up quickly as you begin to work with databases and database objects.

An Access database can contain six types of database objects: tables, queries, forms, reports, macros, and modules. Later in this chapter, you see how to create a database and then explore each of the database objects.

51

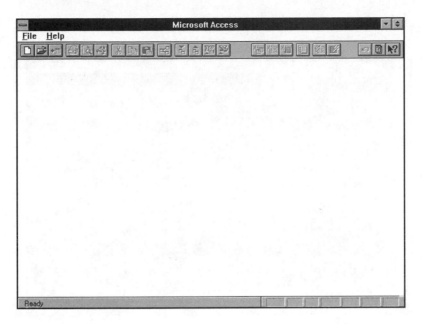

Figure 3.5. The main Access window.

Exiting Access

When you are finished working with a database, exit Access by choosing Exit from the File menu. You also can double-click the Access window's control menu.

When you exit, Access prompts you to save any database objects that have been changed but not saved (see fig. 3.6).

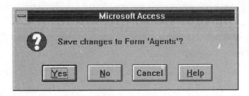

Figure 3.6. Verifying that you want to save your changes.

> **Note:** You may hear a beep when you try to exit Access, which usually means that a dialog box is open: you cannot exit Access when dialog boxes are open. Dialog boxes are *modal*, which means that you cannot move the focus to another window (or exit Access) until you close the dialog box.

Exploring the Main Access Window

Before you open a database, the main Access window contains only a menu bar with the File and Help menus, plus four active buttons that let you create a new database, open an existing database, launch Cue Cards, or open Help (see fig. 3.7).

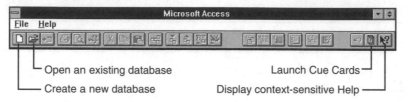

Figure 3.7. The main Access window featuring two menus and a toolbar.

 Note: Only four of the buttons are enabled at this time. The other buttons become enabled after you open a database.

To open an existing database, click the Open Database button on the toolbar or choose Open Database from the File menu. Access displays the Open Database dialog box (see fig. 3.8). Select the desired database file and then click OK.

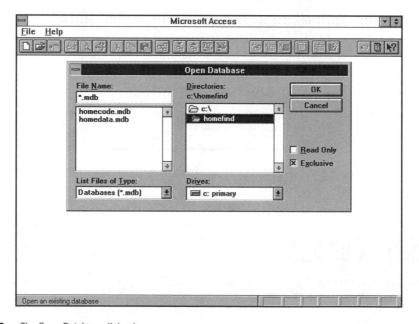

Figure 3.8. The Open Database dialog box.

To open the sample HomeFinder application, select the HOMEFIND directory and click OK. Access displays all the databases (files with an extension of MDB) in the directory. Select HOMECODE.MDB and then click OK a second time to open the database.

Note: The HomeFinder database application contains an AutoExec macro that loads a main menu form. If you want to open the database without running the AutoExec macro, press SHIFT while you click OK.

You can open only one database at a time with the Open Database command. For more information about opening multiple databases using the OpenDatabase method, search Help for "OpenDatabase".

Tip: At the bottom of the File menu, Access displays the names of the four most recently used databases (see fig. 3.9). Open the File menu and select the database name you want.

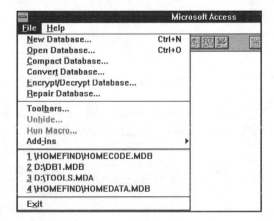

Figure 3.9.   The four most recently opened databases are displayed at the bottom of the File menu.

Creating a Database

To create a database, click the New Database button on the toolbar or choose New Database from the File menu. Access displays the New Database dialog box (see fig. 3.10).

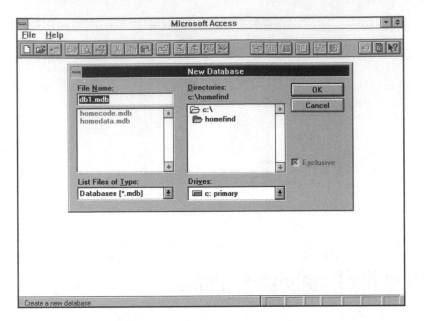

Figure 3.10. The New Database dialog box.

The default file name for new databases is DB1.MDB. You can accept the default or you can replace it with a name you choose. The name you give to the new database is limited to the standard DOS file-name convention of eight characters. If you do not provide an extension, Access adds the MDB extension for you. You can enter the database name in uppercase, lowercase, or mixed case.

The database file name is the only name in Access that is so limited; all the database objects in an Access database can be given longer, descriptive names.

> You also can use the names of directories to help identify your database files. You can create a directory named PERSONAL that contains only personal databases, another named COMPANY that contains only company-related databases, and so on. This system lets you use more than the eight file-name characters to describe the contents of the database.

To create a database named MYDB.MDB, select or enter the correct directory, enter **MYDB** for the database name, and then click OK. Access closes the dialog box and then displays the Database window (see fig. 3.11).

55

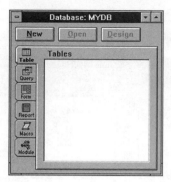

Figure 3.11. The Database window lists all the database objects.

Exploring the Database Window

For each category of database object, the Database window displays a list of all objects in each database.

Note: You may have heard the Database window referred to as the *Database Container*, but this is incorrect.

The different objects that make up a database appear in separate lists, each corresponding to one of the six database object buttons on the left side of the Database window:

- **Tables.** Store data.

- **Queries.** Ask questions about the data and result in dynasets, which frequently form the foundation for forms and reports.

- **Forms.** Display or edit data on-screen.

- **Reports.** Print hard copies of the data.

- **Macros.** Shortcuts for manipulating data and program flow.

- **Modules.** Contain functions (procedures) you use to enhance your database and create database applications.

A typical database has at least one table and one or more forms and reports. In addition, most databases contain queries, macros, and modules. Macros and modules are not limited to complex applications. Even seemingly simple applications can benefit from the use of macros and modules. The rest of this chapter describes the different database objects you can create in the Database window.

Using Database Objects

Six types of database objects exist in Microsoft Access: tables, queries, forms, reports, macros, and modules.

Using Tables

Tables are the most basic of the database objects. Indeed, the reason for even developing a database application is to store, manage, and report on data; tables act as the containers for that data.

Access stores data in tables as records, with each record having one or more fields. You may think of tables as you would a Microsoft Excel spreadsheet: each has multiple rows (in Access, these are called *records*) and columns (in Access, *fields*).

You can open a table and view the records in a familiar row-and-column format called *Datasheet View* (see fig. 3.12) by selecting the table in the Database window and clicking the Open button.

ID	Name	Address	City	State	ZIP	Phone
1	Cantaberry Realty	9202 MLK Blvd.	Seattle	WA	98004	206-555-8256
2	Morningside Real Estate	1200 4th Avenue	Seattle	WA	98002-1002	206-555-7390
3	Judson Realty	235 Union School Drive	Seattle	WA	98005	206-555-9633
4	Pacific Realty	600 NE 8th Avenue	Seattle	WA	98006-2080	206-555-9346
5	Argo Realty, Inc.	5400 N. Maple	Seattle	WA	98002	206-555-0893
6	Equinox Property Company	16135 NE 85th Street	Redmond	WA	98052-2411	206-555-1047
7	Grand Success Realty	16100 Cleveland Street	Redmond	WA	98052	206-555-8346
8	Fisher Group, The	3502 Ridge Lane	Seattle	WA	98005	206-555-8332
9	Plaza Associates	354 BellRed Road	Redmond	WA	98052-2691	206-555-0022
10	Atlantic Property Management	2203 Clinton Road	Seattle	WA	98002	206-555-0473

Table: Agencies — Record: 1 of 10

Figure 3.12. The Agencies table in Datasheet View.

At first glance, Datasheet View appears to be an easy way to present data. As you will see, however, you should avoid direct access to a table and should instead design a form to act as a front end to the data.

You can use a number of field data types to define the table's data: text, number, currency, counter, date/time, yes/no, memo, and OLE object. The following sections describe these and explain when you might choose each of them.

Text Fields

Use text fields to store textual information such as customer names, product names, ZIP codes, and so on. For example, the Agencies table in the HomeFinder application contains a text field to store the names of the various real estate agencies.

You can enter letters, numbers, common punctuation, and even high-bit ANSI characters in a text field. To enter a high-bit character, press and hold down the ALT key and then enter the four-digit ANSI number for the character you want. For a list of ANSI characters, search Help for "ANSI character".

Note: Microsoft Access uses the ANSI character set—not the ASCII character set. If you are accustomed to working with ASCII characters, you may need to compare the two sets of characters to see if there are any conflicts with any existing data you will bring into Access.

Number Fields

Use number fields to store numeric information such as inventory levels, square footage for a house, and quantities; but not dollar or currency amounts (for these, use a currency field, described in the next section).

You can use five kinds of number fields: byte, integer, long integer, double precision, and single precision. Depending on the kind you choose for a field, you can store whole numbers (for example, 200) or fractional values (for example, 200.25).

The numeric range—the lowest and highest value—is different for each specific number type.

Currency Fields

Use currency fields when you need to store large numbers that require rapid calculation, or numbers that require highly accurate rounding. For example, salary amounts and product prices are best stored in currency fields.

Currency fields are accurate to four decimal places.

Counter Fields

You may be unfamiliar with counter fields because they have no counterpart in older database products such as dBASE or Paradox. When you create a counter field, Access assigns consecutive numbers to the field. You can use counter fields to create unique ID numbers. For example, you can use a counter field to produce invoice numbers. Access increments successive counter fields by 1, starting with the value 1. You cannot manually update or otherwise change a counter field.

Access stores counter fields as long integers.

 Note: After you delete a record that contains a counter field, Access does not renumber the counter fields in the remaining records. As a rule, you should not worry about trying to reuse the deleted counter values.

Date/Time Fields

Use date/time fields to store date and time values. Date/time fields can appear in a variety of built-in or user-defined formats. For example, you can choose to display a date/time value as 1/9/62 or January 9, 1962.

You can store date and time data for the years 100AD to 9999AD.

Yes/No Fields

Use Yes/No fields to store information that can have only one of two values, such as Yes or No, True or False, or On or Off. Access stores Yes values as –1 and No values as 0, but when you display Yes/No fields in a datasheet, the words Yes and No appear (see fig. 3.13).

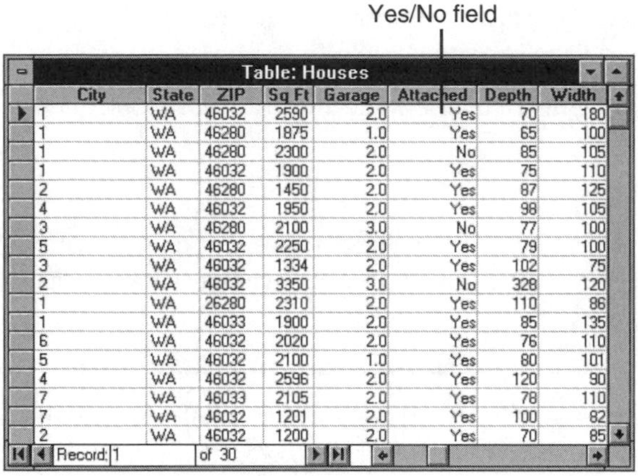

Yes/No field

City	State	ZIP	Sq Ft	Garage	Attached	Depth	Width
1	WA	46032	2590	2.0	Yes	70	180
1	WA	46280	1875	1.0	Yes	65	100
1	WA	46280	2300	2.0	No	85	105
1	WA	46032	1900	2.0	Yes	75	110
2	WA	46280	1450	2.0	Yes	87	125
4	WA	46032	1950	2.0	Yes	98	105
3	WA	46280	2100	3.0	No	77	100
5	WA	46032	2250	2.0	Yes	79	100
3	WA	46032	1334	2.0	Yes	102	75
2	WA	46032	3350	3.0	No	328	120
1	WA	26280	2310	2.0	Yes	110	86
1	WA	46033	1900	2.0	Yes	85	135
6	WA	46032	2020	2.0	Yes	76	110
5	WA	46032	2100	1.0	Yes	80	101
4	WA	46032	2596	2.0	Yes	120	90
7	WA	46033	2105	2.0	Yes	78	110
7	WA	46032	1201	2.0	Yes	100	82
2	WA	46032	1200	2.0	Yes	70	85

Table: Houses — Record: 1 of 30

Figure 3.13.   Yes/No fields display the words Yes or No.

To present Yes/No fields on forms and reports, you usually create check boxes that show the Yes/No, True/False, or On/Off state of the field. When the user selects (checks) a check box, Access stores Yes (–1) in the field; otherwise, Access stores No (0).

Memo Fields

Memo fields are much like text fields: you can use them to store notes, comments, longer descriptions, or anything you care to enter at the keyboard. Unlike text fields, which are limited to 255 characters, memo fields may contain up to 64,000 (slightly less than 64K) characters.

Your decision to use text or memo fields depends largely on two factors:

- **Amount of data.** If you think you will need to store more than 255 characters, go ahead and create a memo field, even if most of the records in the table will not need the extra capacity. Otherwise, you can change a text field to a memo field later on without any loss of data.

- **Searching.** You cannot create an index on memo fields.

OLE Object Fields

You use OLE (Object Linking and Embedding) object fields to embed or link to OLE objects from other Windows-based applications. OLE fields are used most commonly to display graphics, such as Paintbrush pictures, but you may want to embed waveform (.WAV) files to add special touches to your applications. You cannot create an index on an OLE object field.

The Houses table in the HomeFinder application includes an OLE object field to store house photos.

Using Queries

After you create some tables for your database, you will want to pose questions about the data, or you may want to modify the data in the tables. For example, you may want to know which houses meet all of your specified criteria, or which customers have not ordered within the past year. To answer these and other questions, you use queries.

You can use two main categories of queries: select queries and action queries.

Select Queries

Select queries retrieve selected information from tables, but do not change any of the data in the tables. When you run a select query, Access creates a dynaset that you can use as the source of data for forms and reports.

> **Note:** A *dynaset* is a set of records comprised of records from one or more tables. The data and number of records in the dynaset is *dynamic*, which means that the data can change as records are added, changed, or deleted from the underlying tables.

Crosstab queries are a special kind of select query typically used as the basis for charts and graphs. In a crosstab query, you define one row, one or more columns, and the intersecting value (see fig. 3.14).

City	50000: 99999	100000:149999	150000:199999	250000:299999	350000:399999
Bellevue	4			1	1
Fall City	1	1			
Forest Lake		1			
Lynnwood	2	1			
Redmond	2	1	1		
Seattle	2	6	2		
Woodinville	1	2	1		

Figure 3.14. Using crosstab queries to summarize data.

In this example, the crosstab query shows the number of houses in each city that fall into different price ranges.

For more information about select queries in general and crosstab queries in particular, see Chapter 7, "Building the HomeFinder Queries."

Action Queries

Unlike select queries, action queries modify data in the underlying tables. You can use four types of action queries:

- **Make-Table.** Creates a new table.

- **Append.** Adds records from one table to the end of another table.

- **Delete.** Deletes records from a table.

- **Update.** Modifies data according to specified criteria, such as increasing product prices by 5 percent.

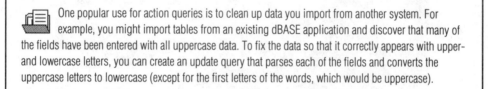 One popular use for action queries is to clean up data you import from another system. For example, you might import tables from an existing dBASE application and discover that many of the fields have been entered with all uppercase data. To fix the data so that it correctly appears with upper- and lowercase letters, you can create an update query that parses each of the fields and converts the uppercase letters to lowercase (except for the first letters of the words, which would be uppercase).

 Tip: Before you can run an action query, it is generally a good idea to create a select query that retrieves the same records. Then, when you are satisfied that the retrieved records really are the ones you want to change, convert the query to an action query.

When you run an action query, Access prompts you to make sure that you want to take the selected action (see fig. 3.15).

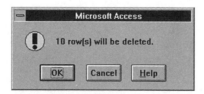

Figure 3.15.   Confirming that you want to delete 10 rows.

Using Forms

You use forms to display and enter information on-screen in a predefined layout. Most databases contain a variety of forms to display data from the underlying tables.

Forms are much like their paper counterparts, but have additional functionality that is available only in Access. You can create forms that contain any combination of text boxes, drop-down lists (combo boxes), check boxes, and graphics (see fig. 3.16). In addition, you can add error checking and data-entry validation to your forms—something that is not possible with paper forms.

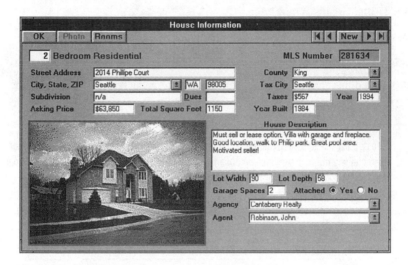

Figure 3.16. The Houses form, with a wide variety of controls and features.

 For more information about creating forms, see Chapter 8, "Building the HomeFinder Forms."

Using Reports

Like forms, reports present information in specific, predetermined layouts. Creating a report is nearly identical to the process you follow to create a form. In fact, you can even create a report directly from an existing form.

Like a form, you can view a report on-screen or create a hard copy on the printer. The essential difference between forms and reports is that reports simply present information—you cannot enter new information in a report like you can in a form. You can also group and summarize information more easily with reports than with forms.

Figures 3.17 and 3.18 illustrate a report based on information in the HomeFinder sample application. This view, called Print Preview, enables you to see what the report will look like before you actually print it.

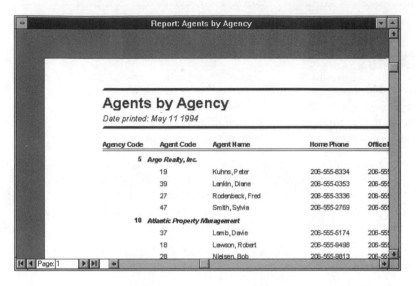

Figure 3.17. Previewing a report on-screen.

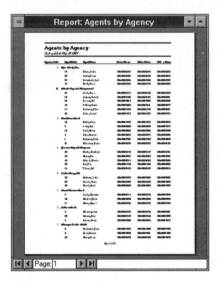

Figure 3.18. Zooming out to view an entire page.

For more information about creating reports, see Chapter 10, "Building the HomeFinder Reports."

Using Macros

If you have used Microsoft Word for Windows or Microsoft Excel, you may be familiar with macros. In those applications, you use macros to record sequences of keystrokes for playback later. This feature lets you define ahead of time the actions the macro takes when you run it. For example, you can automate the process of loading and printing a document.

Access macros work differently than macros in Word for Windows or Excel. Although you cannot directly record keystrokes (there is no macro recorder), you still can define a sequence of events the macro should perform. These events are called *macro actions*. You build a macro by including one or more macro actions that correspond to the desired activity. Macro actions can open forms, find records, and print reports.

Many of the macros you create can be built entirely by selecting items from drop-down lists. Some macro actions require you to enter form names, formatting expressions, and so on, but there is no real programming involved.

 Tip: For all their simplicity, macros do not provide a complete programming environment. Macros offer no error handling, are difficult to debug, and do not provide the debugging capabilities available in modules (see the next section, "Using Modules"). You will use the macro actions, however, in modules, not macros.

 For more information about creating macros, see Chapter 9, "Building the HomeFinder Macros" and Chapter 12, "Migrating from Macros to Modules."

Using Modules

Modules in Microsoft Access are functionally the same as modules in Microsoft Visual Basic and equivalent to programs in dBASE or Paradox. You can think of Access modules as collections of declarations, statements, and procedures written with the Access Basic programming language.

You create modules to contain custom, user-defined function procedures (or functions). For example, you may create a function that determines whether a specified form is loaded:

```
Function csvFormIsLoaded (ByVal MyFormName As String) As Integer

    ' Purpose: Determines whether a specified form is loaded.
    ' Accepts: MyFormName - string that is the form to test.
    ' Returns: True  - the form is loaded.
    '          False - the form is not loaded.
    ' Version: 1.0 23-Mar-94 CSV Initial revision.
    ' ------------------------------------------------------------
    Dim X As String

    On Error Resume Next
    X = Forms(MyFormName).FormName
    If Err Then
        csvFormIsLoaded = False
    Else
        csvFormIsLoaded = True
    End If
    On Error GoTo 0

End Function
```

Because Access does not come with a built-in function that determines whether a form is loaded, you need to create that function yourself.

Function procedures (or functions) are the building blocks for any serious application. You can use functions in forms, reports, and queries, and you can call functions from within macros.

Because functions are so important to your success with Access, you should devote as much time as necessary to acquire a thorough knowledge of Access Basic. You do not need to master Access Basic, but you should develop at least an understanding of when it is necessary to use code and where to look for help.

> It is not within the scope of this book to teach you how to program, but if you can learn by example, you should see Chapter 21, "Useful Functions," for code you can use in your own applications.

Getting Help

Microsoft Access features an award-winning, on-line help system (Help) containing topic discussions beyond that in the printed documentation. Help is always available, even when the printed documentation is not at hand.

You can display Help by pressing the F1 key, by choosing a command from the Help menu, or by clicking the Help button on the toolbar (see fig. 3.19).

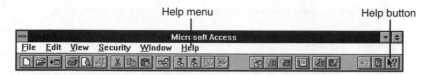

Figure 3.19. Accessing Help.

Using Online Help

The online Help system features a general summary as well as a number of summaries more finely tuned to specific product areas (see fig. 3.20).

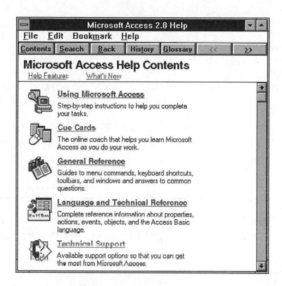

Figure 3.20. Viewing the major categories of help available.

After you press F1, Access displays help that is appropriate to the area of the product you are in, or the action you are trying to perform. For example, if you are building a query and ask for help by pressing F1, Access displays the Queries help topic (see fig. 3.21).

After you click Help on the toolbar, the mouse pointer changes to an arrow with a question mark. Move the mouse pointer to any area on-screen and then click the mouse. Access displays context-sensitive help that relates to the area of the screen on which you just clicked.

While you are coding in the Module window, you can move the insertion point (the I-beam) to any word in the window and then press F1. If the word is a *reserved* word—a word that is built into the Access Basic language—Access displays help for that reserved word.

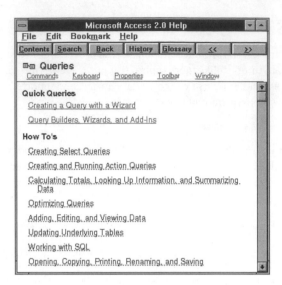

Figure 3.21. Displaying context-sensitive help while building a query.

For example, you may write a function that uses the OpenForm macro action. If you forget details about the action, you can place the insertion point on the word `OpenForm` and then press F1; Access displays the relevant help topic (see fig. 3.22).

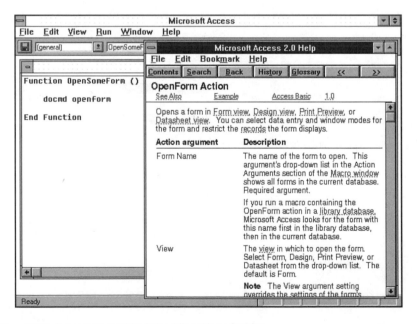

Figure 3.22. Displaying context-sensitive help while writing a function.

Using Cue Cards

The Cue Cards feature guides you through common Access procedures in a step-by-step manner, as if you had your own private tutor. Unlike more typical computer-based tutorials, however, Cue Cards lets you learn about Access while you use your own data, forms, and reports. With Cue Cards, you do not waste time; instead, you perform real work as you learn.

Cue Cards exhibit a few unusual characteristics:

- Cue Cards appear on top of all other windows (not just Access windows), as long as Cue Cards remains loaded and Access is not minimized to an icon. To work effectively with child windows (forms, reports, and so on) in the main Access window, you may have to rearrange your forms, tables, reports, and other objects.

- After you open Cue Cards from Help, Help closes automatically. You can reopen Help after Cue Cards starts.

- You cannot resize the Cue Cards window, but you can move the window, and you can minimize Cue Cards if you need to see what is under the Cue Cards window. Like the Cue Cards window, the Cue Cards icon remains on top of any Access windows.

Cue Cards' unusual characteristics were designed to keep Cue Cards close at hand as you learn how to use Microsoft Access. When you finish studying the Cue Cards relating to an Access topic, close Cue Cards by double-clicking the control menu or by choosing the Close command from the control menu.

You start Cue Cards by choosing Cue Cards from the Help menu or by selecting a Cue Cards topic from any Help topic (see figs. 3.23 and 3.24).

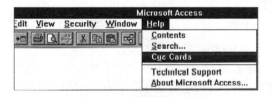

Figure 3.23. Opening Cue Cards from the Help menu.

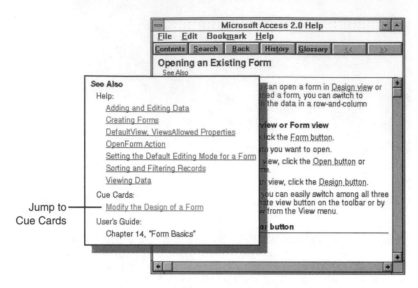

Figure 3.24. Using Help topics featuring direct jumps to Cue Card topics.

Summary

In a network environment, you can install Microsoft Access locally on each workstation or on the network server. Each technique has its advantages and disadvantages, so you should analyze the way you expect to work with Access before you proceed with the installation procedure.

The Microsoft Access development environment is rich with the tools you need to develop a professional database application. You can build powerful queries, usable forms, and highly effective reports quickly and easily. Access also features macros and modules you can create to make your applications more powerful and flexible.

For added effect, you can embed or link a wide variety of OLE objects in your Access databases, including pictures and sounds.

Online Help and Cue Cards are available at the click of a button to help you learn about using Access more efficiently than a more typical trial-and-error approach provides.

4

Customizing the Access Environment

It would be unusual for any off-the-shelf software, including Microsoft Access, to behave exactly as you would like. Because you have your own preferences, Access lets you change the development environment and how the various database objects behave.

You change the way in which Access performs by setting various options. Although many users are pleased with the default settings and will never need to change any of the options, this chapter describes how you can easily change the settings if you want to.

Access offers nine option categories:

- General
- Keyboard
- Printing
- Form & Report Design
- Datasheet
- Query Design
- Macro Design
- Module Design
- Multiuser/ODBC

This chapter discusses each of these categories and offers tips on how you can best set the various options.

The Options Command

When you change option settings, Access writes the changes to a file named SYSTEM.MDA. Any changes you make to the options are global, which means that the changes apply to all databases you open. They also apply to all users in the same workgroup (a workgroup is defined by having users share a common SYSTEM.MDA file).

To change an Access option, you first must open an existing database or create a new database. If you have not created your own database, you can choose the Open Database command from the File menu and then open the HomeFinder sample application.

Choose the Options command from the View menu. Access displays the Options dialog box (see fig. 4.1).

At the top of the dialog box is a list box with the names of the nine option categories (General, Keyboard, and so on). The lower section of the dialog box lists all the settings available for the selected category. In figure 4.1, Access displays all the settings for the General category.

Most of the items feature drop-down lists you can open in order to choose from the valid settings. Other items, however, require you to enter the appropriate value. If you make a mistake and enter an inappropriate value, Access prompts you to correct your entry.

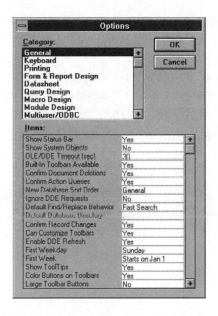

Figure 4.1.   Using the Options dialog box to change system-wide settings.

> **Tip:** In addition to using the Options command, you can also set certain options by choosing commands on various menus. For example, when you are working with forms in Design View, you can quickly turn the ruler on and off by choosing the Ruler command without having to change the default behavior established with the Options command.

To save your changes and close the dialog box, click OK. If you want to close the dialog box without saving any of your changes, click Cancel.

General Options

Figure 4.2 illustrates the General options and their original default values.

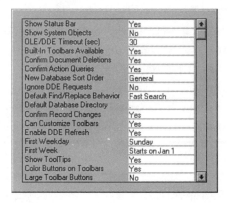

Figure 4.2. The General options.

Set the General options to customize elements common to the entire Access environment, such as whether to prompt the user to confirm the deletion of objects from the database.

Show Status Bar

This option controls whether to display the status bar along the bottom of the Access window (see fig. 4.3). Depending on where you are in Access, the status bar displays different information. For example, when you are in Form View, the status bar displays the status bar text for the active control.

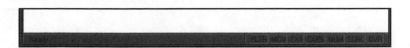

Figure 4.3.   Status bar indicators.

The status bar also displays information about the state of the keyboard. Table 4.1 lists the various indicators Access displays in the status bar.

Table 4.1.   Modes and Locking Keys

Indicator	Description
CAPS	The Caps Lock key is on.
EXT	Extend mode is on (for extending the selection of fields or records). Press Esc to cancel extend mode.
FLTR	A filter for screening records is in effect.
MOV	Move mode is on (for moving columns in a datasheet, in the QBE grid, or in a Filter window). Press Esc to cancel move mode.
NUM	The Num Lock key is on.
OVR	Overtype mode is on. Press the Ins key to cancel overtype mode.
SCRL	The Scroll Lock key is on.

> **Note:** Because the status bar information is so useful, and because it does not take up much screen space, few users turn off the status bar.

Show System Objects

When you set this option to Yes, Access displays system objects in the Database window (see fig. 4.4).

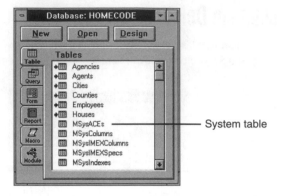

Figure 4.4. Showing system objects in the Database window.

System objects are tables that contain internal Access information about the structure of your database. These tables begin with the letters *MSys*. System objects also include tables and other database objects you create and name with the letters *USys*.

There is usually no reason to display the names of system objects, so most users leave the Show System Objects setting to the default, No.

OLE/DDE Timeout

This option sets the interval after which Access reattempts a failed Object Linking and Embedding (OLE) or Dynamic Data Exchange (DDE) operation.

OLE is a Windows technology that lets you embed or link to documents created in other applications. For example, you can embed a waveform (.WAV) file or link a Microsoft Excel spreadsheet to an Access form.

If you have a particularly slow computer system, or if you are linking to documents located on another system in a network environment, you may need to increase the OLE/DDE Timeout setting to give Access enough time to establish a link. For most stand-alone computers, however, the default setting of 30 (seconds) should be sufficient.

Built-In Toolbars Available

This option controls whether to display the various built-in toolbars along the top of the Access window. This setting does not determine whether your own custom toolbars appear.

Depending on where you are in Access, the built-in toolbars display different buttons and other controls (for example, combo boxes). Most of the toolbars contain Undo and Help buttons.

Confirm Document Deletions

In Microsoft Access, a document is any database object: a table, query, form, report, macro, or module. By default, Access prompts you to confirm document deletions (see fig. 4.5).

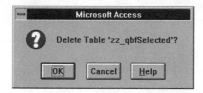

Figure 4.5.   Confirming document deletions.

Although this feature can prevent you from deleting the wrong object, it can slow you down a bit. If you do not think it is likely that you accidentally will delete an object, and you tend to delete objects frequently, you can set this option to No and save a small amount of time. It is probably best, however, to leave Confirm Document Deletions set to Yes.

Confirm Action Queries

By default, whenever you run an action query, Access prompts you to confirm the impending operation (see fig. 4.6).

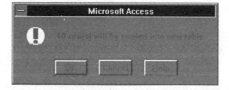

Figure 4.6.   Answering a prompt before running action queries.

Like the Confirm Document Deletions option, this option is a safety feature that you can disable if you want. Because running an action query actually modifies the underlying data, however, you should consider leaving Confirm Action Queries set to the default, Yes.

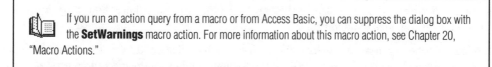

If you run an action query from a macro or from Access Basic, you can suppress the dialog box with the **SetWarnings** macro action. For more information about this macro action, see Chapter 20, "Macro Actions."

New Database Sort Order

This option gives you a choice of 14 alphabetic sort orders for any new databases you create (see fig. 4.7). When you choose a sort order for the database, Access arranges text in the correct alphabetical order for the selected language (different languages have different character sequences), taking into account any special diacritical marks or unique characters in the language.

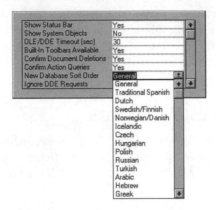

Figure 4.7. Choosing the sort order appropriate for the database you want to create.

 For more information about setting the sort order, and for charts that list the exact character sequences, search Help for "sort order: language specific."

To change the sort order for an existing database, change the New Database Sort Order setting, close the database, and then compact the database by choosing the Compact Database command from the File menu. For more information about compacting a database, see Chapter 23, "Data Compaction, Backups, and Data Recovery."

Ignore DDE Requests

This option offers you a choice of ignoring or accepting DDE (Dynamic Data Exchange) requests from other applications that may try to communicate with Microsoft Access.

If you ignore these requests by setting the option to Yes, other applications produce errors when they try to establish DDE links with Access.

Default Find/Replace Behavior

When you use the Find or Replace dialog boxes, the Default Find/Replace Behavior option offers you two choices:

- **Fast Search**. Searches only the current field and looks for exact matches on the entire field. This process is faster than a general search.

- **General Search**. Examines all fields and matches any part of the field. Depending on how many fields the search involves, this technique can be much slower than the fast search technique. General searching may be necessary, however, if you do not know which field might contain the information you are seeking.

Default Database Directory

This option determines the default directory Access uses when you open databases (you can override the default by navigating the Open Database dialog box). Unless you change the default setting, Access looks in the same directory in which Access was installed. In Access, this directory is represented by a period (.).

You should avoid placing databases in your Access directory, and instead consider creating separate directories for each of your applications. Then, set the default database directory to the location of your most-used database.

Confirm Record Changes

When you set this option to Yes, Access prompts you to confirm before it deletes or pastes records, or makes changes with the Replace command (see fig. 4.8).

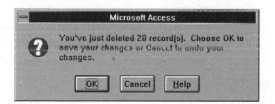

Figure 4.8. Confirming that you want to delete records.

Confirm Record Changes is yet another safety feature that enables you to back out of an unintended deletion or change to data.

Can Customize Toolbars

This option allows or prohibits you from modifying the built-in toolbars, and from creating custom toolbars using the tools in the Toolbars dialog box.

Enable DDE Refresh

This option enables or disables the Refresh Interval setting in the Multiuser/ODBC category.

 Note: The Refresh Interval setting specifies the interval at which Access updates DDE links.

First Weekday

Depending on the country you work in, the first day of the week may be Sunday, Monday, or some other day. The first day of the week in the United States is Sunday, but in Germany it is Monday.

This option directly affects only reports in which the **DateGrouping** property is set to Use Options, or reports that use the **Format**, **DatePart**, or **DateDiff** functions.

You also may find it convenient or even necessary to read the value of the First Weekday option in your own functions. You may create a calendar form that starts each week with the day specified by the user. For more information about determining the option setting, search Help for "GetOption."

First Week

Set this option to indicate what constitutes the first week of a new calendar year. This option affects only the **Format**, **DatePart**, and **DateDiff** functions. Unlike the First Weekday option, the First Week option does not affect reports, queries, or other database objects.

Show ToolTips

You can use this option to enable or disable *ToolTips*—brief descriptions that appear when you move the mouse pointer over buttons or combo boxes on toolbars, the palette, or the toolbox (see fig. 4.9).

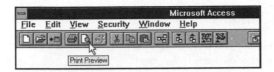

Figure 4.9. Using ToolTips to identify buttons on toolbars.

Color Buttons on Toolbars

You can set this option to display colored toolbar buttons or monochrome buttons. In some screen resolutions, the buttons appear so small that the color elements in the buttons may be annoying. You can turn off the color by setting the Color Buttons on Toolbars option to No, or by enlarging the size of the buttons (see the next section, "Large Toolbar Buttons").

Large Toolbar Buttons

This option lets you display toolbar buttons in a larger, easier-to-read size.

> **Tip:** The larger toolbar buttons are intended for use with screen resolutions higher than regular VGA. If you enable large toolbar buttons on a system using a regular VGA screen driver, some buttons on either end of the toolbar may disappear from view (see fig. 4.10). To see all the buttons, drag the toolbar from its docked position to a convenient location on-screen.

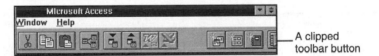

A clipped toolbar button

Figure 4.10. Handling truncated or missing toolbar buttons.

Keyboard Options

Set this option to customize how the keyboard behaves in Access. These choices are a matter of personal preference; users often feel most comfortable with arrow-key and cursor movements similar to other applications they have used before. Figure 4.11 shows the keyboard options and their original default values.

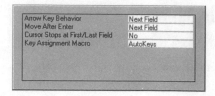

Figure 4.11. The keyboard options.

 Note: The third option (Cursor Stops at First/Last Field) affects keyboard behavior in Datasheet View only.

 Tip: You can change the default keyboard behavior to suit your own preferences, but if you do, another person who uses your system may be confused.

Arrow Key Behavior

You can set this option to Next Character or Next Field. If you choose Next Character, you can press the left- and right-arrow keys to move the caret (the insertion point) to the preceding or next character. If you choose Next Field, you can press the arrow key to move the focus to the preceding (or next) control or field.

Move After Enter

This option determines the action that Access takes after you press ENTER. You can choose from three settings:

- **No**. The focus does not move.
- **Next Field**. The focus moves to the beginning of the next control or field (column).
- **Next Record**. The focus moves to the first control or field in the next record.

Cursor Stops at First/Last Field

This option has two possible settings:

- **Yes**. The cursor (the caret or insertion point) stops at the first or last field in a row, depending on which direction you move with the left- and right-arrow keys.

- **No**. If the cursor is in the last field (column) of the row, you can press the right-arrow key to move the cursor to the first field of the next row. If the cursor is in the first field of the row, you can press the left-arrow key to move the cursor to the last field of the preceding row.

If you are accustomed to the cursor wrapping down to the beginning of the next row after leaving the end of the current row, leave this option set to No. Otherwise, the cursor stops at the end of the row.

Key Assignment Macro

This option enables you to enter the name of a custom key assignment macro. The default key assignment macro name is AutoKeys.

A *key assignment macro* is an optional, special macro group that contains macros that run assigned macro actions after the user presses a specified key sequence. For example, instead of closing the active form, you may want to execute a different sequence of events whenever the user presses Ctrl | F4.

   For more information about the AutoKeys macro, see Chapter 9, "Building the HomeFinder Macros."

Printing Options

Set this option to customize the margins Access uses when you print datasheets, modules, and new forms and reports. The *margin settings* are the distances from the edges of the paper to the sides, top, and bottom of the text or graphics. Figure 4.12 shows the printing options and their default values.

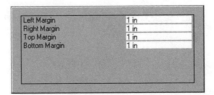

Figure 4.12.   The Printing Options settings.

When you enter the default margin settings, you can enter inches, centimeters, or twips (a *twip* is equal to 1/1440 inch—a very precise unit of measurement).

 Note: These settings affect printing and Print Preview only—not Design View.

Form & Report Design Options

Set the form and report design options to customize the Access workspace you use to design forms and reports. You probably will not need to change to another form or report template, but you may want to adjust the remaining options to suit your preferences. Figure 4.13 shows the form and report design options and their original default values.

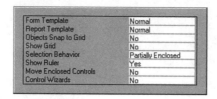

Form Template	Normal
Report Template	Normal
Objects Snap to Grid	No
Show Grid	No
Selection Behavior	Partially Enclosed
Show Ruler	Yes
Move Enclosed Controls	No
Control Wizards	No

Figure 4.13.   The form and report design options.

Form Template

When you create a new form without one of the form wizards (described later in Chapter 8, "Building the HomeFinder Forms"), Access looks to see if you have set the Form Template option to the name of an existing form. If you enter the name of a form, Access uses that form as the template for the new form. This procedure has the same effect as making a copy of the existing form and then renaming it with the new form's name.

Report Template

Much like the Form Template setting, when you create a new report without one of the report wizards, Access looks to see if you have set the Report Template option to the name of an existing report. If you enter the name of a report, Access uses that report as the template for the new report.

Objects Snap to Grid

When set to Yes, this option causes controls on a form or report to "snap" to the grid dots. You easily can align multiple controls because when you drag a control and release the mouse, the control moves to the nearest grid point.

When you resize an item, the edge or corner you drag snaps to the nearest grid point, thus making it easier to make several boxes the same height or width.

For more information about other techniques you can use to align and size multiple controls, see Chapter 8, "Building the HomeFinder Forms."

Show Grid

This option controls the display of grid dots on a form or report in Design View.

When the grid is on and the Objects Snap to Grid option is set to Yes, you can choose the Size to Grid command from the Format menu. This command resizes the selected controls to the nearest grid points.

Selection Behavior

This option determines which controls are selected when you use the mouse to drag a rectangle to enclose a group of controls. You can choose from two settings:

- **Partially Enclosed**. A control is included in the group if any part of the control is inside the selection rectangle.

- **Fully Enclosed**. A control is selected only if it is completely inside the selection rectangle.

Partially Enclosed lets you select a group of relatively large controls by drawing a small rectangle that includes a small part of each control.

In contrast, if you have many controls placed irregularly on your form or report, you may prefer to use Fully Enclosed. Drawing a rectangle around the objects you want to select makes it easier to exclude unwanted controls.

You also can select multiple controls by clicking the mouse on the ruler. For more information about using the ruler, see Chapter 8, "Building the HomeFinder Forms."

84

Show Ruler

This option setting determines whether Access displays the vertical and horizontal rulers in Form and Report Design View (see fig. 4.14).

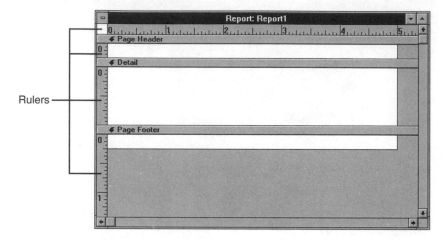

Rulers

Figure 4.14. Displaying rulers in Design View.

You also can toggle the rulers on and off by choosing the Ruler command from the View menu.

Move Enclosed Controls

When you move a control, this option determines whether all other controls completely enclosed within the selected control are moved as well. This situation most often occurs when you select an option group or a rectangle control that has other controls inside it.

Control Wizards

This option setting determines whether the control wizards are active or inactive.

For more information about control wizards, see Chapter 8, "Building the HomeFinder Forms," and Chapter 19, "Creating and Using Libraries."

 Note: This option does not affect the Graph Wizard when you add a graph control to a form or report; the Graph Wizard is always active.

Datasheet Options

Set these options to customize elements that determine how Access displays new or existing query datasheets, and new table and form datasheets. The datasheet format may remind you of spreadsheets because of its familiar row-and-column format. Figure 4.15 shows the datasheet options and their original default values.

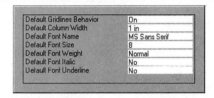

Figure 4.15. The datasheet options.

Default Gridlines Behavior

This option controls whether Access displays gridlines in the datasheet. When the gridlines are on, the datasheet looks similar to a spreadsheet, with visible lines defining the rows and columns.

Default Column Width

You can set the default datasheet column width from 0 to 22 inches (55.87 cm). You can enter the width in inches, centimeters, or twips (1/1440 inch).

> **Tip:** If your datasheets tend to contain mostly numbers, set the default width to smaller values (for example, .5 in) so that you can see more columns at one time. If you often have long text fields, you should set the column width to a larger value.

Text Formatting Options

The remaining datasheet options control the style, size, weight, and emphasis of the text Access uses to display field names and data in datasheets. You can set the following options:

- **Default Font Name**. The default font, MS Sans Serif, is specially designed for optimal screen display, even at smaller font sizes. It is generally the most readable font available on most users' machines, so it is probably best to leave the default font name set to MS Sans Serif.

86

- **Default Font Size**. On a standard VGA system, the 8-point font size is the smallest size that is still legible. If your datasheets tend to be small or if you find the 8-point font size hard to read, select a larger font size.

- **Default Font Weight**. On some displays, the Normal font weight may be too thin; you may want to set the weight to Bold or Semi-Bold to achieve a darker display.

- **Default Font Italic**. On most displays, italic text is not very legible, even at 1024 x 768 resolution; it is almost unusable on a standard (640 x 480) VGA display. Remember that this option setting affects all the text in the datasheet.

- **Default Font Underline**. Like Default Font Italic, the font underline setting applies to all text in the datasheet.

Query Design Options

Set the query design options to customize elements common to the query design environment. Figure 4.16 shows the query design options and their original default values.

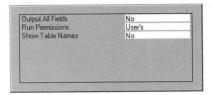

Figure 4.16. The query design options.

Output All Fields

Output All Fields has two possible settings:

- **Yes**. The query includes all the fields from all the query's underlying tables, even if you do not explicitly select the fields.

- **No**. The query output includes only the fields you explicitly select.

> **STOP** **WARNING:** In versions of Microsoft Access prior to release 2.0, this option was called Restrict Available Fields. In those prior releases, you set the option to Yes if you want only the selected fields to appear in the query output, and to No if you want all the fields to appear.

Run Permissions

This option affects only new queries, and only in a multiuser environment with a secure system. This option lets users (who otherwise lack the appropriate permissions to access certain database objects) view forms or run queries. You can choose from two options:

- **Owner's**. Users assume the permissions of the query's owner.

- **User's**. User's own permissions are used.

> You may want to prevent most users from viewing an Employees table that contains salary information. If you have a form based on the Employees table (even a form that does not contain the Salary field), only those users with permission to view the Employees table can open the form. To allow these users to open the form, you set the Run Permissions option to Owner's.

To change the behavior of an existing query, or to override the default behavior established by the Run Permissions option setting, you can set the Run Permissions property that has the same effects.

> For more information about permissions and secure systems, see Chapter 22, "Implementing Security." For more information about setting query properties, see Chapter 7, "Building the HomeFinder Queries."

Show Table Names

When you set this option to Yes, Access displays table names on a separate row in the QBE grid. This method is useful only when the query is based on more than one table, however, and is particularly helpful when you have multiple fields with the same or similar field names.

Macro Design Options

Figure 4.17 shows the macro design options and their original default values.

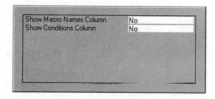

Figure 4.17. The macro design options.

When you set these options to Yes and then create a new macro, Access displays the Macro Name and Condition columns in the Macro window.

To display or hide the columns for an existing macro, choose the Macro Names or Conditions commands from the View menu.

 For more information about the macro design environment, see Chapter 9, "Building the HomeFinder Macros."

Module Design Options

Figure 4.18 illustrates the module design options and their original default values.

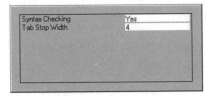

| Syntax Checking | Yes |
| Tab Stop Width | 4 |

Figure 4.18. The module design options.

Set the module design options to customize the Module window and the way in which you write Access Basic code.

- **Syntax Checking**. Like other programming languages, Access Basic has a particular syntax you must follow. This option determines whether Access checks for correct syntax when you enter a line of code. Even if you set this option to No, Access checks all the syntax in your code whenever you compile your modules.

- **Tab Stop Width**. This option controls the number of spaces between tab stops. When you press the Tab key, Access adds enough spaces to advance the caret to the next tab stop, much like on a typewriter.

  You should avoid changing the default Tab Stop Width setting; narrower tab stops result in harder-to-read code, and wider tab stops produce excessively wide blocks of code.

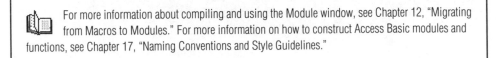 For more information about compiling and using the Module window, see Chapter 12, "Migrating from Macros to Modules." For more information on how to construct Access Basic modules and functions, see Chapter 17, "Naming Conventions and Style Guidelines."

Multiuser/ODBC Options

Set the multiuser/ODBC options to customize the way Access behaves in a multiuser environment and how Access updates records accessed with ODBC (Open Database Connectivity). Figure 4.19 shows the multiuser and ODBC options and their original default values.

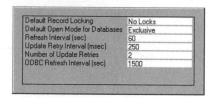

Default Record Locking	No Locks
Default Open Mode for Databases	Exclusive
Refresh Interval (sec)	60
Update Retry Interval (msec)	250
Number of Update Retries	2
ODBC Refresh Interval (sec)	1500

Figure 4.19. The multiuser and ODBC options.

Default Record Locking

This option offers you three settings when you open tables, forms, or queries:

- **No Locks**. No records will be locked.

- **All Records**. All records in the underlying tables will be locked. If you use this setting, you cannot view any records in attached SQL server tables. For more information about attached tables, see Chapter 6, "Building the HomeFinder Tables."

- **Edited Record**. Only the current record being edited will be locked.

Default Open Mode for Databases

After you choose the Open Database command from the File menu, you can open a database in exclusive or nonexclusive mode. The Default Open Mode for Databases option controls the state of the Exclusive check box in the dialog box. You can choose from two settings:

- **Exclusive**. The Exclusive check box is selected (checked).

- **Shared**. The Exclusive check box is cleared (not checked).

Tip: When you open a database exclusively, no other user can open the same database. To allow other users simultaneous access to the same database, set the default open mode to Shared (and leave the Exclusive check box cleared when you choose the Open Database command).

Refresh Settings

The interval options control the timing of several refresh intervals. Depending on the speed of your particular computer system (mostly a hardware consideration), these settings may need to be set to higher values. For the following options, the smaller the setting, the shorter the interval.

- **Refresh Interval**. Sets the interval at which Access refreshes records in the current form or datasheet. Valid values are from 1 to 32,766 (seconds).

- **Update Retry Interval**. Sets the interval at which Access tries to save a changed record that is locked by another user. Valid values are from 0 to 1000 (milliseconds). 1000 milliseconds equal one second.

Number of Update Retries

This option setting determines the number of times Access tries to save a changed record that is locked by another user.

The maximum amount of time it takes to successfully update a record may be calculated by multiplying the Update Retry Interval setting by the Number of Update retries setting. If the interval is set to 250 milliseconds and the number of retries is set to 2, the maximum time will be 500 milliseconds, or one-half second.

Depending on the option settings, Access can take as long as 10 seconds to successfully save one record.

ODBC Refresh Interval

This option controls the interval at which Access refreshes records you are accessing with ODBC. The smaller the setting, the shorter the interval. Valid values are from 1 to 3600 seconds (60 minutes).

Summary

This chapter described ways that you can customize the Access to suit your preferences and the needs of your applications and users.

You can change many of the default option settings at run time by choosing menu commands.

5

The HomeFinder Application

One important task you have as a database developer or administrator is to design a flexible, manageable database. Using a powerful database management system, such as Access, does not guarantee reliable data if the underlying database design is flawed. In many respects, Access is only as useful as the underlying design of the database on which it operates.

Applying a methodical approach to designing an application is important. To help illustrate key concepts, this chapter uses the HomeFinder sample database application included on the disk that accompanies this book.

This chapter covers the following:

- Developing a Design Strategy
- Performing a Needs Analysis
- Identifying the Data Requirements
- Developing a Database Design
- Normalizing the Database
- Creating the New Database

Developing a Design Strategy

Resist the temptation to install Microsoft Access and immediately start developing your application. You get the most out of Access when you develop a design strategy—or road map—of where you intend to go and how you intend to get there.

If you do not define a strategy, you may spend extra time resolving design mistakes. Your application also may not be as efficient and robust as it could be. Figure 5.1 illustrates a typical development strategy.

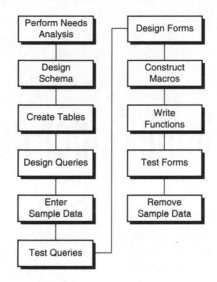

Figure 5.1. A typical development "road map."

The most important thing you can do to ensure the success of your application is to first define the objectives of the application. Many developers start designing tables and forms without a clear understanding of what they are trying to accomplish. For example, a reasonably normalized database supported by efficient queries and user-friendly forms is not usually the objective.

Rather, the objective often is a set of reports, especially if you are computerizing a manual paper system. Remember, users do not care about table design. While they like easy-to-use forms, the real objective is the application's output—what the system does, not how it does it. For this reason, performing a needs analysis is the most important aspect of database development.

Next, define the schema, or structure, for the database. The *schema* is little more than a picture of the relationships among all data. The needs analysis you create makes this step easy because you have already defined the data necessary to implement the application's objectives.

Finally, use Access to implement the database design. This process is much like having to first flowchart a program before you can write a line of code. Most programmers know how to create a flowchart, but few actually do it. It is time-consuming, difficult to do because of the lack of appropriate tools, and hardly anybody ever refers to the flowcharts after the code is written.

Even so, a written strategy for your application makes it much easier to implement your design. Figure 5.1 illustrates an ideal sequence of events. In real life, however, you may back up to previous steps. For example, you may realize that you need to create an additional table to store information you did not anticipate during the needs analysis stage.

Performing a Needs Analysis

To design efficiently, define your information needs and objectives clearly. One way to do this is to analyze the current flow of data. This might be an existing computerized system or a manual system you are computerizing. Consider also the decision-making processes. For example, company executives often need only summary information, while line managers require more detailed information.

Noticing how information is being used is particularly important. If an Access application is to replace a manual or older, computerized system, take a close look at the older database and determine whether it adequately represents the data.

This is a good time to decide whether the current database structure requires changes because it either is not normalized or does not track the kinds of information now needed.

 For more information about normalizing the database, see "Normalizing the Database" later in this chapter.

Next, study the forms, reports, and other output from the existing system to determine their intended purposes and to see whether they should be duplicated in the new Access database. These reports often provide an excellent way to determine which data elements to continue to use and which are obsolete and may be omitted in the new system.

Another key aspect of this identification process is talking with the people who will use the database—the users. Your objective is to determine the specific information they need to maintain and the form in which they intend to use it.

 Note: Although asking users what they want is important, part of your responsibility is to design and implement a usable application that takes all users' needs into account. Unless you are developing an application for one user only, this sometimes means making compromises.

Talking with different users gives you different views of the data. For example, in the HomeFinder application, managers have their own perspective concerning the database and the information it should maintain. Sales representatives have another view, which frequently involves a finer level of detail about houses (see fig. 5.2).

As the database designer, your objective is to consolidate all views so that you can create a single database that satisfies each user's data requirements.

Identifying the Data Requirements

If you have existing forms and reports that you intend to duplicate in Access, you already have a good idea what kind of data you need to maintain. If you have no existing system, then you need to get your users to tell you what their objectives are. Again, this is not quite the same as asking what data they need to store.

For example, do not ask users to provide a list of the fields that need to be in the Houses table. Users cannot be expected to know anything about database design or table structures. Your objective at this development stage is simply to identify the data that needs to be tracked. The next section, "Developing an Initial Database Design," discusses how you can translate this list of needs into a usable structure.

For the HomeFinder application, real estate agents and prospective home buyers were each asked to identify the kinds of things they want to know about houses and house listings. Home buyers said they want to know where a house is located, its asking price, how many bedrooms, and so on. Agents want to know the MLS number, listing date, and expiration date—information that is largely unimportant to home buyers.

The HomeFinder application is intended to be used by both home buyers and real estate agents, so the database design must accommodate both sets of data requirements (see fig. 5.2).

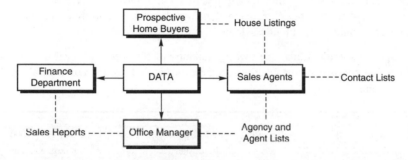

Figure 5.2. Different groups of users have different data needs.

The HomeFinder application must maintain several "sets" of information including houses, their listing agents, the agencies for whom the agents work, and company employees. The following tables list the initial data requirements. As you see in the next sections, however, these lists do not necessarily correspond to the final table definitions.

Table 5.1. Data Requirements for Houses

Requirement
Address
Square Footage
Number of Bedrooms
Number of Bathrooms
Asking Price
Name of Listing Agent
Tax Information
MLS Number

Table 5.2. Data Requirements for Agencies

Requirement
Name
Address
Phone Numbers

Table 5.3. Data Requirements for Agents

Requirement
Name
Name of Agency
Phone Numbers

Table 5.4. Data Requirements for Employees

Requirement
Name
Birthday
Phone Numbers
Hire Date
Job Title
Supervisor's Name

Developing a Database Design

After you identify the specific data needs for the application, you can develop a database design. Consider this an initial design because you will likely make changes as you go along. The following steps outline a general procedure you can follow to design a new database.

1. First, group the various data requirements into broad categories. You will refine these categories and eventually create corresponding tables. In the preceding section, tables 5.1 through 5.4 illustrate four categories of requirements: house-related, agency-related, agent-related, and employee-related.

2. Look at the individual requirements (fields) in your lists and ask the following questions about each field:

   - Does the data requirement specify the need for multiple fields? For example, addresses require separate fields for street addresses, cities, states, and ZIP codes.

   - What is the field's correct name?

   - What kind of information does the field need to store (for example, alphanumeric, numeric, or currency amounts)?

   - If the field is to store textual information (for example, names or addresses), what is the maximum number of characters to be allowed?

   - Does the field have a specific range of valid values? For example, listing prices cannot be less than zero nor more than some reasonable value, perhaps $2 million.

Asking these and other questions of each potential field lets you develop a set of data definitions for each table in the database.

3. The previous step usually results in an expanded and refined list of fields. Some fields rightfully belong in their original categories, but you may discover that others more properly belong in other categories. Update your list and reassign the fields, if necessary. This helps define the tables you need to create.

Table 5.5 contains an expanded list of data requirements for houses.

Table 5.5. Revised Data Requirements for Houses

Requirements for Houses
MLS Number
Name of Listing Agent
Street Address
City
State
ZIP Code
County
Asking Price
Number of Bedrooms
Number of Bathrooms
Number of Garage Spaces
Square Footage
Width of Lot
Depth of Lot
Age of House
Photograph

This list of fields provides the information you need to create a table for houses. Although you can track additional data about each house, this information is enough to get started.

Normalizing the Database

The previous section, "Developing a Database Design," discussed how to define the framework for the database, including table and field listings. Now that you have lists of fields, the next step is to normalize the design. The process of identifying and eliminating redundant data, called *normalization,* is a critical part of the database design process. Normalized databases are more flexible and easier to manage than unnormalized databases, especially when data needs to be changed over time.

Normalizing a database essentially is little more than making sure you do not store the same information twice—or at least minimizing duplicate information. The degree to which you eliminate duplicate information defines the level of normalization. Academics may argue the exact meaning of normalization and may introduce such terms as third normal form (3NF) and projection-join normal form (PJNF). What is most important for you to understand, however, is that normalization pertains to duplicate data, and the less duplicity of data, the better.

Remove Duplicate Data

You normalize a database by eliminating repeating data elements. For example, tables 5.3 and 5.5 each include a field for the name of the listing agent—this is repeating data. To avoid duplicating this data, you can design the house-related table so that it contains a "pointer" to a record in the agent-related table (see fig. 5.3).

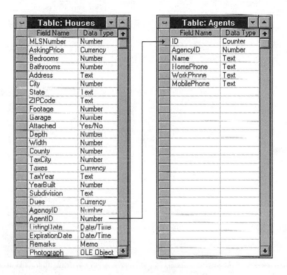

Figure 5.3. The AgentID field "points" to a matching record in the Agents table.

 Note: Figure 5.3 illustrates a number of fields added in Chapter 6, "Building the HomeFinder Tables." The concept illustrated here is that you can avoid duplicating data by pointing to a single location where the data actually is stored.

The Houses table contains a field, AgentID, that corresponds to a matching field in the Agents table. You can minimize (but not eliminate) duplicate data in a relational database system. Although both tables duplicate the agent ID values, they do not duplicate the full names of the listing agents.

You may be wondering why avoiding duplicate data is so important. Long before hardware prices fell and made hard disks relatively inexpensive, you would have wanted to conserve disk space. Today, conserving disk space is still important, but the compelling reason for avoiding duplicate data is that it is much easier and far less work to maintain a single copy of data than multiple copies, as the following examples illustrate:

- *Updating.* If a real estate agency's name changes and the agency's name appears in several tables (or in multiple records in the same table), you must locate and update each instance of the name.

- *Inserting.* When you receive a new house listing, you need to insert data about the listing into the database. If the new information appears in multiple tables, you must insert the new data in each table.

- *Deleting.* When an agent leaves an agency, you may want to delete that agent's record. Again, you would have to locate every instance of data related to the agent to make sure the agency is properly removed from the database.

Creating a Database Schema

You may find it helpful to draw a picture—literally—of what your database will look like. Figure 5.4 illustrates a database schema for the HomeFinder application.

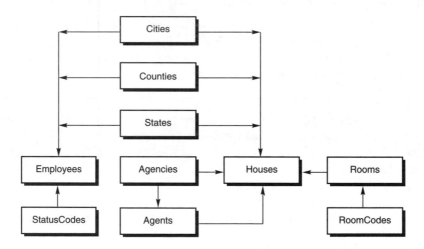

Figure 5.4. Database schema for the tables in the HomeFinder application.

The HomeFinder schema shows the relationships between the tables in the database. In this example, you can see that the Agencies table is related to the Agents and Houses tables. Some tables relate to only one other table; for example, the RoomCodes table relates to only the Rooms table.

A database schema can help you stay focused on the relationships among the various tables. You can also use the diagram later when you begin designing queries and forms to make sure you have provided support for all tables.

Even though you may remember and fully understand all tables and their relationships, a well-drawn database schema is particularly valuable to other developers who review your work and to the technical writer who must document your application.

Creating the New Database

Now that you have a set of table and fields requirements, you can begin implementing your database design. The following procedure outlines the steps you can follow to create a new database.

1. Using the Windows File Manager or at the MS DOS prompt, create a directory named HOMEFIND on your hard disk. If you installed the HomeFinder sample application, you already have a HOMEFIND directory. In this case, create a different directory. Avoid creating databases in the same directory as the Access program files. Instead, create a separate directory, preferably one that is not beneath the Access directory.

    If you would rather open the completed HomeFinder sample application instead of creating a new database at this time, choose the Open Database command, open the HOMEDATA.MDB database (located in a directory named HOMEFIND), and skip ahead to step 3.

2. Choose the New Database command from the File menu. Access displays the New Database dialog box in which you can select a directory and then enter the name of the database, HOMECODE.MDB. By convention, you should name the database file with an extension of MDB, which indicates a Microsoft Access database.

> **Tip:** As a design strategy, create two databases for each application. One is a data database that contains all the tables, and the other is a code database that contains the remaining database objects, such as forms and modules. Later chapters explain why this is an important strategy to follow. For now, worry only about the data database, HOMEDATA.MDB.

3. Access creates the new database and then displays an empty Database window (see fig. 5.5).

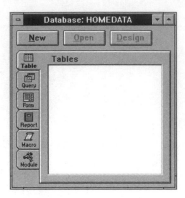

Figure 5.5. The Database window.

To view a list of all database objects in the Database window, click the appropriate button on the left side of the window. To view a list of all forms in the database, click the Form button (or choose the appropriate command from the View menu).

Because HOMEDATA.MDB is a data database, it probably will not contain any objects except tables. Chapter 6, "Building the HomeFinder Tables," explores the table design environment and discusses how to create new tables.

Summary

The most important thing you can do as a developer is ensure the database design incorporates all data requirements. Study the needs of the users, the flow of data from one user to another, and the possible future needs of the users.

Normalize the database design by minimizing duplicity of data between tables.

The time you spend designing the database, even before you start Microsoft Access, is invaluable because a poor design at this stage of development hinders your ability to implement an efficient application later on.

6

Building the HomeFinder Tables

Previous chapters in this book discussed general database design, creating a database schema, and how to create a new database. This chapter explores the next step: creating tables.

Data is the most important element in any application. Think of tables as containers that supply information to other database objects. No amount of forms design or query optimization can save your application from poor table design. Accordingly, invest whatever time is necessary to ensure a good table foundation upon which to build your application.

This chapter covers the following:

- Creating a New Table
- Defining Fields
- Setting Keys
- Saving the New Table
- Entering Sample Data
- Attaching Tables
- Creating Relationships
- Creating a Code Database

Creating a New Table

To create a new table in the HOMEDATA.MDB database, follow these steps:

1. Click the Table button in the Database window and then click the New button. Access displays the New Table dialog box in which you can choose to use the Table Wizard or to create the new table without the wizard.

Note: Wizards are tools you can use to create tables and other database objects, usually in a step-by-step fashion. This book does not illustrate how to use the wizards shipped with Microsoft Access.

 For more information about wizards, see Chapter 19, "Creating and Using Libraries."

2. Click the New Table button. Access displays the table design window. You give the table a real name later, but for now notice in the window's title bar that Access has assigned a temporary table name, Table1 (see fig. 6.1).

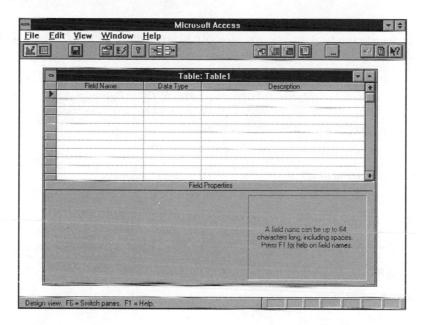

Figure 6.1. Creating a new table.

The table design window features two sections. The top section has three columns where you enter the names of the fields, the data types (defining the kind of data you want to store), and optional descriptions. Each row in the top portion represents one field.

The lower section of the design window provides a place where you can set various field properties. The lower section appears blank until you add fields to the table.

106

Defining Fields

The following procedure outlines the steps you can follow to create a new field in the table.

1. Enter the name of the ID field and select the Counter field data type from the drop-down list (see fig. 6.2).

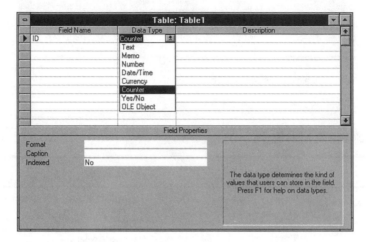

Figure 6.2. Defining a new field.

The default field data type is Text. In the HomeFinder application, however, all ID fields will be counters, which are Access-maintained sequences.

 For more information about the various field data types, see "Using Database Objects" in Chapter 3, "The Access Development Environment."

2. Enter a short description that explains what the field represents, even if the name of the field appears self-explanatory.

3. Set the appropriate field properties (described in the next section, "Setting Field Properties"). At a minimum, be sure you set the **Caption** property.

 Tip: When you create a control by dragging a field from the field list, Access uses the **Caption** property for the control's label. If you do not set the **Caption** property, Access uses the field name. Most field names are short enough to serve as labels, but others are too long to be used on forms and reports and in datasheets.

4. Repeat steps 1 through 3 for each remaining field (see fig. 6.3). Table 6.1 lists the fields in the Agencies table, their field data types, and suggested descriptions.

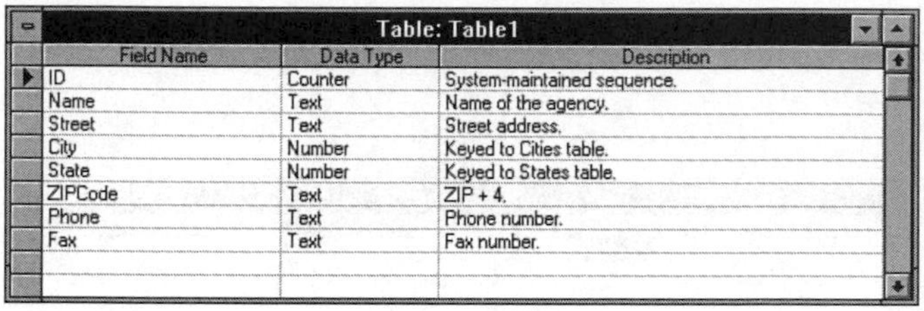

Figure 6.3. The Agencies table contains eight fields.

Table 6.1. Fields in the Agencies Table

Field Name	Data Type	Description
ID	Counter	System-maintained sequence.
Name	Text	Name of the agency.
Street	Text	Street address.
City	Number	Keyed to Cities table.
State	Text	Keyed to States table.
ZIPCode	Text	ZIP + 4.
Phone	Text	Phone number.
Fax	Text	Phone number.

You may expect the City field to be a Text field, but it actually is a pointer to values in another table. This is one way to minimize duplication.

Chapter 5, "The HomeFinder Application," discusses the importance of minimizing data duplicity. Chapter 7, "Building the HomeFinder Queries," explains how to create queries that relate the Agencies, Cities, and States tables.

The next section, "Setting Field Properties," describes how to refine field definitions.

Setting Field Properties

When you create a field and choose a field data type, Access automatically assigns certain default field properties. For example, the default field size for the Text field data type is 50. This defines the maximum number of characters you can enter in a Text field.

Because Microsoft chooses an arbitrary value for each default, you may want to change many of the settings. For example, phone number fields require only 12 characters, but street addresses may require as many as 50 characters.

 For more detailed information about using custom formats and Access Basic to change the appearance of dates, search Help for "formatting dates." For more information about formatting in general, see Chapter 8, "Building the HomeFinder Forms."

As you move from row to row in the table, the names and number of properties in the Field Properties list (in the lower portion of the table design window) changes according to the particular data type. For example, a field defined as a Counter has only three properties (**Format, Caption,** and **Indexed**), number fields have 10 properties, and so on.

For more information about a property, search Help for the particular property name.

Table 6.2 describes the various field properties.

Table 6.2.   Field Properties

Property	Description
AllowZeroLength	For text and Memo fields, determines whether a zero-length string ("") is allowed
Caption	When present, defines the default field label on forms and reports, and as columns in datasheets
DecimalPlaces	For Number fields, determines how many numbers appear to the right of the decimal point
DefaultValue	Value Access automatically enters in the field when you add a new record to the table
FieldSize	For Text fields, defines the maximum number of characters that may be entered; for Number fields, defines the type of number (Byte, Integer, Long Integer, Single, Double)

continues

Table 6.2. Continued

Property	Description
Format	Specifies how data is displayed; use the predefined formats or create your own, custom format using an expression or Access Basic
Indexed	Indicates whether the field is indexed (Yes– No Duplicates, Yes – Duplicates OK, or No)
InputMask	Specifies how data is entered and displayed
Required	For all fields except Counter fields, determines whether an entry is required
Validation Rule	Expression that defines data entry rules and validates the data
Validation Text	Text that appears in a message box when the entered data fails the validation rule

☞ **Note:** Not all properties apply to all data types. For example, the **DecimalPlaces** property does not apply to Text fields and does not appear in the Field Properties list.

Table 6.3 lists the field properties you need to set for each field of the Agencies table. If a property is not listed, you can either leave it blank or enter your own setting, if appropriate.

Table 6.3. Field Property Values for Agencies

Field	Property	Setting
ID	Caption	ID
Name	Caption	Agency
	Required	Yes
Street	Caption	Address
City	Caption	City
	FieldSize	Long Integer
	DefaultValue	0
State	Caption	State
	FieldSize	2
ZIPCode	Caption	ZIP
	FieldSize	10
	InputMask	00000\-9999;0;_

110

Field	Property	Setting
Phone	Caption	Phone
	FieldSize	12
	InputMask	000\-000\-0000;0;_
Fax	Caption	Phone
	FieldSize	12
	InputMask	000\-000\-0000;0;_

Setting Keys

The following sections discuss the two kinds of keys—primary keys and secondary keys. The kind of key you assign to a table depends on the uniqueness of the data and how you intend to use the table.

Setting a Primary Key

A primary key consists of one or more fields that uniquely identify each record in a table. Typically, a primary key is a single, unique field, such as an employee's social security number or a product identification number.

When you create a primary key, Access automatically creates an index on the field. Access can use indexes to quickly locate records, and tables with primary keys are generally more efficient than tables without primary keys.

 For more information about deciding whether to set a primary key, see "Omitting a Primary Key" later in this chapter.

If your table has a field that contains unique values, you can set that field to be the primary key. For example, Counter fields are unique. The ID field in the Agencies table is a Counter and may be set as the primary key.

To set the primary key, click the row containing the desired field and then choose the Set Primary Key command from the Edit menu. Or, click the Set Primary Key button on the toolbar (see fig. 6.4).

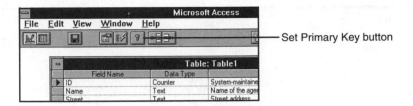

Figure 6.4.   Click the Set Primary Key button to establish a primary key.

Access displays the key field indicator next to the ID field. When you save the table after having set the primary key, Access checks to make sure the field you have selected contains unique values. Remember, a primary key field by definition cannot contain duplicate values.

If you choose a field with duplicate values, Access displays an appropriate message when you try to save the table. Acknowledge the message and select a different field.

Sometimes a table does not have a field representing unique values. In this case, you can add a Counter field to the table and set that field as the primary key.

Setting a Multiple-Field Primary Key

The previous section discussed how you can add a Counter field to create a field with unique values. You may not need to do this, however, if the table has two fields that, when joined, create a unique combination. For example, in a table containing order detail information, the combination of order number and product ID can be used as the primary key.

To set a multiple-field primary key, highlight the desired fields with the mouse and then click the Set Primary Key button on the toolbar.

Omitting a Primary Key

Although it is somewhat unusual, not all tables require a primary key. Database purists may argue that all tables in a relational database system must have a primary key. Base your decision to omit the key on real-world considerations.

For example, if you have a table that has no suitable field (or fields) for a primary key and the number of records is somewhat limited, you may want to forego creating an arbitrary key.

If a table has a key or index (described in the following section), Access can optimize queries and generally perform more efficiently. The tradeoff is that Access must maintain these indexes whenever you add or change records in the table. Consider omitting the primary key, testing the performance of your system, and then adding the key later if performance is unsatisfactory.

Setting Secondary Indexes

You may want to establish additional indexes beyond the one Access automatically creates on the primary key field. For example, if you frequently perform searches on a ZIP code field, you can improve your system performance by setting a secondary index on the ZIP code field.

You establish a secondary index by setting a field's **Indexed** property, selecting one of three choices:

- **No.** The field will not be indexed.

- **Yes (Duplicates OK).** The field will be indexed. You can enter multiple records with the same values in the indexed field.

- **Yes (No Duplicates).** The field will be indexed. You cannot enter records with duplicate values in the index field.

Selecting Yes (No Duplicates) is similar to setting the primary key. One difference is that records appear in primary key sequence when you open the table in Datasheet View. If you set a secondary index and do not set the primary key, the records appear in insertion order (the order in which they were added to the table).

Tip: After the table is open in Datasheet View, you can reorder the records by choosing the Quick Sort command from the Records menu, even if you set the primary key.

Note: Depending on the number of records in a table, the extra overhead may not justify creating another index. Although data retrieval is somewhat faster with an index than without an index, Access must write index information whenever the user enters or changes records in the table. In contrast, changes to non-indexed fields do not require extra file activity. You can search and retrieve data from non-indexed fields.

Saving the New Table

To save the new table, choose the Save As command from the File menu and give the table a meaningful name. For this example, name the table Agencies.

For details about how to name tables and other database objects, see Chapter 17, "Naming Conventions and Style Guidelines."

If you have not set a primary key for the table, Access displays a message, asking whether you want to add one at this time. If you respond by clicking Yes, Access adds a Counter field named ID to the table and makes that field the primary key.

If you already have a Counter field named ID, Access sets that field as the key. If the existing ID field is not a Counter field, Access creates a field named ID1. If you have an existing field named ID1, Access creates ID2, and so on.

Close the Agencies table and then create the remaining nine tables for the HOMEDATA.MDB database. Tables 6.4 through 6.12 list the various field and property settings for each table.

Table 6.4. Field Property Values for Agents

Field	Property	Setting
ID[1]	DataType	Counter
	Description	System-maintained sequence
	Caption	ID
AgencyID	DataType	Number
	Description	Keyed to Agencies table
	FieldSize	Long Integer
	Caption	Agency
	Required	Yes
Name	DataType	Text
	Description	Last, first
	FieldSize	50
	Caption	Name
	Required	Yes
HomePhone	DataType	Text
	Description	Home phone
	FieldSize	12
	Caption	Home Phone
WorkPhone	DataType	Text
	Description	Work phone
	FieldSize	12
	Caption	Work Phone
MobilePhone	DataType	Text
	Description	Mobile/cellular number
	FieldSize	
	Caption	Mobile Phone

[1] *This is the table's primary key field.*

114

Table 6.5. Field Property Values for Cities

Field	Property	Setting
ID[1]	DataType	Counter
	Description	System-maintained sequence.
	Caption	ID
Name	DataType	Text
	Description	Name of city.
	FieldSize	25
	Caption	Name
	Required	Yes
Sequence	DataType	Number
	Description	Sequence in which cities appear in lists.
	FieldSize	Byte
	Caption	Seq

[1] *This is the table's primary key field.*

Table 6.6. Field Property Values for Counties

Field	Property	Setting
ID[1]	DataType	Counter
	Description	System-maintained sequence.
	Caption	ID
Name	DataType	Text
	Description	Name of county.
	FieldSize	25
	Caption	County
	Required	Yes
Sequence	DataType	Number
	Description	Sequence in which counties appear in lists.
	FieldSize	Byte
	Caption	Seq

[1] *This is the table's primary key field.*

115

Table 6.7. Field Property Values for Employees

Field	Property	Setting
ID[1]	DataType	Counter
	Description	System-maintained sequence.
	Caption	ID
SSAN	DataType	Text
	Description	Social security account number.
	FieldSize	11
	Caption	SSAN
	Required	Yes
LastName	DataType	Text
	Description	Last name.
	FieldSize	20
	Caption	Last
	Required	Yes
FirstName	DataType	Text
	Description	First name.
	FieldSize	20
	Caption	First
	Required	Yes
MI	DataType	Text
	Description	Middle initial.
	FieldSize	2
	Caption	MI
Title	DataType	Text
	Description	Employee's title.
	FieldSize	30
	Caption	Title
Birthdate	DataType	Date/Time
	Description	Birthdate.
	Format	Medium Date
	Caption	Birthdate

Field	Property	Setting
HireDate	DataType	Date/Time
	Description	Hire date.
	Format	Medium Date
	Caption	Hire Date
Address	DataType	Text
	Description	Street or post office box.
	Caption	Address
City	DataType	Number
	Description	Keyed to Cities table.
	FieldSize	Long Integer
	Caption	City
State	DataType	Text
	Description	Keyed to States table.
	FieldSize	Long Integer
	Caption	State
	DefaultValue	"WA"
ZIPCode	DataType	Text
	Description	ZIP + 4.
	FieldSize	10
	Caption	ZIP
	DefaultValue	980
County	DataType	Number
	Description	Keyed to Counties table.
	FieldSize	Long Integer
	Caption	County
HomePhone	DataType	Text
	Description	Home phone number, including area code.
	FieldSize	12
	Caption	Home Phone
Extension	DataType	Text
	Description	Internal telephone extension number.
	FieldSize	4
	Caption	Ext.

continues

Table 6.7. Continued

Field	Property	Setting
Photo	DataType	OLE Object
	Description	Picture of employee.
	Caption	Photo
Notes	DataType	Memo
	Description	General information about employee's background.
	Caption	Notes
ReportsTo	DataType	Number
	Description	Keyed to Employees table.
	FieldSize	Long Integer
	Caption	Supervisor
Status	DataType	Number
	Description	Keyed to StatusCodes table.
	FieldSize	Long Integer
	Caption	Status
	Required	Yes

[1] *This is the table's primary key field.*

> **Note:** Check your local laws to make sure you can legally maintain employee birthdates and photos. In the United States, birthdate information may be required for EEO reporting purposes.

Table 6.8. Field Property Values for Houses

Field	Property	Setting
ID[1]	DataType	Counter
	Description	System-maintained sequence.
	Caption	ID
MLSNumber	DataType	Text
	Description	MLS listing number.
	FieldSize	Long Integer
	Caption	MLS Number
	Required	Yes

Field	Property	Setting
AskingPrice	DataType	Currency
	Description	Asking price.
	Format	General Number
	DecimalPlaces	2
	Caption	Price
Bedrooms	DataType	Number
	Description	Number of bedrooms.
	FieldSize	Byte
	Caption	Bedrooms
	DefaultValue	3
Bathrooms	DataType	Number
	Description	Number of bathrooms.
	FieldSize	Single
	Format	Fixed
	DecimalPlaces	1
	Caption	Bathrooms
	DefaultValue	2
Address	DataType	Text
	Description	Street address of house.
	Caption	Street
City	DataType	Number
	Description	Keyed to Cities table.
	FieldSize	Long Integer
	Caption	City
State	DataType	Text
	Description	Keyed to States table.
	FieldSize	2
	Caption	State
	DefaultValue	"WA"
ZIPCode	DataType	Text
	Description	ZIP + 4.
	FieldSize	10
	Caption	ZIP
	DefaultValue	980

continues

Table 6.8. Continued

Field	Property	Setting
Footage	DataType	Number
	Description	Total square feet of living space.
	FieldSize	Integer
	Caption	Sq Ft
Garage	DataType	Number
	Description	Number of parking spaces in garage.
	FieldSize	Byte
	Caption	Garage
	DefaultValue	2
Attached	DataType	Yes/No
	Description	Whether the garage is attached.
	Caption	Attached
	DefaultValue	Yes
Depth	DataType	Number
	Description	Depth of the lot (in feet).
	FieldSize	Integer
	Caption	Depth
Width	DataType	Number
	Description	Width of the lot (in feet).
	FieldSize	Integer
	Caption	Width
County	DataType	Number
	Description	Keyed to Counties table.
	FieldSize	Long Integer
	Caption	County
TaxCity	DataType	Number
	Description	Keyed to Cities table (taxing municipality).
	FieldSize	Long Integer
	Caption	Tax City
Taxes	DataType	Currency
	Description	Net general taxes.
	Caption	Taxes

Field	Property	Setting
TaxYear	DataType	Number
	Description	Tax year (taxes paid through).
	FieldSize	Integer
	Caption	Tax Year
YearBuilt	DataType	Number
	Description	Year house was built (estimated).
	FieldSize	Integer
	Caption	Built
Subdivision	DataType	Text
	Description	Subdivision name.
	FieldSize	25
	Caption	Subdivision
Dues	DataType	Currency
	Description	Subdivision or homeowners association dues.
	Format	General Number
	DecimalPlaces	2
	Caption	Dues
AgencyID	DataType	Number
	Description	Keyed to Agencies table.
	FieldSize	Long Integer
	Caption	Agency
AgentID	DataType	Number
	Description	Keyed to Agents table.
	FieldSize	Long Integer
	Caption	Agent
ListingDate	DataType	Date/Time
	Description	Initial listing date.
	Format	Medium Date
	DefaultValue	=Date$( )
	Caption	List Date

continues

Table 6.8. Continued

Field	Property	Setting
ExpirationDate	DataType	Date/Time
	Description	Expiration date of listing.
	Format	Medium Date
	Caption	Expires
Notes	DataType	Memo
	Description	Notes.
	Caption	Notes
Photo	DataType	OLE Object
	Description	Picture of the house.
	Caption	Photo

[1] This is the table's primary key field.

Table 6.9. Field Property Values for RoomCodes

Field	Property	Setting
RoomCode[1]	DataType	Text
	Description	Room code (5-character identifier).
	FieldSize	5
	Caption	Code
	Required	Yes
Description	DataType	Text
	Description	Room description.
	FieldSize	20
	Caption	Description
	Required	Yes

[1] This is the table's primary key field.

Table 6.10. Field Property Values for Rooms

Field	Property	Setting
HouseID[1]	DataType	Number
	Description	Keyed to Houses table.
	FieldSize	Long Integer
	Caption	House ID
	Required	Yes
RoomCode[1]	DataType	Text
	Description	Keyed to RoomCodes table.
	FieldSize	5
	Caption	Room Code
	Required	Yes
Width	DataType	Number
	Description	Width (in feet).
	FieldSize	Byte
	Caption	Width
Length	DataType	Number
	Description	Length/depth (in feet).
	FieldSize	Byte
	Caption	Length
Features	DataType	Memo
	Description	Special features or notes.
	Caption	Features

[1] *These fields form the table's multiple-field primary key.*

Table 6.11. Field Property Values for States

Field	Property	Setting
Abbreviation[1]	DataType	Text
	Description	Two-letter state abbreviation.
	FieldSize	2
	Caption	State
	Required	Yes

continues

Table 6.11. Continued

Field	Property	Setting
Name	DataType	Text
	Description	Name of state.
	FieldSize	50
	Caption	State Name
	Required	Yes

[1] This is the table's primary key field.

Table 6.12. Field Property Values for StatusCodes

Field	Property	Setting
ID[1]	DataType	Counter
	Description	System-maintained sequence.
	Caption	ID
Description	DataType	Text
	Description	Description.
	FieldSize	50
	Caption	Status
	Required	Yes
Sequence	DataType	Number
	Description	Sequence in which codes appear in lists.
	FieldSize	Byte
	Caption	Seq

[1] This is the table's primary key field.

Entering Sample Data

Now that you have created the required tables, you can enter some sample data. This serves two purposes. First, it provides data you can use to test later elements of your application (for example, queries).

Second, it gives you an opportunity to make sure you are tracking all the information you need in support of the application's objectives. Also, you may discover that a field you added to the table is not really necessary or that you do not have data for enough records to justify maintaining a field.

Open the Agencies table in Datasheet View (if necessary, choose the Datasheet command from the View menu). Access displays the table in a familiar row-and-column format. For most fields, particularly text and number fields, enter the sample data as you would enter data in a spreadsheet.

As you scan the columns, you immediately notice that Access has inserted the value 0 (zero) for the City field. You cannot enter the names of cities because this field is a Number field and is supposed to contain values from a related table that does not yet exist. For now, leave the city entry unchanged.

 Chapter 8, "Building the HomeFinder Forms," describes the technique for resolving this issue.

Embedding OLE Objects

Access supports an OLE Object field data type you can use to store pictures, waveforms, and other OLE objects.

For example, in the HomeFinder application, the Houses table contains a field named Photo that you can use to store pictures of the houses. As designed, the table supports only one photo per house, but you can add additional OLE Object fields to store multiple photos (one of the front, one of the back, interior shots, and so on).

You can create and embed a new OLE object or embed an existing OLE object file.

Embedding a New OLE Object

The following steps outline how to create and embed a new OLE object.

1. Move to the OLE Object field into which you want to embed the object and then choose the Insert Object command from the Edit menu. Access displays the Insert Object dialog box.

2. Select the Create New option button on the left side of the dialog box (see fig. 6.5) and then choose the appropriate object type. In this example, a Paintbrush picture is created.

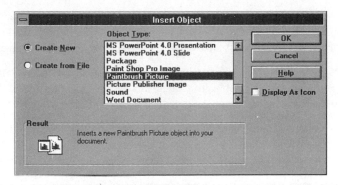

Figure 6.5. Specify the type of OLE object you want to embed.

3. Click OK. Access loads Paintbrush and waits for you to create the desired image. You can paste an existing image into Paintbrush (see fig. 6.6) or draw the image yourself.

Tip: If you choose a different type of OLE object that launches a program that supports direct scanning of photographs, you can scan the image directly into that program.

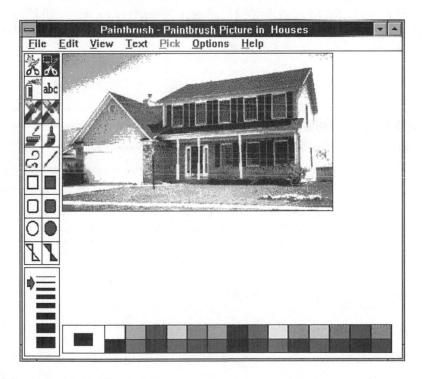

Figure 6.6. A completed Paintbrush picture.

4. When you finish creating the picture, choose the Exit command from the File menu (see fig. 6.7).

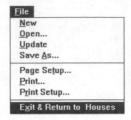

Figure 6.7. Choose the Exit command to save the image and return to Access.

The exact wording for the Exit command may differ in other source programs. For example, in Word for Windows, the Exit command is simply "Exit."

Access displays a message box asking you to decide whether to update the open embedded object (see fig. 6.8). In this case, the open object is an embedded OLE object in an Access table, so choose to update the object.

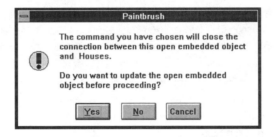

Figure 6.8. You can choose to update the table in Access.

Embedding an Existing OLE Object

To embed an existing OLE object file, follow these steps:

1. Move to the OLE Object field into which you want to embed the object and then choose the Insert Object command from the Edit menu. Access displays the Insert Object dialog box (see fig. 6.9).

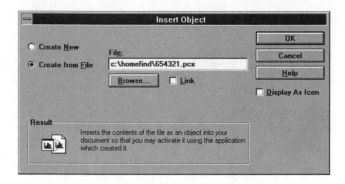

Figure 6.9. Embedding an existing Paintbrush image.

2. Select the Create from File option button on the left side of the dialog box. Access displays a text box in which you can enter the name of the file you want to embed. If necessary, click the Browse button to locate the desired file.

3. Click OK to embed the selected file.

Tip: By default, Access embeds the file into your Access table. If you would rather link the file, select the Link option button in the Import Object dialog box. When you embed a file, Access makes a copy and stores it in your database. When you link a file, only link information is stored in the database. When you link, Access must open the original file whenever you want to access the contents of the file.

Importing Existing Tables

Rather than entering sample data manually, you can import real data from existing tables stored in another database format. When you import, Access converts the data to the Access format.

For example, you may want to import an older dBASE database into Access. Thereafter, you would use Access as the front-end to what used to be dBASE data. Access can import files from a number of database sources, including the following:

- *Microsoft Access.* Databases other than the open database

- *Delimited text.* Values separated by commas, tabs, or other specified characters

- *Fixed-width text.* Values arranged so that each field has a specified width

- *FoxPro.* Version 2.0, 2.5, and 2.6 .DBF files

- *dBASE III and dBASE IV.* .DBF files

- *Microsoft Excel.* Versions 2.x, 3.0, 4.0, and 5.0

128

- *Lotus 1-2-3 or 1-2-3/W.* .WKS, .WK1, and .WK3 files

- *Paradox.* Version 3.x and 4.x .DB files

- *Btrieve.* With the data definition files FILE.DDF and FIELD.DDF

- *SQL databases.* Using ODBC drivers

 For detailed information about importing tables into Access, search Help for "importing data: basics."

Attaching Tables

The preceding section, "Importing Existing Tables," lists a variety of external database sources you can import into Microsoft Access databases. Sometimes, however, importing data from an external database is not practical.

For example, you may want to use Access to manage a dBASE table while other users continue to use dBASE with the same table. In this case, importing the table does not work. If you import the table, changes you make to the table do not affect the other dBASE users—you each are working with a different copy of the dBASE table.

In cases where you must continue to support another program, it is better to attach the external table, not import it.

When you attach a table, the table stays in its original format, but Access uses it almost like a native Access table. At the same time, dBASE users (or other users, depending on the type of file you attach) can continue to add new records and change data in the same table. Attaching the table lets multiple database management systems access the data at the same time.

 For detailed information about attaching tables, see Chapter 7, "Building the HomeFinder Queries," or search Help for "attaching tables: creating the link."

Creating Relationships

Chapter 1, "Database Fundamentals," discusses the value of establishing relationships between tables. When you create a relationship, you tell Access how the records in one table relate to the records in another table.

For example, the Agencies and Agents tables are related because they both have a common field that lets one table refer to the other. When you open the Agents table, note that each record has an agency code (the AgencyID field) that matches an agency code in the Agencies table (the ID field). There can be agencies with no agents, but there cannot be agents without a corresponding agency. This relationship is called one-to-many (one agency to many agents).

The following steps outline the procedure you can follow to create a relationship between two tables.

1. Go to the Database window and choose the Relationships command from the Edit menu. Access displays the Relationships window and immediately opens the Add Table dialog box (see fig. 6.10).

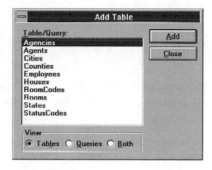

Figure 6.10.   The Add Table dialog box.

2. Add all the tables to the Relationships window (see fig. 6.11), and then close the dialog box.

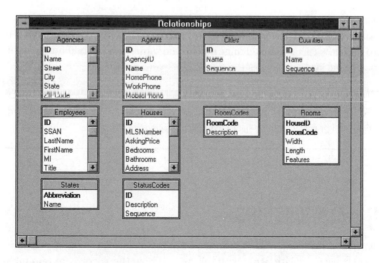

Figure 6.11.   All 10 tables fit in the window.

130

> **Note:** Access displays all primary key fields with a boldface font. For example, all fields named ID appear bold because they are all primary key fields. Most relationships you create involve at least one primary key field. For example, you need to create a relationship between the ID field in the Agencies table (a primary key field) and the AgencyID field in the Agents table.

3. When you drag a field in one table to a field in another table, Access displays the Relationships dialog box in which you can confirm the fields you want to join (you can create multiple joins between the two tables).

4. Click the Join Type button to display the Join Properties dialog box, and then define the join as one-to-one, one-to-many, or many-to-many. For the Agencies-Agents relationship, create a one-to-many relationship by choosing the second option in the dialog box.

5. If you want to permit cascading updates and deletes, select the Enforce Referential Integrity check box.

> For more information about referential integrity, search Help for "referential integrity."

6. Click the Create button. Access closes the dialog box and displays an arrow between the Agencies and Agents tables.

7. Repeat steps 3 through 6 for each relationship required by the database design. Table 6.13 lists all relationships for the tables in the HOMEDATA.MDB database. The first column contains a list of the primary keys you drag to the fields listed in the second column.

Table 6.13. Relationships for Tables in HOMEDATA.MDB

Table/Field	Table/Field
Agencies/ID	Agents/AgencyID
Agencies/ID	Houses/AgencyID
Agents/ID	Houses/AgentID
Cities/ID	Agencies/City
Cities/ID	Employees/City
Cities/ID	Houses/City
Cities/ID	Houses/TaxCity
Counties/ID	Employees/County
Houses/ID	Rooms/HouseID

continues

131

Table 6.13. Continued

Table/Field	Table/Field
RoomCodes/RoomCode	Rooms/RoomCode
States/Abbreviation	Agencies/State
States/Abbreviation	Employees/State
States/Abbreviation	Houses/State
StatusCodes/ID	Employees/Status

Tip: As you can see, given any sufficiently complex database design, the Relationships window quickly becomes cluttered with tables and connecting lines. Try moving the tables around to avoid or minimize crossed lines.

For more detailed information about the Relationships window and how you can display relationships for selected tables only, search Help for "relationships."

Creating a Code Database

Previous chapters discussed the value of separating the tables in your application from forms, queries, modules, and other database objects. Store the tables in the data database (HOMEDATA.MDB) and the other objects in the code database (HOMECODE.MDB).

How you name the actual database files is important only to the extent that you (and other developers) need to be able to distinguish between them. For the HomeFinder application, HOMEDATA and HOMECODE work nicely, but you can name your files anything you like.

Avoid the temptation, however, to use the file name extension (.MDB) as an indicator. For example, do not name a data database HOMEFIND.DAT or HOMEFIND.MDD, or a code database HOMEFIND.COD or HOMEFIND.MDC.

Before you proceed to the next chapters, create another database in the same directory as the HOMEDATA.MDB file. Name the new database HOMECODE.MDB. Then, open the code database and attach all tables from the HOMEDATA.MDB database.

 For more information about attaching tables, search Help for "attaching tables: creating the link."

Summary

This chapter discussed the way you create new tables, define fields for storing data, and define relationships between the various tables.

You can import existing data from external data sources such as FoxPro, dBASE, or Paradox, and you can import or attach tables in another Access database.

7

Building the HomeFinder Queries

A query is a fundamental database object you use to ask questions about the data stored in your database. You use queries to select specific data to display in forms and print in reports. Although it may seem completely obvious to you, it is still worth mentioning that queries represent the most important interaction you have with an Access database. No matter how you store or display data, actual data retrieval occurs only through the Access query mechanism.

This chapter concentrates on the queries you need to support the HomeFinder sample application, but you may find that they represent the kinds of queries you use in your own applications. HomeFinder uses select queries, but action queries are covered here, too.

This chapter covers the following:

- Exploring the Query Window
- Creating a Query Using the QBE Grid
- Exploring Select Queries
- Exploring Action Queries
- Using the SQL Window

Tip: Create and store queries in your application's code database, not in the data database. In the HomeFinder application, the code database is named HOMECODE.MDB.

Exploring the Query Window

The Query window presents a number of features and tools you can use to build powerful queries quickly and easily (see fig. 7.1).

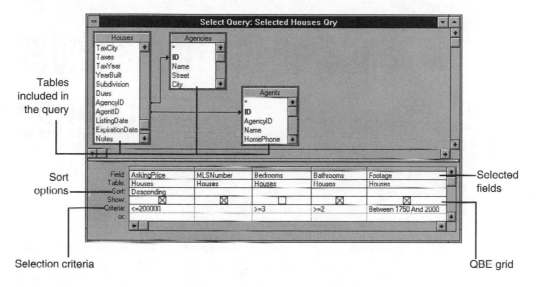

Figure 7.1. The Query window.

To create a query in Access, you use the graphical Query-by-Example (QBE) grid. Unlike other programs that require you to enter complex expressions on a command line or in a programming language, Access enables you to define queries by dragging and dropping table fields from a list to the QBE grid. You then provide the text, numbers, and expressions to match when selecting records—in other words, you provide an example of the data you are looking for.

Many options you may choose for the query (sorting, totaling, and so on) are available in drop-down lists. In most other database programs, these functions are accessible only by entering sometimes confusing command-line expressions or by writing a program. In Access, you can create even seemingly complex queries easily.

You create both select and action queries in the QBE grid. You can view the results of select queries in Datasheet view. In contrast, you cannot view the results of action queries—you can only run action queries. If you want to see which records will be affected by an action query before you actually run the query, change the query to a select query and then open the query in Datasheet view (this process is described later in this chapter).

136

Creating a Query Using the QBE Grid

Select queries are the most fundamental of the query types and are the foundation for all the others. The following procedure outlines the steps you can follow to create a select query, but you can apply these steps to other kinds of queries as well.

1. Go to the Database window, click the Query button, and then click the New button. Access displays the New Query dialog box in which you can choose to use a query wizard or create the new query on your own.

Note: Wizards are tools you can use to create queries and other database objects, usually in a step-by-step fashion. This book does not illustrate how to use the wizards shipped with Microsoft Access.

　For more information about wizards, see Chapter 19, "Creating and Using Libraries."

2. Click the New Query button; Access displays the Query window. Then, Access immediately displays the Add Table dialog box in which you can select all of the tables you want to add to the query.

3. Add the Houses, Agencies, and Agents tables and then close the dialog box. You give the query a real name later, but for now notice in the window's title bar that Access has assigned a temporary table name, Query1.

Tip: Another way to quickly select tables for the query is to drag the table names from the Database window to the upper portion of the Query window.

The Query window features two sections. In the top section are field lists for each table you added to the query. The lower section of the Query window contains the QBE grid, a place where you can enter field names and various query criteria.

The following sections describe ways you can join tables, select fields, set criteria, and view the results of the query.

Joining Tables in Queries

Chapter 6, "Building the HomeFinder Tables," discusses relationships and how you define them by joining a field from one table with a related field in another table. In the top portion of the Query window, Access displays lines that connect these related fields. One benefit, then, to defining relationships is that Access can automatically join tables in the Query window.

Not all pairs of tables have a predefined relationship. You do not, in fact, have to define any relationships at all. However, you otherwise have to define any necessary relationships as you build each query.

The relationships you establish in the Query window have the same effect as relationships you create using the Relationships command, but they remain in effect only as long as the query is running. This means that when you close the query, the relationship no longer exists.

To join two tables in the Query window, drag a field from one table to the matching field in the other table. Access joins the tables on the selected fields and displays a join line such as that between tables in a "real" relationship.

By default, the join you create when you drag a field from one table to another is called an *inner join*.

Sometimes called an *equi-join*, this type of join results in only those records where the matching field value exists in both tables. If a record exists in either table, but does not have a matching record in the other, it is not included in the query's result set.

Most multi-table queries use inner joins. For example, you might join an Orders table with a table containing order details. When you run the query, you want to return only orders that have detail records. Orders that have no detail are not returned by the query.

If an inner join does not produce the desired results, you can choose a different type:

- **Left outer join.** With this type of join, the query returns records from the first table (the table on the left side in the Query window), even if no matching records exist in the second (right side) table.

   For example, you might create a query that uses a left outer join to identify house records that do not have any related agent records.

- **Right outer join.** This has the same effect as a left outer join except that it works in the opposite direction: the query returns records from the second (right side) table, even if no matching records are found in the first table. Depending on which table you add to the query first, you may need to create either a left outer or right outer join.

You can change the type of join in the Query window by double-clicking the join line between the two tables. Access displays the Join Properties dialog box (see fig. 7.2).

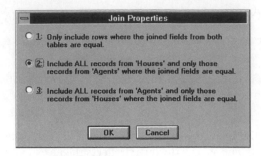

Figure 7.2. Use the Join Properties dialog box to change the type of join.

Select **1** if you want an inner join (the default), **2** for a left outer join, or **3** for a right outer join. When you select an outer join, the join line in the Query window changes from a solid line to a line with an arrowhead that points to the table whose records are returned even when the other table has no matching records. For example, the join line between the Houses and Agencies tables points toward the Agencies table.

Adding Fields to the QBE Grid

Locate all fields you want to include in the query and drag them from the field lists to the Field row in the QBE grid. Table 7.1 lists the fields you need for this example.

Table 7.1. Required Fields

Table	Field
Houses	AskingPrice
	MLSNumber
	Bedrooms
	Bathrooms
	Footage
Agencies	Name
Agents	Name

 Tip: You also can quickly add fields to the QBE grid by double-clicking field names in the field lists.

If you were going to add all the fields from a table, you could do so in any of three ways:

- Double-click or drag each field from the table's field list. Use this technique when the table has few fields.

- Double-click or drag the asterisk that appears at the top of the table's field list box. The asterisk means "all fields." When you use this technique, Access displays an asterisk in the QBE grid.

  The advantage to this technique is that if you later change the table structure (add new fields, rename fields, and so on), the query reflects the new table structure automatically.

- Double-click the table's title bar to highlight all the fields, and then drag the fields to the QBE grid. Access lists each field individually in the grid.

  Use this technique when you want to add most, but not all, of the fields in the table. Add all the fields and then remove the ones you do not need. To delete a field from the query, click on the field selector (the thin, gray row above the field name in each column in the QBE grid) and then press the DEL key or choose the Delete command from the Edit menu.

Using Aliases

Sometimes the table field names are too short, too long, or too cryptic to be useful. For example, you may have a table with field names such as BusName or Addr1 that you would rather call Company Name and Street Address.

To change field names, you can assign an alias. An *alias* is a name you use in place of the real name of an object (a table field, in this case). Aliases are particularly useful because they let you create query results that reflect plain-English column headings instead of the names from the tables.

When you use an alias, you rename fields in the query to make them more meaningful without actually changing the field names in the underlying tables. Not changing the real name means that forms, reports, macros, Access Basic code, and other queries that use the existing name continue to work.

To create an alias, go to the field name in the QBE grid and enter the name of the alias to the left of the existing field name, followed by a colon (see fig. 7.3). In this example, instead of using the actual field name (MLSNumber), the query will use the alias MLS.

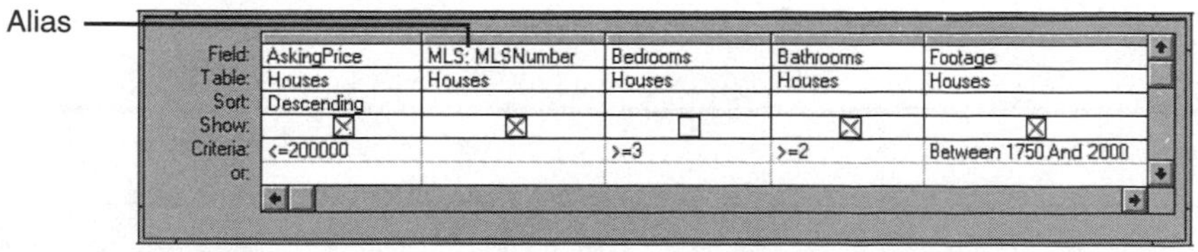

Figure 7.3. Creating an alias.

140

Sorting Queries

Sorting the data in your query in alphabetic or numeric order often makes it easier to interpret and analyze. You can sort the results of the query on one or more fields. For example, you may sort a list of real estate agents in alphabetical order according to their names, or a list of available houses in descending order according to their asking prices.

To sort a query by the contents of a single field, open the drop-down list in the Sort cell for the field you want to sort. Access displays three sort type options: ascending, descending, and not sorted (see fig. 7.4).

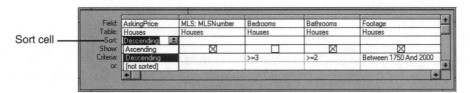

Figure 7.4.   Selecting a sort order.

Unless you choose a sort order, Access does not apply any special sorting rules. If the underlying data is unsorted, the query results also are unsorted. If the underlying data is sorted (as happens when you select a field that is a primary key), then the data may appear in sorted order. As a rule, however, if you want the data sorted in a particular order, choose one of the sort orders instead of relying on Access to sort the data automatically. Choose from three sorting options:

- **Ascending.** Choose this option when you want the data to appear with the lower values first (A–Z, 0–9). For example, if you sort agency names in ascending order, names that begin with A appear before names that begin with B, and so on.

- **Descending.** Choose this option when you want the values to appear with the higher values first (Z–A, 0–9). For example, if you want to prepare a list of house listings where the more expensive houses appear first, select the descending sort order.

- **(not sorted).** Choose this option when you do not want to sort the data on this field. This is the default; that is, Access does not apply any special sorting to fields unless you choose Ascending or Descending.

You can sort on more than one field, each with its own sort order. To sort on multiple fields, move the fields to the left side of the QBE grid so that the most significant field appears first, followed by the other fields.

For example, a prospective home buyer may want to see a list of houses sorted first according to ascending price and then according to descending size of the house. This presents the larger, more affordable houses first and the more expensive, smaller houses last. Change the sort option for the Price field to Ascending and the sort option for the Footage field to descending.

Access sorts the fields from left to right according to their position in the QBE grid. In this example, the fields already are positioned properly. In other queries, you may need to move the columns so that they are in the correct sequence. To move a column in the QBE grid, select and highlight the column by clicking on the field selector and then dragging the field to its new position.

Entering Criteria for Selecting Records

One of Access's greatest strengths is its ability to present information in a usable format. Rather than simply list all data in the underlying tables in an ordered fashion, you can restrict the records to just those that meet certain criteria.

For example, as you add new listings to the Houses table, it quickly grows well beyond the 30 or so records it has today. Over time, the complete listing becomes unmanageable—it is simply too much information to be useful. For example, you might want to concentrate a search for only houses in a particular price range, without having to scan listings for houses beyond your budget (see fig. 7.5).

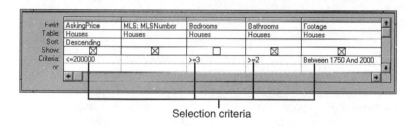

Selection criteria

Figure 7.5. Setting criteria for selecting records.

Not only must the houses cost no more than $200,000, but they must also be within a specified size range (between 1,750 and 2,000 square feet) and have a certain minimum number of bedrooms and bathrooms.

To display the results of the query, click the Datasheet View button on the toolbar or choose the Datasheet command from the View menu. If the query produces too many or too few listings, you can refine the selection criteria.

Saving the Query

After you are satisfied that the query produces the desired records in the proper order, choose Save As from the File menu. Access displays the Save As dialog box in which you can specify the name of the query.

Enter a meaningful name and be sure to add the letters *Qry* to the end. For example, name the query illustrated in the preceding sections "Selected Houses Qry."

All query names should include the Qry suffix.

 For more information about naming queries and other database objects, see Chapter 17, "Naming Conventions and Style Guidelines."

Exploring Select Queries

Select queries are the most common kind of query created in Access. Select queries choose records from one or more tables in the database (or attached tables from other database files such as FoxPro, dBASE, or Paradox) according to various criteria you specify. All queries start out as select queries (until you change them to another type of query).

You can view the selected data directly in a datasheet, or you can use the results as the source of information for forms or reports. When you view the results in a datasheet, you are actually looking at a dynaset. A *dynaset* is a real-time representation of the underlying tables. In a multiuser environment, whenever another user changes the tables, Access updates your view of that same data (hence the name dynaset which comes from *dyna*mic *set*). Likewise, whenever you edit data in the query datasheet, other users see your changes in any forms or datasheets based on the same tables.

Totaling Fields in Queries

Sometimes you need more than just a simple listing of data. For example, you may want to know the average asking price for all the houses in a particular subdivision. This average is a kind of total—a value extracted from all selected records. You can produce a list of all asking prices and then perform the math yourself, but the goal is to get Access to do the work.

If the field is not already part of the query, drag the field you want to total to the QBE grid, and then click the Totals button on the toolbar or choose the Totals command from the View menu. Access displays the Total row in the QBE grid (see fig. 7.6).

Field:	AskingPrice	MLS: MLSNumber	Bedrooms	Bathrooms	Footage
Table:	Houses	Houses	Houses	Houses	Houses
Total:	Group By	Group By	Group By	Group By	Group By
Sort:	Descending				Descending
Show:	☒	☒	☐	☒	☒
Criteria:	<=200000		>=3	>=2	Between 1750 And 2000
or:					

Total row ——

Figure 7.6. Adding totals to a query.

143

Open the drop-down list of available totals:

- **Group By.** Groups records according to the values in the field. This has the same effect as creating a report that has group headers.

 For more information about reports and group headers, see Chapter 10, "Building the HomeFinder Reports."

- **Sum.** Calculates the sum (total) of the values in the field. This option is particularly useful when you combine this with a field totaled with the Group By option.

- **Avg.** Calculates an average of the values in the field. Choose this kind of total to determine the average asking price.

- **Min.** Calculates the minimum (lowest) value.

- **Max.** Calculates the maximum (highest) value.

- **Count.** Calculates a count of the number of records.

- **StDev.** Calculates the standard deviation, a measure of the dispersion of the frequency variation, which is equal to the square root of the variance.

- **Var.** Calculates the variance of the values in the field. This value is equal to the square of the standard deviation.

- **First.** Calculates the value from the first record selected for the query.

- **Last.** Calculates the value from the last record selected for the query.

- **Expression.** Select this option to create a calculated field in the query.

- **Where.** Select this option to specify criteria for a field you are not grouping on. When you select the Where setting, clear the check box on the Show row. When you clear the Show box, Access uses the field to apply the selection criteria but does not include the field in the datasheet or in the query output.

 For more information about using the Expression and Where settings, search Help for "totals: in queries."

Understanding Crosstab Queries

A crosstab (cross-tabulation) query is a special kind of select query you can create to view summarized data in a spreadsheet-like format. In Access, *crosstab* is a term that describes a way to

144

organize information in your database into specific categories. You can calculate, analyze, and compare the data in meaningful ways using values from a field or expression as column headers, often totaling or counting data from individual records. Crosstabs are especially useful when you have a lot of data that you want to condense.

For example, when you create a regular (non-crosstab) select query to view all the orders in an order entry database, it is not easy to see whether one product category is producing better sales results than another. In contrast, you can create a crosstab query that shows sales totals for each product category (see fig. 7.7).

Category	1	2	3	4	5	6	7
Beverages	$52,515.30	$38,542.35	$34,706.80	$32,165.10	$15,089.60	$10,899.90	$16,014.40
Condiments	$14,002.45	$11,989.40	$19,799.50	$6,763.80	$7,829.35	$8,816.90	$8,999.20
Confections	$24,477.55	$24,926.00	$18,438.43	$15,248.40	$10,793.80	$11,745.03	$18,853.10
Dairy Products	$24,314.00	$29,122.20	$42,361.70	$15,705.30	$18,921.40	$16,073.20	$23,002.50
Grains/Cereals	$10,232.85	$6,960.00	$11,533.05	$6,013.70	$10,331.70	$7,194.60	$9,586.05
Meat/Poultry	$30,033.46	$19,357.66	$33,876.12	$4,866.05	$22,801.60	$7,834.20	$9,576.04
Produce	$6,358.00	$11,329.40	$20,496.10	$7,299.00	$7,304.00	$7,162.20	$5,602.80
Seafood	$25,079.84	$13,133.74	$17,443.00	$11,301.30	$4,933.25	$14,872.80	$17,281.00

Crosstab Query: My Crosstab Qry — Record: 1 of 8

Figure 7.7. A crosstab query that summarizes sales information by product by month.

Note: Figure 7.7 illustrates data from the Northwind Traders sample database that ships with Microsoft Access.

As you can see, it is easier to see how the various products have sold during each of 12 months. In other situations, you may want to categorize data by regions or offices, or organize the data by years or calendar quarters.

You can use the same variety of selection criteria and calculation types in a crosstab query that you can when you total fields (for more information, see the preceding section, "Totaling Fields in Queries").

For more information about crosstab queries, search Help for "crosstab queries."

Exploring Action Queries

Unlike select queries that simply retrieve data from the underlying tables, action queries actually change the tables. You can use action queries to add, delete, or change data, and even to create new tables from existing records. For example, you can run an action query to delete obsolete records from a table.

Action queries appear in the Database window with an exclamation point next to their names (see fig. 7.8).

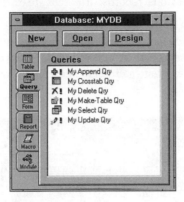

Figure 7.8.   You can easily identify the different types of queries by their icons.

To create an action query, open the Query menu in the Query window and then choose the appropriate command:

- **Make Table.** Make table queries create new tables based on existing data in other tables. These queries are useful particularly when you want to combine information from two tables and create a single table to be used in other database programs.

- **Update.** Update queries change existing records and tables. You create an update query much like the other kinds of queries except that you specify a new value for a specified field. For example, you may want to update a products table by increasing the product prices by five percent, or set a field to the same date when you send a mass mailing to selected customers. Update queries save you the time you would otherwise spend if you had to change each record individually.

- **Append.** Append queries add records to existing tables. When you append data, the tables involved in the query do not have to have the same structure, although the data types of the appended fields must match (except Counter fields, which may be appended to Long Integer fields).

    When you append records to a table, the records in the original table remain intact; Access does not delete the original records. Append queries are particularly useful when you want to merge information from another database.

- **Delete.** Delete queries remove entire records from an existing table. This can save you considerable time when you can identify a certain group of records for deletion. For example, you can create a delete query that removes all of the house listings that have expired.

146

Note: Checking the listing expiration date, Access can determine whether a listing is still active (and keep it) or if it has expired (and delete the record). Real estate listings are valid or in effect for a specific period of time only, usually six months.

You can convert one kind of query into any of the other kinds. For example, you may want to review the records an action query acts upon before you actually run the query. To do this, construct a select query that uses the same selection criteria. Then, open the query in Datasheet view to confirm the correct records have indeed been selected. Once you are satisfied with the criteria, change the select query to the appropriate kind of action query.

Using the SQL Window

When you use the QBE grid to build a query, Access automatically constructs the equivalent SQL (Structured Query Language) statement. If you are familiar with SQL, you may want to construct your queries by entering the SQL statements directly and bypass the QBE grid altogether.

To enter an SQL statement directly, click the SQL button on the toolbar or choose SQL from the View menu. Access displays the SQL window (see fig. 7.9).

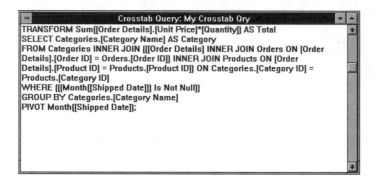

Figure 7.9. You can enter SQL statements directly into the SQL window.

When you make a change in the SQL window, Access automatically updates the QBE grid, and vice versa. This behavior can be useful when you want to create a query using the grid and then copy the SQL statement, especially if you have not mastered SQL.

 For more information about writing your own SQL statements, search Help for "SQL."

147

Entering Text in the SQL Window

Select queries usually are fairly simple and involve only one or two tables. For example, an SQL statement can be as simple as the following:

```
SELECT * FROM Houses
```

This statement retrieves all fields for all records in the Houses table. Most queries are a bit more complicated, however.

```
SELECT DISTINCTROW Houses.AskingPrice, Houses.MLSNumber AS MLS,
Houses.Bathrooms, Houses.Footage, Agencies.Name, Agents.Name
FROM (Houses LEFT JOIN Agencies ON Houses.AgencyID = Agencies.ID) LEFT
JOIN Agents ON Houses.AgentID = Agents.ID
WHERE ((Houses.AskingPrice<=200000) AND (Houses.Bathrooms>=2) AND
(Houses.Footage Between 1750 And 2000) AND (Houses.Bedrooms>=3))
ORDER BY Houses.AskingPrice DESC , Houses.Footage DESC;
```

You can make the SQL statement easier to read by inserting line breaks at strategic points:

```
SELECT DISTINCTROW
    Houses.AskingPrice,
    Houses.MLSNumber AS MLS,
    Houses.Bathrooms,
    Houses.Footage,
    Agencies.Name, Agents.Name
FROM
    (Houses LEFT JOIN Agencies ON Houses.AgencyID = Agencies.ID)
    LEFT JOIN Agents ON Houses.AgentID = Agents.ID
WHERE
    ((Houses.AskingPrice<=200000) AND
    (Houses.Bathrooms>=2) AND
    (Houses.Footage Between 1750 And 2000) AND
    (Houses.Bedrooms>=3))
ORDER BY
    Houses.AskingPrice DESC ,
    Houses.Footage DESC;
```

Access ignores *white space*, including spaces not enclosed in brackets ([ ]) or quotation marks, line feeds and carriage returns. To enter a line break, place the insertion point where you want the break and then press Enter.

 Note: In versions of Microsoft Access prior to 2.0, you had to press Ctrl+Enter.

Where you break the lines depends on the complexity of the SQL statement, its length, plus your own style.

Entering the HomeFinder Queries

Even though you do not know yet how the information will be displayed or printed in reports, you do know that you will need to retrieve information from each table in the HomeFinder data database.

148

Table 7.2 lists some queries used by the HomeFinder sample application. These queries apply no criteria and sort the records according to what right now seem like reasonable fields. You may change some of the queries later on, but for now, create each one by displaying the SQL window, entering the listed SQL statement, and then saving the query with the correct name.

Table 7.2. Initial HomeFinder Queries

Query Name	SQL Statement
Agencies by Name Qry	SELECT DISTINCTROW
	Agencies.Name,
	Agencies.Street,
	Cities.Name AS City,
	Agencies.State,
	Agencies.ZIPCode,
	Agencies.Phone,
	Agencies.Fax
	FROM
	Agencies INNER JOIN Cities ON Agencies.City = Cities.ID
	ORDER BY
	Agencies.Name
	WITH OWNERACCESS OPTION;
Agents by Name Qry	SELECT DISTINCTROW
	Agents.ID,
	Agents.Name,
	Agents.HomePhone,
	Agents.WorkPhone,
	Agents.MobilePhone,
	Agencies.Name
	FROM
	Agents INNER JOIN Agencies ON Agents.AgencyID = Agencies.ID
	ORDER BY
	Agents.Name
	WITH OWNERACCESS OPTION;
Cities by Seq Qry	SELECT DISTINCTROW

continues

Table 7.2.   Continued

Query Name	SQL Statement
	Cities.*
	FROM
	Cities
	ORDER BY
	Cities.Sequence
	WITH OWNERACCESS OPTION;
Counties by Seq Qry	SELECT DISTINCTROW
	Counties.*
	FROM
	Counties
	ORDER BY
	Counties.Sequence
	WITH OWNERACCESS OPTION;
Employees by Name Qry	SELECT DISTINCTROW
	RTrim([LastName] & ", " & [FirstName] & " " & [MI])
	AS Employee,
	Employees.*,
	Cities.Name AS City
	FROM
	Employees LEFT JOIN Cities ON Employees.City − Cities.ID
	ORDER BY
	[LastName] & ", " & [FirstName] & " " & [MI]
	WITH OWNERACCESS OPTION;
Houses by MLS Qry	SELECT DISTINCTROW
	Houses.*
	FROM
	Houses
	ORDER BY
	Houses.MLSNumber
	WITH OWNERACCESS OPTION;
RoomCodes by Code Qry	SELECT DISTINCTROW
	RoomCodes.*

Query Name	SQL Statement
	FROM
	RoomCodes
	ORDER BY
	RoomCodes.RoomCode
	WITH OWNERACCESS OPTION;
States by Abbrev Qry	SELECT DISTINCTROW
	States.*
	FROM
	States
	ORDER BY
	States.Abbreviation
	WITH OWNERACCESS OPTION;
States By Name Qry	SELECT DISTINCTROW
	States.*
	FROM
	States
	ORDER BY
	States.Name
	WITH OWNERACCESS OPTION;
StatusCodes by Seq Qry	SELECT DISTINCTROW
	StatusCodes.*
	FROM
	StatusCodes
	ORDER BY
	StatusCodes.Sequence
	WITH OWNERACCESS OPTION;

Summary

After the data itself, queries are probably the most important part of any database application. You use queries to ask questions about the underlying tables and to base forms and reports on the output produced by queries.

Access provides a wealth of query development tools and features. The Query window and QBE grid make query construction relatively easy, but you can enter SQL statements directly into Access if you want.

8

Building the HomeFinder Forms

Most Microsoft Access applications use forms to display data retrieved from the database and to enter new data into the database. Access forms are like the paper forms you use in a manual record-keeping system. One key difference is that Access forms are connected directly and dynamically to a database.

Forms are based on queries that in turn are based on one or more underlying tables. When a form is bound to a multiple-table query, you can view and enter data more easily than if you had to open each related table individually.

This chapter concentrates on the forms you need to support the HomeFinder sample application—the same kinds of forms you use in your own applications.

This chapter covers the following:

- Exploring the Form Window
- Understanding Access Forms
- Adding Controls
- Creating the Main Menu Form
- Setting Control Properties
- Building the Remaining Forms

Tip: Create and store forms in your application's code database, not in the data database. In the HomeFinder application, the code database is named HOMECODE.MDB.

Exploring the Form Window

When you create a form, you create an interface between the user and the data stored in Access tables. While you can create simple forms that look just like familiar paper forms, you can enhance your forms with visually interesting features—color or shading to set off different sections, pictures or graphs—and a wide variety of controls. Access forms can contain buttons, selection lists, option buttons, and embedded subforms that provide far greater functionality than typical paper forms.

The command buttons, list boxes, and other controls you add to forms ease the effort required to add and extract data. For example, it may be easier and faster for the user to select from a list of valid options than it is to manually type an entry. In addition to making data entry faster, you can help minimize errors by adding validation routines.

The following procedure outlines the steps you can follow to create a form:

1. Go to the Database window, click the Form button, and then click the New button. Access displays the New Form dialog box in which you can enter or select the name of the query on which to base the form. For this example, select the Agencies by Name Qry query.

> **Tip:** Avoid basing forms directly on tables. Because queries offer the ability to restrict the form's records and to sort the records in a specified order, base forms on queries.
>
> If you have not already created a query on which you can base the form, click the Cancel button to close the dialog box and then create the query.

> For more information about creating queries, see Chapter 7, "Building the HomeFinder Queries."

2. You can choose to use a form wizard or create the new form on your own.

> **Note:** Wizards are tools you can use to create forms and other database objects, usually in a step-by-step fashion. This book does not illustrate how to use the wizards shipped with Microsoft Access. For more information about wizards, see Chapter 19, "Creating and Using Libraries."

Click the Blank Form button; Access displays the Form window.

3. Even though the form has no controls, save the new form by choosing the Save As command from the File menu. Name the form Agencies.

4. Display the form's header and footer sections by choosing the Page Header/Footer and Form Header/Footer commands from the Format menu.

Forms are divided into several sections (see fig. 8.1).

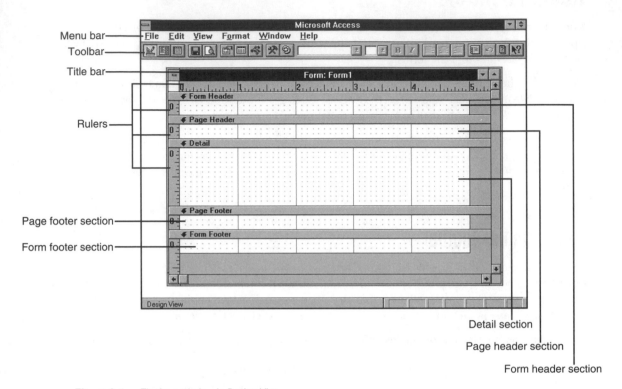

Figure 8.1. The form window in Design View.

 Tip: The size of the Form window varies according to the size of the Access window and the screen resolution. If necessary, change the size of the form by dragging any of the form's borders.

The *title bar* is the colored bar that appears at the top of the Form window. In Design View, the caption displays the name of the form as it appears in the Database window. In Form and Datasheet View, the title bar displays the form's **Caption** property setting, a value the user sees.

The *form header* appears at the top of the form. Typically, you use the form header to hold command buttons or information that applies to all pages in a multiple-page form. *Form footers* appear at the bottom of the form. In a data entry application, you may use a form footer to display summary information, such as the total order amount.

Page headers and footers appear at the top and bottom of each printed page when you print the form, but not in Form or Datasheet View.

155

Adding Controls

Controls are objects on forms that let the user perform such activities as viewing or selecting data, opening other forms, or moving from record to record. In the case of labels, controls help the user by providing visual cues to using forms.

Controls are the equivalent of fields in some form-generating programs. In addition to displaying or selecting data from tables, controls can run macros, call Access Basic functions, and display graphics or other embedded objects such as Microsoft Excel worksheets or charts.

You use two sets of tools to create and modify controls. The toolbar along the top of the Access window has buttons that display various options or switch the form to different viewing modes. The toolbox is a floating window containing buttons that represent the different kinds of controls you can add to a form.

Exploring the Toolbar

Buttons on the toolbar provide shortcuts for menu commands and change according to the operational mode the form is in. For example, when you add a text box control to a form, buttons for selecting font size, alignment, and other font characteristics are enabled on the toolbar. In contrast, when you add an option button to a form, the buttons for text characteristics are not enabled.

The toolbar has different buttons in Design View and in Form or Datasheet View (see figs. 8.2 and 8.3).

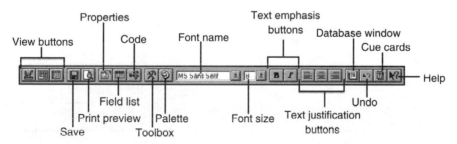

Figure 8.2.   The toolbar (Design View).

Some buttons on the toolbar act as toggles; that is, you click a button once to enable something and click the button again to disable it. For example, click the Toolbox button to alternately display or hide the toolbox.

> **Note:** Almost all the buttons on the toolbar have corresponding menu commands. For example, in Design View you can display or hide the toolbox by choosing the Toolbox command from the View menu.

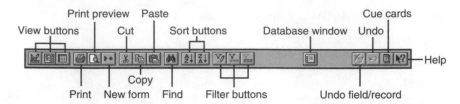

Figure 8.3. The toolbar (Form and Datasheet View).

The following buttons and controls appear on the toolbars:

- *Code Button.* Displays an Access Basic form module in which you can view, enter, or create procedures or run code using the Immediate window

- *Cue Cards Button.* Launches Cue Cards, an on-line coach that walks you through the most common tasks as you work with your own data

- *Cut, Copy, and Paste Buttons.* Cut or copy data or objects to the clipboard or paste data or objects from the clipboard

- *Database Window Button.* Moves the focus to the Database window

- *Field List Button.* Displays or hides the Field List box containing the names of all fields in the form's underlying query or table

- *Filter Buttons.* Create, apply, or remove a filter or sort order

- *Find Button.* Opens a dialog box you can use to search for specific data in the form's underlying query or table

- *Font Name Combo Box.* Sets the font for a control containing text (text boxes, combo boxes, list boxes, and labels)

- *Font Size Combo Box.* Sets the font size for the selected control

- *Help Button.* Displays context-sensitive help

- *Print Button.* Prints the current form

- *Print Preview Button.* Displays a full-page view of the form as it appears when printed

- *Properties Button.* Displays or hides the property sheet to view or change property settings

- *Save Button.* Saves the form

- *Sort Buttons.* Sort the records based on the values in the selected control(s)

- *Text Emphasis Buttons.* Apply or remove bold or italic emphasis to controls containing text

- *Text Justification Buttons.* Apply left, center, and right justification to controls containing text

157

- *Toolbox Button.* Displays or hides the toolbox

- *Undo Button.* Undoes the last design or data change

> **Tip:** Because you can undo only the most recent change to your form, click the Undo button
> (or choose the Undo command from the Edit menu) immediately if you make a mistake.

- *Undo Field/Record Button.* Undoes the last change to a field or form; this button appears
  on the toolbar in Form or Datasheet View only

- *View Buttons.* Display the form in Design, Form, or Datasheet View

Using the Toolbox

In Design View, you add controls by selecting the controls in the toolbox and dragging them to the
form (see fig. 8.4).

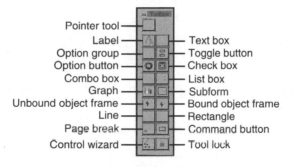

Figure 8.4.   The Toolbox (Design View only).

The following tools appear in the toolbox:

- *Pointer tool.* The Pointer tool resets the cursor to the regular mouse pointer, an arrow. Use
  the arrow to select existing controls on a form in Design View, select sections, and so on.

> **Tip:** You also can click the Pointer tool button to cancel adding a new control. If you start to add a
> control and then change your mind, click the Pointer tool button before you release the mouse button.

- *Label.* Use labels to display titles, instructions, and captions. You cannot move the focus to
  a label, which means users cannot enter data into them.

When you select the Label tool, the mouse pointer turns into a crosshair pointer. Position the pointer at the upper left corner where you want the label to begin and click the mouse. Access draws a narrow rectangle and waits for you to enter the text for the label. To finish creating the label, click ENTER.

- *Text box.* Use text boxes to enter new information and display existing information from the underlying table or query. The text can be numeric or alphanumeric (letters and other characters) and can include special symbols in the Windows ANSI-character set.

  When you select the Text Box tool, the mouse pointer turns into a small crosshair with an attached text box icon. Position the pointer at the upper left corner where you want the text box to begin and click the mouse.

  Because the text box control is one of the controls you can bind (attach) to a field in the underlying query or table, Access automatically updates the underlying table with the data you enter in the text box. Similarly, Access automatically displays the underlying data in the bound text box when the form is in Form or Datasheet View.

- *Option group.* An option group is a group of toggle buttons, option buttons, or check boxes (described later in this section) that represent a limited number of mutually-exclusive choices. The controls in a bound option group supply a numeric value to the option group.

> **Tip:** To make a toggle button, option button, or check box a part of the option group, you must add it to the option group (not simply drag an existing control into the option group). For example, if you create an option button and later decide to make it part of an option group, you must add a new option button directly to the option group and then delete the first option button.

- *Toggle button.* When clicked, a toggle button looks as if it has been pushed down. When clicked again, the button looks like it is back in the up position.

  The way toggle buttons behave depends on whether the buttons are in an option group. A toggle button in an option group has an **OptionValue** property that determines its value when it is pushed or not pushed. In an option group, only one toggle button can be pushed at any one time. The option group has a value that is equal to the **OptionValue** setting of the toggle button that has been pressed.

  A toggle button that is not part of an option group has value that is either True (if the button is pushed) or False (the button is not pushed). Outside an option group, any toggle button can be pushed, and the buttons are not mutually exclusive.

- *Option button.* Option buttons typically represent True/False or Yes/No conditions. When you select an option button, the center of the button turns black. An unselected option button has a white (or clear) center.

Option buttons are usually part of an option group. Option buttons in an option group are mutually exclusive: when you select one button, Access deselects all other option buttons in the same option group.

Option buttons not in an option group are not mutually exclusive. This means you can create multiple option buttons on one form and select all at the same time. Users do not expect this behavior, however. If you want to enable the user to select more than one option, use check boxes instead.

- *Check box.* Like option buttons, check boxes typically represent true and false conditions—true if checked, false if cleared. You can either add check boxes to a form outside an option group or include them in an option group to make them mutually exclusive (although this is generally a poor interface design).

- *Combo box.* A combo box consists of two parts: a text box for entering a new value and a drop-down list that displays a list of values. Use combo boxes to quickly select a choice from a limited set of options or to enter a free text response.

  The combo box's **ListRows** property setting determines the number of rows that appear when you open the list (you should avoid changing the default value, 8). You can scroll the list if there are more rows of data than specified by the **ListRows** property setting (see fig. 8.5).

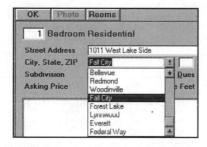

Figure 8.5. A combo box containing city names.

- *List box.* List boxes share many of the same characteristics as combo boxes. Because list boxes do not have a text box section, however, they are inherently limit-to-list: you can choose only exiting entries. Another difference is that list boxes do not have a drop-down section; they are always the same size. This means list boxes occupy more screen space than combo boxes. List boxes do have scroll bars, however, so the number of entries in the list is not limited by the size of the box.

- *Graph.* Graphs are just one variety of OLE (Object Linking and Embedding) object supported by Access. You can base graphs on Access data or on information from other applications such as Microsoft Excel. You create a graph with Microsoft Graph, an application supplied with Access.

160

To create a graph, select the Graph tool from the toolbox and then click the form wherever you want the graph to appear (do not worry about exact size or placement just yet). Access opens the GraphWizard window (see fig. 8.6).

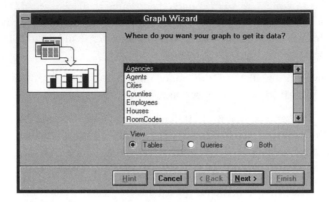

Figure 8.6. Use the Graph Wizard to create a graph or chart in Access.

The Graph Wizard presents a series of dialog boxes in which you can specify the source of the data for the graph, the graph's title, whether there should be a legend, and the type of graph (column, pie, and so on). When you answer all of the questions, Access closes the Graph Wizard and displays the completed graph on the form (see fig. 8.7).

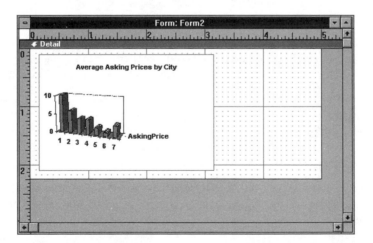

Figure 8.7. The completed graph control.

- *Subform.* Use the subform tool to embed one form (a child form) in another form (the parent or main form). Information in the subform can come from the same query or table, or from a different query or table.

Subforms are used most often to display detail items in a one-to-many relationship. For example, in the HomeFinder database application, the Houses form uses a subform to enter and display room information for a single house (one house to many rooms).

- *Unbound object frame.* Use an unbound object frame to display an OLE object that is not stored in an Access table. The kinds of objects you can embed into an unbound object frame are determined by the custom controls, applications, and drivers installed on your computer.

  Typical OLE objects you may want to embed include Excel charts and worksheets, graphs (Microsoft Graph), Paintbrush pictures, and Word for Windows documents.

- *Bound object frame.* A bound object frame behaves just like an unbound object frame, except that the data is actually bound to a field in the underlying table or query. In the Houses form, the Photo control is a bound object frame.

- *Line.* You can use the Line tool to draw lines and rules. Lines help break up the form into logical sections. For example, you may use a line to separate a data-entry area from a data-display area on the form.

  To draw a line, select the Line tool from the toolbox and then click and drag the mouse from the point where you want the line to start to where you want it to end. Change the line width and color by setting the **BorderWidth** and **BorderColor** properties in the property sheet or by using the palette.

- *Rectangle.* The Rectangle tool works like the Line tool, except that when you drag the mouse you define opposite corners for the rectangle. Drag the mouse diagonally to form the outline of the rectangle and then release the mouse.

  You can use rectangles as outlines to group fields on a form when an option group may be inappropriate. You also can use gray or colored rectangles to form shadows beneath other controls (in fact, one of the form wizards uses gray rectangles to produce a shadowed look).

- *Page break.* Add page breaks if you need to display more information than can fit on the screen at one time. In Form View without page breaks, when you press the PgUp and PgDn keys, Access scrolls the form up or down as if you had used the vertical scroll bar. With page breaks, pressing PgUp and PgDn moves an entire page at a time; with the scroll bar, you can scroll a little bit at a time.

  Page breaks are useful when you want to separate data on a form into logical groups. For example, you might design the first page to enter a company's address and phone numbers, the second page to enter information about the company's products and services, and so on.

  When you add a page break control, Access displays a small, nonresizable dotted line on the far left side of the form. In Form view, this is where the form will break into logical pages.

- *Command button.* You can add command buttons that trigger actions when they are clicked. For example, you can add a command button that closes the form or moves to a new record.

To create a command button, select the Command Button tool from the toolbox and define the button's size by dragging the mouse to form a rectangle on the form. When you release the mouse, Access creates the command button.

- *Control Wizard.* Click this button to turn control wizards on or off before you add a control to a form. When you add a control for which a control wizard exists, you create the control using the wizard. When control wizards are off, or if the control does not have an installed control wizard, you create the control without a wizard.

- *Tool lock.* When you need to add a number of controls of the same type, use the Tool Lock button to prevent Access from selecting the Pointer tool each time you add a control.

   For example, right after you add a text box to a form, Access changes the mouse pointer back to the regular pointer, an arrow. If you want to add a series of text boxes without having to continually select the Text Box tool, click the Tool Lock button.

   The Tool Lock button is a toggle button. When pushed, Access does not reset the mouse pointer. You can change tools while the lock is on. To turn the tool locking off, click the Tool Lock button again.

The next section discusses how you can apply the design tools to create Access forms.

Creating the Main Menu Form

You should draw on paper a rough sketch of how you intend your application to flow. For example, many developers design their applications with a main menu, or switchboard. Users select a major function from the main menu and either go straight to that function or to a secondary menu (see fig. 8.8).

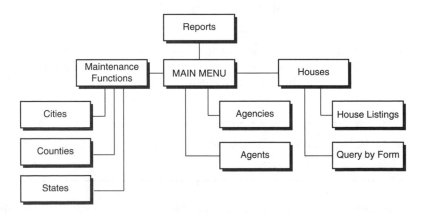

Figure 8.8.   Many applications use a main menu approach to program flow.

To create the Main Menu form for the HomeFinder application, follow these steps:

1. Go to the Database window, click the Form button, and then click the New button. Access displays the New Form dialog box in which you can enter or select the name of the query on which to base the form. The Main Menu is an unbound form (that is, it is not based on any underlying data), so leave the name of the table or query blank.

2. Click the Blank Form button to create the Main Menu on your own without a wizard; Access displays the Form window.

3. Even though the form has no controls, save the new form by choosing Save As from the File menu. Name the form Main Menu.

4. Add four command buttons to the form (see fig. 8.9).

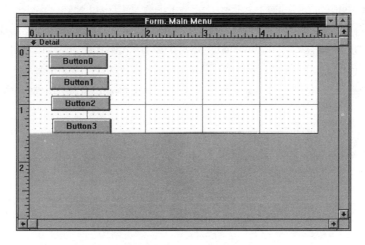

Figure 8.9. The Main Menu uses command buttons to navigate the application.

The HomeFinder application has more than four major functions, of course. The purpose of the Main Menu, however, is to provide access to the most commonly-used functions. For example, you so seldom need to add new states to the system that it makes no sense to provide a command button to open a States form. Instead, access these miscellaneous functions through menu bar commands.

 Chapter 14, "Adding Menu Bars," describes how you can add a custom menu bar to the main menu.

Most command buttons contain a brief, usually single-worded caption. For example, you might create command buttons labeled Houses, Reports, and Exit. To make this application easier to use, however, the captions can be a bit longer, requiring wider command buttons.

The following sections describe how you can complete the Main Menu form by setting a variety of form and control properties and by responding to button presses.

Setting Form and Control Properties

Chapter 15, "Creating a Self-Configuring Application," discusses strategies for automatically setting the form and control colors. For now, set the detail section's **BackColor** property to 12632256.

> **Tip:** Opening the palette and choosing colors is much easier than setting numeric values for colors.

Select the first three command buttons and then change their **ForeColor** property settings to dark blue (8388608). Change the **ForeColor** property setting for the fourth command button to dark red (128). The different color helps distinguish the function of the fourth command button—the one that exits the application.

As a design strategy, make sure you have a consistent amount of *white space* around your controls. For example, the first command button should be 0.125 inches from the top and 0.125 inches from the left edge of the detail section. Left-align the remaining controls with the first command button.

The amount of white space between the command buttons is normally 0.06 inches, but on the Main Menu this results in controls that are a bit too close together. For this form, the white space is 1.25 inches.

The following procedure outlines the steps you can follow to create white space between the command buttons.

1. Set the height for the command buttons to 0.25 inches. For now, do not worry about how wide they are.

2. Total the following to calculate the position for the second command button:

The first command button's **Top** property setting	0.125
Its height	0.25
The amount of white space	0.125

3. The sum (0.5) is the **Top** property setting for the second command button.

4. Perform the same math for the other command buttons to arrive at **Top** property settings of 0.875 and 1.25 inches.

5. Because the last command button performs a different kind of activity (exiting the application), add an additional 0.1 inches of white space and set its **Top** property to 1.3 inches.

165

> **Tip:** At first, the 0.06-inch setting may seem arbitrary but actually is easy to work with on most forms. Because the standard height for most controls is 0.17 inches, all you need to do is add 0.25 inches to a control's **Top** property setting to calculate the next position and still achieve the .06-inch white space.

To identify the major functions of the main menu, change the text that appears atop the command buttons by changing the **Caption** property settings. The first command button should be set to **Find a House**, the second to **House Listings**, the third to **Reports** and, finally, the last command button to **Exit** (see fig. 8.10).

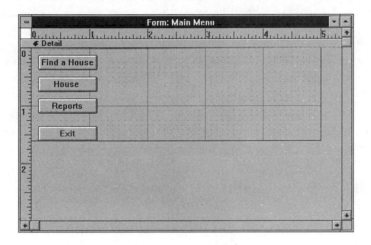

Figure 8.10.   Set the **Caption** property to change a command button's text.

Notice how the caption **House Listings** does not fit the width of the command button. Select all four command buttons by dragging a rectangle through all of the controls and then press ALT+O, S, F (or choose the Size command from the Format menu and then choose the to Fit subcommand).

Access resizes all of the controls to fit the width of their captions, but now the controls are different sizes. Press ALT+O, S, W (or choose the Size command from the Format menu and then choose the to Widest subcommand) to resize the controls to the widest control. In this case, the House Listings command button is the widest.

In resizing for a consistent width, Access also changed the height of the controls to 0.3229 inches. With the controls still selected, open the property sheet and set the **Height** property back to 0.25 inches.

166

Adjust the height of the detail section so that there is 0.1 inch of white space beneath the Exit command button. The easiest way to set the height is to drag the bottom edge of the section up to the bottom of the last control and then add 0.1 inches to the detail section's **Height** property setting. In this example, set the **Height** property to 1.7 inches.

Adjust the width of the detail section so that it has the same amount of white space by dragging the right edge to the right side of the command buttons and then changing the form's **Width** property setting. In this example, you would ordinarily set the **Width** property to 1.4229 inches, but 1.42 is close enough.

> **Note:** Interestingly, Access does not accept a setting of 1.42 inches and instead changes it to 1.4201.

Table 8.1 lists the property settings you need to set for the form. If a property is not listed, its default setting is acceptable.

Table 8.1. Main Menu Form Property Settings

Property	Setting
Caption	Main Menu
Default View	Single Form
Shortcut Menu	No
Scroll Bars	Neither
Record Selectors	No
Navigation Buttons	No
Auto Center	Yes
Modal	Yes
Min Button	No
Max Button	No

Save the Main Menu form, close it, return to the Database window, and then open the form (see fig. 8.11).

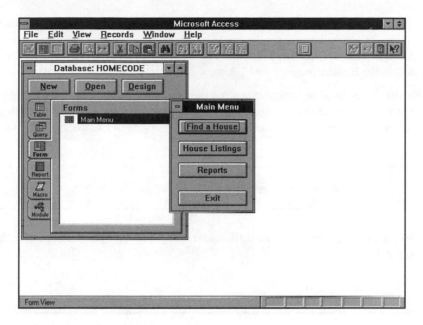

Figure 8.11. The Main Menu form (Form View).

Several things are wrong with the form:

- The form is too narrow.

- The Database window should not be visible.

- The menu bar does not include menus specific to the Main Menu and, in fact, contains menus that have nothing to do with the form.

 See Chapter 14, "Adding Menu Bars," for details on adding a custom menu bar.

- None of the command buttons does anything.

- The toolbar should be hidden because there is nothing on the toolbar the user can use in the current context.

- The text in the status bar reads "Form View," which means nothing to the user.

Most of these issues can be resolved by returning to the form's Design View and then setting various properties or by writing procedures that perform actions, usually in response to events.

Table 8.2 lists the properties you may set for the command buttons on the form.

Table 8.2. Main Menu Control Property Settings

Control	Property	Setting
Find a House	Name	Find
	StatusBarText	Find a house based on the buyer's preferences.
	TabIndex	1
House Listings	Name	Listings
	StatusBarText	Add, display, or change a house listing.
	TabIndex	2
Reports	Name	Reports
	StatusBarText	Display or print a report.
	TabIndex	3
Exit	Name	Exit
	StatusBarText	Exit this application.
	TabIndex	0

Figure 8.12 illustrates how you can enhance the form's appearance by adding an unbound OLE object (a bitmap) behind the command buttons.

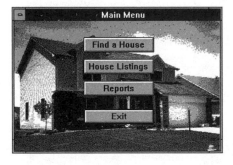

Figure 8.12. Add a bitmap to enhance the form's appearance.

The following procedure outlines the steps you can follow to add a picture already stored in the Houses table included with the HomeFinder sample application.

1. Open the Houses table in Datasheet View.

2. Move to the Photo field for any record and then copy the Paintbrush picture to the clipboard by clicking Ctrl+C.

169

3. Close the Houses table and return to the Main Menu form.

4. Select the detail section and paste the picture by clicking Ctrl+V.

5. Choose the Send To Back command from the Format menu; the picture now appears as a background with the command buttons in front.

The form is more attractive, but it still does not do anything. The following section, "Writing Procedures," describes how you can add code to the form to open other forms or exit the application.

Writing Procedures

The Main Menu has only four functions: load any of three other forms and exit the application. To determine which function to execute, the user clicks a command button, which triggers the *Click* event.

You can respond to a command button's **Click** event by calling a macro, running an Access Basic function, or executing a procedure attached directly to the event. This section describes how you can write a procedure that either opens another, specified form or exits Microsoft Access.

 For more information about creating macros, see Chapter 9, "Building the HomeFinder Macros." For more information about writing functions, see Chapter 12, "Migrating from Macros to Modules."

The following procedure outlines the steps you can follow to create an event procedure.

1. Select the Find a House command button and set its **OnClick** property to [Event Procedure]

2. Right-click the property setting and then choose the Build command; Access displays the form's Module window for the command button's **Click** event. Enter the line of code that opens a form named QBF (see fig. 8.13).

 Note: The QBF form does not yet exist, so the event procedure produces an error if you click the command button while the form is in Form view. After you create the QBF form, however, clicking the command button opens and transfers control to the QBF form.

3. Repeat steps 1 and 2 for the other command buttons. Table 8.3 lists the lines of code you need to add for each event procedure.

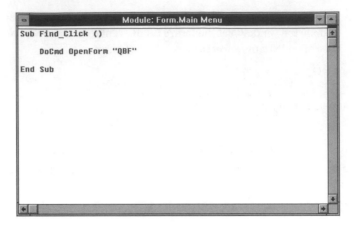

Figure 8.13. This event procedure will load a form named QBF.

Table 8.3. Event Procedure Code

Control	Code
Find a House	DoCmd OpenForm "QBF"
House Listings	DoCmd OpenForm "Houses"
Reports	DoCmd OpenForm "Reports"
Exit	' Application.Quit ' Don't quit until we're code complete.
	DoCmd Close ' Close the form.

Tip: The line of code that normally quits Microsoft Access is commented out with an apostrophe (see Table 8.3). Whenever you press the Exit command button, the event procedure falls through and closes the form. Because the Database window was previously hidden, the Access window becomes empty. To redisplay the Database window, press F11.

For more information about constructing Access Basic procedures, see Chapter 17, "Naming Conventions and Style Guidelines."

171

For now, the only other thing that needs to be done is to hide the Database window when the Main Menu form opens. To hide the window, set the form's **Load** event to [Event Procedure] and then add the following two lines of code to the Form_Load event procedure:

```
Sub Form_Load ()

    DoCmd SelectObject A_FORM, Me.FormName, True
    DoCmd DoMenuItem 1, 4, 3, , A_MENU_VER20

End Sub
```

The first line selects the Main Menu form in the Database window. This has the effect of moving the focus to the Database window. The second line uses the *DoMenuItem* macro action to hide the current window.

Building the Remaining Forms

In addition to the Main Menu form, the 10 tables in the HomeFinder application require their own form for data entry purposes. Also, the application has a Reports form that contains a list of the available reports.

 For more information on reports, see Chapter 10, "Building the HomeFinder Reports."

The following sections discuss important aspects of each form.

Agencies

The Agencies form (see fig. 8.14) provides information about the real estate agencies and the agents that work for each. The subform controls are all disabled and locked, which means the user cannot edit or add agent information. Instead, the user must open the Agents form.

 Tip: You may want to enhance this form by providing a mechanism for selecting an agent and then opening the Agents form to the proper agent. One way of doing this is to add a menu command to a custom menu bar and have the command open the Agents form.

The custom record navigation buttons in the form's header let the user move from record to record. These command buttons call a user-defined function.

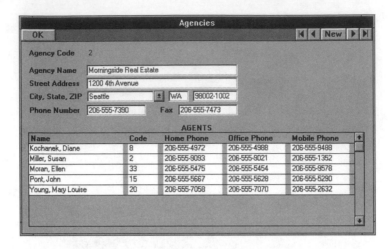

Figure 8.14. The Agencies form features a subform.

 For more information about the CSVGoToRecord() function, see Chapter 12, "Migrating from Macros to Modules."

Another enhancement you may consider is replacing the State text box with a combo box. You can use the States table (currently unused in the HomeFinder application) to fill the combo box.

Agents

You use the Agents form (see fig. 8.15) to enter agent information and to assign agencies to each agent.

Because the Agent Code control is bound to a Counter field in an underlying table, the control is disabled and locked. The **BackStyle** property has been set to Clear so that the control's background appears to be the same as the detail section of the form. Unlike regular sunken text boxes, and as a visual cue to the user that the control is read-only, there is no border around the control.

Cities

The Cities form features an option group with two option buttons for the user to choose the sort order for the cities (see fig. 8.16).

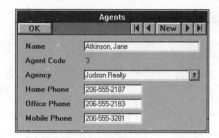

Figure 8.15. The Agents form.

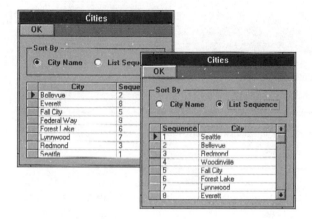

Figure 8.16. Users can choose from two sort orders.

To implement this effect, the form contains two subforms, each the same size and in the same location, one atop the other. Each subform is based on similar queries that differ only in the ORDER BY clause.

Selecting an option button triggers the option group's **AfterUpdate** event. The event procedure makes one of the subforms visible and the other invisible. This has the apparent effect of sorting the list.

Counties

The Counties form (see fig. 8.17) has the same ability to sort the list as the Cities form.

To create the Counties form, you may want to copy the Cities form and then change the form's **Caption** property and a few property settings in the two subforms. The layout of the two forms is the same.

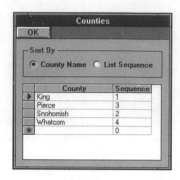

Figure 8.17. The Counties form.

Employees and Status Codes

The HomeFinder application has no Employees form. The Employees table has been included in the HOMEDATA.MDB database for reference purposes, mostly to illustrate certain table concepts.

You can create your own Employees form based on ideas from the Houses form (which includes a photograph) or from the Employees form included in the Northwind Traders sample database that accompanies Microsoft Access.

Likewise, there is no Status Codes form, because the StatusCodes table exists only to support the Employees table.

Houses

The Houses form (see fig. 8.18) is designed primarily for data entry and other internal uses and is intended to be used only by real estate agents. The prospective home buyer uses the QBF form to enter specific home requirements, but does not actually enter information about house listings.

Because this form has to track more information than the other forms in the HomeFinder application, it has the most controls. Even so, the Houses form is easy to use—notice the liberal use of space-saving controls such as combo boxes, option buttons, and a subform.

Tip: The HomeFinder application was developed at standard VGA resolution (640 × 480 pixels × 16 colors). At that resolution, some of the controls on the Houses form had to be placed closer together than would be possible with a higher resolution such as super VGA (800 × 600). If your computer and monitor support a higher resolution, you may want to redesign the forms to take advantage of the extra room and add additional space between the controls. The ideal white space between controls is 0.06 inches.

175

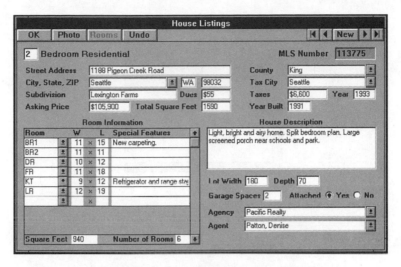

Figure 8.18. The Houses form contains a wide variety of information about house listings.

The Houses form illustrates how you can use a subform control to embed one form in another. The room information section of the form is actually a subform control that gets its information from a form named Houses Sub.

For more information about naming subforms, see Chapter 17, "Naming Conventions and Style Guidelines."

Along the bottom of the subform control is a text box that displays the total square feet for all the rooms listed in the subform. The square footage commonly listed for a house includes dead space, such as hallways and stairways. Because the rooms you list in the subform will be the "real" living space, this figure may be more meaningful as the total square footage figure on the main form. A second text box along the bottom of the subform displays a count of the number of rooms.

Note: Although you can manually enter the room count in the Houses form, having Access calculate the value automatically is much better. Not only is it easier to let the machine do the work, but it is generally a bad idea to store calculated values.

The Houses form tracks more information than can fit on the screen at one time. You have several ways to can handle this, including the following:

- Make the form longer than the physical screen and press the PgUp and PgDn keys; or add a vertical scroll bar to move from page to page. You achieve varying degrees of success when

176

you use this technique because the size of the form is subject to the screen resolution and the size of the window itself.

- Make the form wider than the screen and use the horizontal scroll bar to move from side to side. Scrollbars consume valuable screen real estate, are awkward to use, and require a mouse to operate.

- Make selected information visible or invisible, on demand, even if it means obscuring other data on the form. This is the preferred technique, at least on this form.

In the HomeFinder application, the room information and the house photo share the same screen space in the lower left corner of the form. Only one can be visible at a time.

When you click the Photo command button, the command button's event procedure makes the photo visible and hides the room information (see fig. 8.19). It also hides the label (Room Information) that appears above the subform control so that the text does not show through the photo.

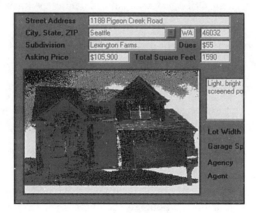

Figure 8.19.   The house photo and room information share the same screen space.

When you click the Rooms command button, the opposite occurs: The photo is made invisible and the room information subform and its label are once again visible.

QBF

Potential home buyers use the QBF (query-by-form) form (see fig. 8.20) to enter their housing preferences. For example, the home buyer can specify a desired city, a price range, and other requirements.

All controls have been assigned default values, but the user can override them by entering new values. When the user clicks the Display command button, the system builds an equivalent SQL WHERE clause that reflects all criteria and then opens the Houses form.

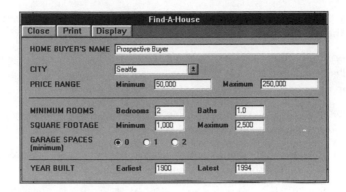

Figure 8.20. The home buyer can enter a variety of selection criteria.

Opening the Houses form from the QBF form is similar to opening the form from the Main Menu, with the following exceptions:

- The Display command button's event procedure applies the WHERE clause to the statement that opens the form. This has the effect of filtering the records.

- The Houses form is read-only; the user cannot edit any of the data.

- As a visual cue that the form is read-only, the style for the text boxes, combo boxes, and option buttons is set to normal, not sunken.

- The New command button is disabled; because the form is read-only, the user cannot add new records.

- The house photograph appears when the form opens; the normal default for the Houses form is to display the room information, not the photo.

When the user clicks the Print command button, the command button's event procedure opens the Selected Houses report and sends it directly to the printer. You ordinarily open the report in Print Preview (and let the user send it to the printer), but the form already has a Display command button to perform that action.

 For complete details about the QBF form, as well as step-by-step instructions on how it was built, see Chapter 16, "Adding Query-by-Form Capability."

Reports

You can create a form that lists all the reports in the system and provides command buttons to either print or display a desired report (see fig. 8.21).

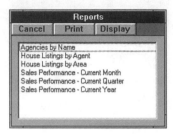

Figure 8.21. Users can identify reports and print them directly from the Reports form.

The list box is dynamic: Whenever you add new reports, change report names, or even delete reports, the Reports form automatically reflects the changes.

Room Codes

The Room Codes form looks a lot like the Cities and Counties forms (see fig. 8.22), but it offers no option to change the sort order of the list (the list appears in sequence according to the room codes).

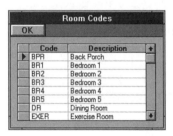

Figure 8.22. The Room Codes form.

States

The States form is nearly identical to the Cities and Counties forms and offers the choice of sorting by name or by abbreviation (see fig. 8.23).

179

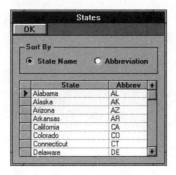

Figure 8.23. The States form.

Summary

As with any complex task, creating forms, especially those such as the Houses form, likely involves a few false starts during the initial development. Expect to make a few mistakes in the beginning, but fewer as you gain experience with the Access form design process.

The forms in the HomeFinder sample application are fairly typical of the ones you may create in your own applications. You can add a wide variety of different controls to improve their efficiency and ease of use.

It is particularly important for you to maintain a consistent style and interface strategy from form to form. A poor, yet consistent, interface is better than a nearly-perfect interface in which the user cannot anticipate what to do.

9

Building the HomeFinder Macros

Regardless of your programming ability, you can use Access macros to make your work easier and more productive. You can use macros to perform such tasks as manipulating database objects, printing reports, validating data, and remapping key settings.

You create Access macros in an interactive environment; defining each step or operation of a macro is easy and straightforward. Many of the macros you create can be built entirely by selecting items from drop-down lists, though some macro actions may require you to enter form names, formatting expressions, and so on.

This chapter concentrates on the macros you need to support the HomeFinder sample application, but you will find that they represent the kinds of macros you will use in your own applications.

This chapter covers the following:

- Using and Avoiding Macros
- Exploring the Macro Window
- Constructing a Macro
- Running a Macro
- Building the AutoExec Macro
- Building the AutoKeys Macro

 Tip: You should create and store macros in your application's code database, and not in the data database. In the HomeFinder application, the code database is named HOMECODE.MDB.

For more information about macros and macro actions, see Chapter 12, "Migrating from Macros to Modules," and Chapter 20, "Macro Actions."

Using and Avoiding Macros

As a rule, you should avoid using macros. For all their simplicity, macros do not provide a complete programming environment. Macros offer no error handling, are difficult to debug, and do not provide the debugging capabilities available in modules.

There are only two situations that demand you use macros:

- To automatically execute a series of operations whenever you first open a database; in this case, you create a macro named AutoExec (described in this chapter)

- To remap specified keys; in this case, you create a macro group named AutoKeys

 To add macros to menu bars, see Chapter 14, "Adding Menu Bars."

In all other cases, you should call Access Basic functions and not macros. For this reason, this chapter is not a complete tutorial on macro construction.

Exploring the Macro Window

You create and modify macros in the Macro window (see fig. 9.1). The Macro window has two sections. The upper section is where you enter the names of the macros, any conditions, the desired macro actions, and optional comments. The lower section is where you enter arguments for the macro actions.

Enter conditions to determine whether to run the macro.   Comments

Use this
column to
create a
macro group.

Select a macro
action from the
drop-down lists.

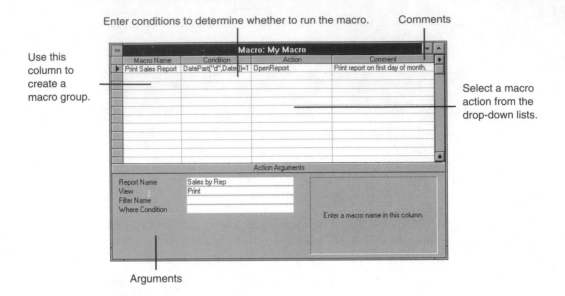

Arguments

Figure 9.1.   The Macro window.

Constructing a Macro

The following procedure outlines the steps you can follow to create a macro.

1. Determine what you want the macro to do, what actions the macro must perform and whether any of the actions depend on conditions (for example, whether a specified form is open).

2. Go to the Database window, click the Macro button, and then click the New button; Access displays the Macro window.

3. If necessary, display the Macro Names and Conditions columns by choosing the appropriate command from the View menu.

How you proceed from here depends greatly on what you want the macro to do. In general, it is as simple as adding whatever macro actions and conditions may be necessary to construct the macro, usually by choosing items from drop-down lists and then setting any arguments required by the macro actions.

Macro Actions

A macro consists of one or more macro actions. The term *action* is equivalent to *commands* or *statements* in other environments, such as Visual Basic or WordBasic. In Microsoft Access, macro actions are not the same as Access Basic functions and statements, although there are equivalent functions for most of the macro actions.

183

You might think of a macro action as an instruction Access carries out to perform a specific operation. For example, the **OpenForm** macro action opens a form. There are other actions that likewise perform specific tasks.

 For more information about the more than 40 macro actions, see Chapter 20, "Macro Actions."

Arguments

Most macro actions have arguments. An *argument* is an attribute or parameter that specifies how Access should execute the macro action. For example, the **OpenReport** macro action needs to know the name of the report you want to open, and how you want to view it (Print, Preview, or Design).

Although some macro arguments are required, many are optional. The hints that appear in the hints section of the Macro window tell you whether you must provide a value for a macro argument.

Conditions

Access typically looks at the first macro action (the first row in the macro), executes it, and then moves to the next row. It continues this process until it reaches the end of the macro (or until it encounters a **StopMacro** or **StopAllMacros** macro action).

At times, you may want to run a macro or a specific macro action only when a certain condition is met. A *condition* is an expression that evaluates to either True or False. When a condition is present, Access executes the macro action only when the condition is True.

For example, you might use the **OpenReport** macro action to print a report, but only if it is the first day of the month. Figure 9.1 illustrates how you can apply a condition to the macro. For more information about entering macro conditions, search Help for "Conditions."

Running a Macro

You can use the following six techniques to run macros:

- *From the Macro Window.* Click the Run button on the toolbar or choose the Run command from the Macro menu.

- *From the Database Window.* Click the Macro button to display a list of macros. Select the desired macro and then click the Run button.

- *Using the Run Macro Command.* Throughout Access, many of the File menus include the Run Macro command; it displays a dialog box in which you can enter or select the name of a macro.

- *From Within Another Macro.* You can use the **RunMacro** macro action to run one macro from another.

- *From a Form, Report, or Control Event.* Set one of the event properties to the name of the macro you want to run (see fig. 9.2).

Access runs this macro whenever the Print command button is clicked.

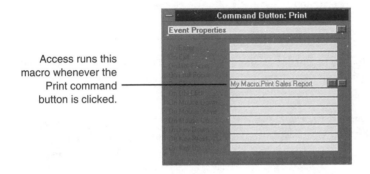

Figure 9.2. Calling a macro from the **Click** event.

There are other events besides **Click**, among them **Close**, **Current**, **DblClick**, and **Enter**. Some of these events apply to command buttons, some to forms, and some to other database objects. For more information about Access events and the objects to which they apply, search Help for "events: reference".

> **Tip:** When you drag a macro from the Database window directly to a form, Access creates a command button and sets the control's **OnClick** property to the name of macro.

- *From Access Basic Code.* You can call macros directly from Access Basic with the **DoCmd** statement:

```
DoCmd RunMacro "Print Sales Report"
```

185

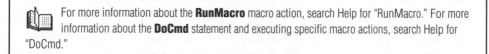

For more information about the **RunMacro** macro action, search Help for "RunMacro." For more information about the **DoCmd** statement and executing specific macro actions, search Help for "DoCmd."

Building the AutoExec Macro

Every time you open a given database, Access checks to see if there is a macro named AutoExec. If this optional macro is present, Access runs it automatically. You create the AutoExec macro like any other macro; the essential difference is that AutoExec runs first, automatically. Each database can have its own AutoExec macro.

For example, you might want to create an AutoExec macro that hides the built-in toolbars, loads a certain startup form (such as the Main Menu form in the HomeFinder application), or performs other macro actions necessary to get the database ready to use.

Tip: Even though the AutoExec macro is designed primarily to be run only when you open the database, you can run the macro at any time like any other macro. For more information, see the preceding section "Running a Macro."

Suppressing the AutoExec Macro

There may be times when you do not want to run the AutoExec macro. For example, you may want to suppress the macro while you are developing and testing it. To prevent Access from running the AutoExec macro, you can do any of several things:

- Change the name of the macro by going to the Database window and then choosing the Rename command from the File menu. When you are ready to run AutoExec again, change the name back to AutoExec.

- Add a **StopMacro** macro action to the top of the AutoExec macro. When you are ready to run AutoExec again, either remove the **StopMacro** action or add a condition, False, to the macro action.

- Press and hold down either Shift key as you open the database containing the AutoExec macro. However, this technique does not work when you open the database using the run-time library supplied with the Access Developers Toolkit (in releases of Access prior to 2.0, this was called the Access Distribution Kit).

Although there is no global AutoExec macro that runs every time you start Access, the /X command-line parameter lets you specify the name of a macro to run in addition to AutoExec (if present). The AutoExec macro runs first, however.

 For more information, see "Starting and Exiting Access" in Chapter 3, "The Access Development Environment."

Exploring the HomeFinder AutoExec Macro

As stated earlier in this chapter and elsewhere in this book, you should avoid using macros for a variety of reasons. However, Access provides no built-in mechanism for automatically calling a function when you open a database, only the AutoExec macro.

Consequently, you should create an AutoExec macro that does only one thing: call a function named AutoExec() (see fig. 9.3).

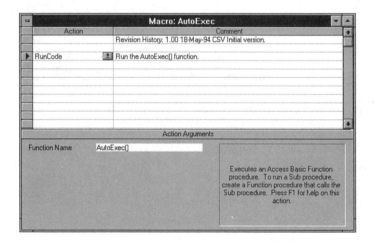

Figure 9.3.   Calling the AutoExec() function from the AutoExec macro.

The AutoExec() function will perform the activities that you would otherwise execute in the AutoExec macro.

The following steps outline the procedure you follow to create the functions called by the AutoExec macro.

1. Go to the Database window, click the Module button, and then click the New button; Access displays the Module window.

2. Save the new module by choosing the Save command from the File menu and name it Initialization.

3. Enter the **Option Explicit** statement (see fig. 9.4).

> For more information about the **Option Explicit** statement, see Chapter 17, "Naming Conventions and Style Guidelines," or search Help for "option."

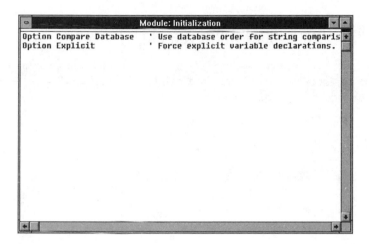

Figure 9.4. Enter the **Option Explicit** statement in every module you create.

4. Enter the following code for the AutoExec() function (when you press Enter at the end of the first line, Access displays a new window in which you can enter the rest of the function):

```
Function AutoExec () As Integer

    Const STARTUPFORM = "Main Menu"
    Dim X As Integer

    X = csvHideToolBars()
    X = csvHideDBWindow()
    DoCmd OpenForm STARTUPFORM

End Function
```

5. Save the Initialization module and then open or create another module named Tools. You will use this module to store generic functions, such as those that hide the toolbars.

Tip: Be sure you enter the **Option Explicit** statement to the new Tools module.

6. Enter the code for the csvHideToolbars() function:

```
Function csvHideToolBars () As Integer

        Application.SetOption "Built-In Toolbars Available", False

    End Function
```

It is generally a bad idea to add language-specific code to your applications. For example, the csvHideToolbars() function has hard-coded text that identifies a specific system option. If you run this function in another language version of Microsoft Access, the function will fail and produce a compile error.

However, application development is an iterative process, and the point of this exercise is to illustrate one way to hide the toolbars.

For more information about designing applications that anticipate international needs, see Chapter 18, "Application Design Guidelines."

7. Enter the code for the csvHideDBWindow() function:

```
Function csvHideDBWindow () As Integer

        csvHideDBWindow = True
        DoCmd Echo False
        DoCmd SelectObject A_MACRO, "AutoExec", True
        DoCmd DoMenuItem 1, 4, 3, , A_MENU_VER20
        DoCmd Echo True

    End Function
```

8. Save the Tools module and then check your work for syntax errors by choosing Compile Loaded Modules from the Run menu. Resolve any reported errors by checking the functions for typing mistakes, and then compile again. Repeat this process until Access no longer produces any error messages.

9. Close both the Tools and Initialization modules.

Test the AutoExec macro by returning to the Database window, selecting the macro, and then clicking the Run button.

Building the AutoKeys Macro

The optional AutoKeys macro stores a set of customized key assignments you can use while you work throughout the Access environment. As you open a database, Access looks to see if there is a macro named AutoKeys. If the macro is present, Access automatically sets the key assignments as it opens the database.

You cannot use the AutoKeys macro to stop or preempt the AutoExec macro. Because AutoExec runs before AutoKeys, do not construct an AutoExec macro that uses the SendKeys macro action or any remapped keys.

 For more information about the **SendKeys** macro action, see Chapter 23, "Macro Actions."

The Microsoft Access AutoKeys macro behaves like similar keyboard macro recorders in other products. The macro lets you assign actions to specified key sequences. For example, instead of displaying the Database window when you press F11, it can display your own form or a message box.

 Tip: Remember that custom key assignments you make with the AutoKeys macro override any built-in key settings. For example, the default behavior for Ctrl+C in most Windows-based applications is to copy the selected text or object to the Clipboard. If you reassign Ctrl+C to mean something else, you cannot use Ctrl+C to copy to the Clipboard. If you remap a key that already has a built-in meaning, such as Ctrl+C, make sure it is not a key otherwise needed to use your database.

Table 9.1 lists the keys you can reassign with the AutoKeys macro.

Table 9.1. AutoKeys Key Sequences

Enter this...	...to assign this key combination
^A or ^4	Ctrl+ any letter or number
{F1}	Any function key (F1-F12)
^{F1}	Ctrl+ any function key
+{F1}	Shift+ any function key
{INSERT}	Ins key
^{INSERT}	Ctrl+Ins key
+{INSERT}	Shift+Ins key

Enter this...	...to assign this key combination
{DELETE} or {DEL}	Del key
^{DELETE} or ^{DEL}	Ctrl+Del key
+{DELETE} or +{DEL}	Shift+Del key

Although the AutoKeys macro uses the same syntax as the **SendKeys** statement in Access Basic, a number of keys cannot be reassigned in AutoKeys. If a key sequence is not listed in Table 9.1, you cannot use it in the AutoKeys macro. For example, you cannot use the Alt, Enter, Home, End, or arrow keys in any key assignment. Further, you cannot use Ctrl or Shift to assign more than one alphanumeric key. For example, ^(XC) is an invalid key assignment.

To define key assignments, enter the desired key code in the Macro Name column, and enter or select the action you want Access to perform (see fig. 9.5).

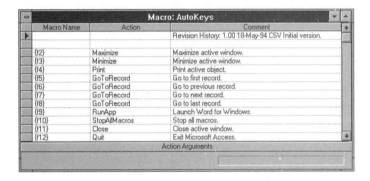

Figure 9.5. Remapping key assignments with the AutoKeys macro.

After you have entered all the key assignments, save the macro and name it AutoKeys. Access maps the key settings immediately. You do not have to run the AutoKeys macro yourself.

Tip: Access does not reserve the name AutoKeys in the same way it does the name AutoExec. Indeed, you can set the name of the AutoKeys macro to anything you want. To change the name of the default key assignment macro, choose the Options command from the View menu, and then select the Keyboard category. In the Key Assignment Macro text box, enter the name of the macro you want to use in place of AutoKeys. The change takes effect immediately.

Summary

Macros are built-in tools you can use to help automate you work. They are somewhat limited in their usefulness, however, because they lack error handling and are difficult to debug.

You should avoid using macros except for the AutoExec macro (which runs automatically when you open the database), the AutoKeys macro (which remaps specified key sequences), and the custom menu bar macros.

10

Building the HomeFinder Reports

Earlier chapters in this book described a typical development process: you perform an analysis to determine the application's data requirements, design a database schema that stores the data, and then implement the design.

Although this process requires much effort, how you develop the application is of little concern to most users; they are mainly interested in the success of your application. The success of your effort is largely determined by whether you have clearly defined the objectives of the application. For most applications, an important objective is the generation of printed reports.

If you are working from an existing printed report, you already have an idea of what the report should look like. However, often users suggest changes to existing printed reports, or you may be working from scratch with no existing design. In either case, you can easily change the design of a report to match the users' requirements more closely.

This chapter illustrates a few of the reports in the HomeFinder sample application, but you will find that they represent the kinds of reports that you will create in your own applications.

This chapter covers the following:

- Exploring the Report Window
- Understanding Access Reports
- Building the Agents by Agency Report
- Building the Remaining Reports

Tip: You should create and store reports in your application's code database, and not in the data database. In the HomeFinder application, the code database is named HOMECODE.MDB.

Exploring the Report Window

A report is much like an Access form: both create an interface between you and the data stored in Access tables. You can create detailed reports that present information at the lowest possible level, or summary reports that consolidate information at the highest levels.

To add controls, you use the same toolbox and procedures as you would for a form. However, some controls do not make sense on a report. For example, it does not make sense to add command buttons and list boxes to a report.

The following procedure outlines the steps that you can follow to create a report:

1. Go to the Database window. Click the Report button and then the New button. Access displays the New Report dialog box in which you can enter or select the name of the query on which to base the report. For this example, however, the report will be based on an SQL statement and not a query, so leave the text box blank.

2. You can choose to use a ReportWizard or create the new report on your own without a wizard.

 Note: Wizards are tools that you can use to create reports and other database objects, usually in a step by step fashion. This book does not illustrate how to use the wizards shipped with Microsoft Access. For more information about wizards, see Chapter 19, "Creating and Using Libraries."

Click the Blank Report button. Access displays the Report window.

3. Even though the report has no controls, save the new report by choosing the Save As command from the File menu. For this example, name the form Agents by Agency.

4. Display the report's header and footer sections by choosing the Report Header/Footer command from the Format menu.

 Note: When you create a report, Access displays the page header and footer automatically.

194

Understanding Access Reports

Reports are divided into several sections (see fig. 10.1).

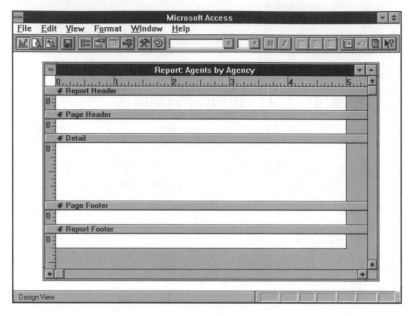

Figure 10.1. The Report window in Design View.

 Tip: The size of the Report window varies according to the size of the Access window and the screen resolution. If necessary, you can change the size of the report to display all the report's sections by dragging any of the report's borders.

In Design View, the Report window's title bar displays the name of the report. For this example, the name displayed is Agents by Agency. In Print Preview and Sample Preview, the title bar displays the value of the report's **Caption** property. If you do not set the report's **Caption** property, Access uses the name of the report.

Report headers appear at the beginning of reports before anything else prints. You use the report header to present information that should appear only once in the report, no matter how many pages are in it. For example, you can use the report header to design a cover page. To do so, add a page break control to the bottom of the Report Header section to make sure that the cover page appears on its own sheet of paper.

Report footers appear at the end of reports and are typically used for grand totals or for footnotes. You may want to include a page break control at the top of the Report Footer section to make sure that the totals or footnotes appear on their own sheet of paper.

Page headers and footers appear at the top and bottom of each printed page. You use the header to present the report title and the date that you printed the report. The page number can go in either the page header or the page footer.

Building the Agents by Agency Report

If you have not already created the blank report, do so now and name the report **Agents by Agency**. (If necessary, refer to the section "Exploring the Report Window" earlier in this chapter.)

This report does not require a report header or footer. If you have not already done so, hide these sections by choosing the Report Header/Footer command from the Format menu.

The following sections describe how you can complete the Agents by Agency report.

Setting the Record Source

The Agents by Agency report is not based on an existing query or table. Instead, specify the report's data source by setting the report's **RecordSource** property to the following SQL statement:

```
SELECT DISTINCTROW
    Agencies.Name,
    Agents.Name,
    Agents.HomePhone,
    Agents.WorkPhone,
    Agents.MobilePhone
FROM
    Agents
    INNER JOIN Agencies ON Agents.AgencyID = Agencies.ID
WITH OWNERACCESS OPTION;
```

Tip: The easiest way to enter a lengthy property setting is to open the Zoom box by pressing Shift+F2. In the Zoom box, you can create line breaks by pressing Ctrl+Enter.

This SQL statement retrieves records from two tables (Agencies and Agents) but does not sort the data in any way. As you will see, you sort records for reports differently than you do for forms.

Setting the Sorting and Grouping

You sort the records on a form by basing the form on a query that contains an ORDER BY clause. To sort the records in a report, you use the Sorting and Grouping dialog box (see fig. 10.2).

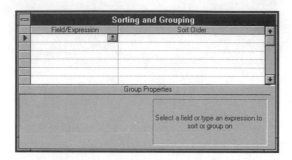

Figure 10.2.   The Sorting and Grouping dialog box.

To open the dialog box, choose the Sorting and Grouping command from the View menu. The following procedure lists the steps that you can follow to specify the sorting and grouping properties for the report:

1. In the Field/Expression column of the first row, enter or select the name of the field that represents the highest sort order. This report will show all agents sorted by agency name, so select the `Agencies.Name` field from the drop-down list.

2. Select the appropriate sort order for the Name field. You want the agency names to appear in alphabetical order, so select `Ascending`.

3. In the lower section of the dialog box, decide whether you want to include a group header, footer, or both. For this report, you need only a group header (see fig. 10.3).

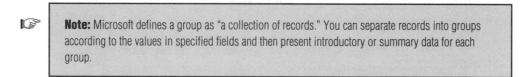

☞   **Note:** Microsoft defines a group as "a collection of records." You can separate records into groups according to the values in specified fields and then present introductory or summary data for each group.

☞   **Note:** You can sort on a field without the field also having a group header or footer. Conversely (but less commonly), you can include a header or footer without also sorting the field.

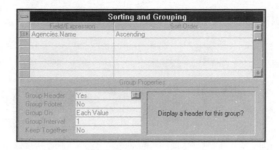

Figure 10.3. The sorting and grouping properties for the agency name field.

4. Within each group (that is, for each agency), the report also needs to sort the individual agents. Select a second field, `Agents.Name`, in the second row of the dialog box, and set the field's sort order option to `Ascending`.

5. You do not need to produce a header or footer for the agent name group, so leave these group properties set to No.

Adding Controls

You add controls to a report in much the same way as you add them to forms. Most of the controls that you add are text boxes, labels, lines, and rectangles. You also can add check boxes to represent Yes/No fields.

The Agents by Agency report features only text boxes, labels, and one line (see fig. 10.4).

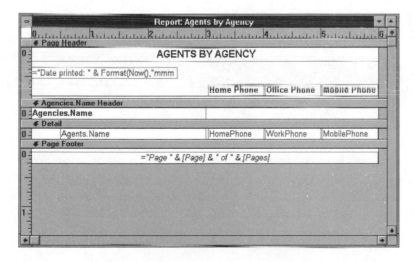

Figure 10.4. The Agents by Agency report (Design View).

198

The Page Header Section

The following procedure outlines the steps you can follow to add the required controls to the form's Page Header section.

1. Add a label control for the report title and set its **Caption** property to the desired text. For most reports, this text is the same as the name of the report.

2. Move the control to the upper-left corner of the section and then set the label's **Width** property to the same width as the report. In this example, the report should be 6 inches wide, so set the label's width to 6 inches.

3. Center the text by setting the control's **TextAlign** property to Center. If you change the title, it will still be centered in the report.

4. For most reports, a sans serif font is desirable because fonts without serifs are easier to read. Set the label's font to Arial or MS Sans Serif.

 Note: If you specify a font that is not installed on the user's machine, Windows substitutes a similar font. For the best results, choose a font that ships with Microsoft Windows, unless you know with certainty that the specified font exists on the user's machine, or that the font that Windows substitutes is satisfactory.

5. Make the text boldface and set the font size to 12 points. This is 2 points larger than the font size for the rest of the text in the report. To avoid mixing more than two different font sizes in the same report, you should apply this 2-point convention as a rule.

 Note: If your report includes footnotes, you can break this rule by setting footnote text to a font size that is 2 points smaller than the rest of the text.

6. Add a text box for the date, set the font size to 10 points, and then set its **ControlSource** property as follows:

   ```
   ="Date printed: " & Format(Date(),"mmmm dd"", ""yyyy")
   ```

   Allow a reasonable amount of white space (approximately 0.06 to 0.1 inches) between the title and the date.

7. Again allowing sufficient white space, add labels for the column headings. Make the labels boldface and set their font size to 10 points.

8. In figure 10.4, note that a line control extends from the left side of the report to the right, just beneath the column headings. The line is 6 inches wide, the same as the width of the report. Set the line's **BorderWidth** property to `Hairline`, and make sure that the **Height** property is set to 0 (this setting yields a horizontal line; increasing the height results in a diagonal line).

199

> **Note:** You also can show separate lines above each of the columns in the report. To do so, create four lines, allowing a bit of white space between the lines and making sure that the lines are all aligned with the bottom of the labels.

9. Set the height of the section so that you have a bit of white space at the bottom. This prevents any text or other visual elements (such as lines or rectangles) in the agencies header from overlapping the lines in the page header.

The *Agencies.Name* Header Section

Previously, you specified that the agency names have a group header. This section appears in the report whenever the value of the group changes. In this case, every time that the name of the agency changes, Access prints a header section.

The following procedure outlines the steps you can follow to add the required controls to the `Agencies.Name` Header section.

1. You want the name of the agency to appear whenever the name changes, so add a text box for the agency name.

2. The agency name is a fairly major grouping that deserves special attention, so present the text in boldface type. Too much boldface type becomes difficult to read, however, so use it sparingly.

> **Tip:** Determining the most effective amount of boldface type is as much a matter of style as common sense, so you may have to experiment to find the right mix of regular and boldface text. As a rule, the title, column headings, and group headers should appear in boldface. The main body of the report and any miscellaneous elements (the date and page numbers, in particular) should be in regular type.

The Detail Section

For every agent in the current agency group, Access prints a detail record. Unless you include so many controls that you start to run out of horizontal space, consider indenting the first text box (the agent name) by 0.5 inches.

Size and align the three phone number text boxes the same as the column headings, but do not make the text boxes boldface.

Each of the text boxes is a bound control; that is, it gets its data from the underlying records produced by the report's SQL statement. In the case of the Agents by Agency report, the data in the table is already formatted properly so that phone numbers print with dashes (for example, 206-555-7947). If you include unformatted data in a report, you may need to enter **Format** property settings for the relevant controls. For more information, search Help for "Format."

☞ **Note:** Notice that the column heading for the work phone text box is not the same as it is for the underlying field. This demonstrates how you can display one thing, yet store another. If you change the column headings, this change does not affect the underlying data nor the database schema in any way; you simply change the caption for the column heading's label.

The Page Footer Section

This page footer section prints the current page number along with the total number of pages in the report. The total page count includes the report header and report footer, if any.

If you include page breaks in the header and footer, you may want to adjust the total page count, as follows:

```
="Page " & [Page] + 1 & " of " & [Pages] - 2
```

In this example, you reduce the total page count by 2 to compensate for page breaks in both the header and footer. If you want to include the final page in the count (and thus "ignore" only the cover page), subtract only 1 from Pages.

 Tip: To compensate for the cover sheet, the preceding example adds one to the current page number, Page. If you include a cover page and add one, the first page following the cover sheet appears as page 1, not page 2.

Set the width of the text box to 6 inches and the alignment to Center.

This report uses an italic font for the page number. As a rule, you should use italic fonts sparingly.

Setting the Report Margins

To specify margins for the report, choose the Print Setup command from the File menu. Access displays the Print Setup dialog box (see fig. 10.5).

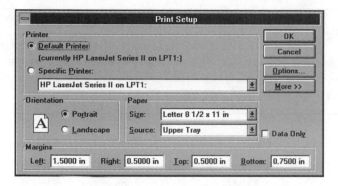

Figure 10.5.   Use the Print Setup dialog box to set the margins.

Along the bottom of the dialog box are four text boxes in which you can enter margin settings. Depending on the specific printer driver that you use (choose the appropriate printer in the top portion of the dialog box), you can set the margins from 0 inches to whatever makes sense for your report.

The following guidelines will help you decide the best margin settings:

- For portrait orientation, set the left margin to at least one inch, and 0.5 inches more than the right margin. For the Agents by Agency report, the left margin is set to 1.5 inches and the right margin is set to 0.5 inches. These settings produce enough white space on the left side so that the report can be three-hole punched without running into any data.

  Set the top and bottom margins to 0.5 and 0.75 inches, respectively.

- For landscape orientation, set the top margin to 1.5 inches and the bottom margin to 0.5 inches.

  Depending on the width of your report and your own preference, either set the left margin to 1 inch (which produces a left-justified report) or set the left and right margins the same to produce a centered report.

Testing the Report

Open the report in either Print Preview or Sample Preview to make sure that you have correctly set the margin settings and the width and height of the report.

If you design a report so that it is wider than the available space on the printed page (taking into account the margins), Access "tiles" the report and prints multiple pages where you expect only one. For example, you might design a report for letter-sized paper that includes 1-inch margins. If the detail section itself is seven inches wide, there obviously will not be enough room for two 1-inch margins plus the 7-inch detail section (1 + 1 + 7 = 9 inches). If necessary, adjust the margins or make the report narrower or shorter.

Resize the Report window so that it nearly fills the Access window, and then save the report. Thereafter, when you open the report in Print Preview or Sample Preview, the report fills most of the screen without any visual clutter from windows appearing beneath the Report window.

Finally, open the Main Menu form, click the Reports button, and then print or preview the report (see fig. 10.6).

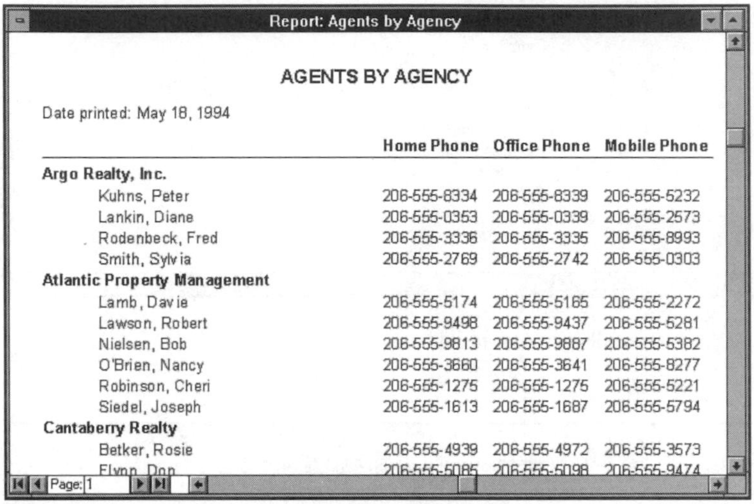

Figure 10.6.   The Agents by Agency report (Print Preview).

Building the Remaining Reports

In addition to the Agents by Agency report, the HomeFinder application includes three other reports. The following sections discuss important aspects of each of them.

Room Codes—1 Column

This report illustrates how you can create a single-column list of data (see fig. 10.7).

This report sorts on the RoomCode field; it includes no group header or footer. Unlike the Agents by Agency report, the page number appears at the top of the report in the page header, not in the page footer.

203

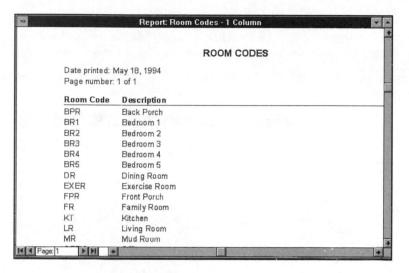

Figure 10.7.   The one-column Room Codes report.

 Tip: You should include a page number on all reports, even one-page reports.

Room Codes—2 Columns

When the data is relatively narrow and you have sufficient horizontal space with which to work, you can create a shorter, two-column report (see fig. 10.8).

This report is nearly identical to the one-column Room Codes report, except that this two-column version presents two columns of data, not just one.

To produce multiple columns of data, choose the Print Setup command from the File menu. Access displays the Print Setup dialog. When you click the More button, Access expands the dialog box to display additional report settings along the bottom (see fig. 10.9).

You use the Items Across text box to specify the number of columns for the report. In this case, two columns are required. Other settings let you to specify how closely to set the columns to each other, how wide the columns will be, and whether Access should arrange the data from left to right (set the Item Layout option to Horizontal) or from top to bottom (set the option to Vertical).

To get your report to appear just right, you may have to try different spacings.

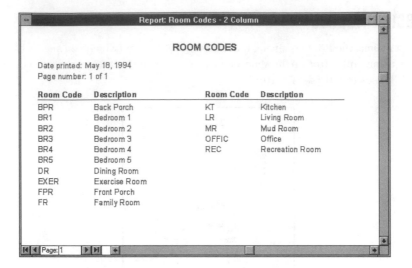

Figure 10.8. A two-column Room Codes report.

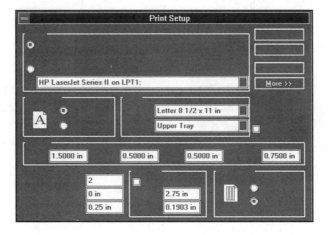

Figure 10.9. Click the More button to set column information.

Note: To create the illustration in figure 10.8, you set the bottom margin to 7.5 inches. This setting makes the Detail section short enough that all the room codes no longer fit in a single column. In your own reports, you will probably want to keep the bottom margin set to 0.75 inches.

205

zz_Selected Houses

When the user clicks the Print command button on the QBF form (which you access by clicking the Find a House command button on the Main Menu), the command button's event procedure prints the zz_Selected Houses report (see fig. 10.10).

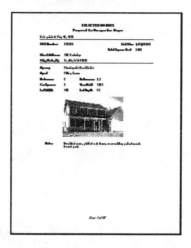

Figure 10.10.   The zz_Selected Houses report (Print Preview).

> **Note:** The Reports form displays a list of all the reports in the system, except those specifically excluded (such as those with a prefix of zz_). The Selected Houses report has been renamed because it depends on the QBF form being open to supply criteria. If the user were allowed to open the report directly from the Reports form, the QBF form would not be open.

To provide enough room for the home buyer to write his own comments, place the Notes control after the photograph.

To ensure that each house listing appears on its own page, place a page break control at the bottom of the Detail section, with no white space beneath the control.

Summary

Reports are much like forms: you create each in a design window, add controls from the toolbox, and set various properties.

The way that you establish the sort order differs, however. In forms you set the sort order in the form's query; in reports you set the sorting order with the Sorting and Grouping dialog box. Unlike forms, reports also offer groupings, group headers, and group footers.

The reports in the HomeFinder sample application are fairly typical of those that you are likely to create in your own applications. You can experiment with the overall design of the reports, but the basic steps of identifying, sorting, and grouping data are pretty much the same from report to report.

As with forms, it is particularly important for you to maintain a consistent style from report to report.

Part II

Nuts and Bolts

11

Enhancing Forms

Most users have high expectations about your applications. For example, they expect a consistent and easy-to-use interface, but they also expect your applications to include advanced features and professional design touches.

The extra steps you take now to add extra value to your forms will go a long way toward satisfying users. It is much easier to build in features than to add them later.

This chapter covers the following:

- Making Forms Modal
- Setting the Initial Focus
- Implementing an Undo Button
- Centering a Form
- Saving and Restoring Form Positions
- Providing Visual Cues
- Creating a Splash Screen
- Exploding Forms

Making Forms Modal

The HomeFinder sample application contains a rather limited number of forms (only 11 that the user sees, although there are 26 in all). Some applications, however, contain dozens of forms, many open at the same time.

The Windows model allows multiple windows (forms) and enables users to move windows around and switch between forms. The ability to move around at will is part of the appeal of Windows. Frequently, however, users become confused about the current context, especially if users have to traverse several forms to get to a certain form. For example, a user might navigate from the Main Menu to a form several levels deep (see fig. 11.1).

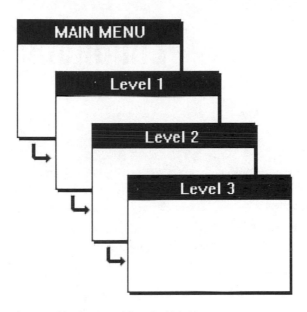

Figure 11.1. Users can be several levels removed from the Main Menu.

From the deepest level in this "chain" of forms, the user can choose any of the open forms. Depending on the application, providing all these choices may not be appropriate because the user may lose context for the current form. If the deepest level depends on values or actions at a higher level, the deepest levels may no longer reflect correct information.

Notwithstanding the Windows model, which allows these multiple windows, you should consider making your forms *modal*. Modal forms require that the user finish one task before moving on to another to prevent simultaneous editing. In the example presented in figure 11.1, the user would have to close each form, in sequence, to return to the Main Menu.

 Tip: Figure 11.1 presents an extreme example. In the real world, you should avoid forms that are more than two levels deep (that is, the Main Menu plus two additional levels) in order to prevent tabbed dialogs.

Even so, sometimes you may want to let the user temporarily open a form higher up the chain, or even a form in a different chain. For example, you may want to enhance the Agencies form by letting the user open the Agents form for the currently selected agent. To do this, provide the user with a command button or menu command that opens the Agents form under program control.

Setting the Initial Focus

When you open a form, Access moves the focus, by default, to the first control in the Detail section. If the first control is a text box (as it often is) and the user starts typing before the form appears on the screen, the user can change the data in the control. Unfortunately, you cannot do much to prevent the user from typing ahead.

In some cases, you should move the focus to the OK or Cancel command button by adding the following line of code to the form's **OnOpen** event procedure:

```
OK.SetFocus
```

Then, if the user happens to press the ENTER key, the OK command button simply closes the form (or performs other actions that you trigger with the command button). This enhancement minimizes the risk of the user typing and unknowingly changing data.

This technique does not anticipate Alt key sequences, however. For example, if you have a custom menu bar that includes a File menu with a Delete Record command, the user could press Alt+F and Alt+D and delete a record, perhaps without knowing it. For this reason, you should provide messages boxes that prompt the user to confirm such actions. The default button for these dialogs should be No, Cancel, or whatever makes sense. The objective is to keep the user from unknowingly changing or deleting data.

Implementing an Undo Button

Most users do not know that pressing the ESC key twice in succession undoes changes to the current record. You can implement the same functionality with a command button or with a custom menu bar.

To add a command button that undoes the current change, add the following code to the command button's **OnClick** event procedure:

```
SendKeys "{esc 2}"
```

To implement similar functionality in a custom menu bar, use the **DoMenuItem** macro action (see fig. 11.2).

As a design convention, all command buttons on a form should have a corresponding menu bar command. To avoid having the undo code in two places (as part of the menu macro and in the command button's **OnClick** event procedure), both the menu and the command button should call a single, generic function:

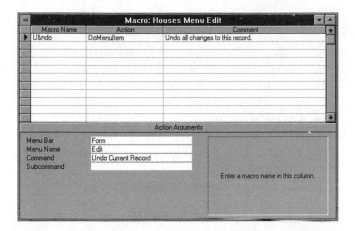

Figure 11.2.   Implementing undo functionality with a menu command.

```
Function csvUndoCurrentRecord () As Integer

    SendKeys "{esc 2}"

End Function
```

Create this function in a global module, not the form's code module. That way, you can call the function from all forms in the application.

> **Note:** The csvUndoCurrentRecord() function uses the **SendKeys** statement, not the **DoMenuItem** macro action. To use the macro action, you must add an error handler to trap the error that would otherwise occur if you use **DoMenuItem** and have nothing to undo.

Centering a Form

When you set a form's **AutoCenter** property to True, Access is supposed to position the form to the center of the Access window. What actually happens, however, is that the form appears centered horizontally, but approximately one third from the top of the window, not centered vertically (see fig. 11.3).

This may seem like a fine distinction, but the effect is even more pronounced when you center one form on top of another. If you want true centering, you must use the csvCenterForm() function (see fig. 11.4).

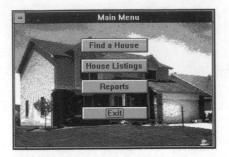

Figure 11.3. Forms that you try to center with **AutoCenter** are not really centered.

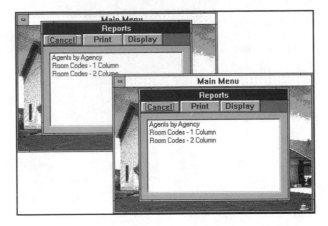

Figure 11.4. Centering with **AutoCenter** (left) and with csvCenterForm() (right).

Call the function from each form's **OnLoad** or **OnOpen** event (in addition to whatever code you are already running):

```
Sub Form_Open (Cancel As Integer)

    Dim X As Integer

    X = csvCenterForm(Me.FormName)

End Sub
```

 You can find a complete code listing and more information about entering the csvCenterForm() function in Chapter 21, "Useful Functions."

Saving and Restoring Form Positions

Many users expect forms to return to the same positions as when the forms were last closed, and not necessarily centered. You can use the csvWindowPosition() function in a form's **OnOpen** event procedure to restore a form to its last-known position:

```
Sub Form_Open (Cancel As Integer)

    Dim X As Integer

    ' Comment out one of the following two lines. Either
    ' center the form or restore its last-known position.
    X = csvCenterForm(Me.FormName)
    X = csvWindowPosition(Me.FormName, "restore")

End Sub
```

When you close a form, save its current position:

```
Sub Form_Close ()

    Dim X As Integer

    X = csvWindowPosition(Me.FormName, "save")

End Sub
```

The csvWindowPosition() function depends on an initialization (.INI) file defined in the function itself. If the file does not exist when you open a form the first time, no action is taken and the form opens wherever you last saved the form in Design view. If the specified .INI file does not exist when you close the form, the function automatically creates the file and saves the form's coordinates.

Tip: The csvWindowPosition() function also saves and restores the form's size. If the user enlarges or shrinks a form, the form reopens with the same dimensions.

To see a complete code listing and more information about entering the csvWindowPosition() function, refer to Chapter 21, "Useful Functions."

Providing Visual Cues

As a rule, you should avoid using color to indicate exceptions, errors, or conditions. For example, do not use the color red alone to indicate negative numbers, because some users cannot distinguish the color red. In the case of negative numbers, if you make them red, also add angle brackets (<>) or a minus sign (−).

However, this rule does not mean that you should not use color creatively and that your applications should be designed in black and white. Indeed, Chapter 15, "Creating a Self-Configuring Application," describes how you can read color settings from the Windows Control Panel and then set your own form colors to match.

You can use color as a visual cue to help the user navigate and use the forms effectively. For example, as users move the focus from control to control, they may find it difficult to determine where the focus is. In most screen resolutions, the insertion point in a text box is quite narrow and difficult to locate even on a form that has few controls. The status bar text provides a clue, but users often do not look to the status bar to find out where the cursor is.

One solution to this problem is to change the background color for the active control. For example, if the default colors for a text box are black on white, you could set the colors to white on black whenever the focus moves to the text box.

 Note: The white-on-black color combination is consistent with combo boxes and list boxes.

To change the colors, open or create the Tools module and enter the `csvInvertColors()` function, as follows:

```
Function csvInvertColors ()

    Dim BackColorSave As Long

    BackColorSave = Screen.ActiveControl.BackColor
    Screen.ActiveControl.BackColor = Screen.ActiveControl.ForeColor
    Screen.ActiveControl.ForeColor = BackColorSave

End Function
```

Then call the `csvInvertColors()` function from the text box's **OnEnter** and **OnExit** event procedures:

```
Sub Home_Enter ()

    Dim X As Integer

    X = csvInvertColors()

End Sub

Sub Home_Exit()

    Dim X As Integer

    X = csvInvertColors()

End Sub
```

Creating a Splash Screen

Many applications, including Microsoft Access, feature a startup "splash screen" that appears when you first load the program. A splash screen typically includes a logo or picture of some sort, the name of the program, as well as copyright and version information (see fig. 11.5). These screens automatically disappear after a few seconds.

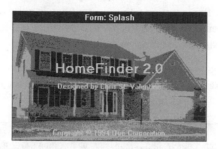

Figure 11.5. A typical splash screen.

You can add your own splash screen by first creating a form that has no title bar, no borders, and no command buttons or other controls that can get the focus.

> **Tip:** You can add a command button to the form and leave the form displayed until the user presses the command button. However, the addition of a command button makes the form a startup screen, not a splash screen. In most applications, either type of form is acceptable.

The following procedure outlines the steps that you can follow to implement your own splash screen:

1. Create a new form with the desired text and image. Be sure that you turn off all unnecessary design elements, such as scroll bars, record navigation buttons, and buttons in the form header.

> **WARNING:** Do not open the splash screen in Form View until you have added code that closes the form. Because the form has no command button and no control menu, the only way to close the form right now is to press Alt+F4, which may close Microsoft Access. This can have unpredictable results. When you finish designing the form, it closes automatically.

2. To remove the title bar from the splash screen, call the `csvRemoveTitleBar()` function from the form's **OnOpen** event procedure, as follows:

```
Sub Form_Open (Cancel As Integer)

    Dim X As Integer

    X = csvCenterForm(Me.FormName)
    X = csvRemoveTitleBar(Me.FormName)
    DoCmd MoveSize , , , Me.Section(0).Height

End Sub
```

The csvRemoveTitleBar() function does nothing to compensate for the now-missing title bar, so the event procedure uses the **MoveSize** macro action to shorten the form so that it matches the height of the detail section.

3. Open or create the Tools module and enter the code for the csvRemoveTitleBar() function, as follows:

```
Function csvRemoveTitleBar (ByVal MyFormName As String) As Integer

    Const csvGWL_STYLE = -16
    Const csvWS_DLGFRAME = &H400000
    Dim OldStyle As Long,
    Dim NewStyle As Long
    Dim WindowHandle As Integer

    On Error Resume Next
    WindowHandle = Forms(MyFormName).hWnd
    If Err Then
        csvRemoveTitleBar = False
    Else
        OldStyle = csvGetWindowLong(WindowHandle, csvGWL_STYLE)
        ' Remove the title bar and all buttons/control menu:
        NewStyle = OldStyle And Not csvWS_DLGFRAME
        OldStyle = csvSetWindowLong(WindowHandle, csvGWL_STYLE, NewStyle)
        csvRemoveTitleBar = True
    End If
    On Error GoTo 0

End Function
```

4. To set the period of time that the splash screen remains on the screen, set the form's **TimerInterval** property to 3000. This setting specifies 3,000 milliseconds, or 3 seconds (1,000 milliseconds = 1 second).

5. When the timer interval elapses (that is, after three seconds), Access automatically executes the event or code specified by the form's **OnTimer** property. Set the **OnTimer** property to [Event Procedure] and then enter the following code in the event's event procedure:

```
Sub Form_Timer ()

    DoCmd Close

End Sub
```

To test your work, close the form, return to the Database window, and then open the splash screen in Form view.

219

Exploding Forms

Another screen effect that you might want to implement is that of an "exploding" form. During a form's **OnOpen** or **OnLoad** events (which occur before the form appears on the screen), you can display a series of rectangles that start small and get progressively larger as they approach the size of the form. If performed quickly enough, this procedure creates an illusion of "exploding" on the screen.

To create an exploding screen effect, open or create the Tools module and then enter the code for the csvExplodeForm() function. For a complete code listing, see Chapter 21, "Useful Functions."

Next, call the csvExplodeForm() function from the form's **OnOpen** or **OnLoad** event procedure, as follows:

```
Sub Form_Load ()

    Const ORIGIN - 0
    Const SPEED = 100
    Dim X As Integer

    X = csvHideDBWindow() ' Will be unnecessary if called from AutoExec().
    X = csvCenterForm(Me.FormName)
    X = csvExplodeForm(Me, ORIGIN, SPEED)

End Sub
```

The last line of code passes two values to the function. First, the ORIGIN argument (0) specifies that the explosion begin from the center of the form (see fig. 11.6). Second, the SPEED argument specifies the speed at which the explosion should occur. Smaller numbers result in a faster effect because the function draws fewer rectangles. To find the speed value that works best on your machine, you probably will have to experiment.

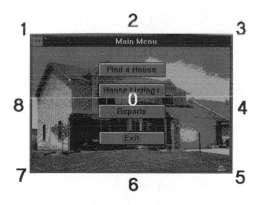

Figure 11.6.   The origin number (0 - 8) determines where the explosion starts.

Summary

You can add many things to your forms to make them easier and, in some cases, more fun to use. As you add new functionality, make sure that you apply new features consistently.

As useful and reliable as your application may be, users often will judge its value by its appearance. Pay particular attention to the look and feel of your applications, and always be prepared to make changes in response to user feedback.

12

Migrating from Macros to Modules

If you have experience developing applications with Microsoft Access, you already know that there are limits to what macros can do. You also know that macros offer no error trapping and can be difficult to debug.

For simple databases, you may not need any greater functionality than that offered by macros. As you begin to develop more serious databases and applications, you use Access Basic to create modules, or functions.

This chapter explores the Module window and how you create functions to extend the functionality of Access and your applications. Many features of serious applications can be implemented only with Access Basic.

This chapter covers the following:

- Exploring the Module Window
- Creating a New Function
- Checking Your Work

Exploring the Module Window

All Access Basic code resides in modules. To create a new module, go to the Database window, click the Module button and then the New button. Access displays a nearly blank Module window (see figure 12.1).

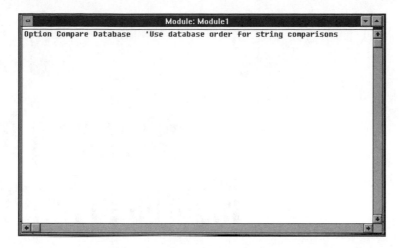

Figure 12.1. The Module window.

As a rule, you should immediately add an **Option Explicit** statement to the module, as shown in figure 12.2.

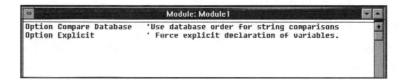

Figure 12.2. Add an **Option Explicit** statement to every module.

The **Option Explicit** statement forces you to declare explicitly all variables in your functions. For more information about **Option Explicit**, see Chapter 17, "Naming Conventions and Style Guidelines."

Note: Do not be overly concerned if you do not understand much of the terminology in this chapter. *Access 2 Power Programming* is not intended to be a full-bodied tutorial on how to program—the amount of material required to treat this topic adequately is beyond the scope of this book. For more detailed information about programming, you should consult other references dedicated to Access Basic.

Entering a New Function

Often in this book you are told to enter code in a module. This means that you should open the Module window and type the lines of code just as you see them listed in the book. As you gain more experience with Access Basic, much of the mystery of entering code will disappear and you will feel more comfortable.

The following procedure lists the steps you follow to enter one of the functions listed in this book:

1. Open the Module window and move the insertion point to the beginning of any line. You do not have to be at the top or bottom of the window, or even in an empty window.

2. Enter the first line of code as follows:

```
Function csvCloseForm (ByVal MyFormName As String) As Integer
```

3. Press the ENTER key. Access displays a new window with your line of code at the top and a new line of code two lines lower:

```
End Function
```

4. Between these two lines, enter whatever other code that the function requires. In this example, the completed function looks like this:

```
Function csvCloseForm (ByVal MyFormName As String) As Integer

    Const FUNCTIONNAME = "csvCloseForm()"

    On Error Resume Next
    DoCmd Close A_FORM, Forms(MyFormName)
    If Err Then
        MsgBox "Couldn't close form '" & MyFormName & "'.",
    ➥csvMB_ICONEXCLAMATION, FUNCTIONNAME
        csvCloseForm = False
    Else
        csvCloseForm = True
    End If
    On Error GoTo 0

End Function
```

Checking Your Work

Check your work by choosing the Compile Loaded Modules command from the Run menu. Compiling the function lets Access check the syntax (structure) of the code and resolve references to global variables, constants, and library routines stored in DLL (Dynamic Link Library) files.

Syntax Errors

If Access finds any syntax errors (typing mistakes, usually), it displays a message (see fig. 12.3). After you close the message box, Access highlights the line of code that produced the error. Resolve the error condition and try compiling again.

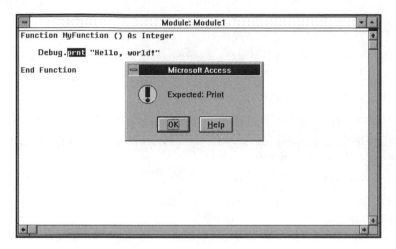

Figure 12.3. Typing mistakes usually produce syntax errors.

Missing Function Declarations

If you encounter an error because Access thinks you are using an undefined function (see fig. 12.4), this usually means that you have omitted a function declaration.

Many of the functions in this book call Windows API (Application Programming Interface) functions. To use an API function, you must enter its function declaration. Appendix A, "Windows API Declarations," lists all the declarations that you need to run the functions in this book and in the HomeFinder application.

To enter a function declaration, open or create the Declarations module and then type the text of the declaration. Save the module and then compile again. For more information about the Declarations module, see Chapter 17, "Naming Conventions and Style Guidelines."

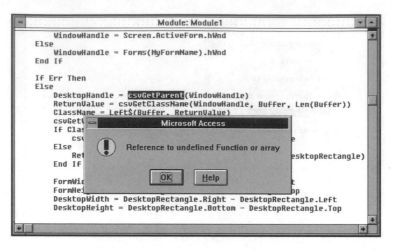

Figure 12.4. This error usually indicates a missing function declaration.

Undefined Functions

If Access continues to produce an error, the function may be calling a second function that you have not yet entered. For example, the `csvFormatDiskLabel()` function calls two other functions: `csvSort()` and `csvMinValue`. Each of these functions might call still another function, and so on.

You can either examine the code to see whether a function calls another function, or simply recompile and let Access do the work of finding the "bad" function calls. Enter the required functions and recompile. Repeat this process until Access no longer produces an undefined function error.

Undefined Constants

You may have entered a function that depends on the existence of a global constant, but you have not yet declared that constant (see fig. 12.5).

 Appendix B, "Constants," lists all the global constants that you need to run the functions in this book and in the HomeFinder application.

To enter a global constant, open or create the Global Constants module and then type the text of the global constant declaration. Save the module and then compile again. For more information about the Global Constants module, see Chapter 17, "Naming Conventions and Style Guidelines."

227

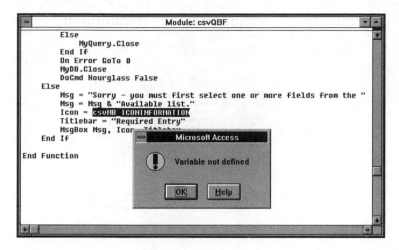

Figure 12.5.   This error usually indicates a missing constant declaration.

Summary

You should avoid using macros and use modules instead, not only because macros offer no error trapping, but also because you can write your own Access Basic functions to extend and enhance the built-in capabilities of Microsoft Access.

228

13

Adding Data Validation

You help the user tremendously when you implement even the most minimal validation at data entry time. For example, a text box designed to store state abbreviations should accept only valid, two-letter abbreviations. Allowing the user to enter anything at all, without such validation, is an invitation to a corrupt and unusable database.

Data validation goes beyond simply making sure the user enters the proper kinds of characters—it means making sure the data withstands a test of reasonableness.

This chapter covers the following:

- Using the **InputMask** Property
- Setting Validation Rules

Using Input Masks

For controls in which the data always has the same format, you can add an input mask to make data entry easier. An input mask lets you determine what kinds of characters (letters or numbers) are valid and the number of characters allowed. You also can specify formatting for separators, such as those that appear in phone numbers and social security numbers.

Input masks do not validate the data—they only ensure that the data meets the minimum requirements of being the proper type and number of characters.

 For more information about validating data, see "Setting Validation Rules" and "Validating Data on Forms" later in this chapter.

To apply an input mask, you set the **InputMask** property. You can set the **InputMask** property for fields in tables, fields in queries, or for text box controls on forms. You can apply the mask using the Input Mask Wizard, or you can set the **InputMask** property manually.

> **Note:** Wizards are tools you can use to create forms and other database objects, usually in a step-by-step fashion. This book does not illustrate how to use the wizards shipped with Microsoft Access.

> For more information about wizards, see Chapter 19, "Creating and Using Libraries."

To set an input mask for a table field, open the data database and then open the desired table in Design View. You also can open the code database and then open the desired query or form.

> **WARNING:** The reason you must open the data database is that from the code database you can change only certain properties of attached tables. When you open the table in Design View from the code database, Access only appears to let you change the **InputMask** property. If you make a change, save the table, and then reopen the table in Design View, you find that the setting has not really been changed. As a rule, always open the data database to make changes to a table's design.

Next, locate the existing **InputMask** property setting:

- *Tables*. Look in the Field Properties section of the Table window (see fig. 13.1).

- *Queries*. Move to the desired field in the QBE grid and then open the property sheet by choosing the Properties command from the View menu (see fig. 13.2).

- *Forms*. Select the desired text box control and then open the property sheet by choosing the Properties command from the View menu (see fig. 13.3).

> **Note:** If you set both the **InputMask** and **Format** properties for a field or control, Microsoft Access uses the input mask when you add or edit data and the **Format** property setting when determining how the data is displayed.

The **InputMask** property setting can contain up to three parts separated by semicolons, as shown here:

```
000\-000\-0000;0;_
```

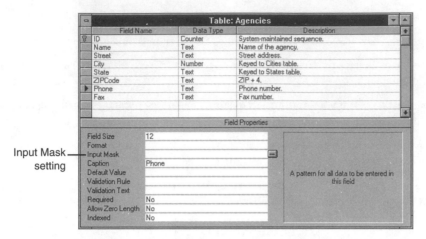

Figure 13.1. The **InputMask** property setting for table fields.

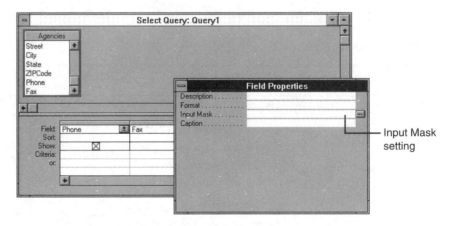

Figure 13.2. The **InputMask** property setting for query fields.

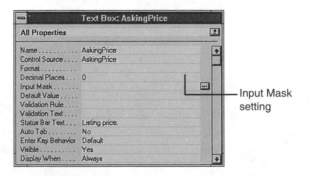

Figure 13.3. The **InputMask** property setting for text box controls.

231

How you set the three parts determines the way Access displays and stores the data.

- *Part 1.* The first part—(999) 000-0000—specifies the input mask itself.

- *Part 2.* The second part—0—specifies whether Access stores the literal display characters in the underlying table.

  Set this part to 0 (zero) if you want Access to store any literal characters appearing in the first part. In this example, the literal characters are the parentheses and the dash.

  If you do not want to store the literal characters, set the second part to 1. Access stores only those characters typed in the field or control.

- *Part 3.* The third part specifies the character Access displays as a placeholder in the input mask. You can specify any character; to display a space, enter a space enclosed in quotation marks (" "). You do not have to enclose any other character with quotation marks.

  If you do not specify the third part, Access uses an underscore (_).

The following table lists the characters you can use to specify the first part of the **InputMask** property setting.

Table 13.1. Input Mask Characters

Character	Description
0	Digit (0–9); entry required
9	Digit or a space; entry optional
#	Digit, space, plus sign (+) or minus sign (-); blank positions are converted to spaces; entry optional
L	Letter (A–Z); entry required
?	Letter; entry optional
Λ	Letter or digit; entry required
a	Letter or digit; entry optional
&	Any character or a space; entry required
C	Any character or a space; entry optional
. , : ; - /	Decimal placeholder and thousand, date, and time separators; these characters are determined by settings from the Windows Control Panel
<	All characters that follow are converted to lowercase (a–z)
>	All characters that follow are converted to uppercase (A–Z)
\	Causes the character that follows to be displayed as the literal character (for example, \A is displayed as just A).

Character	Description
Password	Creates a password entry text box; any character typed in the text box is stored as the typed character but displayed as an asterisk (*); you must enter the word *Password* as the **InputMask** property setting for this to work

> **Note:** The retail documentation for Microsoft Access documents an additional character—the exclamation mark (!). During data entry, this is supposed to cause the input mask to fill from right to left, rather than from left to right. Early copies of Microsoft Access 2.0 do not properly implement the exclamation mark, and you may want to avoid using it.

Fields and controls that have an input mask are always in overtype mode and not in insert mode. Furthermore, pressing the BACKSPACE key to delete a character actually replaces the character with a space.

Only characters the user types directly in the field or text box are affected by the input mask. Access ignores input masks when you attempt the following actions:

- Import data

- Run an action query

- Enter characters in a text box using Access Basic by setting a text box's **Text** property (or making a direct assignment)

- Enter characters using the **SetValue** macro action

Setting Validation Rules

A validation rule is a condition that verifies whether the data in a field, control, or record is valid. Simple validation rules include rules that check to see if a numeric entry is within a specified range.

For example, you might establish a validation rule for house prices to make sure users do not enter unreasonable values. Because a house in a particular housing market does not normally sell for less than $50,000, or more than $500,000, you can set a validation rule to make sure the asking price is within that range.

When the data fails to satisfy the validation rule, Access displays a message box containing the text you enter for the **ValidationText** property. If you do not enter any validation text, Access displays its own message (see figure 13.4).

233

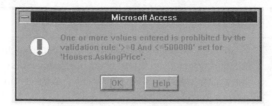

Figure 13.4   Access displays a message when data fails a validation rule.

The most charitable way to describe the message in figure 13.4 is to say it is accurate. The data fails to satisfy the rule (between 0 and 500,000), but the message could be phrased much better by setting the **ValidationText** property (see fig. 13.5).

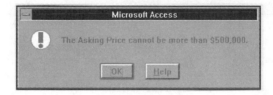

Figure 13.5   Write your own messages by setting the **ValidationText** property

You can set validation rules for table fields, table records, and certain controls on forms.

- *Table fields.* Set this validation rule when you want to validate a specific field in the table (for example, a price range). Open the table in Design View, select the desired field, and then locate the **ValidationRule** property setting in the Field Properties section of the Table window.

- *Table records.* Set the validation rule when you want to validate more than one field (for example, to make sure cities and states match). Open the table in Design View and then display the property sheet by choosing the Properties command from the View menu.

- *Form controls.* Like table fields, set the validation rule for form controls when you want to validate a single control. Open the form in Design View, select the desired control (check box, combo box, list box, option button, option group, text box, or toggle button) and then open the property sheet by choosing the Properties command from the View menu.

Tip: To validate a form record, validate the various fields or controls during the form's **BeforeUpdate** event.

Access applies table field and table record validation rules whether you add or edit data through a form or datasheet, an append or update query, Access Basic code, or by importing data. In contrast, Access applies form control validation rules only when you enter data using the form.

Validation rules can be simple or complex expressions, or even calls to user-defined functions. Table 13.2 lists examples of validation rules.

Table 13.2. Validation Rules

Rule	Description
="WA"	Must equal WA
>0 And <=500000	Must be more than zero, but no more than 500,000
Between 0 And 500000	Must be at least 0, but no more than 500,000
In ("WA", "CA, "OR")	Must match one of the listed states
DLookup("[Abbreviation]", "[States]", "[Abbreviation]=[State]") Is Not Null	The text in the State text box must match an abbreviation in the States table
csvValidatePostalCode()	The return value from the user-defined function must be True

If the expression you enter for the validation rule evaluates to True, the data is accepted as valid. If the expression evaluates to False, the data fails the validation and Access displays a message. When you set a validation rule, you cannot enter invalid data.

Note: You cannot use user-defined functions, domain aggregate functions, SQL aggregate functions, or the **CurrentUser** and **Eval** functions in a table field or table record validation rule.

Summary

You can help prevent introducing invalid data into the database by establishing input masks and validation rules. Access does not permit the user to enter an invalid character or invalid data if the validation rules applied to the fields, records, and controls are stringent enough.

Part III
Fit and Finish

14

Adding Menu Bars

Along the top of most windows, just beneath the title bar, are menu bars. Menu bars are the horizontal bars that contain the names of menus. This chapter discusses the need for custom menu bars and how you can create them. The procedures here are for custom menu bars for forms, but the same techniques apply to reports as well.

This chapter covers the following:

- Exploring Custom Menu Bars
- Understanding Menu Hierarchies
- Creating a Menu

Exploring Custom Menu Bars

Menu bars are context-sensitive for each window. For example, the menu bar for the Database window lists different menus than the menu bar for the Module window (see fig. 14.1).

When you open a form, Access displays the default menu bar that includes the File, Edit, and other menus. You can enhance your application by replacing the built-in menu bars with your own custom menu bars.

Each command button on a form should have a corresponding menu command, but the reverse is not necessarily true. To avoid the visual clutter from having too many command buttons on a form, you may not want to add a command button for every menu command. As a rule, include command buttons for only the most common activities, such as printing, sorting, searching, and similar functions that users are likely to perform on a regular basis.

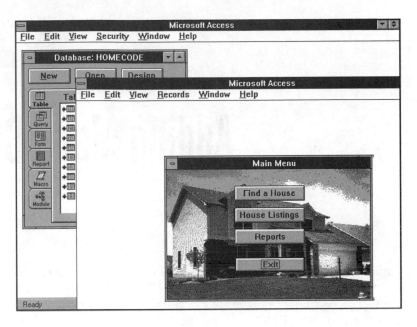

Figure 14.1. Menu bars change according to the current context.

For less common activities, such as configuring the system or setting a password, use menu commands. For example, the Main Menu form does not include command buttons that lead to the Cities or States forms. For these and other miscellaneous, seldom-used forms, menu commands are more appropriate.

Understanding Menu Hierarchies

Ordinarily you should avoid macros in favor of Access Basic modules, but Microsoft Access uses macros to implement custom menu bars. No Access Basic equivalent exists.

You create one macro group for the menu bar itself plus one macro group for each menu. For example, creating a menu bar with File and Help menus requires three macro groups (see fig. 14.2).

The first macro group defines the menu and points to the other macro groups that define the individual File and Help menus. For example, the macro group for the File menu may contain a command for closing the form.

Tip: Create and store menu macros in your application's code database, not in the data database. In the HomeFinder application, the code database is named HOMECODE.MDB.

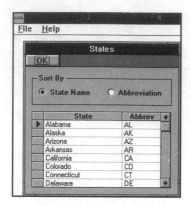

Figure 14.2. It takes three macro groups to implement this menu bar.

Creating a Menu

The preceding section discussed how it takes at least two macro groups to create a custom menu bar: One for the menu bar itself and one for each menu. The first step to creating a menu bar is to organize—on paper—the various menu commands.

For example, the Main Menu form needs menu commands for each command button on the form, plus menu commands that launch the various maintenance forms (see fig. 14.3).

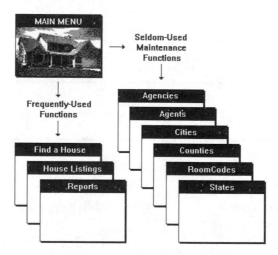

Figure 14.3. The Main Menu requires a number of menu commands.

241

> **Tip:** By convention, all forms should at least have a File menu. Users should be able to close a window by opening the File menu and choosing either a Close or Exit command.

The number of menus and where you place the menu commands varies according to your particular application and your forms. For this exercise, the Main Menu in the HomeFinder application has File, Setup, and Help menus.

You can create a custom menu bar using the Menu Bar Builder, or you can create the menu bar manually.

> Builders are tools you can use to create menus and other database objects, usually in a step-by-step fashion. For more information about builders, see Chapter 19, "Creating and Using Libraries."

Creating the Menu Bar Macro Group

The following procedure outlines the steps you follow to create the menu bar macro group.

1. Go to the Database window, press the Macro button, and then press the New button; Access displays the Macro window.

2. Save the macro and name it Main Menu Menu. This name identifies the form to which the menu applies, plus the fact that it is a menu macro group.

   For example, if you are creating the macro for the Reports form, you would name it Reports Menu.

> For more information about naming macros and other database objects, see Chapter 17, "Naming Conventions and Style Guidelines."

3. In the Action column, enter or select one **AddMenu** macro action for each menu in the menu bar (see fig. 14.4).

4. In the Action Arguments section of the Macro window, enter the name of each menu as you want it to appear in the menu bar (see fig. 14.5).

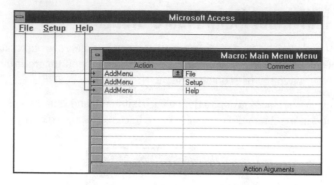

Figure 14.4. Add one **AddMenu** macro action for each menu.

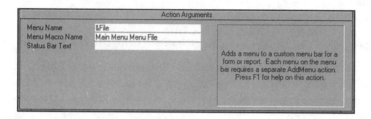

Figure 14.5. The Menu Name entry appears in the menu bar.

To define an access key, enter the name of the menu with an ampersand (&) before the character you want to underline. For example, to define the File menu, enter &File.

 For more information about assigning access keys, see Chapter 18, "Application Design Guidelines."

5. For each menu, enter the name of the menu macro group Access uses when the user opens a menu. For example, when the user opens the File menu, Access uses the Main Menu Menu File macro. This name identifies the form to which the menu applies and the menu name (in this case, File).

For example, if you were to create the File macro for the Reports menu, you would name it Reports Menu File.

The following section describes how you can create the individual menu macro groups.

243

Creating the Individual Menu Macro Groups

The preceding section described how you can create a menu bar macro group that defines a form's custom menu bar. The menu bar macro group uses individual menu macro groups to define the commands that appear when the user opens a menu.

Suppose you create a menu macro group to define the Exit command that appears in the File menu (see fig. 14.6). To add more commands, you add more lines to the macro group.

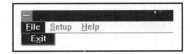

Figure 14.6. The File menu has only one command, Exit.

The following procedure outlines the steps you follow to create a menu macro group.

1. Create a new macro and name it the same as the name you entered in the menu bar macro group. For example, the menu macro group for the File menu is named Main Menu Menu File. The menu macro group that defines the Setup menu is named Main Menu Menu Setup, and so on.

   This consistent naming convention allows all menu macros for one form to appear together in the Database window (see fig. 14.7), and makes it easy to determine what a particular macro group does.

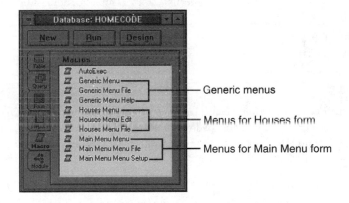

Figure 14.7. Name your menu macro groups consistently.

2. In the Macro window, display the Macro Name column by choosing the Macro Names command from the View menu. In the Macro Name column, enter the name of the first command in the menu. In this case, the menu has only one command, Exit.

244

3. In the Action column, enter or select the appropriate macro action (see fig. 14.8). If the macro action requires any arguments, enter them in the Action Arguments section at the bottom of the Macro window.

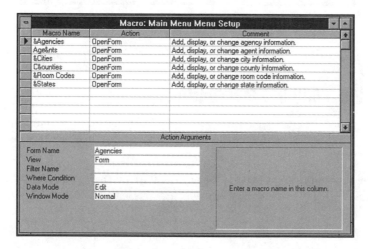

Figure 14.8. This macro group contains only one macro action, **Close**.

 Tip: You may think that the Exit command button on the Main Menu form quits Access, but instead it simply closes the form, which is what you want to do. If you change the action taken by the Exit command button, you also need to change the action taken by the Exit menu command.

4. Repeat steps 2 and 3 for any remaining menu commands.

When you are finished defining the menu commands, save your work, close the macro, and proceed to the next menu macro group. The Setup menu is a bit more ambitious than the File menu (see fig. 14.9).

Figure 14.9. You can define multiple commands for one menu.

The Setup macro group illustrates how you can open another form with the **OpenForm** macro action, but still choose other macro actions. For example, you can open reports (**OpenReport**), print the current form (**Print**), or call an Access Basic function (**RunCode**).

> **Tip:** Whenever possible, consolidate and share menu macro groups. For example, if you have a set of forms that need only a File menu to close the current form, create a generic menu macro with the **Close** macro action only. Then, in each form's menu bar macro, specify the name of the generic menu macro. You can even share a common menu macro to define the File menu.

You can create a Main Menu Menu Help menu macro group if the Help menu is specific to the Main Menu form. Otherwise, create a generic Help menu that you can call from other forms.

In the HomeFinder application, the Generic Menu Help menu macro group contains a single command, About (see fig. 14.10).

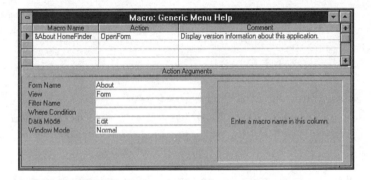

Figure 14.10. A generic Help menu macro.

Attaching the Menu Bar Macro Group

After you have defined the menu bar macro group and all its menu macro groups (one for each menu on the menu bar), you can attach the menu to the form. Open the form in Design view and display the form's property sheet.

Then, set the form's **MenuBar** property to the name of the menu bar macro group. In the case of the Main Menu form, the name of the menu bar macro group is Main Menu Menu (see figure 14.11).

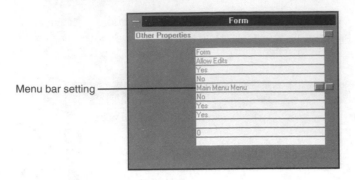

Figure 14.11. Attaching the menu bar macro group.

Testing the Menu Bar Macro Group

Test your work by closing and then reopening the Main Menu form. If Access produces any errors, check for typing mistakes in the macros, especially the macro names.

The menu bar provides access to all maintenance forms, such as Cities and States. However, it does not provide commands for finding a house, the house listings, nor for opening the Reports form.

Add a fourth menu to the form's menu bar macro group to define the menu commands for the command buttons (see fig. 14.12). What you call this menu depends largely on how you describe the options on the Main Menu. For example, you can call them activities or actions. Whatever word you choose is the word that appears in the menu bar.

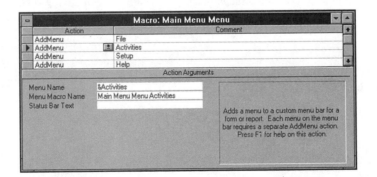

Figure 14.12. The modified menu bar macro group.

The menu commands in the Activities menu should perform the same actions as their corresponding command buttons. In this case, each of the command buttons opens a form, so the menu macro group uses the **OpenForm** macro action (see fig. 14.13).

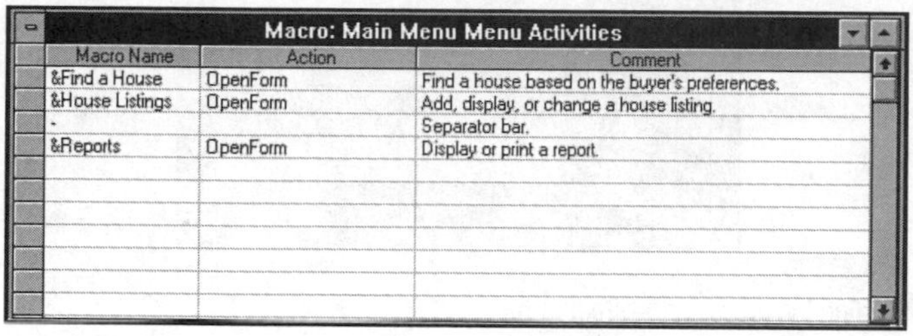

Macro Name	Action	Comment
&Find a House	OpenForm	Find a house based on the buyer's preferences.
&House Listings	OpenForm	Add, display, or change a house listing.
-		Separator bar.
&Reports	OpenForm	Display or print a report.

Figure 14.13. The Activities menu opens any of three forms.

You can add a separator bar in a menu by entering a single dash (–) in place of a macro name. In the case of the Activities menu, a separator appears between the House Listings and Reports commands.

Summary

Custom menu bars add extra value by making your applications more flexible. You can implement seldom-used commands in menus and avoid having to clutter your forms with too many command buttons.

Each menu bar requires one macro group for the menu bar itself, plus one macro group for each menu. You can create common, generic menu macro groups and share them among several forms.

15

Creating a Self-Configuring Application

Unless you work from a comprehensive list of specifications during the design stage of application, you may choose colors, formats, and text that appeal to you, but not to the ultimate users. For example, the HomeFinder application forms are gray with blue text. This may be satisfactory, but if you prefer a different color combination, you have to open each form in Design view, change the colors, and then save your work.

While forms are the most visible elements of any application, the consequences of hard coding extend beyond colors alone. For example, if you are based in the United States but have visions of an international market, you should anticipate the need to change certain currency and date settings.

 Chapter 18, "Application Design Guidelines," discusses these international concerns and suggests ways you can anticipate international and multiuser concerns.

This chapter discusses ways you can self-configure an application so that it changes colors according to the settings in the Windows Control Panel, and text according to the user's language choice.

This chapter covers the following:

- Reading Control Panel Settings
- Setting Form Colors

Reading Control Panel Settings

When you make changes to the Windows environment with the Control Panel, Windows updates various entries in your WIN.INI file. For example, when you set colors (see fig. 15.1), you actually are editing entries in the [colors] section of the WIN.INI file.

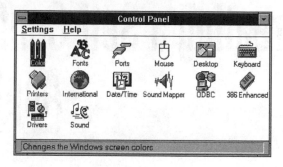

Figure 15.1. The Windows Control Panel.

The [colors] section looks something like the following:

    [colors]

    Background–192 192 192

    AppWorkspace=255 255 255

    Window=255 255 255

    WindowText=0 0 0

    Menu=255 255 255

    MenuText=0 0 0

    ActiveTitle=0 0 128

    InactiveTitle=255 255 254

    TitleText=255 255 255

    ActiveBorder=192 192 192

    InactiveBorder=192 192 192

    WindowFrame=0 0 0

    Scrollbar=192 192 192

    ButtonFace=192 192 192

250

ButtonText=0 0 0

ButtonShadow=128 128 128

GrayText=128 128 128

Hilight=0 0 128

HilightText=255 255 255

InactiveTitleText=0 0 0

ButtonHilight=255 255 255

Reading Color Settings

The preceding WIN.INI example illustrates how each entry defines a separate element of the Windows interface. For example, the ActiveTitle entry (0 0 128) identifies the color for the active window's title bar.

Each color is comprised of three values: a red value, a green value, and a blue value. In this case, the ActiveTitle entry has no red, no green, and some amount of blue. The values can range from 0 to 255. The higher you set a number, the more of that color Windows uses. The combination of red, green, and blue values determines the exact color.

Fortunately, the Control Panel provides an easier way to choose colors than manually editing color values. You can use the Color dialog box to set the various colors stored in the WIN.INI file (see fig. 15.2).

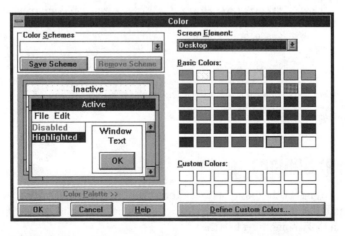

Figure 15.2. The Color dialog box.

When users change color settings in the Color dialog box, they fully expect that all Windows-based applications honor the settings. Unfortunately, Access applications do not automatically detect these color settings. This explains why the colors you set in Design View persist, even after the user changes the colors.

The csvWindowsColor( ) returns the color value for a specific window element. Open or create the Tools module in your code database and then enter the `csvWindowsColor()` function, as shown here:

```
Function csvWindowsColor (ByVal Which As String) As Long

    Const FUNCTIONNAME = 'csvWindowsColor()"
    Const COLOR_APPWORKSPACE = 12   ' Background color for multiple-document
                                    ' interface (MDI) apps.
    Const COLOR_BACKGROUND = 1  ' Background for the desktop.
    Const COLOR_WINDOW = 5      ' Window background.
    Const COLOR_WINDOWTEXT = 8  ' Text in windows.
    Dim AppWorkspace As Long
    Dim Background As Long
    Dim Window As Long
    Dim WindowText As Long

    csvWindowsColor = True

    Select Case LCase$(Which)
        Case "appworkspace"
            csvWindowsColor = csvGetSysColor(COLOR_APPWORKSPACE)
        Case "background"
            csvWindowsColor = csvGetSysColor(COLOR_BACKGROUND)
        Case "window "
            csvWindowsColor = csvGetSysColor(COLOR_WINDOW)
        Case "windowtext"
            csvWindowsColor = csvGetSysColor(COLOR_WINDOWTEXT)
        Case Else
            MsgBox "Invalid argument '" & Which & "'.", csvMB_ICONEXCLAMATION,
FUNCTIONNAME
            csvWindowsColor = False
    End Soloot

End Function
```

The following code returns the color setting for the window background:

```
X = csvWindowsColor ("window")
```

Reading Other Settings

The color settings may not be the only ones that interest you. For example, you may want to determine the language selected by the user. Windows stores the language selection in the [intl] section of the WIN.INI file, which looks something like this:

[intl]

sLanguage=enu

sCountry=United States

iCountry=1

iDate=0

iTime=0

iTLZero=0

iCurrency=0

iCurrDigits=2

iNegCurr=0

iLzero=1

iDigits=2

iMeasure=1

s1159=AM

s2359=PM

sCurrency=$

sThousand=,

sDecimal=.

sDate=/

sTime=:

sList=,

sShortDate=M/d/yy

sLongDate=dddd, MMMM dd, yyyy

You can determine whether a value is a string or an integer by the first character in the entry's name. For example, the sLanguage value is a string. This particular value identifies the selected language: in this case, the enu value identifies English (North American).

You can use the `csvGetIntlInt()` and `csvGetIntlString()` functions to read values from the [intl] section. Be sure you call the correct function according to whether you are looking for an integer or string value.

```
Function csvGetIntlInt (Entry As String) As Integer

    Const ERR_INVALIDARG = "Invalid argument."
    Const TITLEBAR = "Get International Integer"
    Dim Default As Integer
    Dim X As Integer
```

```
        Default = -1
        If Entry <> "" Then
            X = csvGetProfileInt("intl", Entry, Default)
        End If
        If X >= Default Then
            csvGetIntlInt = X
        Else
            MsgBox ERR_INVALIDARG, csvMB_ICONEXCLAMATION, TITLEBAR
            csvGetIntlInt = Default
        End If

    End Function

    Function csvGetIntlString (Entry As String) As String

        Const ERR_INVALIDARG = "Invalid argument."
        Const TITLEBAR = "Get International String"
        Dim Default As String
        Dim Size As Integer
        Dim Text As String * 128
        Dim X As Integer

        Default = ""
        Size = Len(Text)
        If Entry <> "" Then
            X = csvGetProfileString("intl", Entry, Default, Text, Size)
        End If
        If X Then
            csvGetIntlString = Left$(Text, X)
        Else
            MsgBox ERR_INVALIDARG, csvMB_ICONEXCLAMATION, TITLEBAR
            csvGetIntlString = Entry
        End If

    End Function
```

Setting Form Colors

You can use the various color values set in the Control Panel to manipulate the colors in your own applications. For example, if you determine the window color, you can set the background color of a form's Detail section. Then, you can read the window text color and change the foreground color of all the labels on the form.

The following example illustrates one way you can change colors during a form's **OnActivate** event.

```
    Sub Form_Activate ()

        Dim X As Integer

        Section(0).BackColor = csvWindowsColor("window")
        For X = 0 To Me.Count - 1
            If TypeOf Me(X) Is Label Then
                If Me(X).Section = 0 Then
                    Me(X).ForeColor = csvWindowsColor("windowtext")
```

254

```
            End If
        End If
    Next X

End Sub
```

 Note: Do not set colors during the **GotFocus** event. This event occurs only when there are no controls on the form (unlikely) or all controls on the form are disabled (also unlikely).

The preceding code changes the color of the Detail section to match the window color set in the Control Panel. The code then loops through all controls on the form looking for labels. When it finds a label in the Detail section (that is, where the control's **Section** property setting is 0), the code changes the control's foreground to match the window text setting. If you had previously set the **BackStyle** property to Clear, the label appears to have changed colors, with the Detail section's color showing through.

You can expand this code to anticipate other controls. For example, if you have lines or rectangles on a form, you must decide what to do about these controls, too. If you use the same color for lines and rectangles as you do for labels (as in the HomeFinder application), all you need to do is add a test to see if the control is not only a label, but also a line or a rectangle.

If you use different colors, you may have to provide a custom color dialog box. Whenever possible, use the same color settings for all label, line, and rectangle controls.

Summary

Unless there is a compelling reason to use your own color combinations, use the Control Panel settings. You can create a generic function and then call that function from each form's **OnActivate** event procedure.

16

Adding Query-by-Form Capability

Most of the queries you create in Microsoft Access work with specific tables, retrieve specific data, and then sort the data in a specific format. For example, a query you use to supply data to an employee phone book might include all active employees in the Employees table, sorted by last name and first name.

If you wanted to run the same listing, but select a different status, you would ordinarily have to change the underlying query. Although manually editing the query will work, it is both inconvenient and risky to allow end users access to the query in Design View. A better solution would be to determine the desired status at run time.

To resolve these and other dilemmas, this chapter discusses ways you can create dynamic queries that let the user specify the arguments at run time.

This chapter covers the following:

- Creating Parameter Queries

- Implementing Application-Specific Query by Form

- Implementing Application-Independent Query by Form

- Creating the csvQBF Load Form

- Creating the csvQBF Save Form

- Creating the csvQBF Export Form

- Creating the csvQBF SQL Form

- Using csvQBF in Other Applications

Creating Parameter Queries

The easiest way to create a query is to use the QBE (Query by Example) grid. Along the Criteria row you can add selection values that must be satisfied for each record (see fig. 16.1).

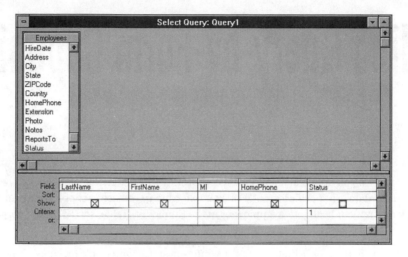

Figure 16.1. In this example, a single criterion has been established for the Status field.

When you run the query, Access checks to see whether an employee's Status field contains a value of 1 (which means the employee is active). If so, the record will be selected (see fig. 16.2).

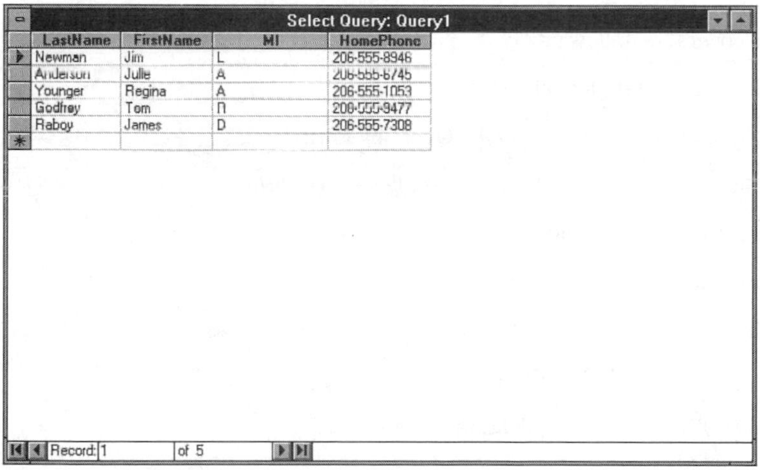

Figure 16.2. When you restrict the Status field, only active employees appear in the output.

Microsoft defines a *parameter query* as one in which arguments to the query are supplied interactively. However, even if you hardcode the criteria (the 1 for the Status field, in this example), you have created a parameter query.

You might also think of a parameter query as one that includes a WHERE clause in its SQL statement. In the query's Design view, choose the SQL command from the View menu to view the SQL statement (see fig. 16.3).

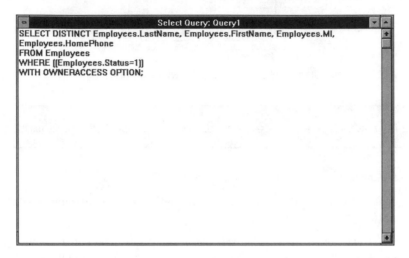

```
Select Query: Query1
SELECT DISTINCT Employees.LastName, Employees.FirstName, Employees.MI,
Employees.HomePhone
FROM Employees
WHERE [[Employees.Status=1]]
WITH OWNERACCESS OPTION;
```

Figure 16.3.   In SQL, the selection criteria, or parameters, appear in the WHERE clause.

This example illustrates how you can hardcode a single parameter, but you could easily add more criteria. In doing so, however, you make the query more specific to one set of circumstances and more difficult to use when your needs change.

The following sections discuss ways you can take a simple parameter query such as this and add query-by-form capability.

User-Supplied Arguments

When you define query parameters, Access prompts you to supply the values you might otherwise hardcode in the query. To add this query-by-form capability to the example single-parameter query (and thus prevent these automatic prompts), you first must remove the 1 from the Criteria row of the query. Then follow these steps:

1. Choose the Parameters command from the Query menu. Access displays the Query Parameters dialog box.

2. Enter the names and types of parameters for the query (see fig. 16.4).

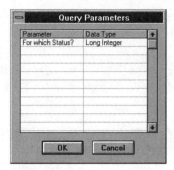

Figure 16.4. In this example, the name of the parameter is **For which Status?**.

 Note: The parameter name also serves as the text that appears in a message box when you run the query.

3. Close the dialog box and return to the QBE grid.

4. Enter in the Criteria row the same text you entered in the Query Parameters dialog box (see fig. 16.5).

   Notice the square brackets on either side of the parameter. If you do not enter square brackets, Microsoft Access treats the parameter name as a string literal.

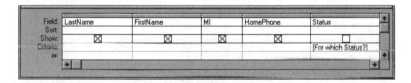

Figure 16.5. For this example, enter **[For which Status?]** below the Status field.

When you run the query, Access displays a dialog box in which you can enter the desired status code, as shown in figure 16.6.

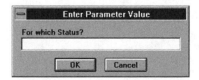

Figure 16.6. Specifying the desired status code.

If you enter **1** and then click the OK button, Access runs the query as if you had hardcoded the same value in the Criteria row. Responding to the dialog box in this manner is a simple version of query-by-form; the query uses the value you enter in a form or, in this case, a dialog box.

Automatic Arguments

The previous section, "User-Supplied Arguments," discussed how you defined parameters and had Access prompt the user for selection criteria at run time. In your applications, you may not want to prompt the user to supply values, at least not with the built-in parameter dialog boxes.

Instead, you may want Access to read values directly from an open form. For example, you might design a Customers form with a command button named Orders that opens an Orders form. When you open the Orders form, you want only the orders for the selected customer to appear. For this to work, you need a control on the Customers form that contains the customer's ID or other key field. Typically, this is a text box, even if the text box is invisible. The following procedure outlines the steps you can use to read values from a form.

1. Select the command button and then open the property sheet. Access displays the properties for the command button.

2. Select [Event Procedure] in the drop-down list, as shown in figure 16.7.

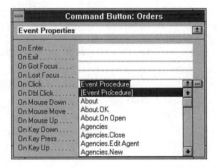

Figure 16.7. Selecting the event procedure.

3. Define an event procedure by right-clicking the property setting and then choosing the Build command from the menu that appears (see fig. 16.8). Access displays the form's Module window for the command button's **OnClick** event.

4. Enter the following line of code in the Orders_Click subprocedure in the Module window:

```
DoCmd OpenForm "Orders", , , "CustID = " & Me![CustID]
```

When the user clicks the Orders command button, Access runs the Orders_Click subprocedure, which in turn opens the Orders form. The form will open and display only those orders where the customer ID for the orders matches the customer ID on the Customers form.

261

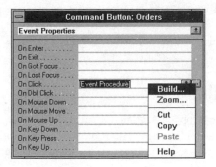

Figure 16.8.   Choose the Build command to create the event procedure.

This technique automatically supplies a value (the customer ID, in this case) to the code that opens the Orders form. This method is also a version of query by form.

Implementing Application-Specific Query by Form

To most users, running a query by form means entering a variety of selection criteria in a form, clicking a command button, and then viewing the results of the query that takes these criteria into account. This section describes how you can implement such a form in the HomeFinder application.

Before you begin creating the query by form mechanism, be sure you clearly define the criteria by which the user will be able to query the database. In the HomeFinder application, there are many fields in the database from which you may choose, but some may not be appropriate fields for the query by form model. For example, you probably would not want to ask for the state if all of your properties are in Washington, or the city if all the houses are in Seattle. In contrast, it may be appropriate to ask for ZIP codes or neighborhoods if you want to restrict searches to certain areas within the same city.

Designing the QBF Form

In the Database window, choose the New command from the File menu and then choose the Form subcommand from the drop-down list. Access displays the New Form dialog box (see fig. 16.9) in which you can enter or select the name of a query or table on which to base the form.

This will be an unbound form, so do not enter or select a query or table name. Because there is no built-in wizard for creating a query by form, click the Blank Form button. Access displays a new blank form. Save the new form and name it "QBF".

The style for all forms in the HomeFinder application includes a form header but no form footer. Choose the Form Header/Footer command from the Layout menu. Access displays both a header and footer section in the new form, but the footer is not needed. Drag the bottom of the form footer up until the Footer section disappears, leaving only the header (see fig. 16.10).

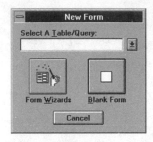

Figure 16.9.   Specifying the record source for the new form.

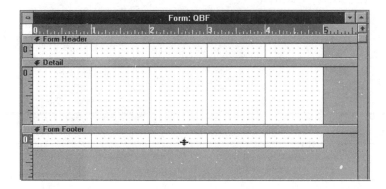

Figure 16.10.   Remove the form footer by dragging its lower border up.

Add the various combo boxes, command buttons, and other controls necessary to implement the query-by-form functionality, as shown in figure 16.11.

In this example, the colors have been set to blue on gray, and the user-editable controls have been given a sunken appearance, but you can choose whatever colors and appearance you find attractive.

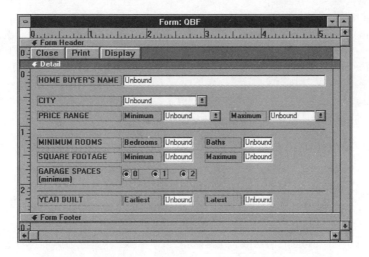

Figure 16.11.   The QBF form in Design View.

Table 16.1 lists the property settings you need to set for the form and each of its controls. If a property is not listed, it means that its default setting is acceptable.

Table 16.1.   QBF Form Properties

Control	Property	Setting
(form)	Caption	Find-A-House
	Default View	Single Form
	Shortcut Menu	No
	Scroll Bars	Neither
	Record Selectors	No
	Navigation Buttons	No
	Auto Resize	Yes
	Auto Center	Yes
	Popup	No
	Modal	Yes
	Min Button	No
	Max Button	No
Close (command button)	Name	Close
	Caption	Close
	Status Bar Text	Close this form and return to the Main Menu.
	On Click	[Event Procedure]

Control	Property	Setting
Print (command button)	Name	Print
	Caption	Print
	Status Bar Text	Print a report containing the selected houses.
	On Click	[Event Procedure]
Display (command button)	Name	Display
	Caption	Display
	Status Bar Text	Display the houses that meet your criteria.
	On Click	[Event Procedure]
Buyer (text box)	Name	Buyer
	Default Value	"Prospective Buyer"
	Status Bar Text	Names of potential home buyers.
City (combo box)	Name	City
	Row Source Type	Table/Query
	Row Source	Cities by Sequence Qry
	Column Count	2
	Column Widths	0;3
	Bound Column	1
	Status Bar Text	The preferred city.
	Default Value	1
Price Min (text box)	Name	PriceMin
	Format	Standard
	Decimal Places	0
	Status Bar Text	Lowest listing price.
	Default Value	50000
	Validation Rule	>=0
	Validation Text	The lowest listing price cannot be less than zero (0).
	Text Align	Left
Price Max (text box)	Name	PriceMax
	Format	Standard
	Decimal Places	0
	Status Bar Text	Highest listing price.
	Default Value	250000
	Validation Rule	>=[PriceMin]
	Validation Text	The highest listing price can't be less than the lowest listing price.
	Text Align	Left

continues

Table 16.1. Continued

Control	Property	Setting
Bedrooms (text box)	Name	BedroomsMin
	Default Value	2
	Validation Rule	>=0
	Validation Text	The minimum number of bedrooms cannot be less than zero.
	Status Bar Text	Minimum number of bedrooms.
Baths (text box)	Name	BathroomsMin
	Format	Fixed
	Decimal Places	1
	Default Value	1
	Validation Rule	>=0
	Validation Text	The minimum number of bathrooms cannot be less than zero.
	Status Bar Text	Minimum number of bathrooms.
Footage Minimum (text box)	Name	FootageMin
	Format	#,###
	Default Value	1000
	Validation Rule	>=0
	Validation Text	The minimum square footage cannot be less than zero.
	Status Bar Text	Minimum square footage.
Footage Maximum (text box)	Name	FootageMax
	Format	#,###
	Default Value	2500
	Validation Rule	>=[FootageMin]
	Validation Text	The maximum square footage cannot be less than the minimum square footage.
	Status Bar Text	Maximum square footage.
Garage Spaces (option group)	Name	GarageSpaces
	Default Value	0
	Status Bar Text	Number of garage/car spaces.
	Border Style	Clear
Zero (option button)	Name	Spaces0
	Option Value	0
	Status Bar Text	No garage necessary.
One (option button)	Name	Spaces1
	Option Value	1
	Status Bar Text	At least one garage space.

Control	Property	Setting
Two (option button)	Name	Spaces2
	Option Value	2
	Status Bar Text	At least two garage spaces.
Earliest (text box)	Name	YearMin
	Decimal Places	0
	Default Value	1980
	Validate Rule	Between 1651 And DatePart("yyyy",Date())
	Validation Text	The year built must be between 1651 and today.
	Status Bar Text	Earliest year of house construction.
Latest (text box)	Name	YearMax
	Decimal Places	0
	Default Value	=DatePart("yyyy",Date())
	Validate Rule	Between [YearMin] And DatePart("yyyy",Date())
	Validation Text	The latest year built must be between the earliest year built and today.
	Status Bar Text	Latest year of house construction.

Figure 16.12 illustrates the QBF form with all its controls and default values.

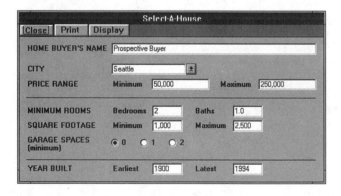

Figure 16.12. Adding default values makes it easier to use the QBF form.

Writing Code for the QBF Form

The Close button should do nothing more than close the form. To open the form's code module, select the Close button, right-click the button's **OnClick** property setting in the property sheet, and then choose the Build command.

Access displays the form's Module window for the command button's **OnClick** event. Enter the following line of code in the Close_Click subprocedure in the Module window:

```
DoCmd Close
```

The Print button should trigger printing a report that lists all the houses that meet the user's criteria. As you did with the Close command button, display the form's Module window for the Print button's **OnClick** event and enter the following line of code in the Print_Click subprocedure:

```
DoCmd OpenReport "Selected Houses", A_NORMAL, , WhereClause()
```

By opening the report with a condition (the fourth argument to the **OpenReport** macro action), this code filters the data so that only those houses that meet the specified criteria will be listed.

> **Tip:** Opening an existing report and applying a filter is an easy way to present a subset of the data without having to rewrite the query or maintain multiple versions of the report.

The WhereClause() function loops through all the controls on the QBF form and builds a string you can use with the **OpenReport** macro action. To create the function, first display the form's code module by choosing the Code command from the View menu. Next, enter the first line of code for the function:

```
Function WhereClause () As String
```

When you press ENTER, Access displays a new window into which you can enter the rest of the code for the WhereClause() function.

```
Function WhereClause () As String

    Dim W As String

    W = ""
    W = W & "City = '" & Me.City & "'"
    W = W & " AND "
    W = W & "AskingPrice BETWEEN " & Me.PriceMin & " AND " & Me.PriceMax
    W = W & " AND "
    W = W & "Bedrooms BETWEEN " & Me.BedroomsMin & " AND " & Me.BedroomsMax
    W = W & " AND "
    W = W & "Footage BETWEEN " & Me.FootageMin & " AND " & Me.FootageMax
    W = W & " AND "
    W = W & "Garage >= " & Me.GarageSpaces
    W = W & " AND "
    W = W & "YearBuilt BETWEEN " & Me.YearMin & " AND " & Me.YearMax

    WhereClause = W


End Function
```

268

Although you should try to avoid cryptic variable names, this function uses "W" instead of something more meaningful (such as "WhereClause") for two reasons. First, "WhereClause" would be unnecessarily lengthy and some lines would extend beyond the width of the Module window in VGA resolution:

```
WhereClause = WhereClause & "Bedrooms BETWEEN " & Me.BedroomsMin & " AND "
➥& Me.BedroomsMax
```

Second, in this example, "WhereClause" is the name of the function. Using a variable name other than "W" would mean having to invent some other name not nearly as good as "WhereClause".

 For details on creating reports, see Chapter 10, "Building the HomeFinder Reports." You also can open a completed Selected Houses report in the sample HomeFinder application (HOMECODE.MDB).

The Display button should display the Houses form. Much like the way the code behind the Print button filters the data by calling the WhereClause() function, so too does the code for the Display button. Enter the following code for the Display button's **OnClick** event:

```
Sub Display_Click ()

    Const MYFORMNAME = "Houses"
    Const csvMB_ICONINFORMATION = 48
    Dim MyForm As Form
    Dim Msg As String
    Dim X As Integer

    DoCmd Hourglass True
    If DCount("*", "Houses", WhereClause()) = 0 Then
        Msg = "Couldn't find any houses meeting your criteria. Refine your "
        Msg = Msg & "selection criteria and try again, or press the Close "
        Msg = Msg & "button to return to the Main Menu."
        DoCmd Hourglass False
        MsgBox Msg, csvMB_ICONINFORMATION, "Find-A-House"
    Else
        DoCmd Echo False
        DoCmd OpenForm MYFORMNAME, , , WhereClause(), A_READONLY
        Set MyForm = Forms("Houses")
        DoEvents
        MyForm.Caption = MyForm![RecordCount] & " House" &
        ➥IIf(MyForm![RecordCount] > 1, "s", "") & " Found"
        MyForm![New].Enabled = False
        X = AppearReadOnly(Me, MYFORMNAME)
        X = csvToggleMenuCommand(0, 0, False)
        DoCmd Echo True
    End If
    DoCmd Hourglass False

End Sub
```

When the user clicks the Display button, the code opens the Houses form, but with only those houses that meet the conditions specified by the WHERE clause.

Once the Houses form appears on the screen, the caption for the form is set so that it displays the number of houses that satisfy the selection criteria. To do this, you need to add a hidden text box to the Houses form. Minimize both the QBF form and the QBF form's Module window and then open the Houses form in Design View. Highlight the form in the Database window and then click the Design button.

Access displays the form in Design View. Add a text box toward the top of the Detail section of the form (see fig. 16.13) and then set the properties for the text box, as listed in table 16.2.

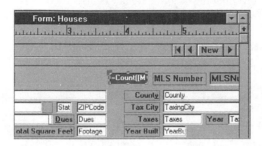

Figure 16.13. Add a hidden text box to store the number of selected homes.

Table 16.2. Control Properties

Control	Property	Setting
RecordCount (text box)	Name	RecordCount
	Visible	No
	Control Source	=Count([MLSNumber])
	Visible	No

Tip: As a visual cue to you and other developers that this is a hidden (invisible) control, change the text box's colors to white on red.

Save the Houses form, but do not close it yet. If you want, you can minimize the form to get it out of the way while you work on the code.

To set the form's caption, you need to know the number of records in the form's underlying recordset, and the **Count** function determines that number. Referring to the value of the RecordCount text box, the following line of the code sets the **Caption** property:

```
MyForm.Caption = MyForm![RecordCount] & " Houses Found"
```

> **Note:** The **DoEvents** statement that precedes setting the caption is there because Access frequently loads and opens the form so quickly that the number of records is not calculated by the time it encounters the line that sets the caption. By inserting this artificial delay, you ensure that Access has calculated the record count before changing the caption. Without the **DoEvents**, the RecordCount text box is Null and the caption of the form is set to "Houses Found."

Next, the function sets the **Enabled** property for the New command button to False. The Houses form actually serves two functions. First, it is the primary means by which you add new and revised data into the system. Second, it provides a way to display the results of the QBF form. When you look for houses, there is no need to add new houses, so the button is disabled.

You must also disable the New command on the form's File menu. To disable a command on a menu, you call the csvToggleMenuCommand() function. If you have not already created this function, do so now. If necessary, see Chapter 21, "Useful Functions," for complete instructions.

Finally, the Display_Click subprocedure calls a function, AppearReadOnly(), that changes the appearance of the form so that it looks like the controls are read-only. As a visual cue, you should make editable controls sunken and read-only fields normal.

> For more information about designing forms, see Chapter 8, "Building the HomeFinder Forms," and Chapter 18, "Application Design Guidelines."

In the Declarations section of the form's code module, enter the first line of the AppearReadOnly() function:

```
Function AppearReadOnly (MyForm As Form, ByVal TargetForm As String,
➡As Integer
```

When you press ENTER, Access displays a new window into which you can enter the rest of the code for the AppearReadOnly() function:

```
Const DETAILSECTION = 0
Const CLEAR = 0
Const NORMAL = 0
Const SUNKEN = 2
Dim Target As Form
Dim X As Integer
Dim DetailBackColor As Long

Set Target = Forms(TargetForm)
DetailBackColor = Target.Section(DETAILSECTION).BackColor
For X = 0 To Target.Count - 1
    If Target(X).Section = DETAILSECTION Then
        On Error Resume Next
        Target(X).SpecialEffect = NORMAL
        Target(X).FillColor = DetailBackColor
```

271

```
            Target(X).BackColor = DetailBackColor
            Target(X).BorderStyle = CLEAR
            On Error GoTo 0
        End If
    Next X
    For X = 1 To 5
        Target("Box" & Trim$(Str$(X))).Visible = True
    Next X
```

To make a control appear as read-only, set the control to normal (versus sunken), set its background and fill colors to the same as the section in which it is located, and set its border style to clear.

Tip: Not all controls have all of these properties. Normally, trying to set a property that does not apply to a given control produces a runtime error. Rather than treating each of the kinds of controls (text box, combo box, and so on) as a special case, and then setting only the relevant properties for each control, this function includes code that essentially ignores any errors.

Check your work for syntax errors by choosing the Compile Loaded Modules command from the Run menu. If you have made any mistakes, correct them and then recompile. Repeat this process until Access no longer produces an error message.

Figure 16.14 illustrates the completed form in Form View. For now, choose the Save command from the File menu to save your work and close the QBF form. This automatically closes the form's code module.

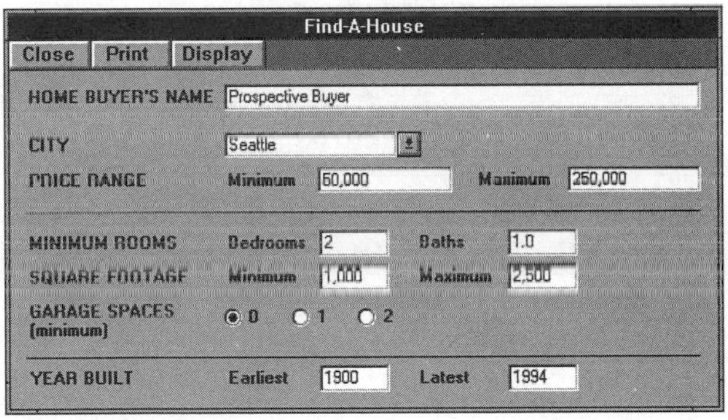

Figure 16.14.   Your completed QBF form will look something like this.

Return to the Houses form, which is still open in Design View. If you minimized the form, click the form's icon and then choose the Restore command.

There are five combo boxes on the Houses form. When the user finds houses, the combo boxes are set to the same color as the Detail section, and the combo box borders are clear. Unless you do something special to the form, however, the drop-down arrows on the combo boxes will still be visible.

To hide the drop-down arrows, add five rectangles, one atop each of the combo boxes' drop-down arrows. The rectangles will be made visible and thus obscure the drop-down arrows. For each rectangle, set the properties listed in table 16.3.

Table 16.3.   Control Properties

Control	Property	Setting
rectangle	Name	Box1*
	Width	.17
	Height	.18

* Create five rectangles named Box1, Box2, Box3, Box4, and Box5.

Position the rectangles so that they completely obscure the drop-down arrows, and then save and close the Houses form.

Testing the QBF Form

If there are any open forms or other windows (except for the Database window), close them. Return to the Database window and then highlight the AutoExec macro. Run the AutoExec macro; Access displays the Main Menu. Click the Find-A-House command button, enter some selection criteria and see how well your form and code work (see fig. 16.15).

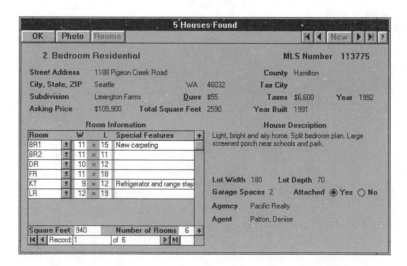

Figure 16.15.   The completed QBF form in Form View.

You may need to adjust the defaults in the QBF form. Depending on the data you have in your Houses table, the default values for the QBF form may result in too many or too few selected homes (see fig. 16.16).

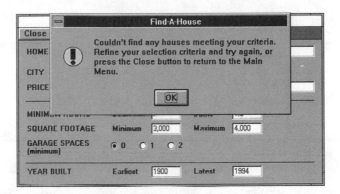

Figure 16.16.   The user may need to refine the selection criteria.

 Tip: Try to make things easy for the user by setting defaults that make sense. In the sample HomeFinder database, for example, the city defaults to Seattle because most prospective buyers tend to look for homes in that city. If you live in an area where a different city preference prevails, change the default.

Enhancing the QBF Form

There are a number of things you may want to implement to make the QBF form easier to use or more flexible:

- Add a user-defined limit to the number of houses returned by the QBF form by including the **TOP** predicate in the where condition when you open the Houses form or the Selected Houses report.

- Add a custom menu bar to the form.

- Provide combo boxes instead of text boxes for the various controls.

- Save the names and selection criteria in case a prospective buyer returns for a subsequent search.

- Provide a mechanism for selecting multiple cities.

- Allow the user to remove any selection criteria by setting the relevant control to Null; modify the WhereClause() function so that it tests for Null before adding the criterion.

Implementing Application-Independent Query by Form

The previous section, "Implementing Application-Specific Query by Form," discussed how you can implement query-by-form capability for a specific application. The QBF form has labels and other controls that make it specific to the HomeFinder application. To make the form work in another application, you have to change not only the form itself, but also its underlying code.

In contrast, you can instead add a generic form and generic code that is not application dependent. Thereafter, you can export the form and code to other applications and, with a minimum of work, implement query-by-form capability in those applications, as well.

Designing the csvQBF Form

Microsoft Access allows only one form with the same name in any given database. If you followed the instructions in the previous sections and created an application-specific form named QBF, you will need to make up a different name for the generic version. For the purposes of this example, the generic form will be named csvQBF.

> **Note:** If you are working in the HomeFinder sample application, you already have a form named csvQBF. If you want to treat this chapter as a tutorial and create the form yourself, either open a different database or rename the existing csvQBF form.

You will probably move the csvQBF form into a library. Forms and other objects in a library should be given names that are not likely to exist in other, non-library databases. The "csv" prefix helps ensure that the name is unique. For more information about libraries, see Chapter 19, "Creating and Using Libraries."

Create a new form by selecting forms in the Database window and then clicking the New button (see fig. 16.17).

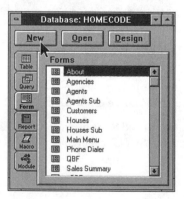

Figure 16.17. Creating a new form.

275

Access displays the New Form dialog box in which you can enter or select the name of a table or query on which to base the form. Like the QBF form presented earlier in this chapter, the csvQBF form will be an unbound form. Do not enter or select a table or query name; just click the Blank Form button. Access displays a new blank form. Save the new form and name it "csvQBF."

As with the QBF and most other forms in the HomeFinder application, there is a form header but no form footer. Choose the Form Header/Footer command from the Layout menu. Access displays both a header and a footer section in the new form, but because the footer is not needed, you should drag the bottom of the form footer up until the Footer section disappears, leaving only the header.

Add the various combo boxes, command buttons, and other controls necessary to implement the query-by-form functionality (see fig. 16.18).

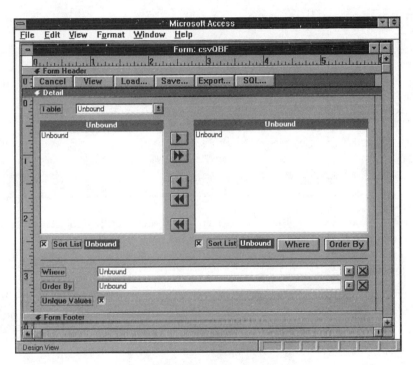

Figure 16.18. The csvQBF form contains a wider variety of controls than the QBF form.

In this example, the colors have been set to blue on gray, and the user-editable controls have been given a sunken appearance, but you can choose other colors and a different appearance.

Table 16.4 lists the property settings you need to set for the form and each of its controls. If a property is not listed, it means that its default setting is acceptable.

Table 16.4. csvQBF Form Properties

Control	Property	Setting
(form)	Caption	Query by Form (QBF)
	Default View	Single Form
	Scroll Bars	Neither
	Navigation Buttons	No
	Auto Center	Yes
	Modal	Yes
	Min Button	No
	Max Button	No
	On Close	[Event Procedure]
Cancel (command button)	Name	Cancel
	Caption	Cancel
	Status Bar Text	Close this form and return to the Main Menu.
	On Click	[Event Procedure]
View (command button)	Name	View
	Caption	View
	Status Bar Text	Accept these parameters and view the results of the query.
	Enabled	No
	On Click	[Event Procedure]
Load (command button)	Name	Load
	Caption	Load...
	Status Bar Text	Load a previously saved query.
	Enabled	Yes
	On Click	[Event Procedure]
Save (command button)	Name	Save
	Caption	Save...
	Status Bar Text	Save this set of criteria as a new query.
	Enabled	No
	On Click	[Event Procedure]
Export (command button)	Name	Export
	Caption	Export...
	Status Bar Text	Export the results of the query to an external file.
	Enabled	No
	On Click	[Event Procedure]

continues

277

Table 16.4. Continued

Control	Property	Setting
SQL (command button)	Name	SQL
	Caption	SQL...
	Status Bar Text	View the SQL statement produced by this query.
	Enabled	No
	On Click	[Event Procedure]
Tables (combo box)	Name	Tables
	Row Source Type	Table/Query
	Row Source	SELECT Name FROM MSysObjects WHERE Type IN (1, 6) AND Left$([Name], 1) <> '~' AND Left$([Name], 2) <> 'zt' AND Left$([Name], 2) <> 'zz' AND Left$([Name], 4) <> 'MSys' AND Left$([Name], 4) <> 'USys' ORDER BY Name;
	Column Count	1
	Status Bar Text	(none)
	Limit To List	Yes
	After Update	[Event Procedure]
	On Enter	[Event Procedure]
	On Exit	[Event Procedure]
Available Fields (label)	Name	AvailableFields
	Caption	AVAILABLE
	Border Style	Clear
	Text Align	Center
Selected Fields (label)	Name	SelectedFields
	Caption	SELECTED
	Border Style	Clear
	Text Align	Center
Available (list box)	Name	Source
	Row Source Type	qbfFillAvailableFields
	Column Count	1
	Status Bar Text	Double-click an entry to add it to the Selected list.
	On Dbl Click	=qbfSelectOne([])

278

Control	Property	Setting
Sort Available (check box)	Name	SortAvailable
	Default Value	0
	Status Bar Text	When selected, sort the entries in the Available list.
	After Update	[Event Procedure]
Selected (list box)	Name	Destination
	Row Source Type	qbfFillSelectedFields
	Column Count	2
	Column Widths	1.5 in; 1.45 in
	Bound Column	1
	Status Bar Text	Double-click an entry to remove it from the Selected list.
	On Dbl Click	=qbfRemoveOne([])
Sort Selected (check box)	Name	SortSelected
	Default Value	0
	Status Bar Text	When selected, sort the entries in the Selected list.
	After Update	[Event Procedure]
Where (command button)	Name	AddWhere
	Caption	Where
	Status Bar Text	Add the highlighted Selected entry to the Where clause.
	Enabled	No
	On Click	[Event Procedure]
Order By (command button)	Name	AddOrderBy
	Caption	Order By
	Status Bar Text	Add the highlighted Selected entry to the Order By clause.
	Enabled	No
	On Click	[Event Procedure]
Where Clause (text box)	Name	WhereClause
	Status Bar Text	Enter the desired conditions; double-click to display the Where Builder.
	Enabled	No

continues

279

Table 16.4. Continued

Control	Property	Setting
Order By Clause (text box)	Name	OrderByClause
	Status Bar Text	Enter the desired sort order; separate entries with a comma.
	Enabled	No
Unique Values (check box)	Name	Unique Values
	Default Value	-1
	Status Bar Text	When selected, only unique (distinct) values will be returned by the query.

Writing Code for the csvQBF Form

The csvQBF form is rather ambitious—it has many controls and there is a lot happening. This section describes the various controls and the events you need to anticipate. There is a fair amount of code, all of it behind the form in the form's code module.

Cancel Command Button

The Cancel command button should do nothing more than close the form—the user has chosen to cancel the query.

Set the command button's **OnClick** property setting in the property sheet to [Event Procedure], and then open the form's code module by clicking the ellipsis that appears to the right of the property setting. Access displays the form's code module in which you can enter the following line of code:

```
Sub Cancel_Click ()
    DoCmd Close
End Sub
```

Close the Module window.

View Command Button

This command button triggers building an SQL statement, running the query, and then displaying the results. It could have been named and labelled "OK", but "View" is more descriptive and more clearly defines what the button does.

Set the command button's **OnClick** property setting in the property sheet to [Event Procedure], and then open the form's code module by clicking the ellipsis that appears to the right of the property setting. Access displays the form's code module in which you can enter the following code:

```
Sub View_Click ()

    Const csvMB_ICONQUESTIONMARK = 32
    Const csvMB_YES = 6
    Const csvMB_YESNO = 4

    If qbfBuildQBFQuery(Me) = True Then
        If MsgBox("This query will produce " & Trim$(Str$(DCount("*",
qbfQUERYNAME))) &
            ➡" records. Continue?",  csvMB_ICONQUESTIONMARK +  csvMB_YESNO,
            ➡"QBF - Results") = csvMB_YES Then
                DoCmd OpenQuery qbfQUERYNAME, A_NORMAL
        End If
    End If

End Sub
```

The first thing the routine does is call a function, `qbfBuildQBFQuery()`, that rebuilds the query using the criteria specified by the user. That function returns either True or False, depending on whether the function was successful.

If successful, the procedure then displays a message box and asks the user whether he wants to continue with the query, producing the number of records indicated.

> **Tip:** You can use the **DCount** function to determine the number of records in a table or the number of records produced or reported on by a query. This is a quick way to validate the criteria and help the user prevent "runaway" queries.

Finally, if the user indicates that he wants to continue, the procedure opens the query in normal, or Datasheet, view.

Take another look at the following line of code:

```
    If MsgBox("This query will produce " & Trim$(Str$(DCount("*",
qbfQUERYNAME))) & " records.",
        ➡65, "QBF - Results") = 6 Then
```

This line uses a literal, 65, that by itself may not mean much to you. The 65 is the second argument to the **MsgBox** function and defines the icons and buttons that will appear in the message box (see fig. 16.19).

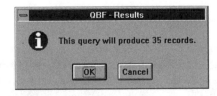

Figure 16.19.   Displaying the number of records.

281

As written, it displays an information icon and the OK command button, but does not otherwise give the user a way to cancel the query. A much more useful message box is shown in figure 16.20.

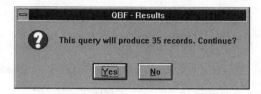

Figure 16.20. Provide a way for the user to cancel the query.

In this example, the message box poses a question and provides Yes and No command buttons. To produce this message box, change the preceding line of code so that it looks like this:

```
If MsgBox("This query will produce " & Trim$(Str$(DCount("*", qbfQUERYNAME))) & "
records.", 32 + 4,
➡"QBF - Results") = 6 Then
```

Still, the numbers 32, 4, and 6 (at the end of the line) do not hold much meaning. For this reason, you should consider using constants:

```
Const csvMB_ICONQUESTIONMARK = 32
Const csvMB_YES = 6
Const csvMB_YESNO = 4
```

The revised subprocedure now looks like this:

```
Sub View_Click ()

    Const csvMB_ICONQUESTIONMARK = 32
    Const csvMB_YES = 6
    Const csvMB_YESNO = 4

    If qbfBuildQBFQuery(Me) = True Then
        If MsgBox("This query will produce " & Trim$(Str$(DCount("*",
qbfQUERYNAME))) & " records.",
        ➡csvMB_ICONQUESTIONMARK + csvMB_YESNO, "QBF - Results") = csvMB_YES Then
            DoCmd OpenQuery qbfQUERYNAME, A_NORMAL
        End If
    End If

End Sub
```

With constants in place, it is easier to see that the message box includes the question mark icon and two command buttons, Yes and No.

The query produced by this subprocedure is defined by a constant, qbfQUERYNAME. If you decide to change the name of the query, it is much easier to change the name of a single constant than every occurrence of the query name. To define the constant, go to the Declarations section of the form's code module and then add the line of code shown in figure 16.21.

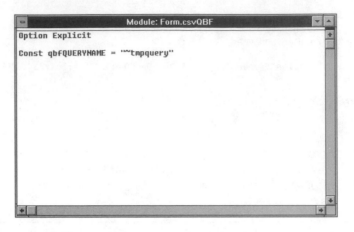

Figure 16.21. A constant that defines the name of the query.

 Note: This is a temporary query, one the user does not normally access directly in the Database window and one whose name should not normally appear in any list. By convention, temporary object names begin with a tilde (~).

You will enter the code for `qbfBuildQBFQuery()` later in this chapter, but for now, close or minimize the code module.

Load Command Button

A useful element of the csvQBF form is that the user can save and load the criteria as a named query. For example, if the user selects a series of tables and fields, sets the sort order, and establishes a WHERE clause, he can save that set of criteria and later retrieve (load) it using the Load command button.

 Note: Unlike the Save command button, the Load command button starts out enabled, and remains enabled, because the user can load (or try to load) a previously saved query without first having to specify any criteria.

Set the command button's **OnClick** property to [Event Procedure] and then open the form's code module. Access displays a nearly blank Module window in which you can enter the following code:

```
Sub Load_Click ()

    Const qbfLOADFORM = "csvQBF Load"
    Const FUNCTIONNAME = "Load_Click()"
    Const csvMB_ICONEXCLAMATION = 48
```

283

```
      On Error Resume Next
      DoCmd OpenForm qbfLOADFORM
      If Err Then
          MsgBox "Couldn't open form '" & qbfLOADFORM & "'.", csvMB_ICONEXCLAMATION,
FUNCTIONNAME
      End If
      On Error GoTo 0

  End Sub
```

> **Tip:** Using a constant for the name of the form (csvQBF Load) makes it easier to change the name of the form later. Rather than search for the name of the form in the body of the subprocedure, you can instead look for the constant.

All of the code for loading a previously saved query is centralized and maintained in the other form, csvQBF Load, so all you need to do here is open that form.

Save Command Button

Once the user has established the tables, fields, and other criteria for the query, he can save the criteria using the Save command button, give it a name, and then later reload the criteria (see the section "Load Command Button").

> **Note:** Unlike the Load command button, the Save command button starts out disabled because there is nothing to save, at least not until the user specifies something (specifically, one or more fields).

Set the command button's **OnClick** property to [Event Procedure] and then open the form's code module. Access displays a nearly blank Module window in which you can enter the following code:

```
  Sub Save_Click ()

      Const qbfSAVEFORM = "csvQBF Save"
      Const FUNCTIONNAME = "Save_Click()"
      Const csvMB_ICONEXCLAMATION = 48

      On Error Resume Next
      DoCmd OpenForm qbfSAVEFORM
      If Err Then
          MsgBox "Couldn't open form '" & qbfSAVEFORM & "'.", csvMB_ICONEXCLAMATION,
FUNCTIONNAME
      End If
      On Error GoTo 0

  End Sub
```

Tip: Using a constant for the name of the form (csvQBF Save) makes it easier to change the name of the form later. Rather than search for the name of the form in the body of the subprocedure, you can instead look for the constant.

This subprocedure is nearly identical to that for the Load command button. All of the code for saving the current criteria as a query is centralized and maintained in the other form, csvQBF Save, so all you need to do here is open that form.

Export Command Button

Once the user has viewed the results of the query (or even without first viewing the results), he can export the results to an external text file, a spreadsheet, or to an Access table for subsequent review, editing, or archiving.

Note: Like the Save command button, the Export command button starts out disabled because there is nothing to export, at least not until the user specifies something (specifically, one or more fields).

Set the command button's **OnClick** property to [Event Procedure] and then open the form's code module. Access displays a nearly blank Module window in which you can enter the following code:

```
Sub Export_Click ()

    Const qbfEXPORTFORM = "csvQBF Export"
    Const FUNCTIONNAME = "Export_Click()"
    Const csvMB_ICONEXCLAMATION = 48

    On Error Resume Next
    DoCmd OpenForm qbfEXPORTFORM
    If Err Then
        MsgBox "Couldn't open form '" & qbfEXPORTFORM & "'.", csvMB_ICONEXCLAMATION,
        ➥FUNCTIONNAME
    End If
    On Error GoTo 0

End Sub
```

Tip: Using a constant for the name of the form (csvQBF Export) makes it easier to change the name of the form later. Rather than search for the name of the form in the body of the subprocedure, you can instead look for the constant.

This subprocedure is nearly identical to that for the Load and Save command buttons. All of the code for exporting the current criteria is centralized and maintained in the other form, csvQBF Export, so all you need to do here is open that form.

285

This statement excludes tables that begin with a tilde, the letters "zt" (temporary tables), the letters "zz" (by convention, hidden tables), as well as system and user tables ("MSys" and "USys"). The list of table names appears in alphabetical order.

WARNING: This function uses the undocumented system table, MSysObjects. Use of the system tables (tables whose names begin with "MSys") is generally discouraged because these tables are subject to changes in their layout and internal values by Microsoft at any time. You must never change anything in any of the internal system tables.

When the user selects a table in the list, you want to perform the following actions:

- Deselect the table name in the combo box.

- Set the status bar text to the name of the selected table.

- Requery the list box containing the names of the available fields.

- Reset the list box to Null (to unhighlight any previously selected field name).

- Update the field count. Above the list box is a label that currently reads "AVAILABLE". At runtime, you want the label to show something like "AVAILABLE—10 Fields", or however many fields exist in the selected table.

Click the ellipsis that appears to the right of the combo box's **AfterUpdate** property setting. Access displays a nearly blank Module window in which you can enter the following code:

```
Sub Tables_AfterUpdate ()

    Const SOURCELISTBOX = "Source"
    Dim X As Integer

    SendKeys "{f2}"                      ' Unhighlight the combo box.
    X = csvSetStatusBarText([Tables])    ' Set status bar text to name of selected
table.
    Me(SOURCELISTBOX).Requery            ' Requery the list of available fields.
    Me(SOURCELISTBOX) = Null             ' Unhighlight the list box.
    X = qbfUpdateListCounts(Me)          ' Update the list counts.

End Sub
```

Note: Because this subprocedure calls two functions that have not been entered, do not try to compile your work yet.

You will want to update the status bar text whenever the user moves into the combo box, even if he does not change the selected table. Click the ellipsis that appears to the right of the **OnEnter** event in the property sheet and then enter the following code:

```
Sub Tables_Enter ()

    Dim X As Integer

    X = csvSetStatusBarText([Tables])

End Sub
```

Now, whenever the user moves into the combo box, the name of the selected table will appear in the status bar. However, if there is no selection, the status bar will be blank, so you might consider changing the code slightly:

```
If IsNull([Tables]) Then
    X = csvSetStatusBarText("Enter or select a table name from the list.")
Else
    X = csvSetStatusBarText([Tables])
End If
```

Note: Because the **AfterUpdate** and **OnEnter** events change the status bar text dynamically, the Tables combo box has no **StatusBarText** property setting (that is, it is Null).

Whenever you change the status bar text with the csvSetStatusBarText() function, make sure you reset the text at some point. If you do not reset the status bar text, even moving to another control will not display the text specified in that control's **StatusBarText** property.

For the combo box's **OnExit** event, click the ellipsis in the property sheet and then enter the following lines of code:

```
Sub Tables_Exit (Cancel As Integer)

    Dim X As Integer

    X = csvResetStatusBarText()

End Sub
```

The csvResetStatusBarText() function calls the built-in **SysCmd** function to reset the status bar text.

Except for the missing functions called from the three subprocedures you just entered, the Tables combo box is now fully functional.

Tip: Even if you followed earlier examples in this book and entered some or all of these functions in a global module, you should enter them again in the csvQBF form's code module. That way, you can export the csvQBF form to another application without having to worry about whether you also need to export functions in some other (global) module. Your goal should be to make the csvQBF form self-contained, at least as much as possible.

Return to the form's code module and go to the Declarations section. There, enter the following line to begin the csvSetStausBarText() function:

```
Function csvSetStatusBarText (ByVal MyText As Variant) As Integer
```

Access displays a nearly blank Module window in which you can enter the rest of the function:

```
Function csvSetStatusBarText (ByVal MyText As Variant) As Integer

    Dim ReturnValue As Variant

    csvSetStatusBarText = True

    If IsNull(MyText) Then
        ReturnValue = csvResetStatusBarText()
    Else
        ReturnValue = SysCmd(4, MyText)
    End If

End Function
```

You might want to replace the 4 in the function with a constant that makes more sense:

```
Const SYSCMD_SETSTATUS = 4
```

The revised function now looks like this:

```
Function csvSetStatusBarText (ByVal MyText As Variant) As Integer

    Const SYSCMD_SETSTATUS = 4
    Dim ReturnValue As Variant

    csvSetStatusBarText = True

    If IsNull(MyText) Then
        ReturnValue = csvResetStatusBarText()
    Else
        ReturnValue = SysCmd(SYSCMD_SETSTATUS, MyText)
    End If

End Function
```

Next, enter the first line of the csvResetStatusBarText() function:

```
Function csvResetStatusBarText () As Integer
```

> **Tip:** You do not have to return to the module's Declarations section to enter a new function. Indeed, you can be on any line, even inside another function, to create the new function.

When you press ENTER, Access displays a nearly blank Module window in which you can enter the rest of the code for the csvResetStatusBarText() function:

```
Function csvResetStatusBarText () As Integer

    Dim ReturnValue As Variant
```

```
csvResetStatusBarText = True

On Error Resume Next
ReturnValue = SysCmd(5)
On Error GoTo 0

End Function
```

You might want to replace the 5 in the function with a constant that makes more sense:

```
Const SYSCMD_CLEARSTATUS = 5
```

The revised function now looks like this:

```
Function csvResetStatusBarText () As Integer

    Const SYSCMD_CLEARSTATUS = 5
    Dim ReturnValue As Variant

    csvResetStatusBarText = True

    On Error Resume Next
    ReturnValue = SysCmd(SYSCMD_CLEARSTATUS)
    On Error GoTo 0

End Function
```

Next, enter the first line of the qbfUpdateListCounts() function:

```
Function qbfUpdateListCounts (MyForm As Form) As Integer
```

When you press ENTER, Access displays a nearly blank Module window which you can enter the rest of the code for the qbfUpdateListCounts() function:

```
Function qbfUpdateListCounts (MyForm As Form) As Integer

    Const MYLABEL = "Entry"
    Const MYLABELPLURAL = "Entries"
    Dim MyControl As Control
    Dim NumberSource As Integer
    Dim NumberDestination As Integer

    qbfUpdateListCounts = True

    On Error Resume Next
    Set MyControl = MyForm![NumberSource]
    If Err Then
        ' An error occurs when this function is called from the
        ' OnClose event of the form; just ignore it.
    Else
        On Error Resume Next
        NumberSource = UBound(qbfFieldArray)
        If Err Then
        Else
            MyForm![NumberSource] = NumberSource
        End If
        NumberDestination = DCount("*", "zz_qbfSelected")
        MyForm![NumberDestination] = NumberDestination
```

```
                MyForm![AvailableFields].Caption = MyForm![NumberSource].DefaultValue & " -
        " &
                ➦MyForm![NumberSource] & If(MyForm![NumberSource] <> 0,
                ➦IMYLABELPLURAL, MYLABEL)
                MyForm![SelectedFields].Caption = MyForm![NumberDestination].DefaultValue &
        " - " &
                ➦MyForm![NumberDestination] & IIf(MyForm![NumberDestination] <> 0,
                ➦MYLABELPLURAL, MYLABEL)
                MyForm![SQL].Enabled = NumberDestination > 0
                MyForm![View].Enabled = NumberDestination > 0
                MyForm![AddWhere].Enabled = NumberDestination > 0
                MyForm![AddOrderBy].Enabled = NumberDestination > 0
                MyForm![Export].Enabled = NumberDestination > 0
                MyForm![Save].Enabled = NumberDestination > 0
                MyForm![WhereClause].Enabled = NumberDestination > 0
                MyForm![OrderByClause].Enabled = NumberDestination > 0
            End If
            On Error GoTo 0

        End Function
```

This function updates the number of available fields and the number of selected fields. These numbers appear in labels above the two list-boxes on the form.

To determine the number of available fields (that is, the number of fields in the selected table), the function needs only to determine the number of entries in the qbfFieldArray. This array is defined in the next section.

To determine the number of selected fields in the Selected list box, the function uses the **DCount** function to count the number of records in the zz_qbfSelected table (this table is explained later in this chapter).

> **Note:** By convention, the letters "zz" at the beginning of an object name indicate that it is a hidden object that does not normally appear in the user interface.

Finally, the function enables or disables the command buttons in the form's header section according to whether the user still has any fields remaining in the Selected list box. For example, if there are no selected fields, the user cannot view the SQL statement and the SQL command's **Enabled** property is set to False.

Available List Box

The entries that appear in this list box are those that are in the table selected in the Tables combo box. If the user has not yet chosen a table, the list box appears without any field names.

To populate the list box, Access calls the `qbfFillAvailableFields()` function. This is a fill function, which follows a specific syntax. Open the form's code module and enter the first line of the `qbfFillAvailableFields()` function:

```
Function qbfFillAvailableFields (MyControl As Control, ID As Variant, Row As Inte-
ger, Col As Integer,
➥Code As Integer)  As Variant

➥As Variant
```

When you press ENTER, Access displays a nearly blank Module window in which you can enter the rest of the qbfFillAvailableFields() function:

```
Function qbfFillAvailableFields (MyControl As Control, ID As Variant, Row As Inte-
ger, Col As Integer,
➥Code As Integer)  As Variant

    Static DefaultWorkspace As WorkSpace
    Static MyDB As Database
    Static MyTable As Recordset
    Static MaxFields As Long
    Dim ReturnValue As Variant
    Dim X As Integer

    Select Case Code
        Case 0 ' Initialize.
            If IsNull([Tables]) Then
                MaxFields = 0
            Else
                Set DefaultWorkspace = DBEngine.Workspaces(0)
                Set MyDB = DefaultWorkspace.Databases(0)
                Set MyTable = MyDB.OpenRecordset([Tables])
                MaxFields = MyTable.Fields.Count
                ReDim qbfFieldArray(MaxFields)
                ' Enumerate all fields in MyTableDef.
                For X = 0 To MaxFields - 1
                    qbfFieldArray(X) = MyTable.Fields(X).Name
                Next X
                MyTable.Close
                MyDB.Close
                If [SortAvailable] = True Then
                    X = csvSortArray(qbfFieldArray(), MaxFields)
                End If
            End If
            ReturnValue = True
        Case 1 ' Open.
            ReturnValue = Timer
        Case 2 ' Not used.
            ReturnValue = Null
        Case 3 ' Rows.
            ReturnValue = MaxFields
        Case 4 ' Columns.
            ReturnValue = 1
        Case 5 ' Column width.
            ReturnValue = -1
        Case 6 ' Data
            If MaxFields > 0 Then
                ReturnValue = qbfFieldArray(Row + 1)
            Else
            End If
        Case 7 ' Not used.
            ReturnValue = Null
```

293

```
        Case 8 ' Not used.
              ReturnValue = Null
        Case 9 ' End.
              ReturnValue = True
  End Select

  qbfFillAvailableFields = ReturnValue

End Function
```

For this function to work, you need to declare an array, `qbfFieldArray`. Since this array must be made available to other functions, you must declare the array to have module-wide scope. Go to the Declarations section of the form's code module and then enter the declaration shown in figure 16.23.

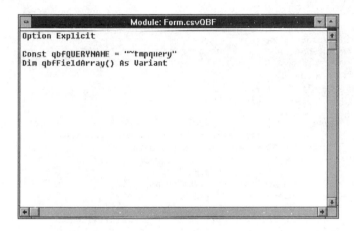

Figure 16.23.   Declaring the qbfFiledArray array.

When you declare the array in the Declarations section, all functions in the same module have access to the array.

Notice that the `qbfFillAvailableFields()` function uses the **Fields** collection introduced in Access 2.0. An older technique that uses the **ListFields** method no longer works since **ListFields** works only with non-attached tables. For more information about using the **Fields** collection and converting older, pre-2.0 code, search Help for "DAO".

Next, you need a routine that sorts the list of field names. Go to the Declarations section of the form's code module and then enter the first line of the `csvSortArray()` function:

```
    Function csvSortArray (Array() As Variant, Upper As Long) As Variant
```

When you press ENTER, Access displays a nearly blank Module window in which you can enter the rest of the `csvSortArray()` function:

```
    Function csvSortArray (Array() As Variant, Upper As Long) As Variant

        Dim I As Long
        Dim J As Long
```

294

```
        Dim K As Long
        Dim L As Long
        Dim M As Long
        Dim N1 As Long
        Dim Z As Variant
        Dim Temp As Variant

        Z = SysCmd(1, "Sorting array...", Upper)
        N1 = Upper
        M = N1

SortArray1:

        M = M \ 2
        If M = 0 Then
            Z = SysCmd(3)
            Exit Function
        End If

        J = 1

SortArray2:

        K = N1 - M
        I = J

SortArray3:

        L = I + M
        Z = SysCmd(2, Abs(L - Upper))
        If LCase(Array(I)) <= LCase(Array(L)) Then
            GoTo SortArray4
        End If
        Temp = Array(I)
        Array(I) = Array(L)
        Array(L) = Temp
        I = I - M
        If I < M Then
            GoTo SortArray4
        End If
        GoTo SortArray3

SortArray4:

        J = J + 1
        If J > K GoTo SortArray1
        GoTo SortArray2

End Function
```

This function calls the **SysCmd** function three times, each time passing it a different literal: 1, 2, or 3. You might instead want to use constants for these literals:

```
Const SYSCMD_INITMETER = 1
Const SYSCMD_UPDATEMETER = 2
Const SYSCMD_REMOVEMETER = 3
```

You also need a version of the `csvSortArray()` function that sorts a two-dimension array. You can either modify the `csvSortArray()` function so that it accepts an argument indicating whether to sort one or two dimensions, or you can enter the following two-dimension sorting function:

```
Function csvSortArray2 (Array() As Variant, Upper As Long) As Variant

    Const SYSCMD_INITMETER = 1
    Const SYSCMD_UPDATEMETER = 2
    Const SYSCMD_REMOVEMETER = 3
    Dim I As Long
    Dim J As Long
    Dim K As Long
    Dim L As Long
    Dim M As Long
    Dim N1 As Long
    Dim Z As Variant
    Dim Temp As Variant

    Z = SysCmd(SYSCMD_INITMETER, "Sorting array...", Upper)
    N1 = Upper
    M = N1

SortArray21:

    M = M \ 2
    If M = 0 Then
        Z = SysCmd(SYSCMD_REMOVEMETER)
        Exit Function
    End If

    J = 1

SortArray22:

    K = N1 - M
    I = J

SortArray23:

    L = I + M
    Z = SysCmd(SYSCMD_UPDATEMETER, Abs(L - Upper))
    If LCase(Array(I, 0)) <= LCase(Array(L, 0)) Then
        GoTo SortArray24
    End If

    Temp = Array(I, 0)
    Array(I, 0) = Array(L, 0)
    Array(L, 0) = Temp

    Temp = Array(I, 1)
    Array(I, 1) = Array(L, 1)
    Array(L, 1) = Temp

    I = I - M
    If I < M Then
        GoTo SortArray24
    End If
```

```
        GoTo SortArray23

SortArray24:

    J = J + 1
    If J > K GoTo SortArray21
    GoTo SortArray22

End Function
```

There are small command buttons between the two list boxes that the user can click to copy entries (field names) to or remove entries from the Selected list box, but it is convenient—and expected behavior—to let the user double-click an entry and have it copy without having to highlight the entry and then click a command button.

When the user double-clicks a field name in the Available list box, the qbfSelectOne() function moves the selected entry to the Selected list box. Go to the Declarations section of the form's code module and then enter the first line of the qbfSelectOne() function:

```
Function qbfSelectOne (MyForm As Form) As Integer
```

When you press ENTER, Access displays a nearly blank Module window in which you can enter the rest of the qbfSelectOne() function:

```
Function qbfSelectOne (MyForm As Form) As Integer

    Dim MyDB As Database
    Dim MySet As Dynaset
    Dim X As Integer

    ' Is there something selected in the Source list box?
    If Not IsNull(MyForm![Source]) Then
        Set MyDB = CurrentDB()
        Set MySet = MyDB.CreateDynaset("zz_qbfSelected")
        ' Make sure it's not already in the Destination list box.
        MySet.FindFirst "[Entry] = '" & MyForm![Source] & "' AND [Subentry] = '" &
MyForm![Tables] &
        ➥"'"
        If MySet.NoMatch Then
            ' It wasn't previously selected, so add it.
            MySet.AddNew
                MySet![Entry] = MyForm![Source]
                MySet![Subentry] = MyForm![Tables]
            MySet.Update
        End If
        MySet.Close
        MyDB.Close
        [Destination].Requery
        X = qbfUpdateListCounts(MyForm)
    End If

End Function
```

Notice that the qbfSelectOne() function uses pre-2.0 methods to manipulate the data access objects (for example, the function uses **CreateDynaset**). While this produces smaller, somewhat faster code, Microsoft nonetheless recommends you use new 2.0-specific techniques. For more information about converting older, pre-2.0 code, search Help for "DAO."

297

If the user double-clicks in an empty Available list box (as might happen if there is no selected table), or if he double-clicks a part of the list box that has no field name, the Available list box will have no value and the function falls through without trying to copy a field name to the Selected list box.

Sort Available Check Box

Beneath the Available list box is a check box that the user can check (or clear) to either sort or not sort the fields in the list box. Particularly if the list of fields is long, sorting the names can make it easier to manage.

Since the list box already takes into account whether the check box is checked, when the user checks or clears the check box, the control's **AfterUpdate** event only needs to requery the list box.

Open the form's code module, go to the Declarations section, and then enter the first line of the csvRequery() function:

```
Function csvRequery(ByVal MyControlName As String) As Integer
```

When you press ENTER, Access displays a nearly blank Module window in which you can enter the rest of the csvRequery() function:

```
Function csvRequery (ByVal MyControlName As String) As Integer

    Const FUNCTIONNAME = "csvRequery()"
    Const csvMB_ICONEXCLAMATION = 48

    csvRequery = False

    If MyControlName = "" Then
        On Error Resume Next
        DoCmd Requery
        If Err Then
            MsgBox "Couldn't requery form.", csvMB_ICONEXCLAMATION, FUNCTIONNAME
        Else
            DoCmd Requery MyControlName
            If Err Then
                MsgBox "Couldn't requery control '" & MyControlName & "'.",
csvMB_ICONEXCLAMATION,
                ➥FUNCTIONNAME
            End If
        End If
        On Error GoTo 0
    End If

End Function
```

Selected List Box

The entries that appear in this list box are those that the user has chosen from the Available list box. If the user has not yet chosen any fields, the list box appears without any field names.

To populate the list box, Access calls the `qbfFillSelectedFields()` function. This is a fill function, much like the preceding `qbfFillAvailableFields()` function, which follows a specific syntax. Open the form's code module and enter the first line of the `qbfFillSelectedFields()` function:

```
Function qbfFillSelectedFields (MyControl As Control, ID As Variant, Row As Integer,
Col As Integer,
➥Code As Integer) As Variant
```

When you press ENTER, Access displays a nearly blank Module window in which you can enter the rest of the `qbfFillSelectedFields()` function:

```
Function qbfFillSelectedFields (MyControl As Control, ID As Variant, Row As Integer,
Col As Integer, Code As Integer)
➥As Variant

    Static MyDB As Database
    Static MySnap As Snapshot
    Static MaxFields As Long
    Dim X As Integer
    Dim ReturnValue As Variant

    Select Case Code
        Case 0 ' Initialize.
            Set MyDB = CurrentDB()
            Set MySnap = MyDB.CreateSnapshot("zz_qbfSelected")
            On Error Resume Next
            MySnap.MoveLast
            If Err Then
                MaxFields = 0
            Else
                MaxFields = MySnap.RecordCount
                ReDim qbfSelectedFieldArray(MaxFields, 1)
                MySnap.MoveFirst
                For X = 1 To MaxFields
                    qbfSelectedFieldArray(X, 0) = MySnap![Entry]
                    qbfSelectedFieldArray(X, 1) = MySnap![Subentry]
                    MySnap.MoveNext
                Next X
                If [SortSelected] = True Then
                    X = csvSortArray2(qbfSelectedFieldArray(), MaxFields)
                End If
            End If
            MySnap.Close
            MyDB.Close
            ReturnValue = True
        Case 1 ' Open.
            ReturnValue = Timer
        Case 2 ' Not used.
            ReturnValue = Null
        Case 3 ' Rows.
            ReturnValue = MaxFields
        Case 4 ' Columns.
            ReturnValue = 1
        Case 5 ' Column width.
            ReturnValue = -1
        Case 6 ' Data
            If MaxFields > 0 Then
                ReturnValue = qbfSelectedFieldArray(Row + 1, Col)
```

299

```
            End If
      Case 7 ' Not used.
            ReturnValue = Null
      Case 8 ' Not used.
            ReturnValue = Null
      Case 9 ' End.
            ReturnValue = True
   End Select

   qbfFillSelectedFields = ReturnValue

End Function
```

Like the `qbfFillAvailableFields()` function, this function uses an array to populate the list box. Go to the Declarations section of the form's code module and enter a second declaration for an array (see fig. 16.24).

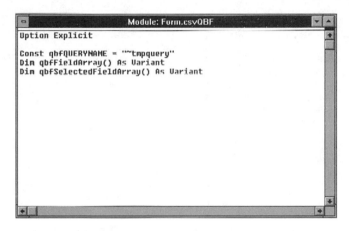

Figure 16.24. Declaring the qbfFillAvailableFields array.

In addition, this fill function depends on there being a table, zz_qbfSelected, to store the names of the selected fields and the tables from which they came.

To create this table, return to the Database window, choose New from the File menu, and then choose the Table subcommand. Next, create the new table with two fields (see fig. 16.25).

Tip: Although the fields will eventually be used to store field and table information, you should name the fields Entry and Subentry, not Field and Table. This temporary table may some day be used for other purposes, and the generic Entry/Subentry field names will make more sense. Indeed, you might want to rename the table zz_Selected (instead of zz_qbfSelected). If so, be sure you change all references to the old table name.

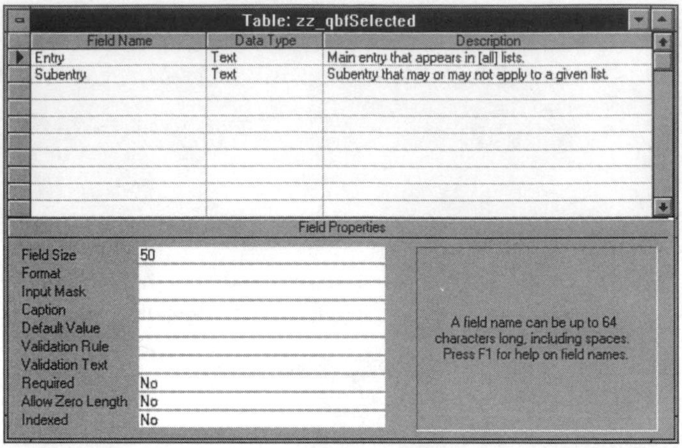

Figure 16.25. Creating the zz_qbfSelected table.

Save and close the table (naming it zz_qbfSelected) and return to the csvQBF form.

When the user double-clicks a field name in the Selected list box, the qbfRemoveOne() function removes the selected entry from the Selected list box. Go to the Declarations section of the form's code module and then enter the first line of the qbfRemoveOne() function:

```
Function qbfRemoveOne (MyForm As Form) As Integer
```

When you press ENTER, Access displays a nearly blank Module window in which you can enter the rest of the qbfRemoveOne() function:

```
Function qbfRemoveOne (MyForm As Form) As Integer

    Dim MyDB As Database
    Dim MySet As Dynaset
    Dim X As Integer

    ' Is there something selected in the Destination list box?
    If Not IsNull[Destination]) Then
        Set MyDB = CurrentDB()
        Set MySet = MyDB.CreateDynaset("zz_qbfSelected")
        MySet.FindFirst "[Entry] = '" & [Destination] & "' AND [Subentry] = '" &
        ➡[Destination].Column(1)  & "'"
        If Not MySet.NoMatch Then
            MySet.Delete
        End If
        MySet.Close
        MyDB.Close
        [Destination].Requery
        X = qbfUpdateListCounts(MyForm)
    End If

End Function

                MsgBox Msg, Icon, Titlebar
```

301

Note: Unlike preceding examples that used snapshots, this function creates a dynaset because a record may have to be removed from the underlying table, zz_qbfSelected. You cannot edit or remove records from a snapshot, but you can from a dynaset.

Movement Command Buttons

In the center of the form are five command buttons that either copy field names from the Available list box to the Selected list box, or remove field names from the Selected list box (see fig. 16.26).

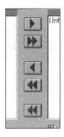

Figure 16.26. Click these buttons to move entries back and forth.

The top command button copies one entry from the Available list box to the Selected list box. To do this, set the command button's **OnClick** property, as shown in figure 16.27.

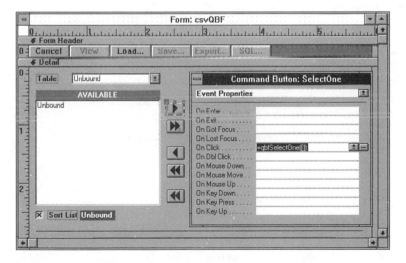

Figure 16.27. Calling a function from the **OnClick** event.

When the user clicks the button, the **OnClick** event calls the same qbfSelectOne( ) function as the Available list box's **OnDblClick** event.

 Note: This and the other functions described later in this section test to see if a field already exists in the Selected list box and automatically prevents duplicate entries.

The second command button from the top copies all of the fields from the Available list box to the Selected list box. Set this button's **OnClick** property, as shown in figure 16.28.

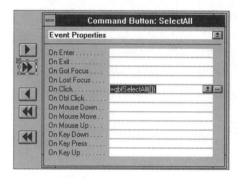

Figure 16.28. Calling the `qbfSelectAll()` function.

As you did with the preceding `qbfSelectOne()` function, enter the following code in the form's code module:

```
Function qbfSelectAll (MyForm As Form) As Integer

    Dim MyDB As Database
    Dim MySet As Dynaset
    Dim X As Integer

    ' Are there any fields in the Source list box (there will be if there
    ' is a table selected in the Tables combo box)?
    If csvSomethingIn(MyForm![Tables]) Then
        DoCmd Hourglass True
        DoCmd Echo True, "Processing..."
        Set MyDB = CurrentDB()
        Set MySet = MyDB.CreateDynaset("zz_qbfSelected")
        For X = 1 To UBound(qbfFieldArray)
            ' Make sure it's not already in the Destination list box.
            MySet.FindFirst "[Entry] = '" & qbfFieldArray(X) & "' AND [Subentry] =
            ➥'" & MyForm![Tables] & "'"
            If MySet.NoMatch Then
                ' It wasn't previously selected, so add it.
                MySet.AddNew
```

```
                    MySet![Entry] = qbfFieldArray(X)
                    MySet![Subentry] = MyForm![Tables]
                MySet.Update
            End If
        Next X
        MySet.Close
        MyDB.Close
        [Destination].Requery
        X = qbfUpdateListCounts(MyForm)
        DoCmd Hourglass False
    End If

    End Function
```

This function introduces another generic function, csvSomethingIn(), that determines whether there is something in a specified control (it is not sufficient to check for whether a control is Null, since the user may have entered, and then deleted, an entry). Go to the Declarations section of the form's code module and enter the first line of the csvSomethingIn( ) function:

```
Function csvSomethingIn (MyControl As Control) As Integer
```

When you press ENTER, Access displays a nearly blank Module window in which you can enter the rest of the csvSomethingIn( ) function:

```
Function csvSomethingIn (MyControl As Control) As Integer

    csvSomethingIn = True

    If IsNull(MyControl) Then              ' Control is Null.
        csvSomethingIn = False
    Else
        If IsEmpty(MyControl) Then         ' Control is Empty.
            csvSomethingIn = False
        Else
            If MyControl = "" Then         ' Control is zero-length.
                csvSomethingIn = False
            End If
        End If
    End If

    End Function
```

The third command button from the top removes one entry from the Selected list box. When the user clicks the button, the **OnClick** event calls the same qbfRemoveOne() function as the Selected list box's **OnDblClick** event.

The fourth command button from the top removes all of the fields for the currently selected table. For example, if the user selects the Houses table in the Tables combo box, clicking the fourth command button from the top removes any (all) fields from the Selected list box that were selected from the Houses table. To remove all of the fields for a given table, the user can either remove them individually, or select the desired table and then click this fourth button.

Add the following code for the fourth command button's **OnClick** event:

```
Function qbfRemoveAll (MyForm As Form) As Integer

    Dim X As Integer

    DoCmd SetWarnings False
    DoCmd RunSQL "DELETE * FROM zz_qbfSelected WHERE Subentry = '" & [Tables] & "'"
    DoCmd SetWarnings True
    X = csvRequery("Destination")
    X = qbfUpdateListCounts(MyForm)

End Function
```

This is a rather easy function to write, since all that really needs to happen is that all (any) records previously added to the zz_qbfSelected table need to be deleted. The simplest way to delete records is with the **RunSQL** macro action. The field names are then removed from the screen by requerying the list box.

The fifth button, which appears in the sample database with a red bitmap, removes all of the fields from the Selected list box, no matter which table has been selected in the Tables combo box (see fig. 16.29).

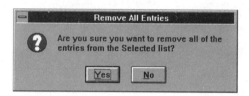

Figure 16.29.   Prompt the user before you remove all the entries.

The function that removes all of the entries is remarkably similar to that for the command button that removes all of the fields for only the selected table. Set the fifth command button's **OnClick** property and then enter the qbfClearAll() function in the form's code module, as shown in figure 16.30.

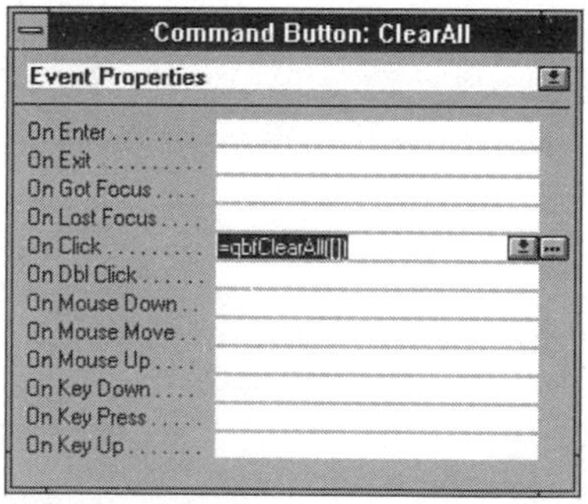

Figure 16.30.   Calling the qbfClearAll() function.

305

Go to the Declarations section of form's code module and enter the following function:

```
Function qbfClearAll (MyForm As Form) As Integer

    Const csvMB_ICONQUESTIONMARK = 32
    Const csvMB_YES = 6
    Const csvMB_YESNO = 4
    Dim Msg As String
    Dim Icon As Integer
    Dim Titlebar As String
    Dim Response As Integer
    Dim X As Integer

    ' Are there even any fields to remove?
    If DCount("*", "zz_qbfSelected") > 0 Then
        Msg = "Are you sure you want to remove all of the entries from the "
        Msg = Msg & "Selected list?"
        Icon = csvMB_ICONQUESTIONMARK + csvMB_YESNO
        Titlebar = "Remove All Entries"
        If MsgBox(Msg, Icon, Titlebar) = csvMB_YES Then
            ' Remove all of the fields from the SelectedFields list, no matter
            ' which table(s) they came from.
            DoCmd SetWarnings False
            DoCmd RunSQL "DELETE * FROM zz_qbfSelected"
            DoCmd SetWarnings True
            X = csvRequery("Destination")
            X = qbfUpdateListCounts(MyForm)
        End If
    End If

End Function
```

 Tip: Each of the command buttons calls a function that checks to see whether there is any action required. For example, if there is no field name selected in the Available list box, the `qbfSelectOne()` function falls through without any further action. You may want to display a message when the user tries to do something like this, but keep in mind that too many messages can be annoying. You may be better off simply ignoring such button clicks. When the user sees that the button does not "do" anything, he will stop clicking it, even if you do not display a message. In any case, avoid beeping the computer's speaker.

 Be sure to read about new coding techniques in Appendix D, "Converting Old Code."

Where Command Button

This command button, located beneath the Selected list box, is actually named AddWhere because that is what it does: it adds the selected field in the Selected list box to the WHERE clause of the SQL statement.

The command button appends the name of the highlighted field to the contents of the WhereClause text box. The contents of the WhereClause text box will eventually be read and added to the SQL statement. To do this, set the command button's **OnClick** property to [Event Procedure] and then add the following code for the event:

```
Sub AddWhere_Click ()

    Const csvMB_ICONINFORMATION = 64
    Dim X As Integer
    Dim Response As Integer
    Dim Msg As String
    Dim Icon As Integer
    Dim Titlebar As String

    If csvSomethingIn([Destination]) Then
        [WhereClause] = [WhereClause] & " AND [" & [Destination].Column(1) & "].[" &
[Destination]
        ➥& "] = "
        If Left$([WhereClause], 5) = " AND " Then
            [WhereClause] = Mid$([WhereClause], 5)
        End If
        [WhereClause].SetFocus
        SendKeys "{f2}" ' Unhighlight the WhereClause text box.
    Else
        Msg = "Sorry - you must first select an entry in the Selected list."
        Icon = csvMB_ICONINFORMATION
        Titlebar = "Required Entry"
        MsgBox Msg, Icon, Titlebar
        AddWhere = False
    End If

End Sub
```

 Be sure to read about new coding techniques in Appendix D, "Converting Old Code."

 Note: In this function, the decision is made to display a message when the user clicks the command button but there is nothing to do (that is, there is no highlighted field to add to the WhereClause text box). It is difficult and largely academic to state a rule that would dictate whether to display a message. If you are concerned with application consistency, either avoid displaying a message here, or add an appropriate message to each of the functions that copy and remove field names from the list boxes.

Order By Command Button

This command button, also located beneath the Selected list box, is actually named AddOrderBy because that is what it does: it adds the selected field in the Selected list box to the ORDER BY clause of the SQL statement.

The command button appends the name of the highlighted field to the contents of the OrderByClause text box. The contents of the OrderByClause text box will eventually be read and added to the SQL statement. To do this, set the command button's **OnClick** property to [Event Procedure] and then add the following code for the event:

```
Sub AddOrderBy_Click ()

    Const csvMB_ICONINFORMATION = 64
    Dim Response As Integer
    Dim Msg As String
    Dim Icon As Integer
    Dim Titlebar As String

    If csvSomethingIn([Destination]) Then
        [OrderByClause] = [OrderByClause] & ", [" & [Destination].Column(1) & "].["
& [Destination]
        ➥& "]"
        If Left$([OrderByClause], 2) = ", " Then
            [OrderByClause] = Mid$([OrderByClause], 3)
        End If
    Else
        Msg = "Sorry - you must first select an entry in the Selected list."
        Icon = csvMB_ICONINFORMATION
        Titlebar = "Required Entry"
        MsgBox Msg, Icon, Titlebar
    End If

End Sub
```

 Be sure to read about new coding techniques in Appendix D, "Converting Old Code."

 Note: As with the preceding AddWhere_Click subprocedure, you should decide whether you are concerned with application consistency. If so, either avoid displaying a message here (when the user clicks the command button without first highlighting a field name in the Selected list box), or add an appropriate message to each of the functions that copy and remove field names from the list boxes.

This subprocedure does not check to see if the field the user is adding already exists in the OrderByClause text box. Even so, there is no real harm in having a field appear multiple times (it does not affect the sort order), other than possibly increasing the time it takes to run the query.

Zoom Command Buttons

There are two small command buttons located to the right of the WhereClause and OrderByClause text boxes (see fig. 16.31). When clicked, these command buttons move the focus to the appropriate text box and then trigger F2 to open the Zoom box. This is a convenience to users who do not know

the Zoom box may be opened with F2. You might consider widening the boxes so that you can change the captions to the word "zoom." In the HomeFinder sample application, a single "z", set in Small Fonts (5 points) yields a satisfactory appearance.

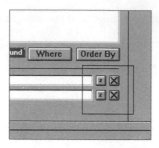

Figure 16.31. The Zoom and Clear buttons provide extra convenience to the user.

For the first zoom command button (next to the WhereClause text box), set its **OnClick** property to [Event Procedure] and then enter the following code for its **OnClick** event:

```
Sub ZoomWhere_Click ()

    [WhereClause].SetFocus
    SendKeys "+{f2}", True

End Sub
```

The subprocedure first moves the focus to the WhereClause text box and then uses the **Sendkeys** statement to open the Zoom box.

The property setting for the next zoom command button (next to the OrderByClause text box), also is [Event Procedure]. Its **OnClick** subprocedure looks like this:

```
Sub ZoomOrderBy_Click ()

    [OrderByClause].SetFocus
    SendKeys "+{f2}", True

End Sub
```

Clear Command Buttons

The other two small command buttons, located to the right of the zoom command buttons, clear the contents of the WhereClause and OrderByClause text boxes. This lets the user click a command button instead of having to highlight the relevant text and then clicking the DEL key.

For the first clear command button, set its **OnClick** property to [Event Procedure] and then enter the following code for its **OnClick** event:

309

```
Sub ClearWhereClause_Click ()

    [WhereClause] = Null

End Sub
```

Set the **OnClick** property setting for the second clear command button to [Event Procedure] and then enter its **OnClick** event code:

```
Sub ClearOrderBy_Click ()

    [OrderByClause] = Null

End Sub
```

> **Tip:** These command buttons are perhaps too easy to use, since neither subprocedure prompts the user to confirm that the text should, indeed, be deleted. You might consider adding an "Are you sure?" message box to these subprocedures.

Unique Values Check Box

The only remaining control on the csvQBF form that may require your attention is the check box that appears along the bottom of the form. When checked, the resulting query produces only unique values (more precisely, the query includes a DISTINCTROW predicate).

If unique values are typically the result you want, leave the **DefaultValue** property set at −1. Otherwise, set the check box's **DefaultValue** property to 0 (zero).

Adding the Remaining Code

There are several other functions, mostly called from subprocedures triggered by the user clicking command buttons or selecting field names. Enter each of these functions by first going to the Declarations section of the csvQBF form's code module and then typing the code as you see it listed here.

qbfBuildQBFQuery()

```
Function qbfBuildQBFQuery (MyForm As Form) As Integer

    Const qbfMYQUERYNAME = "~tmpquery"
    Const FIELDLIMIT = 10
    Const csvMB_ICONQUESTIONMARK = 32
    Const csvMB_ICONEXCLAMATION = 48
    Const csvMB_YESNO = 4
    Const csvMB_YES = 6
    Dim MyDB As Database
    Dim MyQuery As QueryDef
```

```
       Dim Msg As String
       Dim Icon As Integer
       Dim Titlebar As String
       Dim NumberDestination As Integer

       qbfBuildQBFQuery = True

       ' Were any entries selected (and, if so, is the number reasonable)?
       ' Check this only if the user *didn't* press the SQL button.
       If csvSomethingIn([NumberDestination]) Then
           NumberDestination = Val([NumberDestination])
           If NumberDestination > FIELDLIMIT And Screen.ActiveControl.ControlName <>
       ➥ "SQL" Then
               Msg = "Are you sure you want to report on "
               Msg = Msg & Trim$(Str$(NumberDestination)) & " fields?"
               Icon = csvMB_ICONQUESTIONMARK + csvMB_YESNO
               Titlebar = "Excessive Fields"
               If MsgBox(Msg, Icon, Titlebar) <> csvMB_YES Then
                   qbfBuildQBFQuery = False
                   Exit Function
               End If
           End If
           ' The user said OK, or the number of selected fields is reasonable.
           DoCmd Echo True, "Processing..."
           DoCmd Hourglass True
           Set MyDB = CurrentDB()
           On Error Resume Next
           Set MyQuery = MyDB.OpenQueryDef(qbfMYQUERYNAME)
           If Err Then
               Set MyQuery = MyDB.CreateQueryDef(qbfMYQUERYNAME)
               qbfBuildQBFQuery = False
           End If
           On Error GoTo 0
           On Error Resume Next
           MyQuery.SQL = qbfSQLStmt(MyForm)
           If Err Then
               Titlebar = "Build QBF Query"
               MsgBox "Sorry - couldn't update query, probably because the WHERE clause
       ➥or ORDER BY clause is invalid.", csvMB_ICONEXCLAMATION, Titlebar
               qbfBuildQBFQuery = False
           Else
               MyQuery.Close
           End If
           On Error GoTo 0
           MyDB.Close
           DoCmd Hourglass False
       Else
           Msg = "Sorry - you must first select one or more fields from the "
           Msg = Msg & "Available list."
           Icon = csvMB_ICONINFORMATION
           Titlebar = "Required Entry"
           MsgBox Msg, Icon, Titlebar
       End If

End Function
```

qbfSQLStmt()

```
Function qbfSQLStmt (MyForm As Form) As String

    Const qbfFIELDLIMIT = 10
    Const csvMB_ICONQUESTIONMARK = 32
    Const csvMB_YES = 6
    Dim MyDB As Database
    Dim MySnap As Snapshot
    Dim NumberDestination
    Dim Criteria As String
    Dim Msg As String
    Dim Icon As Integer
    Dim Titlebar As String
    Dim X As Integer
    Dim Y As Integer
    Dim CRLF As String
    Dim Pos As Integer
    Dim Temp As String
    Dim S As String
    Dim SelectStmt As String
    Dim FromClause As String
    Dim WhereClause As String
    Dim OrderByClause As String
    ReDim TableArray(0) As String

    CRLF = Chr$(13) & Chr$(10)
    ' --------------------------------------------------------------
    ' Were any entries selected (and, if so, is the number reasonable)?
    ' --------------------------------------------------------------
    If csvSomethingIn([NumberDestination]) Then
        NumberDestination = Val([NumberDestination])
        If NumberDestination > qbfFIELDLIMIT And Screen.ActiveControl.ControlName <>
        ➥"SQL" Then
            Msg = "Are you sure you want to report on "
            Msg = Msg & Trim$(Str$(NumberDestination)) & " fields?"
            Icon = csvMB_ICONQUESTIONMARK + csvMB_YESNO
            Titlebar = "Excessive Fields"
            If MsgBox(Msg, Icon, Titlebar) <> csvMB_YES Then
                qbfSQLStmt = ""
                Exit Function
            End If
        End If
    End If
    ' --------------------------------------------------------------
    ' The user said OK, or the number of selected fields is reasonable.
    ' --------------------------------------------------------------
    DoCmd Echo True, "Processing..."
    DoCmd Hourglass True
    Set MyDB = CurrentDB()
    SelectStmt = " SELECT " & IIf(Forms![csvQBF]![UniqueValues] = False, "",
    ➥"DISTINCTROW")
    SelectStmt = SelectStmt & CRLF
    ' --------------------------------------------------------------
    ' Determine which fields were selected and build Select statement.
    ' --------------------------------------------------------------
    Set MySnap = MyDB.CreateSnapshot("SELECT [Entry] As FieldName, [Subentry] As
    ➥TableName FROM zz_qbfSelected")
```

```
Do Until MySnap.EOF
    SelectStmt = SelectStmt & "    [" & MySnap![TableName] & "]."
    SelectStmt = SelectStmt & "[" & MySnap![FieldName] & "], " & CRLF
    MySnap.MoveNext
Loop
SelectStmt = Left$(SelectStmt, Len(SelectStmt) - 4) ' Strip the trailing ",
➥"/CRLF.
' Determine which tables have been selected for the query. To do
' this, create a snapshot containing distinct [Subentry] values
' from the zz_qbfSelected table. Then, add them to the TableArray array.
Set MySnap = MyDB.CreateSnapshot("SELECT DISTINCT [Subentry] As TableName
➥FROM zz_qbfSelected")
Do Until MySnap.EOF ' Look at each entry.
    ReDim Preserve TableArray(UBound(TableArray) + 1)
    TableArray(UBound(TableArray)) = MySnap![TableName]
    MySnap.MoveNext
Loop
' -----------------------------------------------------------------
' Build the FROM clause.
' -----------------------------------------------------------------
FromClause = " FROM " & CRLF
For X = 1 To UBound(TableArray)
    FromClause = FromClause & "    [" & TableArray(X) & "], " & CRLF
Next X
' -----------------------------------------------------------------
' Handle the joins, if any.
' -----------------------------------------------------------------
If UBound(TableArray) > 1 Then
    Set MySnap = MyDB.CreateSnapshot("zz_qbfJoins")
    For X = 1 To UBound(TableArray)
        MySnap.FindFirst "TableLeft = '[" & TableArray(X) & "]'"
        If Not MySnap.NoMatch Then
        ' Look for an entry in TableRight that is also in the
        ' TableArray array.
            For Y = 1 To UBound(TableArray)
                Criteria = "TableLeft = '[" & TableArray(X) & "]'"
                Criteria = Criteria & " AND "
                Criteria = Criteria & "TableRight = '[" & TableArray(Y) &
                ➥"]'"
                MySnap.FindFirst Criteria
                If Not MySnap.NoMatch Then
                    ' Get the join info and exit the loop.
                    FromClause = FromClause & "    " & MySnap![TableLeft] & " "
                    FromClause = FromClause & MySnap![Join] & " JOIN "
                    FromClause = FromClause & MySnap![TableRight] & " ON " &
                    ➥CRLF
                    FromClause = FromClause & "        " & MySnap![FieldLeft]
                    ➥& " = "
                    FromClause = FromClause & MySnap![FieldRight] & ", " &
                    ➥CRLF
                    Exit For
                End If
            Next Y
        End If
    Next X
End If
Do Until Right$(FromClause, 4) <> ", " & CRLF
```

continues

313

```
        FromClause = Left$(FromClause, Len(FromClause) - 4)
Loop
If Right$(FromClause, 2) <> CRLF Then
    FromClause = FromClause & CRLF
End If
' ----------------------------------------------------------------
' Parse and then build the WHERE clause. UNDONE
' ----------------------------------------------------------------
WhereClause = IIf(IsNull([WhereClause]), "", [WhereClause])
WhereClause = IIf(WhereClause = "", "", " WHERE " & CRLF & "    " &
➥Trim$(WhereClause) & " " & CRLF)
' Check to see if there are any ambiguous fields in the clause.
' To do this, parse the line and see how many occurrences exist
' in the snapshot (the snapshot contains all of the fields). The
' rules for this block are simple:
'
' o field names may be delimited with brackets, but don't
'   have to be
' o the first word is the name of a field (or table.field)
' o field names are defined as characters appearing between
'   commas and the following space that is not enclosed in
'   a bracket
' o all other words are ignored
' Parse the WHERE clause and look for ambiguous references. UNDONE
'Pos = 1 ' Start looking at the first position of the clause.
'Do Until InStr(Pos, WhereClause, ",") = 0
'    Temp = Mid$(WhereClause, Pos + 1)
'    For X = 1 To Len(Temp)
'
'    Next X
'Loop
' ----------------------------------------------------------------
' Parse and then build the ORDER BY clause. UNDONE
' ----------------------------------------------------------------
OrderByClause = IIf(IsNull([OrderByClause]), "", [OrderByClause])
If OrderByClause <> "" Then
    Temp = Trim$(OrderByClause)
    If Right$(Temp, 1) = "," Then
        Temp = Left(Temp, Len(Temp) - 1)
    End If
    OrderByClause = " ORDER BY " & CRLF
    ' Now, add all of the fields (delimited by commas).
    Do Until InStr(Temp, ",") = 0
        OrderByClause = OrderByClause & "    " & Trim$(Left$(Temp,
        ➥InStr(Temp, ","))) & CRLF
        Temp = Trim$(Mid$(Temp, InStr(Temp, ",") + 1))
    Loop
    If Len(Trim$(Temp)) <> 0 Then
        OrderByClause = OrderByClause & "    " & Temp
    End If
    If Right$(OrderByClause, 2) <> CRLF Then
        OrderByClause = OrderByClause & CRLF
    End If
End If
' ----------------------------------------------------------------
' Set the SQL property and save the query.
' ----------------------------------------------------------------
```

```
            S = SelectStmt & " " & CRLF & FromClause
            S = S & WhereClause & OrderByClause
            S = S & " WITH OWNERACCESS OPTION;"
            MySnap.Close
            MyDB.Close
            DoCmd Hourglass False
            qbfSQLStmt = S
        Else
            Msg = "Sorry - you must first select one or more fields from the "
            Msg = Msg & "Available list."
            Icon = csvMB_ICONINFORMATION
            Titlebar = "Required Entry"
            MsgBox Msg, Icon, Titlebar
            qbfSQLStmt = ""
        End If

    End Function
```

> 📖 Be sure to read about new coding techniques in Appendix D, "Converting Old Code."

Testing the csvQBF Form

Open the csvQBF form in Form View and then select a table from the Tables combo box (see fig. 16.32).

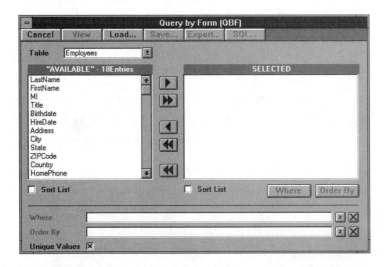

Figure 16.32. The csvQBF form needs some adjustments.

315

In this example, the user has chosen the Employees table. The label above the Available list box shows the proper number of fields (18), but the caption is faulty: it has two quotation marks and the number of fields runs into the word "Entries". To fix this, open the form in Design View, open the form's code module, and then locate the code that sets the caption.

> **Tip:** Since you know you are going to be changing a caption, you can choose the Find command from the Edit menu and then look for the word "caption." Or, if you first determine the name of the label, you can search for "[AvailableFields].Caption".

The function that needs to be corrected is the `qbfUpdateListCounts()` function. The specific line of code that sets the caption looks like this:

```
MyForm![AvailableFields].Caption = MyForm![NumberSource].DefaultValue & " - " &
➥MyForm![NumberSource] &
➥IIf([NumberSource] <> 0, MYLABELPLURAL, MYLABEL)
```

The problems here are:

- The default value for the NumberSource control has quotation marks that should be ignored.

- There should be a space between the number and the label (MYLABELPLURAL or MYLABEL).

To ignore the quotation marks, you can change the line to this:

```
MyForm![AvailableFields].Caption = Mid(MyForm![NumberSource].DefaultValue, 2,
➥Len(MyForm![NumberSource].DefaultValue)
➥- 2) & " - " & MyForm![NumberSource] & IIf([NumberSource] <> 0, MYLABELPLURAL,
➥MYLABEL)
```

With this change, the code takes the characters from the second position through the next to last character, effectively ignoring the quotation marks.

> **Note:** This technique works only if you want to ignore exactly one leading and one trailing character.

To insert a space between the number and the label, change the code so that it now looks like this:

```
MyForm![AvailableFields].Caption = Mid(MyForm![NumberSource].DefaultValue, 2,
➥Len(MyForm![NumberSource].DefaultValue)
➥- 2) & " - " & MyForm![NumberSource] & " " & IIf([NumberSource] <> 0,
➥MYLABELPLURAL, MYLABEL)
```

Although you haven't yet selected any fields from the Available list box, you should already anticipate that the label appearing above the Selected list box is also faulty. Change the other label's code as shown here:

```
MyForm![SelectedFields].Caption = Mid(MyForm![NumberDestination].DefaultValue, 2,
➥Len(MyForm![NumberDestination].
```

```
➡DefaultValue) - 2) & " - " & MyForm![NumberDestination] & " " &
➡IIf([NumberDestination] <> 0,
➡MYLABELPLURAL, MYLABEL)
```

Again open the form in Form View, select a table, and then double-click a few field names to test copying field names to the Selected list box (see fig. 16.33).

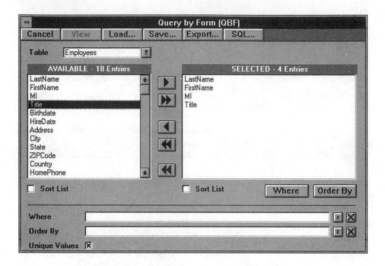

Figure 16.33. Testing the csvQBF form (Form View).

In this example, the field count is correct and the caption above the Selected list box correctly shows four fields have been selected.

Now, try selecting and then removing field name entries. As you move to the bottom of either list box, you see a blank line (see fig. 16.34).

There is something wrong with the fill functions that populate the lists, so take a look first at the `qbfFillAvailableFields()` function. The error lies in this block of code:

```
For X = 0 To MaxFields - 1
    qbfFieldArray(X) = MyTable.Fields(X).Name
Next X
```

The `qbfFieldArray()` array is one-based, which means the zero element is not used. The loop counter in this block, X, begins with 0 (zero), however, which means the array is being populated beginning with 0, not 1. To fix it, change the block of code so that it reads as shown here:

```
For X = 0 To MaxFields - 1
    qbfFieldArray(X + 1) = MyTable.Fields(X).Name
Next X
```

Adding one to the array element should fix not only the blank line but also the fact that the first field name was not displayed in the Available list box (see fig. 16.35).

317

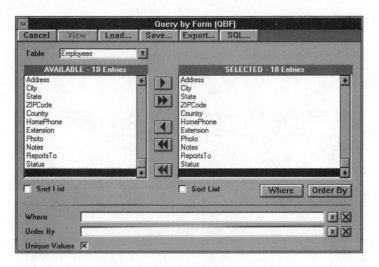

Figure 16.34.   Each list box has an unwanted blank line.

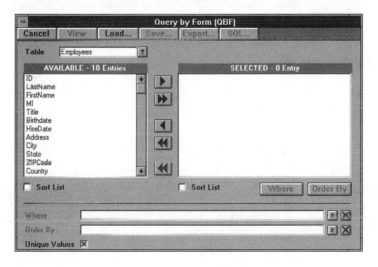

Figure 16.35.   When you correct the fill function, the first field, ID, appears.

The qbfFillSelectedFields() function was handled a bit differently:

```
For X = 1 To MaxFields
    qbfSelectedFieldArray(X, 0) = MySnap![Entry]
    qbfSelectedFieldArray(X, 1) = MySnap![Subentry]
    MySnap.MoveNext
Next X
```

In this block of code, the loop counter started with 1, not 0, so the problem of being 0-based versus 1-based does not arise. This block is unlike the one in the `qbfFillAvailableFields()` function because of the technique used to obtain the field names.

Take a look again at figure 16.35 and you see that there is still a problem with the label appearing above the Selected list box. When no fields have been selected, the label should either say simply "SELECTED" or "SELECTED - 0 Entries". "0 Entry" is grammatically incorrect and should be fixed. Return to the `qbfUpdateListCounts()` function and locate the incorrect code:

```
MyForm![AvailableFields].Caption = Mid(MyForm![NumberSource].DefaultValue, 2,
➥Len(MyForm![NumberSource].DefaultValue) - 2) & " - " & MyForm![NumberSource] & " "
&
➥IIf([NumberSource] <> 0, MYLABELPLURAL, MYLABEL)
MyForm![SelectedFields].Caption = Mid(MyForm![NumberDestination].DefaultValue, 2,
➥Len(MyForm![NumberDestination].DefaultValue) - 2) & " - " &
MyForm![NumberDestination] &
➥" " & IIf([NumberDestination] <> 0, MYLABELPLURAL, MYLABEL)
```

Apparently, `NumberSource` or `NumberDestination` can be Null. The code, however, does not check for a Null condition, only that the values are not 0 (zero). The labels should have plural captions if their corresponding values (numbers) are greater than 0. Change both occurrences of <> **0** to <> **1**.

Take another look at the Selected list box and you see that the list box should display not only the names of the selected fields, but also the names of the tables from which they came. Go to the `qbfFillSelectedFields()` function and look at this block of code:

```
        Case 4 ' Columns.
            ReturnValue = 1
```

If `ReturnValue` is set to 1, Access creates a single-column list box (or combo box). Since the Selected list box should indeed display two columns, change the value from 1 to 2:

```
        Case 4 ' Columns.
            ReturnValue = 2
```

Open the form in Form View and notice that the Selected list box now displays field names and table names (see fig. 16.36).

 Note: It does not matter that the **ColumnCount** property for the list box was previously set to 2. The fill function must "know" that it needs to return two columns of data.

Figure 16.37 shows the results of selecting the Employees table and three of its fields and then clicking the View command button.

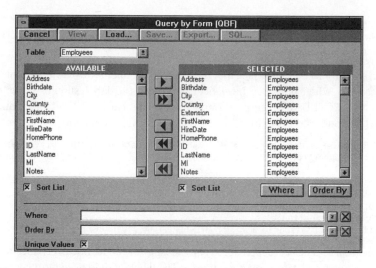

Figure 16.36. Including table names in the Selected list box.

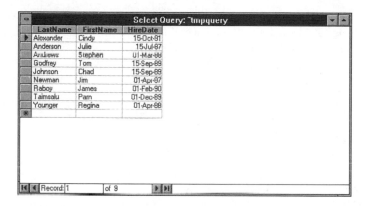

Figure 16.37. Access displays the results of the query in Datasheet View.

 Note: Later sections in this chapter describe how you can implement the Load, Save, Export, and SQL command buttons.

Handling Multiple Tables and Join Operations

When you include multiple tables in a query, you need to add the appropriate join operations. For example, if you were to choose fields from the Agencies table and the Agents table, a simple SQL statement might look like this:

```
SELECT DISTINCTROW Agencies.Name, Agents.Name
FROM Agencies INNER JOIN Agents ON Agencies.ID = Agents.AgencyID;
```

The inner join operation must somehow be created based only on knowledge of the two table names. In the QBE grid, Microsoft Access itself makes a best guess as to which fields should be joined. Typically, selecting two tables in which each has a counter field results in a join between the two counters. This is rarely the desired result, however, so you must find some other way to determine the joins. You have at least two options:

- Provide a text box into which the user can type the exact syntax for the join operation. This is not an attractive option because most users do not possess the training and experience to specify join information correctly.

- Add a separate table to the application that stores the join information.

Maintaining a separate table is better than making the user specify the joins, and better than performing a best guess as Access does in the QBE grid. It does, however, mean that you will need to determine all of the possible joins in advance. It also means that whenever the user creates or adds new tables to the application that your table will have to be updated.

To create the table, return to the Database window, choose New from the File menu, and then choose the Table subcommand. Next, create the new table with six fields, as shown in figure 16.38.

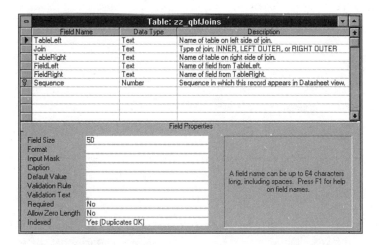

Figure 16.38. Creating a table to store join information.

Save the table and name it zz_qbfJoins. Open the table in Table View, and define the required joins by adding records to the table. For example, figure 16.39 illustrates how you can define the join between the Agencies table and the Agents table, a one-to-many relationship.

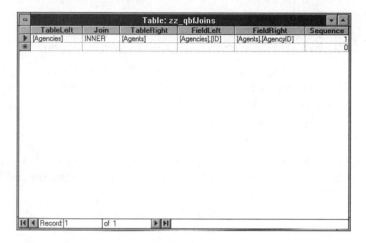

Figure 16.39. Define relationships by adding records to the zz_qbfJoins table.

To test the joins, return to the cqvQBF form and open it in Form View. Immediately, you see that there are selected fields in the Selected list box. These fields are still in the zz_qbfSelected table and thus appear in the list box when you first open the form.

To fix this, closing the form should trigger the same code as clicking the Clear All command button. Open the form in Design View, open the form's code module, and then enter the following code for the form's **OnClose** event:

```
Sub Form_Close ()

    Dim X As Integer

    X = qbfClearAll(Me)

End Sub
```

 Be sure to read about new coding techniques in Appendix D, "Converting Old Code."

Now, whenever the user closes the form, the **OnClose** event will call the `qbfClearAll()` function. However, this has the annoying effect of prompting the user to confirm that the entries should be removed, even when the form is being closed. You can resolve this by adding code to the `qbfClearAll()` function that detects whether the function is being called from the **OnClose** event (in which case the message should be suppressed), or you can duplicate just that portion of the `qbfClearAll()` function that actually removes the field names:

```
Sub Form_Close ()

    DoCmd SetWarnings False
    DoCmd RunSQL "DELETE * FROM zz_qbfSelected"
    DoCmd SetWarnings True

End Sub
```

> **Tip:** As a rule, you should try to avoid duplicating functionality. In this example, however, it seems innocent enough to duplicate the code in a second subprocedure to avoid having to add special code in the `qbfClearAll()` function to handle one exception.

Open the form in Form View, select fields from both the Agencies table and the Agents table (see fig. 16.40), and then click the View command button to confirm that the join information is properly stored and retrieved.

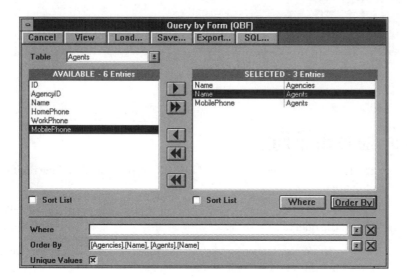

Figure 16.40.   Selecting fields from multiple tables.

323

In this example, the query should produce a sorted list of agencies and their corresponding agents and mobile phone numbers (see fig. 16.41).

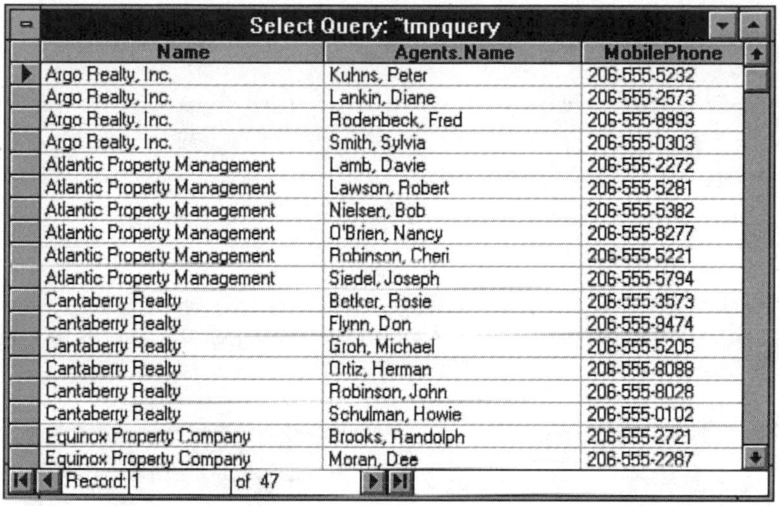

Select Query: ~tmpquery

Name	Agents.Name	MobilePhone
Argo Realty, Inc.	Kuhns, Peter	206-555-5232
Argo Realty, Inc.	Lankin, Diane	206-555-2573
Argo Realty, Inc.	Rodenbeck, Fred	206-555-8993
Argo Realty, Inc.	Smith, Sylvia	206-555-0303
Atlantic Property Management	Lamb, Davie	206-555-2272
Atlantic Property Management	Lawson, Robert	206-555-5281
Atlantic Property Management	Nielsen, Bob	206-555-5382
Atlantic Property Management	O'Brien, Nancy	206-555-8277
Atlantic Property Management	Robinson, Cheri	206-555-5221
Atlantic Property Management	Siedel, Joseph	206-555-5794
Cantaberry Realty	Betker, Rosie	206-555-3573
Cantaberry Realty	Flynn, Don	206-555-9474
Cantaberry Realty	Groh, Michael	206-555-5205
Cantaberry Realty	Ortiz, Herman	206-555-8088
Cantaberry Realty	Robinson, John	206-555-8028
Cantaberry Realty	Schulman, Howie	206-555-0102
Equinox Property Company	Brooks, Randolph	206-555-2721
Equinox Property Company	Moran, Dee	206-555-2287

Record: 1 of 47

Figure 16.41. Viewing the query results.

Enhancing the csvQBF Form

However powerful and flexible the generic query by form may be, there are still some things you might add to make it even more useful:

- Add a user-defined limit to the number of records returned by the form by including the **TOP** predicate in the query.
- Create builders for the WhereClause and OrderByClause text boxes. For more information, see Chapter 19, "Creating and Using Libraries."
- Add a custom menu bar to the form.
- Add error checking to make sure the user has selected a field in the Selected list box before clicking the Where or Order By command buttons.
- Provide mechanisms for handling more than just the WHERE and ORDER BY clauses (for example, GROUP BY and HAVING).
- Use the Relations collection to see if you can avoid having to maintain a manual list of relationships between tables in the database. For more information, search Help for "Relations."

Creating the csvQBF Load Form

Create a new form the user can use to load a previously saved query. Name the form csvQBF Load and add several command buttons to the form's header and a single list box to the Detail section (see fig. 16.42).

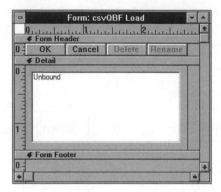

Figure 16.42. The csvQBF Load form (Design View).

Table 16.5 lists the property settings you need to set for the form and each of its controls. If a property is not listed, it means its default setting is acceptable.

Table 16.5. csvQBF Load Form Properties

Control	Property	Setting
(form)	Caption	Load Query
	Default View	Single Form
	Shortcut Menu	No
	Scroll Bars	Neither
	Record Selectors	No
	Navigation Buttons	No
	Auto Resize	Yes
	Auto Center	Yes
	Popup	No
	Modal	Yes
	Min Button	No
	Max Button	No

continues

325

Table 16.5. Continued

Control	Property	Setting
OK (command button)	Name	OK
	Caption	OK
	Status Bar Text	Load the selected query.
	On Click	[Event Procedure]
Cancel (command button)	Name	Cancel
	Caption	Cancel
	Status Bar Text	Close this form and return to the previous form.
	On Click	[Event Procedure]
Delete (command button)	Name	Delete
	Caption	Delete
	Status Bar Text	Delete the selected query.
	On Click	[Event Procedure]
	Enabled	No
Rename (command button)	Name	Rename
	Caption	Rename
	Status Bar Text	Rename the selected query.
	On Click	[Event Procedure]
	Enabled	No
Queries (list box)	Name	Queries
	Row Source Type	Table/Query
	Row Source	SELECT DISTINCTROW Mid(Name, 5) FROM MSysObjects WHERE Type = 5 AND Left(Name, 4) = "qbf_" AND Right(Name, 4) <> "0000" ORDER BY Name;
	Column Count	1
	Column Widths	3 in.
	Bound Column	1
	Status Bar Text	Select the desired query.
	On Dbl Click	[Event Procedure]

Writing Code for the csvQBF Load Form

The csvQBF Load form has a limited number of controls and few functions.

OK Command Button

The OK command button should accept the name of the highlighted query, parse the query, and then place onto the csvQBF form all of the selected tables and fields. Enter the following code for the command button's **OnClick** event:

```
Sub OK_Click ()

    Dim X As Integer

    X = qbfLoadQuery()

End Sub
```

> **Tip:** This subprocedure calls a function that actually loads the desired query. The reason for calling a function instead of placing the code here in this subprocedure is so the user can double-click the query in the list box and have that list box's **OnDblClick** event call the same code.

Go to the Declarations section and then enter the code for the qbfLoadQuery() function:

```
Function qbfLoadQuery () As Integer

    Const csvMB_ICONEXCLAMATION = 48
    Const csvMB_ICONINFORMATION = 64
    Dim MyDB As Database
    Dim MyQuery As QueryDef
    Dim QueryName As Control
    Dim MyQueryName As String
    Dim Msg As String
    Dim Icon As Integer
    Dim Titlebar As String
    Dim SQLStmt As String
    Dim SelectStmt As String
    Dim FromClause As String
    Dim WhereClause As String
    Dim OrderByClause As String
    Dim FromPosition As Integer
    Dim WherePosition As Integer
    Dim OrderByPosition As Integer
    Dim OwnerPosition As Integer
    Dim X As Integer
    Dim CRLF As String

    CRLF = Chr$(13) & Chr$(10)

    qbfLoadQuery = False
    Set QueryName = [Queries]
```

```
If IsNull(QueryName) Then
    Msg = "Sorry - you must first select a query from the list."
    Icon = csvMB_ICONINFORMATION
    Titlebar = "Required Entry"
    DoCmd Echo True
    MsgBox Msg, Icon, Titlebar
    [Queries].SetFocus
Else
    MyQueryName = "qbf_" & QueryName
    DoCmd Hourglass True
    DoCmd Echo False, "Processing..."
    Set MyDB = CurrentDB()
    On Error Resume Next
    Set MyQuery = MyDB.OpenQueryDef(MyQueryName)
    If Err Then
        On Error GoTo 0
        Msg = "Couldn't open query '" & QueryName & "'."
        Icon = csvMB ICONEXCLAMATION
        Titlebar = "Load Query"
        DoCmd Hourglass False
        DoCmd Echo True
        MsgBox Msg, Icon, Titlebar
    Else
        On Error GoTo 0
        SQLStmt = MyQuery.SQL
        MyQuery.Close

        ' Parse SQL statement and set relevant controls on QBF form.
        FromPosition = InStr(SQLStmt, CRLF & "FROM ")
        WherePosition = InStr(SQLStmt, CRLF & "WHERE ")
        OrderByPosition = InStr(SQLStmt, CRLF & "ORDER BY ")
        OwnerPosition = InStr(SQLStmt, CRLF & "WITH ")

        SelectStmt = Left(SQLStmt, InStr(SQLStmt, CRLF & "FROM ") - 1)

        If WherePosition <> 0 Then
            X = WherePosition
        End If
        If WherePosition = 0 And OrderByPosition <> 0 Then
            X = OrderByPosition
        End If
        If WherePosition = 0 And OrderByPosition = 0 Then
            X = OwnerPosition
        End If
        FromClause = Mid(SQLStmt, FromPosition, X - FromPosition)

        If OrderByPosition <> 0 Then
            X = OrderByPosition
        Else
            X = OwnerPosition
        End If
        If WherePosition <> 0 Then
            WhereClause = Mid(SQLStmt, WherePosition + 8, X - WherePosition - 8)
        End If

        If OrderByPosition <> 0 Then
            OrderByClause = Mid(SQLStmt, OrderByPosition + 11, OwnerPosition -
            ➥OrderByPosition - 11)
        End If
```

```
            X = qbfUpdateSelected(SelectStmt)
            Forms![csvQBF]![WhereClause] = WhereClause
            Forms![csvQBF]![OrderByClause] = OrderByClause
            DoCmd Echo True
            qbfLoadQuery = True
        End If
        MyDB.Close
        DoCmd Hourglass False
    End If

End Function
```

The `qbfLoadQuery()` function calls the `qbfUpdateSelected()` function to update the list of selected fields:

```
Function qbfUpdateSelected (ByVal SelectStmt As String) As Integer

    Dim MyDB As Database
    Dim MySet As Dynaset
    Dim X As Integer
    Dim MyFieldName As String
    Dim MyTableName As String
    Dim DotPosition As Integer
    Dim CommaPosition As Integer
    Dim S As String

    DoCmd SetWarnings False
    DoCmd RunSQL "DELETE * FROM zz_qbfSelected"
    DoCmd SetWarnings True

    Set MyDB = CurrentDB()
    Set MySet = MyDB.CreateDynaset("zz_qbfSelected")
    S = SelectStmt

    Do Until InStr(S, ".") = 0
        DotPosition = InStr(S, ".")
        MyFieldName = Mid(S, DotPosition + 2, InStr(DotPosition, S, "]")) -
        ➥DotPosition - 2)
        MyTableName = Mid(S, InStr(S, "[") + 1, InStr(S, "]") - InStr(S, "[") - 1)
        MySet.AddNew
            MySet![Entry] = MyFieldName
            MySet![Subentry] = MyTableName
        MySet.Update
        CommaPosition = InStr(S, ",")
        If CommaPosition <> 0 Then
            S = Mid(S, CommaPosition + 1)
        Else
            S = ""
        End If
    Loop

    MySet.Close
    MyDB.Close
    Forms![csvQBF]![Destination].Requery
    X = qbfUpdateListCounts(Forms![csvQBF])

End Function
```

Be sure to read about new coding techniques in Appendix D, "Converting Old Code."

The `qbfUpdateSelected()` function calls the `qbfUpdateListCounts()` function. However, you have already entered the code for `qbfUpdateListCounts()` in the code module for the csvQBF form. You have to decide whether you want to repeat that code in the csvQBF Load form or move the existing function into a global module to which both forms have access.

 Tip: As a rule, you should try to avoid duplicating functionality. In this example, it is better to move the code into a global module. If there were only a few lines of code involved, it might make more sense to repeat the code.

Open the csvQBF form in Design View and locate the `qbfUpdateListCounts()` function. Cut the code from the form's code module. Next, Return to the Database window and create a new module. Paste the just cut code into the module's Declarations section and then save the module as csvQBF. Do not close the module just yet.

If you choose the Compile Load Modules command from the Run menu, you will see that the `qbfFieldArray` array does not "exist" in the newly-created module. Indeed, it is declared in the csvQBF form's code module. The `qbfFieldArray` array needs to be declared a global array, so return to the Declarations section of the csvQBF form's code module and locate the array declarations:

```
Option Explicit

Const qbfQUERYNAME = "~tmpquery"
Dim qbfFieldArray() As Variant
Dim qbfSelectedFieldArray() As Variant
```

The last two lines declare two arrays that have module scope; only procedures in the same module can "see" them. Cut both lines from the Declarations section and paste them to the Declarations section of the csvQBF module. Notice, however, that they must now be global declarations:

```
Option Compare Database    'Use database order for string comparisons
Option Explicit

Global qbfFieldArray() As Variant
Global qbfSelectedFieldArray() As Variant
```

 Tip: Access automatically inserts the **Option Compare Database** statement. As a rule, you should add the **Option Explicit** statement to each/every function you use or create.

Cancel Command Button

The Cancel command button should do nothing more than close the form; the user has chosen to cancel the query. Enter the following code for the command button's **OnClick** event:

```
Sub Cancel_Click ()

    DoCmd Close

End Sub
```

Delete Command Button

The Delete command button is currently disabled and left as an exercise for you to implement. The command button should accept the highlighted query, prompt the user to confirm the action, and then delete the query.

Be sure you requery the list box to reflect that the query has been deleted.

Rename Command Button

The Rename command button is currently disabled and left as an exercise for you to implement. The command button should accept the highlighted query, prompt the user for the new name (checking to see that the new name does not already exist), and then rename the query.

Be sure you requery the list box to reflect the new query name.

Queries List Box

As a convenience, the user can double-click the name of a query in the Queries list box and have the query loaded automatically. This has the same effect as highlighting the desired query and then clicking the OK command button.

You have already entered the code for the function that actually loads the query (see "OK Command Button" earlier in this section). To call the function, enter the following code for the list box's **OnDblClick** event:

```
Sub Queries_DblClick (Cancel As Integer)

    Dim X As Integer

    X = qbfLoadQuery()

End Sub
```

Testing the csvQBF Load Form

Figure 16.43 illustrates the completed csvQBF Load form.

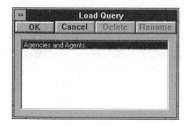

Figure 16.43. Only previously-saved QBF queries appear in the list box.

Creating the csvQBF Save Form

Create a new form the user can use to save the current set of criteria. Name the form csvQBF Save. Add two command buttons to the form's header, and a single text box to the Detail section, as shown in figure 16.44.

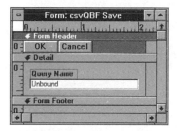

Figure 16.44. The csvQBF Save form (Design View).

Table 16.6 lists the property settings for the form and each of its controls. If a property is not listed, its default setting is acceptable

Table 16.6. csvQBF Save Form Properties

Control	Property	Setting
(form)	Caption	Save Query
	Default View	Single Form
	Shortcut Menu	No
	Scroll Bars	Neither
	Record Selectors	No
	Navigation Buttons	No

Control	Property	Setting
	Auto Resize	Yes
	Auto Center	Yes
	Popup	No
	Modal	Yes
	Min Button	No
	Max Button	No
OK (command button)	Name	OK
	Caption	OK
	Status Bar Text	Save this query using the specified name.
	On Click	[Event Procedure]
Cancel	Name	Cancel
(command button)	Caption	Cancel
	Status Bar Text	Close this form and return to the previous form.
	On Click	[Event Procedure]
Query Name (text box)	Name	QueryName
	Status Bar Text	Enter a name for this query (no more than 50 characters).

Writing Code for the csvQBF Save Form

The csvQBF Save form is fairly simple and straightforward. It has only one subprocedure of consequence: the **OnClick** subprocedure for the OK command button.

OK Command Button

The OK command button should accept the name of the query and then save the query. Enter the following code for the command button's **OnClick** event:

```
Sub OK_Click ()

    Const csvMYQUERYNAME = "~tmpquery"
    Const csvMB_ICONQUESTIONMARK = 32
    Const csvMB_ICONEXCLAMATION = 48
    Const csvMB_ICONINFORMATION = 64
    Const csvMB_YES = 6
    Const csvMB_YESNO = 4
    Dim MyDB As Database
    Dim MyQuery As QueryDef
```

333

```
Dim TempQuery As QueryDef
Dim QueryName As Control
Dim MyQueryName As String
Dim Msg As String
Dim Icon As Integer
Dim Titlebar As String
Dim Response As Variant
Dim QueryExists As Integer
Dim X As Integer

Set QueryName = [QueryName]

If IsNull(QueryName) Then
    Msg = "Sorry - you must first enter a name for the query."
    Icon = csvMB_ICONINFORMATION
    Titlebar = "Required Entry"
    MsgBox Msg, Icon, Titlebar
    [QueryName].SetFocus
    Exit Sub
Else
    MyQueryName = QueryName
    If Left$(QueryName, 1) = "~" Or Left$(QueryName, 3) = "zz_" Or
➡Left$(QueryName, 4) = "qbf_" Then
        Msg = "Sorry - query names cannot begin with '~', 'zz_' or 'qbf_'."
        Icon = csvMB_ICONINFORMATION
        Titlebar = "Invalid Query Name"
        MsgBox Msg, Icon, Titlebar
        [QueryName].SetFocus
        Exit Sub
    End If
End If

' Prepend 'qbf_' to the query name.
MyQueryName = "qbf_" & MyQueryName

' Check for an existing query with the same name.
DoCmd Hourglass True
Set MyDB = CurrentDB()
On Error Resume Next
Set MyQuery = MyDB.OpenQueryDef(MyQueryName)
If Err Then                                     ' It doesn't exist.
    Set MyQuery = MyDB.CreateQueryDef(MyQueryName)
Else                                            ' It does exist.
    On Error GoTo 0
    Msg = "A query with the name '" & QueryName & "' already "
    Msg = Msg & "exists. Do you want to delete it?"
    Icon = csvMB_ICONQUESTIONMARK + csvMB_YESNO
    Titlebar = "Replace Query"
    DoCmd Hourglass False
    Response = MsgBox(Msg, Icon, Titlebar)
    If Response <> csvMB_YES Then               ' Leave it intact.
        [QueryName].SetFocus
        MyQuery.Close
        MyDB.Close
        Exit Sub
    End If
End If
DoCmd Hourglass True
```

```
    If qbfBuildQBFQuery(Forms![csvQBF]) = False Then
        MsgBox "Couldn't build temporary query.", csvMB_ICONEXCLAMATION, "Save
        ➥Query"
        Err = 1 ' Any error will do.
    Else
        On Error Resume Next
        Set TempQuery = MyDB.OpenQueryDef(csvMYQUERYNAME)
        MyQuery.SQL = TempQuery.SQL
    End If
    MyQuery.Close
    TempQuery.Close
    MyDB.Close
    DoCmd SetWarnings True
    DoCmd Echo True
    DoCmd Hourglass False
    '----------------------------------------------------------------------
    If Err Then
        Msg = "Sorry - couldn't save query '" & QueryName & "'."
        Icon = csvMB_ICONEXCLAMATION
    Else
        Msg = "Query '" & QueryName & "' has been saved. If you want, you can "
        Msg = Msg & "base a new report on this query."
        Icon = csvMB_ICONINFORMATION
        DoCmd Close
        [Cancel].SetFocus
    End If
    On Error GoTo 0
    MsgBox Msg, Icon, "Save Query"

End Sub
```

This subprocedure calls the `qbfBuildQBFQuery()` function that you previously entered in the code module for the csvQBF form. Open the csvQBF form in Design View and locate the `qbfBuildQBFQuery()` function. Highlight and cut the entire function.

Return to the Database window and open the csvQBF module. Paste the previously-cut function into the csvQBF module, and then choose the Compile Loaded Modules command from the Run menu to confirm that there are no errors.

Immediately, you see that the compiler produces an error when it gets to the line of code that refers to the NumberDestination control:

```
    If Not IsNull([NumberDestination]) Then
```

Before, when the function existed behind the csvQBF form, there was an implicit form reference. Now that the function is in a global module, all of the references to the NumberDestination control must be fully-qualified:

```
    If Not IsNull(MyForm![NumberDestination]) Then
```

Choose the Compile Loaded Modules command again and check for any additional reference errors. Add "MyForm!" to the beginning of each reference to NumberDestination.

Even when all of the control references are fixed, Access will produce a compile error. The `qbfBuildQBFQuery()` function calls another function, `qbfSQLStmt()`, which also was entered into the csvQBF form's code module. Move the `qbfSQLStmt()` function into the csvQBF module and compile again.

335

As with the `qbfBuildQBFQuery()` function, you will need to fully qualify all of the references to the NumberDestination control, the WhereClause control, and the OrderByClause control.

> **Tip:** As you can see, the ability to refer controls by their names (only) in a form's code module can be both a good thing and a not-so-good thing. It is good in that you do not have to refer explicitly to any one form (or the **Me** property). However, if you should have to move a block of code to a global module, as in this example, fully qualifying the controls is a better idea.

Once there are no compile errors, you can open the csvQBF form in Form View, enter some criteria, and then save the query (see fig. 16.45).

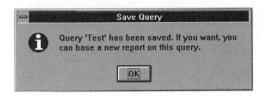

Figure 16.45.   Saving the criteria as a new query.

Cancel Command Button

The Cancel command button should do nothing more than close the form: the user has chosen not to save the query at this time. Enter the following code for the command button's **OnClick** event:

```
Sub Cancel_Click ()

    DoCmd Close

End Sub
```

Creating the csvQBF Export Form

Create a new form the user can use to export the current set of criteria. Name the form csvQBF Export; add two command buttons to the form's header, and a single text box to the Detail section, as shown in figure 16.46.

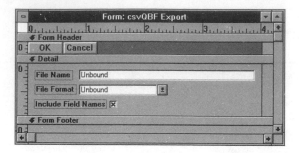

Figure 16.46.   The csvQBF Export form (Design View).

Table 16.7 lists the property settings you need to set for the form and each of its controls. If a property is not listed, its default setting is acceptable.

Table 16.7.   csvQBF Export Form Properties

Control	Property	Setting
(form)	Caption	Export Query
	Default View	Single Form
	Shortcut Menu	No
	Scroll Bars	Neither
	Record Selectors	No
	Navigation Buttons	No
	Auto Resize	Yes
	Auto Center	Yes
	Popup	No
	Modal	Yes
	Min Button	No
	Max Button	No
	On Open	[Event Procedure]
OK (command button)	Name	OK
	Caption	OK
	Status Bar Text	Accept these parameters and export the query results.
	On Click	[Event Procedure]

continues

337

Table 16.7. Continued

Control	Property	Setting
Cancel	Name	Cancel
(command button)	Caption	Cancel
	Status Bar Text	Close this form without exporting the results.
	On Click	[Event Procedure]
File Name (text box)	Name	FileName
	Status Bar Text	Enter the name of the output file (including path).
	After Update	[Event Procedure]
File Format (combo box)	Name	FileFormat
	Row Source Type	Value List
	Row Source	1;Lotus (WKS);2;Lotus (WK1);0; Microsoft Excel (XLS);3;Text File (TXT);4; Access Table
	Column Count	2
	Bound Column	1
	Column Widths	0 in.; 3 in.
	Status Bar Text	Select the desired output file format.
	Limit To List	Yes
Field Names (check box)	Name FieldNames	
	Default Value	1

Writing Code for the csvQBF Export Form

Much like the csvQBF Save form, the csvQBF Export form is fairly simple and straightforward. This form has only two subprocedures of consequence, the **OnOpen** subprocedure for the form itself and the **OnClick** subprocedure for the OK command button.

OnOpen Event

The form's **OnOpen** event should set the default value for the file format. Enter the following code for the form's **OnOpen** event:

```
Sub Form_Open (Cancel As Integer)
```

```
        [FileFormat] = 0

    End Sub
```

This has the effect of choosing Microsoft Excel (XLS) as the default file format for the output.

You may want to make Excel 5.0 the default. If so, change the preceding line of code as shown here:

```
        [FileFormat] = 5
```

For this to work, however, you must include Microsoft Excel 5.0 in the list of available file formats. Change the **RowSource** property for the FileFormat combo box as shown here:

```
1;Lotus (WKS);2;Lotus (WK1);0;Microsoft Excel (XLS);5;Microsoft Excel 5.0 (XLS);3;
➥Text File (TXT);4;Access Table
```

> **Tip:** Before you decide on the default file format, try to determine the file format most users will be choosing—most of the time. The reason for establishing a default is so the user will not have to do or choose anything. Selecting the appropriate default can be difficult, especially with a generic form or routine, so you may want to enhance the csvQBF Export form by reading the default setting from an .INI file.

OK Command Button

The OK command button should accept the name of the output file, the desired file format, and the decision to include field names so that it can then export the query. Enter the following code for the command button's **OnClick** event:

```
Sub OK_Click ()

    Const csvMYQUERYNAME = "~tmpquery"
    Const EXPORTFORMNAME = "csvQBF Export"
    Const TABLEPREFIX = "~"
    Const csvMB_CANCEL = 2
    Const csvMB_NO = 7
    Const csvMB_YES = 6
    Const csvMB_RETRY = 4
    Const csvMB_YESNOCANCEL = 3
    Const csvMB_ICONQUESTIONMARK = 32
    Dim Msg As String
    Dim Response As Integer
    Dim CloseForm As Integer
    Dim Icon As Integer
    Dim Titlebar As String
    Dim MyFileName As String
    Dim FileExists As Integer
    Dim TableExists As Integer
    Dim CRLF As String
    Dim X As Integer
    Dim S As String
    Dim HasFieldNames As Integer
    Dim InputQueryName As String
    '------------------------------------------------------------------
```

339

```
CRLF = Chr$(13) & Chr$(10)
CloseForm = False

If IsNull([FileName]) Then
    Msg = "Sorry - you must first enter a file name for the output."
    Icon = csvMB_ICONINFORMATION
    MsgBox Msg, Icon, "Output File Name"
Else
    MyFileName = [FileName]
    Response = csvMB_YES
    Select Case Val([FileFormat])
        Case 0, 1, 2, 3 ' File.
            FileExists = csvFileExists(MyFileName)
        Case 4 ' Table.
            If Left$(MyFileName, Len(TABLEPREFIX)) <> TABLEPREFIX Then
                Msg = "Sorry - the table name must begin with the "
                Msg = Msg & "following character(s):"
                Msg = Msg & CRLF & CRLF & Space(27) & TABLEPREFIX
                Msg = Msg & CRLF & CRLF & "I will add these character(s) "
                Msg = Msg & "for you."
                Icon = csvMB_ICONINFORMATION
                Titlebar = "Invalid Table Name"
                MsgBox Msg, Icon, Titlebar
                [FileName].SetFocus
                SendKeys "{f2}"
                SendKeys "{" & TABLEPREFIX & "}", True
                Exit Sub
            Else
                TableExists = csvObjectExists(MyFileName, "table")
            End If
    End Select
    ' ------------------------------------------------------------------------
    If FileExists Then
        Msg = "File '" & MyFileName & "' already exists. "
        Msg = Msg & "Do you want to replace the existing file?"
        Icon = csvMB_ICONQUESTIONMARK + csvMB_YESNOCANCEL
        Response = MsgBox(Msg, Icon, "File Exists")
        Select Case Response
            Case csvMB_NO
            Case csvMB_CANCEL
                CloseForm = True
            Case csvMB_YES
                ' User intends to replace the existing file.
                Response = csvMB_RETRY
                Do While Response = csvMB_RETRY
                    On Error Resume Next
                    Kill MyFileName
                    If Err Then
                        Msg = "Couldn't delete file '"
                        Msg = Msg & MyFileName & "'."
                        Icon = csvMB_ICONEXCLAMATION + csvMB_RETRYCANCEL
                        Response = MsgBox(Msg, Icon, "ExportResults()")
                    Else
                        Response = csvMB_YES
                    End If
                    On Error GoTo 0
                Loop
        End Select
    End If
```

```
' ----------------------------------------------------------------
If TableExists Then
    Msg = "Table '" & MyFileName & "' already exists. "
    Msg = Msg & "Do you want to replace the existing table?"
    Icon = csvMB_ICONQUESTIONMARK + csvMB_YESNOCANCEL
    Response = MsgBox(Msg, Icon, "Table Exists")
    Select Case Response
        Case csvMB_NO
        Case csvMB_CANCEL
            CloseForm = True
        Case csvMB_YES
            ' User intends to replace the existing table.
            Response = csvMB_RETRY
            Do While Response = csvMB_RETRY
                DoCmd Echo False
                On Error Resume Next
                DoCmd SelectObject A_TABLE, MyFileName, True
                DoCmd SetWarnings False
                SendKeys "{del}", True
                DoCmd SetWarnings True
                SendKeys "%wh", True
                If Err Then
                    Msg = "Couldn't replace table '"
                    Msg = Msg & MyFileName & "'."
                    Icon = csvMB_ICONEXCLAMATION + csvMB_RETRYCANCEL
                    Response = MsgBox(Msg, Icon, "Export Results()")
                Else
                    Response = csvMB_YES
                End If
                On Error GoTo 0
            Loop
    End Select
End If
' ----------------------------------------------------------------
If Response = csvMB_YES Then
    DoCmd Hourglass True
    DoCmd Echo False, "Exporting results.."
    HasFieldNames = [FieldNames]
    InputQueryName = csvMYQUERYNAME
    On Error Resume Next
    Select Case Val([FileFormat])
        Case 0, 1, 2, 5 ' Spreadsheet (one of four formats).
            DoCmd TransferSpreadsheet A_EXPORT, Val([FileFormat]),
            ➥InputQueryName, MyFileName, HasFieldNames
        Case 3 ' Delimited text (listed on form as Text File).
            DoCmd TransferText A_EXPORTDELIM, , InputQueryName, MyFileName
        Case 4 ' Access database table (listed as Access Table).
            DoCmd SetWarnings False
            S = "SELECT DISTINCTROW [" & InputQueryName & "].* "
            S = S & "INTO [" & MyFileName & "] FROM "
            S = S & "[" & InputQueryName & "] "
            S = S & "WITH OWNERACCESS OPTION;"
            DoCmd RunSQL S
            DoCmd SetWarnings True
    End Select
    DoCmd Echo True
    DoCmd Hourglass False
```

```
                If Err Then
                    Msg = "Couldn't export results to file"
                    Icon = csvMB_ICONEXCLAMATION
                    Titlebar = "Export Error"
                Else
                    Msg = "The results have been written to " & IIf(Val([FileFormat]) =
                    ➥4, "table", "file")
                    Icon = csvMB_ICONINFORMATION
                    Titlebar = "Export Results"
                    CloseForm = True
                End If
                On Error GoTo 0
                Msg = Msg & " '" & MyFileName & "'."
                MsgBox Msg, Icon, Titlebar
            End If
        End If
        If CloseForm Then
            DoCmd Close
        End If

    End Sub
```

This subprocedure calls either of two functions that determine whether the specified file or table exists. Open the csvQBF module (or your own Tools or Utilities module, if it exists) and then enter the csvFileExists() and csvObjectExists() functions:

```
    Function csvFileExists (ByVal MyFileName As String) As Integer

        Dim FileNumber As Integer

        FileNumber = FreeFile
        On Error Resume Next
        Open MyFileName For Input As FileNumber
        If Err Then
            csvFileExists = False
        Else
            csvFileExists = True
        End If
        On Error GoTo 0
        Close

    End Function

    Function csvObjectExists (ByVal MyObjectName As String, ByVal MyObjectType As
    String) As Integer

        Const FUNCTIONNAME = "csvObjectExists()"
        Dim MyDB As Database
        Dim ObjectList As Snapshot
        Dim ObjectName As String
        Dim ObjectType As Integer

        If LCase$(MyObjectType) = "table" Then
            csvObjectExists = (csvTableType(MyObjectName) <> 0)
            Exit Function
        End If

        Set MyDB = CurrentDB()
        Set ObjectList = MyDB.CreateSnapshot("MSysObjects")
```

342

```
    ObjectName = LCase$(MyObjectName)
    Select Case LCase$(MyObjectType)
        Case "form": ObjectType = -32768
        Case "macro": ObjectType = -32766
        Case "module": ObjectType = -32761
        Case "query": ObjectType = 5
        Case "report": ObjectType = -32764
        Case Else
            MsgBox "Invalid argument '" & MyObjectType & "'.",
csvMB_ICONEXCLAMATION, FUNCTIONNAME
    End Select

    ObjectList.MoveFirst
    csvObjectExists = False
    Do Until ObjectList.EOF
        If LCase$(ObjectList![Name]) = MyObjectName And ObjectList![Type] =
        ➥MyObjectType Then
            csvObjectExists = True
            Exit Do
        End If
        ObjectList.MoveNext
    Loop

End Function
```

> **🛑 WARNING:** The `csvObjectExists()` function uses the undocumented system table,
> MSysObjects. Use of the system tables (tables whose names begin with "MSys") is generally
> discouraged because these tables are subject to changes in their layout and internal values by Microsoft
> at any time. You must never change anything in any of the internal system tables.

The `csvObjectExists()` function in turn calls the `csvTableType()` function to determine whether the
table is attached.

```
Function csvTableType (ByVal MyTableName As String) As Integer

    Dim MyDB As Database
    Dim TableList As Snapshot
    Dim TempTableName As String

    TempTableName = LCase$(MyTableName)
    Set MyDB = CurrentDB()
    Set TableList = MyDB.ListTables()

    csvTableType = 0
    TableList.MoveFirst
    Do Until TableList.EOF
        If LCase$(TableList.Name) = TempTableName Then
            Select Case TableList.TableType
                Case DB_TABLE
                    csvTableType = 1                    ' Native table.
                Case DB_ATTACHEDTABLE
                    csvTableType = 2                    ' Attached table.
```

```
                      Case Else
                End Select
                Exit Do
           End If
        TableList.MoveNext
    Loop

    TableList.Close
    MyDB.Close

End Function
```

File Name Text Box

You should make at least a minimal attempt to validate the file name entered by the user. Enter the following code for the text box's **AfterUpdate** event:

```
Sub FileName_AfterUpdate ()

    Const DEFAULTPATH = "c:\"
    Dim X As Variant

    [FileName] = UCase([FileName])

    ' For file transfers, see that a directory has been specified.
    If [FileFormat] <> 4 Then
        If InStr([FileName], "\") = 0 Then
            [FileName] = DEFAULTPATH & [FileName]
        End If
    End If

End Sub
```

Testing the csvQBF Export Form

Figure 16.47 illustrates the completed csvQBF Export form.

A message box appears if there are any problems encountered during the export (see fig. 16.48).

Enhancing the Export Form

There are a few things you may want to implement to make the export form easier or more flexible to use:

- Typical problems during the export process include invalid file names, drive letters, or table names. You can include a more rigorous file name parsing routine.

- Provide a default file name for the output, perhaps read from an .INI file or a user-maintainable table.

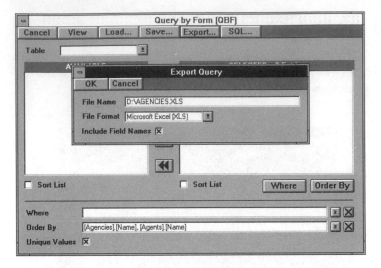

Figure 16.47.   Enter a file name, choose a file format, and then export the results of the query.

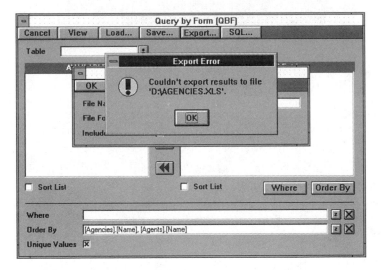

Figure 16.48.   The function displays a message if there was an error.

- Add a file name parsing routine to the file format combo box's **AfterUpdate** event, so that it adds the appropriate file name extension to the entry in the text box.

- Modify the csvObjectExists( ) function so that it no longer accesses the MSysObjects table directly and instead uses the various TableDefs, QueryDefs, and other DAO collections.

345

Creating the csvQBF SQL Form

Create a new form the user can use to view the current set of criteria expressed as an SQL statement. Name the form csvQBF SQL and add one command button to the form's header and a single text box to the Detail section, as shown in figure 16.49.

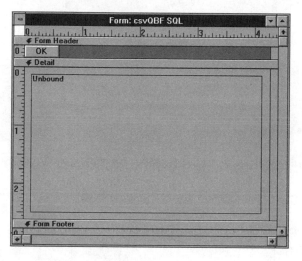

Figure 16.49. The csvQBF SQL form (Design View).

Table 16.8 lists the property settings you need to set for the form and each of its controls. If a property is not listed, its default setting is acceptable.

Table 16.8. csvQBF View Form Properties

Control	Property	Setting
(form)	Caption	QBF - SQL
	Default View	Single Form
	Shortcut Menu	No
	Scroll Bars	Neither
	Record Selectors	No
	Navigation Buttons	No
	Auto Resize	Yes
	Auto Center	Yes
	Popup	No

346

Control	Property	Setting
	Modal	Yes
	Min Button	No
	Max Button	No
OK (command button)	Name	OK
	Caption	OK
	Status Bar Text	Close this form and return to the QBF form.
	On Click	[Event Procedure]
SQL Statement (text box)	Name	SQLStmt
	Default Value	=qbfSQLStmt([])
	Status Bar Text	Use the arrow keys to scroll the SQL statement up and down.
	Locked	Yes

Writing Code for the csvQBF SQL Form

The csvQBF SQL form allows no user input and has only two controls.

OK Command Button

The OK command button should do nothing more than close the form: the user has chosen to close the form and return to the csvQBF form. Enter the following code for the command button's **OnClick** event:

```
Sub OK_Click ()

    DoCmd Close

End Sub
```

SQLStmt Text Box

The SQLStmt text box can get the focus (that is, it is enabled), but it is locked so the user cannot make any changes. This is a read-only control, and you do not need to trap any events.

Testing the csvQBF SQL Form

Open the csvQBF form in Form View and then load a previously saved query, or specify new selection criteria. Then, click the SQL command button to view the SQL statement.

347

Immediately, Access produces an error message and highlights the following line of code from the
qbfSQLStmt() function:

```
If Not IsNull(MyForm![NumberDestination]) Then
```

The specific error message is "Invalid reference to field 'NumberDestination'." In this example, the
form referred to by **MyForm** does not contain a field named **NumberDestination**. You have already
modified this function once (having moved it from the csvQBF form's code module to a global module,
csvQBF), but now must change it again to explicitly refer to the csvQBF form. To fix the function,
replace all occurrences of **MyForm** to **Forms![csvQBF]**, as shown in this example:

```
If Not IsNull(Forms![csvQBF]![NumberDestination]) Then
```

> **Tip:** Do not change the **MyForm** that appears in the first line of the function:
>
> ```
> Function qbfSQLStmt (MyForm As Form) As String
> ```

Figure 16.50 illustrates the completed csvQBF SQL form.

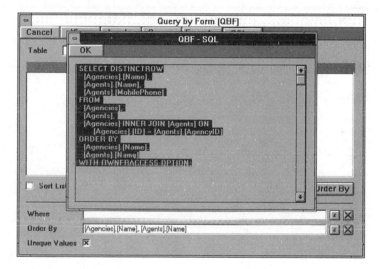

Figure 16.50. The user cannot change the SQL statement, but he can copy it to the clipboard.

Unless you tell Access to behave otherwise, the first control in the Detail section receives the focus.
Further, a text box that receives the focus appears highlighted (see fig. 16.50). To fix this and have
the SQL statement appear normally, you can either use the **SendKeys** statement to send F2 to the
form (which toggles the highlight off), or you can move the focus to the OK command button.

For this example, the focus will be moved to the OK command button:

1. Open the csvQBF SQL form in Design View.

2. Change the form's **OnOpen** property setting to [Event Procedure].

3. Open the form's code module.

4. Enter the following code for the form's **OnOpen** event:

```
Sub Form_Open (Cancel As Integer)

    [OK].SetFocus

End Sub
```

Reopen the csvQBF form and view the SQL statement again:

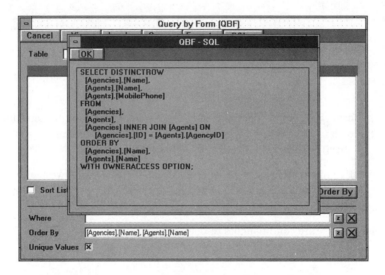

Figure 16.51. The revised csvQBF SQL form with the focus on the OK command button.

The SQL statement no longer appears highlighted, but neither does the vertical scroll bar. If the SQL statement happens to extend beyond the limits of the text box, the user will have to know that he can scroll the SQL statement by first clicking the SQL statement.

For this reason, you may want to consider leaving the focus on the text box and using the **SendKeys** statement as previously suggested.

349

Using csvQBF in Other Applications

As much as possible, all of the forms, tables, and modules have been made generic and application-independent. To use the query by form capabilities found in HomeFinder, export these database objects to the other application:

- **Tables.** zz_qbfJoins and zz_qbfSelected

- **Forms.** csvQBF, csvQBF Export, csvQBF Load, csvQBF Save, and csvQBF SQL

- **Modules.** csvQBF

Note: In addition, if you added any QBF functions to a Tools or Utilities module instead of to the csvQBF module, copy those functions, too.

Summary

Adding query-by-form capability to an application is one way to increase the value and utility of an application, often without much work on your part. Once implemented, not only can a user define queries on-the-fly, but the user can do so without your help.

You can implement application-specific query-by-form capability in which you tailor the forms and code to one application, or you can implement application-independent query by form that you can then copy and paste to other applications without making significant changes.

You can combine the features and benefits of one technique with those of the other to create the appropriate interface and add the required functionality for any given application.

Part IV

Reference

17

Naming Conventions and Style Guidelines

Whether you are a professional programmer or just getting started with database development, good programming practice requires a consistent, maintainable, and readable coding style. Months or even years from now, you will want to be able to look back at the objects and code you create today and understand them immediately, without having to spend extra time deciphering your work.

If you work in an environment where more than one person contributes to an application, it is even more important to adopt a consistent style. If all developers write with the same guidelines in mind, it is easier to incorporate code, share work, and improve the efficiency of your applications.

This chapter explores a number of naming and style issues; in adopting these guidelines, keep in mind that you may not always be the only one who has to work with your applications. While some users will be experienced, professional developers—perhaps fluent in one or more programming languages—most users are not so experienced and may look to your applications as examples of good design.

This chapter covers the following:

- Naming Database Objects and Controls
- Laying Out Modules—What Goes Where
- Designing a Function Procedure
- Adding Comments and Documenting Your Work
- Choosing between Modules and Macros
- Exploring Miscellaneous Issues

Naming Database Objects and Controls

Implementing a consistent database object naming convention makes it easier for users to find and identify objects and you and other developers to write and decipher code. This section outlines a number of techniques you should adopt as you develop your own applications and applications you distribute to others.

This section is based largely on the CSV conventions widely circulated among Access developers. What follows is the result of many years of research, usability testing, and sometimes heated debate among BASIC and Access programmers both inside and outside the walls of Microsoft.

Tables and Queries

Table names should be descriptive, yet relatively short (see fig. 17.1). They should be I-capped, which means each word begins with a capital letter, but without underscores (_) or spaces. Underscores are difficult for most people to locate on the keyboard, and names with underscores or all uppercase letters are more difficult to read.

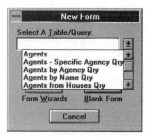

Figure 17.1. Name your tables and queries so that they appear together in drop-down lists

 One exception to using underscores relates to temporary objects. For more information, see the section "Temporary, Unfinished, and To-Be-Deleted Objects" later in this chapter.

Most other software platforms do not allow spaces in table names. If you someday decide to move your tables to such a platform (for example, the SQL Server), you have to rename your tables, plus change any forms, reports, queries, macros, and modules that refer to those tables. Because Access does not support the concept of a data dictionary and has no global search and replace, this results in a significant amount of work on your part.

Depending on your application, table names should be plural: Agencies, Agents, Cities (and not Agency, Agent, or City), and so on (see fig. 17.2).

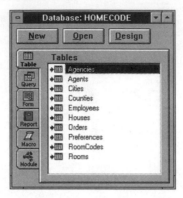

Figure 17.2. Try to use plurals for your table names.

For tables that merge data from more than one table (an intersection table designed to create a many-to-many relationship), choose a name that is descriptive and, where appropriate, includes the names of both or all tables. For example, a table that combines values from a Students table and a Classes table could be named StudentsClasses (see fig. 17.3).

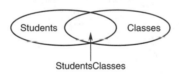

Figure 17.3. StudentsClasses is an intersection table.

You can often base the name of a query on the names of the source tables for the query. For example, Agencies by Name Qry identifies a query based on the Agencies table. Similarly, Listings by MLS Qry identifies a query based on the Listings table, and so on. If you adopt this strategy, when you list the queries in the Database window, all queries based on any particular table will appear together. In lists that combine table and query names (for example, the RecordSource drop-down list in a form's Design view), you will see the table and all its queries listed together alphabetically (see fig. 17.4).

As with tables, query names should be descriptive yet brief. Remember that you cannot scroll the Database window (and certain other lists) horizontally, so to view all of an exceptionally long name you must enlarge the window (see fig. 17.5).

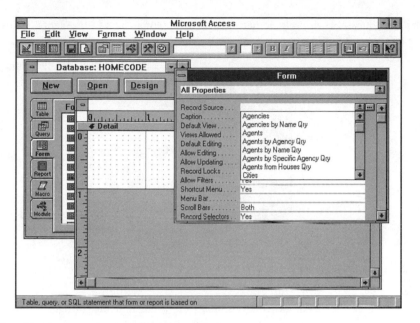

Figure 17.4.   All of the agent-related queries appear together.

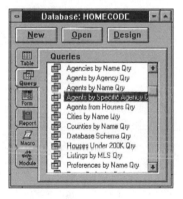

Figure 17.5.   Try to avoid particularly long object names.

Differentiating between Tables and Queries

Tables and queries share the same name space—you cannot have a table and a query with the same name. Because tables and queries appear in the same lists several places in the user interface, it is important to be able to tell the difference between tables and queries. To differentiate between tables

and queries, add a suffix, Qry, to the names of queries. For example, Sales for 1991 Qry and Customers by Name Qry.

You may be accustomed to prefixing table names with "tbl" and queries with "qry," or some other prefix. However, queries already are identified with a suffix and therefore there is no need to uniquely identify tables with either a prefix or suffix. It is the absence of a suffix that identifies a given object (in a list of tables and queries) as a table.

It is not particularly important to achieve consistency in using suffixes among all of your object names. What is important is only the need to differentiate tables and queries. Adding suffixes to other objects is largely unnecessary and adds nothing to the readability or utility of these other names.

Table Fields

As with table names, field names should be descriptive, yet relatively short. The names should be I-capped, using upper- and lowercase letters but no underscores or spaces (remember, most other software platforms do not allow spaces in either table or field names). Avoid unnecessary abbreviations, but do not make them so long that they become tedious to type.

Most fields can be described with a single word. Avoid naming fields with concatenated words that include the name of the table as well as the particular field. For example, in a table named Shippers, you can name fields Name, State, and so on. Because the name of the table already identifies that you are working with shippers, the field names do not need to be ShipperName, ShipperState, and so on. Wherever the name of the field might otherwise appear in Access, the name of the table also appears.

> **Note:** Avoid special characters in field names; use only letters (az, AZ) and perhaps numbers (0-9). Specifically, do not use number signs (#), dashes (-), or ampersands (&). In certain contexts, the presence of these special characters in a field name can be ambiguous or confusing. For example, you use the number sign to delimit date/time values and the ampersand to perform string concatenation.

Avoid special characters when you define your field names.

Controls

Unless you create a control by dragging and dropping a field name from the Field List, the default control name assigned by Microsoft Access looks something like Text12, Field5, and so on. You should rename all controls to something more meaningful, such as State or Birthdate. To understand the value of giving your controls "real" names, consider the following expressions.

```
If Not csvSomethingIn(Forms![Customers]![Field5]) Then...
If Not csvSomethingIn(Forms![Customers]![ZIP]) Then...
```

Clearly, an expression that refers to ZIP is easier to work with than one that refers to Field5. Further, you should rename labels, even if you do not think you will ever refer to them in code or in expressions. If you later decide to document (see fig. 17.6) your application by listing all of the controls on your forms, you will want to avoid lists with meaningless names.

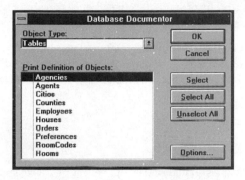

Figure 17.6.   Use the Database Documentor to create documentation for your tables.

Control names should be I-capped, using upper- and lowercase letters, but no underscores; avoid any special characters such as numbers signs, dashes, and ampersands. For example, a control that refers to a customer's company name might be named, appropriately enough, CompanyName.

In contrast, you should avoid naming the control CoNam because that name is unnecessarily cryptic.

> **Tip:** Even though you may be accustomed to adding prefixes, or tags, to control names to identify the control type, you should *avoid* such tags (except for label controls, discussed later in this section). For example, you might have created a text box named txtState or a combo box named cboShippers. The txt and cbo identify the control type as a text box or combo box, but in most contexts the control type is either unimportant or is apparent from its name or usage.

On occasion, you may even want to change the type of a control. For example, you may design a form that uses a text box to enter the state in a customer's address. If you name the control txtState and later decide you would rather use a combo box, you will either have to name the combo box txtState (which conflicts with the prefix naming scheme) or somehow locate and change every occurrence of the name throughout your application to reflect the new control name (but remember, there is no global search and replace mechanism).

Although `Forms!Customers!State` is an otherwise valid reference to a control named State (Access *requires* brackets only when there are spaces), the preferred syntax is nonetheless `Forms![Customers]![State]`.

> **Tip:** Even though Access allows you to insert spaces in control names, you should avoid using spaces. Always use brackets when you refer to controls and other user-defined names, even though they do not contain spaces. The following table shows examples of satisfactory and unsatisfactory control references:
>
> | Code Example | Satisfactory | Comments |
> |---|---|---|
> | `Forms![Customers]![CompanyName]` | Yes | |
> | `Forms!Customers![Company Name]` | No | Missing brackets; contains space |
> | `Forms![Customers]![State]` | Yes | |
> | `Forms!Customers!State` | No | Missing brackets |

Bound controls (that is, controls that have a **ControlSource** property setting) should be named the same as the fields to which they are bound, except in those cases where a naming conflict arises in a calculated control. In these cases, rename the control. For example, you might create a text box named City that is actually the concatenation of a record's city, state, and ZIP code. The control source for the text box might look something like this:

```
=[City] & ", " & [State] & " " & [ZIPCode]
```

Naming the control City will not work because it creates a circular reference: the control is based, in part, on itself. Access cannot resolve the name City, so you have to change the name of the control to something else (perhaps CityEtc).

Generally, label controls should be named the same as their captions with a suffix, Lbl (an abbreviation for label). For example, you might create a label with the caption Company Name. Its control name would be CompanyNameLbl (notice the absence of spaces). You would not name the label CompanyName because that would likely conflict with a text box with the same name, the very text box to which the label refers.

Forms and Reports

Name your forms and reports with descriptive names using uppercase and lowercase letters. In contrast with tables, fields, and controls, however, form and report names should include spaces between words. In particular, report names frequently appear in the user interface in your applications (see fig. 17.7) and thus having readable names is a much-desired convenience. Because forms and reports cannot be used outside the Access environment, the usual restriction against using spaces does not apply.

Try not to make your names so long that they do not fit in the Database window. Most form names can be single words (Agencies, Houses, and so on) that adequately describe the form's purpose. Since most forms deal with multiple records, most form names are plural, not singular. For example, you would not name a form Agency or House.

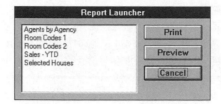

Figure 17.7. You can create a form that lists only report objects.

Reports typically represent a subset of table information and thus warrant more descriptive names than do tables or forms (see fig. 17.8). For example, avoid naming a report Agencies when Agencies by Name more clearly identifies the report. Name a report according to the data it represents and, where appropriate, its layout. For example, a report named Sales Report, although accurate, is not nearly as good as Sales Report by Sales Rep.

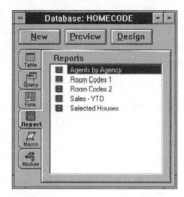

Figure 17.8. Create reports with meaningful names: not too short, not too long.

Name your subforms and subreports, when they are not also used as stand-alone forms and reports, the same as the main, or parent, form or report with an additional suffix, Sub. For example, a form named Customers might contain a subform named Customers Sub. In the Database window, such forms are easily recognized as subforms by this suffix. In the Northwind Traders sample database, the Orders form contains a subform named Order Details; although this is an otherwise valid form name, it would be better named Orders Sub.

Avoid prefixes in form and report names, because using a prefix prevents similarly named forms and reports from appearing together in lists. For example, Customers and Customers Sub would appear together in the Database window listing of forms. Naming the subform with a prefix (for example, Sub Customers) would likely cause the subform to appear elsewhere in the list of forms, away from the entry for Customers.

Macros

All except the AutoExec, AutoKeys, and custom menu macros should be in macro groups, even if a given macro group contains only one macro.

There are three kinds of macro groups: form- and report-specific macros, menu bar macro groups, and general-purpose macros.

Form- and Report-Specific Macro Groups

Generally, create one macro group per form or report, and include all of the relevant macros in those groups. Name the macro group the same as the form or report using the same upper- and lowercase letters and spaces. For example, a form named Agencies would have its own macro group named Agencies, Houses would have one named Houses, and so on.

Within the macro group, name the individual macros according to either the name of the control or event that triggers the macro, or a name that describes what the macro does.

For example, you might create a form with a command button named Close that calls a macro to close the form. The macro itself should be named Close because that is the name of the control that calls the macro (it also happens to describe the macro's action).

Most macros, however, can be named even more descriptively. For example, a form named Orders might need to update a TotalSales control with a running total each time a product is added, a quantity changes, or a line price changes. Rather than call three separate macros, you can create a single macro named Update Total. In this example, Update Total is more descriptive than the name of any of the controls that might trigger the macro.

The decision to use the names of the calling controls or more descriptive names depends on your particular application and the macros you call. In either case, be sure you document the macros by adding a comment that explains or identifies the events that call the macro (see fig. 17.9).

Menu Bar Macro Groups

In addition to the single macro group for each form or report, adding custom menu bars requires additional, multiple macro groups. For example, to add File, Edit, and Help menu commands to a custom menu bar requires four menu groups (see fig. 17.10).

You should adopt a consistent naming convention for these menu macro groups as you would any other macro group. The recommended naming convention uniquely and concisely identifies menu macro groups and their functions:

> form name **Menu** menu name

In the preceding example, the menu bar macro groups have been named the same as the form, Customers, followed by the words Menu and the name of the menu (Edit, File, and Help).

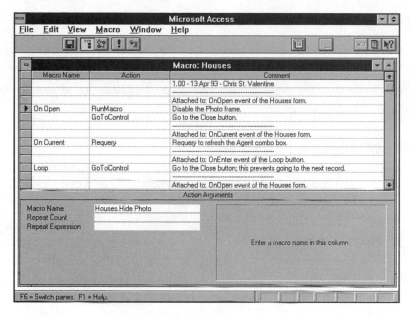

Figure 17.9. Add comments to document your macros.

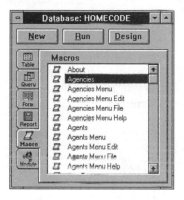

Figure 17.10. Consistently named menu macro groups appear together in the Database window.

The macro group names should be I-capped, using upper- and lowercase letters, with spaces separating the words but no underscores. Menu bar macro groups named in this fashion will appear in the Database window following the form's primary macro group (in this example, Customers).

General-Purpose Macro Groups

Depending on your application, you should create additional general-purpose macro groups beyond those specifically designed for your forms and reports. These general-purpose macro groups typically contain macros called from multiple forms or, in some cases, from Access Basic.

Examples of general-purpose macro groups include the AutoExec and AutoKeys macros. You might also create a macro group containing record navigation macros, form closing macros, or other macros called from multiple places.

The names you choose for such general-purpose macro groups will likely vary according to your application. Typical names include Generic (when the macros are truly generic), String Manipulation (or simply Strings), Mail, and so on (see fig. 17.11). The names are descriptive, but generally short enough to be viewed in the normal Database window.

Name the macro groups with upper- and lowercase letters and insert spaces between words.

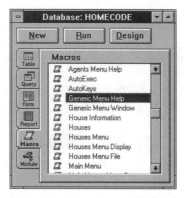

Figure 17.11.   You may be able to call generic macros from multiple forms.

Temporary, Unfinished, and To-Be-Deleted Objects

Objects in the Database window and in a variety of drop-down list boxes appear in alphabetical order. The following table illustrates how you can use this feature when you want to locate certain database objects that represent work-in-progress, that are created for some temporary purpose, or are objects you intend to delete.

Prefix	Example	Comments
_ (underscore)	_Customers	Use an underscore to prefix work-in-progress or other incomplete objects that need additional changes before they can be fully implemented. This technique is most useful for modules because you do not refer to module names anywhere in Access and renaming a module will not break anything. Objects with a leading underscore appear first in the Database window and in list boxes.

continues

363

Prefix	Example	Comments
zt	ztMonthlySales	Use zt to prefix temporary objects you create in code; for example, queries you create in Access Basic. The letters zt cause the objects to sort to the end of the Database window (except for objects beginning with zz, see below).
zz	zzCustomers	Rather than deleting a database object, consider renaming it with the zz prefix. That way, you have an opportunity to change your mind and recover the "deleted" object. Often, you will want to scavenge code, macros, or controls from the object.

After your application is finished, review all the lists in the Database window to make sure you have no underscore or zz database object names (see fig. 17.12).

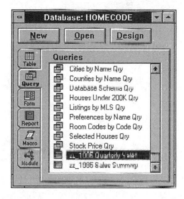

Figure 17.12. Temporary and to-be-deleted objects appear at the end of lists in the Database window.

Laying Out Modules—What Goes Where

How you organize a module (and the individual function procedures within them) can make it easier or harder to navigate through your code, especially if you share code in a multiuser development environment.

In a typical module, global variables and constants appear in the Declarations section along with function (API) declarations. Once an application has grown beyond just a few functions, however, a more organized structure is required.

For example, your application should have separate modules for global constants, variables, function declarations, and user-defined type declarations. The following table lists the minimum modules most applications use:

Module	Contains
Globals	Global constants and global variables
Declarations	Function (API) declarations and user-defined type declarations
Messages	Text for messages that appear in the user interface

Depending on your particular application, you may have additional modules dedicated to specific uses. For example, you might create a module named Strings that contains routines for manipulating strings, another named Validation that contains general-purpose validation routines, and yet another named Forms and Controls that contains form- and control-related functions. Not only does naming the modules according to the functions they contain make it easier to locate any particular functions, it also makes it easier to share code between applications because you can export an entire module to another database and know that you are copying only relevant functions.

For modules that contain only form- or report-specific code, name the module the same as the form or report. For example, a module that contains functions used only by an Orders form would itself be named Orders. This technique follows the same strategy as creating a single macro group for each form and naming it the same as the form.

Designing a Function Procedure

Within a function procedure, a consistent layout makes it easy to locate specific elements of the module. The following example illustrates a function designed with an easy-to-read format that includes many of the elements you are likely to encounter in a procedure.

```
Function csvGetWindowsColors () As Integer

    ' Purpose: Determines color settings set in the
    '          Control Panel.
    ' Accepts: (nothing)
    ' Returns: True  - successful
    '          False - unsuccessful
    ' ------------------------------------------------
    Const COLOR_APPWORKSPACE = 12 ' Background.
    Const COLOR_BACKGROUND = 1    ' Desktop background.
    Const COLOR_WINDOW = 5        ' Window background.
    Const COLOR_WINDOWTEXT = 8    ' Text in windows.
    Dim AppWorkspace As Long, Background As Long
    Dim Window As Long, WindowText As Long, X As Integer
```

```
        csvGetWindowsColors = True      ' Assume success.
        ' Enable error handling.
        On Error GoTo Err_GetWindowsColors
        ' Get the various Windows color settings.
        AppWorkspace = csvGetSysColor(COLOR_APPWORKSPACE)
        Background = csvGetSysColor(COLOR_BACKGROUND)
        Window = csvGetSysColor(COLOR_WINDOW)
        WindowText = csvGetSysColor(COLOR_WINDOWTEXT)
        ' Disable error handling.
        On Error GoTo 0

        ' Additional code that saves or uses the colors would
        ' go here.

    Exit_GetWindowsColors:

        Exit Function

    Err_GetWindowsColors:

        X = csvDisplayMsg(CANTREADCOLORS,
        ➥csvMB_ICONEXCLAMATION, "Colors")
        csvGetWindowsColors = False    ' Function failed.
        Resume Exit_GetWindowsColors

    End Function
```

Order of Elements in a Function

As a general rule, add elements to your own procedures in the following order:

- A "header" that describes the purpose of the procedure, the arguments it accepts (if any) and the procedure's possible return values.

  While the procedure is still in development (that is, before so-called code complete), consider adding other notes that document the progress of the procedure, remaining work left to be done, or perhaps notes about the revision level and the names of the developers.

- Local constant declarations (**Const** statements)

- Variable declarations (**Dim** statements)

- Procedure initialization code (for example, setting counters to 0)

- Remaining code (the bulk of the procedure)

- Error-handling code (if any)

Naming Functions

Function names should be as long as necessary to convey meaning without unnecessary abbreviations and, where possible, without requiring comments. Conversely, however, try to avoid particularly long function names that would otherwise require a lot of typing (for example, GetDailyTasksByPriority).

Avoid using underscores in function names; instead, use upper- and lowercase letters:

Satisfactory	*Unsatisfactory*
GetWindowText	Get_Window_Text
InitGlobals	INITGLOBALS
FormIsLoaded	Loaded

In general, name your functions according to their function or context. For example, you might name a function GetWindowText because that is what it does—it gets the window text. Still, you might create another function that calculates a shipping charge that might best be named ShippingCharges, not CalculateShipping, even though that is what the function does:

```
SalesTotal = OrderAmount + CalculateShipping() ' Bad example.
SalesTotal = OrderAmount + ShippingCharges() ' Good example.
```

In this second example, the name of the function is appropriate given its context. Name your functions according to how and where they will be used.

Using and Avoiding Subprocedures

Generally, create user-defined subprocedures only when you know (with reasonable certainty) the procedures will *never* be needed outside of Access Basic. Consider that you cannot call subprocedures from outside Access Basic, but you can call function procedures from queries and expressions on forms as record sources for controls, in reports, and from macros—from anywhere in your application. Therefore, use function procedures, even if the utility of a function's return value is not immediately apparent. If you were later to decide you need to call a Sub procedure from outside Access Basic, you would have to convert it to a function. Having created a function in the first place is better than having to make the conversion.

Declaring Private Procedures

Unless you need to call a Function procedure from outside the module in which it appears, declare it to be a private procedure:

```
Private Function GetScreenType() As Integer
```

Private procedures are limited in scope, which means the function can be "seen" only from within the module in which it appears. The effect of this is that you cannot call the function from outside the module itself. At first this may seem like a useless or unnecessary limitation, but in some cases this is a desired effect. One benefit to creating private procedures is that there is no chance of a name conflict with other functions since only non-private procedures are visible, or have scope, throughout an application. In contrast, a private procedure in one module can have the same name as another private procedure in a second module.

Procedures inside form modules are automatically private and do not require the **Private** reserved word. Consequently, they may be called only from the corresponding form. If you want to be able to call one of these functions from someplace other than the form or the form module in which it appears, you need to create a general-purpose function (in other than a form module) instead of a private function.

Indenting Code

You should indent all lines except the function declaration itself, the **End Function** statement, and any line labels (most functions do not have line labels). You may be accustomed to placing comments or declarations (**Dim** statements) to the far left of the Module window but doing so disrupts the ability to quickly determine where blocks of code begin and end.

The default tab stop width in Microsoft Access is four spaces; you should avoid changing this default for several reasons:

- Narrower tab stop widths (fewer than four spaces) result in more compact, often harder-to-read code.

- Wider tab stops (more than four spaces) result in longer lines that tend to extend beyond the limits of the Module window, thus requiring excessive scrolling. In addition, longer lines also tend to wrap when you print your code (unless you print in landscape mode, something other developers will not expect).

- Especially in a multiple-developer environment, the standard tab stop width is essential to presenting a unified application that also matches what other non-developer users are accustomed to using.

Within a function, you should indent additional levels:

- All lines in a loop

- Lines in an **If...Then...Else** construct

- Cases in a **Select Case** block

- All lines within a **Case** of a **Select Case** block

- All lines between an **AddNew** or **Edit** method and its corresponding **Update** or **Rollback** method

Line Spacing

As the preceding example procedure illustrates, you should add blank lines to increase the readability of your code. Insert blank lines before and after declarations, between significant blocks of code (you decide what is significant), and before and after loops and similar block constructs. The amount of

368

such "white space" can vary greatly depending on the particular procedure. The goal of blank lines is to isolate major sections to increase the readability of your code.

Naming Constants

Generally, constants should be all uppercase with allowable underscores. Examples of satisfactory constants include IGNORECASE and HOTPINK. Depending on the application, you also may want to include a prefix that identifies the kind or category of constant, as in the case of message box-related constants that would otherwise start with MB_ (for example, MB_ICONEXCLAMATION).

Avoid same-name constants that have conflicting scope. For example, avoid naming a global constant and a module-level constant with the same name. Many new users may not understand the implications of scope and may become confused at how Microsoft Access "ignores" a seemingly good global constant when there is a scoping conflict.

Declaring and Naming Variables

If you have included the **Option Explicit** statement in every module (and you should), you must explicitly declare each variable:

```
Dim MyDB As Database, MyTable As Table
Dim MyControl As Control
Dim SalesTotal As Currency, X As Integer
```

Avoid type-declaration characters. For example, although X% is an otherwise valid variable name, you should avoid using the percent sign (%). One reason for avoiding type-declaration characters is that not all data types have a type-declaration character: For example, Variants.

Another reason for omitting type-declaration characters is that they add only marginal utility to variable names at the expense of making the variables harder to read. Moreover, most function procedures are so short that, if you should have to determine a variable's data type, you can look through the procedure's **Dim** statements. If your variables have meaningful names, you probably will not need to determine the data type at all. For example, you can generally assume a variable named City is a string, SalesTotal is a currency variable, and NumRecords is a long integer. In contrast, City$, SalesTotal@, and NumRecords& are unnecessarily harder to read and add little, if any, value.

For the same reasons that they add little utility and make your code harder to read, you also should avoid the so-called Hungarian notation, or prefixes. For example, you would not name these same variables strCity, curSalesTotal, or lngNumRecords. Again, if you need to make sure of a variable's data type, look for its **Dim** statement.

Generally, group the variable declarations by function; that is, group the database object variables together, looping control variables together, and so on. Within each group, declare the variables alphabetically.

Variable names should be as long as necessary to convey meaning without undue confusion or unnecessary abbreviations. For example, Org is a poor abbreviation for Original. If you decide to abbreviate, choose abbreviations that are intuitive to general users and not necessarily developers (remember, you may not always be the only one who has to look at your code). In this example, Orig is a better abbreviation than Org, which could be mistaken to mean Organization.

Tip: By convention, only constants and user-defined types appear in all uppercase. Avoid using underscores in variable names; instead, use upper- and lowercase letters:

Satisfactory	Unsatisfactory
SalesTotal	Sales_Total
RecordsFound	RECORDSFOUND
X	x

As with constants, avoid same-name variables that have conflicting scope.

To make better use of memory, try to avoid declaring large, static arrays. Instead, programmatically determine how large the array needs to be and use the **ReDim** statement to declare the array.

Tip: When you are done using a static array, **ReDim** the array to zero elements. In the case of a dynamic array, use the **Erase** statement to free the memory used by the array.

Adding Comments and Documenting Your Work

No matter how intuitively you name database objects and variables, nothing can replace descriptive, clear, and concise comments. Long after you have worked on your code, you or other developers (or users) will return to the application. One goal of commenting your work is to minimize the time it takes to figure out what your code does and how it works.

Earlier in this chapter, "Order of Elements in a Function" discussed using a "header" that describes the purpose of the procedure, the arguments it accepts (if any), and the procedure's possible return value(s). These general notes are intended to document *what* the procedure does but not necessarily *how* it works.

Most function procedures contain sufficiently complex code requiring additional comments in the body of the procedure. For some sections of code, particularly **Select...Case** and **If...Then** constructs, a *block comment* is appropriate. A block comment describes the actions or results of a

block of code (hence the name block comment). A block comment begins in the same column as the block to which it applies.

```
' Loop through the records looking for all Sales
' representatives and change their titles to Account
' Executive.
Do Until MySet.EOF
...
Loop
```

For many other lines of code, including lines otherwise documented with a block comment, you can add comments to the end of the line, aligned in the same column whenever possible.

```
Function csvNullToZero (Number As Variant) As Variant

    If Not IsNull(Number) Then  ' If it isn't Null...
        csvNullToZero = Number  ' ...return same value.
    Else
        csvNullToZero = 0       ' Otherwise, return 0.
    End If

Loop
```

Tip: As you try to align comments in the Module window, it is sometimes difficult to tell which column you are in, especially if previous comments earlier in the procedure have scrolled off the screen. Consider maximizing the Module window and then using the TAB key to move the insertion point to a reference point on the toolbar. For example, you might position the insertion point at the tab position immediately before or after the Run button.

Whether a line requires a comment depends on the particular function the line appears in, the function's construction, and the comments around and near the line. All comments should end with trailing punctuation, usually a period.

Choosing between Modules and Macros

The decision to choose modules over macros (or vice versa) depends greatly on your particular application, any product elements you may be trying to illustrate (if you are creating a teaching application), as well as the need for consistency among all of your applications.

As you decide when and whether to use either modules or macros, try to remember that typical users must first acquire a full understanding of macro actions before they can fully implement the power of Access Basic. Remember, too, that most users are familiar with macros but not Basic.

Even so, there are some easily identified situations in which either modules or macros are the better choice.

371

Choose macros in the following situations:

- When you do not require error handling; that is, the actions in the macro cannot possibly create a run-time error condition.

- To create an AutoExec macro that runs each time users run your application. Depending on the complexity of the macro and whether you require any error handling, consider creating a single-action AutoExec macro that uses the **RunCode** macro action to call a function named AutoExec.

- For quick prototyping when speed of development is paramount or when you are testing ideas for application task flow.

- To create custom menu bars, something you cannot do in Access Basic code.

- To create an AutoKeys macro that remaps, or reassigns, keys.

- When the actions you want to take are simple, fairly straightforward, and well-defined.

- When it is practical, makes sense, and does not require elaborate branching to other macros, does not involve loops, and is easy to follow.

Choose modules in the following situations:

- When you require error handling.

- When a macro starts to get too involved because of excessive jumping around between macros (using the **RunMacro** macro action).

- When a condition to a macro action is complex or particularly lengthy, making it hard to read; in this case, convert the macro to a function.

- When the user interface elements prove inadequate and the required macro action does not exist.

- To implement transactions.

- To process data one record at a time (for example, looping through a recordset).

- To create new database objects.

- To call a Windows API function or a function in a Dynamic Link Library (DLL).

Miscellaneous Issues

Supplementing the issues raised earlier in this chapter, the following collection of guidelines summarizes additional miscellaneous standards you should consider as you develop your applications.

- Always use the **Option Explicit** statement. Including **Option Explicit** requires you to declare every variable. Among the goals and effects of this statement are to prevent misspellings and to make sure you properly declare the variable data types. Notice, however, that **Option Explicit** is effective only in the module in which it appears, so you must add the statement to every module, even such modules as Global Constants, Declarations, and Messages (just in case you or someone else adds executable code to these modules).

- Use the plus sign (+) for math operations and the ampersand (&) for string concatenation. Avoid using the plus sign to handle strings; as it relates to null values, if you want to reproduce the effects of using the plus sign, create a function that handles this correctly.

- Use the reserved words **True** and **False**, and not the values–1 and 0.

- To improve the speed performance of your application, open all modules, choose the Compile Loaded Modules command from the Run menu and then explicitly save each module. This technique ensures that none of your code has to be compiled at runtime.

- As you work on your code, certain elements remain work-in-progress. To identify these unfinished areas, add a comment formatted like that shown here:

      ' UNDONE

  Follow a single apostrophe with a single space and the word UNDONE and any additional, optional comments. Adopting this guideline not only lets you quickly search for any unfinished code, but also lets others know whether code is broken or simply incomplete.

- "If you turn it on, turn it off. If you turn it off, turn it back on."

  If you turn echo off, be sure you turn echo back on; if you enable error trapping, disable it when you are finished with it. The same holds true for enabling and disabling system warnings toggled with the **SetWarnings** macro action. Do not rely on Microsoft Access to turn these settings back on for you.

- When you want to manipulate or work with strings, use the $ forms of functions. Use the non-$ forms when you work with or manipulate Variants. Such functions include **Left[$]**, **Right[$]**, and **Format[$]**.

- Generally, place only one statement on a line. Exceptions include simple assignments such as initialization code at the beginning of a procedure.

      X = 0: Y = 0

  One other exception is combining multiple variable declarations on a single line:

      Dim X As Integer, Y As Integer

Summary

Adopting a consistent naming convention is not just about making your code pretty and compliant with somebody else's guidelines. Rather, a carefully thought-out and readable style is essential to making your applications easy to design and easy to maintain. Indeed, even if you do not agree with all of the guidelines described in this chapter, you should adopt the ones that make sense in the context of your own applications.

Whereas this chapter has concerned itself largely with behind-the-scenes issues, the next chapter, "Application Design Guidelines," discusses ways you can make your applications more attractive and usable.

18

Application Design Guidelines

The previous chapter, "Naming Conventions and Style Guidelines," discussed a variety of strategies for writing clean, logical code, designing efficient macros, and naming your database objects with meaningful names. Still, your applications will not be used if they do not look good or simply are not usable.

This chapter covers the following:

- Designing the User Interface

- Dealing with International Issues

- Exploring Miscellaneous Design Issues

- Accommodating Disabled Users

- Reading the Control Panel Settings

Designing the User Interface

As you build your databases, keep in mind that the user interface—the things the user sees—is the most important part of your application (at least to the user). Although the underlying logic, code, and algorithms also are important, your consistent use of appropriate screen elements directly affects the user's ability to use your application. It is true that image is everything: Create an application that is pleasant to look at and easy to use, and users will use it.

Consistency within an application (and between multiple applications) makes it easier to learn your current applications and minimizes the time it takes to learn a new application. Consistency also reduces confusion that otherwise arises when different applications perform similar functions, but in different ways.

This section discusses some of the major issues related to the Windows environment in general and the Access database environment in particular. For more detailed information about designing effective interfaces for Windows and Access, see *The Windows Interface—An Application Design Guide* (MS Press).

Using and Avoiding Icons

Icons, especially those on toolbars and attached to command buttons, can be an effective means by which users can identify and invoke certain actions. Typical icons include printers (to print the current form or report), disks (to save the current record), and so on. Icons are most useful, however, when they are instantly understood and unambiguous (see fig. 18.1).

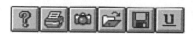

Figure 18.1. Choose icons that make sense and are not confusing.

An icon that is not understood and intuitive often results in either of two user responses:

- First, the user presses the button just to see what happens (and might not like the consequences).

- Second, and more frequently, the button remains unused simply because the user is afraid of what *might* happen.

To be effective elements of your application, icons must make sense, not just to you but to other users, as well. You may not be able to represent all actions with an icon, and not every possible action can be represented with a single picture, at least not the size of an icon. Depending on your application, consider not using icons at all. Instead, set the **Caption** properties for the command buttons (see fig. 18.2).

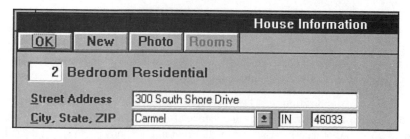

Figure 18.2. Use captions when an icon will not work.

In figure 18.2, the captions on the New and OK buttons clearly indicate their functions. Even though a suitable icon for each button might exist (for example, a new document and an open door), it is important for your application to use icons or captions consistently. If one form uses captions, they all should. Similarly, if you use icons in one form, other forms also should use icons.

Providing Menu Commands

Users like applications with uncluttered, easy to read screens. Throughout your application, you may be tempted to include a command button for every available function. On a sufficiently complex form, however, there may not be room for all the buttons (see fig. 18.3).

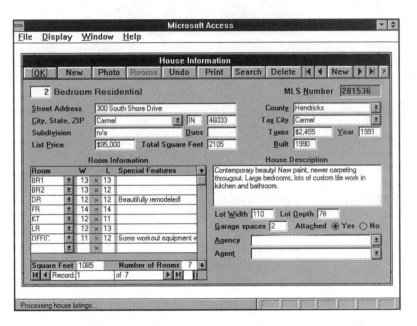

Figure 18.3.   Avoid adding too many buttons to complex forms.

To avoid this clutter, each command button on a form should have a corresponding menu command, but not every menu command necessarily requires a command button. You should include buttons for only the most frequent activities, such as printing, sorting, searching, and similar functions. For less frequent activities, such as configuring the system or setting a password, use menu commands (see fig. 18.4).

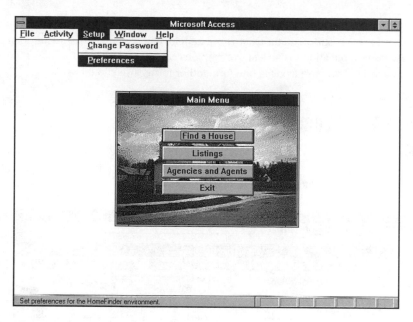

Figure 18.4. Place seldom-used commands in menus.

Providing Mouse and Keyboard Support

Wherever practical, provide both mouse and keyboard equivalents. Not only should all command buttons on a form have an equivalent menu command, but all mouse actions should have a menu command. You might, for example, create a text box the user can double-click to open a second pop-up form. You should make that action available through a menu command, as well, since not all users are able to operate a mouse and some have difficulty managing the double-click.

Most users are accustomed to using the keyboard and, except for drawing programs and other applications that demand precise positioning, requiring a mouse is an unnecessary restriction placed on the user. View the mouse as an enhancement to your application, not a requirement.

Using and Avoiding Access Keys

Access keys are key sequences the user can press to either open menus or move to specific controls on a form. Figure 18.5 illustrates a form that has a number of access keys, identified by underscores in their labels.

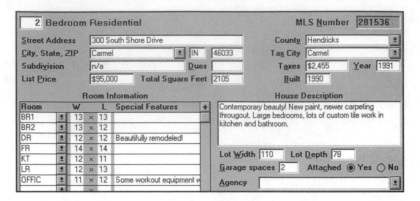

Figure 18.5. You can use access keys to let users navigate from control to control.

Menu Access Keys

The user can open any of the menus in a menu bar by clicking them with the mouse or by pressing the corresponding access key. For example, pressing Alt+F would open the File menu without the user having to move his hands from the keyboard to the mouse. Although you are not required to define access keys for menus, it is a Windows standard to include them.

As you define your menu access keys, keep them consistent from form to form. For example, if you use Alt+F for the File menu, do so throughout your application. Do not use Alt+F on one form and Alt+O on another. Table 18.1 lists some of the more common menu access keys you might use in your own applications.

Table 18.1. Common Menu Access Keys

Menu	Access Key
File	F
Edit	E
Format	T
Help	H
New	N
Open	O
Search	S
View	V
Window	W

In most cases, menu access keys are the first letter of the menu name. The access key for the File menu, for example, is **F**. However, where you have multiple menus beginning with the same letter, you have to choose another letter for the second menu. For example, if you have a File menu (that already uses the letter **F**), a Format menu in the same menu bar uses a different letter, in this case **T**.

You should use the same access keys from form to form. If a menu bar includes a Format menu but no File menu, you would still use Alt+T, even though Alt+F would otherwise be available.

Control Access Keys

In figure 18.5, pressing Alt+S lets the user move the focus to the Street Address text box, Alt+P moves to the List Price text box, and so on. Access keys let the user navigate quickly from control to control, as opposed to having to press the Tab key repeatedly.

As useful as they might seem, you should *avoid* access keys for form controls because you will quickly run out of letters. For example, if you have already used Alt+H for a Help menu, you cannot use it for a form control named HomePhone. For that control, you have to choose a different letter, perhaps **P**. However, that might also conflict with an access key for a menu named Preferences. You could choose the letter **O**, but that might conflict with a menu access key for Options, and so on.

Even if you do not have a conflict with any of your menu access keys, the number of letters left over will likely be far too little to accommodate all of the controls on the form. This means you will have to assign access keys to some controls, but not others. Users expect consistency, and not assigning an access key to each control will lead to confusion, or at least to the question of why some controls have access keys and some do not. For most applications, you are probably better off not using control access keys at all.

Reassigning Function Keys

You can use the AutoKeys macro to reassign certain key sequences, usually to automate operations or to inhibit normal program behavior. When the user presses the F11 key, for example, Access displays the Database window. Because most developers want to keep the Database window hidden, you will want to reassign the F11 key so that it either does something else or nothing at all. You might consider reassigning F11 so that it displays a message like that shown in figure 18.6.

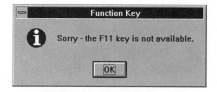

Figure 18.6.   You can prevent users from displaying the Database window by reassigning the F11 key.

You also might want to reassign other functions keys that have special meanings in Access. Table 18.2 lists some of the function keys you should consider reassigning.

Table 18.2. Selected Function Key Assignments

Key	Purpose
F1	Displays context-sensitive help (reassign if you have not provided your own custom help file)
Ctrl+F4	Closes the active window
F11	Displays the Database window
Alt+F1	(same as F11)
F12	Displays the Save As dialog box
Alt+F2	(same as F12)
Shift+F12	Saves the current database object (usually a form or report)
Alt+Shift+F2	(same as Shift+F12)
F7	Displays the Find dialog box

You should consider reassigning these function keys because their default behavior is not normally needed outside the development environment. For example, you may not want your users to close forms using Ctrl+F4 and might instead want them to press your own OK or Cancel buttons. Figure 18.7 illustrates one way you can reassign the Ctrl+F4 key sequence.

> **Tip:** You also might want to reassign some of the default function key assignments to implement your own functionality. For example, the F12 key normally opens the Save As dialog box, something to which most users do not need access. Rather than leave this key enabled and available to the unwary user, you can have it insert the current date. In the AutoKeys macro, enter F12 for the macro name and use the **SendKeys** macro action to send Ctrl+; (semicolon). It is far easier to explain to users that they can press F12 to insert today's date than it is to explain how to press Ctrl+; (this is further complicated on some keyboards because the semicolon may require pressing the Shift key, as well as the Ctrl and semicolon keys).

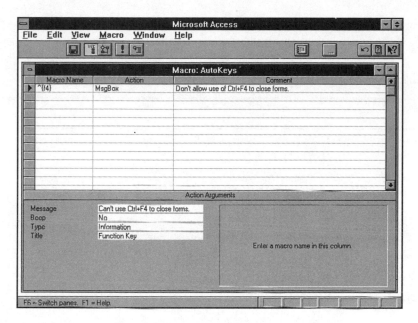

Figure 18.7. Inhibit users from closing forms by remapping the Ctrl+F4 key sequence.

Dealing with International Issues

To compete successfully in international markets, you should ensure that your applications can be easily adapted to accommodate differences in language, culture, and hardware. In addition, your applications should take into account specific user preferences.

With commercially distributed applications where users typically see only the forms and reports in your applications, you can usually design the underlying expressions, queries, macros, and modules pretty much any way you like. You can be neat and orderly, or you can be less concerned with the appearance of your code.

For example, your users do not know or care whether you used abbreviations and contractions or chose to spell names out. Still, your applications may be used not only as fully functional applications but also as learning tools. As such, every aspect of your applications will be closely inspected by the users. Your sensitivity to international issues can help facilitate acceptance of your applications.

This section explores these and other issues that affect your ability to create and distribute international-aware applications.

Handling the Interface Text

Even if users do not care about an application's underlying code, they are keenly aware and concerned about the text that appears in the application's interface: on forms, in message boxes, and in reports.

> **Tip:** As you design your application, keep in mind that it may someday be localized into any number of languages. When translated, some text expands to much larger strings. For example, German text is generally 40% longer than the equivalent English text. You should design your application with this in mind and allow plenty of room for somewhat lengthy translations by making labels, text boxes, combo boxes, and list boxes wider than usual.

Other Text

The interface text includes other elements that are just as important as the text on forms and reports. Specifically, the names of forms, tables, reports, queries, and modules may be localized since these names appear in the Database window and in various lists and combo boxes. Particularly important are the names you give to table fields, since these appear throughout the application in queries, list boxes, and in modules. As a guideline, choose names that make sense to the user, and not necessarily to just developers. Avoid field names that are unnecessarily abbreviated or cryptic.

> For more information, see the section "Naming Database Objects and Controls" in Chapter 17, "Naming Conventions and Style Guidelines."

Your Application as a Template

In addition to anticipating various foreign languages, you also might consider that your application may be used as a template for other applications. For example, you might develop an order entry system that labels a customer's name Customer Name. A user might take this system and create another that requires an entirely different label, perhaps Subscriber. Allowing enough room for translations generally provides room for such alternate text.

Creating Sample Data

If your application includes sample data, you should anticipate the international nature of your users and include data that does not reflect bias toward or against any one country. An order-entry system, for example, should include data that includes customers from around the world, not from just one

country (see fig. 18.8). The data included with the Northwind Traders database is a good model for sample data because it shows how you can include customers and suppliers from many countries.

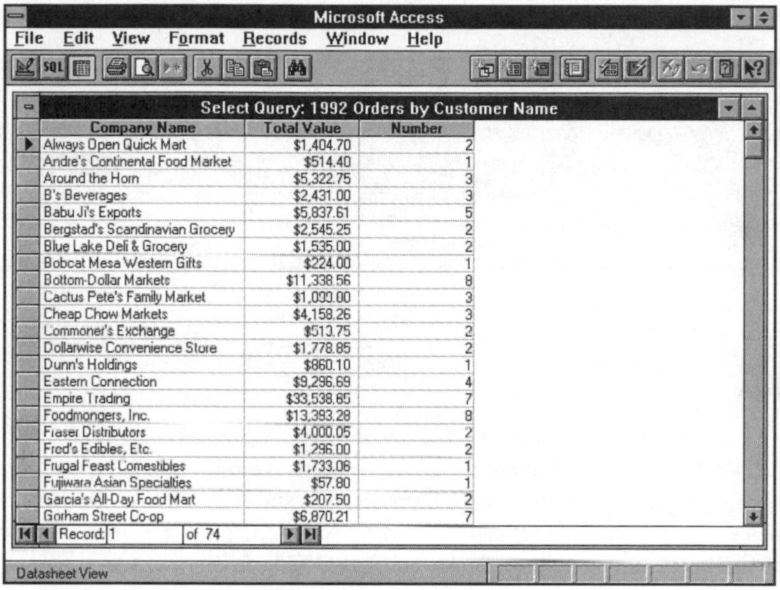

Figure 18.8. Include enough sample data in your database to make demonstrations meaningful.

Create enough sample data to fully illustrate your application's capabilities. An order-entry application should have enough order-detail records and product-detail records to make the sample orders meaningful. An order with several items is far more illustrative than an order with only one item.

Other applications, such as the HomeFinder sample application included with this book, do not require an extensive amount of sample data to show how the system works.

Anticipating Different Hardware and Formats

If your applications will be used in different countries, your users' hardware and formatting requirements may not be the same as yours.

Hardware

Throughout the world, display, printer, and keyboard hardware is not dominated by United States standards. Whenever possible, you should design your applications knowing they may be run on a wide variety of equipment.

Displays

You should design your forms, dialog boxes, and other interface elements so that they maintain their aesthetic appeal in various resolutions and screen-aspect ratios. If possible, change your video display driver to see how your application looks in different configurations, especially the more common ones, VGA (640 x 480) and SVGA (800 x 600).

Particularly important is to make sure that you do not create forms that look fine in one resolution but either too small or too large in another. Figure 18.9 illustrates the effect of having designed a form in regular VGA resolution and then running it in SVGA resolution.

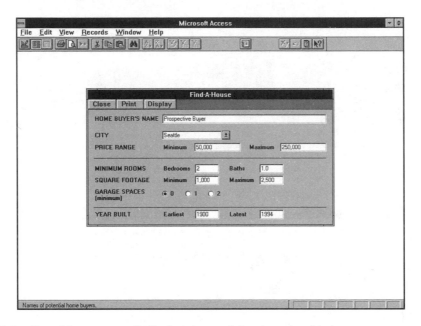

Figure 18.9. If possible, run your application in various resolutions to see how it looks.

The form in figure 18.9 appears smaller than expected; in many cases this is acceptable, especially if you have centered the form (by having set its **AutoCenter** property to Yes). Although it is possible to detect the screen resolution and resize the form to fit the Access window, that will not resize any of the controls on the form (see fig. 18.10).

If you create a form in a higher resolution and then run it in a lower resolution, the effect is the opposite: forms appear much larger than intended (see fig. 18.11).

> **Tip:** If you are unhappy with the appearance of your forms in various resolutions, you can detect the current screen resolution and then change the size and position of all the controls on the form. Although it is time-consuming to determine the exact coordinates, sizes, and fonts, this is probably better than having to maintain multiple versions of each form, one for each resolution you intend to support.

385

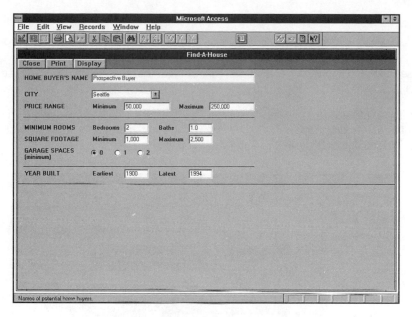

Figure 18.10.   Access does not resize controls when you enlarge the form window.

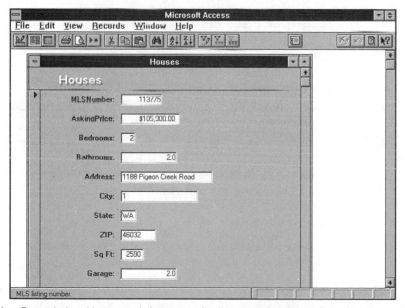

Figure 18.11.   Forms designed in one resolution may not fit when run under other configurations.

Printers

When you design reports, forms, or other objects the user is likely to print, format them for the United States standard letter-sized paper (8 1/2 x 11 in) even though the international standard is A4 paper (210 x 297 mm). If you do this, reports still fit on the larger A4 paper without having to adjust report layouts. It is better to design for smaller paper (letter-sized) and have it print on larger paper (A4) than it is to have a report not fit.

To set the paper size, open each report or other object in Design view, choose the Print Setup command from the File menu, and then select the A4 paper size (see fig. 18.12).

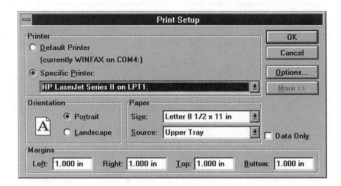

Figure 18.12   You set the paper size in the Print Setup dialog box.

Keyboards

International keyboards also may differ from those in the United States. In particular:

- If you have decided to use Access keys (see "Avoiding Access Keys" earlier in this chapter), choose Alt+key combinations carefully because some international keyboards use them to enter certain characters.

- Choose shortcuts that use punctuation marks carefully because some punctuation marks (for example, braces and brackets) are frequently not found on international keyboards or are available only in combination with the Alt key.

- Any documentation that describes the position of keys should take into account that not all keyboards have the same letters and characters in the same position. For example, you can expect to find the Y key along the top row of letter keys on a United States keyboard, but along the bottom row on a Swiss French keyboard.

Formats

Different countries often use substantially different formats for dates, time, currency, numbers, measurements, and telephone numbers. As a result, international-aware applications should allow

these formats to be changed easily. The Setup program for your application should set the default formats based on the settings obtained from the Windows Control Panel. Your application may also allow the formats to be changed whenever necessary during the normal use of the application. Such changes should not affect the system defaults.

Table 18.3 lists the most common format categories and the variables in each that may differ from country to country.

Table 18.3. International Formats

Category	Format considerations
Date	Order, separator, and long/short formats
Time	Separator and cycle (12-hour vs. 24-hour)
Physical quantity	Metric vs. English measurement system
Currency	Symbol and format (for example, trailing vs. preceding symbol)
Separators	List, decimal, and thousands separator
Telephone numbers	Separator for area codes and exchanges
Paper sizes	United States vs. European paper sizes

Wherever you determine the format for a date or currency field or a control, use the settings that the user has already set in the Control Panel (see "Reading the Control Panel Settings" later in this chapter).

Calendars

If your application contains calendar or date functions, you may need to consider that in some parts of the world, weeks do not always begin on the same day. In the United States the week begins on Sunday and ends on Saturday. In some other countries, however, the first day of the week is not on Sunday. For example, in Germany weeks begin on Monday and end on Sunday. Design your application so that the user can configure the beginning day of the week.

Exploring Miscellaneous Design Issues

The following collection of guidelines summarizes additional miscellaneous standards you should consider as you design your application and its interface.

- Avoid screen clutter; where practical, limit the amount of information that appears on a single form and use multiple pages or secondary (or pop-up) forms to present the less critical or important information.

- Allow sufficient "white space" around labels and other controls. Do not make buttons so short or narrow that their captions appear to touch the edges of the buttons.

  If necessary, either change the caption or make the button taller or wider (see fig. 18.13).

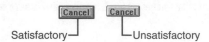

Satisfactory┘   └Unsatisfactory

Figure 18.13.   Avoid controls that are too short or too narrow.

- Try to limit the number of items or choices the user has at any given time. For example, try to avoid including more than eight selections on a main menu. If you have more selections than that, try to find a way to categorize them into major functions that reveal minor functions when chosen. Similarly, try to limit the size (height) of combo boxes and list boxes to eight items (the default for combo boxes is eight rows).

- Choose fonts that are likely to exist on users' systems. For example, Arial and Times New Roman are common fonts furnished with Microsoft Windows and you can safely assume these fonts have been installed. In contrast, avoid fonts that most users do not have. For example, the Tekton font might otherwise be suitable for a given application, but few users have the Tekton font installed. When you use an unavailable font, Windows substitutes a different (although not always equivalent) font, often with undesirable results.

- Avoid adding colons to labels and column headings (see fig. 18.14).

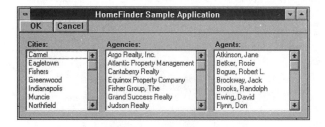

Figure 18.14.   Colons usually add nothing to the design of your forms.

- Unless you intend to leave the Database window open and visible to your users, hide the Database window as soon as possible. For more information, see Chapter 21, "Useful Functions."

- Make sure that every control that can get the focus has its **StatusBarText** property set and every toolbar button has ToolTips.

- Use the sunken effect to indicate that a control can get the focus and can be changed by the user. The sunken appearance is a visual cue to the user that the control is editable. Contrast this with a normal, unsunken control that is read-only (see fig. 18.15). For more information about the sunken effect and other visual cues, see Chapter 8, "Building the HomeFinder Forms."

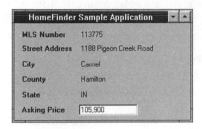

Figure 18.15. Use the sunken effect to indicate an editable control.

- Users expect that raised areas on a form can be pressed. For example, command and toggle buttons are raised and provide a visual cue that the control can be pressed. Avoid creating raised surfaces that cannot be pressed. For example, raised frames or option groups that enclose related controls should be either sunken or normal, but not raised (see fig. 18.16).

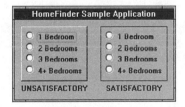

Figure 18.16. Raised areas appear, in this example erroneously, as if they can be pressed.

- Remove the Minimize button from modal forms by setting the **MinButton** property to **False**.

- Remove the Maximize button from forms that do not benefit from being maximized by setting the **MaxButton** property to **False**.

- When you remove the Minimum or Maximize buttons from a form, Access automatically removes the corresponding the Minimize and Maximize commands from the Control menu. However, you might consider removing the Control menu altogether on forms for which you provide an OK, Cancel, or Close button that closes the form. You can remove the Control menu by setting the **ControlBox** property to **False**.

Accommodating Disabled Users

Depending on your application, there may be some design decisions you can make to help disabled users adjust the interface. For example, you might include a configuration option that lets visually impaired users set a larger font size. Your application can further accommodate disabled users by observing these guidelines:

- Avoid using audio cues, such as beeps or other tones, for any situation that absolutely requires the user's attention.

  Certain users cannot hear the sound, while some systems are situated such that the computer's speaker cannot be heard at all.

- Similarly, use color to accentuate or highlight, but do not rely on color alone to provide essential information. Some users cannot distinguish certain color combinations.

  For example, do not rely on the color red to indicate a negative number. Instead, use a format that includes a minus sign (–12.00) or angle brackets (<$12.00>).

- Color settings should be configurable by the user without having to open forms and reports in Design View. You should include a function in your application that reads the colors previously set by the user in the Control Panel and sets form colors accordingly. You might like blue text on a gray background, but your monochrome laptop users might have a hard time seeing the screen.

- Do not require rapid responses; avoid time-out situations that require the user to respond quickly (except in the case of game applications).

  If you must include a time-out period, as in the case of a logon screen, make the time-out period long, permit the user to run the application in "slow" mode, or consider allowing the user to configure the rate at which your timer routine runs.

- Avoid rapid flashing of any screen element, including the title bar; rapid flashing can cause seizures in some users.

  If you include flashing, make the flashing rate no faster than two times per second and, where practical, allow the user to set the rate.

Reading the Control Panel Settings

Some of the user-definable settings you use in your application should, in fact, be the same as the Windows system settings. To display or change these settings, you open the Control Panel and choose an appropriate category (see fig. 18.17).

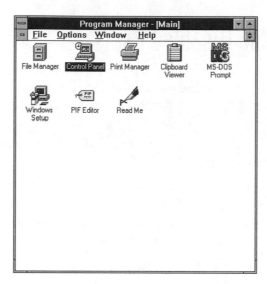

Figure 18.17.   Open the Control Panel to edit Windows settings.

For example, to set the date, time, and currency formats, you choose the International category. The International dialog box appears (see fig. 18.18).

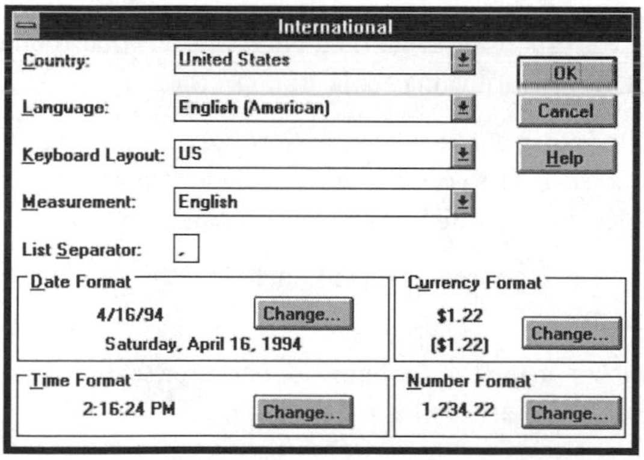

Figure 18.18.   You can set a wide variety of formats in the International dialog box.

When the user makes changes to the international settings, what he is really doing is modifying entries in the [intl] section of his WIN.INI file. A typical [intl] section looks like this:

```
[intl]
sLanguage=enu
sCountry=United States
iCountry=1
iDate=0
iTime=0
iTLZero=0
iCurrency=0
iCurrDigits=2
iNegCurr=0
iLzero=1
iDigits=2
iMeasure=1
s1159=AM
s2359=PM
sCurrency=$
sThousand=,
sDecimal=.
sDate=/
sTime=:
sList=,
sShortDate=M/d/yy
sLongDate=dddd, MMMM dd, yyyy
```

To read the international Control Panel settings directly from the INI file, you need to call two Windows API functions, csvGetProfileInt (for numeric entries such as iCurrDigits) and csvGetProfileString (for string entries such as sCurrency). You can use the following user-defined functions to read the desired entries from the [intl] section.

```
Function csvGetIntlInt (Entry As String) As Integer

    Const TITLEBAR = "csvGetIntlInt"
    Dim Msg As String, Default As Integer, X As Integer

    Default = -1
    If Entry <> "" Then
        X = csvGetProfileInt("intl", Entry, Default)
    End If
    If X >= Default Then
        csvGetIntlInt = X
    Else
        Msg = "Invalid argument '" & Entry & "'."
        MsgBox Msg, csvMB_ICONEXCLAMATION, TITLEBAR
        csvGetIntlInt = Default
    End If

End Function
Function csvGetIntlString (Entry As String) As String

    Const TITLEBAR = "csvGetIntlString"
    Dim Msg As String, Default As String, Size As Integer
    Dim Text As String * 128, X As Integer

    Default = ""
```

```
    Size = Len(Text)
    If Entry <> "" Then
        X = csvGetProfileString("intl", Entry, Default,
        [IconCont]Text, Size)
    End If
    If X Then
        csvGetIntlString = Left$(Text, X)
    Else
        Msg = "Invalid argument '" & Entry & "'."
        MsgBox Msg, csvMB_ICONEXCLAMATION, TITLEBAR
        csvGetIntlString = Default
    End If

End Function
```

 Note: You need both functions because the csvGetProfileInt API function returns only integers and csvGetProfileString returns only strings. The WIN.INI file contains both integer and string entries.

The following example illustrates how you can format a currency field using the currency symbol (sCurrency) and number of decimal places (iCurrDigits) defined with the Control Panel.

```
= Format([My Field], Left$(csvGetIntlString("sCurrency")
[IconCont] & "0.000000000", csvGetIntlInt("iCurrDigits") + 3))
```

Summary

A consistent, easy to use interface is among the most important and visible element of a successful application. Your choice of icons, menu bars, and toolbars will go a long way toward improving your applications both as commercial releases and as teaching tools for other developers.

International and disabled users will benefit greatly from your having anticipated their unique needs. Accommodating the different hardware standards in use throughout the world will make it easier for a wider variety of users to run your applications. In addition, many of the settings you might otherwise code into your applications can instead be read from the Control Panel and the user's WIN.INI file.

The next chapter, "Creating and Using Libraries," discusses how you can use libraries to minimize the amount of application-specific code required for your applications.

19

Creating and Using Libraries

An Access library database (library) is a collection of database objects that you can install and then have available to all applications. When you create a library, you typically include only general-purpose objects that need to be shared across multiple applications, not just one.

You create libraries to store usually generic, general-purpose forms, macros, Access Basic Function procedures, toolbars, and other database objects. Once installed and loaded, these objects are available to all applications as if they were part of the applications themselves.

This chapter covers the following:

- Libraries
- Wizards
- Builders
- Add-In Libraries

Libraries

A *library database* (or *library*) typically contains forms and code that perform application-independent functions. For example, you might create a library that contains generic tools and utilities that all applications can share. You do not add application-specific forms or code to a library because only one application would need them. Although it would not otherwise cause other applications to work any less efficiently, the extra overhead of the library would waste memory.

Part of the appeal of library databases is that their code and other objects are available from within all applications. If you have multiple applications that use common forms or routines, it may make sense to place them in a library and reduce the amount of duplicity across all your applications. Later sections in this chapter discuss strategies for deciding what you should include in your libraries.

Tip: You can create and install multiple libraries. For example, you might have a form-only library, a code-only library, or some combination. Usually, however, you create and install only one library that contains all the desired objects.

There are five steps to creating and using a library:

1. Decide what will eventually go into the library and then create those objects (usually just code, but it could include forms and other objects, as well).

2. Test the objects to make sure they do or perform as you expect.

3. Create the library.

4. Install the library in your MSACC20.INI file.

5. Test the objects once more to make sure they perform properly as a library.

The following sections discuss these steps in detail.

Creating Objects for a Library

A library database is much like any code database, except that libraries are usually generic and do not refer to objects in a code database by name. For example, a library would not explicitly refer to the Customers table in the Northwind Traders database. However, the same library might accept the name of a table as an argument to a library function.

> Throughout most of your applications, you are likely to find that you call on a variety of functions all the time. For example, you might have functions that determine whether a form is loaded or that validate a state abbreviation, or even play a specified waveform (.WAV) file. For these and other common, generic functions, it is convenient to add the code somewhere only once and have it available to all applications.

The following steps outline the procedure you can follow to create a library containing functions you frequently use:

1. Open an existing database (but not the HomeFinder sample application) that you can use to test the functions. If you do not already have an existing database, create a new one.

> For details on how to create a new database, see Chapter 5, "The HomeFinder Application."

2. Create a new module that contains the functions you want. Follow the guidelines in Chapter 17, "Naming Conventions and Style Guidelines," and be sure to add the **Option Explicit** statement to the Declarations section.

3. Save the new module and name it Tools or some other name that you will remember as identifying generic, application-independent tools or utilities. Later, you will move this module to the library, but for now, you need it in the current database for testing purposes.

4. Next, create a new function that tests to see whether a form is loaded. For this example, name the function csvFormIsLoaded. The csv prefix identifies this as a function in a library, but you can use whatever prefix you like.

> **Tip:** All function names, whether they identify functions in the current database or in any loaded library, share the same *name space*. This simply means that you cannot have two functions with the same name, even if one is in a regular database and the other is in a library database. For example, if you have a library with a function named FormIsLoaded(), you cannot have a function in the current, regular database with the same name. For this reason, you will want to add a prefix to create a name that is unlikely to exist in any regular, non-library database.

5. Complete the csvFormIsLoaded( ) function by typing the following code in the Module window:

```
Function csvFormIsLoaded (ByVal MyFormName As String) As Integer

    ' Purpose: Determines whether a specified form is loaded.
    ' Accepts: MyFormName - string that is the form to test.
    ' Returns: True  - the form is loaded.
    '          False - the form is not loaded.
    ' Version: 1.0 23-Mar-94 CSV Initial revision.

    Dim X As String

    On Error Resume Next
    X = Forms(MyFormName).FormName
    If Err Then
        csvFormIsLoaded = False
    Else
        csvFormIsLoaded = True
    End If
    On Error GoTo 0

End Function
```

6. Make sure that you have no errors by choosing the Compile Loaded Modules command from the Run menu. If necessary, correct any mistakes in the function and try recompiling until Access no longer produces any error messages.

Testing the Objects

So far, only one object is to be included in the library, a function named csvFormIsLoaded(). To test this function, follow these steps:

1. Open the Immediate window and then call the function, passing to it the name of a form you know is not loaded (see fig. 19.1).

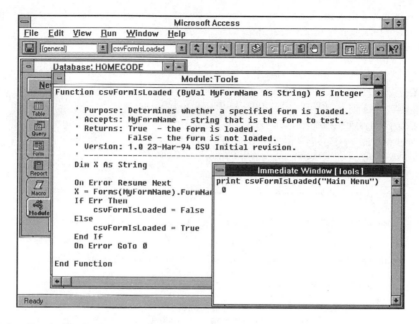

Figure 19.1. Test the function by calling it from the Immediate window.

As expected, the function returns 0 (False), which indicates the specified form is not loaded.

2. Next, open an existing form, and then call the function again. This time, specify the name of the loaded form.

> See Chapter 8, "Building the HomeFinder Forms," for instructions on how to create a form.
>
> You might take a look in Chapter 21, "Useful Functions," to see if there are any more generic, application-independent functions you want to add to the library. If you add more functions, be sure to test each one after you type it into the module.

3. The function returns 1 (True), which indicates that the specified form is loaded (see fig. 19.2). This test confirms that the function performs as expected.

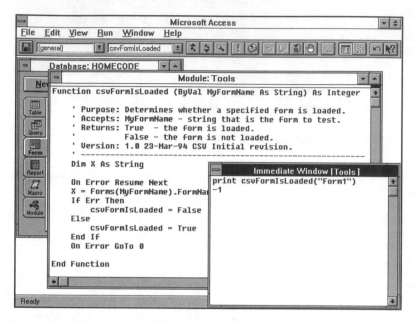

Figure 19.2. The function returns -1 (True) when you specify a loaded form.

Creating a Library

As discussed earlier in this chapter, libraries, or library databases, are pretty much the same as any other Access database, except that the objects in libraries are available to all applications. To create a library, you first create a new Access database.

> **Tip:** Although Microsoft recommends that you store your libraries in the same directory as the Access program files, you should store them in a separate directory named LIB beneath the Access directory instead. This strategy lets you easily identify which files are part of the standard Access installation and which files you created yourself. If necessary, return to the Windows Program Manager, load the File Manager, and then create the new LIB directory.

To create a new Access database, follow these steps:

1. Choose New Database from the File menu. Access displays the New Database dialog box (see fig. 19.3).

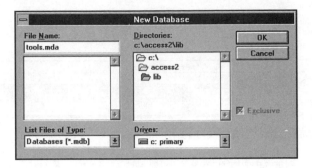

Figure 19.3. Specify the name of the new database in the New Database dialog box.

2. Select the destination for the library database and enter TOOLS.MDA for the name of the database.

   In this example, the TOOLS.MDA library database will be created in the LIB directory beneath the Access directory.

3. Click OK, or press Enter.

> **Note:** Although you can name library databases with whatever extension you like, by convention non-library code and data databases have an extension of .MDB and library databases have an extension of .MDA.

Now that you have a new database, you can import all the objects that will make it a library. Follow these steps:

1. Choose Import from the File menu. Access displays the Import dialog box listing a variety of data sources (see fig. 19.4).

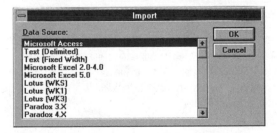

Figure 19.4. Use the Import dialog box to import database objects from other databases.

400

☞ **Note:** Your list of data sources is likely to differ from this example because you may have chosen different options when you installed Access.

2. Choose Microsoft Access and then click OK. Access displays the Select Microsoft Access Database dialog box.

3. In the File Name list box, select the database that contains the objects you want to import into the library and then click OK. Access displays the Import Objects dialog box (see fig. 19.5).

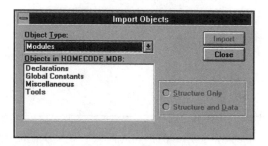

Figure 19.5. Select the specific object you want to import.

4. Choose Modules from the Object Type combo box, and then select the Tools module from the list of objects. (If you named your module something other than Tools, select the appropriate module.)

5. Click the Import button to import the module into the new TOOLS.MDA database. Access displays a message letting you know that the import was successful. Click OK to return to the Import Objects dialog box.

6. If you created other modules that need to be imported into the library database, select them from the list of module names and click the import button.

7. When you finish importing, click the Close button to close the dialog box.

Before you close the database and install it as a library, check once more to make sure there are no compile errors. Follow these steps:

1. In the Database window, click the Module button to display a list of all the modules in the database.

2. Select the Tools module and then click the Design button.

3. Choose the Compile Loaded Modules command from the Run menu. You must resolve any compile errors before you can install the library.

401

Tip: If you follow the guidelines in Chapter 17, "Naming Conventions and Style Guidelines," you may create separate modules for function declarations and global constants. If you do not import these modules, you may find that functions in the Tools module no longer compile without error.

Installing a Library

Access maintains all its library settings in your MSACC20.INI file. You install or remove libraries by adding or removing entries in the [Libraries] section. If you chose to include the Access wizards when you installed Access, your [Libraries] section probably looks like this:

```
[Libraries]
wzlib.mda=rw
wzTable.mda=rw
wzQuery.mda=rw
wzfrmrpt.mda=rw
wzbldr.mda=rw
```

Note: MSACC20.INI is in your Windows directory; you can open and edit this file with Notepad or any text editing program, even while Access is running.

The first part of each entry, to the left of the equal sign, identifies the name of the library database, and the second part following the equal sign indicates whether the library is to be opened for read/write access (rw) or for read-only access (ro). In the preceding example, wzlib.mda is a library opened for read/write access.

Tip: If a library does not need to create or change any objects in its own database, open the library for read-only access. Libraries opened for read-only access are somewhat faster and more efficient than those opened for read/write access.

Install the Tools library by adding a new entry to the [Libraries] section:

```
[Libraries]
wzlib.mda=rw
wzTable.mda=rw
wzQuery.mda=rw
wzfrmrpt.mda=rw
wzbldr.mda=rw
c:\access2\lib\tools.mda=ro
```

In this example, the new line at the bottom of the section installs the TOOLS.MDA database as a library. You can use any combination of uppercase or lowercase letters, and the order of entries in the [Libraries] section is not significant.

Note: If the library database is located in the same directory as the Access files, you do not need to specify a path to the database. If the library is located in a different directory, as in the preceding example, you must include the path in order for Access to locate the file.

Save the changes, but do not close Notepad until you are sure the functions in the newly-installed library function properly. If you have to uninstall the library during the next phase—debugging—you will already have the MSACC20.INI file available for editing.

Access reads the [Libraries] section only when you start the program, so restart Microsoft Access to let the system know the Tools library is now available.

Debugging a Library

As you built the library, you worked on it as you would any regular, non-library database. Once installed and loaded as a library, however, the rules are a bit different. You can no longer simply open the database and browse through its objects (code, forms, and so on). Indeed, the library is essentially hidden except that you can call on the objects in the library to perform whatever actions or functions you built into them.

There are two ways you can debug a library database:

- Disable the library so that you can open it as a regular database.
- Enable library debugging.

The following sections discuss each of these options in detail.

Disabling a Library

Disable a library by either removing its entry in the [Libraries] section of the MSACC20.INI file, or by inserting a semicolon (;) to the left of the entry (which comments out the entry). After you relaunch Access, you can then open the library database as a regular database.

 Tip: Commenting the library entry is better than removing it altogether. When you finish debugging the database, you can reinstall it as a library by removing the semicolon instead of retyping the entire line. Remember, you must restart Access to complete the reinstallation process.

Enabling Library Debugging

Because certain behaviors of the database may be different while the database is a library (and those are the behaviors you should test), a second method of debugging a library is probably better. With

403

this alternate technique, the database is allowed to remain loaded as a library but can be opened, inspected, and changed. Follow these steps:

1. Open your MSACC20.INI file using Notepad or another text editing program and locate the [Options] section. The [Options] section will typically appear at the beginning of the file and looks something like this:

```
[Options]
SystemDB=C:\ACCESS\system.mda
UtilityDB=C:\ACCESS\utility.mda
AllowCustomControls=1
AllowOLE1LinkFormat=0
```

2. To enable debugging of library databases, add a new line to the bottom of the [Options] section:

```
DebugLibraries=True
```

3. Save the changes and restart Access. Leave Notepad open, as you may want to return to the file to disable library debugging. To disable library debugging, change the "True" to "False", save the changes, and then restart Access.

> **Tip:** When you enable library debugging using this technique, all the libraries are available to you in the Module window. Although this provides a great deal of flexibility (because you can browse all of the library code), it also incurs a performance penalty when you choose the Compile Loaded Modules command from the Run menu or when you search for text with the Find or Replace commands from the Edit menu. In contrast, when you disable library debugging, Access compiles the library code only when you first start Microsoft Access.

Locating Function Procedures in a Library Database

When you open a module in Design view, you can choose the Procedures command from the View menu (or press F2) to display the View Procedures dialog box. The dialog includes a combo box from which you can select a module, along with a list box from which you choose the function procedure you want. Notice that the combo box lists only modules in the current database (see fig. 19.6).

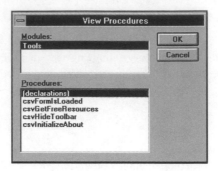

Figure 19.6. Display the View Procedures dialog box to locate modules and procedures.

You may need to view or edit a library database while it is installed as a library. After you enable library debugging, you can browse and edit modules in the current database plus any of the library databases (see fig. 19.7). When you select a database from the combo box along the bottom of the dialog box, Access displays the modules (and procedures) in that database.

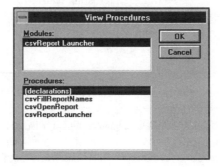

Figure 19.7. When you enable library debugging, you can choose a specific database.

> You can view and edit procedures in any module for which you otherwise have permissions. For more information about security and assigning permissions, see Chapter 22, "Implementing Security."

If you previously installed the Tools library, you can select the TOOLS.MDA database to view a list of the available modules.

Again, remember that because enabling library debugging degrades performance, you should disable debugging when you are sure that your libraries are functioning properly.

Wizards

Wizards are libraries that perform more complex operations or activities than the kinds of libraries discussed earlier in this chapter. Wizards are regular Access databases with the same common database objects: forms, modules, macros, and, to a lesser extent, tables.

Unlike regular libraries, wizards require the user's attention and commonly consist of forms and related code. For example, the Form Wizard included with Microsoft Access is a wizard that includes a series of dialog boxes. When the user successfully navigates to the end of the last dialog, the wizard creates a new form.

This step-by-step interface is one of the things that distinguishes wizards from regular libraries, but not all wizards contain multiple forms or dialog boxes. Indeed, if you have a generic form that seems to appear in all your applications, consider moving it from the various applications and into a wizard library.

> Sooner or later, you will probably create a runaway query, a query that returns far more records than you thought. This can happen when the query is improperly constructed, does not contain valid joins, or does not include sufficient criteria to limit the number of records. For example, you might construct a query against a multimillion-record Sales table but—innocently enough—fail to include a date criterion that would otherwise restrict the records. One solution is to write a function that determines the number of records that will be returned by the query, but before the query actually returns any data or before you print a report based on the query (if left unattended, such a report could easily consume a large amount of paper).

Creating the Report Launcher Wizard

The following steps describe how you can create the Report Launcher, a wizard that determines the number of records and gives the user the opportunity to continue or cancel a report. After this wizard is installed as a library, you will be able to call the wizard from any application. You can choose to create a new library database for the wizard, or you can add to an existing library.

Creating a New Library for the Wizard

To create a new library database for the wizard, follow these steps:

1. Choose New Database from the File menu, or click the New Database button on the toolbar (see fig. 19.8). Access displays the New Database dialog box.

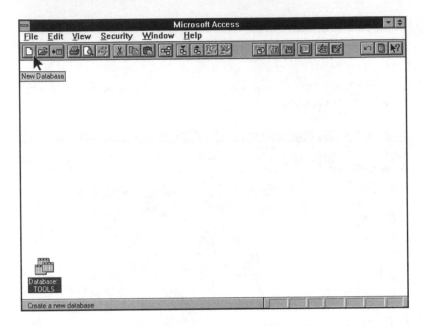

Figure 19.8. Choose the New Database button to create a new library database.

> If you created a subdirectory beneath Access named LIB, choose that directory. If you did not create a subdirectory, select the Access directory. For more information about the LIB subdirectory, see "Creating a Library" earlier in this chapter.

2. Name the new database RPTLNCH.MDA, or some other name you will recognize as containing the Report Launcher wizard.

Adding the Wizard to an Existing Library

If you want, you can add the Report Launcher to an existing library. For example, if you have already created a Tools library (TOOLS.MDA), it may make sense to add the Report Launcher to that library instead of creating yet another, smaller library.

To add to the Tools library, you must first disable the library. For more information, see "Disabling a Library" earlier in this chapter.

Creating the Report Launcher Form

The Report Launcher requires a form to provide a user interface. The following steps outline the procedure you can follow to create the form (see fig. 19.9):

1. Create a new, unbound form and save it with the name **csvReport Launcher**. Then add a list box and three command buttons.

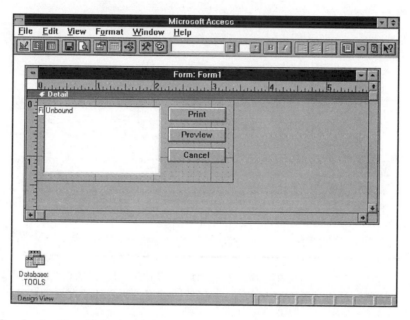

Figure 19.9. Create a form with these controls.

2. Remove the list box's attached label by first selecting the label and then pressing Delete.

3. Next, open the property sheet and set the following properties for the form:

Property	Setting
Caption	Report Launcher
Default View	Single Form
Shortcut Menu	No

Property	Setting
Scroll Bars	Neither
Record Selectors	No
Navigation Buttons	No
Auto Center	Yes
Modal	Yes
Border Style	Dialog
Control Box	No

Note: Setting the **BorderStyle** property to Dialog automatically removes the Minimize and Maximize buttons.

4. Set the following properties for the first command button, Print:

Property	Setting
Name	Print
Caption	Print
Status Bar Text	Print the selected report.
Tab Index	2
On Click	=csvOpenReport([ ], "print")

Note: In the **OnClick** property setting, two square brackets are inside the parentheses. This is "short-hand" for the current form and avoids having to specify a more lengthy Forms![csvReport Launcher].

5. Set the following properties for the second command button, Preview:

Property	Setting
Name	Preview
Caption	Preview
Status Bar Text	Preview the selected report.

continues

409

Property	Setting
Tab Index	3
On Click	=csvOpenReport([], "preview")

6. Set the following properties for the third command button, Cancel:

Property	Setting
Name	Cancel
Caption	Cancel
Status Bar Text	Close this form without printing a report.
Tab Index	0

7. Unlike the Print and Preview buttons, do not set the Cancel button's **OnClick** property by typing the name of a function. Instead, you specify an event procedure by clicking toward the right side of the On Click property text box and then selecting [Event Procedure] from a drop-down list (see fig. 19.10).

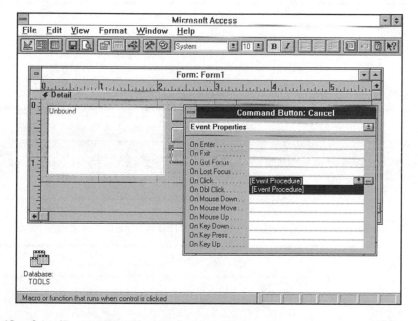

Figure 19.10. Select [Event Procedure] from the drop-down list.

8. After you select [Event Procedure], click the button just to the right of the drop-down arrow. Access displays a Module window and the Cancel_Click Sub procedure.

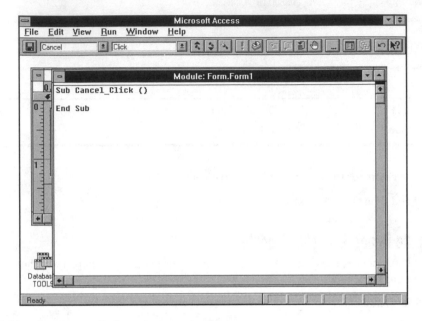

Figure 19.11. Access automatically creates an empty procedure.

9. When the user clicks the Cancel button, you want Access to call the Cancel_Click procedure and close the form. Unless you enter code that actually closes the form, however, the procedure does not do anything; it is an empty procedure. Modify the procedure by adding the following line of code between the other two lines of code:

```
DoCmdClose
```

10. Set the following properties for the Reports list box:

Property	Setting
Name	Reports
Row Source Type	csvFillReportNames
Status Bar Text	Select the desired report from the list.
Tab Index	1
Width	2 in
Height	1.1701 in
Special Effect	Sunken
On Dbl Click	=csvOpenReport([ ], "print")

411

Note: If you would rather preview a report when the user double-clicks the name of a report, set the **OnDblClick** property to =csvOpenReport([], "preview").

11. Set the following properties for the Detail section:

Property	Setting
Name	DetailSection
Height	1.4299 in

12. Choose colors for the Detail section and the controls.

13. Save and then close the form.

Creating the Report Launcher Module

The Report Launcher requires a module to supply all the code necessary to implement the wizard. The module contains three functions:

- csvReportLauncher( )

  You call this function to open the csvReport Launcher form.

- csvOpenReport( )

  The form calls this function whenever the user clicks the Print or Preview button.

- csvFillReportNames( )

  Access calls this function to fill the Reports list box with the names of all the reports in the current database.

The following steps outline the procedure you can follow to create the module.

1. Create a new module and save it with the name **csvReport Launcher**.

2. In the Declarations section, enter the **Option Explicit** statement (see fig. 19.12).

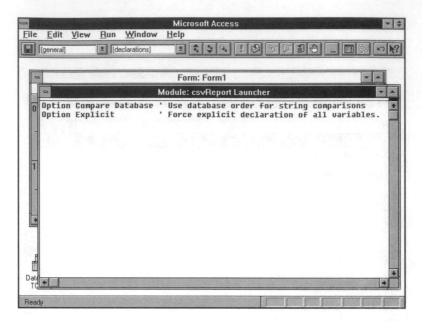

Figure 19.12. Always enter the Option Explicit statement.

3. Move to the next line in the Module window and enter the first line of the csvReportLauncher( ) function:

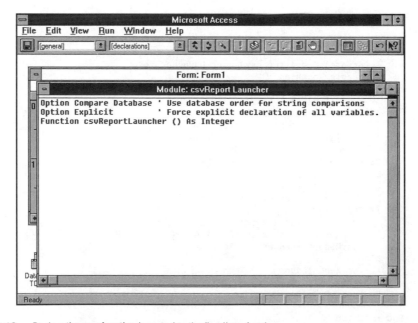

Figure 19.13. Declare the new function by entering the first line of code.

As soon as you enter the first line and press Enter, Access displays what appears to be a
new window with only the first and last lines of the function:

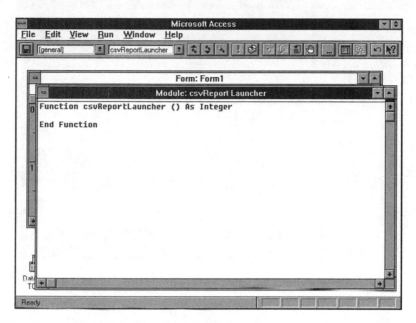

Figure 19.14.   Access automatically creates an empty Function procedure.

4. Enter the rest of the function as follows:

```
Function csvReportLauncher () As Integer

    ' Purpose: Opens the csvReport Launcher form.
    ' Accepts: nothing
    ' Returns: True  - successful
    '          False - unsuccessful
    ' Version: 1.00 29-Mar-94  CSV
    '                Initial revision.
    ' -----------------------------------------------
    Const csvMB_ICONEXCLAMATION = 48
    Const TITLEBAR = "Open Report Launcher"
    Dim Msg As String
    On Error Resume Next
    DoCmd OpenForm "csvReport Launcher"
    If Err Then
        Msg = "Couldn't open form 'csvReport Launcher'."
        MsgBox Msg, csvMB_ICONEXCLAMATION, TITLEBAR
        csvReportLauncher = False
    Else
        csvReportLauncher = True
    End If
    On Error GoTo 0

End Function
```

5. Check to make sure you have no errors by choosing the Compile Loaded Modules command from the Run menu. If necessary, correct any mistakes in the function and try recompiling until Access no longer produces any error messages.

6. Next, enter the csvOpenReport( ) function:

```
Function csvOpenReport (MyForm As Form,
➥ByVal OpenMode As String) As Integer

    ' Purpose: Opens a specified report.
    ' Accepts: MyForm   - forms object identifying form
    '                     calling this function
    '          OpenMode - "print" or "preview"
    ' Returns: 0 - unsuccessful (error)
    '          1 - unsuccessful (no records in report)
    '          2 - unsuccessful (user cancelled)
    '          3 - successful   (bound report)
    '          4 - successful   (unbound report)
    ' Version: 1.00 29-Mar-94  CSV
    '                  Initial revision.
    ' ------------------------------------------------
    Const TITLEBAR = "Open Report"
    Const csvMB_ICONEXCLAMATION = 48
    Const csvMB_ICONINFORMATION = 64
    Const csvMB_ICONQUESTION = 32
    Const csvYESNO = 4
    Const csvNO = 7
    Dim MaxRecords As Long, MyRecordSource As Variant
    Dim MyReport As Control
    Dim Msg As String

    Set MyReport = MyForm![Reports]

    If IsNull(MyReport) Then
        Msg = "You must first select a report from "
        Msg = Msg & "the list.",
        MsgBox Msg, csvMB_ICONINFORMATION, TITLEBAR
        csvOpenReport = False
    Else
        DoCmd Echo False
        DoCmd OpenReport MyReport, A_DESIGN
        MyRecordSource = Reports(MyReport).RecordSource
        DoCmd Close A_REPORT, MyReport
        DoCmd Echo True
        On Error Resume Next
        If Not IsNull(MyRecordSource) Then
            MaxRecords = DCount("*", MyRecordSource)
        Else
            MaxRecords = -1
        End If
        If Err Then
            Msg = "Couldn't open report '" & MyReport
            Msg = Msg & "'."
            MsgBox Msg, csvMB_ICONEXCLAMATION, TITLEBAR
            csvOpenReport = 0
```

continues

415

```
                        On Error GoTo 0
                        Exit Function
                End If

                On Error GoTo 0
                If MaxRecords = 0 Then
                    Msg = "Couldn't open report '" & MyReport
                    Msg = Msg & "' because there is no data."
                    MsgBox Msg, csvMB_ICONINFORMATION, TITLEBAR
                    csvOpenReport = 1
                Else
                    If MaxRecords > 0 Then
                        Msg = "There " & IIf(MaxRecords = 1,
                        ➥"is", "are")
                        Msg = Msg & " " & Trim$(Str$(MaxRecords))
                        Msg = Msg & " record"
                        Msg = Msg & IIf(MaxRecords = 1, "", "s")
                        Msg = Msg & " in this report. Continue?"
                        If MsgBox(Msg, csvMB_ICONQUESTION +
                        ➥csvYESNO, MyReport) = csvNO
                        ➥Then
                            csvOpenReport = 2
                            Exit Function
                        Else
                            csvOpenReport = 3
                        End If
                    Else
                        csvOpenReport = 4
                    End If
                    DoCmd OpenReport MyReport,
                    ➥IIf(LCase$(OpenMode) = "print",
                    ➥A_NORMAL, A_PREVIEW)
                End If
            End If

        End Function
```

7. Again, check to make sure you have no errors by choosing the Compile Loaded Modules command from the Run menu.

8. When Access no longer produces any error messages, enter the csvFillReportNames( ) function:

```
Function csvFillReportNames (MyControl As Control,
➥ID As Variant, Row As Integer, Col As Integer, ➥Code As Variant) As Variant

    ' Purpose: Fills specified control with names of
    '          reports in the current database.
    ' Accepts: various
    ' Returns: various
    ' Version: 1.00 29-Mar-94  CSV
    ' -------------------------------------------
    Const EXCLUDEPREFIX1 = "zt"
    Const EXCLUDEPREFIX2 = "zz"
    Dim DefaultWorkspace As WorkSpace
    Dim CurrentDatabase As Database
    Dim MyContainer As Container, MyReportName As String
```

416

```
        Dim X As Long
        Static ReportArray(), ReportCount As Long
        Static ShowUSysObjects As Variant

        Select Case Code
            Case LB_INITIALIZE
                    Set DefaultWorkspace =
                    ➥DBEngine.Workspaces(0)
                    Set CurrentDatabase =
                    ➥DefaultWorkspace.Databases(0)
                    Set MyContainer =
                    ➥CurrentDatabase.Containers("Reports")
                    ShowUSysObjects =
                    ➥Application.GetOption("Show System Objects")
                    ReportCount = 0
                    For X = 0 To MyContainer.Documents.Count - 1
                        MyReportName =
                        ➥MyContainer.Documents(X).Name
                        If LCase$(Left$(MyReportName,
                        ➥Len(EXCLUDEPREFIX1)))
                        ➥<> EXCLUDEPREFIX1 And
                        ➥LCase$(Left$(MyReportName,
                        ➥Len(EXCLUDEPREFIX2))) <>
                        ➥EXCLUDEPREFIX2 And
                        ➥((ShowUSysObjects = True) Or
                        ➥(ShowUSysObjects = False And
                        ➥LCase$(Left$(MyReportName, 4))
                        ➥<> "usys")) Then
                            ReportCount = ReportCount + 1
                            ReDim Preserve
                            ➥ReportArray(ReportCount)
                            ReportArray(ReportCount) =
                            ➥MyReportName
                        End If
                    Next X
                    csvFillReportNames = True
            Case LB_OPEN
                    csvFillReportNames = Timer
            Case LB_GETROWCOUNT ' Number of rows.
                    csvFillReportNames = ReportCount
            Case LB_GETCOLUMNCOUNT ' Number of columns.
                    csvFillReportNames = 1
            Case LB_GETCOLUMNWIDTH ' Column width.
                    csvFillReportNames = -1 ' Automatic.
            Case LB_GETVALUE ' Assign data.
                    csvFillReportNames = ReportArray(Row + 1)
            Case LB_END ' End.
                    Erase ReportArray
                    csvFillReportNames = True
            Case Else ' Unknown or not used.
                    csvFillReportNames = True
        End Select

    End Function
```

417

Tip: The csvFillReportNames() function excludes temporary reports with names beginning with the characters specified by the EXCLUDEPREFIX1 and EXCLUDEPREFIX2 constants. In this example, reports that begin with the letters "zt" and "zz" are excluded from the list.

 For more information about naming temporary reports and other objects, see Chapter 17, "Naming Conventions and Style Guidelines."

10. Make a final check to ensure that you have no errors by choosing the Compile Loaded Modules command from the Run menu. Save and then close the module and return to the Database window.

Installing the Report Launcher Wizard

You might want to take this opportunity to create a few blank reports to test the functionality of the Report Launcher before you install it as a library. When you are satisfied with the form's appearance and know that the code functions properly, delete any of these temporary reports.

 Note: Compacting the database will remove previously-deleted objects.

 Close the RPTLNCH.MDA database and then compact the database by choosing the Compact Database command from the File menu. For more information about compacting databases, see Chapter 23, "Data Compaction, Backups, and Data Recovery."

Edit your MSACC20.INI file using Windows Notepad or another text editing program and locate the [Libraries] section. In the following example, the last line installs the Report Launcher as a wizard library.

```
[Libraries]
wzlib.mda=rw
wzQuery.mda=rw
wzfrmrpt.mda=rw
wzbldr.mda=rw
wzTable.mda=rw
c:\access2\lib\rptlnch.mda=rw
```

Save the changes to MSACC20.INI, close Notepad, and then restart Microsoft Access. From now on, you can call the Report Launcher wizard from any application by calling the csvReportLauncher( ) function.

Where Access Looks for Objects

You might find it interesting to note that when you execute library code, and Access tries to locate an object, it looks in libraries first, before it looks in the current database (see fig. 19.15). For example, if you have a form named My Form in an installed library and a form in the current database also named My Form, Access will always load the library copy of My Form.

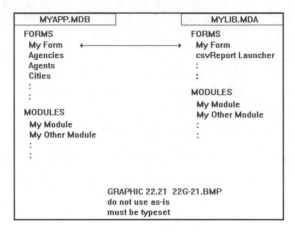

Figure 19.15. You can have same-named objects in library and on-library databases.

When you execute a line of code that opens My Form, Access loads the copy stored in the library. You cannot specify in code or in a macro which particular My Form to open. In this example, the only way for the user to open the form stored in the current database is to return to the Database window and manually open the form.

> **Tip:** Because Access allows these same-named objects, make sure you choose your library object names carefully. This book illustrates using a prefix, "csv." Consider adopting a similar strategy for identifying your own library objects.

Builders

Like wizards, *builders* are libraries that provide a user interface. Unlike wizards, which may present a series of dialog boxes, builders usually present only a single form or dialog box.

Because wizards provide pretty much the same functionality as builders, you may not have much need to create your own builders and can instead use wizards. Remember that builders are most useful as design tools and have limited value to users.

419

Examples of builders include the ones that come with Microsoft Access—for example, a Menu Builder that you can use as you are designing a form. The builder steps you through the process of adding a custom menu bar to the form. In this sense, a builder is a somewhat more specialized than a wizard.

Creating a Builder

The easiest way to create a builder on your own is to copy one of the existing builders and make whatever modifications are necessary. For example, you might want to modify the Menu Builder so that it skips the initial dialog box (where you are asked to select a template).

WARNING: It is a good idea to copy an existing builder and make changes to the copy instead of modifying the original.

For information about how to install your new builder, see "Installing a Library" earlier in this chapter.

Add-In Libraries

An *add-in* is not a type of library so much as it is a classification. In reality, all libraries, no matter what they do, may be classified as add-in libraries. The primary difference between a library that is an add-in and one that is not an add-in is that add-in libraries appear in a variety of lists. For example, the Database Documentor add-in appears when you choose Add-Ins from the File menu (see fig. 19.16).

You can have your own wizard or other library routine appear in this list of add-ins. The ability to choose an add-in from the Add-Ins submenu makes add-ins ideal for routines you want the user to be able to invoke upon demand. If your users do not need to invoke a certain library or routine from the list of add-ins, do not make it an add-in.

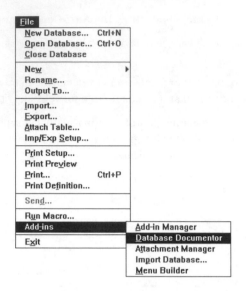

Figure 19.16. Choose the Add-Ins command to display a list of the installed add-ins.

Creating an Add-In

You create the desired library database, wizard, or builder following the steps outlined earlier in this chapter. Although there are no special procedures or rules for creating an add-in, you should adopt some general guidelines to make sure that your add-ins are consistent and easy to use.

> **Tip:** You can change a regular library into an add-in, which exposes it to the user, or remove it from any list of add-ins, at any time.

Although Microsoft recommends that you design your add-ins to look and behave like the rest of the Access system and its add-ins, you should instead design your add-ins to look and behave like the rest of your application. Most users have no need or desire to look behind the scenes, and most do not even care that you used Microsoft Access to create the application.

Wherever practical, however, you should adopt the same guidelines Microsoft used to develop their add-ins:

- Center add-in forms on the screen by setting the **AutoCenter** property to Yes.

- Avoid record selectors, scroll bars, and navigation buttons because they amount to visual clutter.

- Use modal or dialog forms. This prevents users from moving to other forms without first completing steps on one form that may be required for subsequent actions.

To the user, add-ins should be just another part of the application, not separate tools with a different look and feel. To help achieve this effect of integration, adopt the same style, labeling, color scheme, and choice of wording as the rest of your application.

Types of Add-Ins

You can create five kinds of add-ins in Microsoft Access:

- **Menu**

    These add-ins are the kind you are most likely to create. These add-ins appear in a list when you choose the Add-Ins command on the File menu (see fig. 19.17). For example, you might create a menu add-in that launches Microsoft Excel. The Add-In command and its list are not available unless a database is open; that is, they are not available in the Startup window.

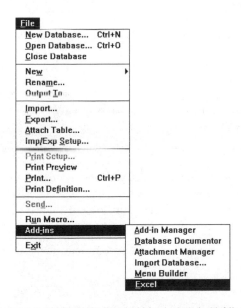

Figure 19.17.   You can add your own add-ins to the list of add-ins included with Microsoft Access.

- **Table or query wizard**

  When you create a new table or query and click the Wizard button, Access displays a list of available table or query wizards (see fig. 19.18). Unless you have special needs not already handled by the wizards included with Access, you probably do not need to create any table or query wizards on your own.

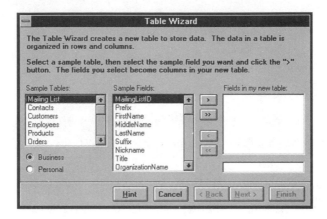

Figure 19.18. When you create a new table or query, you can choose from among the available wizards.

- **Form or report wizard**

  When you create a new form or report and click the Wizard button, Access displays a list of available form or report wizards (see fig. 19.19). Your need to create a special form or report wizard may be greater than the need to create special table or query wizards. As a developer, you may find it just as convenient (or more so, considering the work it takes to create a wizard) to create new forms without benefit of a wizard.

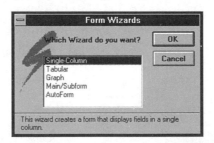

Figure 19.19. When you create a new form or report, you can choose from among the available wizards.

- **Property builder or wizard**

  In the property sheet, you can invoke any of the available builders or wizards by clicking the Builder button beside the appropriate property. The Choose Builder dialog box appears (see fig. 19.20). You probably will not need to create your own property builder or wizard unless you also create or include custom controls in your application.

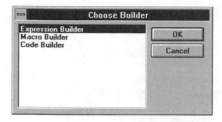

Figure 19.20. When you invoke a property builder, Access displays a list of builders.

- **Control builder or wizard**

  If you first choose the Control Wizards command on the View menu, Access automatically displays a list of the available builders and wizards when you add a control to a form or report (see fig. 19.21). You also can invoke a builder or wizard for an existing control by clicking the desired control with the right mouse button and then choosing the Build command from the shortcut menu (see fig. 19.22).

The following descriptions identify these types of add-ins, when and why you might want to create and use them, and how you invoke them in your applications.

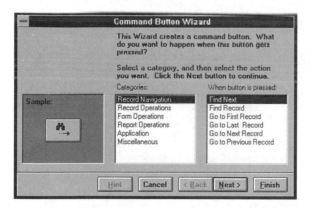

Figure 19.21. When you create a new control, Access loads the appropriate wizard.

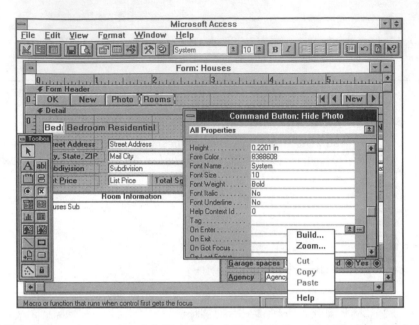

Figure 19.22. When you invoke a property builder with the right mouse button, Access displays a list of wizards.

Installing an Add-In

After you create and test your add-in, you can install it either of two ways:

- Manually by editing your MSACC20.INI file

- Automatically using the Microsoft Access Add-In Manager

The following sections describe the procedures for each of these techniques.

Manually Installing an Add-In

Especially while you are developing and testing, you will probably find it faster and more convenient to manually install (and uninstall) your add-ins by editing your MSACC20.INI file.

> **Tip:** You should still be familiar with using the Add-In Manager to automatically install your add-ins, however, because this is what your users will be using. For more information, see "Using the Add-In Manager," later in this chapter.

The procedure for editing your MSACC20.INI file depends on the kind of add-in you are creating. For more information about library settings, see "Installing a Library" earlier in this chapter.

Menu

For each menu add-in you want to appear in the Add-In submenu, add an entry to the [Libraries] section. In the following example, the last line installs one or more add-ins that are stored in the MYADDIN.MDA file.

```
[Libraries]
wzlib.mda=rw
wzTable.mda=rw
wzQuery.mda=rw
wzfrmrpt.mda=rw
wzbldr.mda=rw
c:\access2\lib\myaddin.mda=ro
```

 Tip: As previously discussed in "Installing a Library," the second part of each entry following the equal sign indicates whether the library is to be opened for read/write access or for read-only access. If your add-in does not write to any objects in its own library database, make the add-in read-only (ro). Only if the add-in writes to objects in its own database you should make it available for read/write access (rw).

If you place your library databases in the same directory as Access, you do not need to specify the complete path. In the preceding example, though, the add-in entry includes a complete path because the library database is in a subdirectory beneath the ACCESS2 directory. Consider creating your own subdirectory for such files, and avoid placing custom or user-defined files in the same directory as your Access program files.

Next, add an entry to your MSACC20.INI file so that the add-in appears in the list of add-ins when the user chooses the Add-Ins command from the File menu. The following example shows how you can display the name of an add-in in the list by adding an entry to the [Menu Add-Ins] section.

```
[Menu Add-Ins]
&Add-in Manager==Wm_Entry()
&Database Documentor==Doc_PrintDataBase()
A&ttachment Manager==Am_Entry()
Im&port Database...==Doc_ImportDatabase()
&Menu Builder==CustomMenuBuilder()
&Excel==csvLaunchExcel()
```

In this example, the last entry identifies the Excel add-in. The text that appears to the left of the double equal signs (==) is what appears in the list of add-ins:

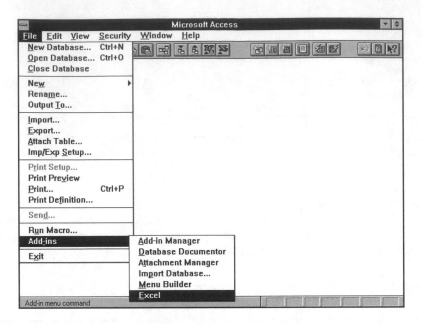

Figure 19.23. Use an ampersand (&) to view the add-in menu command list.

Including an ampersand (&) in the text indicates an access key. Even though access key assignments are optional, you should include them for consistency throughout your application. For the Excel add-in, E is the access key. If the name of your add-in happens to include an ampersand, use two ampersands. For example, to display "Search & Replace" in the list, the entry would be something like this:

```
Search && Replace==csvSearchReplace()
```

At runtime, the double ampersands display a single ampersand without creating what would otherwise be an access key.

The text that appears to the right of the double equal signs is the name of the function in the library that starts the add-in. In the preceding examples, the names of the functions are csvLaunchExcel( ) and csvSearchReplace( ). Enter any function arguments inside the parentheses; if a function does not accept any arguments, you must still include the parentheses.

Table or Query Wizard

For each table or query wizard you want to make available, add an entry to the [Libraries] section of your MSACC20.INI file. This procedure is the same one you would follow for a menu add-in. In the following example, the last line installs one or more table wizards that are stored in the TBLWIZ.MDA library.

```
[Libraries]
wzlib.mda=rw
wzTable.mda=rw
wzQuery.mda=rw
wzfrmrpt.mda=rw
wzbldr.mda=rw
c:\access2\lib\tblwiz.mda=rw
```

 Make the add-in read/write or read-only, as appropriate. Avoid placing wizards or any add-in in the same directory as your Access files. For more information, see "Installing a Library" earlier in this chapter.

Next, add another entry to your MSACC20.INI file so that the wizard appears in the list of wizards when the user creates a new table or query. The following example shows how you can display the name of a table wizard by adding an entry to the [Table Wizards] section.

```
[Table Wizards]
Table=TW_Entry,,'This wizard creates a new table to...'
Lookup Table=csvLookupWizard,,'Create a new lookup...'
```

Note: The process for installing query wizards is similar to that for table wizards, except that you edit the [Query Wizards] section instead of the [Table Wizards] section.

The syntax for adding an entry is:

```
displayname=functionname[,,statusbartext]
```

The *displayname* argument is a string that is the name that will appear in the list of wizards. In the preceding example, the display name is Lookup Table.

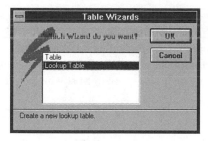

Figure 19.24. The display name appears in the list of wizards.

The *functionname* argument is a string that identifies the name of the function called by the wizard.

The *statusbartext* argument is a string that specifies the text that appears in the dialog box's form footer whenever the user highlights the wizard in the list of add-ins (see fig. 19.25). Notice that the text is delimited with apostrophes ('), but the apostrophes do not appear in the list.

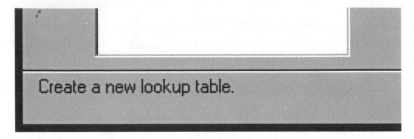

Figure 19.25.   The status bar text appears in the form footer.

> **Tip:** Depending on the resolution, lengthy status bar messages do not display properly on some screens. Save space by providing concise and relatively short status bar text, usually starting with a verb such as **Create** or **Change**. In particular, do not begin the status bar text with **This wizard will...**because it is clear that the wizard will do whatever follows in the message.

The status bar text is optional, but include it for consistency throughout your application. If you decide not to include the status bar text, do not include the double commas, as shown here:

```
Lookup Table=csvLookupWizard
```

> **Note:** Unlike menu add-ins, notice that you enter only one equal sign, and that you do not follow the *functionname* argument with parentheses.

Form or Report Wizard

For each form or report wizard you want to make available, add an entry to the [Libraries] section of your MSACC20.INI file. This procedure is the same one you would follow for a menu add-in or a table or query wizard. In the following example, the last line installs one or more form wizards that are stored in the FORMWIZ.MDA file.

```
[Libraries]
wzlib.mda=rw
wzTable.mda=rw
wzQuery.mda=rw
wzfrmrpt.mda=rw
wzbldr.mda=rw
c:\access2\lib\formwiz.mda=rw
```

Make the add-in read/write or read-only, as appropriate. Avoid placing wizards or any add-in in the same directory as your Access files. For more information, see "Installing a Library" earlier in this chapter.

Next, add another entry to your MSACC20.INI file so that the wizard appears in the list of wizards when the user creates a new form or report. The following example shows how you can display the name of a form wizard by adding an entry to the [Form Wizards] section.

```
[Form Wizards]
Single-Column=zwForm, 1,'This wizard creates a form...'
Tabular=zwForm, 2,'This wizard creates a form that...'
Graph=zwGraph,, 'This wizard creates a form that...'
Main/Subform=zwMainSub,, 'This wizard creates...'
AutoForm=zwAutoForm,, 'AutoForm automatically creates...'
Standard=csvStandardForm, 1,'Create a new...'
```

Note: The process for installing report wizards is similar to that for form wizards, except that you edit the [Report Wizards] section instead of the [Form Wizards] section.

The syntax for adding an entry is as follows:

```
displayname=functionname[, [wizardid][,statusbartext]]
```

The *displayname* argument is a string that is the name that will appear in the list of wizards. In the following example, the display name is Standard.

```
Standard=csvStandardForm, 1,'Create a new...'
```

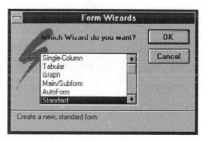

Figure 19.26. The new wizard appears in the list of available wizards.

The *functionname* argument is a string that identifies the name of the function called by the wizard.

The second argument, *wizardid*, is an integer that identifies an optional value you can pass to the function identified by the *functionname* argument. A number of form wizards included with Access use a single function to launch multiple wizards, and the *wizardid* argument provides a mechanism

for determining which wizard to start. For most custom form and report wizards, however, you should probably create separate functions that start the appropriate wizard. If you decide to use the *wizardid* argument, remember that you can specify only integer values.

 Note: The function identified by the *functionname* argument must accept a string argument, which is the name of the table to be created. Access provides the value for this argument automatically. In addition, if you specify the *wizardid* argument in the [Form Wizards] entry, the function must also accept an integer argument.

The *statusbartext* argument is a string that specifies the text that appears in the dialog box's form footer whenever the user highlights the wizard in the list of add-ins. Notice that the text is delimited with apostrophes ('), but the apostrophes do not appear in the list (see fig. 19.27).

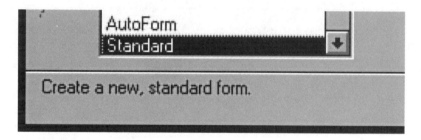

Figure 19.27. You can specify the text that appears in the footer of the dialog box.

The status bar text is optional, but include it for consistency throughout your application. If you decide not to include the status bar text, you can still specify the *wizardid* argument, as shown here:

```
Standard=csvStandardForm, 1
```

If you specify the *statusbartext* argument but do not specify a *wizardid* argument, you must still include the comma, as shown here:

```
Standard=csvStandardForm,,'Create a new, standard form.'
```

 Note: Unlike menu add-ins, notice that you enter only one equal sign and do not follow the *functionname* argument with parentheses.

Property Builder or Wizard

For each property builder or wizard you want to make available, add an entry to the [Libraries] section of your MSACC20.INI file. This procedure is the same one as you would follow for a menu add-in or

any of the previously-described wizards. In the following example, the last line installs one or more property builders or wizards that are stored in the BUILDWIZ.MDA file.

```
[Libraries]
wzlib.mda=rw
wzTable.mda=rw
wzQuery.mda=rw
wzfrmrpt.mda=rw
wzbldr.mda=rw
c:\access2\lib\buildwiz.mda=ro
```

 Make the add-in read/write or read-only, as appropriate. Avoid placing wizards or any add-in in the same directory as your Access files. For more information, see "Installing a Library" earlier in this chapter.

Tip: Because they perform such similar functions, consider combining control and property builders and wizards in the same .MDA file.

Next, add another entry to your MSACC20.INI file so that the add-in appears in the list of builders and wizards when the user invokes the property builders. The following example shows how you can display the name of a property builder by adding an entry to the [Property Wizards] section.

```
[Property Wizards]
MSMenuBarBuilder=Menubar, MenuBar Builder, MB_ENTRY,rw
MSInputMaskWizard=InputMask, Input Mask Builder,
➥IM_ENTRY,rw
MSForeColorBuilder=ForeColor, ForeColor Builder,
➥CP_ENTRY,rw
MSBackColorBuilder=BackColor, BackColor Builder,
➥CP_ENTRY,rw
MSBorderColorBuilder=BorderColor, BorderColor Builder,
➥CP_ENTRY,rw
MSPictureBuilder=Picture, Picture Builder, PP_ENTRY,rw
MSFieldBuilder=FieldName,Field Builder,tw_FieldEntry, rw
csvEffectBuilder=SpecialEffect, Effect Builder, csvEffectBuilder,rw
```

The syntax for adding an entry is as follows:

```
uniquename=propertyname, displayname, functionname, readwriteflag
```

The *uniquename* argument is a string that is a unique name for the builder or wizard (unique in the sense that it does not otherwise appear in the list of builders and wizards in the [Property Wizards] section of your MSACC20.INI file). In the preceding example, the last line installs a builder with a unique name of csvEffectBuilder.

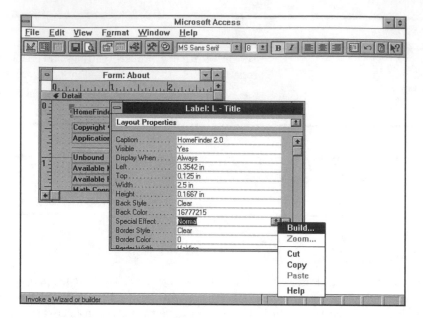

Figure 19.28.   You display a list of available builders by first choosing the Build command.

The *propertyname* argument is a string that identifies the property for which the builder or wizard is designed. In the preceding example, csvEffectBuilder is designed for the **SpecialEffect** property.

The *displayname* argument is a string that is the name that will appear in the list of builders and wizards. In the preceding example, the display name is Effect Builder.

 Note: Unlike display names for form and report wizards, you do not delimit display names for property builders and wizards with apostrophes.

The *functionname* argument is a string that identifies the name of the function called by the builder or wizard.

The *readwriteflag* argument is a string that identifies whether the user can use the builder or wizard to change existing property settings or can only use the builder or wizard to create new property settings:

Read/Write Flag	Effect
rw	User can create new property settings and change existing property settings to which the builder or wizard applies.
w	User can only modify existing property settings to which the builder or wizard applies.

Note: Unlike menu add-ins, notice that you enter only one equal sign and do not follow the *functionname* argument with parentheses.

Control Builder or Wizard

For each control builder or wizard you want to make available, add an entry to the [Libraries] section of your MSACC20.INI file. This procedure is the same one you would follow for a menu add-in or any of the previously-described wizards. In the following example, the last line installs one or more control builders or wizards that are stored in the BUILDWIZ.MDA file.

```
[Libraries]
wzlib.mda=rw
wzTable.mda=rw
wzQuery.mda=rw
wzfrmrpt.mda=rw
wzbldr.mda=rw
c:\access2\lib\buildwiz.mda=ro
```

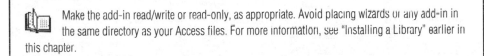

Make the add-in read/write or read-only, as appropriate. Avoid placing wizards or any add-in in the same directory as your Access files. For more information, see "Installing a Library" earlier in this chapter.

Next, add another entry to your MSACC20.INI file so that the wizard appears in the list of wizards when the user invokes the control builders. The following example shows how you can display the name of a control builder by adding an entry to the [Control Wizards] section.

```
[Control Wizards]
MSListBoxWizard=ListBox, List Box Builder, LST_ENTRY,w
MSComboBoxWizard=ComboBox, ComboBox Wizard, CMB_ENTRY,w
MSOptionGroupWizard=OptionGroup, OptionGroup Wizard,
➥OGrp_ENTRY,w
MSCommandButtonWizard=CommandButton, CommandButton
➥Wizard, BW_ENTRY,w
csvGraphBuilder=Graph, Graph Builder, csvGraphBuilder,w
```

The syntax for adding an entry is as follows:

```
uniquename=controltype, displayname, functionname, readwriteflag
```

The *uniquename* argument is a string that is a unique name for the builder or wizard (unique in the sense that it does not otherwise appear in the list of builders and wizards in the [Control Wizards] section of your MSACC20.INI file). In the preceding example, the last line installs a builder with a unique name of csvGraphBuilder (see fig. 19.29).

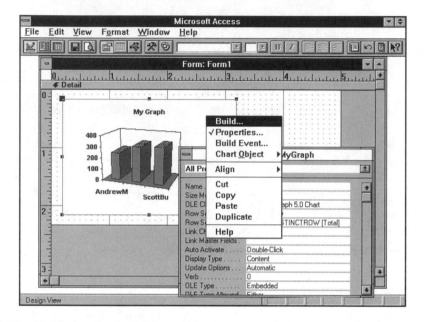

Figure 19.29. You display a list of available control builders by first choosing the Build command.

The *controltype* argument is a string that identifies the type of control to which the builder or wizard applies. Valid control types are:

- Combo Box
- Command Button
- Graph
- List Box
- Option Group

In the preceding example, csvGraphBuilder applies to graphs.

The *displayname* argument is a string that is the name that will appear in the list of builders and wizards. In the preceding example, the display name is Graph Builder.

Note: Unlike display names for form and report wizards, you do not delimit display names for control builders and wizards with apostrophes.

The *functionname* argument is a string that identifies the name of the function called by the builder or wizard.

The *readwriteflag* argument is a string that identifies whether the user can use the builder or wizard to change existing controls or can only use the builder or wizard to create new controls:

Read/Write Flag	Effect
rw	User can create new controls and change existing controls to which the builder or wizard applies.
w	User can only modify existing controls to which the builder or wizard applies.

Note: Unlike menu add ins, notice that you enter only one equal sign and do not follow the *functionname* argument with parentheses.

Using the Add-In Manager

The previous section discussed how you can install add-ins by manually editing your MSACC20.INI file. As a developer, this is probably a good technique for you because you are experienced and comfortable with editing .INI files. Most users, however, do not have your level of experience and often feel more comfortable with a more automated process.

The Add-In Manager is an ideal end-user tool. The Add-In Manager, which is itself an add-in, provides a more user-friendly interface (see fig. 19.30) and takes care of editing your MSACC20.INI file. Indeed, you may even want to use the Add-In Manager yourself.

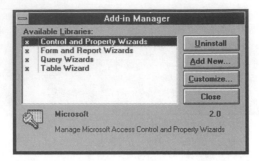

Figure 19.30.   Use the Add-In manager to install or uninstall the add-ins supplied with Access.

To install an add-in using the Add-In Manager, follow these steps:

1. Open the Add-In Manager dialog box by choosing the Add-In Manager command from the Add-Ins submenu. The Add-In Manager dialog box appears.

2. Choose the desired add-in from the list of available libraries, and then click the Install button. Access places an "x" to the left of the library name to indicate the add-in has been installed, and changes the caption on the Install button to Uninstall.

3. If the name of the add-in library you want to install does not appear in the list, click the Add New button to display the Add New Library dialog box.

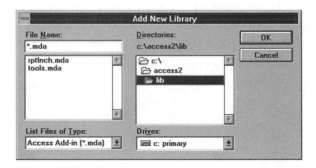

Figure 19.31.   Use this dialog box to add new add-ins to your system.

4. Locate the desired library file and then click the OK button. Access installs the library and adds it to the list of installed add-ins.

Note: When you install a library using the Add New Library dialog, Access makes a copy of the library file and places the copy in the same directory as Access. Only add-in libraries located in the same directory as Access appear in the list of available libraries. If you have placed your custom add-in libraries in a subdirectory beneath Access as suggested earlier in this chapter, this somewhat limits the usefulness of the Add-In Manager since your own add-ins will not appear in the list.

To uninstall an add-in library, highlight the library in the Add-In Manager dialog box, and then click the Uninstall button. Access removes the "x" from the left of the library name and changes the caption on the Uninstall button to Install. The name of the library remains in the list even though it is no longer installed. To remove a library from the list, you must delete the library file from your Access directory.

Role of the USysAddIns Table

When you use the Add-In Manager, Access looks for a table named USysAddIns in the library file. Although this table is optional, creating one for each library file makes it possible for Access to display useful information in the Add-In Manager dialog box.

For example, you can specify such information as your company name or other identification, a version number, plus an icon to display whenever the user selects the library. The USysAddIns table can also include information that identifies the kind of add-in (for example, whether it is a form wizard or perhaps a control builder).

The easiest way to create a USysAddIns table is to make a copy of the table from an existing add-in library. For example, you could import the USysAddIns table from the WZQUERY.MDA file and modify it as necessary to reflect the information that is specific to your add-in.

Note: Table names that begin with the letters "USys" or "MSys" are known as system tables (user system tables and Microsoft system tables, respectively). These tables can be viewed only if you have enabled viewing system objects.

To create a USysAddIns table by making a copy of the table from an existing add-in library, follow these steps:

1. If you have not already done so, enable viewing system objects by choosing the Options command from the View menu. The Options dialog box appears. Set the Show System Objects setting to Yes (see fig. 19.32).

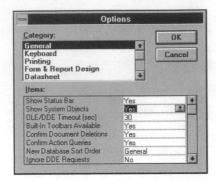

Figure 19.32. Choose the Options command from the View menu to enable viewing system tables.

2. Choose the Import command from the File menu. The Import dialog box appears (see fig. 19.33).

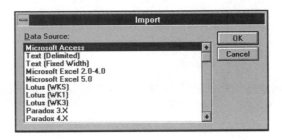

Figure 19.33. You can import from a variety of data sources.

3. Select Microsoft Access from the list of available data sources. Access displays a dialog box where you can select the WZQUERY.MDA file (see fig. 19.34).

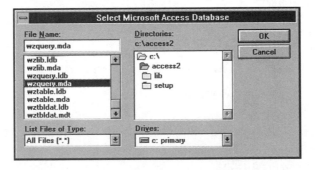

Figure 19.34. Select the database that contains the table you want to import.

439

4. When you click OK, Access displays the Import Objects dialog box, where you can select the type and name of the object you want to import (see fig. 19.35).

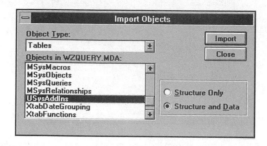

Figure 19.35. Select the desired table from the list of tables in the database.

5. Import both the structure and data of the table into your add-in library database. Close the Import Objects dialog box.

6. Open the USysAddIns table in Design view in order to examine the table structure. Each record in the table contains ten fields, one named PropertyName plus a series of generic fields named Val1 through Val9 (see fig. 19.36).

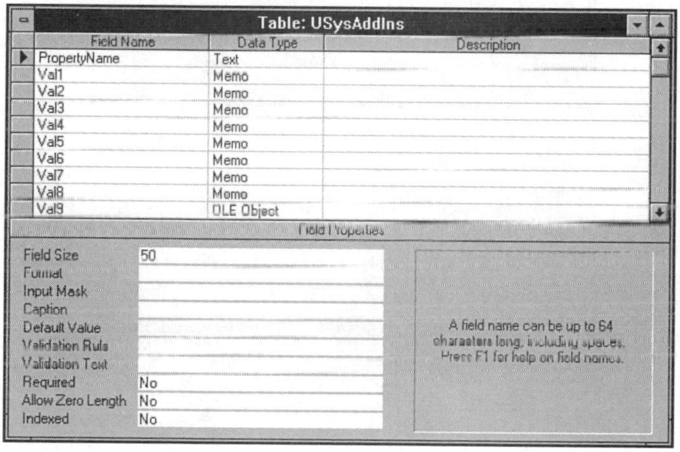

Figure 19.36. Each record in the UsysAddIns table contains ten fields.

7. Each record contains a value in the PropertyName field and at least one of the generic value fields. To see the kinds of values for each record and field, open the table in Datasheet view (see fig. 19.37).

440

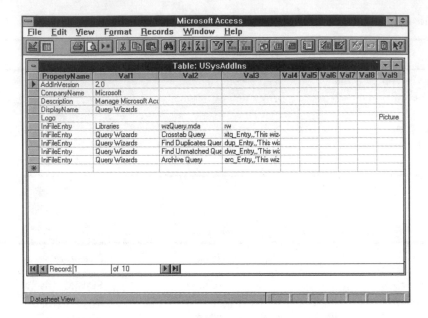

Figure 19.37. Access maintains settings for all the add-ins in the USysAddIns table.

The values in the table are those for the WZQUERY.MDA library; replace these settings with those for your own add-in. The following tables describe various properties and the kinds of values Access expects for each.

AddInVersion

Purpose	Value Fields Used	Example
Identifies the version of the library that appears in the bottom of the dialog box.	Val1—version number or text	1.0

CompanyName

Purpose	Value Fields Used	Example
Identifies the company name or other identification that appears in the bottom portion of the dialog box; do not enter any more text than will fit on one line.	Val1—company name or other identification	Quick Software

Description

Purpose	Value Fields Used	Example
Specifies the text that appears in the bottom portion of the dialog box; do not enter any more text than will fit on a single line.	Val1—text to appear in the bottom portion of the dialog box	Start Microsoft Excel

DisplayName

Purpose	Value Fields Used	Example
Specifies the name that will appear in the list of available add-in libraries.	Val1—name that will appear in the list	Excel

Logo

Purpose	Value Fields Used	Example
Displays a picture in the lower section of the dialog box; typically a .WMF, .BMP, or .PCX image, the picture should be no larger than 32 x 32 pixels (the size of a standard icon).	Val9—picture	

FunctionToCallOnCustomize

Purpose	Value Fields Used	Example
Identifies the description and name of the function to be called when the user clicks the Customize button in the Dialog box; there can be more than one such record with this property name value (but usually only if you have more than one add-in allowing customization).	Val1—text that appears in the Customize Add-In dialog box	Customize Report Launcher
	Val2—name of the function to be called from the Customize Add-In dialog box, followed by parentheses	csvCustomizeLauncher( )

IniFileEntry

Purpose	Value Fields Used	Example
Creates an entry in your MSACC20.INI file; depending on the type of add-in, you may have more than one such record (for example, if you are specifying a form wizard, you will have one record for the entry in the [Libraries] section and another record for the entry in the [Form Wizards] section.	Val1—name of the section in which the entry is to be made	Libraries
	Val2—add-in display name, unique name, or library name (the text that appears to the left of the equal sign in the entry)	MYADDIN.MDA
	VAl3—value (the text that appears to the right of the equal sign)	ro

 Note: The preceding IniFileEntry illustrates the [Libraries] section entry only. You will need additional records for the other entries. For example, installing a menu add-in requires another record for the [Menu Add-Ins] section entry.

443

Summary

Access library databases (libraries) are collections of database objects you install and make available to all applications—automatically. Libraries typically contain forms and code that perform application-independent functions, as opposed to functions unique to only one or two applications. When you have multiple applications that use otherwise common forms or routines, consider placing these common elements in a library.

20
Macro Actions

Macro actions are instructions that Access carries out to perform specific operations, and these can be very useful in your application. For example, you can use the **OpenForm** macro action to open a form.

Previous chapters explained some of the reasons why you should generally avoid macros themselves: they offer no error handling, are difficult to debug, and do not provide the debugging capabilities available in modules. This does not mean, however, that you will not need to use the same macro actions you would otherwise use to build macros.

The various macro actions may be grouped into these seven categories:

- *Navigating*
- *Searching* and *sorting*
- *Object-manipulation*
- *Form-* and *window-manipulation*
- *Macro* and *code*
- *Importing* and *exporting*
- *Miscellaneous*

Some of the macro actions require arguments, some allow optional arguments, and still others accept no arguments at all. For example, to use the **OpenForm** macro action you must specify the name of the form (a required argument), but you do not have to specify the type of view (an optional argument). The **Beep** macro action accepts no arguments whatsoever.

Few applications will need all of the more than forty macro actions available in Microsoft Access. Indeed, you may find that you frequently use only a small subset of them and never use others. This chapter describes the more commonly-used macro actions in greater detail than the ones you are likely to use only infrequently. For more information about any macro action, search Help for the name of the desired macro action.

Navigating Macro Actions

You use the navigating macro actions to move to a specified control, page, or record in a form or report:

- **GoToControl**
- **GoToPage**
- **GoToRecord**

GoToControl

You use the **GoToControl** macro action to move the *input focus* to a specified control on a form or in a datasheet. A control with the input focus can receive user input (typing at the keyboard or clicking with the mouse).

Syntax

    DoCmd GoToControl controlname

The **GoToControl** macro action accepts the following required argument:

Argument	Required	Comments
controlname	Yes	This is the name of the control that is to receive the input focus.

Example

Figure 20.1 illustrates how you can move the input focus to a command button named "OK."

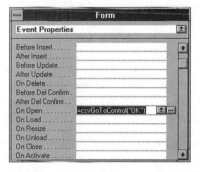

Figure 20.1.   Calling a function that uses the **GoToControl** macro action.

446

```
Function csvGoToControl (ByVal MyControlName) As Integer

    ' Purpose: moves the focus to the specified control.
    ' Accepts: MyControlName - name of the desired
    '          control.
    ' Returns: True  - successful
    '          False - unsuccessful
    ' Version: 1.00 01-Apr-94  CSV
    ' -------------------------------------------
    Const csvMB_ICONEXCLAMATION = 48
    Dim Msg As String, Icon As Integer
    Dim Titlebar As String

    Titlebar = "csvGoToControl"
    On Error Resume Next
    DoCmd GoToControl MyControlName
    If Err Then
        Msg = "Couldn't go to control '" & MyControlName
        Msg = Msg & "'."
        Icon = csvMB_ICONEXCLAMATION
        MsgBox Msg, Icon, Titlebar
        csvGoToControl = False
    Else
        csvGoToControl = True
    End If
    On Error GoTo 0

End Function
```

Remarks

The control identified by the *controlname* argument must be on the currently-active database object. For example, to go to a control on the Customers form, the Customers form must already have the focus. If necessary, use the **SelectObject** macro action to make the Customers form active and then use the **GoToControl** macro action (see fig. 20.2).

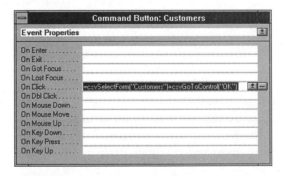

Figure 20.2. Calling two user-defined functions during one event.

In this example, control passes to the Customers form and the input focus moves to the OK command button.

```
Function csvSelectForm (ByVal MyFormName As String) As Integer

    ' Purpose: selects a specified form.
    ' Accepts: MyFormName - name of the desired form.
    '          InWindow   - True : in Database window
    '                       False: not in Database window
    ' Returns: True  - successful
    '          False - unsuccessful
    ' Version: 1.00 01-Apr-94  CSV
    ' --------------------------------------------
    Const csvMB_ICONEXCLAMATION = 48
    Dim Msg As String, Icon As Integer
    Dim Titlebar As String

    Titlebar = "csvSelectForm"
    On Error Resume Next
    DoCmd SelectObject A_FORM, MyFormName
    If Err Then
        Msg = "Couldn't select form  '" & MyFormName
        Msg = Msg & "'."
        Icon = csvMB_ICONEXCLAMATION
        MsgBox Msg, Icon, Titlebar
        csvSelectObject = False
    Else
        csvSelectObject = True
    End If
    On Error GoTo 0

End Function
```

GoToPage

On a multipage form (a form that has one or more Page Break controls), you can use the **GoToPage** macro action to go to a specified page.

Syntax

DoCmd GoToPage *pagenumber, right, down*

The **GoToPage** macro action accepts the following required and optional arguments:

Argument	Required	Comments
pagenumber	Yes	This is the number of the page to which you want to move.
right	No*	This is the distance, in twips (from the left edge of the page), to which you want to move. A twip is 1/1440 of an inch.

Argument	Required	Comments
down	No*	This is the distance, in twips (from the top edge of the page), to which you want to move.

* If you specify either the right or down argument, however, you must specify both arguments.

Example

The following example illustrates how you can go to the second page of a form.

```
DoCmd GoToPage 2
```

Remarks

The input focus moves to the first control (according to the form's tab order) on the page.

If you specify a page number that does not exist (for example, page 3 when the form has only two pages), Access displays an error message and the macro action fails.

> **Tip:** The *right* and *down* arguments to the **GoToPage** macro action are useful only if you create forms that are larger than the physical screen. The *right* and *down* arguments specify the specific area of the page that will be displayed. For example, you can specify that after going to page 2 of a form, Access displays the part of the page whose upper-left corner is offset by the distances specified for the arguments.

When you go to a new page, Access places the input focus on the first control in the form's tab order. If this is not the effect you want, you can either use the **GoToControl** macro action to go to a different control or you can change the tab order. There are two ways you can view or set a form's tab order:

- Choose the Tab Order command from the Edit menu while the form is in Design View and adjust the tab order as necessary.

- Inspect each of the control's **TabIndex** property settings and make whatever changes are necessary.

 You might design an Employees form with a series of command buttons. When the user presses a command button with the caption "Salary" you can call a function that uses the **GoToPage** macro action to move to the page containing salary information (see fig. 20.3).

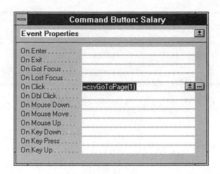

Figure 20.3. Moving the focus to a specified page.

```
Function csvGoToPage (ByVal MyPageNumber As Integer) As Integer

    ' Purpose: moves to specified page number on a form.
    ' Accepts: MyPageNumber - desired page (1 to X).
    ' Returns: True  - successful
    '          False - unsuccessful
    ' Version: 1.00 02-Apr-94   CSV
    ' ---------------------------------------------
    Const csvMB_ICONEXCLAMATION = 48
    Dim Msg As String
    Dim Icon As Integer
    Dim Titlebar As String

    Titlebar = "csvGoToPage"
    On Error Resume Next
    DoCmd GoToPage MyPageNumber
    If Err Then
        Msg = "Couldn't go to page "
        Msg = Msg & Trim$(Str$(MyPageNumber))
        Msg = Msg & "' on form '"
        Msg = Msg & Screen.ActiveForm.FormName & "'."
        Icon = csvMB_ICONEXCLAMATION
        MsgBox Msg, Icon, Titlebar
        csvGoToPage = False
    Else
        csvGoToPage = True
    End If
    On Error GoTo 0

End Function
```

Other buttons could go to other pages containing personal or EEO status, emergency contact data, or other employee information.

GoToRecord

You use the **GoToRecord** macro action to move the focus to a specified record.

Syntax

    DoCmd GoToRecord objecttype, objectname, record, offset

The **GoToRecord** macro action accepts the following optional arguments:

Argument	Required	Comments
objecttype	No*	This is the type of database object that contains the record you want to go to. Valid values are A_TABLE, A_QUERY, and A_FORM.
		If you want to move to a record in the current database object (that is, the object that has the focus), you can leave this argument blank. This argument is optional unless you are moving to a record in a different database object (for example, on a different form). In that case, you must specify the object type.
objectname	No*	This is the name of the specific database object. Like the *objecttype* argument, you can leave this argument blank if you are moving to another record in the current database object.
record	No	This argument identifies which record you want to go to. Valid values are A_PREVIOUS, A_NEXT, A_FIRST, A_GOTO, and A_NEWREC.
		If you do not specify the *record* argument, Access uses A_NEXT. If you specify A_GOTO, Access uses the value of the *offset* argument to determine which record to make current.
offset	No**	When you specify A_GOTO for the *record* argument, Access uses the value of the *offset* argument to determine which record to go to.
		If you specify A_PREVIOUS or A_NEXT for the *record* argument, Access uses *offset* to determine how many records to back up or go forward from the current record position.

* *If you specify either the* right *or* down *argument, however, you must specify both arguments.*

** *If you specify A_GOTO for the* record *argument, however, you must also supply an* offset *argument.*

451

Example

The following example illustrates how you can move to the previous record on a form:

```
DoCmd GoToRecord A_PREV
```

Remarks

The value of the *offset* argument must be a whole number or an expression that evaluates to a whole number. If you enter an expression, you must precede it with an equal sign (=).

If the value of the *offset* argument causes Access to try to move beyond the beginning or end of the records, Access displays an error message and the function fails.

> You may want to disable the built-in navigation buttons along the bottom of a form, yet still provide a way for users to navigate from record to record. First, add small command buttons to the form's header (see fig. 20.4).

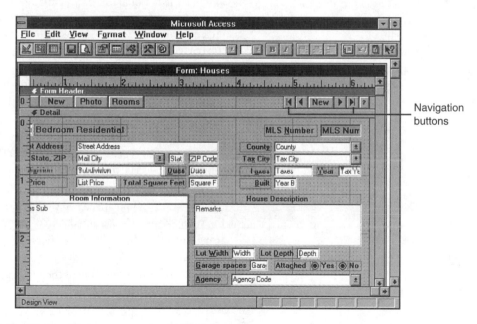

Figure 20.4. You can add your own record navigation buttons.

Set each button's **OnClick** property to call a function that uses the **GoToRecord** macro action to move to the appropriate record (see fig. 20.5).

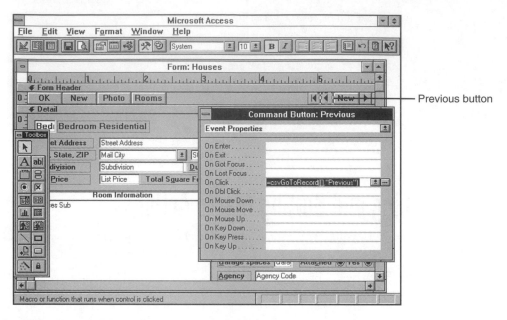

— Previous button

Figure 20.5. Calling the csvGoToRecord() function from the **OnClick** event.

```
Function csvGoToRecord (MyForm As Form,
➥ByVal Direction As String) As Variant

    ' Copyright © 1993 by Chris St. Valentine
    ' Purpose: moves the focus to a specified record.
    ' Accepts: Direction - string identifying which
    '                      direction to move:
    '                      "first"    first record
    '                      "last"     last record
    '                      "previous" previous record
    '                      "next"     next record
    '                      "new"      new record
    ' Returns: non-Null - successful
    '          Null     - unsuccessful
    ' Version: 1.00 15-Mar-93  CSV
    ' ----------------------------------------
    Const csvMB_ICONEXCLAMATION
    Dim Msg As String, Icon As Integer
    Dim Titlebar As String, X As Integer

    Titlebar = "csvGoToRecord"
    X = (InStr(1,
➥"first   last    previous next    new       ",
➥Direction, 1) + 7) \ 8
    If X <> 0 Then
        X = Choose(X, A_FIRST, A_LAST, A_PREVIOUS,
        ➥A_NEXT, A_NEWREC)
        On Error Resume Next
```

continues

453

```
        DoCmd GoToRecord A_FORM, MyForm.FormName, X
        On Error GoTo 0
        csvGoToRecord = X
    Else
        Msg = "Invalid direction argument '"
        Msg = Msg & Direction & "'."
        Icon = csvMB_ICONEXCLAMATION, Titlebar
        MsgBox Msg, Icon, Titlebar
        csvGoToRecord = Null
    End If

End Function
```

Searching and Sorting Macro Actions

The searching and sorting macro actions let you search for specified data and sort the data once you find it:

- **ApplyFilter**
- **FindNext**
- **FindRecord**
- **Requery**
- **RunSQL**
- **ShowAllRecords**

ApplyFilter

You use the **ApplyFilter** macro action to both filters and sort the records from a specified table or query used by a form or report.

Syntax

```
DoCmd ApplyFilter filtername, wherecondition
```

The **ApplyFilter** macro action accepts the following optional arguments:

Argument	Required	Comments
filtername	No*	This is either the name of a query or the name of a filter that you have saved as a query.
wherecondition	No*	This is any otherwise valid SQL Where clause, an expression that restricts the records you want to see in the form or report. Do not include the word "where."

* Although neither argument is required, you must provide at least one of them.

Example

The following example illustrates how you can show only records where the city control contains "Redmond."

```
DoCmd ApplyFilter , "City = 'Redmond'"
```

Remarks

You can use the **ApplyFilter** macro action with forms in either Form view or Datasheet View. When applied to a report, you can use **ApplyFilter** only during the **OnOpen** event of the report.

ApplyFilter has the same effect as pressing the Apply Filter/Sort button on the toolbar or choosing the Apply Filter/Sort command from the Records menu.

 You might add an option group named Region with check boxes that let the user specify that only domestic or international (or both) customers be included in the form (see fig. 20.6).

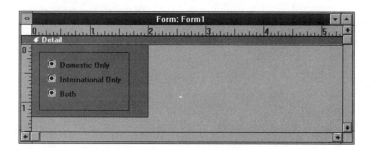

Figure 20.6. Whenever practical, provide users with choices.

In this example, the first check box, Domestic Only, has an **OptionValue** property setting of 1. International Only has a value of 2, and Both has a value of 3. By referring to this option group, you can avoid having to hard code the criterion:

```
Function csvApplyDomesticIntl (MyForm As Form) As Integer

    ' Purpose: restricts records to Domestic, International, or both.
    ' Accepts: MyForm - Forms object identifying form calling function.
    ' Returns: True
    ' Version: 1.00 02-Apr-94  CSV
    ' --------------------------------------------
    Const HOMECOUNTRY = "USA"
    Dim Criterion As String

    csvApplyDomesticIntl = True
```

continues

455

```
    Select Case MyForm![Region]
        Case 1 ' domestic only.
            Criterion = "Country = '" & HOMECOUNTRY
            Criterion = Criterion & "'"
        Case 2 ' international only.
            Criterion = "Country <> '" & HOMECOUNTRY
            Criterion = Criterion & "'"
            DoCmd ApplyFilter , Criterion
        Case 3 ' both.
            DoCmd ShowAllRecords
            Exit Function
    End Select
    DoCmd ApplyFilter , Criterion

End Function
```

FindNext

You use the **FindNext** macro action to search for the next record that matches the criterion set in the last call to the **FindRecord** macro action, or in the last use of the Find command on the Edit menu.

Syntax

```
DoCmd FindNext
```

The **FindNext** macro action accepts no arguments.

Example

The following example illustrates how you can find the next record matching the previously set or defined criterion.

```
DoCmd FindNext
```

Remarks

If there is no next record that matches the previously-specified criterion, Access displays an error message and the function fails.

FindRecord

You use the **FindRecord** macro action to move to the first record that satisfies the specified criteria.

Syntax

```
DoCmd FindRecord findwhat, where, matchcase, direction, asformatted, searchin,
findfirst
```

The **FindRecord** macro action accepts the following required and optional arguments:

Argument	Required	Comments
findwhat	Yes	This identifies the data you want to find in the record. It can be text, a number, a date, or an expression preceded by an equal sign (=). The entry you type can include any of the following wildcard characters: * (asterisk) ? (question mark) # (number sign) [ ] (left and right brackets) ! (exclamation point) - (hyphen)
where	No	This specifies the portion of the field that must match. Valid values are A_ANYWHERE, A_ENTIRE, and A_START. **A_ANYWHERE** looks for the data anywhere in the field. This is the slowest technique, but the most flexible if you are not sure where the text might be found. **A_ENTIRE** satisfies the conditions of the macro action; the data must match the entire field character-for-character. **A_START** looks for the data at the beginning of the field. This is the fastest technique. If you do not specify the *where* argument, Access uses **A_ENTIRE**.
matchcase	No	This specifies whether the search will be case-sensitive. Valid values are True and False. If you specify False and search for "chris," Access will find "Chris." If you specify True, searching for "chris" will fail to find "Chris" because the case of the characters is not an exact match. If you do not specify the *matchcase* argument, Access uses False.

continues

457

Argument	Required	Comments
direction	No	Use this argument to specify in which direction you want to search. Value values are A_UP (search toward the beginning of the records) and A_DOWN (search toward the end of the records).
		If you do not specify the *direction* argument, Access uses A_DOWN.
asformatted	No	This determines whether the search will match the format of the underlying data. Valid values are True and False.
		True. Access looks for a match the way the data appears, not how it is stored internally. For example, on forms dates usually appear formatted (10-Jan-56), but are actually stored internally as double precision numbers (20464). To find January 10, 1956, the value of the *findwhat* argument must be in the same format as it appears on the form.
		False. The value of the *findwhat* argument does not have to be in the same format as the underlying data. To find the same January 10 record, *findwhat* could be Jan-10-56, January 10, 1956, or #1-1-56#.
		If you do not specify the *asformatted* argument, Access uses False.
searchin	No	Use this argument to specify where the search should be conducted. Valid values are A_CURRENT and A_ALL.
		A_CURRENT is the faster technique since Access searches only in the current field. You may have to use the **GoToControl** macro action before you use **FindRecord**.
		A_ALL looks for a match in every (any) field of every record.
		If you do not specify the *searchin* argument, Access uses A_CURRENT.

Argument	Required	Comments
findfirst	No	Use this argument to specify whether the search starts at the current record or at the first (or last) record. Valid values are True and False.
		True. Begin the search from the beginning or end of the records, depending on the *direction* argument. If *direction* is A_DOWN, Access begins the search from the beginning of the records; if *direction* is A_UP, the search begins from the end of the records.
		False. Searches from the current record position and looks in the direction specified by the *direction* argument.
		If you do not specify the *findfirst* argument, Access uses True.

Example

The following example illustrates how you can find the next customer whose residence is in Washington. Because the *matchcase* argument is not specified and False is the default, the search will find the next match whether it is "wa" or "WA."

```
DoCmd FindRecord "WA", A_START
```

Remarks

 For more information about using wildcard characters as part of the *findwhat* argument, search Help for "wildcard characters."

FindRecord has the same effect as choosing the Find command from the Edit menu.

Requery

You use the **Requery** macro action to rerun the query that originally filled a database object or a control (typically a combo box or list box) with data.

Syntax

```
DoCmd Requery controlname
```

The **Requery** macro action accepts the following optional argument:

Argument	Required	Comments
controlname	No	This is the name of the control you want to requery.
		If you do not specify the controlname argument, Access requeries the active database object (usually a form).

Example

The following example illustrates how you can requery a combo box to retrieve current values.

```
:
X = csvRequeryControl(Forms![MyForm], "MyComboBox")
:


Function csvRequeryControl (MyForm As Form,
↪ByVal MyControlName As String) As Integer

    ' Purpose: requeries the current object or a
    '          specified control.
    ' Accepts: MyForm - Forms object identifying form
    '                       calling function.
    '          MyControlName - name of the desired
    '                          object.
    ' Returns: True
    ' Version: 1.00 02-Apr-94  CSV
    ' --------------------        ...........
    csvRequeryControl = True
    DoCmd Requery MyControlName

End Function
```

Remarks

Controls that can be based on queries include subforms, combo boxes, list boxes, OLE objects (for example, graphs and pictures), and any control whose control source includes one of the domain aggregate functions (for example, **DAvg** or **DSum**).

You use the **Requery** macro action most often to make sure the most current information is displayed on a form. For example, you might open several forms, each displaying the same information in perhaps slightly different formats. To make sure information changed in one form appears in the other forms, requery the other forms.

> **Note:** The **Requery** macro action has been made obsolete by the **Requery** method, and you should use the method instead of the macro action.

```
Function csvRequery (MyForm As Form, ByVal MyControlName As String) As Integer

    ' Purpose: requeries the current object or a specified control.
    ' Accepts: MyForm - Forms object identifying form calling function.
    '          MyControlName - name of the desired object.
    ' Returns: True
    ' Version: 1.00 02-Apr-94  CSV
    ' --------------------------------------------
    csvRequery = True
    If MyControlName <> "" Then
        MyForm(MyControlName).Requery
    Else
        MyForm.Requery
    End If

End Function
```

Requery has the same effect as pressing Shift+F9.

RunSQL

You use the **RunSQL** macro action to execute an SQL statement.

Syntax

DoCmd RunSQL *sqlstatement*

The **RunSQL** macro action accepts the following required argument:

Argument	Required	Comments
sqlstatement	Yes	This is an otherwise valid SQL statement that would create an append, delete, make-table, or update query.

Example

The following example illustrates how you can delete all inactive customers from a table.

```
DoCmd SetWarnings False
DoCmd RunSQL "DELETE * FROM Customers WHERE Status = 'I';"
DoCmd SetWarnings True
```

461

Remarks

The **RunSQL** macro action lets you achieve the same effect as action queries without having to first create and save a query. You can use this macro action to create new tables from query dynasets, update tables, delete records, or append records to existing tables or to query dynasets.

Be sure you use the **SetWarnings** macro action to suppress the prompt Access normally displays when you use **RunSQL** (see fig. 20.7).

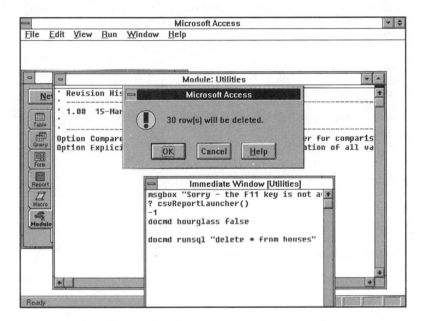

Figure 20.7. Access normally prompts you to confirm action queries.

 Tip: To view and then copy the SQL statement from a previously-saved action query, open the query in Design View and then choose the SQL command from the View menu. Highlight the entire SQL statement, copy it to the clipboard, and then paste it into your function (you will probably have to adjust for line breaks).

ShowAllRecords

You use the **ShowAllRecords** macro action to remove any filters from the active form and display all the records in the form's source query.

Syntax

```
DoCmd ShowAllRecords
```

The **ShowAllRecords** macro action accepts no arguments.

Example

The following example illustrates how you can remove the filter from the currently-active form.

```
DoCmd ShowAllRecords
```

Remarks

When you use **ShowAllRecords** to display all records, Access displays any changed records, plus any new records added to the underlying tables. It forces a requery of the underlying table or query dynaset as if you had also used the **Requery** macro action or **Requery** method.

ShowAllRecords has the same effect as choosing the Show All Records command from the Records menu.

Object-Manipulation Macro Actions

The object-manipulation macro actions select or change database objects or, in the case of the **SetValue** macro action, change controls on a database object:

- **CopyObject**
- **DeleteObject**
- **Print**
- **Rename**
- **RepaintObject**
- **SelectObject**
- **SetValue**

CopyObject

You use the **CopyObject** macro action to copy the currently-selected database object from one database to another, or from one location to another (but with a new name) within the same database.

Syntax

```
DoCmd CopyObject destination, newname
```

The **CopyObject** macro action accepts the following optional arguments:

Argument	Required	Comments
destination	No*	This is the name of the database (including path, if necessary) to which you want to copy the database object.
		If you do not specify the *destination* argument, Access uses the path and name of the current database.
newname	No*	This is the new name for the database object that will be copied.
		If you do not specify the *newname* argument, Access uses the same name as the database object you are copying.

* You must provide at least one of these arguments.

Example

The following example illustrates how you can make a backup of the Customers table by copying it from the current database to another database.

```
DoCmd SelectObject A TABLE, "Customers", True
DoCmd CopyObject "K:\MYDATA.MDB"
```

In this example, a second database named MYDATA.MDB had previously been created to hold back-up copies of database objects.

Remarks

Depending on the macro action arguments you provide, **CopyObject** has the same effect as:

- Selecting a database object in the Database window, choosing the Copy command from the Edit menu, and then choosing the Paste command from the Edit menu.

- Opening an existing database object, choosing the Save As command from the File menu, and then typing a new name for the database object.

- Opening a different database, choosing the Import command from the File menu, and then importing the desired database object into the database.

DeleteObject

You use the **DeleteObject** macro action to delete a database object.

Syntax

```
DoCmd DeleteObject objecttype, objectname
```

The **DeleteObject** macro action accepts the following optional arguments.

Argument	Required	Comments
objecttype	No*	This is the type of database object you want to delete. Valid values are A_TABLE, A_QUERY, A_FORM, A_REPORT, A_MACRO, and A_MODULE.
		If you do not specify the *objecttype* argument, do not specify the *objectname* argument, either.
objectname	No*	This is the name of the specific database object you want to delete.
		If you do not specify the *objectname* argument, do not specify the *objecttype* argument, either.

* If you specify either argument, however, you must specify both.

> **STOP**
>
> **WARNING:** When you omit both of the arguments to the **DeleteObject** macro action, Access deletes the currently-selected database object in the Database window—without notice and without warning. You should always specify both arguments to **DeleteObject**.

Example

The following example illustrates how you can delete a specified query.

```
DoCmd DeleteObject A_QUERY, "zt_Temp Qry"
```

Remarks

DeleteObject has the same effect as selecting a database object in the Database window and then pressing the Del key or choosing the Delete command from the Edit menu. Unlike these techniques, however, when you supply both arguments to the **DeleteObject** macro action you do not have to select the database object in the Database window.

Print

You use the **Print** macro action to print the active datasheet, form, or report.

Syntax

DoCmd Print *printrange, printfrom, printto, printquality, copies, collate*

The **Print** macro action accepts the following optional arguments:

Argument	Required	Comments
printrange	No	Specifies whether you want to print all or part of the selected database object. Valid values are A_PRINTALL, A_SELECTION, and A_PAGES.
		A_PRINTALL prints the entire database object (all pages).
		A_SELECTION prints only the selected area (click and drag to highlight the area you want to print before you call the function that uses **Print**).
		A_PAGES prints the pages specified by the *pagefrom* and *pageto* arguments.
		If you do not specify the *printrange* argument, Access uses A_PRINTALL.
printfrom	No*	This identifies the first page to print; printing begins at the top of the specified page.
		This argument has meaning only when the *printrange* argument has been set to A_PAGES.
printto	No*	This identifies the last page to print.
		This argument has meaning only when the *printrange* argument has been set to A_PAGES.
printquality	No	This determines the quality of the print. Valid values are A_HIGH, A_MEDIUM, A_LOW, and A_DRAFT.
		Generally, the higher the quality, the slower the speed. Draft quality is the fastest, but produces lesser quality (this may be satisfactory for internal company uses, however). Depending on your printer driver, you may not see a significant difference between some of these settings.
		If you do not specify the *printquality* argument, Access uses A_HIGH.

Argument	Required	Comments
copies	No	This determines the number of copies to print.
		If you do not specify the *copies* argument, Access uses 1.
collate	No	When you specify more than 1 for the copies argument, this specifies the way page collating is handled. Valid values are True and False.
		True collates the pages; to print 2 copies of a three-page report, Access prints pages 1, 2, 3, 1, 2, and 3, in that order.
		False does not collate the pages; to print 2 copies of a three-page report, Access prints pages 1, 1, 2, 2, 3, and 3, in that order. Specify False to print at a faster speed.
		If you do not specify the *collate* argument, Access uses True.

* *The* printfrom *and* printto *arguments are required if you specify A_PAGES for the* printrange *argument.*

Example

The following example illustrates how you can print two collated copies of the currently active database object.

```
DoCmd Print , , , , 2, True
```

Remarks

Print has the same effect as selecting a database object and then choosing the Print command from the File menu.

Rename

You use the **Rename** macro action to rename the currently-selected database object.

Syntax

```
DoCmd Rename newname, objecttype, objectname
```

The **Rename** macro action accepts the following required and optional arguments:

Argument	Required	Comments
newname	Yes	This is the new name for the database object.
objecttype	No*	This is the type of database object you want to rename. Valid values are A_TABLE, A_QUERY, A_FORM, A_REPORT, A_MACRO, and A_MODULE.
		If you do not specify the *objecttype* argument, do not specify the *objectname* argument, either.
objectname	No*	This is the name of the specific database object you want to rename. This is the old name.
		If you do not specify the *objectname* argument, do not specify the *objecttype* argument, either.

* If you specify either argument, however, you must specify both.

> **STOP** **WARNING:** When you omit the *objecttype* and *objectname* arguments to the **RenameObject** macro action, Access renames the currently-selected database object in the Database window—without notice and without warning. You should always specify all three arguments to **RenameObject**.

Example

The following example illustrates how you can rename an existing query.

```
DoCmd Rename "Custom Qry", A_QUERY, "zt_Temp Qry"
```

Remarks

> **Tip:** You cannot rename an open database object.

> The **Rename** macro action simply gives the database object a new name; it does not make a copy of the object. To make a copy, see the **CopyObject** macro action earlier in this section.

Rename has the same effect as selecting an object in the Database window and then choosing the Rename command from the File menu.

RepaintObject

You use the **RepaintObject** macro action to redraw the selected or active database object on the screen, and force any pending recalculations of the controls in that object to be performed.

Syntax

```
DoCmd RepaintObject objecttype, objectname
```

The **RepaintObject** macro action accepts the following optional arguments:

Argument	Required	Comments
objecttype	No*	This is the type of database object that you want to repaint. Valid values are A_TABLE, A_QUERY, A_FORM, A_REPORT, A_MACRO, and A_MODULE.
		If you do not specify the *objecttype* argument, do not specify the *objectname* argument, either.
objectname	No*	This is the name of the specific database object you want to repaint.
		If you do not specify the *objectname* argument, do not specify the *objecttype* argument, either.

* *If you specify either argument, however, you must specify both.*

Example

The following example illustrates how you can repaint the Customers form.

```
DoCmd RepaintObject A_FORM, "Customers"
```

Remarks

If you do not specify the *objecttype* and *objectname* arguments, Access repaints the active window.

> **Tip:** Use the **RepaintObject** macro action when Access is not updating fields as quickly as you want. For example, if a number of fields on a form receive data through **SetValue** macro actions, explicitly repainting the objects causes the recalculation of those fields to occur more quickly. You can use **RepaintObject** to make sure that all information in an object is current and complete.

The **RepaintObject** macro action does not cause a requery of the source object, and it does not show changed, new, or deleted records. To show newly-changed or added records, use the **Requery** or **ShowAllRecords** macro actions described earlier in this chapter.

RepaintObject has an effect similar to selecting an object and then choosing the Refresh command from the Records menu. However, the Refresh command, which is actually a combination of the **RepaintObject** and **Requery** macro actions, shows any changes that were made to the displayed records.

RepaintObject has the same effect as clicking F9 to recalculate.

SelectObject

You use the **SelectObject** macro action to select a database object and make it the active object.

Syntax

DoCmd SelectObject *objecttype, objectname, indbwindow*

The **SelectObject** macro action accepts the following required and optional arguments:

Argument	Required	Comments
objecttype	Yes	This is the type of database object that you want to select. Valid values are A_TABLE, A_QUERY, A_FORM, A_REPORT, A_MACRO, and A_MODULE.
		If you do not specify the *objecttype* argument, do not specify the *objectname* argument, either.
objectname	Yes	This is the name of the specific database object you want to select.
		If you do not specify the *objectname* argument, do not specify the *objecttype* argument, either.
indbwindow	No	This indicates whether to select the database object in the Database window. Valid values are True and False.
		True. Select the database object in the Database window; the database object may be open or closed.
		False. Do not select the object in the Database window; the database object must be open.
		If you do not specify the *indbwindow* argument, Access uses False.

Example

The following example illustrates how you can select the Customers form in the Database window.

```
DoCmd SelectObject A_FORM, "Customers", True
```

Remarks

When you select a hidden database object, Access makes the object visible. For example, when you select a hidden form, its **Visible** property is automatically set to True. Also, with forms, the **SelectObject** macro action uses whatever form properties you previously set for the form. For example, if the form is a pop-up form, **SelectObject** opens the form as a pop-up form.

If the object is not open, and you do not set the *indbwindow* argument to True, Access displays an error message and the function fails.

SetValue

You use the **SetValue** macro action from within a macro to set the value of a field, control, or property to a specified value.

The **SetValue** macro action accepts the following required arguments:

Argument	Required	Comments
item	Yes	This is the name of the field, control, or property on a form or report, or in a datasheet whose value you want to set.
value	Yes	This is the value or expression that becomes the new value for the item specified by *item*.

 You can use **SetValue** only from within a macro and not in Access Basic. For more information about the **SetValue** macro action, along with examples of its use, search Help for "SetValue."

Form- and Window-Manipulation Macro Actions

The form- and window-manipulation macro actions provide control over forms and windows in the Access environment:

- **AddMenu**
- **Close**
- **Maximize**
- **Minimize**
- **MoveSize**
- **OpenForm**
- **OpenModule**
- **OpenQuery**
- **OpenReport**
- **OpenTable**
- **Restore**

AddMenu

You use the **AddMenu** macro action from within a macro to add menus to a custom menu bar attached to a form or report.

The **AddMenu** macro action accepts the following required and optional arguments:

Argument	Required	Comments
menuname	Yes	This is the name of the menu that appears along the menu bar. Examples of menu names include File, Edit, and Help.
macroname	Yes	This is the name of the macro group that contains the individual macros that define the commands within the menu.
statusbartext	No	This the text that appears in the status bar when the user clicks on the menu name.

Remarks

The status bar text has limited value since it appears in the status bar only while the user clicks the menu. As soon as the user releases the mouse button, however, the status bar text disappears. In its place, Access either displays the status bar text for whatever control has the focus on the current form, or the status bar text for a menu command (if the user clicks on a menu command).

You can use **AddMenu** only from within a macro and not in Access Basic. For more information about the **AddMenu** macro action, along with examples of its use, search Help for "AddMenu."

Tip: When you add a custom menu bar, you replace the standard Access menu bar. To retain some of the Access commands on the custom menu bar, add the **DoMenuItem** macro action for each standard command you want to include in the custom menu bar.

Close

You use the **Close** macro action to close a specified window or, if no window is specified, the active window.

Syntax

```
DoCmd Close objecttype, objectname
```

The **Close** macro action accepts the following optional arguments:

Argument	Required	Comments
objecttype	No*	This is the type of database object you want to close. Valid values are A_TABLE, A_QUERY, A_FORM, A_REPORT, A_MACRO, and A_MODULE.
		If you do not specify the *objecttype* argument, do not specify the *objectname* argument, either.
objectname	No*	This is the name of the specific database object you want to close.
		If you do not specify the *objectname* argument, do not specify the *objecttype* argument, either.

* If you specify either argument, however, you must specify both.

473

Example

The following example illustrates how you can close the Customers form.

```
DoCmd Close A_FORM, "Customers"
```

Remarks

When you specify a specific database object, Access closes the window that contains the object. If you specify an object that is not currently open, or an object that does not exist, no error occurs and the function does not fail.

If you do not specify the *objecttype* and *objectname* arguments, Access closes the active window.

> One typical use of the **Close** macro action is to close the current form when the user presses a command button named OK or Cancel. To trigger the macro action, set the button's **OnClick** property to the name of a function that uses the **Close** macro action.
>
> **Close** has the same effect as choosing the Close command from the File menu or clicking Ctrl+F4.

Maximize

You use the **Maximize** macro action to resize the active window so that it fills the Access window.

Syntax

```
DoCmd Maximize
```

The **Maximize** macro action accepts no arguments.

Example

The following example illustrates how you can select and then maximize a form named Customers.

```
DoCmd SelectObject, A_FORM, "Customers"
DoCmd Maximize
```

Remarks

> The preceding example first used the **SelectObject** macro action to make the Customers form the active window. For more information, see the **SelectObject** macro action earlier in this chapter.

Maximize has the same effect as clicking the Maximize button in the window you want to enlarge.

Minimize

You use the **Minimize** macro action to reduce a window to an icon (see fig. 20.8).

Syntax

```
DoCmd Minimize
```

The **Minimize** macro action accepts no arguments.

Example

The following example illustrates how you can minimize a form named Main Menu (see fig. 20.8).

```
DoCmd SelectObject, A_FORM, "Main Menu"
DoCmd Minimize
```

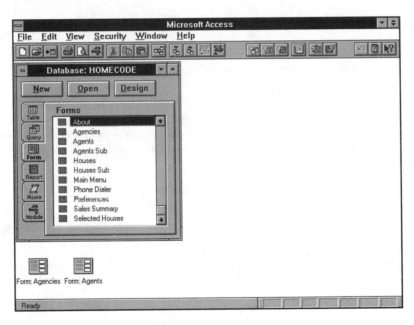

Figure 20.8. Use the **Minimize** macro action to reduce a form to an icon.

Remarks

 The preceding example first used the **SelectObject** macro action to make the Main Menu form the active window. For more information, see the **SelectObject** macro action earlier in this chapter.

Minimize has the same effect as clicking the Minimize button in the window you want to reduce to an icon.

MoveSize

You use the **MoveSize** macro action to either move or resize (or both) the active window.

Syntax

```
DoCmd MoveSize right, down, width, height
```

The **MoveSize** macro action accepts the following optional arguments:

Argument	Required	Comments
right	No*	This is the distance, in twips, that you want to move the window from the left edge of the Access window. A twip is 1/1440 of an inch.
down	No*	This is the distance, in twips, that you want to move the active window from the top edge of the Access window.
width	No*	This is the width, in twips, to which you want to resize the active window.
height	No*	This is the height, in twips, to which you want to resize the active window.

* Although each argument is optional, you must specify at least one of them.

Example

The following example illustrates how you can resize the active window to 3 inches wide and 2 inches high, plus move the window so that there is a half-inch of white space above and to the left.

```
DoCmd MoveSize 720, 720, 4320, 2880
```

Remarks

Because the **MoveSize** macro action works with the active window, you may need to first select the desired object (usually a form). For more information, see the **SelectObject** macro action earlier in this chapter.

OpenForm

You use the **OpenForm** macro action to open a specified form.

Syntax

```
DoCmd OpenForm formname, view, filtername, wherecondition, datamode, windowmode,
openargs
```

The **OpenForm** macro action accepts the following required and optional arguments:

Argument	Required	Comments
formname	Yes	This is the name of the form you want to open.
view	No	This is the view in which you want to open the form. Valid values are A_NORMAL, A_DESIGN, A_PREVIEW, and A_FORMDS (Datasheet View).
		If you do not specify the view argument, Access uses A_NORMAL.
filtername	No	This is the name of an existing filter or a filter that has been saved as a query. It determines which records to display, the sort order in which to display the records, or both.
wherecondition	No	This is a string that is an otherwise valid WHERE clause (without the word WHERE) that determines which records from the form's underlying recordset to show in the form.
datamode	No	This is the mode in which the form will be opened. Valid values are A_ADD, A_EDIT, and A_READONLY.
		A_ADD. You can add records but not edit existing records, to the form.
		A_EDIT. You can edit existing records, plus add new records.
		A_READONLY. You can view, but not change, any existing record. You cannot add new records.
		If you do not specify the datamode argument, Access uses A_EDIT.
windowmode	No	This describes the type of window in which the form will be opened. Valid values are A_NORMAL, A_HIDDEN, A_ICON, and A_DIALOG.
		A_NORMAL The form opens using whatever properties you set for the form in Design View.
		A_HIDDEN The form opens with the properties set in Design View, except the form is hidden (invisible). To display the form, set the form's Visible property to True.

continues

Argument	Required	Comments
		A_ICON. The form opens but is minimized to an icon. This has the same effect as opening the form using A_NORMAL and then using the **Minimize** macro action.
		A_DIALOG. The form opens with its **Modal** and **Pop-up** properties set to True.
		If you do not specify the *windowmode* argument, Access uses A_NORMAL.
openargs	No	You use this string argument to set the form's **OpenArgs** property. This argument may be used only in Access Basic and not in a macro.

Example

The following example illustrates how you can open a form named csvReport Launcher.

```
DoCmd OpenForm "csvReport Launcher"
```

Remarks

When you use the **OpenForm** macro action on a form that is already open, Access reopens the form using whatever arguments you specify to the macro action.

> The most common use for the **OpenForm** macro action is to open one form from another. For example, you might have a form named Orders containing a command button named History. When the user clicks the button, you can open a second form showing all of the relevant customer's sales history. To do this, specify the *wherecondition* argument to the macro action:
>
> ```
> DoCmd OpenForm "History", , ,"[OrderID] = '" &
> ➡Forms![Orders]![ID] & '"
> ```

If you specify the *openargs* argument, you can later determine the value of that argument by inspecting the form's **OpenArgs** property. For example, you might specify an *openargs* argument that is the ID for a particular customer. Once the form is open, you can then use the **FindRecord** macro action to go to that customer's record:

```
DoCmd OpenForm "Customers", , , , , , Forms![Lookup]![CustID]
DoCmd GoToControl "CustID"
DoCmd FindRecord Forms![Lookup]![CustID]
```

> **Tip:** In the preceding example, notice that specifying the *openargs* argument is not quite the same as specifying the *wherecondition* argument. When you specify the where condition, you limit the records. When you specify the *openargs* argument, you are simply passing along a string—a sort of comment—that you can later refer to in order to perform some other action (in this example, to position to a particular record).

OpenForm has the same effect as selecting a form in the Database window and then pressing either the Design or Open button.

OpenModule

You use the **OpenModule** macro action to open a specified module or procedure.

Syntax

```
DoCmd OpenModule modulename, procedurename
```

The **OpenModule** macro action accepts the following optional arguments:

Argument	Required	Comments
modulename	No*	This is the name of the module you want to open or, if you also specify the *procedurename* argument, it is the name of the module containing the desired procedure.
procedurename	No*	This is the name of the Function, Sub, or event procedure you want to open.
		If you do not specify the *procedurename* argument, Access opens the module specified by the *modulename* argument and displays the module's Declarations section.

* Although neither argument is required, you must specify one of them.

Example

The following example illustrates how you can open a module named Utilities and then go to the csvGoToRecord( ) function.

```
DoCmd OpenModule "Utilities", "csvGoToRecord"
```

Remarks

If you specify only the *procedurename* argument, Access looks for the desired procedure among all the global modules. Library modules are searched only if you have enabled library debugging. For more information, see Chapter 19, "Creating and Using Libraries."

OpenModule has the same effect as selecting a module in the Database window and then clicking the Design button. In addition, specifying the *procedurename* argument has the same effect as locating the desired procedure once the module has been opened.

OpenQuery

You use the **OpenQuery** macro action to open a select query or execute an action query (including pass-through queries that act like select and action queries).

Syntax

```
DoCmd OpenQuery queryname, view, datamode
```

The **OpenQuery** macro action accepts the following required and optional arguments:

Argument	Required	Comments
queryname	Yes	This is the name of the query you want to open (select queries) or run (action queries).
view	No	This is the view in which you want to open the query. Valid values are A_NORMAL (Datasheet view), A_DESIGN, and A_PREVIEW.
		If you do not specify the *view* argument, Access uses A_NORMAL.
datamode	No	This is the mode in which the query will be opened. Valid values are A_ADD, A_EDIT, and A_READONLY.
		A_ADD. You can add records to, but not edit existing records in, the datasheet.
		A_EDIT. You can edit existing records, plus add new records.
		A_READONLY. You can view, but not change, any existing record. You cannot add new records.
		If you do not specify the *datamode* argument, Access uses A_EDIT.

Example

The following example illustrates how you can open a query named Customers by Name Qry.

```
DoCmd OpenQuery "Customers by Name Qry"
```

Remarks

OpenQuery has the same effect as selecting a query in the Database window and then pressing either the Design or Open button.

OpenReport

You use the **OpenReport** macro action to open a specified report.

Syntax

```
DoCmd OpenReport reportname, view, filtername, wherecondition
```

The **OpenReport** macro action accepts the following required and optional arguments:

Argument	Required	Comments
formname	Yes	This is the name of the report you want to open.
view	No	This is the view in which you want to open the report. Valid values are A_NORMAL, A_DESIGN, and A_PREVIEW.
		If you do not specify the view argument, Access uses A_NORMAL, which prints the report.
filtername	No	This is the name of an existing filter or a filter that has been saved as a query. It determines which records to include in the report, the sort order in which to print the records, or both.
wherecondition	No	This is a string that is an otherwise valid WHERE clause (without the word WHERE) that determines which records from the report's underlying recordset to include in the report.

Example

The following example illustrates how you can open a report named Customers by Name.

```
DoCmd OpenReport "Customers by Name"
```

Remarks

When you print a report with the **OpenReport** macro action, Access prints the report without first displaying the Print dialog box. Instead, Access uses the most recent printer settings.

> **Tip:** If you want, you can use the **Print** macro action to define the printer settings. To make sure that the printer settings are correct before printing, you can use both the **OpenReport** macro action to open the report in Print Preview and then use the **Print** macro action to actually print the report.

OpenReport has the same effect as selecting a report in the Database window and then clicking either the Design or Preview button.

OpenTable

You use the **OpenTable** macro action to open a specified native or attached table.

Syntax

```
DoCmd OpenTable tablename, view, datamode
```

The **OpenTable** macro action accepts the following required and optional arguments:

Argument	Required	Comments
tablename	Yes	This is the name of the table you want to open.
view	No	This is the view in which you want to open the table. Valid values are A_NORMAL (Datasheet view), A_DESIGN, and A_PREVIEW.
		If you do not specify the *view* argument, Access uses A_NORMAL.
datamode	No	This is the mode in which the table will be opened. Valid values are A_ADD, A_EDIT, and A_READONLY.
		A_ADD. You can add records to, but not edit existing records in, the table.
		A_EDIT. You can edit existing records, plus add new records.
		A_READONLY. You can view, but not change, any existing record. You cannot add new records.
		If you do not specify the *datamode* argument, Access uses A_EDIT.

Example

The following example illustrates how you can open a table in Datasheet View.

```
DoCmd OpenTable "Customers", A_NORMAL
```

Remarks

There is not much demand for opening a table directly via Access Basic. The **OpenForm**, **OpenReport**, and **OpenQuery** macro actions are far more useful than **OpenTable**. You should think of tables more as sources of data for forms, reports, and queries, and not as objects you manipulate directly.

OpenTable has the same effect as selecting a table in the Database window and then pressing the Design or Open button.

Restore

You use the **Restore** macro action to restore a window to its previous size and position.

Syntax

```
DoCmd Restore
```

The **Restore** macro action accepts no arguments.

Example

The following example illustrates how you can first select and then restore a previously-minimized form.

```
DoCmd SelectObject A_FORM, "Main Menu"
DoCmd Restore
```

Remarks

The **Restore** macro action restores the window that contains the active object. If necessary, first select the window using the **SelectObject** macro action.

If the window has not been minimized (that is, it is not an icon), **Restore** has the same effect as clicking the Restore button in the upper right corner of the window. If the window has been reduced to an icon, using the **Restore** macro action has the same effect as choosing the Restore command from the window's control menu (see fig. 20.9).

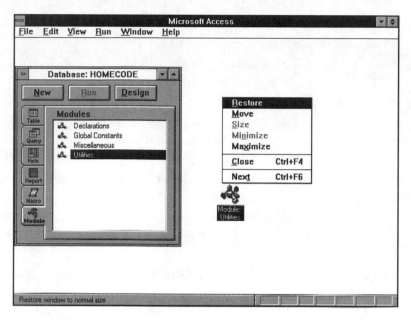

Figure 20.9. Users can choose the Restore command to restore the form.

Macro and Code Macro Actions

The macro and code macro actions let you control the execution of other macro actions or the execution of other programs:

- **CancelEvent**
- **DoMenuItem**
- **RunApp**
- **RunCode**
- **RunMacro**
- **StopAllMacros**
- **StopMacro**

CancelEvent

You use the **CancelEvent** macro action to cancel an event.

Syntax

```
DoCmd CancelEvent
```

The **CancelEvent** macro action accepts no arguments.

Example

The following example illustrates how you can cancel updating a record.

```
Function csvCheckForRequired (MyForm As Form) As Integer

    Dim AllFields As Integer

    ' Check to see if all required fields have been filled in.
    :
    If Not AllFields Then
        DoCmd CancelEvent
    End If
    csvCheckForRequired = AllFields

End Function
```

Remarks

The **CancelEvent** macro action has an effect only when you use it in a function called from an event such as **BeforeUpdate**.

You normally use **CancelEvent** when you want to stop an event under certain conditions. For example, you may not want to save a record if it does not pass all of your data validation checks. You can call a function with your data validation routines from the **BeforeUpdate** event of the form. If the form fails the validation, you can use the **CancelEvent** macro action to cancel the update.

Not all events may be canceled with **CancelEvent**, however. Table 20.1 lists the events to which this macro action applies.

Table 20.1. Events You Can Cancel

Event

BeforeDelConfirm

BeforeInsert

BeforeUpdate

DblClick

Delete

Exit

Format

KeyPress

MouseDown

Open

Print

Unload

> **STOP** **WARNING:** If a form's **OnUnload** event calls a function or event procedure that uses the **CancelEvent** macro action, the form will not close—**CancelEvent** cancels the close. To close the form under these conditions, you must resolve the condition that causes the **CancelEvent** macro action to run, or remove the **CancelEvent** macro action from the function or event procedure. If the form is a modal form (that is, you have set the form's **Modal** property to True), however, you will not be able to open the module containing the **CancelEvent**. For this reason, fully debug your application before you make your forms modal.

DoMenuItem

You use the **DoMenuItem** macro action to execute a built-in Access menu command as if the command had been chosen manually from a menu.

Syntax

```
DoCmd DoMenuItem menubar, menuname, command, subcommand, version
```

The **DoMenuItem** macro action accepts the following required and optional arguments:

Argument	Required	Comments
menubar	Yes	This is a number that identifies the menu bar that contains the command you want to execute. For Access 2.0, valid values are from 0 to 13.
		0 Form
		1 Database
		2 Filter
		3 Form Design
		4 Startup
		5 Module
		6 Query
		7 Report
		8 Macro
		9 Table Design
		10 Form Datasheet
		11 Table Datasheet
		12 Query Datasheet
		13 System Relationships
menu	Yes	This is a number that identifies the desired menu on the menu bar specified by the *menubar* argument. Valid values range from 0 to the number of menus available in the selected menu bar. To specify the first menu, enter 0 for the *menu* argument; to specify the second menu, enter 1, and so on.
command	Yes	This is a number that identifies the desired command within the menu specified by the *menu* argument. Valid values range from 0 to the number of commands available in the selected menu. To specify the first command, enter 0 for the *command* argument; to specify the second command, enter 1, and so on.
subcommand	No*	This is a number that identifies the desired subcommand for the selected command. Valid values range from 0 to the number of subcommands available for the command specified by the *command* argument.
		Not all menu commands have subcommands.

continues

Argument	Required	Comments
version	No	This determines whether the macro action will use the Access 1.X or Access 2.0 numbering scheme. Valid values are A_MENU_VER1X and A_MENU_VER20.
		A_MENU_VER1X. Values specified for the macro action refer to the number and order of menus and commands found in Access 1.0 and 1.1.
		A_MENU_VER20. Values specified for the macro action refer to the number and order of menus and commands found in Access 2.0.
		If you do not specify the *version* argument, Access uses A_MENU_VER1X.

* *This is required, however, whenever the command specified by the* command *argument has subcommands.*

Example

The following example illustrates how you can use **DoMenuItem** to select the current record.

```
DoCmd DoMenuItem 0, 1, 8, , A_MENU_VER20
```

Remarks

You must specify a command that is appropriate for the active object and the view. For example, if you are in Design View for a report, you cannot use **DoMenuItem** to run the Refresh command from the Records menu because that command is not appropriate for the current context.

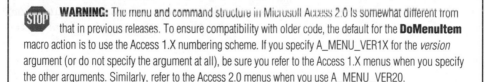

WARNING: The menu and command structure in Microsoft Access 2.0 is somewhat different from that in previous releases. To ensure compatibility with older code, the default for the **DoMenuItem** macro action is to use the Access 1.X numbering scheme. If you specify A_MENU_VER1X for the *version* argument (or do not specify the argument at all), be sure you refer to the Access 1.X menus when you specify the other arguments. Similarly, refer to the Access 2.0 menus when you use A_MENU_VER20.

 You can use **DoMenuItem** to add one of the built-in Access commands to custom menu bar. For more information, see the **AddMenu** macro action earlier in this chapter.

RunApp

You use the **RunApp** macro action to launch a Windows-based or DOS-based application.

The **RunApp** macro action accepts the following required argument:

Argument	Required	Comments
commandline	Yes	This is the name of the command used to start the desired application, including the path and any command-line arguments.

 You can use **RunApp** only from within a macro and not in Access Basic. For more information about the **RunApp** macro action, along with examples of its use, search Help for "RunApp."

RunApp has the same effect as using the **Shell** function. For more information about the **Shell** function, search Help for "shell."

RunCode

You use the **RunCode** macro action to call a function procedure from within a macro.

The **RunCode** macro action accepts the following required argument:

Argument	Required	Comments
functionname	Yes	This is the name of the function, followed by any arguments required by the function enclosed in parentheses. If the function does not accept any arguments, you must still include the parentheses.

 You can use **RunCode** only from within a macro and not in Access Basic. For more information about the **RunCode** macro action, along with examples of its use, search Help for "RunCode."

OutputTo

You use the **OutputTo** macro action to transfer data from a specified database object to an external file in another format.

Syntax

    DoCmd OutputTo *objecttype*, *objectname*, *outputformat*, *outputfile*, *autostart*

The **OutputTo** macro action accepts the following optional arguments:

Argument	Required	Comments
objecttype	No	This is the type of database object you want to output. Valid values are A_TABLE, A_QUERY, A_FORM, A_REPORT, and A_MODULE.
		You cannot use the **OutputTo** macro action to output the contents of a macro.
		If you do not specify the *objecttype* argument, Access uses the type of the current database object. For example, if a form is active when you use **OutputTo**, Access uses A_FORM.
objectname	No	This is the name of the database object you want to output. If specified, it must be the name of an object of the same type identified by the *objecttype* argument.
		If you do not specify the *objectname* argument, Access uses the name of the current database object.
outputformat	No	This identifies the format of the file you want to create. Valid values are A_FORMATXLS, A_FORMATRTF, and A_FORMATTXT.
		A_FORMATXLS creates a Microsoft Excel 3.0-compatible file.
		A_FORMATRTF creates a Rich Text Format (RTF) file.
		A_FORMATTXT creates an MS-DOS text file. If the *objecttype* argument identifies a module (or if you do not specify the *objecttype* argument and the current object is a module), then you may only output to an MS-DOS file.
		If you do not specify the *outputformat* argument, Access prompts you for the format.

492

Argument	Required	Comments
outputfile	No	This is the full name, including the path, of the file you want to create.
		If you do not specify the *outputfile* argument, Access prompts you for the file name.
autostart	No	This determines whether you want to launch an applicable application to load the output file. Valid values are True and False.
		True. Launch the application associated with the output file's extension. For example, if the output file is named OUTPUT.RTF, launch Microsoft Word for Windows.
		False. Do not launch the application.
		If you do not specify the *autostart* argument, Access uses False.

Example

The following example illustrates how you can transfer the contents of the Customers List report to a Rich Text Format (RTF) file.

```
MyReportName = "Customers List"
MyOutputFile = "C:\TEMP\CUSTLIST.RTF"
DoCmd OutputTo A_REPORT, MyReportName, A_FORMATRTF, MyOutputFile
```

Remarks

The following additional rules apply when you use the **OutputTo** macro action:

- If the output file contains OLE objects (for example, embedded graphs or bitmaps), the fields containing those objects appear blank.

- Fields based on Yes/No values (for example, toggle buttons and option buttons) appear as –1 (for True values) or 0 (for False values).

- When you transfer the data from a report using Excel format, Access transfers only text boxes. If you use the RTF or text formats, Access transfers only text boxes and labels.

- Access does not transfer subforms or subreports.

The **OutputTo** macro action has the same effect as choosing the Output To command from the File menu. The arguments to **OutputTo** correspond to the settings in the Output To dialog boxes.

SendObject

You use the **SendObject** macro action to include the data from a specified database object in a mail message and send that message.

Syntax

```
DoCmd SendObject objecttype, objectname, outputformat, to, cc, bcc, subject,
messagetext, editmessage
```

The **SendObject** macro action accepts the following optional arguments:

Argument	Required	Comments
objecttype	No*	This is the type of database object you want to include in the mail message. Valid values are A_TABLE, A_QUERY, A_FORM, A_REPORT, and A_MODULE.
		You cannot use the **SendObject** macro action to output the contents of a macro.
		If you do not specify the *objecttype* argument, Access uses the type of the current database object. For example, if a form is active when you use **SendObject**, Access uses A_FORM.
objectname	No*	This is the name of the database object you want to include. If specified, it must be the name of an object of the same type identified by the *objecttype* argument.
		If you do not specify the *objectname* argument, Access uses the name of the current database object, but only if you specify the *objecttype* argument (see the note below).
outputformat	No	This identifies the format of the file you want to create. Valid values are A_FORMATXLS, A_FORMATRTF, and A_FORMATTXT.
		A_FORMATXLS includes a Microsoft Excel 3.0-compatible file.
		A_FORMATRTF includes a Rich Text Format (RTF) file.

Argument	Required	Comments
		A_FORMATTXT includes an MS-DOS text file. If the *objecttype* argument identifies a module (or if you do not specify the *objecttype* argument and the *objectname* argument identifies a module), then you may only format the object as an MS-DOS file.
		If you do not specify the *outputformat* argument, Access prompts you for the format.
to	No	This is a string that identifies the list of people to whom you want to send the message. Separate the names with a semicolon (;).
		If you do not specify the *to* argument, Access prompts you for the list of recipients.
cc	No	Like the *to* argument, this is a string that identifies the list of people to whom you want to send the message. The *cc* recipients, however, receive carbon copies of the message.
bcc	No	Like the *to* argument, this is a string that identifies the list of people to whom you want to send the message. The *bcc* recipients, however, receive blind carbon copies of the message.
subject	No	This is the text that will appear in the subject line of the message.
messagetext	No	This is the text that will appear along with the embedded database object in the body of the message.
editmessage	No	This indicates whether Access should launch the mail application with the message loaded. Valid values are True and False.
		True. Launch the mail application and allow you to edit the message before sending it.
		False. Do not launch the mail application and send the message immediately.
		If you do not specify the *editmessage* argument, Access uses False.

* *If you do not specify either argument, Access sends the message but does not include any database object.*

Example

The following example illustrates how you can send a mail message to Regina Younger that includes a copy of the Daily Sales report in Microsoft Excel format.

```
DoCmd SendObject A_REPORT, "Daily Sales", A_FORMATXLS,
➥"Regina Younger", , , "Today's Report", "Call
➥me if you have any questions."
```

Remarks

You can use the **SendObject** macro action only if you have a MAPI-compliant mail system installed on your computer.

The following additional rules apply when you use the **SendObject** macro action:

- If the selected database object contains OLE objects (for example, embedded graphs or bitmaps), those objects appear blank.

- Fields based on Yes/No values (for example, toggle buttons and option buttons) appear as −1 (for True values) or 0 (for False values).

- When you send a report object using Excel format, Access includes only text boxes. If you use the RTF or text formats, Access includes only text boxes and labels.

- Access does not include subforms or subreports.

> **Note:** If the mail application cannot identify the names you specify in the *to*, *cc*, or *bcc* arguments, the message will not be sent.

SendObject has the same effect as choosing the Send command from the File menu. The arguments to **SendObject** correspond to the settings in the Send dialog boxes.

TransferDatabase

You use the **TransferDatabase** macro action to import or export data or database objects to another database, or to attach a table in another database.

Syntax

```
DoCmd TransferDatabase transfertype, databasetype, databasename, objecttype, source,
destination, structureonly, saveloginid
```

The **TransferDatabase** macro action accepts the following required and optional arguments:

Argument	Required	Comments
transfertype	No	This identifies the type of transfer you want to perform. Valid values are A_IMPORT, A_EXPORT, and A_ATTACH.
		A_IMPORT copies data from the source database.
		A_EXPORT copies data to the destination database.
		A_ATTACH establishes a link between two databases; you can use the data, but it continues to reside in the source database.
		If you do not specify the *transfertype* argument, Access uses A_IMPORT.
databasetype	Yes	This is a string that identifies the type of database you want to work with. Valid values may include "Microsoft Access" and "FoxPro 2.5."
		For a complete list of the available database types (determined by the drivers you selected when you installed Access), create a new macro, select the **TransferDatabase** macro action, and then open the drop-down list for the database type.
databasename	Yes	This is the name, including the complete path, of the database you want to use.
objecttype	No	This identifies the type of database object you want to import, export, or attach. Valid values are A_TABLE, A_QUERY, A_FORM, A_REPORT, A_MACRO, and A_MODULE.
		If you specify any argument other than A_TABLE, the *databasetype* argument must be "Microsoft Access."
		To export the results of a query to another Access database, specify A_QUERY. To export the results to another type of database other than Microsoft Access, specify A_TABLE.
		If you do not specify the *objecttype* argument, Access uses A_TABLE.
source	Yes	This is the name of the database object whose data you want to import, export, or attach.

continues

497

Argument	Required	Comments
destination	Yes	This is the name of the database object in the "other" database.
structureonly	No	This identifies whether only the structure of the object is to be imported or exported. Valid values are True and False.
		True. Import or export only the structure; do not include any data.
		False. Import or export not only the structure, but the data as well.
		If you do not specify the *strutureonly* argument, Access uses False.
saveloginid	No	This indicates whether login and password information for an SQL database should be stored for an attached table. Valid values are True and False.
		True. Store the user ID and password when you attach the table; Access does not prompt for the ID or password when the user uses the attached table.
		False. Do not store the user ID and password; each time the user uses the attached table, Access prompts for the ID and password.
		If you do not specify the *saveloginid* argument, Access uses False.

Example

The following example illustrates how you can import the Utilities module from another Access database and copy it to the Tools module.

```
DoCmd TransferDatabase A_IMPORT, "Microsoft Access",
➡"C:\ACCESS\LIB\TOOLS.MDA", A_MODULE,
➡"Utilities", "Tools"
```

Remarks

Even if you specify True for the *savelogin* argument, the administrator of an SQL database can disable this feature on the backend and require users to enter an ID and password each time they connect to the SQL database.

If you are importing, and an existing Access object already has that name, Access uses the same name but adds a number to the end of the name. If you are exporting and the name already exists, Access automatically overwrites (replaces) the existing table or object with the one you are exporting.

> ▣ Use the **TransferDatabase** macro action when you maintain data in one environment yet have access to it in another. For example, your invoice system may exist in dBASE format. To maintain a list of customers in a Microsoft Access table, you can either import the existing dBASE customer database into Access and leave the original customer database in dBASE, or you can attach the customer database to Access and use the original in both dBASE and Access. If you attach instead of import, whenever you add new customers from either Access or dBASE both environments will "see" the new customers without having to enter the data twice. **TransferDatabase** has the same effect as choosing the Import, Export, or Attach Table commands from the File menu.

TransferSpreadsheet

You use the **TransferSpreadsheet** macro action to import or export data between Microsoft Access and a spreadsheet.

Syntax

```
DoCmd TransferSpreadsheet transfertype, spreadsheettype, tablename, filename,
hasfieldnames, range
```

The **TransferSpreadsheet** macro action accepts the following required and optional arguments:

Argument	Required	Comments
transfertype	No	This identifies the type of transfer you want to perform. Valid values are A_IMPORT and A_EXPORT.
		A_IMPORT copies data from the specified spreadsheet file.
		A_EXPORT copies data to the specified spreadsheet file.
		If you do not specify the *transfertype* argument, Access uses A_IMPORT.
spreadsheettype	No	This identifies the type of spreadsheet you want to work with. Valid values are 0, 1, 2, 3, 4, and 5.
		0 Microsoft Excel versions 2.x, 3.x, and 4.x
		1 Lotus 1-2-3 (WKS format)
		2 Lotus 1-2-3 (WK1 format)
		3 Lotus 1-2-3 (WK3 format)

continues

Syntax

```
DoCmd TransferText transfertype, specificationname, tablename, filename,
hasfieldnames
```

The **TransferText** macro action accepts the following required and optional arguments:

Argument	Required	Comments
transfertype	No	This identifies the type of transfer you want to perform. Valid values are A_IMPORTDELIM, A_IMPORTFIXED, A_EXPORTDELIM, A_EXPORTFIXED, and A_EXPORTMERGE.
		A_IMPORTDELIM copies data from the specified file; the fields are separated by a special character, usually a comma.
		A_IMPORTFIXED copies data from the specified file; the fields are not separated by any special character, but rather have predefined widths. Each row has the same width and each field begins and ends at the same position within its row.
		A_EXPORTDELIM copies data to the specified file; the fields will be separated by a delimiter, usually a comma.
		A_EXPORTFIXED copies data to the specified file; the fields will not be separated by any special character, but rather will have fixed row lengths and field widths.
		A_EXPORTMERGE copies data to a Microsoft Word for Windows mail merge data file.
		If you do not specify the *transfertype* argument, Access uses A_IMPORTDELIM.
specificationname	No*	This is the name of a previously-defined import or export specification in the current database.
tablename	Yes	This is the name of the Microsoft Access table into which you want to import the data, or from which you want to export data.
		If you are importing and the specified table already exists, Access appends the data to the table.
		If you are exporting, the *tablename* argument can also be the name of a select query.

Argument	Required	Comments
filename	Yes	This is the name, including the complete path, of the file you want to work with.
		If you are exporting and the specified file already exists, Access replaces the existing file.
hasfieldnames	No	This identifies whether the file has field names in the first row. Valid values are True and False.
		True. If importing a file, the first row contains field names; the field names in the file must match the field names in the Access table. If exporting to a file, Access will insert field names in the first row of data.
		False. If importing a file, the first row contains data, not field names; if exporting to a file, Access will place data in the first row, not field names.
		Access ignores this argument if the *transfertype* argument is A_EXPORTMERGE. In this case, the first row of data must contain field names.
		If you do not specify the *hasfieldnames* argument, Access uses False.

* This argument is required when the transfertype *argument is A_IMPORTFIXED or A_EXPORTFIXED.*

Example

The following example illustrates how you can export the Customer Phone Book report to a delimited text file.

```
DoCmd TransferText A_EXPORTDELIM, , "Customer PhoneBook", "C:\TEMP\FONEBOOK.TXT"
```

Remarks

Microsoft Access provides several methods for sharing complex data when you are uncertain about the hardware and software others might use to read the data.

> You might create a series of columnar reports on different computer systems, print them to files and download them to your computer. Then, use the **TransferText** macro action to import the files into an Access table as fixed-width text. If you want to share data with other users, and you do not know for certain what software may be used on the other systems, you can be reasonably sure that exported, delimited text will be readable on those other systems. Most software can import data from a delimited text file.

TransferText has the same effect as choosing the Import or Export command from the file menu.

Miscellaneous Macro Actions

The following sections describe ways to use miscellaneous macro actions in Microsoft Access:

- **Beep**
- **Echo**
- **Hourglass**
- **MsgBox**
- **Quit**
- **SendKeys**
- **SetWarnings**
- **ShowToolbar**

Beep

You use the **Beep** macro action to emit an audible tone.

Syntax

```
DoCmd Beep
```

The **Beep** macro action accepts no arguments.

Example

The following example illustrates how you can produce a beep on the computer's speaker.

```
DoCmd Beep
```

Remarks

Use the **Beep** macro action to alert the user to special conditions such as errors when you display a message box. Avoid using sounds alone, however, because some users cannot hear and some computers may be situated where the speaker cannot be heard.

The user can turn off the speaker via the Windows Control Panel by disabling system sounds (see fig. 20.10).

Hourglass

You use the **Hourglass** macro action to display or turn off the hourglass mouse pointer (refer to fig. 20.12).

Syntax

```
DoCmd Hourglass status
```

The **Hourglass** macro action accepts the following required argument:

Argument	Required	Comments
status	Yes	This indicates whether the mouse pointer should be an hourglass.

Example

The following example illustrates how you can change the mouse pointer to an hourglass (see fig. 20.12) while deleting records from a table.

```
DoCmd Hourglass True
DoCmd SetWarnings False
DoCmd RunSQL "DELETE * FROM Customers WHERE Status = 'I';"
DoCmd SetWarnings True
DoCmd Hourglass False
```

Figure 20.12. You can use the **Hourglass** macro action to change the shape of the mouse pointer.

Remarks

Use the **Hourglass** macro action whenever you perform an activity or call a function that will take more than just a few seconds complete. Setting the mouse pointer to an hourglass will help prevent unwanted computer rebooting because it lets the user know the system is in use and is not locked up.

MsgBox

You use the **MsgBox** macro action to display a message box with specified text and an optional icon.

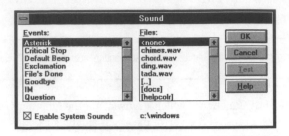

Figure 20.10. Use the Control Panel to enable system sounds.

Echo

You use the **Echo** macro action to suppress or enable updating of the screen, or to set the text that appears in the status bar.

Syntax

```
DoCmd Echo status, statusbartext
```

The **Echo** macro action accepts the following required and optional arguments:

Argument	Required	Comments
status	Yes	This identifies whether screen updating will be enabled. Valid values are True and False.
		True enables screen updating.
		False disables screen updating.
statusbartext	No	This is the text that will be displayed in the status bar.
		If you do not specify the *statusbartext* argument, the status bar text remains unchanged.

Example

The following example illustrates how you can suppress screen updating.

```
DoCmd Echo False
```

Remarks

 For more information about using the **Echo** macro action, search Help for "Echo."

Using **Echo** does not affect the function in which it is used, nor the function's results. You cannot use the **Echo** macro action to suppress certain error messages and dialog boxes, however. To suppress dialog boxes, use the **SetWarnings** macro action.

You can use **Echo** more than once in a single function and thus change the status bar text to indicate the progress of the function (see fig. 20.11).

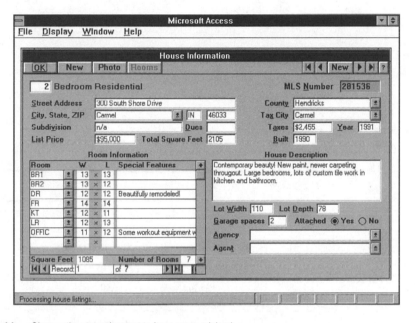

Figure 20.11. Change the status bar text to keep users advised.

 Note: You can also use the **SysCmd** function to set the status bar text. For more information about the **SysCmd** function, search Help for "SysCmd."

 Tip: If you use the **Echo** macro action to suppress screen updating, consider using the **Hourglass** macro action to turn the mouse pointer into an hourglass; this provides the user with a visual cue that the system is running your function and is not locked up.

Syntax

DoCmd MsgBox *message*, *icon*, *titlebar*

The **MsgBox** macro action accepts the following required and optional arguments:

Argument	Required	Comments
message	Yes	This is the text that will appear in the message box. It can be a literal string or an expression that evaluates to a string.
icon	No	This integer value defines not only the type of icon that appears in the message box, but also the number and types of buttons.
		If you do not specify the *icon* argument, Access displays a single command button with the caption, "OK."
titlebar	No	This identifies the caption that will appear in the title bar.
		If you do not specify the *titlebar* argument, Access displays "Microsoft Access" in the title bar.

Example

The following example illustrates how you can display a message box with a custom message, icon, and caption in the titlebar.

```
    :
    Msg = "Report '" & MyReportName & "' has been printed."
    Icon = csvMB_ICONINFORMATION ' 64.
    Titlebar = "Print Report"
    DoCmd MsgBox Msg, Icon, Titlebar
    :
```

Remarks

The following tables list the values you can use for the *icon* argument. Table 20.2 lists the values you can specify to add buttons to a message box, table 20.3 lists values for the icons, and table 20.4 lists the values for setting the default button.

Table 20.2. Button Values

Value	Meaning
0	Display an OK button only.

Value	Meaning
1	Display OK and Cancel buttons.
2	Display Abort, Retry, and Ignore buttons.
3	Display Yes, No, and Cancel buttons.
4	Display Yes and No buttons.
5	Display Retry and Cancel buttons.

Table 20.3.   Icon Values

Value	Meaning	Icon
0	Display no icon.	
16	Display a stop sign.	
32	Display a question mark.	
48	Display an exclamation mark.	
64	Display an information icon.	

Table 20.4.   Default Button Values

Value	Meaning
0	The first button is the default button.
256	The second button is the default button.
512	The third button is the default button.

Note: The *icon* argument values are additive, which means you can combine values to achieve different effects. For example, specifying a value of 4 for the *icon* argument will display both a Yes and No button, but no icon. If you are asking a question, however, you should also display a question mark. The value for a question mark icon is 32, so the combined icon value is 36 (4 + 32 = 36). This produces a message box with a question mark icon and two command buttons.

Message boxes are modal and retain their focus until the user clicks one of the command buttons.

> **Tip:** You can use the **MsgBox** function to determine which button the user clicked. For more information about using the **MsgBox** macro action or the **MsgBox** function, search Help for "MsgBox."

Quit

You use the **Quit** macro action to leave (quit) Access.

Syntax

```
DoCmd Quit option
```

The **Quit** macro action accepts the following optional arguments:

Argument	Required	Comments
option	No	This specifies whether Access prompts the user to save unsaved changes. Valid values are A_PROMPT, A_SAVE, and A_EXIT.
		A_PROMPT. The user will be prompted to save any unsaved changes.
		A_SAVE. Any changes will automatically be saved without prompting the user.
		A_EXIT. Quits Access without saving any changes.
		If you do not specify the *option* argument, Access uses A_SAVE.

Example

The following example illustrates how you can exit Microsoft Access after first prompting the user to save any unsaved changes.

```
DoCmd Quit A_PROMPT
```

Remarks

The most common way to use the **Quit** macro action is on a main menu form that has an Exit command button. To trigger the macro action, set the command button's **OnClick** property to the name of a function that uses the **Quit** macro action (see fig. 20.13).

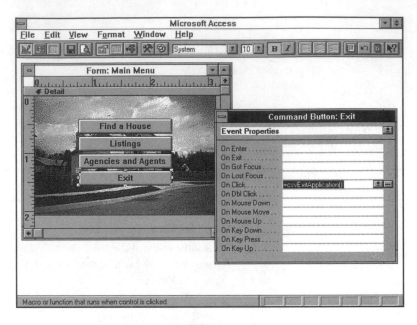

Figure 20.13. You can call a function that uses the **Quit** macro action.

```
Function csvExitApplication () As Integer

    ' Purpose: exits Access after first saving all
    '          unsaved changes.
    ' Accepts: nothing
    ' Returns: True  - successful
    '          False - unsuccessful
    ' Version: 1.00 02-Apr-94  CSV
    ' -------------------------------------------
    Const csvMB_ICONINFORMATION = 64
    Dim Msg As String, Icon As Integer
    Dim Titlebar As String

    Titlebar = "csvExitApplication"
    On Error Resume Next
    DoCmd Quit
    If Err Then
        Msg = "Couldn't exit application."
        Icon = csvMB_ICONEXCLAMATION
        MsgBox Msg, Icon, Titlebar
        csvExitApplication = False
    Else
        csvExitApplication = True
    End If
    On Error GoTo 0

End Function
```

Quit has the same effect as choosing the Exit command from the File menu.

SendKeys

You use the **SendKeys** macro action to send keystrokes directly to Access or to an active Windows application as if the user had typed them directly at the keyboard.

Syntax

    DoCmd SendKeys *keystrokes*, *wait*

The **SendKeys** macro action accepts the following required and optional arguments:

Argument	Required	Comments
keystrokes	Yes	This is a string that contains the keys you want to "send" to the keyboard.
wait	No	This indicates whether Access should wait until the keystrokes have been processed. Valid values are True and False.
		True. Wait until the keystrokes have been processed before continuing.
		False. Do not wait before continuing.
		If you do not specify the *wait* argument, Access uses False.

Remarks

 You can use **SendKeys** only from within a macro and not in Access Basic. For more information about the **SendKeys** macro action, along with examples of its use, search Help for "SendKeys."

SetWarnings

You use the **SetWarnings** macro action to suppress certain system messages.

Syntax

    DoCmd SetWarnings *state*

The **SetWarnings** macro action accepts the following required argument:

Argument	Required	Comments
state	Yes	This indicates whether certain system messages should be suppressed. Valid values are True and False.
		True. Display system messages.
		False. Do not display system messages.

Example

The following example illustrates how you can suppress the system message that normally appears when you use the **RunSQL** macro action.

```
DoCmd SetWarnings False
DoCmd RunSQL "DELETE * FROM Customers WHERE Status = 'I';"
DoCmd SetWarnings True
```

Remarks

No matter how you specify the *state* argument, Access always displays untrapped error messages.

> **Tip:** To make sure a function runs properly with warnings suppressed, first call the function with the *state* argument set to True. If you press OK or Yes in all the warning or message boxes, you can then set the *state* argument to True. However, if you press No or Cancel in any of the warning or message boxes, you do not want to use the **SetWarnings** macro action to suppress the messages.

ShowToolbar

You use the **ShowToolbar** macro action to display or hide a built-in or custom toolbar.

Syntax

```
DoCmd ShowToolbar toolbarname, show
```

The **ShowToolbar** macro action accepts the following required and optional arguments:

Argument	Required	Comments
toolbarname	Yes	This is the name of one of the built-in toolbars or the name of a custom toolbar you have created.
show	No	This indicates whether and when the specified toolbar will be made visible. Valid values are A_TOOLBAR_YES, A_TOOLBAR_WHERE_APPROP, and A_TOOLBAR_NO. **A_TOOLBAR_YES** displays the toolbar at all times, no matter which window has the focus. **A_TOOLBAR_WHERE_APPROP.** If the toolbar specified by the *toolbarname* argument is a built-in toolbar, the toolbar will be visible only when the active window would normally display the toolbar. If the toolbar is a custom toolbar, the toolbar will be visible no matter which window has the focus (that is, it will be as if you had specified A_TOOLBAR_YES). **A_TOOLBAR_NO** does not display the specified toolbar. If you do not specify the *show* argument, Access uses A_TOOLBAR_NO.

Example

The following example illustrates how you can display a custom toolbar named Customers Toolbar when the Customers form is opened.

```
DoCmd OpenForm, "Customers"
DoCmd ShowToolbar "Customers Toolbar", A_TOOLBAR_YES
```

Remarks

If the Built-In Toolbars Available item in the General category in the Options dialog box is set to No, you can use the **ShowToolbar** macro action to display and hide only custom toolbars.

> **Tip:** Unlike the preceding example, it may be better to display a custom toolbar as part of a form's **GotFocus** event. That way, whenever the form receives the focus (not just when it is first opened) the toolbar will become visible. Similarly, you might hide the toolbar as part of the form's **LostFocus** event. Use **ShowToolbar**, specifying A_TOOLBAR_NO for the *show* argument.

ShowToolbar has the same effect as choosing the Toolbars command from the View menu, selecting a toolbar, and choosing the Show or Hide button.

21

Useful Functions

This chapter includes the source code for more than 100 user-defined functions you can use to provide extended functionality and flexibility to your applications.

Many of these functions call other user-defined functions, Windows API functions, or refer to global constants you must declare in your own Declarations or Global Constants modules. For more information about these modules, see Chapter 17, "Naming Conventions and Style Guidelines."

> **Tip:** The easiest way to determine whether a function requires a declaration (or calls another function) is to enter the function from this chapter and then choose the Compile Loaded Modules command from the Run menu. Access highlights and identifies any missing declaration or function. Appendix A, "Windows API Declarations," and Appendix B, "Constants," contain the API function declarations and global constant declarations.

This chapter includes the functions described in Table 21.1.

Table 21.1. Useful Functions and Their Purposes

Function	Purpose
csvActivateApp()	Makes another application active.
csvBinarySearch()	Quickly locates an element in a sorted array.
csvCapture()	Copies a specified area of the screen to the clipboard.
csvCaptureForm()	Copies a specified form to the clipboard.
csvCaptureScreen()	Copies the entire screen to the clipboard.

continues

Table 21.1. Continued

Function	Purpose
csvCenterForm()	Centers a form on-screen.
csvCheckMenuCommand()	Checks or unchecks a menu command.
csvCloneControls()	Saves or restores the values from a set of controls.
csvCloseForm()	Closes a specified form.
csvConnectTo()	Connects to a specified network resource.
csvCopyObject	Copies a specified database object.
csvCreateTextFile()	Creates a specified text (MS-DOS) file.
csvDeleteAllRecords()	Removes (deletes) all records from a specified table.
csvDeleteObject()	Deletes a specified database object.
csvDialPhone()	Dials a specified phone number.
csvDisableControl()	Disables a specified control.
csvDoDblClick()	Executes the macro or function specified by a control's **OnDblClick** property.
csvDriveType()	Returns the type of drive for a specified device.
csvEcho()	Enables or disables echoing of screen updates.
csvEnableControl()	Enables a specified control.
csvExecuteCommand()	Executes a built-in MS-DOS command.
csvExecuteProgram()	Executes (launches) a Windows-based application.
csvExitWindows()	Exits Microsoft Windows.
csvExplodeForm()	Creates an exploding form effect when a form first opens.
csvExportTable()	Exports the contents of a specified table (or query) to an external MS-DOS text file.
csvFieldDataType()	Determines the data type for a specified field in a specified table.
csvFileExists()	Determines whether a specified external MS-DOS file exists.
csvFillDeviceCharacteristics()	Fills a combo box or list box with a variety of characteristics for a specified device.
csvFillDisplayCharacteristics()	Fills a combo box or list box with a variety of characteristics for the display device.
csvFillFileNames()	Fills a combo box or list box with the file names for a specified directory.

Function	Purpose
csvFormatDiskLabel()	Formats a report with the names of files on a specified drive.
csvFormIsLoaded()	Determines whether a specified form is loaded.
csvGetDiskSpaceFree()	Returns the amount of available space on a specified drive.
csvGetFreeResources()	Returns the amount of available system resources.
csvGetINIText()	Returns an entry from a specified .INI file.
csvGetIntlInt()	Returns a numeric entry from the [Intl] section of the WIN.INI file.
csvGetIntlString()	Returns a string entry from the [Intl] section of the WIN.INI file.
csvGoToControl	Moves the focus to a specified control and optionally to a specified form.
csvGoToForm()	Moves the focus to a specified open form.
csvGoToPage()	Moves the focus to a specified page.
csvGoToRecord()	Moves the focus to a specified record.
csvHideControl()	Hides (makes invisible) a specified control.
csvHideForm()	Hides (makes invisible) a specified form.
csvHighWord()	Returns the high word for a specified numeric value.
csvHourglass()	Enables or disables the hourglass mouse pointer.
csvICap()	Returns a string that is initial-capped.
csvIsEnabled()	Determines whether a specified control is enabled.
csvKeyboardInfo()	Determines a variety of information about the keyboard.
csvLogError()	Writes selected error information to an external MS-DOS text file.
csvLowWord()	Returns the low word for a specified numeric value.
csvMakeDirectory	Creates a new directory on a specified drive.
csvMathChipPresent()	Determines whether a math chip (coprocessor) is installed.
csvMaximize()	Maximizes the current window.
csvMaxValue()	Returns the larger of two values.
csvMinimize()	Minimizes the current window.
csvMinValue()	Returns the smaller of two values.

continues

517

Table 21.1. Continued

Function	Purpose
csvMoveToForm()	Moves the focus to a specified form.
csvMultiCap()	Returns a string in which each word is initial-capped.
csvNullToChar()	Returns a value in which a Null value is replaced with a specified value (or string).
csvObjectExists()	Determines whether a specified object exists.
csvOpenForm()	Opens a specified form.
csvOperatingMode()	Determines the current operating mode (for example, 386 Enhanced).
csvParseArticles()	Returns a string in which the articles *a*, *an*, and *the* are moved to the end of the string.
csvPlayWaveform()	Plays a specified waveform (.WAV) file.
csvQuit()	Quits (exits) Microsoft Access.
csvRecordCount()	Returns the number of records in a specified table or returned by a specified query.
csvRemoveAccessMenu()	Removes the menu bar from the Access window.
csvRemoveCloseCommand()	Removes the Close command from the control menu.
csvRemoveTitleBar()	Removes the title bar from a specified form.
csvRename()	Renames a specified database object.
csvRequery()	Requeries the current form or a specified control.
csvResetStatusBarText()	Resets the status bar text.
csvResizeForm()	Resizes a specified form.
csvRestore()	Restores the current window.
csvRound()	Returns the rounded equivalent for a specified numeric value.
csvScreenDimension()	Returns the width or height for the current display.
csvSearchAndReplace()	Returns a string in which specified characters are replaced with other specified characters.
csvSetAppTitleBar()	Sets the caption for the Access window.
csvSetStatusBarText()	Sets the status bar text to a specified string.
csvSetTitleBar()	Sets the caption for a specified form.
csvSetToNull()	Sets a specified control to Null.
csvSizeWindow()	Saves the current size/position of a form or restores the previously saved size/position.

Function	*Purpose*
csvSomethingIn()	Determines whether anything is in a specified control.
csvSort()	Sorts an array.
csvSortArray()	Sorts an array (specifying the upper limit).
csvSound()	Plays a sound (frequency) through the computer's speaker.
csvStackForms()	Centers all open forms, creating a stacked appearance.
csvStartupDirectory()	Returns the startup directory for the current database.
csvStripCtrlChars()	Returns a string in which all the control characters have been removed.
csvSystemResources()	Returns the amount of available system resources or the amount of available memory.
csvTableType	Determines whether a specified table is native or attached.
csvTempFileName()	Creates a text file with a temporary file name.
csvToggleControlMenu()	Hides or shows the control menu on a specified form.
csvToggleMenuCommand()	Enables or disables a specified menu command.
csvToggleMinMax()	Hides or shows the minimize and maximize buttons on a specified form.
csvToggleToolbars()	Hides or displays the built-in toolbars.
csvUnhighlightControl()	Unhighlights a specified control by sending F2 and, optionally, HOME.
csvUsedErrors()	Creates an external MS-DOS text file listing all the internal Access Basic error codes.
csvValidatePostalCode()	Determines whether a specified postal code is valid.
csvValidState()	Determines whether a specified state abbreviation is valid.
csvWait()	Pauses for a specified period of time.
csvWaitToExecute()	Pauses for a specified period of time and then executes a specified command or launches a specified application.
csvWindowPosition()	Saves or restores the position of a specified form.
csvWindowsColor()	Returns a specified color previously set with the Control Panel.
csvWindowsVersion()	Returns the Microsoft Windows version.
csvWindowText()	Returns the text (caption) for a specified form.

519

csvActivateApp()

Use the csvActivateApp() function to make another running application active. For example, from Microsoft Access you can move the focus to the Windows Calendar application or to Microsoft Excel.

```
Function csvActivateApp (ByVal AppName As String, ByVal ClassName As String) As
➡Integer

    Const TITLEBAR = "Activate Application"
    Dim WindowHandle As Integer
    Dim X As Integer
    Dim Found As Integer

    If AppName <> "" Then
        WindowHandle = csvFindWindow(0&, AppName)
    Else
        WindowHandle = csvFindWindow(ClassName, 0&)
    End If

    If WindowHandle <> 0 Then
        X = csvSetActiveWindow(WindowHandle)
    End If

    Found = (WindowHandle <> 0)
    If Not Found Then
        MsgBox "Couldn't activate '" & Trim$(AppName & "   " & ClassName) & "',",
csvMB_ICONINFORMATION,
        [IconCont]TITLEBAR
    End If

    csvActivateApp = Found

End Function
```

You must supply either the *AppName* or *ClassName* argument. Table 21.2 lists class names for some common applications.

Table 21.2. Common Application Class Names

Application	Class Name
Access (MSACCESS.EXE)	OMain
Calculator (CALC.EXE)	SciCalc
Calendar (CALENDAR.EXE)	CalWndMain
Cardfile (CARDFILE.EXE)	Cardfile
Clock (CLOCK.EXE)	Clock
Control Panel (CONTROL.EXE)	CtlPanelClass
Notepad (NOTEPAD.EXE)	Notepad
Paintbrush (PBRUSH.EXE)	PbParent

Application	Class Name
Print Manager (PRINTMAN.EXE)	PrintManager
File Manager (WINFILE.EXE)	WFS_Frame
Windows Help (WINHELP.EXE)	MW_WINHELP
Write (WRITE.EXE)	MSWRITE_MENU

csvBinarySearch()

There are two ways you can search an array: linear and binary.

Linear Search

In a linear search, you look for a match in the first element of the array. If you find a match, stop. If you do not find a match, look at the next element and continue until you find a match or reach the end of the array.

In an array of 1000 elements, you may need to look through all 1000 elements before you can tell whether the element you want exists.

When you use a linear search, the array does not need to be sorted.

Binary Search

 A binary search works only if the array is sorted. For more information about sorting an array, see the `csvSortArray()` function later in this chapter.

In a binary search, you look at the middle element, and if you find a match, stop. If you find no match, determine whether the element you want should be in the first half or second half of the array. This eliminates half the elements from consideration.

For example, if an array has 1000 elements, look at the middle element. If you find no match, ignore the first 500 or the last 500 elements. Next, check the middle element in the half that remains, continuing this process until you find a match or run out of elements to check.

Table 21.3 illustrates the maximum number of searches necessary to find (or not find) an element and how much more efficient a binary search is when you work with sorted arrays.

Table 21.3.   Comparison of Linear and Binary Searches

Number of Elements	Linear Search	Binary Search
500	500	10
1000	1000	11
2000	2000	12
5000	5000	14
10,000	10,000	15
20,000	20,000	16
100,000	100,000	18

Searching an unsorted array larger than about 100 elements is impractical. If the array is sorted, however, you can realistically perform a binary search no matter how many elements are in the array. Doubling the number of elements to search adds only one more comparison, so even a million-element array requires no more than 21 comparisons.

```
Function csvBinarySearch (Array() As Variant, ByVal FindString As Variant) As Long

    Dim Minimum As Long
    Dim Maximum As Long
    Dim FindLength As Integer
    Dim Possible As Long

    Minimum = LBound(Array)
    Maximum = UBound(Array)
    FindLength = Len(FindString)

    csvBinarySearch = 0
    Do
        Possible = (Maximum + Minimum) \ 2
        If Len(Array(Possible)) = FindLength Then
            If Array(Possible) = FindString Then
                csvBinarySearch = Possible
                Exit Do
            End If
        End If
        If Array(Possible) > FindString Then
            Maximum = Possible - 1
        Else
            Minimum = Possible - 1
        End If
    Loop While Maximum > Minimum

End Function
```

csvCapture()

You can use the csvCapture() function to copy all or part of the screen to the clipboard. This function accepts four coordinates (expressed in pixels) that define the upper left and lower right corners of the area you want to copy.

Both the csvCaptureForm() and csvCaptureScreen() functions call this function, but you may find that capturing selected portions of a form is useful.

```
Function csvCapture (ByVal X1 As Integer, Y1 As Integer, X2 As Integer, Y2 As
Integer, ByVal MyWindowHandle
➥As Integer) As Integer

    Dim RectWidth As Integer
    Dim RectHeight As Integer
    Dim SourceDC As Integer
    Dim DestDC As Integer
    Dim BitmapHandle As Integer
    Dim WindowHandle As Integer
    Dim ReturnValue As Integer

    RectWidth = X2 - X1
    RectHeight = Y2 - Y1
    SourceDC = csvCreateDC("DISPLAY", "", "", "")
    DestDC = csvCreateCompatibleDC(SourceDC)
    BitmapHandle = csvCreateCompatibleBitmap(SourceDC, RectWidth, RectHeight)
    ReturnValue = csvSelectObject(DestDC, BitmapHandle)
    ReturnValue = csvBitBlt(DestDC, 0, 0, RectWidth, RectHeight, SourceDC, X1, Y1,
    ➥csvSRCCOPY)

    If MyWindowHandle = 0 Then
        WindowHandle = Screen.ActiveForm.hWnd
    Else
        WindowHandle = MyWindowHandle
    End If

    ReturnValue = csvOpenClipboard(WindowHandle)
    ReturnValue = csvEmptyClipboard()
    ReturnValue = csvSetClipboardData(csvCF_BITMAP, BitmapHandle)
    ReturnValue = csvCloseClipboard()
    ReturnValue = csvDeleteDC(DestDC)
    ReturnValue = csvReleaseDC(BitmapHandle, SourceDC)

End Function
```

csvCaptureForm()

In MDI (multiple document interface) applications such as Microsoft Access, pressing Alt+Prtsc copies not only the active window but also the active window's parent.

For example, if you are on a form and press Alt+Prtsc, Windows copies both the form and the Access window to the clipboard. You can use the csvCaptureForm() function to copy only the active form.

Note: This result of pressing Alt+Prtsc is a feature of not only Access, but also other MDI applications such as Microsoft Word for Windows.

```
Function csvCaptureForm (ByVal MyFormName As String) As Integer

    Const TITLEBAR = "Capture Form"
    Dim FormRectangle As csvRECT
    Dim X1 As Integer
    Dim Y1 As Integer
    Dim X2 As Integer
    Dim Y2 As Integer

    csvGetWindowRect Forms(MyFormName).hWnd, FormRectangle
    X1 = csvMaxValue(FormRectangle.Left, 0)
    Y1 = csvMaxValue(FormRectangle.Top, 0)
    X2 = csvMinValue(FormRectangle.Right, csvGetSystemMetrics(csvSM_CXSCREEN) - 1)
    Y2 = csvMinValue(FormRectangle.Bottom, csvGetSystemMetrics(csvSM_CYSCREEN) - 1)

    If csvCapture(X1, Y1, X2, Y2, Forms(MyFormName).hWnd) Then
        MsgBox "Couldn't capture '" & MyFormName & "'", csvMB_ICONEXCLAMATION,
        ➥TITLEBAR
        csvCaptureForm = False
    Else
        csvCaptureForm = True
    End If

End Function
```

 You may want to provide a command button or menu command that automatically captures a copy of the active form, launches Paintbrush, and pastes the image so the user can then save or edit the image.

csvCaptureScreen()

In DOS-based applications, pressing the Prtsc key sends a copy of the screen to the printer. In Windows-based applications such as Microsoft Access, pressing the Prtsc key sends a copy of the screen to the clipboard.

Many users do not know they can make a copy of the screen in this manner, so you may want to add a command button or menu command that calls the csvCaptureScreen() function. Then the user can launch Paintbrush and paste the image for subsequent editing.

```
Function csvCaptureScreen () As Integer

    Const TITLEBAR = "Capture Screen"
    Dim X1 As Integer
    Dim Y1 As Integer
    Dim X2 As Integer
    Dim Y2 As Integer

    X1 = 0
    Y1 = 0
    X2 = csvGetSystemMetrics(csvSM_CXSCREEN) - 1
    Y2 = csvGetSystemMetrics(csvSM_CYSCREEN) - 1

    If csvCapture(X1, Y1, X2, Y2, csvGetParent(Screen.ActiveForm.hWnd)) Then
        MsgBox "Couldn't capture screen.", csvMB_ICONINFORMATION, TITLEBAR
        csvCaptureScreen = False
    Else
        csvCaptureScreen = True
    End If

End Function
```

csvCenterForm()

The **AutoCenter** property positions a form to the near-center of the screen when a form first opens. If the user moves the form, however, no built-in property or function exists to move the form back to the center.

Use the csvCenterForm() function to position a form to the actual center of the screen.

```
Function csvCenterForm (ByVal MyFormName As String) As Integer

    Const TITLEBAR = "Center Form"
    Const POPUP = "OFormPopup"
    Dim WindowHandle As Integer
    Dim DesktopHandle As Integer
    Dim Buffer As String * 255
    Dim ClassName As String
    Dim FormRectangle As csvRECT
    Dim DesktopRectangle As csvRECT
    Dim ReturnValue As Integer
    Dim FormHeight As Integer
    Dim FormWidth As Integer
    Dim DesktopWidth As Integer
    Dim DesktopHeight As Integer
    Dim X As Integer
    Dim Y As Integer

    ReturnValue = 0

    On Error Resume Next
    If MyFormName = "" Then
        WindowHandle = Screen.ActiveForm.hWnd
```

continues

```
        Else
            WindowHandle = Forms(MyFormName).hWnd
        End If

        If Err Then
        Else
            DesktopHandle = csvGetParent(WindowHandle)
            ReturnValue = csvGetClassName(WindowHandle, Buffer, Len(Buffer))
            ClassName = Left$(Buffer, ReturnValue)
            csvGetWindowRect WindowHandle, FormRectangle
            If ClassName = POPUP Then
                csvGetWindowRect DesktopHandle, DesktopRectangle
            Else
                ReturnValue = csvGetClientRect(DesktopHandle, DesktopRectangle)
            End If

            FormWidth = FormRectangle.Right - FormRectangle.Left
            FormHeight = FormRectangle.Bottom - FormRectangle.Top
            DesktopWidth = DesktopRectangle.Right - DesktopRectangle.Left
            DesktopHeight = DesktopRectangle.Bottom - DesktopRectangle.Top

            If ClassName = POPUP Then
                X = DesktopRectangle.Left + (DesktopWidth - FormWidth) \ 2
                Y = DesktopRectangle.Top + (DesktopHeight - FormHeight) \ 2
            Else
                X = (DesktopWidth - FormWidth) \ 2
                Y = (DesktopHeight - FormHeight) \ 2
            End If

            ReturnValue = csvMoveWindow(WindowHandle, X, Y, FormWidth, FormHeight, True)
        End If

        If ReturnValue = 0 Then
            MsgBox "Couldn't center '" & MyFormName & "'.", csvMB_ICONEXCLAMATION,
TITLEBAR
        Else
            csvCenterForm = ReturnValue
    End If

    End Function
```

csvCheckMenuCommand()

If you provide menu commands that act as toggles, you should check those commands when they are "on" and uncheck them when they are "off."

The csvCheckMenuCommand() function accepts three arguments, all of which are required:

MenuCommand	This number, starting with zero, indicates which menu you want to affect. The leftmost menu, usually the File menu, is zero.
MenuSubCommand	This number, also starting with zero, indicates the particular menu command in the menu. The first menu command is zero, the second is one, and so on. Separator bars, if any, count.
State	This string indicates whether you want to check ("on") or uncheck ("off") the menu command.

```
Function csvCheckMenuCommand (ByVal MenuCommand As Integer, ByVal MenuSubCommand As
Integer,
➥ByVal State As String) As Integer
    Const CLASSNAME = "OMain"
    Const NULLCHAR = 0&
    Dim AppWindow As Integer
    Dim TopMenu As Integer
    Dim SubMenu As Integer
    Dim ReturnValue As Integer

    AppWindow = csvFindWindow(CLASSNAME, NULLCHAR)
    TopMenu = csvGetMenu(AppWindow)
    SubMenu = csvGetSubMenu(TopMenu, MenuCommand)

    Select Case LCase$(State)
        Case "on"
            ReturnValue = csvCheckMenuItem(SubMenu, MenuSubCommand,
            ➥csvMF_BYPOSITION Or csvMF_CHECKED)
        Case "off"
            ReturnValue = csvCheckMenuItem(SubMenu, MenuSubCommand,
            ➥csvMF_BYPOSITION Or csvMF_UNCHECKED)
    End Select

End Function
```

The following example illustrates how you can check the third command in the fourth menu (see also fig. 21.1).

```
X = csvCheckMenuCommand(3, 2, "on")
```

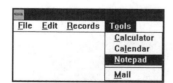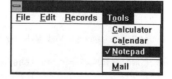

Figure 21.1. Check a menu command to indicate an "on" status.

csvCloneControls()

This function illustrates how you can keep track of the values from one record and transfer them to another record.

By calling the function with the *Flag* argument set to "from", you can copy the values from selected controls. Calling the function with the *Flag* argument set to "to" pastes the previously saved values.

You need one hidden control for each control you want to track.

```
Function csvCloneControls (ByVal Flag As String) As Integer

    Const FUNCTIONNAME = "csvCloneControls()"
    Const MYFORMNAME = "My Form Name Goes Here"
    Dim MyForm As Form
    Static ControlValue(4) As Variant

    Set MyForm = Forms(MYFORMNAME)

    Select Case Flag
        Case "to"
                MyForm![First Field] = ControlValue(1)
                MyForm![Second Field] = ControlValue(2)
                MyForm![Third Field] = ControlValue(3)
                MyForm![Fourth Field] = ControlValue(4)
        Case "from"
                ControlValue(1) = MyForm![First Field]
                ControlValue(2) = MyForm![Second Field]
                ControlValue(3) = MyForm![Third Field]
                ControlValue(4) = MyForm![Fourth Field]
        Case Else
                MsgBox "Invalid Flag argument '" & Flag & "'.",
csvMB_ICONEXCLAMATION, FUNCTIONNAME
    End Select

End Function
```

csvCloseForm()

Use the csvCloseForm() function to close a specified form. To close the active (current) form, call the function like this:

```
X = csvCloseForm(Screen.ActiveForm.FormName)
```

```
Function csvCloseForm (ByVal MyFormName As String) As Integer

    Const FUNCTIONNAME = "csvCloseForm()"

    On Error Resume Next
    DoCmd Close A_FORM, Forms(MyFormName)
    If Err Then
```

```
        MsgBox "Couldn't close form '" & MyFormName & "'.", csvMB_ICONEXCLAMATION,
FUNCTIONNAME
        csvCloseForm = False
    Else
        csvCloseForm = True
    End If
    On Error GoTo 0

End Function
```

csvConnectTo()

You can use the `csvConnectTo()` function to connect to a network resource. The following examples illustrate how you can connect to a network drive at the MS-DOS prompt and from within Access basic.

```
C:\net use \\wpguser1\dpg e:
```

```
NetworkDrive = csvConnectTo("\\wpguser1\dpg", "mypassword")
```

If the network drive or device has no password, pass a zero-length string rather than a password:

```
NetworkDrive = csvConnectTo("\\wpguser1\public", "")
```

```
Function csvConnectTo (ByVal Resource As String, ByVal Password As String) As
➥Variant

    Dim DriveNumber As Integer
    Dim FirstDrive As Integer
    Dim DriveLetter As Variant

    DriveNumber = 0

    Do
        DriveNumber = DriveNumber + 1
        FirstDrive = csvGetDriveType(DriveNumber)
    Loop Until FirstDrive = 0 Or DriveNumber = 27

    If FirstDrive <> 0 Then
        DriveLetter = Chr$(FirstDrive + 65) & ":"
        If csvWNetAddConnection(Resource, Password, DriveLetter) <> csvWN_SUCCESS
Then
            DriveLetter = Null
        End If
    Else
        DriveLetter = Null
    End If

    csvConnectTo = DriveLetter

End Function
```

csvCopyObject()

You can use the csvCopyObject() function to copy an existing database object to the current database or to another specified database. To copy to the same database, set the *DestinationDB* argument to a zero-length string ("").

```
Function csvCopyObject (ByVal DestinationDB, ByVal NewName As String, ByVal
MyObjectType,
➥ByVal MyObjectName) As Integer

    Const FUNCTIONNAME = "csvCopyObject()"
    Dim ObjectType As Integer

    csvCopyObject = False

    Select Case LCase$(MyObjectType)
        Case "table"
            ObjectType = A_TABLE
        Case "query"
            ObjectType = A_QUERY
        Case "form"
            ObjectType = A_FORM
        Case "report"
            ObjectType = A_REPORT
        Case "macro"
            ObjectType = A_MACRO
        Case "module"
            ObjectType = A_MODULE
        Case Else
            MsgBox "Invalid argument '" & MyObjectType & "'." &
csvMB_ICONEXCLAMATION, FUNCTIONNAME
            Exit Function
    End Select

    On Error Resume Next
    If DestinationDB = "" Then
        DoCmd CopyObject, NewName, ObjectType, ObjectName
    Else
        DoCmd CopyObject DestinationDB, NewName, ObjectType, ObjectName
    End If
    If Err Then
        MsgBox "Couldn't copy object '" & MyObjectName & "'." &
csvMB_ICONEXCLAMATION, FUNCTIONNAME
    Else
        csvCopyObject = True
    End If
    On Error GoTo 0

End Function
```

csvCreateTextFile()

You may find that working with an external MS-DOS text file is convenient or even necessary. The csvCreateTextFile() function determines whether the specified file already exists and allows the user to overwrite it.

```
Function csvCreateTextFile (ByVal FileName As String, ByVal Overwrite As Integer) As
Integer

    Const TITLEBAR = "Create Text File"
    Const QUOTE = """"
    Dim FileNumber As Integer

    csvCreateTextFile = False

    FileNumber = FreeFile
    On Error Resume Next
    Open FileName For Input As FileNumber
    Close FileNumber
    If Err = 0 And Not Overwrite Then
        If MsgBox(QUOTE & FileName & QUOTE & " exists. Overwrite it?",
csvMB_ICONQUESTIONMARK +
        ➥csvMB_YESNO, TITLEBAR) = csvMB_NO Then
            On Error GoTo 0
            Exit Function
        End If
    End If

    FileNumber = FreeFile
    Open FileName For Output As FileNumber
    If Err Then
        MsgBox "Couldn't create " & QUOTE & FileName & QUOTE & ".",
CSVMB_ICONEXCLAMATION, TITLEBAR
    Else
        Close FileNumber
        csvCreateTextFile = True
    End If

    On Error GoTo 0

End Function
```

csvDeleteAllRecords()

You can use the csvDeleteAllRecords() function to remove all the records in a specified table. If the table has no records or the table does not exist, the function displays an appropriate message. Otherwise, the function asks the user to confirm the pending deletions (see fig. 21.2).

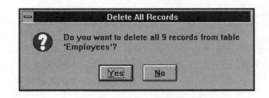

Figure 21.2. You should ask the user to confirm record deletions.

```
Function csvDeleteAllRecords (ByVal MyTableName As String) As Integer

    Const TITLEBAR = "Delete All Records"
    Dim MaxRecords As Long
    Dim ReturnValue As Variant
    Dim X As Long

    csvDeleteAllRecords = False

    On Error Resume Next
    MaxRecords = DCount("*", MyTableName)
    If Err Then
        MsgBox "Couldn't get record count from table '" & MyTableName & "'.",
csvMB_ICONEXCLAMATION,
        ➥TITLEBAR
    Else
        Select Case MaxRecords
            Case 0
                MsgBox "There are no records in table '" & MyTableName & "'.",
csvMB_ICONINFORMATION,
                ➥TITLEBAR
            Case Else
                If MsgBox("Do you want to delete all " & MaxRecords & " records
from table '" &
                    ➥MyTableName & "'?", csvMBICONEXCLAMATION +
                    ➥CSVMB_YESNO, TITLEBAR) - csvMB_YES Then
                        ReturnValue = SysCmd(csvSB_SETTEXT, "Deleting records...")
                        DoCmd RunSQL "DELETE * FROM " & MyTableName & ";"
                        ReturnValue = SysCmd(csvSB_REMOVE)
                        csvDeleteAllRecords = True
                End If
        End Select
    End If
    On Error GoTo 0
End Function
```

csvDeleteObject()

Use the csvDeleteObject() function to delete a database object from the current database.

```
Function csvDeleteObject (ByVal ObjectName As String, ByVal ObjectType As String) As
Integer

    Const TITLEBAR = "Delete Object"
```

```
        Dim X As Integer

        csvDeleteObject = False

        X = Int(InStr("table query form  reportmacro module", ObjectType) / 6) + 1
        X = Choose(X, A_TABLE, A_QUERY, A_FORM, A_REPORT, A_MACRO, A_MODULE)
        On Error Resume Next
        DoCmd DeleteObject X, ObjectName
        If Err Then
            MsgBox "Couldn't delete '" & ObjectName & "'.", csvMB_ICONEXCLAMATION,
TITLEBAR
        Else
            csvDeleteObject = True
        End If
        On Error GoTo 0

    End Function
```

csvDialPhone()

If the computer is equipped with a modem, you can use the csvDialPhone() function to automate dialing a phone number. The function performs simple validation of the number before dialing.

```
    Function csvDialPhone (ByVal InPhoneNumber As Variant) As Integer

        Const TITLEBAR = "Dial Phone Number"
        Dim CommPortID As Integer
        Dim PhoneLength As Integer
        Dim X As Integer
        Dim CommPortName As String
        Dim Internal As Integer
        Dim InternalPrefix As String
        Dim ExternalPrefix As String
        Dim Char As String
        Dim PhoneNumber As String
        Dim ReceiveBufferSize As Integer
        Dim Flag As Integer
        Dim RemarkDelimiter As String
        Dim CR As String

        CR = Chr$(13)
        CommPortName = "COM1:"
        InternalPrefix = ""
        ExternalPrefix = "9-"
        RemarkDelimiter = "'"

        ReceiveBufferSize = 128 ' Arbitrary, as we don't know what modem returns.

        csvDialPhone = False
        If IsNull(InPhoneNumber) Then
            MsgBox "Missing telephone number.", csvMB_ICONINFORMATION, TITLEBAR
        Else
            If InStr(InPhoneNumber, RemarkDelimiter) Then
                PhoneNumber = Trim$(UCase$(Left$(InPhoneNumber, InStr(InPhoneNumber,
RemarkDelimiter) - 1)))
```

continues

```
            Else
                PhoneNumber = Trim$(UCase$(InPhoneNumber))
            End If
            PhoneNumber = Trim(UCase$(PhoneNumber))
            If InStr(PhoneNumber, "Q") Or InStr(PhoneNumber, "Z") Then
                MsgBox "Telephone number '" & PhoneNumber & "' can't contain the letters
'Q' or 'Z'.",
                ➥csvMB_ICONINFORMATION, TITLEBAR
            Else
                For X = 1 To Len(PhoneNumber)
                    Char$ = Mid$(PhoneNumber, X, 1)
                    If Char$ >= "A" And Char$ <= "Y" Then
                        Mid$(PhoneNumber, X, 1) =
Trim$(Str$(Val(Mid$("2223334445555666777888999",
                        ➥InStr("ABCDEFGHIJKLMNOPRSTUVWXY", Char$), 1))))
                    End If
                Next X
                PhoneNumber = IIf(Internal, InternalPrefix, ExternalPrefix) &
InPhoneNumber & CR
                PhoneLength = Len(PhoneNumber)
                Flag = csvRETRY
                Do While Flag = csvRETRY
                    CommPortID = csvOpenComm(CommPortName, ReceiveBufferSize,
PhoneLength)
                    If CommPortID < 0 Then
                        Flag = MsgBox("Couldn't open communications port '" &
CommPortName & "'.",
                        ➥csvMB_ICONINFORMATION + csvMB_RETRYCANCEL, TITLEBAR)
                    Else
                        Flag = csvCANCEL
                        If csvWriteComm(CommPortID, PhoneNumber, PhoneLength) < 0 Then
                            Flag = MsgBox("Couldn't dial '" & InPhoneNumber & "'.",
csvMB_ICONINFORMATION +
                            ➥csvMB_RETRYCANCEL, TITLEBAR)
                        Else
                            MsgBox "Press OK to disconnect the computer from the mo-
dem.", , TITLEBAR
                            X = csvCloseComm(CommPortID)
                            csvDialPhone = True
                        End If
                    End If
                Loop
            End If
    End If

End Function
```

> **Tip:** The csvDialPhone() function has hardcoded values for the communications port, the phone prefixes, and the delimiter(s). You can enhance this function by instead maintaining these settings in an .INI file and reading them from disk when you first call the function.

csvDisableControl()

Depending on the form, you may find it convenient and intuitive to temporarily disable a control. Suppose that you have a command button named Edit which, depending on how you may have enabled record locking, may not be appropriate at any given time. If so, use the csvDisableControl() function to disable the control.

```
Function csvDisableControl (MyForm As Form, ByVal MyControlName As String) As
➡Integer

    Const FUNCTIONNAME = "csvDisableControl()"

    On Error Resume Next
    MyForm(MyControlName).Enabled = False
    If Err Then
        MsgBox "Couldn't disable control '" & MyControlName & "'.",
csvMB_ICONEXCLAMATION, FUNCTIONNAME
        csvDisableControl = False
    Else
        csvDisableControl = True
    End If
    On Error GoTo 0

End Function
```

csvDoDblClick()

You can use the csvDoDblClick() function to perform whatever action may be specified by the **OnDblClick** property of a control (except for code in an event procedure). For example, you may want a menu command to do the same thing as double-clicking a particular control.

```
Function csvDoDblCLick () As Integer

    Dim PropSetting As Variant
    Dim X As Variant

    csvDoDblCLick = False
    On Error Resume Next
    PropSetting = Screen.ActiveControl.OnDblClick
    If Err Then
    Else
        If Not IsNull(PropSetting) Then
            If Left$(PropSetting, 1) = "=" Then
                X = Eval(Mid$(PropSetting, 2))
            Else
                DoCmd RunMacro MacroName
            End If
            csvDoDblCLick = True
        End If
    End If
    On Error GoTo 0

End Function
```

535

csvDriveType()

The csvDriveType() function returns a number that identifies the type of drive:

- 1   removable

- 2   fixed (not removable)

- 3   remote (network drive)

- 0   unknown (or an error was detected)

```
Function csvDriveType (ByVal DriveLetter As String) As Integer

    Const TITLEBAR = "Drive Type"
    Dim X As String

    X = UCase$(Left$(DriveLetter, 1))
    Select Case csvGetDriveType(Asc(UCase$(Left$(DriveLetter, 1))) - 65)
        Case csvDRIVE_REMOVABLE
            csvDriveType = 1
        Case csvDRIVE_FIXED
            csvDriveType = 2
        Case csvDRIVE_REMOTE
            csvDriveType = 3
        Case Else
            csvDriveType = 0
    End Select

End Function
```

csvEcho()

To suppress updating the screen while other code is executing (for example, when you select objects in the Database window or open objects in Design view), call the csvEcho() function with the *State* argument set to False.

 Note: Be sure you turn echoing back on by calling csvEcho() with the *State* argument set to True.

```
Function csvEcho (ByVal State As Integer) As Integer

    csvEcho = True

    DoCmd Echo State

End Function
```

csvEnableControl()

This function, the companion to `csvDisableControl()`, enables a specified control.

```
Function csvEnableControl (MyForm As Form, ByVal MyControlName As String) As Integer

    Const FUNCTIONNAME = "csvEnableControl()"

    On Error Resume Next
    MyForm(MyControlName).Enabled = True
    If Err Then
        MsgBox "Couldn't enable control '" & MyControlName & "'.",
csvMB_ICONEXCLAMATION, FUNCTIONNAME
        csvEnableControl = False
    Else
        csvEnableControl = True
    End If
    On Error GoTo 0

End Function
```

csvExecuteCommand()

You can use the `csvExecuteCommand()` function to execute an internal MS-DOS command such as COPY.

The *ShowFlag* argument indicates how the resulting window will be displayed:

- `csvSW_HIDE`   hidden

- `csvSW_MAXIMIZE`   maximized

- `csvSW_MINIMIZE`   minimized

- `csvSW_SHOWNORMAL`   normal

```
Function csvExecuteCommand (ByVal CommandText As String, ByVal ShowFlag As Integer)
As Integer

    Dim ComSpec As String
    Dim Msg As String
    Dim Reason As String
    Dim X As Integer
    Dim CRLF As String

    CRLF = Chr$(13) & Chr$(10)
    csvExecuteCommand = True

    ComSpec = Environ$("comspec")
    ComSpec = IIf(ComSpec = "", "command.com", ComSpec)

    If CommandText <> "" Then
        ComSpec = ComSpec & " /c " & CommandText
```

continues

```
        End If

        X = csvWinExec(ComSpec, ShowFlag)
        If X < 32 Then
            Select Case X
                Case 0: Reason = "Out of memory"
                Case 2: Reason = "File not found"
                Case Is < 32
                        Reason = "Error code" & Str$(X)
            End Select
            Msg = "Couldn't execute" & CRLF & "'" & ComSpec & "'." & CRLF & CRLF &
"Reason: " & Reason
            MsgBox Msg, csvMB_ICONINFORMATION, "Execute Command"
            csvExecuteCommand = False
        End If

End Function
```

csvExecuteProgram()

Use the csvExecuteProgram() function to launch another application and, optionally, wait until it closes before returning to your application (by setting the *Wait* argument to True).

If you set the *OtherEvents* argument to True, the other application allows other events to occur while it is running. If you set the *OtherEvents* argument to False, the other application runs exclusively.

```
    Function csvExecuteProgram (ByVal ProgramName As String, ByVal ShowFlag As Integer,
    ByVal Wait As Integer,
    ➡ByVal OtherEvents As Integer) As Integer

        Const TITLEBAR = "Execute Program"
        Dim WindowHandle As Integer

        If csvWinExec(ProgramName, ShowFlag) >= 32 Then
            WindowHandle = csvGetActiveWindow()
            If Wait Then
                Do While csvIsWindow(WindowHandle)
                    If OtherEvents Then
                        DoEvents
                    End If
                Loop
            End If
        Else
            MsgBox "Couldn't execute '" & ProgramName & "'.", csvMB_ICONINFORMATION,
TITLEBAR
        End If

    End Function
```

csvExitWindows()

Usually, the user must return to the Program Manager (or other Windows shell) to quit, but you may find it convenient to allow the user to quit Microsoft Windows from within your application.

When Microsoft Windows closes, it sends a value, or return code, back to MS-DOS. If appropriate, and you are testing the value when you return to MS-DOS, you should set the *ReturnCode* argument to an appropriate value. If not, set the *ReturnCode* argument to zero (0).

```
Function csvExitWindows (ByVal ReturnCode As Integer) As Integer

    Const TITLEBAR = "Exit Windows"

    csvExitWindows = True
    If csvExitWindows(0&, ReturnCode) = 0 Then
        MsgBox "Couldn't exit Windows - one or more applications couldn't or
wouldn't exit.",
        ➥csvMB_ICONINFORMATION, TITLEBAR
        csvExitWindows = False
    End If

End Function
```

csvExplodeForm()

Use the csvExplodeForm() function to create an exploding form effect. Depending on the value of the *Origin* argument, the explosion can appear to start from any corner, side, or from the center of the form:

- 1   upper left to bottom right
- 2   top to bottom
- 3   upper right to bottom left
- 4   right to left
- 5   bottom right to upper left
- 6   bottom to top
- 7   bottom left to upper right
- 8   left to right
- (else)   center to edges

The *Speed* argument determines the speed at which the explosion occurs; the smaller the number, the faster the explosion appears. On a 386/20 machine, try a setting of 25. On a faster machine such as a 486/66, try 200.

Tip: Consider adding a routine, run during your startup code, that determines the speed of the machine or reads the speed setting from an .INI file. This routine should be machine-specific, not application-specific, because different users of the same application in a network environment may have different machines with different speeds.

```
Function csvExplodeForm (MyForm As Form, ByVal Origin As Integer, ByVal Speed As
Integer) As Integer

    Dim FormRectangle As csvRECT
    Dim FullWidth As Integer
    Dim FullHeight As Integer
    Dim Cx As Integer
    Dim Cy As Integer
    Dim I As Integer
    Dim X As Integer
    Dim Y As Integer
    Dim ScreenDeviceContext As Integer
    Dim BrushHandle As Integer
    Dim ReturnValue As Integer

    ' Get form's window position.
    csvGetWindowRect MyForm.hWnd, FormRectangle
    ' Calculate width & height.
    FullWidth = FormRectangle.Right - FormRectangle.Left
    FullHeight = FormRectangle.Bottom - FormRectangle.Top

    ' Get device context for the whole screen.
    ScreenDeviceContext = csvGetDC(0)
    ' Set brush color based on background color of detail section.
    BrushHandle = csvCreateSolidBrush(MyForm.Section(0).BackColor)
    ReturnValue = csvSelectObject(ScreenDeviceContext, BrushHandle)

    ' Draw progressively larger rectangles, up to size of form.
    For I = 1 To Speed
        Cx = FullWidth * (I / Speed)
        Cy = FullHeight * (I / Speed)
        Select Case Origin
            Case 1 ' upper left corner
                X = FormRectangle.Left
                Y = FormRectangle.Top
            Case 2 ' top to bottom
                X = FormRectangle.Left
                Y = FormRectangle.Top
                Cx = FormRectangle.Right - X
                Cy = FullHeight * (I / Speed)
            Case 3 ' upper right corner
                X = FormRectangle.Right
                Y = FormRectangle.Top
                Cx = -Cx
            Case 4 ' right to left
                X = FormRectangle.Right
                Y = FormRectangle.Top
                Cx = -FullWidth * (I / Speed)
                Cy = FormRectangle.Bottom - Y
```

```
                    Case 5 ' bottom right corner
                            X = FormRectangle.Right
                            Y = FormRectangle.Bottom
                            Cx = -Cx
                            Cy = -Cy
                    Case 6 ' bottom to top
                            X = FormRectangle.Left
                            Y = FormRectangle.Bottom
                            Cx = FormRectangle.Right - X
                            Cy = -FullHeight * (I / Speed)
                    Case 7 ' bottom left corner
                            X = FormRectangle.Left
                            Y = FormRectangle.Bottom
                            Cy = -Cy
                    Case 8 ' left to right
                            X = FormRectangle.Left
                            Y = FormRectangle.Top
                            Cx = FullWidth * (I / Speed)
                            Cy = FormRectangle.Bottom - Y
                    Case Else ' center
                            X = FormRectangle.Left + (FullWidth - Cx) / 2
                            Y = FormRectangle.Top + (FullHeight - Cy) / 2
            End Select
            csvRectangle ScreenDeviceContext, X, Y, X + Cx, Y + Cy
        Next I

        ' Release device context and brush.
        ReturnValue = csvReleaseDC(0, ScreenDeviceContext)
        csvDeleteObject BrushHandle

    End Function
```

csvExportTable()

You may want to provide the ability to export a table to an external MS-DOS text file for subsequent editing or analysis.

 Note: The `csvExportTable()` function actually exports both tables and queries. Because tables and queries share the same name space in Microsoft Access, no special code is necessary to accommodate either type of database object.

```
Function csvExportTable (ByVal MyTableName As String, ByVal OutputFileName As
String,
➥ByVal IncludeFieldNames As Integer) As Integer

    csvExportTable = True

    On Error Resume Next
    DoCmd TransferText A_EXPORTDELIM,, MyTableName, OuputFileName, IncludeFieldNames
```

continues

```
        If Err Then
            MsgBox "Couldn't export '" & MyTableName & "'.", csvMB_ICONINFORMATION,
TITLEBAR
            csvExportTable = False
        End If
        On Error GoTo 0

End Function
```

csvFieldDataType()

You may find it convenient to know whether a given field in a table is a numeric, string, or date/time field. The csvFieldDataType() function returns a number that indicates the data type for a specified field in a specified table:

- 1   text
- 2   date/time
- 3   numeric
- 0   unknown or function was unsuccessful

> **STOP** **WARNING:** This function uses the undocumented system table MSysColumns. Use of the system tables (tables whose names begin with "MSys") is generally discouraged because these tables are subject to changes in their layout and internal values by Microsoft at any time. You must never change anything in any of the internal system tables.

```
Function csvFieldDataType (ByVal MyTableName As String, ByVal MyFieldName As String)
As Integer

    Dim MyDB As Database
    Dim MySnap As Snapshot
    Dim Msg As String
    Dim Icon As Integer
    Dim Titlebar As String
    Dim S As String
    Dim X As Integer

    S = "SELECT DISTINCTROW MSysColumns.ColTyp "
    S = S & "FROM MSysObjects, MSysColumns, "
    S = S & "MSysObjects INNER JOIN MSysColumns ON "
    S = S & "MSysObjects.Id = MSysColumns.ObjectId "
    S = S & "WHERE MSysObjects.Type IN (1, 4) AND "
    S = S & "MSysObjects.Name = '" & MyTableName & "' AND "
    S = S & "MSysColumns.Name = '" & MyFieldName & "' "

    Set MyDB = CurrentDB()
    Set MySnap = MyDB.CreateSnapshot(S)
    On Error Resume Next
    MySnap.MoveLast
    If Err Then
        csvFieldDataType = 0 ' No such table or field.
```

```
        Else
            If MySnap.RecordCount <> 1 Then
                If csvEnableDebug Then
                    Msg = "Multiple values for field '" & MyFieldName & "' in "
                    Msg = Msg & "table '" & MyTableName & "'."
                    Icon = csvMB_ICONEXCLAMATION
                    Titlebar = "csvFieldDataType()"
                    X = csvDisplayMsg(Msg, Icon, Titlebar)
                End If
                csvFieldDataType = 0 ' Invalid function.
            Else
                Select Case MySnap![ColTyp]
                    Case 10: csvFieldDataType = 1
                    Case 8:  csvFieldDataType = 2
                    Case 7:  csvFieldDataType = 3
                    Case Else
                        If csvEnableDebug Then
                            Msg = "Unexpected column type '" & MySnap![ColTyp]
                            Msg = Msg & "'."
                            Icon = csvMB_ICONEXCLAMATION
                            Titlebar = "csvFieldDataType()"
                            X = csvDisplayMsg(Msg, Icon, Titlebar)
                        End If
                        csvFieldDataType = 0
                End Select
            End If
        End If
        On Error GoTo 0
        MySnap.Close
        MyDB.Close

End Function
```

 Be sure to read about new coding techniques in Appendix D, "Converting Old Code."

---

csvFileExists()

The csvFileExists() function determines whether a specified file exists by trying to open it for input access. Be sure you specify a complete path as part of the *MyFileName* argument.

```
Function csvFileExists (ByVal MyFileName As String) As Integer

    Dim FileNumber As Integer

    FileNumber = FreeFile

    On Error Resume Next
    Open MyFileName For Input As FileNumber
    If Err Then
        csvFileExists = False
    Else
        csvFileExists = True
    End If
    On Error GoTo 0

End Function
```

csvFillDeviceCharacteristics()

The csvFillDeviceCharacteristics() function fills a combo box or list box (see fig. 21.3) with a variety of information about the screen device, although you could check another device by assigning a different device context:

```
DeviceContext = csvGetWindowDC(Screen.ActiveForm.hWnd)

Function csvFillDeviceCharacteristics (MyListBox As Control, ID As Variant, Row As
Integer, Col As Integer,
➥Code As Variant) As Variant

    Dim X As String
    Dim Y As Integer
    Dim DeviceContext As Integer
    Dim ReturnValue As Integer

    Select Case Code
        Case 0
            csvFillDeviceCharacteristics = True        ' Initialize.
        Case 1
            csvFillDeviceCharacteristics = Timer       ' Open.
        Case 3
            csvFillDeviceCharacteristics = 28          ' Number rows.
        Case 4
            csvFillDeviceCharacteristics = 2           ' Number columns.
        Case 5
            csvFillDeviceCharacteristics = -1          ' Column width.
        Case 6
            Select Case Row                            ' Get data.
                Case 1: Y = csvDRIVERVERSION
                        X = "Device driver version - DRIVERVERSION"
                Case 2: Y = csvTECHNOLOGY
                        X = "Device technology - TECHNOLOGY"
                Case 3: Y = csvHORZSIZE
                        X = "Width of physical display (millimeters) - HORZSIZE"
                Case 4: Y = csvVERTSIZE
                        X = "Height of physical display (millimeters) - VERTSIZE"
                Case 5: Y = csvHORZRES
                        X = "Width of the display (pixels) - HORZRES"
                Case 6: Y = csvVERTRES
                        X = "Height of the display (raster lines) - VERTRES"
                Case 7: Y = csvBITSPIXEL
                        X = "Number of adjacent color bits for each pixel -
                        ➥BITSPIXEL"
                Case 8: Y = csvPLANES
                        X = "Number of color planes - PLANES"
                Case 9: Y = csvNUMBRUSHES
                        X = "Number of device-specific brushes - NUMBRUSHES"
                Case 10: Y = csvNUMPENS
                        X = "Number of device-specific pens - NUMPENS"
                Case 11: Y = csvNUMFONTS
                        X = "Number of device-specific fonts - NUMFONTS"
                Case 12: Y = csvNUMCOLORS
                        X = "Number of entries in the device's color table -
                        ➥NUMCOLORS"
```

544

```
      Case 13: Y = csvPDEVICESIZE
               X = "Size of the PDEVICE internal data structure -
               ➡PDEVICESIZE"
      Case 14: Y = csvCURVECAPS
               X = "Bitmask containing curve capabilities - CURVECAPS"
      Case 15: Y = csvLINECAPS
               X = "Bitmask containing line capabilities - LINECAPS"
      Case 16: Y = csvPOLYGONALCAPS
               X = "Bitmask containing polygonal capabilities -
               ➡POLYGONALCAPS"
      Case 17: Y = csvTEXTCAPS
               X = "Bitmask containing text capabilities - TEXTCAPS"
      Case 18: Y = csvCLIPCAPS
               X = "Clipping capabilities (0 = no / 1 = yes) - CLIPCAPS"
      Case 19: Y = csvRASTERCAPS
               X = "Raster capabilities - RASTERCAPS"
      Case 20: Y = csvASPECTX
               X = "Relative width of the device pixel used for line
               ➡drawing - ASPECTX"
      Case 21: Y = csvASPECTY
               X = "Relative height of the device pixel used for line
               ➡drawing - ASPECTY"
      Case 22: Y = csvASPECTXY
               X = "Diagonal width of the device pixel used for line
               ➡drawing - ASPECTXY"
      Case 23: Y = csvLOGPIXELSX
               X = "Number of logical pixels per inch along the display
               ➡width - LOGPIXELSX"
      Case 24: Y = csvLOGPIXELSY
               X = "Number of logical pixels per inch along the display
               ➡height - LOGPIXELSY"
      Case 25: Y = csvSIZEPALETTE
               X = "Number of entries in the system palette -
               ➡SIZEPALETTE"
      Case 26: Y = csvNUMRESERVED
               X = "Number of reserved entries in the system palette -
               ➡NUMRESERVED"
      Case 27: Y = csvCOLORRES
               X = "Actual color resolution (bits per pixel) - COLORRES"
      Case Else
End Select

If Row = 0 Then
    If Col = 0 Then
        csvFillDeviceCharacteristics = "CHARACTERISTIC"
    Else
        csvFillDeviceCharacteristics = "VALUE"
    End If
Else
    If Col = 0 Then
        csvFillDeviceCharacteristics = X
    Else
        DeviceContext = csvGetWindowDC(Screen.ActiveForm.hWnd)
        csvFillDeviceCharacteristics = csvGetDeviceCaps(DeviceContext,
        ➡Y)
        ReturnValue = csvReleaseDC(Screen.ActiveForm.hWnd,
        ➡DeviceContext)
```

continues

```
                End If
            End If
        Case 9                                      ' End.
    End Select

End Function
```

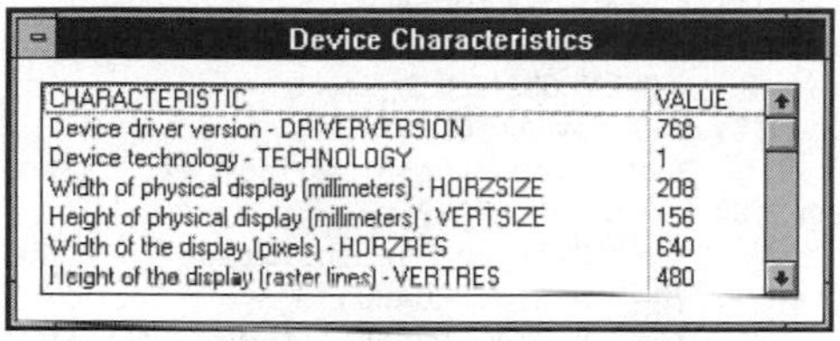

Figure 21.3. Displaying the device characteristics.

csvFillDisplayCharacteristics()

The csvFillDisplayCharacteristics() function fills a combo box or list box with a variety of information about the screen device (see fig. 21.4).

```
Function csvFillDisplayCharacteristics (MyListBox As Control, ID As Variant, Row As
Integer,
➥Col As Integer, Code As Variant) As Variant

    Dim X As String
    Dim Y As Integer

    Select Case Code
        Case 0
            csvFillDisplayCharacteristics = True      ' Initialize.
        Case 1
            csvFillDisplayCharacteristics = Timer     ' Open.
        Case 3
            csvFillDisplayCharacteristics = 12        ' Number rows.
        Case 4
            csvFillDisplayCharacteristics = 2         ' Number columns.
        Case 5
            csvFillDisplayCharacteristics = -1        ' Column width.
        Case 6
            Select Case Row                           ' Get data.
                Case 1
                    Y = csvSM_CXSCREEN: X = "Width of screen"
                Case 2
                    Y = csvSM_CYSCREEN: X = "Height of screen"
                Case 3
                    Y = csvSM_CYCAPTION: X = "Height of caption"
                Case 4
                    Y = csvSM_CXICON: X = "Width of icon"
                Case 5
```

```
                                    Y = csvSM_CYICON: X = "Height of icon"
                            Case 6
                                    Y = csvSM_CXCURSOR: X = "Width of cursor"
                            Case 7
                                    Y = csvSM_CYCURSOR: X = "Height of cursor"
                            Case 8
                                    Y = csvSM_CXMIN: X = "Minimum width of window"
                            Case 9
                                    Y = csvSM_CYMIN: X = "Minimum height of window"
                            Case 10
                                    Y = csvSM_MOUSEPRESENT: X = "Mouse present (0 = no / non-zero
                                    ➥= yes)"
                            Case 11
                                    Y = csvSM_SWAPBUTTON
                                    X = "Left and right mouse buttons swapped (0 = no /non-zero =
                                    ➥yes)"
                            Case 12
                                    Y = csvSM_DEBUG
                                    X = "Debug Windows is running (0 = no / non-zero = yes)"
                            Case Else
                    End Select
                    If Row = 0 Then
                        If Col = 0 Then
                            csvFillDisplayCharacteristics = "CHARACTERISTIC"
                        Else
                            csvFillDisplayCharacteristics = "VALUE"
                        End If
                    Else
                        If Col = 0 Then
                            csvFillDisplayCharacteristics = X
                        Else
                            csvFillDisplayCharacteristics = csvGetSystemMetrics(Y)
                        End If
                    End If
            Case 9                                           ' End.
        End Select

    End Function
```

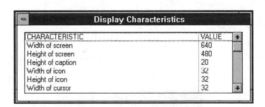

Figure 21.4. Displaying the display characteristics.

csvFillFileNames()

The csvFillFileNames() function fills a combo box or list box with a list of files in a specified path (see fig. 21.5). In this example, the path is specified by the constant, FILEPATH, although you can (and probably should) instead refer to a global variable.

```
Function csvFillFileNames (MyListBox As Control, ID As Variant, Row As Integer, Col
As Integer,
➥Code As Variant) As Variant

    Const FILEPATH = "c:\windows\*.*"
    Const MAXFILES = 255
    Static FileArray(255)
    Static FileCount As Long

    Select Case Code
        Case 0 ' Initialize.
            FileCount = 1
            FileArray(1) = Dir(FILEPATH)
            Do Until FileArray(FileCount) = "" Or FileCount >= MAXFILES
                FileCount = FileCount + 1
                FileArray(FileCount) = Dir
            Loop
            FileCount = FileCount - 1
            ' Sort the array, else the file names will appear in the order
            ' they appear in the directory.
            csvFillFileNames = csvSortArray(FileArray(), FileCount)
            csvFillFileNames = True
        Case 1 ' Open.
            csvFillFileNames = Timer
        Case 3 ' Number of rows.
            csvFillFileNames = FileCount
        Case 4 ' Number of columns.
            csvFillFileNames = 1
        Case 5 ' Column width
            csvFillFileNames = -1
        Case 6 ' Got data.
            csvFillFileNames = FileArray(Row + 1)
        Case 9 ' End.
            Erase FileArray
    End Select

End Function
```

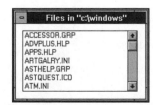

Figure 21.5. Displaying a file list.

Tip: You can use the `csvSetTitleBar()` function to set the form's caption to the name of the directory.

csvFormatDiskLabel()

You can create a report the size of a diskette label and then call the `csvFormatDiskLabel()` function to format the label with the names of all the files on the disk. Call the function from the **OnFormat** event of the report's Detail section.

Be sure you set the *Path* argument to the complete path of the disk or directory for which the label applies.

```
Function csvFormatDiskLabel (ByVal Path As String) As Integer

    Dim FileCount As Long
    Dim X As Integer
    ReDim FileArray(1)

    csvFormatDiskLabel = True

    FileCount = 1
    FileArray(1) = Dir(Path)
    Do Until FileArray(FileCount) = ""
        FileCount = FileCount + 1
        ReDim Preserve FileArray(FileCount)
        FileArray(FileCount) = Dir
    Loop
    X = csvSort(FileArray())

    Screen.ActiveReport.FontName = "Courier New"
    Screen.ActiveReport.FontSize = 8
    Screen.ActiveReport.CurrentY = 1440
    For X = 1 To csvMinValue(33, FileCount)    ' No more than 33 names will fit.
        Screen.ActiveReport.Print Left$(FileArray(X) & Space$(13), 13);
        If X Mod 3 = 0 Then
            Screen.ActiveReport.Print
        End If
    Next X

    Erase FileArray

End Function
```

csvFormIsLoaded()

The `csvFormIsLoaded()` function determines whether a specified form is loaded, no matter which view (Form, Datasheet, or Design).

549

```
Function csvFormIsLoaded (ByVal MyFormName As String) As Integer

    Dim X As Integer

    csvFormIsLoaded = False
    For X = 0 To Forms.Count - 1
        If Forms(X).FormName = MyFormName Then
            csvFormIsLoaded = True
            Exit For
        End If
    Next X

End Function
```

csvGetDiskSpaceFree()

You can use the csvGetDiskSpaceFree() function with an About... form to let the user know how much free space remains on a specified drive.

> **Note:** The routine called by this function, csvGetDiskSpaceFree(), resides in a wide variety of third-party libraries. In particular, the SETUPKIT.DLL file that ships with Microsoft's Visual Basic and other applications includes this routine.

```
Function csvGetDiskSpaceFree (ByVal Drive As String) As Long

    Dim CurrentDrive As String

    CurrentDrive = Left$(CurDir$, 1)
    ChDrive Drive
    csvGetDiskSpaceFree = csvDiskSpaceFree()
    ChDrive CurrentDrive

End Function
```

csvGetFreeResources()

You can call the csvGetFreeResources() function to approximate the amount of free system resources (as a percentage). Generally, falling below about 30 percent results in poor system performance.

```
Function csvGetFreeResources (ByVal ModuleName As String) As Long

    Dim ResourceSpace As Long
    Dim TotalSpace As Long
```

```
    ResourceSpace = csvGetHeapSpaces(csvGetModuleHandle(ModuleName))
    TotalSpace = csvHighWord(ResourceSpace)
    csvGetFreeResources = csvLowWord(ResourceSpace) * 100 \ TotalSpace

End Function
```

csvGetINIText()

Use the `csvGetINIText()` function to retrieve an entry from an .INI file.

Tip: in this function, the .INI file has been defined by the `FILEPATH` constant, although you can modify the function to accept the name of the .INI file (or refer instead to a global variable).

```
Function csvGetINIText (Section As String, Entry As String) As String

    Const FILEPATH = "c:\mydir\myini.ini"
    Const ERR_INVALIDARGS = "Invalid arguments."
    Const TITLEBAR = "Get INI Text"
    Dim Default As String
    Dim FileName As String
    Dim Size As Integer
    Dim Text As String * 128
    Dim X As Integer

    Default = ""
    Size = Len(Text)

    If Len(Section) * Len(Entry) Then
        X = csvGetPrivateProfileString(Section, Entry, Default, Text, Size,
        ➥FILEPATH)
    End If
    If X Then
        csvGetINIText = Text
    Else
        MsgBox ERR_INVALIDARGS, csvMB_ICONEXCLAMATION, TITLEBAR
        csvGetINIText = Section & " - " & Entry
    End If

End Function
```

csvGetIntlInt()

The `csvGetIntlInt()` function retrieves a numeric entry from the [Intl] section of the user's WIN.INI file. You might use this function as part of a routine that handles international issues such as the number of decimal places to use in a currency field or control.

```
Function csvGetIntlInt (Entry As String) As Integer

    Const ERR_INVALIDARG = "Invalid argument."
    Const TITLEBAR = "Get International Integer"
    Dim Default As Integer
    Dim X As Integer

    Default = -1
    If Entry <> "" Then
        X = csvGetProfileInt("intl", Entry, Default)
    End If
    If X >= Default Then
        csvGetIntlInt = X
    Else
        MsgBox ERR_INVALIDARG, csvMB_ICONEXCLAMATION, TITLEBAR
        csvGetIntlInt = Default
    End If

End Function
```

csvGetIntlString()

The csvGetIntlString() function is a companion to the csvGetIntlInt() function; csvGetIntlString() retrieves a string value.

```
Function csvGetIntlString (Entry As String) As String

    Const ERR_INVALIDARG = "Invalid argument."
    Const TITLEBAR - "Get International String"
    Dim Default As String
    Dim Size As Integer
    Dim Text As String * 128
    Dim X As Integer

    Default = ""
    Size = Len(Text)
    If Entry <> "" Then
        X = csvGetProfileString("intl", Entry, Default, Text, Size)
    End If
    If X Then
        csvGetIntlString = Left$(Text, X)
    Else
        MsgBox ERR_INVALIDARG, csvMB_ICONEXCLAMATION, TITLEBAR
        csvGetIntlString = Entry
    End If

End Function
```

552

csvGoToControl()

You can use the csvGoToControl() function to move the focus to a specified control.

```
Function csvGoToControl (ByVal MyFormName As String, ByVal MyControlName As Control)
As Integer

    Const FUNCTIONNAME = "csvGoToControl()"

    csvGoToControl = False

    If MyFormName <> "" Then
        If csvGoToForm(MyFormName) = False Then
            Exit Function
        End If
    End If

    On Error Resume Next
    DoCmd GoToControl MyControlName
    If Err Then
        MsgBox  "Couldn't go to control '" & MyControlName & "'.",
csvMB_ICONEXCLAMATION, FUNCTIONNAME
    Else
        csvGoToControl = True
    End If
    On Error GoTo 0

End Function
```

Depending on the context, you may instead be able to use the **SetFocus** method:

```
Forms![My Form Name]![MyControlName].SetFocus
```

csvGoToForm()

You can use the csvGoToForm() function to move the focus to a specified open form.

```
Function csvGoToForm (ByVal MyFormName As String) As Integer

    Const FUNCTIONNAME = "csvGoToForm()"

    csvGoToForm = True

    On Error Resume Next
    DoCmd SelectObject A_FORM, MyFormName, False
    If Err Then
        MsgBox "Couldn't go to form '" & MyFormName & "'.", csvMB_ICONEXCLAMATION,
FUNCTIONNAME
        csvGoToForm = False
    End If
    On Error GoTo 0

End Function
```

Depending on the context, you may instead be able to use the **SetFocus** method:

```
Forms![My Form Name].SetFocus
```

 Be sure to read about new coding techniques in Appendix D, "Converting Old Code."

csvGoToPage()

On a multipage form (a form with page break controls), you can use the csvGoToPage() function to navigate from page to page.

```
Function csvGoToPage (ByVal PageNumber As Integer) As Integer

    Const FUNCTIONNAME = "csvGoToPage()"

    csvGoToPage = True

    On Error Resume Next
    DoCmd GoToPage PageNumber
    If Err Then
        MsgBox "Couldn't go to page " & PageNumber & ".", csvMB_ICONEXCLAMATION,
FUNCTIONNAME
        csvGoToPage = False
    End If
    On Error GoTo 0

End Function
```

 Be sure to read about new coding techniques in Appendix D, "Converting Old Code."

csvGoToRecord()

If you provide your own record navigation buttons to replace those usually found at the bottom of forms, you can use the csvGoToRecord() function to avoid the message that normally appears when you try to move beyond the beginning or end of the current set of records.

You can place your custom navigation buttons in the form's header or footer, or in the form's toolbar.

```
Function csvGoToRecord (ByVal Direction As String) As Variant

    Const FUNCTIONNAME = "csvGoToRecord()"
    Dim X As Integer

    X = (InStr(1, "First   Last    PreviousNext    New     ", Direction,
➥csvCASEINSENSITIVE) + 7) \ 8
    If X <> 0 Then
        X = Choose(X, A_FIRST, A_LAST, A_PREVIOUS, A_NEXT, A_NEWREC)
```

```
        On Error Resume Next
        DoCmd GoToRecord A_FORM, Screen.ActiveForm.FormName, X
        On Error GoTo 0
        csvGoToRecord = X
    Else
        MsgBox "Invalid argument '" & Direction & ".", csvMB_ICONEXCLAMATION,
FUNCTIONNAME
        csvGoToRecord = Null
    End If

End Function
```

csvHideControl()

Use the csvHideControl() function to hide a specified control.

> **Tip:** Because you cannot hide the active (current) control, you may need to first call the csvGoToControl() function to move the focus to another control.

```
Function csvHideControl (MyForm As Form, ByVal MyControlName As String) As Integer

    Const FUNCTIONNAME = "csvHideControl()"

    On Error Resume Next
    MyForm(MyControlName).Visible = False
    If Err Then
        MsgBox "Couldn't hide control '" & MyControlName & "'.",
csvMB_ICONEXCLAMATION, FUNCTIONNAME
        csvHideControl = False
    Else
        csvHideControl = True
    End If
    On Error GoTo 0

End Function
```

csvHideForm()

Use the csvHideForm() function to hide a specified form.

> **Tip:** Because you cannot hide the active (current) form, you may need to first call the csvGoToForm() function to move the focus to another form.

```
Function csvHideForm (MyForm As Form, MyFormName As String) As Integer

    Const FUNCTIONNAME = "csvHideForm()"

    On Error Resume Next
    Forms(MyFormName).Visible = False
    If Err Then
        MsgBox = "Couldn't hide form '" & MyFormName & "'.", csvMB_ICONEXCLAMATION,
FUNCTIONNAME
        csvHideForm = False
    Else
        csvHideForm = True
    End If
    On Error GoTo 0
End Function
```

csvHighWord()

The csvHighWord() function returns the high word portion of a specified numeric value.

```
Function csvHighWord (ByVal Value As Long) As Long

    Dim X As Long

    X = Value \ &H10000
    csvHighWord = IIf(X < 0, X + &H10000, X)

End Function
```

csvHourglass()

You can use the csvHourglass() function to change the mouse pointer to an hourglass (by setting the *State* argument to True) or to an arrow (by setting the *State* argument to False).

```
Function csvHourglass (ByVal State As Integer) As Integer

    csvHourglass = True

    DoCmd Hourglass State

End Function
```

csvICap()

The `csvICap()` function returns a string in which only the first character is capitalized and all remaining characters are lowercase. For example, you may find this function useful if you want to capitalize a person's name (see fig. 21.6).

```
Function csvICap (ByVal InString As Variant) As Variant

    Dim ANSI As Integer
    Dim Temp As Variant
    Dim X As Integer

    Temp = LCase(InString)                      ' Start with lowercase.
    If Len(Temp) > 0 Then                       ' If not empty string.
        Mid(Temp, 1, 1) = UCase(Left(Temp, 1))  ' I-cap first character.
    End If
    csvICap = Temp

End Function
```

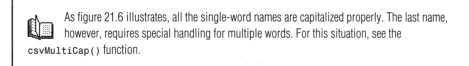

Figure 21.6. Testing the results of the `csvICap()` function.

As figure 21.6 illustrates, all the single-word names are capitalized properly. The last name, however, requires special handling for multiple words. For this situation, see the `csvMultiCap()` function.

csvIsEnabled()

Before you move the focus to a given control, you can use the `csvIsEnabled()` function to determine whether that control is enabled.

```
Function csvIsEnabled (MyControl As Control) As Variant

    Const FUNCTIONNAME = "csvIsEnabled()"

    On Error Resume Next
    csvIsEnabled = MyControl.Enabled
    If Err Then
        MsgBox "Couldn't determine enabled state of control.",
        ➥csvMB_ICONEXCLAMATION, FUNCTIONNAME
        csvIsEnabled = Null
    End If
    On Error GoTo 0

End Function
```

csvKeyboardInfo()

The csvKeyboardInfo() function displays a message box containing a variety of information about the keyboard. You can modify the function so it returns the type of keyboard, the subtype, or the number of function keys.

```
Function csvKeyboardInfo () As Integer

    Const TITLEBAR = "Keyboard Information"
    Dim Msg As String
    Dim CRLF As String

    CRLF = Chr$(13) & Chr$(10)

    csvKeyboardInfo = True

    Select Case csvGetKeyboardType(0)
        Case 1
            Msg = "IBM PC/XT (83-key)"
        Case 2
            Msg = "Olivetti (102-key)"
        Case 3
            Msg = "IBM AT (84-key)"
        Case 4
            Msg = "IBM enhanced (101- or 102-key)"
        Case 5
            Msg = "Nokia 1050 or similar"
        Case 6
            Msg = "Nokia 9140 or similar"
    End Select

    Msg = "Keyboard Type: " & Msg & CRLF
    Msg = Msg & "Keyboard Subtype Value: " & csvGetKeyboardType(1) & CRLF
    Msg = Msg & "Number of Function Keys: " & csvGetKeyboardType(2)
    MsgBox Msg, csvMB_ICONINFORMATION, TITLEBAR

End Function
```

csvLogError()

If you are trapping runtime errors, you may want to use the csvLogError() function to log, or record, the errors by writing selected information to an external MS-DOS text file.

```
Function csvLogError (ByVal Module As String, ByVal Procedure As String, ByVal
Number As Long,
➥ByVal Comment As String) As Integer

    Const OUTPUTFILE = "C:\TEMP\ERRORS.TXT"
    Dim FileNumber As Integer
    Dim T As String

    T = Chr$(9)
    FileNumber = FreeFile

    On Error GoTo Err_LogError
    Open OUTPUTFILE For Append As FileNumber
    Print #FileNumber, Module; T; Procedure; T; Number; T; Comment
    Close FileNumber
    On Error GoTo 0

    csvLogError = True
    Exit Function

Err_LogError:

    MsgBox "Couldn't write to ERRORS.LOG.", csvMB_ICONEXCLAMATION, "Disk Error"
    csvLogError = False
    On Error GoTo 0

End Function
```

csvLowWord()

The csvLowWord() function returns the low word portion of a specified numeric value.

```
Function csvLowWord (ByVal Value As Long) As Long

    Dim X As Long

    X = Value Mod &H10000
    csvLowWord = IIf(X < 0, X + &H10000, X)

End Function
```

csvMakeDirectory()

The csvMakeDirectory() function creates a specified directory, returning False if the directory already exists or if the specified name is invalid. Be sure you include a complete path for the *NewDirectory* argument.

```
Function csvMakeDirectory (ByVal NewDirectory As String) As Integer

    Const TITLEBAR = "Make Directory"

    csvMakeDirectory = True

    On Error Resume Next
    MkDir NewDirectory
    If Err Then
        MsgBox "Couldn't create directory '" & NewDirectory & "'.",
csvMB_ICONEXCLAMATION, TITLEBAR
        csvMakeDirectory = False
    End If
    On Error GoTo 0

End Function
```

csvMathChipPresent()

The csvMathChipPresent() function determines whether a math chip (coprocessor) is present. This information is most useful when displayed in an About... screen.

```
Function csvMathChipPresent () As Integer

    csvMathChipPresent = ((csvGetWinFlags() And csvWF_8087) \ csvWF_8087) = 1

End Function
```

csvMaximize()

Use the csvMaximize() function to maximize the current window.

```
Function csvMaximize () As Integer

    csvMaximize = True

    DoCmd Maximize

End Function
```

csvMaxValue()

The csvMaxValue() function returns the larger of two values, numeric or string.

```
Function csvMaxValue (ByVal X As Variant, ByVal Y As Variant) As Variant

    Const FUNCTIONNAME = "csvMaxValue()"

    If IsNumeric(X) * IsNumeric(Y) Then
        csvMaxValue = X + (X - Y) * (X < Y)
    Else
        MsgBox "Invalid numeric argument.", csvMB_ICONEXCLAMATION, FUNCTIONNAME
        csvMaxValue = Null
    End If

End Function
```

csvMinimize()

Use the csvMinimize() function to minimize the current window.

```
Function csvMinimize () As Integer

    csvMinimize = True

    DoCmd Minimize

End Function
```

csvMinValue()

The csvMinValue() function returns the smaller of two values, numeric or string.

```
Function csvMinValue (ByVal X As Variant, ByVal Y As Variant) As Variant

    Const FUNCTIONNAME = "csvMinValue()"

    If IsNumeric(X) * IsNumeric(Y) Then
        csvMinValue = X + (X - Y) * (X > Y)
    Else
        MsgBox "Invalid numeric argument.", csvMB_ICONEXCLAMATION, FUNCTIONNAME
        csvMinValue = Null
    End If

End Function
```

csvMoveToForm()

Use the csvMoveToForm() function to move the focus to a specified form. Using this function is similar in effect to using the **SelectObject** macro action or the **OpenForm** macro action.

 Note: This function is nearly identical to the csvGoToForm() function and is included for completeness and consistency in naming.

```
Function csvMoveToForm (ByVal MyFormName As String) As Integer

    Const FUNCTIONNAME = "csvMoveToForm()"

    csvMoveToForm = True

    On Error Resume Next
    DoCmd SelectObject A_FORM, MyFormName
    If Err Then
        MsgBox "Couldn't move to form '" & MyFormName & "'.", csvMB_ICONEXCLAMATION,
FUNCTIONNAME
        csvMoveToForm = False
    End If
    On Error GoTo 0

End Function
```

csvMultiCap()

This function is similar to csvICap(), except that csvMultiCap() capitalizes multiple words in a single string (see fig. 21.7).

```
Function csvMultiCap (ByVal InString As Variant) As Variant

    Dim ANSI As Integer
    Dim Temp As Variant
    Dim X As Integer

    Temp = LCase(InString)                       ' Start with lowercase.

    If Len(Temp) > 0 Then                        ' If not empty string.
        Mid(Temp, 1, 1) = UCase(Left(Temp, 1))   ' I-cap first character.
        For X = 2 To Len(Temp) - 1               ' Check other characters.
            ANSI = Asc(Mid(Temp, X, 1))          ' Obtain ANSI values.
            If ANSI < 65 Or ANSI > 122 Or (ANSI > 90 And ANSI < 97) Then
                Mid(Temp, X + 1, 1) = UCase(Mid(Temp, X + 1, 1))
            End If
        Next X
    End If

    csvMultiCap = Temp

End Function
```

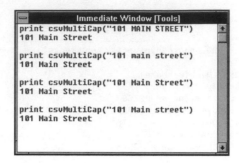

Figure 21.7.   Testing the results of the `csvMultiCap()` function.

csvNullToChar()

Depending on the context, you may want to replace Null values with a different, specified value. The replacement character can be a numeric value (usually zero) or a string value (often a zero-length string).

```
Function csvNullToChar (ByVal Number As Variant, ByVal NewChar As Variant) As
➡Variant

    If Not IsNull(Number) Then      ' Assume not Null.
        csvNullToZero = Number       ' Return same value.
    Else
        csvNullToZero = NewChar      ' Return new character, not Null.
    End If

End Function
```

csvObjectExists()

Use the `csvObjectExists()` function to determine whether a specified object exists.

```
Function csvObjectExists (ByVal MyObjectName As String, ByVal MyObjectType As
String) As Integer

    Const FUNCTIONNAME = "csvObjectExists()"
    Dim MyDB As Database
    Dim ObjectList As Snapshot
    Dim ObjectName As String
    Dim ObjectType As Integer

    If LCase$(MyObjectType) = "table" Then
        csvObjectExists = (csvTableType(MyObjectName) <> 0)
        Exit Function
```

continues

563

```
        End If

    Set MyDB = CurrentDB()
    Set ObjectList = MyDB.CreateSnapshot("MSysObjects")

    ObjectName = LCase$(MyObjectName)
    Select Case LCase$(MyObjectType)
        Case "form": ObjectType = -32768
        Case "macro": ObjectType = -32766
        Case "module": ObjectType = -32761
        Case "query": ObjectType = 5
        Case "report": ObjectType = -32764
        Case Else
            MsgBox "Invalid argument '" & MyObjectType & "'.",
csvMB_ICONEXCLAMATION, FUNCTIONNAME
    End Select

    ObjectList.MoveFirst
    csvObjectExists = False
    Do Until ObjectList.EOF
        If LCase$(ObjectList![Name]) = MyObjectName And ObjectList![Type] =
MyObjectType Then
            csvObjectExists = True
            Exit Do
        End If
        ObjectList.MoveNext
    Loop

End Function
```

 Be sure to read about new coding techniques in Appendix D, "Converting Old Code."

csvOpenForm()

You can open a specified form with the csvOpenForm() function. The *Action* argument indicates what happens to the current (active) form:

- invisible   make the current form invisible
- visible   make the current form visible
- minimize   minimize the current form
- maximize   maximize the current form
- close   close the current form
- ""   do nothing

```
    Function csvOpenForm (ByVal MyFormName As String, ByVal Action As String) As String

    Dim MyForm As Form
    Dim X As Integer

    csvOpenForm = False
```

```
On Error Resume Next
Set MyForm = Screen.ActiveForm
On Error GoTo 0

Select Case LCase(Action)
    Case ""
        ' Do nothing.
    Case "invisible"
        X = MyForm.Visible = False
    Case "visible"
        X = MyForm.Visible = True
    Case "minimize"
        X = csvMinimize(MyForm.FormName)
    Case "maximize"
        X = csvMaximize(MyForm.FormName)
    Case "close"
        DoCmd Close A_FORM, MyForm.FormName
    Case Else
        MsgBox "Invalid argument '" & Action & "'.", csv_MB_ICONEXCLAMATION,
FUNCTIONNAME
        Exit Function
End Select

On Error Resume Next
DoCmd OpenForm MyFormName
If Err Then
    MsgBox "Couldn't open form '" & MyFormName & "'.", csvMB_ICONEXCLAMATION,
FUNCTIONNAME
Else
    csvOpenForm = True
End If
On Error GoTo 0

End Function
```

csvOperatingMode()

You can use the `csvOperatingMode()` function to determine the current operating mode. This information is most useful in an About... screen.

```
Function csvOperatingMode () As String

    Dim Flags As Long
    Dim Match As Integer
    Dim X As String

    Flags = csvGetWinFlags()

    Match = 1
    Select Case Match
        Case (Flags And csvWF_CPU486) \ csvWF_CPU486
            X = "486"
        Case (Flags And csvWF_CPU386) \ csvWF_CPU386
```

continues

565

```
                X = "386"
        Case Else
                X = "286"
    End Select

    If Flags And csvWF_ENHANCED Then
        X = X & " Enhanced"
    Else
        X = X & " Standard"
    End If

    csvOperatingMode = X & " Mode"

End Function
```

csvParseArticles()

Use the csvParseArticles() function to strip strings of the leading articles *a*, *an*, and *the*. When you sort strings that begin with these characters, the strings sort out of sequence. Stripping the articles and placing them at the end causes the strings to sort properly.

```
Function csvParseArticles (ByVal InString As Variant) As Variant

    Dim X As Variant
    Dim Y As Integer
    Dim Z As Integer

    If Not IsNull(InString) Then
        X = UCase(Left(InString, 4))
        Y = InStr(X, " ")
        Z = Y
        If Y Then
            Y = (LCase(Left(X, 2)) = "a ") + (LCase(Left(X, 3)) = "an ") + (LCase(X)
= "the ")
        End If
        If Y Then
            csvParseArticles = Mid(InString, Z + 1) & ", " & Left(InString, Z - 1)
        Else
            csvParseArticles = InString
        End If
    Else
        csvParseArticles = Null
    End If

End Function
```

csvPlayWaveform()

If your computer has a sound card or compatible speaker driver, you can use the `csvPlayWaveform()` function to play a specified waveform (.WAV) file. Valid values for the *PlayHow* argument include these numbers:

- 0   synchronous

- 1   synchronous

- 8   loop (continuously)

```
Function csvPlayWaveform (ByVal FileName As String, ByVal PlayHow As Integer) As
Integer

    csvPlayWaveform = csvSndPlaySound(FileName, How)

End Function
```

csvQuit()

You can use the `csvQuit()` function to let the user exit your application, even if the user is not at a top-level form such as a main menu.

```
Function csvQuit (ByVal Action As String) As Integer

    Const FUNCTIONNAME = "csvQuit()"
    Dim X As Integer

    csvQuit - True

    Select Case LCase$(Action)
        Case "prompt"
            X = A_PROMPT
        Case "save"
            X = A_SAVE
        Case "exit"
            X = A_EXIT
        Case Else
            MsgBox "Invalid argument '" & Action & "'.", csvMB_ICONEXCLAMATION,
FUNCTIONNAME
            csvQuit = False
            Exit Function
    End Select

    Application.Quit X

End Function
```

csvRecordCount()

You can use the csvRecordCount() function to determine the number of records in a table or the number of records a specified query will return.

> **Tip:** This function is particularly useful because you can see how many records a query will return without actually having to run the query. If you use the csvRecordCount() function as part of a query-by-form routine, you can prevent running a runaway query.

```
Function csvRecordCount (ByVal MyTableQueryName As String) As Variant

    Const TITLEBAR = "Record Count"

    On Error Resume Next
    csvRecordCount = DCount("*", MyTableQueryName)
    If Err Then
        MsgBox "Couldn't determine record count for '" & MyTableQueryName & "'.",
csvMB_ICONEXCLAMATION,
        ➡TITLEBAR
        csvRecordCount = Null
    End If
    On Error GoTo 0

End Function
```

csvRemoveAccessMenu()

You can use the csvRemoveAccessMenu() function to remove the menu bar that normally appears whenever there is no form or other window with the focus (this would normally happen only when the Database window has the focus) or when you open a form that has no custom menu bar.

```
Function csvRemoveAccessMenu () As Integer

    Const CLASSNAME = "OMain"
    Dim X As Integer

    X = csvSetMenu(csvFindWindow(CLASSNAME, 0&), 0&)

End Function
```

csvRemoveCloseCommand()

If you have provided the user with an OK, Close, or Cancel command button on a form, you may want to use the csvRemoveCloseCommand() function to remove the Close command from the Control menu.

```
Function csvRemoveCloseCommand () As Integer

    Const COMMANDPOSITION = 6
    Dim WindowHandle As Integer
    Dim ControlMenuHandle As Integer
    Dim X As Integer

    WindowHandle = Screen.ActiveForm.hWnd
    ControlMenuHandle = csvGetSystemMenu(WindowHandle, 0)

    For X = 1 To 2
        csvRemoveCloseCommand = csvDeleteMenu(ControlMenuHandle, COMMANDPOSITION,
csvMF_BYPOSITION)
    Next X

End Function
```

csvRemoveTitleBar()

You can use the csvRemoveTitleBar() function to remove the title bar (see fig. 21.8). If you use this function, be sure you then call the csvResizeForm() function to compensate for the area of the form that no longer exists.

```
Function csvRemoveTitleBar (MyForm As Form) As Integer

    Dim OldStyle As Long
    Dim NewStyle As Long
    Dim WindowHandle As Integer

    On Error Resume Next
    WindowHandle = MyForm.hwnd
    If Err Then
        csvRemoveTitleBar = False
    Else
        OldStyle = csvGetWindowLong(WindowHandle, csvGWL_STYLE)
        NewStyle = OldStyle And Not csvWS_CAPTION
        OldStyle = csvSetWindowLong(WindowHandle, csvGWL_STYLE, NewStyle)
        csvRemoveTitleBar = True
    End If
    On Error GoTo 0

End Function
```

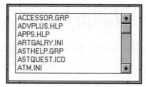

Figure 21.8. A form with no titlebar.

csvRename()

You can use the csvRename() function to rename an existing database object (table, query, form, and so on).

```
Function csvRename (ByVal ObjectType As String, ByVal OldName As String, ByVal
NewName As String)
➥As Integer

    Const FUNCTIONNAME = "csvRename()"
    Const TITLEBAR = "Rename Object"
    Dim X As Integer

    csvRename = False

    Select Case LCase$(ObjectType)
        Case "table"
            X = A_TABLE
        Case "query"
            X = A_QUERY
        Case "form"
            X = A_FORM
        Case "report"
            X = A_REPORT
        Case "macro"
            X = A_MACRO
        Case "module"
            X = A_MODULE
        Case Else
            MsgBox "Invalid argument '" & ObjectType & "'.", csvMB_ICONEXCLAMATION,
FUNCTIONNAME
            Exit Function
    End Select

    On Error Resume Next
    DoCmd RenameObject NewName, X, OldName
    If Err Then
        MsgBox "Couldn't rename '" & OldName & "'.", csvMB_ICONINFORMATION, TITLEBAR
    Else
        csvRename = True
    End If
    On Error GoTo 0

End Function
```

csvRequery()

Use the `csvRequery()` function to requery a form (by setting the *MyControlName* argument to a zero-length string) or a specified control on the current (active) form.

```
Function csvRequery (ByVal MyControlName As String) As Integer

    Const FUNCTIONNAME = "csvRequery()"

    csvRequery = False

    If MyControlName = "" Then
        On Error Resume Next
        DoCmd Requery
        If Err Then
            MsgBox "Couldn't requery form.", csvMB_ICONEXCLAMATION, FUNCTIONNAME
        Else
            DoCmd Requery MyControlName
            If Err Then
                MsgBox "Couldn't requery control '" & MyControlName & "'.",
csvMB_ICONEXCLAMATION,
                ➥FUNCTIONNAME
            End If
        End If
        On Error GoTo 0
    End If

End Function
```

 Be sure to read about new coding techniqes in Appendix D, "Converting Old Code.'

csvResetStatusBarText()

If you have set the status bar text using the `csvSetStatusBarText()` function, use the `csvResetStatusBarText()` function to reset it.

```
Function csvResetStatusBarText () As Integer

    Dim ReturnValue As Variant

    csvResetStatusBarText = True

    On Error Resume Next
    ReturnValue = SysCmd(5)
    On Error GoTo 0

End Function
```

571

csvResizeForm()

Use the csvResizeForm() function to change the size of an open form. As written, the function assumes you will be passing the new width and height in the form of inches. If necessary, change the value of the FACTOR constant to compensate for units other than inches.

```
Function csvResizeForm (ByVal MyFormName As String, ByVal NewWidth As Integer, ByVal
NewHeight As Integer)
➥As Integer

    Const FUNCTIONNAME = "csvResizeForm()"
    Const FACTOR = 1440

    csvResizeForm = True

    On Error Resume Next
    DoCmd MoveSize ,, NewWidth * FACTOR, NewHeight * FACTOR
    If Err Then
        MsgBox "Couldn't resize form '" & MyFormName & "'.", csvMB_ICONEXCLAMATION,
FUNCTIONNAME
        csvResizeForm = False
    End If
    On Error GoTo 0

End Function
```

csvRestore()

Use the csvRestore() function to restore the current window to its original shape and position before the window was minimized or maximized.

```
Function csvRestore () As Integer

    Const FUNCTIONNAME = "csvRestore()"

    On Error Resume Next
    DoCmd Restore
    If Err Then
        MsgBox "Couldn't restore form.", csvMB_ICONEXCLAMATION, FUNCTIONNAME
        csvRestore = False
    Else
        csvRestore = True
    End If
    On Error GoTo 0

End Function
```

csvRound()

Unlike setting the **Format** property for a control, which affects only the way a numeric value appears, the csvRound() function changes a numeric value by rounding it to a specified number of decimal places.

```
Function csvRound (ByVal Number As Variant, ByVal Decimals As Integer) As Variant

    Const TITLEBAR = "Round"

    If Decimals >= 0 Then
        csvRound = Int(Number * 10 ^ Decimals + .5) / 10 ^ Decimals
    Else
        MsgBox "Invalid decimal places '" & Decimals & "'.", csvMB_ICONEXCLAMATION,
TITLEBAR
        csvRound = Number
    End If

End Function
```

csvScreenDimension()

You can use the csvScreenDimension() function to determine the width or height of the current display. You may want to use these dimensions to calculate the factor used to scale forms and controls so they properly fit the screen.

```
Function csvScreenDimension (ByVal Which As String) As Variant

    Const FUNCTIONNAME = "csvScreenDimension()"

    Select Case LCase$(Which)
        Case "width"
            csvScreenDimension = csvGetSystemMetrics(0)
        Case "height"
            csvScreenDimension = csvGetSystemMetrics(1)
        Case Else
            MsgBox "Invalid argument '" & Which & "'.", csvMB_ICONEXCLAMATION,
FUNCTIONNAME
            csvScreenDimension = Null
    End Select

End Function
```

csvSearchAndReplace()

Use the csvSearchAndReplace() function to parse a string and replace one substring with another (see fig. 21.9). The replacement string specified by the *NewChar* argument does not need to contain the same number of characters as the substring you want to replace (specified by the *OldChar*

argument). You even can remove selected characters by setting the *NewChar* argument to a zero-length string ("").

```
Function csvSearchAndReplace (ByVal InString As Variant, ByVal OldChar As Variant,
➥ByVal NewChar As Variant) As Variant

    Dim X As Integer
    Dim OldCharLength As Integer
    Dim NewCharLength As Integer
    Dim Position As Integer

    If Not IsNull(InString) Then
        OldChar = IIf(IsNull(OldChar), "", OldChar)
        NewChar = IIf(IsNull(NewChar), "", NewChar)
        OldCharLength = Len(OldChar)
        NewCharLength = Len(NewChar)
        Position = 1
        X = InStr(Position, InString, OldChar)
        Do While X
            InString = Left(InString, X - 1) & NewChar & Mid(InString, X +
OldCharLength)
            Position = X + NewCharLength
            X = InStr(Position, InString, OldChar)
        Loop
    End If

    csvSearchAndReplace = InString

End Function
```

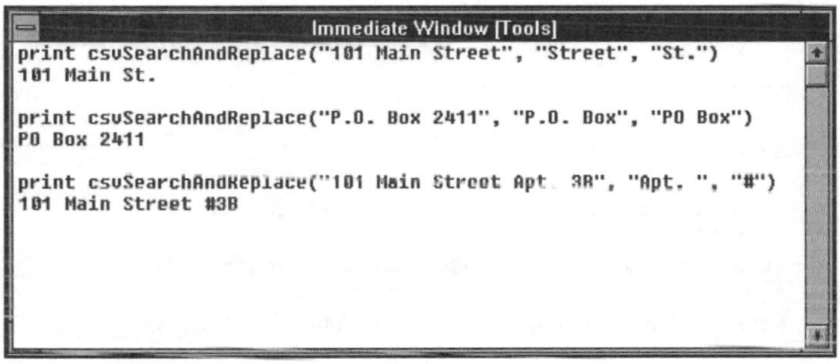

Figure 21.9.   Testing the results of the csvSearchAndReplace() function.

As figure 21.9 illustrates, you need to call csvSearchAndReplace() more than one time if you want to replace more than one substring.

csvSetAppTitleBar()

You can use the `csvSetAppTitleBar()` function to replace the *Microsoft Access* that normally appears in the Access window title bar (see fig. 21.10).

```
Function csvSetAppTitleBar (ByVal MyTitle As Variant) As Integer

    Const DEFAULT = "Microsoft Access"
    Const CLASSNAME = "OMain"

    csvSetAppTitleBar = True

    csvSetWindowText csvFindWindow(CLASSNAME, 0&), IIf(IsNull(MyTitle), DEFAULT,
MyTitle)

End Function
```

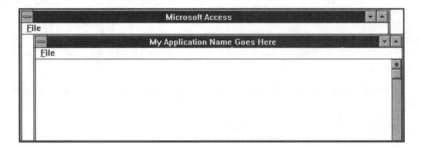

Figure 21.10.   Changing the caption in the Access window title bar.

Tip: If you set the *MyTitle* argument to Null, the `csvSetAppTitleBar()` function resets the title bar to the default (*Microsoft Access* in this example).

csvSetStatusBarText()

When you set a control's **StatusBarText** property, the specified text appears in the status bar only when the control has the focus. You can use the `csvSetStatusBarText()` function to set the status bar text at any time.

If you set the *MyText* argument to Null, the function resets the status bar text (which has the same effect as calling the `csvResetStatusBarText()` function).

```
Function csvSetStatusBarText (ByVal MyText As Variant) As Integer

    Dim ReturnValue As Variant

    csvSetStatusBarText = True

    If IsNull(MyText) Then
        ReturnValue = csvResetStatusBarText()
    Else
        ReturnValue = SysCmd(4, MyText)
    End If

End Function
```

csvSetTitleBar()

Depending on your application, you may want to use the csvSetTitleBar() function to change the caption that appears in a form's title bar. For example, you may want to display a secondary form that shows detail for a customer's main form. You can set the secondary form's caption so it displays the customer's name.

```
Function csvSetTitleBar (ByVal MyFormName As String, ByVal MyTitle As String) As
Integer

    Const FUNCTIONNAME - "csvSetTitleBar()"

    csvSetTitleBar = False

    On Error Resume Next
    Forms(MyFormName).Caption = MyTitle
    If Err Then
        MsgBox "Couldn't set title bar for '" & MyFormName & "'.",
csvMB_ICONEXCLAMATION, FUNCTIONNAME
    Else
        csvSetTitleBar = True
    End If
    On Error GoTo 0

End Function
```

csvSetToNull()

Use the csvSetToNull() function to set a specified control to Null.

```
Function csvSetToNull (MyForm As Form, ByVal MyControlName As String) As Integer

    Const FUNCTIONNAME = "csvSetToNull()"

    On Error Resume Next
    MyForm(MyControlName) = Null
```

```
        If Err Then
            MsgBox "Couldn't set '" & MyControlName & "' to Null.",
csvMB_ICONEXCLAMATION, FUNCTIONNAME
            csvSetToNull = False
        Else
            csvSetToNull = True
        End If
        On Error GoTo 0

    End Function
```

csvSizeWindow()

Use the csvSizeWindow() function to resize a form, usually in response to having detected the current screen resolution.

```
    Function csvSizeWindow (ByVal FormName As String, ByVal State As String) As Integer

        Const FUNCTIONNAME = "csvSizeWindow()"
        Dim WindowHandle As Integer
        Dim ReturnValue As Integer

        If FormName = "" Then
            WindowHandle = csvGetParent(csvGetActiveWindow())
        Else
            WindowHandle = Forms(FormName).hWnd
        End If

        Select Case LCase$(Left$(State, 3))
            Case "res", "restore" ' Restore.
                ReturnValue = csvShowWindow(WindowHandle, csvSW_RESTORE)
            Case "min", "minimize" ' Minimize.
                ReturnValue = csvShowWindow(WindowHandle, csvSW_SHOWMINIMIZED)
            Case "max", "maximize" ' Maximize.
                ReturnValue = csvShowWindow(WindowHandle, csvSW_SHOWMAXIMIZED)
            Case Else
                MsgBox "Invalid argument '" & State & "'.", csvMB_ICONEXCLAMATION,
FUNCTIONNAME
        End Select

    End Function
```

csvSomethingIn()

You can use the csvSomethingIn() function to determine if anything is in a specified control. This function does not distinguish between Null, Empty, or zero-length string values.

```
Function csvSomethingIn (MyControl As Control) As Integer

    csvSomethingIn = True

    If IsNull(MyControl) Then              ' Control is Null.
        csvSomethingIn = False
    Else
        If IsEmpty(MyControl) Then          ' Control is Empty.
            csvSomethingIn = False
        Else
            If MyControl = "" Then          ' Control is zero-length.
                csvSomethingIn = False
            End If
        End If
    End If

End Function
```

csvSort()

Use the csvSort() function to sort all elements in a single-dimension, zero-based array.

```
Function csvSort (Array() As Variant) As Variant

    Dim I As Long
    Dim J As Long
    Dim K As Long
    Dim L As Long
    Dim M As Long
    Dim N1 As Long
    Dim Z As Variant
    Dim Temp As Variant

    Z = SysCmd(1, "Sorting array...", UBound(Array))
    N1 = UBound(Array)
    M = N1

Sort1:

    M = M \ 2
    If M = 0 Then
        Z = SysCmd(3)
        Exit Function
    End If

    J = 1

Sort2:

    K = N1 - M
    I = J

Sort3:
```

```
        L = I + M
        Z = SysCmd(2, Abs(L - UBound(Array)))
        If LCase(Array(I)) <= LCase(Array(L)) Then
            GoTo Sort4
        End If
        Temp = Array(I)
        Array(I) = Array(L)
        Array(L) = Temp
        I = I - M
        If I < M Then
            GoTo Sort4
        End If
        GoTo Sort3

Sort4:

        J = J + 1
        If J > K GoTo Sort1
        GoTo Sort2

End Function
```

csvSortArray()

Use the csvSortArray() function to sort a specified number of elements in a single-dimension, zero-based array. This function is similar to csvSort().

```
    Function csvSortArray (Array() As Variant, Upper As Long) As Variant

        Dim I As Long
        Dim J As Long
        Dim K As Long
        Dim L As Long
        Dim M As Long
        Dim N1 As Long
        Dim Z As Variant
        Dim Temp As Variant

        Z = SysCmd(1, "Sorting array...", Upper)
        N1 = Upper
        M = N1

SortArray1:

        M = M \ 2
        If M = 0 Then
            Z = SysCmd(3)
            Exit Function
        End If

        J = 1

SortArray2:
```

continues

579

```
        K = N1 - M
        I = J

SortArray3:

        L = I + M
        Z = SysCmd(2, Abs(L - Upper))
        If LCase(Array(I)) <= LCase(Array(L)) Then
            GoTo SortArray4
        End If
        Temp = Array(I)
        Array(I) = Array(L)
        Array(L) = Temp
        I = I - M
        If I < M Then
            GoTo SortArray4
        End If
        GoTo SortArray3

SortArray4:

        J = J + 1
        If J > K GoTo SortArray1
        GoTo SortArray2

End Function
```

csvSound()

If you have a sound card or compatible speaker driver, you can use the csvSound() function to play a specified sound (frequency). You can combine calls to csvSound() to produce tunes or entire songs.

```
Function csvSound (ByVal Frequency As Single, ByVal Duration As Single) As Integer

    Dim F As Long
    Dim ReturnValue As Integer

    F = Frequency * 2 ^ 16
    If csvOpenSound() <> 0 Then
        If csvSetVoiceSound(1, F, 400 * Duration) = 0 Then
            csvSound = csvStartSound()
            While csvWaitSoundState(0)
            Wend
            csvSound = csvCloseSound()
        End If
    End If

End Function
```

csvStackForms()

Figure 21.11 shows the built-in commands that tile or cascade all open windows.

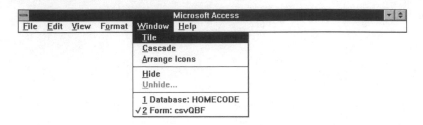

Figure 21.11. Choosing the Tile and Cascade commands.

You can use the csvStackForms() function to center all forms, no matter where they exist on-screen. The forms then appear to be stacked one atop the other.

```
Function csvStackForms () As Integer

    Dim X As Integer
    Dim ReturnValue As Integer

    csvStackForms = True

    For X = 0 To Forms.Count - 1
        ReturnValue = csvCenterForm (Forms(X).FormName))
    Next X

End Function
```

 Note: You may need to use the csvMoveToForm() function to make a specific form appear on top of the stack.

csvStartupDirectory()

Use the csvStartupDirectory() function to determine the directory in which the current (code) database exists.

```
Function csvStartupDirectory (ByVal FileName As String) As Variant

    Dim Buffer As String * 255

    If csvGetModuleFileName(csvGetModuleHandle(FileName), Buffer, Len(Buffer)) = 0
```

continues

```
Then
        csvStartupDirectory = Null
    Else
        csvStartupDirectory = Buffer
    End If

End Function
```

csvStripCtrlChars()

You can use the csvStripCtrlChars() function to remove specific ranges of characters. This function is especially helpful if you work with imported files from other environments. As written, the function removes characters whose ANSI values fall below 32 or higher than 122.

```
Function csvStripCtrlChars (ByVal InString As Variant) As Variant

    Const LOW = 32
    Const HIGH = 122
    Dim Done As Integer
    Dim ANSI As Integer
    Dim X As Integer
    Dim Temp As Variant

    Temp = ""
    For X = 1 To Len(InString)
        ANSI = Asc(Mid(InString, X, 1))
        If ANSI >= LOW And ANSI <= HIGH Then
            Temp = Temp & Mid(InString, X, 1)
        End If
    Next X

    csvStripCtrlChars = Trim(Temp)

End Function
```

csvSystemResources()

Use the csvSystemResources() function to determine the minimum amount of available system resources. This information is most useful in an About... screen.

```
Function csvSystemResources (ByVal Which As String) As Variant

    Const FUNCTIONNAME = "csvSystemResources()"
    Dim GDIFree As Long
    Dim UserFree As Long
    Dim Msg As String
    Dim CRLF As String

    CRLF = Chr$(13) & Chr$(10)
```

```
Select Case LCase$(Which)
    Case "resource", "resources"
        GDIFree = csvGetFreeResources("GDI")
        UserFree = csvGetFreeResources("User")
        csvSystemResources = csvMinValue(GDIFree, UserFree)
    Case "mem", "memory"
        csvSystemResources = csvGetFreeSpace(0)
    Case Else
        MsgBox "Invalid argument '" & Which & "'.", csvMB_ICONEXCLAMATION,
FUNCTIONNAME

End Function
```

csvTableType()

You can use the csvTableType() function to determine whether a specified table is an attached table or a native (non-attached) table.

```
Function csvTableType (ByVal MyTableName As String) As Integer

    Dim MyDB As Database
    Dim TableList As Snapshot
    Dim TempTableName As String

    TempTableName = LCase$(MyTableName)
    Set MyDB = CurrentDB()
    Set TableList = MyDB.ListTables()

    csvTableType = 0
    TableList.MoveFirst
    Do Until TableList.EOF
        If LCase$(TableList.Name) = TempTableName Then
            Select Case TableList.TableType
                Case DB_TABLE
                    csvTableType = 1              ' Native table.
                Case DB_ATTACHEDTABLE
                    csvTableType = 2              ' Attached table.
                Case Else
            End Select
            Exit Do
        End If
        TableList.MoveNext
    Loop

    TableList.Close
    MyDB.Close

End Function
```

 Be sure to read about new coding techniqes in Appendix D, "Converting Old Code.'

csvTempFileName()

Use the csvTempFileName() function to create an external MS-DOS text file on a specified drive. If the specified drive contains the path specified by the TEMP environment variable, the file is created in that directory; otherwise, the file is created in the default directory in the specified drive.

The *Prefix* argument specifies the letters Windows uses to create the file name. Specify between one and three characters.

The *Unique* argument, if True, indicates that a unique file name will be generated. Otherwise, a non-unique file name will be generated each time you call the function.

```
Function csvTempFileName (ByVal DriveLetter As Integer, ByVal Prefix As String,
ByVal Unique As Integer)
➥As String

    Dim Buffer As String * 255
    Dim ReturnValue As Integer

    ReturnValue = csvGetTempFileName(DriveLetter, Prefix, Unique, Buffer)
    csvTempFileName = Left$(Buffer, InStr(Buffer, Chr$(0)) - 1)

End Function
```

csvToggleControlMenu()

You can remove a form's Control menu by setting its **ControlBox** property to False, but only while the form is in Design view. In Form or Datasheet view, you can use the csvToggleControlMenu() function to add the Control menu (by setting the *State* argument to True) or remove the menu (by setting the *State* argument to False).

```
Function csvToggleControlMenu (ByVal MyFormName As String, By Val State As String)
As Integer

    Const FUNCTIONNAME = "csvToggleControlMenu()"
    Dim OldStyle As Long
    Dim NewStyle As Long
    Dim WindowHandle As Integer
    Dim Okay As Integer

    csvToggleControlMenu = False
    On Error Resume Next
    WindowHandle = Forms(MyFormName).hWnd
    If Err Then
    Else
        Okay = True
        Forms(MyFormName).Painting = False
        OldStyle = csvGetWindowLong(WindowHandle, csvGWL_STYLE)
        Select Case LCase$(State)
            Case "on"
                NewStyle = OldStyle And csvWS_SYSMENU
            Case "off"
                NewStyle = OldStyle And Not csvWS_SYSMENU
```

584

```
            Case Else
                MsgBox "Invalid argument '" & State & "'.", csvMB_ICONEXCLAMATION,
FUNCTIONNAME
                Okay = False
        End Select
        Forms(MyFormName).Painting = True
        If Okay Then
            OldStyle = csvSetWindowLong(WindowHandle, csvGWL_STYLE, NewStyle)
            csvToggleControlMenu = True
        End If
    End If
    On Error GoTo 0

End Function
```

csvToggleMenuCommand()

Depending on your application, you may want to use the `csvToggleMenuCommand()` function to enable a menu command (by setting the *State* argument to True) or disable a command (by setting the *State* argument to False). Figure 21.12 illustrates this command.

The *MenuCommand* argument is an integer that identifies the menu containing the command you want to toggle. Begin counting at the first menu, usually the File menu. The first menu is 0, the second menu is 1, and so on.

The *MenuSubCommand* argument is also an integer that identifies the command in the menu. The first command is 0, the second command is 1, and so on.

```
Function csvToggleMenuCommand (ByVal MenuCommand As Integer, ByVal MenuSubCommand As
Integer, ByVal State
➥As Integer) As Integer

    Const CLASSNAME = "OMain"
    Const NULLCHAR = 0&
    Dim AppWindow As Integer
    Dim TopMenu As Integer
    Dim SubMenu As Integer
    Dim ItemID As Integer
    Dim ReturnValue As Integer

    AppWindow = csvFindWindow(CLASSNAME, NULLCHAR)
    TopMenu = csvGetMenu(AppWindow)
    SubMenu = csvGetSubMenu(TopMenu, MenuCommand)

    If State = True Then
        csvToggleMenuCommand = csvEnableMenuItem(SubMenu, MenuSubCommand,
csvMF_ENABLED Or
        ➥csvMF_BYPOSITION)
    Else
        csvToggleMenuCommand = csvEnableMenuItem(SubMenu, MenuSubCommand,
csvMF_GRAYED Or csvMF_BYPOSITION)
    End If

End Function
```

```
        T = Chr$(9)
        X = 0
        FileNumber = FreeFile
        On Error Resume Next
        Open OUPUTFILE For Output As FileNumber
        If Err Then
            csvUsedErrors = False
        Else
            Do While True
                X = X + 1
                If LCase(Left(Error(X), 18)) <> USERDEFINED Then
                    If Err Then
                        Exit Do
                    End If
                    Print #FileNumber, X; T; Frror(X)
                End If
            Loop
            Close FileNumber
            csvUsedErrors = True
        End If
        On Error GoTo 0

End Function
```

csvValidatePostalCode()

You can use the csvValidatePostalCode() function to determine whether a given postal code withstands a test of reasonableness.

As written, this function assumes that you are calling the function from the current (active) form and that the form has controls named Country and PostalCode.

```
Function csvValidatePostalCode () As Integer

    Const TITLEBAR = "Invalid Postal Code"
    Dim MyForm As Form
    Dim MyCountry As Control
    Dim MyPostalCode As Control
    Dim Msg As String
    Dim OK As Integer
    Dim PostalCodeLength As Integer
    Dim X As Integer
    Dim Margin As String
    Dim CRLF As String
    Dim ProposedPostalCode As Variant

    Margin = Space$(10)
    CRLF = Chr$(13) & Chr$(10)

    Set MyForm = Screen.ActiveForm
    Set MyCountry = MyForm![Country]
    Set MyPostalCode = MyForm![PostalCode]
    ProposedPostalCode = MyPostalCode
```

```
    Msg = "The postal code for " & MyCountry & " must "

    On Error Resume Next
    PostalCodeLength = Len(MyPostalCode)
    If Err Then
        csvValidatePostalCode = True
        Exit Function
    End If
    On Error GoTo 0
    OK = True

    Select Case LCase(MyCountry)
        Case "usa"
            Select Case PostalCodeLength
                Case 5, 9, 10
                    If PostalCodeLength = 9 Then
                        ProposedPostalCode = Left(MyPostalCode, 5) & "-" &
Right(MyPostalCode, 4)
                    End If
                    For X = 1 To PostalCodeLength
                        If (Mid(ProposedPostalCode, X, 1) < "0" Or
Mid(ProposedPostalCode, X, 1) > "9")
                            ➥And X <> 6 Then
                            OK = False
                            Exit For
                        End If
                    Next X
                    If OK And PostalCodeLength = 10 Then
                        If Mid(ProposedPostalCode, 6, 1) <> "-" Then
                            OK = False
                        End If
                    End If
                Case Else
                    OK = False
            End Select
            Msg = Msg & "be in one of these formats:" & CRLF & CRLF & Margin &
"xxxxx" & CRLF & Margin &
                ➥"xxxxx-xxxx" & CRLF & CRLF & "where 'x' is a number."
        Case "canada"
            Select Case PostalCodeLength
                Case 6, 7
                    If PostalCodeLength = 7 Then
                        ProposedPostalCode = Left(MyPostalCode, 3) &
Right(MyPostalCode, 3)
                    End If
                    For X = 1 To 5 Step 2
                        If Mid(ProposedPostalCode, X, 1) < "a" Or
Mid(ProposedPostalCode, X, 1) > "z"
                            ➥Then
                            OK = False
                            Exit For
                        End If
                    Next X
                    For X = 2 To 6 Step 2
                        If Mid(ProposedPostalCode, X, 1) < "0" Or
Mid(ProposedPostalCode, X, 1) > "9"
                            ➥Then
```

continues

```
                                    OK = False
                                    Exit For
                              End If
                         Next X
                  Case Else
                         OK = False
            End Select
            Msg = Msg & "be in one of these formats:" & CRLF & CRLF & Margin &
"LNLNLN" & CRLF & Margin &
               ➥"LNL NLN" & CRLF & CRLF & "where 'L' is a letter and 'N' is a number."
         Case "australia", "singapore"
               If PostalCodeLength <> 4 Then
                  OK = False
               End If
         Case "france", "italy", "spain"
               If PostalCodeLength <> 5 Then
                  OK = False
               End If
         Case Else
      End Select

      If Not OK Then
         MsgBox Msg, csvMB_ICONEXCLAMATION, TITLEBAR
      End If
      csvValidatePostalCode = OK

End Function
```

csvValidState()

You can use the csvValidState() function to determine whether a state abbreviation is valid.

As written, the function allows the user to enter *DC* (District of Columbia), *PR* (Puerto Rico), and *VI* (Virgin Islands). To add other abbreviations, add the appropriate two-letter abbreviations to the vs (valid state) variable.

```
Function csvValidState (ByVal InState As Variant) As Integer

      Const TITLEBAR = "Invalid State Abbreviation"
      Const FUNCTIONNAME = "csvidState()"
      Const INVALIDSTATE = 32000
      Const STATETOOSHORT = 32001
      Const STATETOOLONG = 32002
      Dim Msg As String
      Dim Temp As Variant
      Dim Valid As Integer
      Dim VS As String
      Dim X As Integer

      ' Define the valid, two-letter state abbreviations.
      VS = "ALAKAZARCACOCTDEDCFLGAHIIDILINIAKSKYLAMEMDMAMIMNMSMOMT"
      VS = VS & "NENVNHNJNMNYNCNDOHOKORPAPRRISCSDTNTXUTVTVIVAWAWVWIWY"

      On Error GoTo Err_ValidState            ' Enable error trapping.
```

```
        If Len(InState) = 2 Then
            Temp = UCase(InState)
            For X = 1 To Len(VS) - 1 Step 2
                If Mid(VS, X, 2) = Temp Then
                    Valid = True                ' Entry is valid.
                    Exit For
                End If
            Next X
            If Not Valid Then
                Error INVALIDSTATE              ' Entry is invalid.
            End If
        ElseIf Len(InState) > 2 Then            ' Entry is too long.
            Error STATETOOLONG
        Else
            Error STATETOOSHORT                 ' Entry is too short.
        End If

        On Error GoTo 0                         ' Disable error trapping.
        csvValidState = Valid
        Exit Function

    Err_ValidState:

        Msg = "The state abbreviation '" & InState & "' is"
        Select Case Err
            Case INVALIDSTATE
                Msg = Msg & "n't valid."
            Case STATETOOSHORT
                Msg = Msg & " too short."
            Case STATETOOLONG
                Msg = Msg & " too long."
            Case Else
                Msg = "Error (" & Err & ": " & Error & ") in " & FUNCTIONNAME & "."
        End Select

        MsgBox Msg, csvMB_ICONEXCLAMATION, TITLEBAR
        Valid = False
        Resume Next

    End Function
```

csvWait()

You can use the csvWait() function to introduce an arbitrary delay (a specified number of seconds).

```
    Function csvWait (ByVal Seconds As Long) As Integer

        Dim StartTicks As Long

        csvWait = True
        StartTicks = csvGetTickCount()
        Do Until csvGetTickCount() >= StartTicks + Seconds * 1000
            DoEvents
        Loop

    End Function
```

591

csvWaitToExecute()

The csvWaitToExecute() function is similar to the csvWait() function except that csvWaitToExecute() executes another application (or triggers some other activity) when a specified date and time occur.

```
Function csvWaitToExecute (ByVal ExecutionDateTime As String) As Integer

    csvWaitToExecute = True

    Do Until Str$(Now) >= ExecutionDateTime
        DoEvents
    Loop

    MsgBox "A timed event can go here...", , "Wait to Execute"

End Function
```

csvWindowPosition()

You can use the csvWindowPosition() function to save the coordinates for a specified form (by setting the *Action* argument to "save") or restore the coordinates (by setting the *Action* argument to "restore").

For example, many users expect forms to appear in the positions in which the forms were last opened. You can use the csvWindowPosition() function in the **OnOpen** and **OnClose** events to save and restore forms' positions.

```
Function csvWindowPosition (ByVal MyFormName As String, ByVal Action As String) As
Integer

    Const FUNCTIONNAME = "csvWindowPosition()"
    Const INIFILENAME = "d:\myini.ini"
    Const SWP_NOZORDER = &H4
    Dim XOffset As Integer
    Dim YOffset As Integer
    Dim FormWidth As Integer
    Dim FormHeight As Integer
    Dim CurrentFormName As String
    Dim FormRectangle As csvRECT
    Dim ParentRectangle As csvRECT
    Dim WindowHandle As Integer
    Dim Buffer As String * 128
    Dim Size As Integer
    Dim ReturnValue As Integer

    CurrentFormName = LCase$(IIf(MyFormName = "", Screen.ActiveForm.FormName,
MyFormName))

    WindowHandle = Forms(CurrentFormName).hWnd
    csvGetWindowRect csvGetParent(WindowHandle), ParentRectangle

    Select Case LCase$(Action)
```

```
        Case "save" ' Save coordinates relative to parent window.
              csvGetWindowRect WindowHandle, FormRectangle
              XOffset = FormRectangle.Left - ParentRectangle.Left
              YOffset = FormRectangle.Top - ParentRectangle.Top
              FormWidth = FormRectangle.Right - FormRectangle.Left
              FormHeight = FormRectangle.Bottom - FormRectangle.Top
              ReturnValue = csvWritePrivateProfileString(CurrentFormName, "left",
Trim$(Str$(XOffset)),
              ➡INIFILENAME)
              ReturnValue = csvWritePrivateProfileString(CurrentFormName, "top",
Trim$(Str$(YOffset)),
              ➡INIFILENAME)
              ReturnValue = csvWritePrivateProfileString(CurrentFormName, "width",
Trim$(Str$(FormWidth)),
              ➡INIFILENAME)
              ReturnValue = csvWritePrivateProfileString(CurrentFormName, "height",
Trim$(Str$(FormHeight)),
              ➡INIFILENAME)
        Case "restore" ' Restore relative to parent window's current location.
              XOffset = csvGetPrivateProfileInt(CurrentFormName, "left", 0,
INIFILENAME)
              YOffset = csvGetPrivateProfileInt(CurrentFormName, "top", 0,
INIFILENAME)
              FormWidth = csvGetPrivateProfileInt(CurrentFormName, "width", 0,
INIFILENAME)
              FormHeight = csvGetPrivateProfileInt(CurrentFormName, "height", 0,
INIFILENAME)
              csvSetWindowPos WindowHandle, 0, XOffset, YOffset, FormWidth,
FormHeight, SWP_NOZORDER
        Case Else
              MsgBox "Invalid argument.", csvMB_ICONEXCLAMATION, FUNCTIONNAME
    End Select

End Function
```

csvWindowsColor()

You can use the csvWindowsColor() function as part of a form-initialization routine to retrieve the screen colors previously set by the user in the Windows Control Panel.

```
    Function csvWindowsColor (ByVal Which As String) As Integer

        Const FUNCTIONNAME = 'csvWindowsColor()"
        Const COLOR_APPWORKSPACE = 12    ' Background color for multiple-document
                                         ' interface (MDI) apps.
        Const COLOR_BACKGROUND = 1  ' Background for the desktop.
        Const COLOR_WINDOW = 5      ' Window background.
        Const COLOR_WINDOWTEXT = 8  ' Text in windows.
        Dim AppWorkspace As Long
        Dim Background As Long
        Dim Window As Long
        Dim WindowText As Long

        csvWindowsColor = True
```

continues

```
      Select Case LCase$(Which)
          Case "appworkspace"
              csvWindowsColor = csvGetSysColor(COLOR_APPWORKSPACE)
          Case "background"
              csvWindowsColor = csvGetSysColor(COLOR_BACKGROUND)
          Case "window "
              csvWindowsColor = csvGetSysColor(COLOR_WINDOW)
          Case "windowtext"
              csvWindowsColor = csvGetSysColor(COLOR_WINDOWTEXT)
          Case Else
              MsgBox "Invalid argument '" & Which & "'.", csvMB_ICONEXCLAMATION,
FUNCTIONNAME
              csvWindowsColor = False
      End Select

End Function
```

csvWindowsVersion()

You can use the csvWindowsVersion() function to determine the version of Windows under which your application is run.

```
Function csvWindowsVersion () As Double

    Dim X As Integer
    Dim Minor As Integer
    Dim Major As Integer

    X = csvGetVersion()
    Major = X And 255
    Minor = (X And &HFF00) \ 256
    csvWindowsVersion = Major + Minor * .01

End Function
```

csvWindowText()

Use the csvWindowText() function to determine the current contents of a form's **Caption** property. You may want to save the contents before you change it with the csvSetTitleBar() function.

```
Function csvWindowText (ByVal MyFormName) As Variant

    On Error Resume Next
    csvWindowText = Forms(MyFormName).Caption
    If Err Then
        MsgBox "Couldn't read caption for form '" & MyFormName & "'.",
csvMB_ICONEXCLAMATION, FUNCTIONNAME
        csvWindowText = Null
    End If
    On Error GoTo 0

End Function
```

22

Implementing Security

Security means far more than just making sure the computer itself is protected from damage or theft. In Microsoft Access, it also means making sure only authorized users gain access to your data and perform only authorized operations. Finally, proper security also means protecting the various database objects in your application from unauthorized users.

This chapter covers the following areas:

- Administering Users and Workgroups
- Analyzing the Need for Security
- Securing an Access System
- Administering User and Group Accounts
- Encrypting and Decrypting a Database

Administering Users and Workgroups

This section explores the SYSTEM.MDA file and the role it plays in establishing workgroups. A *workgroup* is a collection of users who share data in a multiuser environment, a common SYSTEM.MDA file, and the right to open specified databases shared by the workgroup. A workgroup is not quite the same as a *group account,* which is also a collection of related users: workgroups contain group accounts. Figure 22.1 illustrates the relationship between workgroups and group accounts.

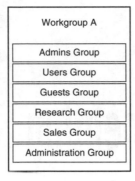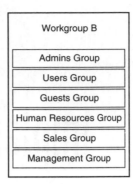

Figure 22.1. Each workgroup contains its own group accounts.

Workgroups contain group accounts that contain lists of individual users. The specific names of the group accounts are not particularly significant. For example, the preceding figure shows two Sales group accounts. In reality, these two groups are separate, each with its own list of users. Information about one workgroup is separate (both physically and logically) from every other workgroup.

The Role of *SYSTEM.MDA*

Microsoft Access stores system-wide security information in the SYSTEM.MDA file. SYSTEM.MDA contains user names, passwords, and assigned permissions. When a user logs on to a secure system, Access searches the SYSTEM.MDA file to determine whether the specified user name and password are valid. If so, Access allows the user to continue.

The SYSTEM.MDA file itself defines a workgroup. That is, Access stores all information about a particular workgroup in a single SYSTEM.MDA file. When you launch Access from the Program Manager, Access searches the MSACC20.INI file in your Windows directory for the location of the SYSTEM.MDA it should use. Even if you do not join a workgroup when you first install Access, Access creates one for you automatically.

> **STOP** **WARNING:** In a secure system, the SYSTEM.MDA file that was used to create a database and all its objects is required to open and use that database. For this reason, you should maintain a current backup copy of any SYSTEM.MDA files you create.

Sharing Information between Systems

Depending on your user and group accounts, as well as the systems under which the various databases are created, you may need to allow users to share information between two or more systems.

For example, you might want to launch Access with one workgroup and then use tables in a database created in another workgroup. To do this, create the same group account on both systems, specifying the same name and same PID (personal identification number) for each. Thereafter, you will be able to open databases and access data in either system, regardless of which SYSTEM.MDA you use to launch Access.

Changing Workgroups

When you first install Microsoft Access, you can choose to join an existing workgroup (see fig. 22.2). If you decide on an existing workgroup, be prepared to supply the complete path and name for the SYSTEM.MDA file you intend to use. Remember, a workgroup is defined by a SYSTEM.MDA file.

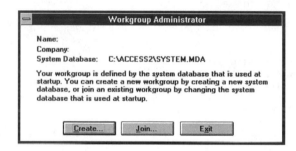

Figure 22.2. You can join an existing workgroup when you install Microsoft Access.

Or you can choose to install a local, standalone copy of Access that is not part of an existing workgroup. If so, Access creates a new SYSTEM.MDA file. If you want, you can change your mind at some future date and join another workgroup. You can belong to any number of workgroups, all at the same time.

Creating Workgroup Directories

Because a workgroup is defined by a SYSTEM.MDA file, creating multiple workgroups means creating multiple SYSTEM.MDA files. However, MS-DOS does not permit duplicate file names in the same directory; you must store the various SYSTEM.MDA files in separate directories or, less commonly, on separate drives.

For example, you might create separate systems and databases in support of both your Sales and Human Resources departments. To do this, you can create a separate directory for sales information (C:\DATA\SALES) and another for personnel information (C:\DATA\HR). Place the appropriate SYSTEM.MDA file in each directory.

Note: The directories that contain the SYSTEM.MDA files (typically the same as the databases to which they apply) must not be marked read-only by the network operating system, even if the users are not allowed to change data in the databases.

Switching between Workgroups

To switch from one workgroup to another, be prepared to specify the complete path and name of the SYSTEM.MDA file you intend to use.

The workgroup Access uses is defined by an entry in the [Options] section of your MSCC20.INI file:

```
[Options]
SystemDB=C:\ACCESS2\system.mda
UtilityDB=C:\ACCESS2\utility.mda
AllowCustomControls=1
AllowOLE1LinkFormat=0
DebugLibraries=True
```

In this example, the SystemDB entry points to the SYSTEM.MDA file in the C:\ACCESS2 directory. You can change the SystemDB entry in two ways:

- Open the MSACC20.INI file with Windows Notepad or another text-editing program, edit the entry so that it points to the desired SYSTEM.MDA file, and save the changes.

- Run the Workgroup Administrator Utility (WRKGADM.EXE in your Access directory). You use this utility to change workgroups.

When you first install Microsoft Access, the Setup program creates an icon in the Program Manager that launches the Workgroup Administrator Utility (see fig. 22.3).

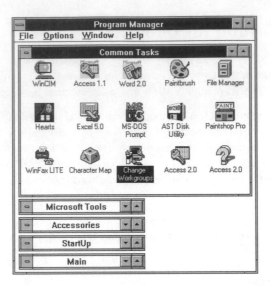

Figure 22.3. Change workgroups by choosing the Change Workgroups icon in the Program Manager.

When you run the Workgroup Administrator Utility, Access displays the Workgroup System Database dialog box in which you can specify the path and name of the desired SYSTEM.MDA file (see fig. 22.4).

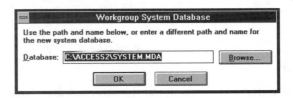

Figure 22.4. Specifying the desired workgroup's SYSTEM.MDA file.

Restarting Microsoft Access

Whether you edit the MSACC20.INI file manually or run the Workgroup Administrator Utility, you must close and then relaunch Microsoft Access in order for the new SystemDB entry to take effect.

599

Analyzing the Need for Security

With Microsoft Access, you can establish a fully secure system in which only authorized users can gain access and view or change data, or you can establish an open system in which there is little, if any, system-level protection. There are additional degrees of protection between these two extremes.

The level of security you need, and the techniques required to implement it, depend greatly on the kind of information you store and the nature of the various database objects you want to protect. For example, an application that maintains human resource or payroll information justifies a higher level security than an application that stores information about your personal CD collection. Generally, the applications you develop for your own personal use probably do not require any security protection, but applications you develop for other users or clients do.

Access uses the terms *secure* and *unsecure* to describe whether a system has its security enabled. The following sections describe the characteristics of each kind of system.

Unsecure Systems

An unsecure system is the default: you do not have to do anything special to have an unsecure system. In an unsecure system, Access logs you on as the Admin user automatically. The Admin user has unlimited access to all database objects and has the rights and privileges to read and modify data, and to execute all queries and code in Access Basic modules.

If you are developing an application for personal use, an unsecure system is probably satisfactory.

Secure Systems

Unlike an unsecure system, a secure system imposes restrictions on the kinds of operations a user may perform and restricts the database objects to which users have access. For example, you can determine which users can execute certain queries or open certain forms (such as payroll forms).

Even in a secure system, however, you can establish so-called *superusers*, or administrators, that have unlimited access to all database objects.

In a secure system, each user has a user name, a PID (a personal identification number much like those designed for automatic teller machines), and a password. The combination of name and number uniquely identifies each user of the system.

In addition, you can establish groups of users, usually related by function. For example, you might create a group for users who work in the Sales department, another group for Human Resources employees, yet another for Administration users, and so on.

There are two kinds of security information:

- *Permissions.* This category defines the rights each user has to the various database objects. Access stores permissions information in each database (.MDB file).

- *System.* This category defines all remaining security information. It includes user names and passwords, names of groups, and so on. In other words, this category includes system-wide security information, not database-specific security information. Access stores system security information in the SYSTEM.MDA file. Users who share a common SYSTEM.MDA file in a network (multiuser) environment are said to belong to the same workgroup. For more information about workgroups, see "Administering Users and Workgroups" earlier in this chapter.

Securing an Access System

You create a secure Microsoft Access system by activating the logon procedure, by establishing user accounts, and by assigning passwords for each user.

Activating the Logon Procedure

In an unsecure system, Access assumes you are the Admin user and have unlimited rights. Because you have unrestricted access, you are not prompted for either a user name or a password.

The default password for the Admin user is blank; that is, no password exists. To activate the logon procedure and to have Access prompt you for your name and password, you need only assign a password to the Admin user.

Open any database (or create a new database) and then choose the Change Password command from the Security menu (see fig. 22.5).

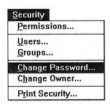

Figure 22.5.   Choose the Change Password command to assign or change your password.

Access displays the Change Password dialog box in which you can select a user and enter the new password (see fig. 22.6).

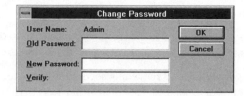

Figure 22.6. Specifying a user password.

In the case of the Admin user, no password exists, so you can leave the Old Password text box blank. Enter a new password in the New Password text box and in the Verify text box. As you type the passwords, Access displays asterisks rather than the actual characters you type. Finally, click the OK button to accept the changes. The next time you launch Microsoft Access, the system will prompt you to enter your name and password (see fig. 22.7).

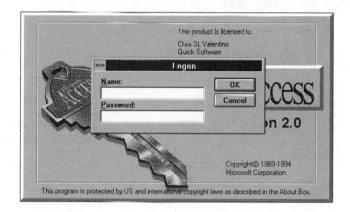

Figure 22.7. In a secure system, you must enter your name and password before you can use Access.

Creating a Replacement Admin Account

Every Microsoft Access system includes an Admin user account in the Admins group account. Every user in the Admins group account has unlimited access rights. To prevent unauthorized users from gaining access to your system, replace the default Admin user account with a new account—even though you may have assigned a password to the Admin user account.

> To create a replacement Admin account, you must first be logged on as the Admin user or another user who is a member of the Admins group. For more information about user groups, see "Administering User and Group Accounts" later in this chapter.

Open any database (or create a new database) and then choose the Users command from the Security menu (see fig. 22.8).

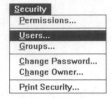

Figure 22.8. Choose the Users command to add or delete user accounts.

Access displays the Users dialog box in which you can add or delete users, remove passwords, and administer group memberships (see fig. 22.9).

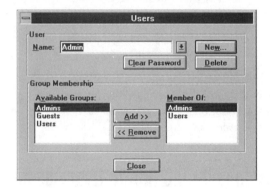

Figure 22.9. Maintain user information with the Users dialog box.

To create a new user account, click the New button; Access displays the New User/Group dialog box (see fig. 22.10).

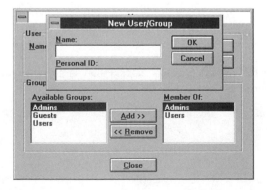

Figure 22.10. Adding a new user to the system.

Enter the new user's name and personal identification number (between 4 and 20 characters). The combination of name and number uniquely identifies the user's account.

> **Note:** As you add new users to the system, make sure you enter unique names and that the combinations of names and personal identification numbers are unique across all systems with which you intend to share information.
>
> Do not track this information in an Access table; experience suggests security information should not be stored in a database to which users otherwise have access. If you must store a list of names, identification numbers, and passwords, store the list apart from the computer, preferably in a secure location (for example, a bank vault). You may need this information later if you should have to re-create a user account.

When you click OK to close the dialog box, Access adds the new user account to the system. Next, identify the groups to which the new user will belong. Specifically, make sure the new user belongs to at least the Admins group.

Select the Admins group from the list of available groups (Access automatically creates the Admins, Guests, and Users groups) and then click the Add button.

Finally, click OK to close the Users dialog box and return to the Database window. Relaunch Microsoft Access and log on as the new system administrator (in this example, CSV). The password is blank (that is, no password exists); you should add a password to the user account. For more information about adding passwords, see "Administering Users and Workgroups" earlier in this chapter.

Removing Permissions for the Admin User Account

Now that you have a new system administrator (CSV), remove all the permissions for the existing Admin user account. This step is essential to creating a secure Microsoft Access system.

> **WARNING:** If you do not remove all permissions for the existing Admin user account, anyone who can get to your database files with a different Access installation will be able to access all your data and database objects.

If you have not relaunched Microsoft Access and logged on as the new system administrator, do so before you change the permissions.

For more information about removing or assigning permissions, see the next section, "Administering User and Group Accounts."

Administering User and Group Accounts

You perform three primary administrative tasks to support your applications:

- Maintain user names and passwords

- Create user groups and assign users to them

- Assign various permissions

User Names and Passwords

To either add a new user or delete an existing user from the system, choose the Users command from the Security menu. Access displays the Users dialog box in which you can select an existing user or click the New button to add a new user.

 For more information about adding new users using the Users dialog box, see "Creating a Replacement Admin Account" earlier in this chapter.

Using the CreateUser Method

You may find it convenient or even necessary to add new users to the system programmatically; that is, using Access Basic and not the interactive Users dialog box. If so, you can use the **CreateUser** method to add new users.

The syntax for using the **CreateUser** method is:

```
Set variable = object.CreateUser(name, pid, password)
```

The **CreateUser** method accepts the following required and optional arguments:

Argument	Required	Comments
variable	Yes	Variable declared as type User.
object	Yes	Group or workspace object.
name	Yes	String that uniquely identifies the new user's name. The name must contain between 1 and 20 characters and can include alphabetic characters, accented characters, numbers, spaces, and symbols, with the following exceptions: The characters " / \ [ ] : ¦ < > + = ; , ? * Leading spaces Control characters (ANSI 0 to ANSI 31)

continues

Continued

Argument	Required	Comments
pid	No	String that is the personal identification number (PID) of the new user account. The identifier must contain between 4 and 20 alphanumeric characters.
		If you do not specify the *pid* argument, you must set the **PID** property for the group or workspace object before you append the new account to the Users group.
password	No	String that is the password for the new user account. If you specify the *password* argument, it must contain between 1 and 14 characters. It can include any characters except the ANSI character 0 (null).
		If you do not specify the *password* argument, the new user account will be blank (that is, it will have no password).

STOP **WARNING:** If you should have to re-create a user account that was created in a different workgroup (or perhaps was accidentally deleted), the user name you specify for the *name* argument must be an exact case-sensitive match of the original name. For this reason, you may want to maintain a separate list of user account names and store that list in a secure location apart from the computer.

The following example illustrates how you can add a new user account, set its **Password** and **PID** properties, and then append the account to the Users group.

```
Function csvAddUser (ByVal MyName As String, ByVal MyPassword As String,
➥By MyPID As String) As Integer

    Dim MyUser As User

    csvAddUser = False

    On Error Resume Next
    ' Create a new user account.
    Set MyUser = DBEngine.Workspaces(0).CreateUser(MyName)
    If Err Then
    Else    ' Set properties of MyUser.
        MyUser.PID = MyPID
        If Err Then
        Else
            MyUser.Password = MyPassword
            If Err Then
```

```
            Else ' Save user account by appending to
                ' Users collection.
               DBEngine.Workspaces(0).Users.Append
               ➡MyUser
               If Err Then
               Else ' Add user to predefined Users
                   ' group.
                  MyUser.Groups.Append
                  ➡MyUser.CreateGroup("Users")
                  If Err Then
                  Else
                      csvAddUser = True
                  End If
               End If
            End If
         End If
      End If
      On Error GoTo 0

   End Function
```

Setting Passwords

Microsoft Access has no default passwords. Or, more precisely, the default password is no password at all. An account with no password is secure only if the user's name is secret. Often, however, user names are easy to figure out: sometimes they are the users' first names, E-mail aliases, nicknames, children's names, and so on. To fully protect a user account, you should assign passwords.

To assign or change a password, choose the Change Password command from the Security menu. Access displays the Change Password dialog box and shows the name of the current user (see fig. 22.11).

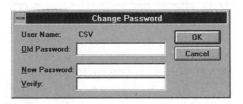

Figure 22.11.   Specifying a new password.

 Note: You cannot change the password for another user without first logging on using that user's name and password.

Enter your current password in the Old Password text box and then enter the new password in both the New Password text box and the Verify text box. When you click the OK button, Access saves the change to your password and closes the dialog box. The next time you log on, you must provide the new password.

Note: Although you cannot change another user's password, you can remove the password if you are the system administrator or any other member of the Admins group. Choose the Users command from the Security menu, select the desired user account, and then click the Clear Password button.

Using the NewPassword Method

As with creating new user accounts, you may find it convenient or even necessary to change existing passwords using Access Basic. If so, you can use the **NewPassword** method to change a password.

The syntax for using the **NewPassword** method is:

```
object.NewPassword(oldpassword, newpassword)
```

The **NewPassword** method accepts the following required arguments:

Argument	Required	Comments
object	Yes	User object that identifies the user account whose password you want to change.
oldpassword	Yes	String that is the current, existing password.
newpassword	Yes	String that is the new password for the new user account. The new password must contain between 1 and 14 characters and can include any characters except the ANSI character 0 (null).

The following example illustrates how you can change an existing password.

```
Function csvChangePassword (ByVal MyUserName As String,
➥OldPassword As String, ByVal NewPassword As String) As Integer

    Const csvMB_ICONEXCLAMATION = 48
    Dim Msg As String, Icon As Integer
    Dim Titlebar As String
    Dim CRLF As String

    CLF = Chr$(13) & Chr$(10)

    On Error Resume Next
    DBEngine.Workspaces(0).Users(MyName).NewPassword OldPassword, NewPassword
    If Err Then
        Msg = "Couldn't change password for user '"
        Msg = Mg & MyUserName & "'. "
        Msg = Msg & "Probable causes: " & CRLF & CRLF
        Msg = Msg & "o the specified user name does not exist"
        Msg = Msg & CRLF & CRLF
        Msg = Msg & "o the old password does not match"
```

```
            Msg = Msg & CRLF & CRLF
            Msg = Msg & "o the new password is not valid"
            Icon = csvMB_ICONEXCLAMATION
            Titlebar = "Change Password"
            MsgBox Msg, Icon, Titlebar
            csvChangePassword = False
        Else
            csvChangePassword = True
        End If
        On Error GoTo 0

    End Function
```

Group Accounts

You may find it convenient to organize your users into groups, especially if the number of users is large or if they have clearly defined data processing needs. For example, users who take orders or prepare sales quotes could easily fall into a group of sales personnel. Similarly, users who perform administrative tasks could form a second group, personnel employees a third, and so on.

One advantage to creating these groups of users is that as the needs of the groups change, you can easily modify the group's rights rather than modify individual user accounts. In addition, it is easy to move a user from one group to another. For example, if an employee moves from the Administrative department to the Sales department, you can remove the user from the Administration group and add the user to the Sales group account.

 Note: Users in a group account assume all rights and privileges of the group, plus their own individual rights. If the group rights are more restrictive, a user's rights take precedence. In contrast, if the user's rights are more restrictive, the user gains the more encompassing or more powerful rights of the group account.

To create a new group account, choose the Groups command from the Security menu (see fig. 22.12).

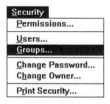

Figure 22.12. Choose the Groups command to add, delete, and maintain group accounts.

Access displays the Groups dialog box (see fig. 22.13).

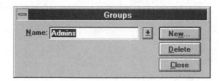

Figure 22.13. Administering a group account.

Click New to display the New User/Group dialog box (see fig. 22.14).

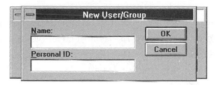

Figure 22.14. Adding a new group account.

Enter the name of the new group account in the Name text box and the group's personal identification number in the Personal ID text box. Finally, click the OK button to add the new group account. Access closes the New User/Group dialog box and returns you to the Groups dialog box. If you have other groups to add, click the New button. When you are finished adding groups, click the OK button to close the Users dialog box.

Using the CreateGroup Method

As with creating new user accounts and setting passwords, you may find it convenient, or even necessary, to add a new group account using Access Basic. If so, you can use the **CreateGroup** method to add a a new group.

The syntax for using the **CreateGroup** method is:

```
Set variable = object.CreateGroup(groupname, pid)
```

The **CreateGroup** method accepts the following required and optional arguments:

Argument	Required	Comments
variable	Yes	Variable declared as type Group.
object	Yes	User or workspace object.

610

Argument	Required	Comments
groupname	No	User object that identifies the group account you want to create.
		If you do not specify the *groupname* argument, you must set the group's **Name** property before you can append the new group account to the Groups collection.
pid	No	String that is the personal identification number (PID) of the new group account. The identifier must contain between 4 and 20 alphanumeric characters.
		If you do not specify the *pid* argument, you must set the **PID** property for the group or workspace object before you append the new group account to the Groups collection.

If the *name* argument identifies a group account that already exists, Access produces a trappable run-time error when you use the **Append** method to save the new account.

The following example illustrates how you can add a new group account.

```
Function csvCreateGroup (ByVal MyGroupName As String,
[IconCont]ByVal MyPID As String) As Integer

    Const csvMB_ICONEXCLAMATION = 48
    Dim MyGroup As Group
    Dim Msg As String, Icon As Integer
    Dim Titlebar As String
    Dim CRLF As String

    CLF = Chr$(13) & Chr$(10)
    Icon = csvMB_ICONEXCLAMATION
    Titlebar = "Create Group"
    Msg = "Couldn't create group '" & MyGroupName & "'. "
    Msg = Msg & "Probable causes: " & CRLF & CRLF

    csvCreateGroup = False

    On Error Resume Next
    Set MyGroup = DBEngine.Workspaces(0).CreateGroup (MyGroupName, MyPID)
    If Err Then
        Msg = Msg & "o the specified group name is not valid"
        Msg = Msg & CRLF & CRLF
        Msg = Msg & "o the PID is not valid"
        Icon = csvMB_ICONEXCLAMATION
        Titlebar = "Create Group"
        MsgBox Msg, Icon, Titlebar
```

continues

611

```
        Else ' Create the new group by appending to the
             ' Groups collection.
            DBEngine.Workspaces(0).Groups.Append MyGroup
            If Err Then
                Msg = Msg & "o the specified group name
                ⮕already exists"
                MsgBox Msg, Icon, Titlebar
            Else
                csvCreateGroup = True
            End If
        End If
        On Error GoTo 0

    End Function
```

Permissions

Beyond creating users and groups and assigning passwords, a key aspect to establishing adequate database security is granting permissions for the various database objects. Your primary concern should be making sure only authorized users can get to your data (that is, your tables), but each of the other database objects is just as important and deserves the same consideration.

> For example, you might create any number of forms that act as the interface to the underlying data in your system. Leaving the forms unprotected will otherwise allow users unrestricted access to the "protected" tables.

To restrict the objects to which users have access and the activities users can perform, you assign permissions. A *permission* is an access right you grant to a user or to a group:

- Read Definitions
- Modify Definitions
- Read Data
- Modify Data
- Execute
- Full Permissions

The level of permission you grant to users or groups depends greatly on the kind of data and objects you are trying to protect, as well as to whether your system is susceptible to so-called *hackers*.

Individual users assume the rights and permissions of the groups to which they belong, even if the user's account does not otherwise have the same rights. Access combines the individual rights and permissions with those of the group.

Table 22.1 lists the various permissions and their applications.

Table 22.1. Access Permissions

This permission...	Enables you to...	And applies to...
Read Definitions	View objects	All objects
Modify Definitions	View, replace, and delete objects	All objects
Read Data	View data	Tables, queries, and forms
Modify Data	View and modify data	Tables, queries, and forms
Execute	Use, run, or execute object	Forms, reports, and macros
Full Permissions	(all rights)	All objects

Note: Some permissions imply other permissions. For example, if you grant Modify Data permission to a user, that user also assumes the Read Data and Read Definitions permissions.

To assign permissions, choose the Permissions command from the Security menu (see fig. 22.15).

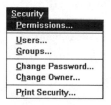

Figure 22.15. Choose the Permissions command to assign permissions to users and groups.

Access displays the Permissions dialog box in which you can select the user or group to which you want to assign permissions, plus the specific database objects to which those permissions are to apply (see fig. 22.16).

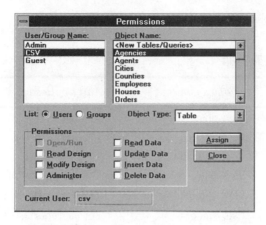

Figure 22.16.   Administering permissions.

Select the desired user or group, and then select the database object category (tables, queries, forms, reports, macros, or modules) for the relevant database object. As you assign permissions to individual users or groups of users, you assign these permissions for individual database objects.

Next, specify the permissions you want to grant by selecting or clearing the appropriate check boxes at the bottom of the dialog box.

> **Note:** Users inherit the rights of the groups to which they belong. In a large database with many database objects, you may find it faster and more convenient to assign permissions to groups rather than to individual users. For example, you might have 20 database objects, two groups, and a total of 10 users. To assign permissions for each user, you will have to go through the permission-assignment process 200 times (20 objects x 10 users). If you assign permissions to groups, however, you need go through the process only 40 times (20 objects x 2 groups).
>
> You must assign permissions for each database object separately and cannot assign permissions for groups of objects.

Encrypting and Decrypting a Database

No matter what security steps you take—assigning passwords and permissions—Microsoft Access databases are still MS-DOS files and thus are susceptible to prying eyes, file editing utilities, and ordinary word processors. For example, you can load an Access database into a file editing program that lets you view and modify the data (see fig. 22.17).

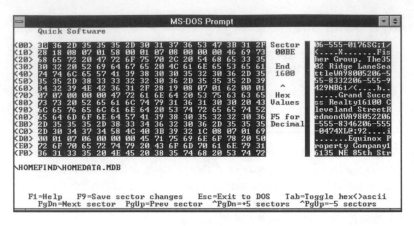

Figure 22.17. Unprotected databases may be edited with DOS-based utilities.

In the preceding example, the unprotected data is clearly visible. When you edit an Access database file, or practically any MS-DOS file, in this manner, you can view names, phone numbers, salary figures, and other sensitive information.

To protect your data from even file editing programs, you can encrypt your database files. When you encrypt a database, Access makes the file virtually indecipherable and unusable outside the Access environment.

> **WARNING:** Encryption alone does not protect a database within the Access environment. Unless you also assign permissions, a user can import your encrypted objects into another database. For more information about permissions, see "Permissions" earlier in this chapter.

> You might want to encrypt your databases before you transmit them by modem or before you store them (usually for archival or other long-term storage purposes) on disk or tape.

> **Tip:** Because encrypted databases are slower to work with than nonencrypted databases, you will want to make sure you need the added protection provided by encryption before you encrypt the working copies of your databases.

Encrypting a Database

You use the Encrypt Database command to encrypt a database file. In an application that involves multiple Access databases, you must encrypt each database separately.

To encrypt a database, you must be its owner; that is, you must be logged on as the user who created the database.

> **STOP** **WARNING:** To encrypt a database in a multiuser environment, you must make sure no user has the database open. If you try to encrypt a database while it is open, Access will produce unpredictable results and could corrupt the database beyond repair. This warning does not apply if you are running in a single-user environment, however, because you cannot choose the Repair Database command unless you have closed the current database.

When you close the current database, Access closes the Database window and automatically enables the Encrypt/Decrypt Database command (see fig. 22.18).

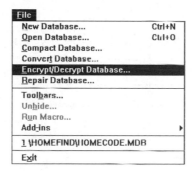

Figure 22.18. Choose the Encrypt/Decrypt Database command to protect your databases.

Choose the Encrypt/Decrypt Database command from the File menu; Access displays the Encrypt/Decrypt Database dialog box in which you can enter or select the name of the database you want to encrypt (see fig. 22.19).

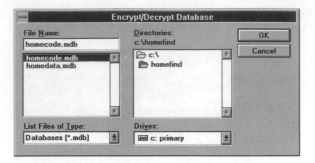

Figure 22.19.   Selecting the database to be encrypted.

In this example, the HOMECODE.MDB database will be encrypted. When you click OK, Access displays the Encrypt Database As dialog box in which you can enter or select the name of the encrypted version of the database you want to create (see fig. 22.20).

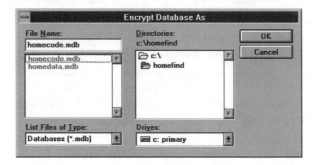

Figure 22.20.   Specifying the name of the encrypted version of the database.

At this point, you can choose to replace the existing copy of the database (the database you are encrypting) with the encrypted copy, or you can choose to create a copy of the existing database by entering a different name.

> **Tip:** If you are replacing the existing database, you can click the name of the database in the list of file names. Even though the names are dimmed and appear to be disabled, you can click one of them to select an existing database.

If you choose to replace an existing database, Access displays a message box and asks you to confirm that this is what you want to do (see fig. 22.21).

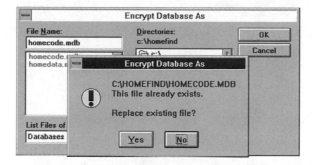

Figure 22.21. Access prompts you before overwriting an existing database.

 Note: When you encrypt a database, you must have at least as much free disk space as the space required by the new database, even if you are replacing an existing database. Microsoft Access creates the new database and then deletes the old version before renaming the encrypted version.

When you click OK, Access initiates the encryption process and displays a progress indicator in the status bar. Access automatically compacts the encrypted version of the database. When the encryption process is finished, Access displays a message only if a problem occurred.

 Tip: You may find it convenient or even necessary to encrypt a database programmatically; that is, using Access Basic and not the interactive Encrypt/Decrypt command. If so, you can use the **CompactDatabase** method to encrypt a database. For more information about the **CompactDatabase** method, see "Compacting a Database" in Chapter 23, "Data Compaction, Backups, and Data Recovery."

Decrypting a Database

The previous section, "Encrypting a Database," discussed how an encrypted Access database is virtually unusable outside the Microsoft Access environment. If there is a downside to working with encrypted databases, it is that they are slower than nonencrypted databases.

When you retrieve data from an encrypted table or load an encrypted form, Access must decrypt the data or object on-the-fly. Similarly, when you save data or an object, Access must encrypt it on its way back to the database. This process takes time, but how much time depends greatly on the amount and nature of the data or object.

To decrypt a database and all objects in it (you cannot encrypt or decrypt individual database objects), you choose the Encrypt/Decrypt command from the Security menu. Access displays the Encrypt/Decrypt Database dialog box in which you can enter or select the name of the database you want to decrypt.

When you select or enter the name of the database, Access automatically determines whether the database is already encrypted. If so, Access displays the Decrypt Database As dialog box in which you can enter or select the name of the encrypted version of the database you want to create (see fig. 22.22).

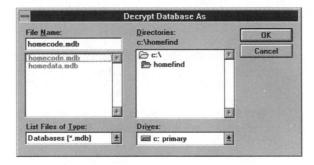

Figure 22.22.   Specifying the name of the decrypted version of the database.

At this point, you can choose to replace the existing copy of the database (the database you are decrypting) with the decrypted copy, or you can choose to create a copy of the existing database by entering a different name.

Tip: If you are replacing the existing database, you can click the name of the database in the list of file names. Even though the names are dimmed and appear to be disabled, you can click one of them to select an existing database.

If you choose to replace an existing database, Access displays a message box and asks you to confirm that this is what you want to do.

Summary

Determining the required security needs for your application is a key element in administrating and maintaining your Access databases. You can then choose to create a fully secure system in which each user (or group of users) has specific permissions, or you can create an open, unsecure, and unprotected system in which all users have unrestricted access.

Between these two extremes lies partial system security, which may be adequate for your system. Depending on the data you maintain and the nature of the various database objects, you may choose to protect certain objects and leave others unsecure.

In a secure system, each user has a name and password, as well as a personal identification number, with each combination uniquely identifying a user account. Users can belong to group accounts when the users share common data processing needs. Especially in systems involving many users, such group accounts can make security administration easier by letting you assign rights and permissions to a more limited number of group accounts rather than to many more user accounts.

Each user or group account may be granted a wide variety of permissions, including read-only and modify definitions. The permissions you grant depend on the specific needs of the individual users or groups.

You can add extra protection to your data by encrypting your databases. Although they are somewhat slower than nonencrypted databases, encrypted databases offer the ultimate protection against unauthorized use outside the Access environment.

23

Data Compaction, Backups, and Data Recovery

Your responsibilities as an application developer may not end when you finish creating tables, designing forms, and writing code. If you are also the system or database administrator, you must also consider several maintenance issues.

As the administrator, you must make sure your applications are backed up regularly and are in optimum working order.

This chapter covers the following:

- Compacting a Database
- Creating and Maintaining Backups
- Recovering Data

Compacting a Database

When you create a Microsoft Access database, Access allocates 64K of disk space for the new file, even before you add any tables, forms, or other database objects. As you add tables and data, the database begins to fill up in roughly direct proportion to the amount of data you enter (see fig. 23.1).

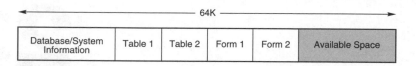

Figure 23.1. Access allocates a minimum of 64K to each database.

Queries, forms, reports, and modules also occupy space in the database. Eventually, you will exhaust the space in the initial 64K space. When this happens, Access allocates an additional 32K block of disk space. You can continue to add more objects or data until you reach the end of the 96K block (the initial 64K plus the extra 32K block). At that time, Access allocates yet another 32K. This process continues until you either stop adding new objects and data, or reach the maximum size for an Access database (one gigabyte, or about one billion bytes).

Note: Even though a single database is limited to one gigabyte, Microsoft Access allows you to attach tables from other databases. Because you can have up to 32,768 attached tables, the total size for an application is practically unlimited (32,768 × 1 gigabyte). The real limitation, then, is the storage capacity of your computer.

During the development phase of your application, and certainly while you are first learning how to use Microsoft Access, you will experiment with the various parts of the system, creating and then deleting objects. For example, you may create and then discard any number of tables and forms before you arrive at the final tables and forms your application will use.

As figure 23.2 illustrates, Table1 and Form1 have been deleted from the database. As you can see, Access does not automatically reclaim the space previously occupied by the deleted objects. This means that when you delete an object, the space occupied by the object is still marked "used" by Access, even though the space appears to be available.

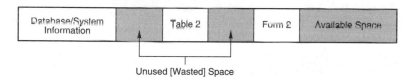

Figure 23.2. Deleted objects continue to occupy space in a database.

If you subsequently create a third table, Access checks to see if there is enough room at the end of the database (in the "available space"); if not, Access allocates another 32K block of disk space for the database.

Because Access adds new objects to the end of the database, any new records will be separate (physically) from the rest of their respective tables, resulting in fragmented data.

To reclaim all of this database space, and to defragment the tables, you should compact the database. When you compact a database, Access moves the remaining objects to the beginning of the database and consolidates each table's data into one contiguous chunk. Then, Access resets the length of the database to the space actually used (subject to the same 64K/32K rules). This process often results in a smaller database that is not only more efficient but also occupies less disk space and takes less time to back up.

How often you should compact your databases depends in large part on how much activity goes on in the databases. For example, if you have a great deal of data entry activity in a particular database, you may want to compact that database more frequently than a database that sees little activity. Also, the more objects you add and delete during application development, the more fragmented your databases will be and the more frequently you should compact the databases.

> As a rule, consider compacting your databases once a week as part of a weekly backup procedure. For more information about backing up your databases, see "Creating and Maintaining Backups" later in this chapter.

The Compact Database Command

You use the Compact Database command to compact and defragment a database file. In an application that involves multiple Access databases, you must compact each database separately.

> **WARNING:** To compact a database in a multiuser environment, you must make sure no user has the database open. If you try to compact a database while it is open, Access will produce unpredictable results and could corrupt the database beyond repair. This warning does not apply if you are running in a single-user environment, however, because you cannot choose the Compact Database command unless you have closed the current database.

When you close the current database, Access closes the Database window and enables the Compact Database command (see fig. 23.3).

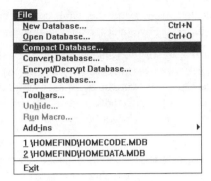

Figure 23.3. Choose the Compact Database command to compact a Microsoft Access database.

Choose the Compact Database command from the File menu; Access displays the Database to Compact From dialog box (see fig. 23.4) in which you can enter or select the name of the database you want to compact.

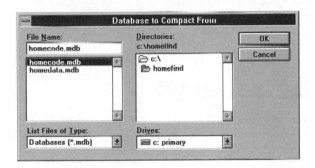

Figure 23.4. Select the database you want to compact.

As figure 23.4 illustrates, the HOMECODE.MDB database will be compacted. When you click the OK button, Access displays the Database to Compact Into dialog box (see fig. 23.5) in which you can enter or select the name of the database you want to create (the compacted version).

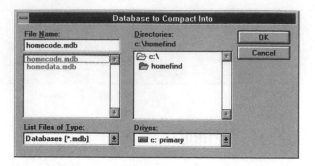

Figure 23.5.   Choosing the name of the compacted database.

You can either replace the existing copy of the database (the database you are compacting) with the compacted, defragmenting copy, or you can create a copy of the existing database by entering a different name.

Tip: If you are replacing the existing database, you can click the name of the database in the list of file names. Even though the names are dimmed and appear to be disabled, you can click one of them to select an existing database.

If you choose to replace an existing database, Access displays a message box and asks you to confirm that this is what you want to do (see fig. 23.6).

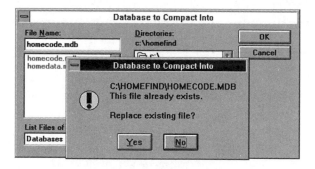

Figure 23.6.   Access prompts you before overwriting the existing database.

Note: When you use the Compact Database command, you must have at least as much free disk space as the space required by the new database, even if you are replacing an existing database. Microsoft Access creates the new database and then deletes the old version before renaming the compacted version.

The CompactDatabase Method

Much like the Compact Database command, you can use the **CompactDatabase** method to compact and defragment a specified database. Both the command and the method operate on closed databases; both techniques recover unused space and consolidate table data.

There are two significant differences between the Compact Database command and the **CompactDatabase** method:

- Unlike the command, which you must invoke manually, you use the method in a function within Access Basic.

- When you use the command, you can replace the old database with the new, compacted database. When you use the method, you can only create a new database. To replace the old version, you must create the new database, delete the old version, and then rename the new database to the old name.

The syntax for using the **CompactDatabase** method is:

```
DBEngine.CompactDatabase sourcedb, destinationdb, ocale, options
```

The **CompactDatabase** method accepts the following required and optional arguments:

Argument	Required	Comments
sourcedb	Yes	This is the name, including the complete path, of the database you want to compact and defragment. The database must already exist and must be closed.
destinationdb	Yes	This is the name, including the complete path, of the new, compacted database. The new database cannot be the same as the database identified by the sourcedb argument.
locale	No	This identifies the collating order for the new database. Valid values are listed in Table 23.1.
options	No	This is any combination of values that determine whether to encrypt or decrypt the source database, and the data format to use in the new database.
		Valid values for encrypting and decrypting are A_ENCRYPT and A_DECRYPT.

Argument	Required	Comments
		A_ENCRYPT. Create an encrypted destination database. The source database does not have to be encrypted.
		A_DECRYPT. Decrypt the source database and create a decrypted destination database.
		Valid values for determining the data format of the destination database are DB_VERSION10, DB_VERSION11, and DBVERSION20.
		DB_VERSION10. Create a database that uses the 1.0 database engine.
		DB_VERSION11. Create a database that uses the 1.1 database engine.
		DB_VERSION20. Create a database that uses the 2.0 database engine.

Specifying the Locale Argument

If you do not specify the locale argument, Access uses the same collating order as source database.

 For more information about setting the collating order, search Help for "sort order."

Table 23.1. Constants for Specifying the Collating Order

Constant	Description
DB_LANG_GENERAL	English, German, French, Portuguese, Italian, and Modern Spanish
DB_LANG_ARABIC	Arabic
DB_LANG_CZECH	Czech
DB_LANG_CYRILLIC	Russian
DB_LANG_DUTCH	Dutch
DB_LANG_GREEK	Greek
DB_LANG_HEBREW	Hebrew
DB_LANG_HUNGARIAN	Hungarian

continues

Table 23.1. Continued

Constant	Description
DB_LANG_ICELANDIC	Icelandic
DB_LANG_NORDIC	Nordic Languages (Access 1.x databases only)
DB_LANG_NORWDAN	Norwegian and Danish
DB_LANG_POLISH	Polish
DB_LANG_SWEDFIN	Swedish and Finnish
DB_LANG_SPANISH	Traditional Spanish
DB_LANG_TURKISH	Turkish

Specifying the Options Argument

You can specify an encryption value, a version value, or both. The following example encrypts an Access 1.1 database and creates a 2.0-compatible data format at the same time.

```
DBEngine.CompactDatabase "C:\DATA\OLDDB.MDB",
[IconCont]"C:\DATA\NEWDB.MDB", , DB_ENCRYPT + DB_VERSION20
```

If you do not specify the options argument, Access applies the same encryption or decryption as exists in the source database. In addition, the new database will have the same data format as the source database.

> **Note:** You can create a new database only with the same or a higher-numbered data format. For example, you can compact an Access 1.1 database and create a 2.0 version, but you cannot compact a 2.0 database and create a 1.1 compatible version. Changing the data format does not change the format of forms, reports, or other database objects. To change the format of these objects, choose the Convert Database command from the File menu.

Automating the Compaction Process

One advantage the **CompactDatabase** method has over the Compact Database command is that you can write a function that automates the entire process. Instead of responding to a series of dialog boxes, the user can trigger a function that performs the necessary actions.

The csvCompactDatabase( ) function illustrates how you can use the **CompactDatabase** method to compact a database.

```
Function csvCompactDatabase (ByVal SourceDB As String,
[IconCont]ByVal DestinationDB As String) As Integer

    Const csvMB_ICONEXCLAMATION = 48
    Const csvMB_ICONINFORMATION = 64
    Dim Msg As String, Icon As Integer
    Dim Titlebar As String

    csvCompactDatabase = True
    Msg = "Couldn't compact '" & SourceDB & "'"
    Icon = csvMB_ICONINFORMATION
    Titlebar = "Compact Database"

    On Error Resume Next
    DBEngine.CompactDatabase SourceDB, DestinationDB
    If Err Then
        Select Case Err
            Case 3196
                    Msg = Msg & ", probably because the "
                    Msg = Msg & "database is in use."
            Case 3204
                    Msg = Msg & " because the new "
                    Msg = Msg & "database '" & DestinationDB
                    Msg = Msg & "' already exists."
            Case Else
                    Msg = Msg & "; unexpected error "
                    Msg = Msg & Trim$(Str$(Err)) & "."
                    Icon = csvMB_ICONEXCLAMATION
        End Select
        MsgBox Msg, Icon, Titlebar
        csvCompactDatabase = False
    End If
    On Error GoTo 0

End Function
```

☞ **Note:** Because the database you want to compact and copy must be closed, you cannot use csvCompactDatabase() to compact the current database.

Creating and Maintaining Backups

You should make periodic backup copies of your databases as insurance against software or hardware failures—or user error. Having a current backup will help minimize the impact of such a failure or mistake.

For example, the Access program itself could "crash" and you could lose data, or your application could even become unusable. Even though Microsoft Access includes a Repair command, you cannot depend on Access to always recover your data fully.

629

A more common occurrence, however, is a power failure at the very moment you try to write data to the hard disk. If the power goes out, you could lose not only Access data but data in other applications as well.

To protect against these and other possibilities, make backup copies of all your databases on a regular basis.

Making Backups

Your choice of programs to make backup copies are many and varied. If a particular database is small enough to fit on a single disk, you can use the built-in MS-DOS command, COPY. If the database file is too large to fit on a single disk, you can use the MS-DOS backup utility (BACKUP.EXE) or a third-party utility. Most of these third-party tools allow you backup to either disk or tape.

> Although Microsoft Access does not include a backup command, you can use the Compact Database command or **CompactDatabase** method to make a copy of a database. For more information, see "Compacting a Database" earlier in this chapter.

> **WARNING:** Making a backup copy of a database on the same hard disk is not a good backup technique. Although this protects you against software failure (and user error), it does not protect you against hardware failure. If the hard disk should fail, you may lose not only the original data, but the backup as well.

You should store the backup copy separate from the computer that maintains the primary, working copy. This is known as off-site storage and insures you against fire or theft of the computer itself. If you store the backup copy near the computer, remember that a fire will likely destroy the disks or tapes along with the computer. Also consider that when a computer is stolen, disks and tapes are often taken as well.

Establishing a Backup Schedule

How often you should make backups depends on how often your databases change and how much risk you are willing to assume. In developing your own backup schedule, you might take into account how much data you are willing to reenter and how many new database objects (for example, new forms or code) you are willing to re-create.

One strategy for creating backups requires three sets of disks (or tapes). With this technique, you rotate the disks and use each one on subsequent days. Figure 23.7 illustrates a three-set backup schedule.

Mon	Tue	Wed	Thu	Fri
Set 1	Set 2	Set 3	Set 1	Set 2
Set 3	Set 1	Set 2	Set 3	Set 1
Set 2	Set 3	Set 1	Set 2	Set 3

Figure 23.7. A three-set backup schedule.

In this case, you would use Set 1 on the first day, Set 2 on the second day, and so on. On the fourth day you would reuse Set 1, thus rotating the sets of disks. Once you get started, you will have a set of disks that is two days old, a set that is one day old, plus the current backup set.

You should store the oldest set off-site, perhaps in a bank vault (some users take this set home with them). The next-oldest set should also be stored away from the computer, but not necessarily off-site. Finally, the current backup may be stored alongside the computer.

> **STOP**
>
> **WARNING:** Test your backup copies periodically to make sure the backup procedure is creating valid backups and that the backup medium (disk or tape) is functioning properly. Do not assume the disks or tapes you are creating are, in fact, valid backups.
>
> Perhaps the easiest way to validate a backup is to restore the backup copy to a different directory than the original and then try to open the database. Microsoft Access validates the integrity of the database automatically when you open the database. If there is no error, you may safely assume the backup is valid. If the backup is invalid, however, you should resolve the cause of the error before you rely on the backup procedure and medium.
>
> Do not restore the backup copy to the working directory. If the backup copy is corrupted and cannot be repaired, you will have lost your original, working database.

Preventing Power-Related Problems

One inexpensive solution to power-related problems is to install an *uninterruptible power supply* (UPS). These are essentially battery devices that fit between your power source—typically a wall socket—and the computer.

When the UPS senses a disruption in the incoming power, it automatically switches over to its internal battery and continues to run your system. The amount of time the UPS can operate your system depends on how much power the system draws from the battery, as well as the battery's capacity.

You can expect a UPS to cost less than $300 and provide up to 30 minutes of emergency power. If yours is a multiuser environment and you are on a limited budget, protect the file server first and then install additional UPS units on other machines.

Recovering Data

Sooner or later, disaster will strike and you or another user will inadvertently delete or change data, or one of the databases in your application will become corrupted. This can be the result of a software or hardware failure, but how the database became corrupted or otherwise unusable is not really important.

The most important part of a disaster recovery plan is to be able to recover from such a condition. This means making regular, periodic backups so that you can restore a copy of the data and, if necessary, the application itself. For more information about making backup copies, see "Creating and Maintaining Backups" earlier in this chapter.

Sometimes the database itself becomes corrupted. A corrupt database is one in which one or more database objects (for example, a table) becomes unreadable. When this happens, Microsoft Access will not be able to open the database. Rather than restoring a backup copy of the database, you can attempt to repair the database. If successful, this is better than restoring a backup copy because any newly entered information will remain intact.

The Repair Database Command

If a database becomes corrupted or otherwise unusable, you should attempt to repair it before you consider any other recovery technique. You use the Repair Database command to attempt the repair.

> **STOP** **WARNING:** To repair a database in a multiuser environment, you must make sure no user has the database open. If you try to repair a database while it is open, Access will produce unpredictable results and could corrupt the database beyond repair. This warning does not apply if you are running in a single-user environment, however, because you cannot choose the Repair Database command unless you have closed the current database.

When you close the current database, Access closes the Database window and enables the Repair Database command (see fig. 23.8).

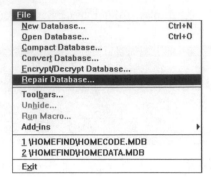

Figure 23.8. Choose the Repair Database command to repair corrupted Access databases.

Choose the Repair Database command from the File menu; Access displays the Repair Database dialog box in which you can enter or select the name of the database you want to repair (see fig. 23.9).

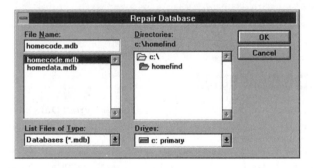

Figure 23.9. Selecting the database you want to repair.

In this case, the HOMECODE.MDB database will be repaired. When you click the OK button, Access attempts to repair the database. If successful, Access displays a message box informing you that the database has been repaired (see fig. 23.10).

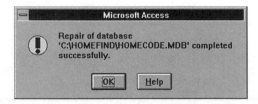

Figure 23.10. If successful, your database should be intact and ready to use.

If the repair is unsuccessful, Access displays a different message box (see fig. 23.11).

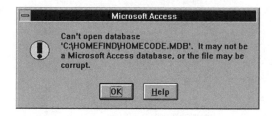

Figure 23.11. On occasion, Microsoft Access will not be able to fully recover a corrupted database.

Tip: Even if Access cannot repair the database, you may still be able to recover some or all the objects in the database. Create a new database and then attempt to import all the database objects (tables, queries, forms, reports, macros, and modules) in the corrupted database. If this is successful, delete the old, corrupted database and then rename the new database.

The RepairDatabase Method

Much like the Repair Database command, you can use the **RepairDatabase** method to repair a specified database. Both the command and the method operate on closed databases.

The significant difference between the Repair Database command and the **RepairDatabase** method is that while you must invoke the command manually, you use the method in a function within Access Basic.

The syntax for using the **RepairDatabase** method is:

```
DBEngine.RepairDatabase sourcedb
```

The **RepairDatabase** method accepts the following required argument:

Argument	Required	Comments
sourcedb	Yes	This is the name, including the complete path, of the database you want to repair. The database must already exist and must be closed.

Automating the Repair Process

One advantage the **RepairDatabase** method has over the Repair Database command is that you can write a function that automates the entire process. Instead of responding to a series of dialog boxes, the user can trigger a function that performs the necessary actions.

The csvRepairDatabase() function illustrates how you can use the **RepairDatabase** method to repair a database.

```
Function csvRepairDatabase (ByVal MyDB As String) As Integer

    Const csvMB_ICONEXCLAMATION = 48
    Const csvMB_ICONINFORMATION = 64
    Dim Msg As String, Icon As Integer
    Dim Titlebar As String

    csvRepairDatabase = True
    Msg = "Couldn't repair '" & MyDB & "'"
    Icon = csvMB_ICONINFORMATION
    Titlebar = "Repair Database"

    On Error Resume Next
    DBEngine.RepairDatabase MyDB
    If Err Then
        Select Case Err
            Case 3196
                Msg = Msg & ", probably because the "
                Msg = Msg & "database is in use."
            Case Else
                Msg = Msg & "; unexpected error "
                Msg = Msg & Trim$(Str$(Err)) & "."
                Icon = csvMB_ICONEXCLAMATION
        End Select
        MsgBox Msg, Icon, Titlebar
        csvRepairDatabase = False
    End If
    On Error GoTo 0

End Function
```

 Note: Because the database you want to repair must be closed, you cannot use csvRepairDatabase() to repair the current database.

Restoring a Database

If you know the specific database object you want to recover, you can import that object from a previously saved backup copy of the database. But, even if you need to recover an entire database, starting from a backup copy is better than having to re-create the database from scratch.

You also may need to restore a backup copy of a database when the Repair Database command is unsuccessful in recovering the database.

To restore selected database objects or an entire database, first copy or restore the backup copy. The technique you use to restore the backup depends on how you created the backup. For example, if you used the MS-DOS backup utility (BACKUP.EXE), you would use the restore utility (RESTORE.EXE). If you used the built-in COPY command, use the COPY command a second time to copy the database back to the hard disk. If you used a third-party backup utility, use its corresponding restoration utility or program.

> **Tip:** If you used the MS-DOS COPY command to create the backup, you may not need to copy the backup copy to the hard disk. If you intend to import selected objects from the backup, simply import them from the disk.

> **WARNING:** If you are trying to recover individual database objects, do not restore the backup copy to the working directory. If you do, you will overwrite and lose the valid objects in the current version of the database.

A backup represents a "snapshot" of the database at the time you made the backup. Any data or database objects you add or change after you make the backup will be lost if you restore the backup copy. Because of this, consider making frequent backups. As a rule, make backup copies of your databases each day.

Summary

Designing and creating the various databases in an application is just part of the application development process. Making regular, periodic backups is your best insurance against hardware and software failure, as well as user error.

You can use the built-in Compact Database command or **CompactDatabase** method to make a copy of a database, and then use a wide variety of MS-DOS and third-party tools to copy the database to a disk or tape.

If the Repair Database command is unsuccessful in repairing a database, you can restore individual database objects (or an entire database), underscoring the importance of making regular, periodic backups.

Part V

Appendixes

Windows API Declarations

This appendix lists declarations for all the Windows API functions used throughout this book and the sample applications on the accompanying disk, as well as other API functions you may find useful in your own applications.

Each of these declarations may be found on the disk in the file API.TXT. Use Windows Notepad or another text editing program to open the file, copy the desired declaration, and then paste it into the Declarations module of your application.

User-Defined Type Declarations

This section lists some of the user-defined type declarations you need when you use certain API functions.

```
Type csvMAPIFILE
    Reserved As Long
    Flags As Long
    Position As Long
    PathName As String
    FileName As String
    FileType As String
End Type

Type csvMAPIMESSAGE
    Reserved As Long
    Subject As String
    NoteText As String
    MessageType As String
    DateReceived As String
    ConversationID As String
    Flags As Long
    RecipCount As Long
    FileCount As Long
End Type
```

```
Type csvMAPIRECIP
    Reserved As Long
    RecipClass As Long
    Name As String
    Address As String
    EIDSize As Long
    EntryID As String
End Type

Type csvOPENFILENAME
    StructureSize As Long
    OwnerHandle As Integer
    Instance As Integer
    Filter As String
    CustomFilter As String
    MaxCustomFilters As Long
    FilterIndex As Long
    File As String
    MaxFile As Long
    FileTitle As String
    MaxFileTitle As Long
    InitialDirectory As String
    Title As String
    Flags As Long
    FileOffset As Integer
    FileExtension As Integer
    DefaultExtension As String
    CustomData As Long
    Hook As Integer
    TemplateName As String
End Type

Type csvRECT
    Left As Integer
    Top As Integer
    Right As Integer
    Bottom As Integer
End Type
```

API Function Declarations

Some of the API function declarations refer to user-defined types. For example, the csvGetClientRect function uses the csvRECT user-defined type. If you copy any of these function declarations, be sure you also copy the required type declarations.

Each of the API functions has been given an alias. For more information about aliases, see Chapter 19, "Creating and Using Libraries."

```
Declare Function csvAnyPopup Lib "User"
Alias "AnyPopup"
() As Integer
```

```
Declare Function csvArc Lib "GDI"
Alias "Arc"
(ByVal DeviceContext As Integer, ByVal X1 As Integer,
ByVal Y1 As Integer, ByVal X2 As Integer, ByVal Y2 As Integer,
ByVal X3 As Integer, ByVal Y3 As Integer, ByVal X4 As Integer,
ByVal Y4 As Integer) As Integer

Declare Function csvBitBlt Lib "GDI"
Alias "BitBlt"
(ByVal DestDeviceContext As Integer, ByVal X As Integer,
ByVal Y As Integer, ByVal BitmapWidth As Integer,
ByVal BitmapHeight As Integer, ByVal SourceDC As Integer,
ByVal XSrc As Integer, ByVal YSrc As Integer,
ByVal RasterOp As Long) As Integer

Declare Function csvBMAPIAddress Lib "MAPI.DLL"
Alias "BMAPIAddress"
(Info As Long, ByVal Session As Long, ByVal UIParam As Long,
Caption As String, ByVal EditFields As Long, Label As String,
Recipients As Long, Recip As csvMAPIRECIP, ByVal Flags As Long,
ByVal Reserved As Long) As Long

Declare Function csvBMAPIGetAddress Lib "MAPI.DLL"
Alias "BMAPIGetAddress"
(ByVal Info As Long, ByVal NumRecipients As Long,
Recipients As csvMAPIRECIP) As Long

Declare Function csvBMAPIGetReadMail Lib "MAPI.DLL"
Alias "BMAPIGetReadMail"
(ByVal Msg As Long, Message As csvMAPIMessage,
Recip As csvMAPIRECIP, File As csvMAPIFILE,
Originator As csvMAPIRECIP) As Long

Declare Function csvBMAPIReadMail Lib "MAPI.DLL"
Alias "BMAPIReadMail"
(Msg As Long, Recipients As Long, Files As Long,
ByVal Session As Long, ByVal UIParam As Long, MessageID As String,
ByVal Flag As Long, ByVal Reserved As Long) As Long

Declare Function csvCheckMenuItem Lib "User"
Alias "CheckMenuItem"
(ByVal MenuHandle As Integer, ByVal MenuItem As Integer,
ByVal CheckFlag As Integer) As Integer

Declare Function csvChord Lib "GDI"
Alias "Chord"
(ByVal DeviceContext As Integer, ByVal X1 As Integer,
ByVal Y1 As Integer, ByVal X2 As Integer, ByVal Y2 As Integer,
ByVal X3 As Integer, ByVal Y3 As Integer, ByVal X4 As Integer,
ByVal Y4 As Integer) As Integer

Declare Function csvCloseClipboard Lib "User"
Alias "CloseClipboard"
() As Integer

Declare Function csvCloseComm Lib "User"
Alias "CloseComm"
(ByVal CommPortID As Integer) As Integer
```

```
Declare Function csvCloseSound Lib "SOUND.DRV"
Alias "CloseSound"
() As Integer

Declare Function csvCommDlgExtendedError Lib "COMMDLG.DLL"
Alias "CommDlgExtendedError"
() As Long

Declare Function csvCreateCompatibleBitmap Lib "GDI"
Alias "CreateCompatibleBitmap"
(ByVal DeviceContext As Integer, ByVal BitmapWidth As Integer,
ByVal BitmapHeight As Integer) As Integer

Declare Function csvCreateCompatibleDC Lib "GDI"
Alias "CreateCompatibleDC"
(ByVal DeviceContext As Integer) As Integer

Declare Function csvCreateDC Lib "GDI"
Alias "CreateDC"
(ByVal DriverName As String, ByVal DeviceName As String,
ByVal OutputPort As String, ByVal InitData As String) As Integer

Declare Function csvCreatePen Lib "GDI"
Alias "CreatePen"
(ByVal PenStyle As Integer, ByVal PenWidth As Integer,
ByVal PenColor As Long) As Integer

Declare Function csvCreateSolidBrush Lib "GDI"
Alias "CreateSolidBrush"
(ByVal COLOR As Long) As Integer

Declare Function csvDeleteDC Lib "GDI"
Alias "DeleteDC"
(ByVal DeviceContext As Integer) As Integer

Declare Function csvDeleteMenu Lib "User"
Alias "DeleteMenu"
(ByVal MenuHandle As Integer, ByVal Position As Integer,
ByVal Flags As Integer) As Integer

Declare Function csvDiskSpaceFree Lib "SETUPKIT.DLL"
Alias "DiskSpaceFree"
() As Long

Declare Function csvDrawText Lib "GDI"
Alias "DrawText"
(ByVal DeviceContext As Integer, ByVal lpStr As String,
ByVal MyCount As Integer, Rectangle As csvRECT,
ByVal MyFormat As Integer)
As Integer

Declare Function csvEllipse Lib "GDI"
Alias "Ellipse"
(ByVal DeviceContext As Integer, ByVal X1 As Integer,
ByVal Y1 As Integer, ByVal X2 As Integer, ByVal Y2 As Integer)
As Integer
```

```
Declare Function csvEmptyClipboard Lib "User"
Alias "EmptyClipboard"
() As Integer

Declare Function csvEnableMenuItem Lib "User"
Alias "EnableMenuItem"
(ByVal MenuHandle As Integer, ByVal ItemID As Integer,
ByVal State As Integer) As Integer

Declare Function csvExitWindows Lib "User"
Alias "ExitWindows"
(ByVal ReservedCode As Long, ByVal ReturnCode As Integer) As Integer

Declare Function csvFindWindow Lib "User"
Alias "FindWindow"
(ByVal ClassName As Any, ByVal Caption As Any) As Integer

Declare Function csvFlashWindow Lib "User"
Alias "FlashWindow"
(ByVal WindowHandle As Integer, ByVal State As Integer) As Integer

Declare Function csvFloodFill Lib "GDI"
Alias "FloodFill"
(ByVal DeviceContext As Integer, ByVal X As Integer,
ByVal Y As Integer, ByVal crColor As Long) As Integer

Declare Function csvGetActiveWindow Lib "User"
Alias "GetActiveWindow"
() As Integer

Declare Function csvGetCaretBlinkTime Lib "User"
Alias "GetCaretBlinkTime"
() As Integer

Declare Function csvGetClassName Lib "User"
Alias "GetClassName"
(ByVal WindowHandle As Integer, ByVal Buffer As String,
ByVal Size As Integer) As Integer

Declare Function csvGetClientRect Lib "User"
Alias "GetClientRect"
(ByVal WindowHandle As Integer, Rectangle As csvRECT) As Integer

Declare Function csvGetCurrentPosition Lib "GDI"
Alias "GetCurrentPosition"
(ByVal DeviceContext As Integer) As Long

Declare Function csvGetDC Lib "User"
Alias "GetDC"
(ByVal WindowHandle As Integer) As Integer

Declare Function csvGetDesktopWindow Lib "User"
Alias "GetDesktopWindow"
() As Integer

Declare Function csvGetDeviceCaps Lib "GDI"
Alias "GetDeviceCaps"
(ByVal DeviceContext As Integer, ByVal IndexNum As Integer) As Integer
```

```
Declare Function csvGetDriveType Lib "Kernel"
Alias "GetDriveType"
(ByVal DriveNumber As Integer) As Integer

Declare Function csvGetFreeSpace Lib "Kernel"
Alias "GetFreeSpace"
(ByVal Flags As Integer) As Long

Declare Function csvGetHeapSpaces Lib "Kernel"
Alias "GetHeapSpaces"
(ByVal ModuleHandle As Integer) As Long

Declare Function csvGetKeyboardType Lib "Keyboard"
Alias "GetKeyboardType"
(ByVal TypeFlag As Integer) As Integer

Declare Function csvGetMenu Lib "User"
Alias "GetMenu"
(ByVal WindowHandle As Integer) As Integer

Declare Function csvGetMenuItemID Lib "User"
Alias "GetMenuItemID"
(ByVal MenuHandle As Integer, ByVal Position As Integer) As Integer

Declare Function csvGetModuleFileName Lib "Kernel"
Alias "GetModuleFileName"
(ByVal ModuleHandle As Integer, ByVal FileName As String,
ByVal Size As Integer) As Integer

Declare Function csvGetModuleHandle Lib "Kernel"
Alias "GetModuleHandle"
(ByVal AppName As String) As Integer

Declare Function csvGetModuleUsage Lib "Kernel"
Alias "GetModuleUsage"
(ByVal ModuleHandle As Integer) As Integer

Declare Function csvGetNumTasks Lib "Kernel"
Alias "GetNumTasks"
() As Integer

Declare Function csvGetOpenFileName Lib "COMMDlG.DLL"
Alias "GetOpenFileName"
(X As csvOPENFILENAME) As Integer

Declare Function csvGetParent Lib "User"
Alias "GetParent"
(ByVal WindowHandle As Integer) As Integer

Declare Function csvGetPrivateProfileInt Lib "Kernel"
Alias "GetPrivateProfileInt"
(ByVal Section As String, ByVal Entry As String,
ByVal Default As Integer, ByVal FileName As String) As Integer

Declare Function csvGetPrivateProfileString Lib "Kernel"
Alias "GetPrivateProfileString"
(ByVal Section As String, ByVal Entry As String,
ByVal Default As String, ByVal ReturnString As String,
ByVal Size As Integer, ByVal FileName As String) As Integer
```

644

```
Declare Function csvGetProfileInt Lib "Kernel"
Alias "GetProfileInt"
(ByVal Section As String, ByVal Entry As String,
ByVal Default As Integer) As Integer

Declare Function csvGetProfileString Lib "Kernel"
Alias "GetProfileString"
(ByVal Section As String, ByVal Entry As String,
ByVal Default As String, ByVal ReturnString As String,
ByVal Size As Integer) As Integer

Declare Function csvGetSaveFileName Lib "COMMDLG.DLL"
Alias "GetSaveFileName"
(X As csvOPENFILENAME) As Integer

Declare Function csvGetStockObject Lib "GDI"
Alias "GetStockObject"
(ByVal IndexNum As Integer) As Integer

Declare Function csvGetSubMenu Lib "User"
Alias "GetSubMenu"
(ByVal MenuHandle As Integer, ByVal Position As Integer) As Integer

Declare Function csvGetSysColor Lib "User"
Alias "GetSysColor"
(ByVal IndexNum As Integer) As Long

Declare Function csvGetSysModalWindow Lib "User"
Alias "GetSysModalWindow"
() As Integer

Declare Function csvGetSystemMenu Lib "User"
Alias "GetSystemMenu"
(ByVal WindowHandle As Integer, ByVal Revert As Integer) As Integer

Declare Function csvGetSystemMetrics Lib "User"
Alias "GetSystemMetrics"
(ByVal IndexNum As Integer) As Integer

Declare Function csvGetTempDrive Lib "Kernel"
Alias "GetTempDrive"
(ByVal DriveLetter As Integer) As Integer

Declare Function csvGetTempFileName Lib "Kernel"
Alias "GetTempFileName"
(ByVal DriveLetter As Integer, ByVal Prefix As String,
ByVal Unique As Integer, ByVal TempFileName As String) As Integer

Declare Function csvGetTextAlign Lib "GDI"
Alias "GetTextAlign"
(ByVal DeviceContext As Integer) As Integer

Declare Function csvGetTickCount Lib "User"
Alias "GetTickCount"
() As Long

Declare Function csvGetVersion Lib "Kernel"
Alias "GetVersion"
() As Integer
```

645

```
Declare Function csvGetWindow Lib "User"
Alias "GetWindow"
(ByVal WindowHandle As Integer, ByVal Relationship As Integer)
As Integer

Declare Function csvGetWindowDC Lib "User"
Alias "GetWindowDC"
(ByVal WindowHandle As Integer) As Integer

Declare Function csvGetWindowExt Lib "GDI"
Alias "GetWindowExt"
(ByVal DeviceContext As Integer) As Long

Declare Function csvGetWindowLong Lib "User"
Alias "GetWindowLong"
(ByVal WindowHandle As Integer, ByVal IndexNum As Integer) As Long

Declare Function csvGetWindowsDirectory Lib "Kernel"
Alias "GetWindowsDirectory"
(ByVal Buffer As String, ByVal Size As Integer) As Integer

Declare Function csvGetWindowText Lib "User"
Alias "GetWindowText"
(ByVal WindowHandle As Integer, ByVal Buffer As String,
ByVal Size As Integer) As Integer

Declare Function csvGetWinFlags Lib "Kernel"
Alias "GetWinFlags"
() As Long

Declare Function csvIsIconic Lib "User"
Alias "IsIconic"
(ByVal WindowHandle As Integer) As Integer

Declare Function csvIsWindow Lib "User"
Alias "IsWindow"
(ByVal WindowHandle As Integer) As Integer

Declare Function csvIsZoomed Lib "User"
Alias "IsZoomed"
(ByVal WindowHandle As Integer) As Integer

Declare Function csvLineTo Lib "GDI"
Alias "LineTo"
(ByVal DeviceContext As Integer, ByVal X As Integer,
ByVal Y As Integer) As Integer

Declare Function csvMAPIDeleteMail Lib "MAPI.DLL"
Alias "MAPIDeleteMail"
(ByVal Session As Long, ByVal UIParam As Long, ByVal MsgID As String,
ByVal Flags As Long, ByVal Reserved As Long) As Long

Declare Function csvMAPIDetails Lib "MAPI.DLL"
Alias "BMAPIDetails"
(ByVal Session As Long, ByVal UIParam As Long,
Recipient As csvMAPIRECIP, ByVal Flags As Long,
ByVal Reserved As Long) As Long
```

```
Declare Function csvMAPIFindNext Lib "MAPI.DLL"
Alias "BMAPIFindNext"
(ByVal Session As Long, ByVal UIParam As Long, MsgType As String,
SeedMsgID As String, ByVal Flag As Long, ByVal Reserved As Long,
MsgID As String) As Long

Declare Function csvMAPILogoff Lib "MAPI.DLL"
Alias "MAPILogoff"
(ByVal Session As Long, ByVal UIParam As Long, ByVal Flags As Long,
ByVal Reserved As Long) As Long

Declare Function csvMAPILogon Lib "MAPI.DLL"
Alias "MAPILogon"
(ByVal UIParam As Long, ByVal Test As String,
ByVal Password As String, ByVal Flags As Long, ByVal Reserved As Long,
Session As Long) As Long

Declare Function csvMAPIResolveName Lib "MAPI.DLL"
Alias "BMAPIResolveName"
(ByVal Session As Long, ByVal UIParam As Long,
ByVal UserName As String, ByVal Flags As Long, ByVal Reserved As Long,
Recipient As csvMAPIRECIP) As Long

Declare Function csvMAPISaveMail Lib "MAPI.DLL"
Alias "BMAPISaveMail"
(ByVal Session As Long, ByVal UIParam As Long,
Message As csvMAPIMessage, Recipient As csvMAPIRECIP,
File As csvMAPIFILE, ByVal Flags As Long, ByVal Reserved As Long,
MsgID As String) As Long

Declare Function csvMAPISendDocuments Lib "MAPI.DLL"
Alias "MAPISendDocuments"
(ByVal UIParam As Long, ByVal DelimStr As String,
ByVal FilePaths As String, ByVal FileNames As String,
ByVal Reserved As Long) As Long

Declare Function csvMAPISendMail Lib "MAPI.DLL"
Alias "BMAPISendMail"
(ByVal Session As Long, ByVal UIParam As Long,
Message As csvMAPIMessage, Recipient As csvMAPIRECIP,
File As csvMAPIFILE, ByVal Flags As Long, ByVal Reserved As Long)
As Long

Declare Function csvModifyMenu Lib "User"
Alias "ModifyMenu"
(ByVal MenuHandle As Integer, ByVal Position As Integer,
ByVal WinFlags As Integer, ByVal IDNewItem As Integer,
ByVal NewItem As Long) As Integer

Declare Function csvMoveTo Lib "GDI"
Alias "MoveTo"
(ByVal DeviceContext As Integer, ByVal X As Integer,
ByVal Y As Integer) As Long

Declare Function csvMoveWindow Lib "User"
Alias "MoveWindow"
(ByVal WindowHandle As Integer, ByVal WindowLeft As Integer,
ByVal WindowTop As Integer, ByVal WindowWidth As Integer,
ByVal WindowHeight As Integer, ByVal RepaintFlag As Integer)
As Integer
```

```
Declare Function csvOpenClipboard Lib "User"
Alias "OpenClipboard"
(ByVal WindowHandle As Integer) As Integer

Declare Function csvOpenComm Lib "User"
Alias "OpenComm"
(ByVal PortName As String, ByVal InQueueSize As Integer,
ByVal OutQueueSize As Integer) As Integer

Declare Function csvOpenSound Lib "SOUND.DRV"
Alias "OpenSound"
() As Integer

Declare Function csvPie Lib "GDI"
Alias "Pie"
(ByVal DeviceContext As Integer, ByVal X1 As Integer,
ByVal Y1 As Integer, ByVal X2 As Integer, ByVal Y2 As Integer,
ByVal X3 As Integer, ByVal Y3 As Integer, ByVal X4 As Integer,
ByVal Y4 As Integer) As Integer

Declare Function csvReleaseDC Lib "User"
Alias "ReleaseDC"
(ByVal WindowHandle As Integer, ByVal DeviceContext As Integer)
As Integer

Declare Function csvRestoreDC Lib "GDI"
Alias "RestoreDC"
(ByVal DeviceContext As Integer, ByVal SavedDC As Integer) As Integer

Declare Function csvRoundRect Lib "GDI"
Alias "RoundRect"
(ByVal DeviceContext As Integer, ByVal X1 As Integer,
ByVal Y1 As Integer, ByVal X2 As Integer, ByVal Y2 As Integer,
ByVal X3 As Integer, ByVal Y3 As Integer) As Integer

Declare Function csvSaveDC Lib "GDI"
Alias "SaveDC"
(ByVal DeviceContext As Integer) As Integer

Declare Function csvSelectObject Lib "GDI"
Alias "SelectObject"
(ByVal DeviceContext As Integer, ByVal ObjectHandle As Integer)
As Integer

Declare Function csvSetActiveWindow Lib "User"
Alias "SetActiveWindow"
(ByVal WindowHandle As Integer) As Integer

Declare Function csvSetBkMode Lib "GDI"
Alias "SetBkMode"
(ByVal DeviceContext As Integer, ByVal BackgroundMode As Integer)
As Integer

Declare Function csvSetClipboardData Lib "User"
Alias "SetClipboardData"
(ByVal ClipFormat As Integer, ByVal Mem As Integer) As Integer
```

648

```
Declare Function csvSetFocus Lib "User"
Alias "SetFocus"
(ByVal WindowHandle As Integer) As Integer

Declare Function csvSetPixel Lib "GDI"
Alias "SetPixel"
(ByVal DeviceContext As Integer, ByVal X As Integer,
ByVal Y As Integer, ByVal crColor As Long) As Long

Declare Function csvSetSysModalWindow Lib "User"
Alias "SetSysModalWindow"
(ByVal WindowHandle As Integer) As Integer

Declare Function csvSetTextAlign Lib "GDI"
Alias "SetTextAlign"
(ByVal DeviceContext As Integer, ByVal wFlags As Integer) As Integer

Declare Function csvSetTextColor Lib "GDI"
Alias "SetTextColor"
(ByVal DeviceContext As Integer, ByVal crColor As Long) As Long

Declare Function csvSetVoiceNote Lib "SOUND.DRV"
Alias "SetVoiceNote"
(ByVal Voice As Integer, ByVal Value As Integer,
ByVal Length As Integer, ByVal Dots As Integer) As Integer

Declare Function csvSetVoiceQueueSize Lib "SOUND.DRV"
Alias "SetVoiceQueueSize"
(ByVal Voice As Integer, ByVal Size As Integer) As Integer

Declare Function csvSetVoiceSound Lib "SOUND.DRV"
Alias "SetVoiceSound"
(ByVal Source As Integer, ByVal Frequency As Long,
ByVal Duration As Integer) As Integer

Declare Function csvSetWindowLong Lib "User"
Alias "SetWindowLong"
(ByVal WindowHandle As Integer, ByVal IndexNum As Integer,
ByVal Style As Long) As Long

Declare Function csvShowWindow Lib "User"
Alias "ShowWindow"
(ByVal WindowHandle As Integer, ByVal State As Integer) As Integer

Declare Function csvSndPlaySound Lib "MMSYSTEM.DLL"
Alias "SndPlaySound"
(ByVal FileName As String, ByVal Flag As Integer) As Integer

Declare Function csvStartSound Lib "SOUND.DRV"
Alias "StartSound"
() As Integer

Declare Function csvSysErrorBox Lib "User"
Alias "SysErrorBox"
(ByVal Message As String, ByVal Titlebar As String,
ByVal Button1 As Integer, ByVal Button2 As Integer,
ByVal Button3 As Integer) As Integer
```

```
Declare Function csvTextOut Lib "GDI"
Alias "TextOut"
(ByVal DeviceContext As Integer, ByVal X As Integer,
ByVal Y As Integer, ByVal MyString As String,
ByVal CharCount As Integer) As Integer

Declare Function csvTrackPopupMenu Lib "User"
Alias "TrackPopupMenu"
(ByVal MenuHandle As Integer, ByVal Flags As Integer,
ByVal X As Integer, ByVal Y As Integer, ByVal Reserved1 As Integer,
ByVal WindowHandle As Integer, Reserved2 As Any) As Integer

Declare Function csvWaitSoundState Lib "SOUND.DRV"
Alias "WaitSoundState"
(ByVal State As Integer) As Integer

Declare Function csvWinExec Lib "Kernel"
Alias "WinExec" (ByVal ApplicationName As String,
ByVal State As Integer) As Integer

Declare Function csvWinHelp Lib "User"
Alias "WinHelp"
(ByVal WindowHandle As Integer, ByVal HelpFile As String,
ByVal HelpCommand As Integer, Context As Any) As Integer

Declare Function csvWNetAddConnection Lib "User"
Alias "WNetAddConnection"
(ByVal NetPath As String, ByVal Password As String,
ByVal LocalName As String) As Integer

Declare Function csvWNetCancelConnection Lib "User"
Alias "WNetCancelConnection"
(ByVal LocalName As String, ForceClose As Integer) As Integer

Declare Function csvWriteComm Lib "User"
Alias "WriteComm"
(ByVal CommPortID As Integer, ByVal Buffer As String,
ByVal BufferSize As Integer) As Integer

Declare Function csvWritePrivateProfileString Lib "Kernel"
Alias "WritePrivateProfileString"
(ByVal Section As String, ByVal Entry As String,
ByVal Value As String, ByVal FileName As String) As Integer
```

API Subroutine Declarations
Even though, as a rule, you should avoid creating your own, user-defined Sub procedures, there are number of built-in Windows API subroutines you may find useful.

For more information about choosing between Function and Sub procedures, see chapter17, "Naming Conventions and Style Guidelines."

```
Declare Sub csvDeleteObject Lib "GDI"
Alias "DeleteObject"
(ByVal ObjectHandle As Integer)

Declare Sub csvGetWindowRect Lib "User"
Alias "GetWindowRect"
(ByVal WindowHandle As Integer, Rectangle As csvRECT)
```

```
Declare Sub csvRectangle Lib "GDI"
Alias "Rectangle"
(ByVal DeviceContext As Integer, ByVal X1 As Integer,
ByVal Y1 As Integer, ByVal X2 As Integer, ByVal Y2 As Integer)

Declare Sub csvScrollWindow Lib "User"
Alias "ScrollWindow"
(ByVal WindowHandle As Integer, ByVal XAmount As Integer,
ByVal YAmount As Integer, FormRectangle As csvRECT,
ClipRectangle As csvRECT)

Declare Sub csvSetBkColor Lib "GDI"
Alias "SetBkColor"
(ByVal DeviceContext As Integer, ByVal COLOR As Long)

Declare Sub csvSetCaretBlinkTime Lib "User"
Alias "SetCaretBlinkTime"
(ByVal Milliseconds As Integer)

Declare Sub csvSetSysColors Lib "User"
Alias "SetSysColors"
(ByVal NumberChanges As Integer, SysColor As Integer,
ColorValues As Long)

Declare Sub csvSetWindowPos Lib "User"
Alias "SetWindowPos"
(ByVal WindowHandle As Integer, ByVal InsertAfterWindow As Integer,
ByVal X As Integer, ByVal Y As Integer, ByVal NewWidth As Integer,
ByVal NewHeight As Integer, ByVal Flags As Integer)

Declare Sub csvSetWindowText Lib "User"
Alias "SetWindowText"
(ByVal WindowHandle As Integer, ByVal Title As String)

Declare Sub csvShowScrollBar Lib "User"
Alias "ShowScrollBar"
(ByVal WindowHandle As Integer, ByVal WhichBar As Integer,
ByVal ShowState As Integer)
```

B

Constants

This appendix lists all the intrinsic (built-in) constants available in Access Basic, the constants used throughout this book and the sample applications on the accompanying disk, as well as other constants you may find useful in your own applications.

Each of these constants may be found on the disk in the file CONSTANT.TXT. Except for the intrinsic constants, you can use Windows Notepad or another text editing program to open the file, copy the desired constant, and then paste it into the Declarations module of your application.

 Note: Because the intrinsic constants are always available, there should be no need for you to copy them. They are included in this appendix for reference.

Intrinsic Constants

Access automatically declares the intrinsic constants whenever you start the program. Access defines these constants in the UTILITY.MDA file.

```
Global Const A_ADD = 0
Global Const A_ALL = 14
Global Const A_ANYWHERE = 0
Global Const A_ATTACH = 2
Global Const A_COPY = 3
Global Const A_CURRENT = 0
Global Const A_CUT = 2
Global Const A_DELETE = 6
Global Const A_DELETE_V2 = 7
Global Const A_DESIGN = 1
Global Const A_DIALOG = 3
Global Const A_DOWN = 1
```

```
Global Const A_DRAFT = 3
Global Const A_EDIT = 1
Global Const A_EDITMENU = 1
Global Const A_ENTIRE = 1
Global Const A_EXIT = 2
Global Const A_EXPORT = 1
Global Const A_EXPORTDELIM = 2
Global Const A_EXPORTFIXED = 3
Global Const A_EXPORTMERGE = 4
Global Const A_FILE = 0
Global Const A_FIRST = 2
Global Const A_FORM = 2
Global Const A_FORMATRTF = "Rich Text Format (*.rtf)"
Global Const A_FORMATTXT = "MS-DOS Text (*.txt)"
Global Const A_FORMATXLS = "Microsoft Excel (*.xls)"
Global Const A_FORMBAR = 0
Global Const A_FORMDS = 3
Global Const A_GOTO = 4
Global Const A_HIDDEN = 1
Global Const A_HIGH = 0
Global Const A_ICON = 2
Global Const A_IMPORT = 0
Global Const A_IMPORTDELIM = 0
Global Const A_IMPORTFIXED = 1
Global Const A_LAST = 3
Global Const A_LOW = 2
Global Const A_MACRO = 4
Global Const A_MEDIUM = 1
Global Const A_MENU_VER1X = 11
Global Const A_MENU_VER20 = 20
Global Const A_MODULE = 5
Global Const A_NEW = 0
Global Const A_NEWREC = 5
Global Const A_NEXT = 1
Global Const A_NORMAL = 0
Global Const A_OBJECT = 14
Global Const A_OBJECTUPDATE = 3
Global Const A_OBJECTVERB = 0
Global Const A_PAGES = 2
Global Const A_PASTE = 4
Global Const A_PREVIEW = 2
Global Const A_PREVIOUS = 0
Global Const A_PRINTALL = 0
Global Const A_PROMPT = 0
Global Const A_QUERY = 1
Global Const A_READONLY = 2
Global Const A_RECORDSMENU = 3
Global Const A_REFRESH = 2
Global Const A_REPORT = 3
Global Const A_SAVE = 1
Global Const A_SAVEFORM = 2
Global Const A_SAVEFORMAS = 3
Global Const A_SAVERECORD = 4
Global Const A_SELECTALLRECORDS = 8
Global Const A_SELECTALLRECORDS_V2 = 9
Global Const A_SELECTION = 1
Global Const A_SELECTRECORD = 7
Global Const A_SELECTRECORD_V2 = 8
```

```
Global Const A_START = 2
Global Const A_TABLE = 0
Global Const A_TOOLBAR_NO = 2
Global Const A_TOOLBAR_WHERE_APPROP = 1
Global Const A_TOOLBAR_YES = 0
Global Const A_UNDO = 0
Global Const A_UNDOFIELD = 1
Global Const A_UP = 0
Global Const ALT_MASK = 4
Global Const CTRL_MASK = 2
Global Const DATA_ERRADDED = 2
Global Const DATA_ERRCONTINUE = 0
Global Const DATA_ERRDISPLAY = 1
Global Const DB_APPENDONLY = &H8
Global Const DB_ATTACHEDODBC = &H20000000
Global Const DB_ATTACHEDTABLE = &H40000000
Global Const DB_ATTACHEXCLUSIVE = &H10000
Global Const DB_ATTACHSAVEPWD = &H20000
Global Const DB_AUTOINCRFIELD = &H10
Global Const DB_BINARY = 9
Global Const DB_BOOLEAN = 1
Global Const DB_BYTE = 2
Global Const DB_CONSISTENT = &H20
Global Const DB_CURRENCY = 5
Global Const DB_DATE = 8
Global Const DB_DECRYPT = 4
Global Const DB_DENYREAD = &H2
Global Const DB_DENYWRITE = &H1
Global Const DB_DESCENDING = &H1
Global Const DB_DOUBLE = 7
Global Const DB_ENCRYPT = 2
Global Const DB_FAILONERROR = &H80
Global Const DB_FIXEDFIELD = &H1
Global Const DB_FORWARDONLY = &H100
Global Const DB_FREELOCKS = 1
Global Const DB_HIDDENOBJECT = &H1&
Global Const DB_IGNORENULL = 8
Global Const DB_INCONSISTENT = &H10
Global Const DB_INTEGER = 3
Global Const DB_LANG_ARABIC = ";LANGID=0x0401;CP=1256;COUNTRY=0"
Global Const DB_LANG_CYRILLIC = ";LANGID=0x0419;CP=1251;COUNTRY=0"
Global Const DB_LANG_CZECH = ";LANGID=0x0405;CP=1250;COUNTRY=0"
Global Const DB_LANG_DUTCH = ";LANGID=0x0413;CP=1252;COUNTRY=0"
Global Const DB_LANG_GENERAL = ";LANGID=0x0409;CP=1252;COUNTRY=0"
Global Const DB_LANG_GREEK = ";LANGID=0x0408;CP=1253;COUNTRY=0"
Global Const DB_LANG_HEBREW = ";LANGID=0x040D;CP=1255;COUNTRY=0"
Global Const DB_LANG_HUNGARIAN = ";LANGID=0x040E;CP=1250;COUNTRY=0"
Global Const DB_LANG_ICELANDIC = ";LANGID=0x040F;CP=1252;COUNTRY=0"
Global Const DB_LANG_NORDIC = ";LANGID=0x041D;CP=1252;COUNTRY=0"
Global Const DB_LANG_NORWDAN = ";LANGID=0x0414;CP=1252;COUNTRY=0"
Global Const DB_LANG_POLISH = ";LANGID=0x0415;CP=1250;COUNTRY=0"
Global Const DB_LANG_SPANISH = ";LANGID=0x040A;CP=1252;COUNTRY=0"
Global Const DB_LANG_SWEDFIN = ";LANGID=0x040B;CP=1252;COUNTRY=0"
Global Const DB_LANG_TURKISH = ";LANGID=0x041F;CP=1254;COUNTRY=0"
Global Const DB_LONG = 4
Global Const DB_LONGBINARY = 11
Global Const DB_MEMO = 12
Global Const DB_NONULLS = 3
```

```
Global Const DB_OLE = 11
Global Const DB_OPEN_DYNASET = 2
Global Const DB_OPEN_SNAPSHOT = 4
Global Const DB_OPEN_TABLE = 1
Global Const DB_OPTIONINIPATH = 1
Global Const DB_PRIMARY = 2
Global Const DB_PROHIBITNULL = 4
Global Const DB_QACTION = &HF0
Global Const DB_QAPPEND = &H40
Global Const DB_QCROSSTAB = &H10
Global Const DB_QDDL = &H60
Global Const DB_QDELETE = &H20
Global Const DB_QMAKETABLE = &H50
Global Const DB_QSELECT = &H0
Global Const DB_QSETOPERATION = &H80
Global Const DB_QSPTBULK = &H90
Global Const DB_QSQLPASSTHROUGH = &H70
Global Const DB_QUERYDEF = 5
Global Const DB_QUPDATE = &H30
Global Const DB_READONLY = &H4
Global Const DB_RELATIONDELETECASCADE = &H1000&
Global Const DB_RELATIONDONTENFORCE = &H2&
Global Const DB_RELATIONINHERITED = &H4&
Global Const DB_RELATIONLEFT = &H1000000
Global Const DB_RELATIONRIGHT = &H2000000
Global Const DB_RELATIONUNIQUE = &H1&
Global Const DB_RELATIONUPDATECASCADE = &H100&
Global Const DB_SEC_CREATE = &H1&
Global Const DB_SEC_DBCREATE = &H1&
Global Const DB_SEC_DBEXCLUSIVE = &H4&
Global Const DB_SEC_DBOPEN = &H2&
Global Const DB_SEC_DELETE = &H10000
Global Const DB_SEC_DELETEDATA = &H80&
Global Const DB_SEC_FRMRPT_EXECUTE = &H100&
Global Const DB_SEC_FRMRPT_READDEF = &H4&
Global Const DB_SEC_FRMRPT_WRITEDEF = &H8& + DB_SEC_FRMRPT_READDEF + DB_SEC_DELETE
Global Const DB_SEC_FULLACCESS = &HFFFFF
Global Const DB_SEC_INSERTDATA = &H20&
Global Const DB_SEC_MAC_EXECUTE = &H10&
Global Const DB_SEC_MAC_READDEF = &HA&
Global Const DB_SEC_MAC_WRITEDEF = &H6& + DB_SEC_DELETE
Global Const DB_SEC_MOD_READDEF = &H2&
Global Const DB_SEC_MOD_WRITEDEF = &H4& + DB_SEC_MOD_READDEF + DB_SEC_DELETE
Global Const DB_SEC_NOACCESS = &H0&
Global Const DB_SEC_READDEF = &H4&
Global Const DB_SEC_READSEC = &H20000
Global Const DB_SEC_REPLACEDATA = &H40&
Global Const DB_SEC_RETRIEVEDATA = &H10& Or DB_SEC_READDEF
Global Const DB_SEC_WRITEDEF = &H8& Or DB_SEC_READDEF Or DB_SEC_DELETE
Global Const DB_SEC_WRITEOWNER = &H80000
Global Const DB_SEC_WRITESEC = &H40000
Global Const DB_SINGLE = 6
Global Const DB_SORTARABIC = 267
Global Const DB_SORTCYRILLIC = 263
Global Const DB_SORTCZECH = 264
Global Const DB_SORTDUTCH = 259
Global Const DB_SORTGENERAL = 256
Global Const DB_SORTGREEK = 269
```

```
Global Const DB_SORTHEBREW = 268
Global Const DB_SORTHUNGARIAN = 265
Global Const DB_SORTICELANDIC = 262
Global Const DB_SORTNORWDAN = 261
Global Const DB_SORTPDXINTL = 4096
Global Const DB_SORTPDXNOR = 4098
Global Const DB_SORTPDXSWE = 4097
Global Const DB_SORTPOLISH = 266
Global Const DB_SORTSPANISH = 258
Global Const DB_SORTSWEDFIN = 260
Global Const DB_SORTTURKISH = 270
Global Const DB_SORTUNDEFINED = -1
Global Const DB_SQLPASSTHROUGH = &H40
Global Const DB_SYSTEMOBJECT = &H80000002
Global Const DB_TABLE = 1
Global Const DB_TEXT = 10
Global Const DB_UNIQUE = 1
Global Const DB_UPDATABLEFIELD = &H20
Global Const DB_VARIABLEFIELD = &H2
Global Const DB_VERSION10 = 1
Global Const DB_VERSION11 = 8
Global Const DB_VERSION20 = 16
Global Const DELETE_CANCEL = 1
Global Const DELETE_OK = 0
Global Const DELETE_USER_CANCEL = 2
Global Const LB_CLOSE = 8
Global Const LB_END = 9
Global Const LB_GETCOLUMNCOUNT = 4
Global Const LB_GETCOLUMNWIDTH = 5
Global Const LB_GETFORMAT = 7
Global Const LB_GETROWCOUNT = 3
Global Const LB_GETVALUE = 6
Global Const LB_INITIALIZE = 0
Global Const LB_OPEN = 1
Global Const LEFT_BUTTON = 1
Global Const MIDDLE_BUTTON = 4
Global Const OBJSTATE_DIRTY = 2
Global Const OBJSTATE_NEW = 4
Global Const OBJSTATE_OPEN = 1
Global Const OLE_CHANGED = 0
Global Const OLE_CLOSED = 2
Global Const OLE_RELEASE = 5
Global Const OLE_RENAMED = 3
Global Const OLE_SAVED = 1
Global Const RIGHT_BUTTON = 2
Global Const SHIFT_MASK = 1
Global Const SOA_Abort = 102
Global Const SOA_Close = 101
Global Const SOA_ctypFormula = -1
Global Const SOA_ctypLabel = 2
Global Const SOA_ctypNil = 0
Global Const SOA_ctypPB = 3
Global Const SOA_ctypText = 1
Global Const SOA_DocFtr = 2
Global Const SOA_DocHdr = 1
Global Const SOA_Dtl = 0
Global Const SOA_FirstBlFtr = 6
Global Const SOA_FirstBlHdr = 5
```

```
Global Const SOA_ftypFormula = -1
Global Const SOA_ftypNil = 0
Global Const SOA_ftypNum = 7
Global Const SOA_ftypText = 10
Global Const SOA_IDERR = -1
Global Const SOA_LastBlFtr = 24
Global Const SOA_LastBlHdr = 23
Global Const SOA_PgFtr = 4
Global Const SOA_PgHdr = 3
Global Const SOA_RptSectMax = 25
Global Const SOA_Start = 100
Global Const SOA_TA_CENTER = 6
Global Const SOA_TA_LEFT = 0
Global Const SOA_TA_RIGHT = 2
Global Const SYSCMD_ACCESSDIR = 9
Global Const SYSCMD_ACCESSVER = 7
Global Const SYSCMD_CLEARHELPTOPIC = 11
Global Const SYSCMD_CLEARSTATUS = 5
Global Const SYSCMD_GETOBJECTSTATE = 10
Global Const SYSCMD_INIFILE = 8
Global Const SYSCMD_INITMETER = 1
Global Const SYSCMD_REMOVEMETER = 3
Global Const SYSCMD_RUNTIME = 6
Global Const SYSCMD_SETSTATUS = 4
Global Const SYSCMD_UPDATEMETER = 2
Global Const V_CURRENCY = 6
Global Const V_DATE = 7
Global Const V_DOUBLE = 5
Global Const V_EMPTY = 0
Global Const V_INTEGER = 2
Global Const V_LONG = 3
Global Const V_NULL = 1
Global Const V_SINGLE = 4
Global Const V_STRING = 8
```

User-Defined Constants

This section lists some user-defined constants you may find useful in your own applications. Unlike the intrinsic constants, Access does not automatically declare user-defined constants. You must enter or copy them into your Global Constants module.

For more information about constants and the Global Constants module, see Chapter 17, "Naming Conventions and Style Guidelines."

```
Global Const csvABORT = 3
Global Const csvANSI_FIXED_FONT = 11
Global Const csvANSI_VAR_FONT = 12
Global Const csvAPPNAME = "MSACCESS.EXE"
Global Const csvASPECTX = 40
Global Const csvASPECTXY = 44
Global Const csvASPECTY = 42
Global Const csvBITSPIXEL = 12
Global Const csvBLACK = 0
Global Const csvBLACK_BRUSH = 4
```

```
Global Const csvBLACK_PEN = 7
Global Const csvBLUE = 16711680
Global Const csvCANCEL = 2
Global Const csvCASEINSENSITIVE = 1
Global Const csvCF_BITMAP = 2
Global Const csvCF_DIB = 8
Global Const csvCF_DIF = 5
Global Const csvCF_METAFILEPICT = 3
Global Const csvCF_OEMTEXT = 7
Global Const csvCF_PALETTE = 9
Global Const csvCF_SYLK = 4
Global Const csvCF_TEXT = 1
Global Const csvCF_TIFF = 6
Global Const csvCLIPCAPS = 36
Global Const csvCOLOR_ACTIVEBORDER = 10
Global Const csvCOLOR_ACTIVECAPTION = 2
Global Const csvCOLOR_APPWORKSPACE = 12
Global Const csvCOLOR_BACKGROUND = 1
Global Const csvCOLOR_BTNFACE = 15
Global Const csvCOLOR_BTNSHADOW = 16
Global Const csvCOLOR_BTNTEXT = 18
Global Const csvCOLOR_CAPTIONTEXT = 9
Global Const csvCOLOR_ENDCOLORS = 18
Global Const csvCOLOR_GRAYTEXT = 17
Global Const csvCOLOR_HIGHLIGHT = 13
Global Const csvCOLOR_HIGHLIGHTTEXT = 14
Global Const csvCOLOR_INACTIVEBORDER = 11
Global Const csvCOLOR_INACTIVECAPTION = 3
Global Const csvCOLOR_MENU = 4
Global Const csvCOLOR_MENUTEXT = 7
Global Const csvCOLOR_SCROLLBAR = 0
Global Const csvCOLOR_WINDOW = 5
Global Const csvCOLOR_WINDOWFRAME = 6
Global Const csvCOLOR_WINDOWTEXT = 8
Global Const csvCOLORRES = 108
Global Const csvCURVECAPS = 28
Global Const csvDEFAULT_PALETTE = 15
Global Const csvDEVICE_DEFAULT_FONT = 14
Global Const csvDKGRAY_BRUSH = 3
Global Const csvDRIVE_FIXED = 3
Global Const csvDRIVE_REMOTE = 4
Global Const csvDRIVE_REMOVABLE = 2
Global Const csvDRIVERVERSION = 0
Global Const csvDT_BOTTOM = &H8
Global Const csvDT_CALCRECT = &H400
Global Const csvDT_CENTER = &H1
Global Const csvDT_CHARSTREAM = 4
Global Const csvDT_DISPFILE = 6
Global Const csvDT_EXPANDTABS = &H40
Global Const csvDT_EXTERNALLEADING = &H200
Global Const csvDT_INTERNAL = &H1000
Global Const csvDT_LEFT = &H0
Global Const csvDT_METAFILE = 5
Global Const csvDT_NOCLIP = &H100
Global Const csvDT_NOPREFIX = &H800
Global Const csvDT_PLOTTER = 0
Global Const csvDT_RASCAMERA = 3
Global Const csvDT_RASDISPLAY = 1
```

```
Global Const csvDT_RASPRINTER = 2
Global Const csvDT_RIGHT = &H2
Global Const csvDT_SINGLELINE = &H20
Global Const csvDT_TABSTOP = &H80
Global Const csvDT_TOP = &H0
Global Const csvDT_VCENTER = &H4
Global Const csvDT_WORDBREAK = &H10
Global Const csvGRAY = 12632256
Global Const csvGRAY_BRUSH = 2
Global Const csvGREEN = 32768
Global Const csvGW_CHILD = 5
Global Const csvGWL_STYLE = -16
Global Const csvHOLLOW_BRUSH = 5
Global Const csvHORZRES = 8
Global Const csvHORZSIZE = 4
Global Const csvHOTPINK = 16711935
Global Const csvIGNORE = 5
Global Const csvLINECAPS = 30
Global Const csvLOGPIXELSX = 88
Global Const csvLOGPIXELSY = 90
Global Const csvLTGRAY_BRUSH = 1
Global Const csvMAPI_AB_NOMODIFY = &H400
Global Const csvMAPI_BCC = 3
Global Const csvMAPI_BODY_AS_FILE = &H200
Global Const csvMAPI_CC = 2
Global Const csvMAPI_DIALOG = &H8
Global Const csvMAPI_E_AMBIGUOUS_RECIPIENT = 21
Global Const csvMAPI_E_ATTACHMENT_NOT_FOUND = 11
Global Const csvMAPI_E_ATTACHMENT_OPEN_FAILURE = 12
Global Const csvMAPI_E_ATTACHMENT_WRITE_FAILURE = 13
Global Const csvMAPI_E_BAD_RECIPTYPE = 15
Global Const csvMAPI_E_BLK_TOO_SMALL = 6
Global Const csvMAPI_E_DISK_FULL = 4
Global Const csvMAPI_E_FAILURE = 2
Global Const csvMAPI_E_INSUFFICIENT_MEMORY = 5
Global Const csvMAPI_E_INVALID_MESSAGE = 17
Global Const csvMAPI_E_INVALID_SESSION = 19
Global Const csvMAPI_E_LOGIN_FAILURE = 3
Global Const csvMAPI_E_NO_MESSAGES = 16
Global Const csvMAPI_E_TEXT_TOO_LARGE = 18
Global Const csvMAPI_E_TOO_MANY_FILES = 9
Global Const csvMAPI_E_TOO_MANY_RECIPIENTS = 10
Global Const csvMAPI_E_TOO_MANY_SESSIONS = 8
Global Const csvMAPI_E_TYPE_NOT_SUPPORTED = 20
Global Const csvMAPI_E_UNKNOWN_RECIPIENT = 14
Global Const csvMAPI_ENVELOPE_ONLY = &H40
Global Const csvMAPI_FORCE_DOWNLOAD = &H1000
Global Const csvMAPI_GUARANTEE_FIFO = &H100
Global Const csvMAPI_LOGON_UI = &H1
Global Const csvMAPI_NEW_SESSION = &H2
Global Const csvMAPI_OLE = &H1
Global Const csvMAPI_OLE_STATIC = &H2
Global Const csvMAPI_ORIG = 0
Global Const csvMAPI_PEEK = &H80
Global Const csvMAPI_SUPPRESS_ATTACH = &H800
Global Const csvMAPI_TO = 1
Global Const csvMAPI_UNREAD_ONLY = &H20
Global Const csvMAPI_USER_ABORT = 1
```

```
Global Const csvMB_ABORTRETRYIGNORE = 2
Global Const csvMB_ICONEXCLAMATION = 48
Global Const csvMB_ICONINFORMATION = 64
Global Const csvMB_ICONQUESTIONMARK = 32
Global Const csvMB_ICONSTOPSIGN = 16
Global Const csvMB_NO = 7
Global Const csvMB_RETRYCANCEL = 5
Global Const csvMB_YES = 6
Global Const csvMB_YESNO = 4
Global Const csvMF_BITMAP = 4
Global Const csvMF_BYCOMMAND = 0
Global Const csvMF_BYPOSITION = &H400
Global Const csvMF_CHECKED = 8
Global Const csvMF_DISABLED = 2
Global Const csvMF_ENABLED = 0
Global Const csvMF_GRAYED = 1
Global Const csvMF_UNCHECKED = 0
Global Const csvNULL_BRUSH = 5
Global Const csvNULL_PEN = 8
Global Const csvNUMBRUSHES = 16
Global Const csvNUMCOLORS = 24
Global Const csvNUMFONTS = 22
Global Const csvNUMMARKERS = 20
Global Const csvNUMPENS = 18
Global Const csvNUMRESERVED = 106
Global Const csvOEM_FIXED_FONT = 10
Global Const csvOFN_ALLOWMULTISELECT = &H200
Global Const csvOFN_CREATEPROMPT = &H2000
Global Const csvOFN_ENABLEHOOK = &H20
Global Const csvOFN_ENABLETEMPLATE = &H40
Global Const csvOFN_ENABLETEMPLATEHANDLE = &H80
Global Const csvOFN_EXTENSIONDIFFERENT = &H400
Global Const csvOFN_FILEMUSTEXIST = &H1000
Global Const csvOFN_HIDEREADONLY = &H4
Global Const csvOFN_NOCHANGEDIR = &H8
Global Const csvOFN_NOREADONLYRETURN = &H8000
Global Const csvOFN_NOTESTFILECREATE = &H10000
Global Const csvOFN_NOVALIDATE = &H100
Global Const csvOFN_OVERWRITEPROMPT = &H2
Global Const csvOFN_PATHMUSTEXIST = &H800
Global Const csvOFN_READONLY = &H1
Global Const csvOFN_SHAREAWARE = &H4000
Global Const csvOFN_SHAREFALLTHROUGH = 2
Global Const csvOFN_SHARENOWARN = 1
Global Const csvOFN_SHAREWARN = 0
Global Const csvOFN_SHOWHELP = &H10
Global Const csvOPAQUE = 2
Global Const csvPDEVICESIZE = 26
Global Const csvPLANES = 14
Global Const csvPOLYGONALCAPS = 32
Global Const csvPS_DASH = 1
Global Const csvPS_DASHDOT = 3
Global Const csvPS_DASHDOTDOT = 4
Global Const csvPS_DOT = 2
Global Const csvPS_INSIDEFRAME = 6
Global Const csvPS_NULL = 5
Global Const csvPS_SOLID = 0
Global Const csvRASTERCAPS = 38
```

661

```
Global Const csvRC_BANDING = 2
Global Const csvRC_BITBLT = 1
Global Const csvRC_BITMAP64 = 8
Global Const csvRC_DI_BITMAP = &H80
Global Const csvRC_DIBTODEV = &H200
Global Const csvRC_FLOODFILL = &H1000
Global Const csvRC_GDI20_OUTPUT = &H10
Global Const csvRC_PALETTE = &H100
Global Const csvRC_SCALING = 4
Global Const csvRC_STRETCHBLT = &H800
Global Const csvRC_STRETCHDIB = &H2000
Global Const csvRED = 255
Global Const csvRETRY = 4
Global Const csvSB_BOTH = 3
Global Const csvSB_CTL - 2
Global Const csvSB_HORZ = 0
Global Const csvSB_VERT = 1
Global Const csvSIZEPALETTE = 104
Global Const csvSM_CMETRICS = 36
Global Const csvSM_CXBORDER = 5
Global Const csvSM_CXCURSOR = 13
Global Const csvSM_CXDLGFRAME = 7
Global Const csvSM_CXFRAME = 32
Global Const csvSM_CXFULLSCREEN = 16
Global Const csvSM_CXHSCROLL = 21
Global Const csvSM_CXHTHUMB = 10
Global Const csvSM_CXICON = 11
Global Const csvSM_CXMIN = 28
Global Const csvSM_CXMINTRACK = 34
Global Const csvSM_CXSCREEN = 0
Global Const csvSM_CXSIZE = 30
Global Const csvSM_CXVSCROLL = 2
Global Const csvSM_CYBORDER = 6
Global Const csvSM_CYCAPTION = 4
Global Const csvSM_CYCURSOR = 14
Global Const csvSM_CYDLGFRAME = 8
Global Const csvSM_CYFRAME = 33
Global Const csvSM_CYFULLSCREEN = 17
Global Const csvSM_CYHSCROLL = 3
Global Const csvSM_CYICON = 12
Global Const csvSM_CYKANJIWINDOW = 18
Global Const csvSM_CYMENU = 15
Global Const csvSM_CYMIN = 29
Global Const csvSM_CYMINTRACK = 35
Global Const csvSM_CYSCREEN = 1
Global Const csvSM_CYSIZE = 31
Global Const csvSM_CYVSCROLL = 20
Global Const csvSM_CYVTHUMB = 9
Global Const csvSM_DEBUG = 22
Global Const csvSM_MOUSEPRESENT = 19
Global Const csvSM_RESERVED1 = 24
Global Const csvSM_RESERVED2 = 25
Global Const csvSM_RESERVED3 = 26
Global Const csvSM_RESERVED4 = 27
Global Const csvSM_SWAPBUTTON = 23
Global Const csvSRCCOPY = &HCC0020
Global Const csvSUCCESS_SUCCESS = 0
Global Const csvSW_HIDE = 0
```

```
Global Const csvSW_MAXIMIZE = 3
Global Const csvSW_MINIMIZE = 6
Global Const csvSW_NORMAL = 1
Global Const csvSW_RESTORE = 9
Global Const csvSW_SHOW = 5
Global Const csvSW_SHOWMAXIMIZED = 3
Global Const csvSW_SHOWMINIMIZED = 2
Global Const csvSW_SHOWMINNOACTIVE = 7
Global Const csvSW_SHOWNA = 8
Global Const csvSW_SHOWNOACTIVE = 4
Global Const csvSW_SHOWNORMAL = 1
Global Const csvSYSTEM_FIXED_FONT = 16
Global Const csvSYSTEM_FONT = 13
Global Const csvTA_BASELINE = 24
Global Const csvTA_BOTTOM = 8
Global Const csvTA_CENTER = 6
Global Const csvTA_LEFT = 0
Global Const csvTA_NOUPDATECP = 0
Global Const csvTA_RIGHT = 2
Global Const csvTA_TOP = 0
Global Const csvTA_UPDATECP = 1
Global Const csvTEAL = 8421376
Global Const csvTECHNOLOGY = 2
Global Const csvTEXTCAPS = 34
Global Const csvTRANSPARENT = 1
Global Const csvVALIDACCOUNTHIGH = 9999
Global Const csvVALIDACCOUNTLOW = 1000
Global Const csvVERTRES = 10
Global Const csvVERTSIZE = 6
Global Const csvVK_RETURN = &HD
Global Const csvWF_8087 = &H400
Global Const csvWF_CPU286 = &H2
Global Const csvWF_CPU386 = &H4
Global Const csvWF_CPU486 = &H8
Global Const csvWF_ENHANCED = &H20
Global Const csvWF_STANDARD = &H10
Global Const csvWHITE = 16777215
Global Const csvWHITE_BRUSH = 0
Global Const csvWHITE_PEN = 6
Global Const csvWN_BAD_PASSWORD = 6
Global Const csvWN_NET_ERROR = 2
Global Const csvWN_SUCCESS = 0
Global Const csvWS_CAPTION = &HC00000
Global Const csvWS_MAXIMIZEBOX = &H10000
Global Const csvWS_MINIMIZEBOX = &H20000
Global Const csvWS_SYSMENU = &H80000
Global Const csvYELLOW = 65535
```

Access Error Messages

This appendix lists all of the numbered Access error messages. When you enable error handling, you can trap these run-time errors and, if necessary, display either the default text, or your own custom messages.

Some of the error messages listed here contain placeholders. For example, the message for error 2008 is `Document '|' is open; you must close it before deleting it`. At run time, Access inserts a document name in place of the vertical bar (|) placeholder and displays a dialog box similar to figure C.1.

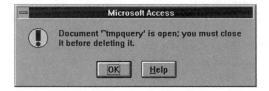

Figure C.1. At run time, Access inserts a literal in place of the placeholder.

Some messages contain multiple placeholders, and some messages are nothing but placeholders used by other error messages.

The number and range of error numbers varies with the version of Microsoft Access you are running. For example, this appendix lists the errors for Access 2.0. If you are running a previous or future version of Access, however, your list will be different. For details on how you can create a revised list for any version, see the csvUsedErrors( ) function in Chapter 21, "Useful Functions."

> **Tip:** Some error numbers are reserved for future use by Microsoft. These are identified by the message "Reserved Error" and extend in Access 2.0 from 3 to 7999. You should avoid creating your own custom errors that use numbers below 8000. Indeed, you should consider numbering custom errors much higher, perhaps starting with 30,000 (currently, error numbers can reach as high as 32,767). This allows for possible future expansion of the product's built-in error messages.

Table C.1. Access Error Codes and Messages

Error code	Message
3	Return without GoSub
5	Illegal function call
6	Overflow
7	Out of memory
9	Subscript out of range
10	Duplicate definition
11	Division by zero
13	Type mismatch
14	Out of string space
16	String formula too complex
17	Can't continue
19	No Resume
20	Resume without error
28	Out of stack space
35	Sub or Function not defined
48	Error in loading DLL
49	Bad DLL calling convention
51	Internal error
52	Bad file name or number
53	File not found
54	Bad file mode
55	File already open
57	Device I/O error
58	File already exists
59	Bad record length
61	Disk full
62	Input past end of file
63	Bad record number
64	Bad file name
67	Too many files
68	Device unavailable
70	Permission denied

Error code	Message
71	Disk not ready
74	Can't rename with different drive
75	Path/File access error
76	Path not found
90	Compile error
91	Object variable not Set
92	For loop not initialized
93	Invalid pattern string
94	Invalid use of Null
95	Cannot destroy active form instance
280	DDE channel not fully closed; awaiting response from the other application.
281	No more DDE channels are available.
282	Can't open DDE channel; Microsoft Access couldn't find the specified application and topic.
283	Can't open DDE channel; more than one application responded.
284	DDE channel is locked.
285	The other application won't perform the DDE method or operation you attempted.
286	Timeout while waiting for DDE response.
287	Operation terminated because Esc key was pressed before completion.
288	The other application is busy.
289	Data not provided when requested in DDE operation.
290	Data supplied in a DDE conversation is in the wrong format.
291	The other application quit.
292	DDE conversation closed or changed.
293	DDE method invoked with no channel open.
294	Invalid link format; can't create link to the other application.
295	Message queue filled; DDE message lost.
296	PasteLink already performed on this control.
297	Can't set LinkMode; invalid LinkTopic.
298	The DDE transaction failed. Check to ensure you have the correct version of DDEML.DLL.
2000	Not enough memory to start Cue Cards.

continues

Table C.1. Continued

Error code	Message
2001	Operation cancelled.
2002	Not Yet Implemented.
2003	¦ Not Yet Implemented.
2004	Out of memory.
2005	Not enough memory to start Microsoft Access.
2006	Not a valid document name: '¦'.
2007	You already have an open document named '¦'; you must close it before you can save or rename another document under the same name.
2008	Document '¦' is open; you must close it before deleting it.
2009	Document '¦' is open; you must close it before renaming it.
2010	Document '¦' is open; you must close it before cutting it.
2011	Not a valid password.
2012	This copy of Microsoft Access has expired. Please get a new copy from your Microsoft distributor.
2013	This copy of Microsoft Access hasn't been personalized properly. Please reinstall using the provided Setup program.
2014-2039	Reserved Error
2040	Incompatible version of 'WIN87EM.DLL'; Microsoft Access can't run.
2041	Reserved Error
2042	Can't start Microsoft Access. Please try again.
2043	Can't find file: '¦'. Please verify that the correct path and file name are given.
2044	Currently unable to quit Microsoft Access.
2045	An argument in the command line used to start Microsoft Access wasn't valid and was ignored.
2046	Command not available: ¦.
2047	Incompatible version of 'MSABC200.DLL'; Microsoft Access can't run.
2048	Not enough memory to open '¦'.
2049	Name '¦' contains invalid characters or is too long.
2050	OLE/DDE Timeout must be from 0 to 300 seconds.
2051	"The new name, '¦', is too long. Microsoft Access object names can't exceed 64 characters."
2052	Not enough system resources to update display.
2053	Wildcard characters aren't allowed in file name.

Error code	Message
2054	Can't change to directory; path too long.
2055	Expression not valid: '¦'.
2056	Can't supply context-sensitive Help.
2057	Not enough stack memory left.
2058	Incompatible version of '¦'; Microsoft Access can't run.
2059	The selected name is too long for Microsoft Access.
2060	Can't create a field list on an action query: '¦'.
2061	Negative numbers aren't allowed.
2062	msacc20.ini is missing or isn't the correct version. Import/Export isn't available.
2063	"Can't create, open, or write to index file '¦'."
2064	Not a valid menu bar value: '¦'.
2065	"Not a valid name for a menu, command, or subcommand."
2066	A display driver resolution of at least 400 x 340 pixels is required to run Microsoft Access.
2067	The AddMenu action can be used only in a macro specified as the MenuBar property setting.
2068	Help isn't available for this item.
2069	The key combination '¦1' in '¦2' isn't valid and will be ignored.
2070	The key combination '¦1' in '¦2' is also assigned to another macro. Only the first one will be used.
2071	Cue Cards couldn't be started because of an incomplete setup.
2072	Outdated '¦' file. Please reinstall Microsoft Access.
2073	Specification doesn't exist in this database or has no columns defined.
2074	There was an error while attempting to communicate with Cue Cards.
2075	The other application couldn't be found in any of the directories in your PATH.Please check your AUTOEXEC.BAT file.
2076	The other application couldn't be started because the .EXE file isn't valid.
2077	This database currently has no import/export specifications.
2078	Help isn't available due to lack of available memory or improper installation of Windows or Microsoft Access.
2079	Entry Required!
2080	Microsoft Access is corrupted. Reinstall from the original disks.

continues

669

Table C.1. Continued

Error code	Message
2081	Specification has too many columns for that table.
2082	Specification column '¦' doesn't match a table column.
2083	Database is read-only — cannot create specification tables.
2084	Start and width must be greater than 0.
2085	ODBC Refresh Interval must be in the range of 1-3600 seconds.
2086	Some Add-In menu entries couldn't be loaded because too many were specified.
2087	Add-In menu expression '¦' is too long and will be ignored.
2088	Add-In menu expression is empty and will be ignored.
2089	Can't display a submenu twice in the same menu hierarchy.
2090	An action within the current global menu's macro group can't change the global menu bar.
2091	Invalid name '¦'.
2092	Invalid variant type for this option setting.
2093	Invalid option setting. Valid settings are 0 to ¦.
2094	Unknown toolbar '¦'.
2095	Can't switch to ¦.
2096	Can't load MSTOOLBR.DLL.
2097	Can't create import/export specification for a Microsoft Access database stored in an out-of-date format.
2098	Reserved Error
2099	Reserved Error
2100	Can't place item at this location.
2101	The setting you entered isn't valid for this property.
2102	There is no form named '¦'.
2103	There is no report named '¦'.
2104	You already have something named '¦'.
2105	Can't go to specified record.
2106	¦ errors occurred while loading.
2107	The value you entered is prohibited by the validation rule set for this field.
2108	The GoToControl action can't be executed until the field being edited is saved.

Error code	Message
2109	There is no control named '¦'.
2110	Can't move to control ¦.
2111	"Couldn't save the changes you made. Click OK to try again, or click Cancel to undo your changes."
2112	Can't paste item.
2113	The value you entered isn't appropriate for this field.
2114	Invalid file format; can't load bitmap from file¦.
2115	Field or record can't be saved while it's being validated.
2116	Can't restore field's previous value; choose Undo Current Record or Undo Current Field from the Edit menu.
2117	Text too long.
2118	The Requery action can't be executed until the field is saved.
2119	The Requery action can't be used on control ¦.
2120	You must select an existing table or query to use a Form or Report Wizard.
2121	Can't open form ¦.
2122	Can't view a form as a continuous form if it contains a subform or an unbound OLE object.
2123	Not a valid control name.
2124	Not a valid form name.
2125	The setting for FontSize must be from 1 to 127.
2126	The setting for ColumnCount must be from 1 to 255.
2127	The setting for BoundColumn can't be greater than the number of columns set with the ColumnCount property.
2128	"The setting for RowSourceType must be Table/Query, Value List, Field List, or the name of a valid Access Basic fill function."
2129	"The setting for DefaultEditing must be Allow Edits, Read Only, Data Entry, or Can't Add Records."
2130	The setting for GridX or GridY must be from 1 to 64.
2131	"An expression can't be longer than 2,048 characters."
2132	The setting for DecimalPlaces must be from 0 to 15. You also can enter Auto (-1) for the default.
2133	"A form can't be a subform within itself, and a report can't be a subreport within itself."
2134	The setting for Width must be from 0 to 22 inches (55.87 cm).

continues

Table C.1. Continued

Error code	Message
2135	Can't set this property; it's read-only.
2136	This property can be set only in Design view; it's read-only otherwise.
2137	Can't use Find or Replace for one of the following reasons: There are no fields to search; fields have no data; data in fields can't be searched.
2138	Can't search field because there was an error getting its value.
2139	Can't replace current value of field.
2140	Couldn't save field. Please undo and then choose Find or Replace.
2141	No match to replace in current field.
2142	The FindRecord action requires a FindWhat argument.
2143	Search Criteria wasn't specified; use the FindRecord action or the Find command.
2144	The setting for ListRows must be from 1 to 255.
2145	"ColumnWidths must be one or more values from 0 to 22 inches (55.87 cm), separated by ';' or the list separator."
2146	Couldn't save field. Please undo and then choose the Allow Editing command.
2147	Controls can be created only in Design view.
2148	The section ID is invalid.
2149	The item type is invalid.
2150	This control can't contain other controls.
2151	This control can't contain that type of control.
2152	Group levels can be created only in reports.
2153	Maximum number of group levels exceeded.
2154	Can't execute this function with the Sorting and Grouping box open.
2155	Access Basic compile error.
2156	Access Basic compile error. View error in context?
2157	The sum of the top and bottom margins and page header and footer heights is greater than the page length.
2158	Print and graphics methods and their associated properties can be used only while printing or previewing a report.
2159	Not enough memory to initialize print or graphics methods.
2160	An error occurred while initializing print or graphics methods.
2161	FindWhat argument contains an invalid expression.

Error code	Message
2162	Can't search data using current FindRecord action arguments.
2163	Page number given as an argument for the GoToPage action is out of range.
2164	Can't disable the control that has the focus.
2165	Can't hide the control that has the focus.
2166	Can't lock the control that has the focus.
2167	Can't set this property; it's read-only.
2168	The setting for this property can be changed only with the Object/Change Link command on the Edit menu.
2169	"The record being edited can't be saved. If you close the form, the changes you've made to the record will be lost. Close anyway?"
2170	Can't retrieve data for the list box.
2171	Subforms can't be nested more than three deep.
2172	The crosstab query underlying a subform or subreport must have fixed column headings.
2173	Can't search in current field '¦'.
2174	Can't end browse mode from this form event.
2175	Out of memory during search.
2176	The setting for this property is too long.
2177	"Reports may only be embedded in other reports, not in forms."
2178	Can't add section. Doing so would exceed maximum combined section size limit. You must shrink one of the existing sections first.
2179	Couldn't open Palette.
2180	Couldn't open toolbox.
2181	Can't perform a Quick Sort on a calculated field.
2182	"Can't perform a Quick Sort on this field, or within a subform."
2183	"Invalid setting for TimerInterval property; correct values are from 0 to 65,535 milliseconds."
2184	Invalid setting for TabIndex property; correct values are from 0 to ¦.
2185	This property is available only when the control has the focus.
2186	This property isn't available in Design view.
2187	This property is available only in Design view.
2188	Section width is greater than page width and there are no items in the additional space. Some pages may be blank.
2189	Syntax error or missing Control Wizard.

continues

Table C.1. Continued

Error code	Message
2190	This property has been replaced by a new property; use the new property instead.
2191	Can't set property '¦' after printing has started.
2192	Must be a device-independent bitmap (DIB).
2193	The left and right margins are wider than the page.
2194	Can't set PictureData property in Datasheet view.
2195	Not a valid section name.
2196	"Can't obtain this property setting. The property may not be available in this view, or an error may have occurred."
2197	Can't set the subform control's SourceObject property to Null while displaying the main form in Form view.
2198	Reserved Error
2199	Reserved Error
2200	Not a valid number.
2201	An error occurred while attempting to retrieve printer information for the ¦1 on ¦2
2202	There is no default printer. Select or install one using the Windows Control Panel.
2203	COMMDLG.DLL failed: error code '0x¦'.
2204	The 'device=¦' entry in the WIN.INI file isn't valid.
2205	The default printer driver '¦.DRV' wasn't found. Reinstall using the Windows Control Panel.
2206	Not a valid page number.
2207	Can't print macros.
2208	The sum of the left and right margins is greater than the width of the selected paper size.
2209	The sum of the top and bottom margins is greater than the length of the selected paper size.
2210	Can't print or preview; page size larger than .75inches.
2211-2219	Reserved Error
2220	Couldn't open file '¦'.
2221	Text would be too long; change cancelled.
2222	This control is read-only and can't be modified.
2223	The file name '¦' is too long.

Error code	Message
2224	Name '¦' contains invalid characters or is too long.
2225	Couldn't open the Clipboard.
2226	Can't paste.
2227	Data format error; can't paste.
2228	Can't load or save object.
2229	Can't start object application.
2230	Reserved Error
2231	Errors encountered during OLE operation. The problem ID is '¦'.
2232-2233	Reserved Error
2234	There is no object in this control.
2235-2236	Reserved Error
2237	The text you enter must match an entry in the list.
2238	Reserved Error
2239	"'¦' is corrupted or isn't a Microsoft Access database file. To repair, clear the Read Only check box before opening the database, or use the Repair Database command."
2240	Unexpected data exchange error.
2241	The ¦ object is corrupted and might not be displayed properly.
2242	Reserved Error
2243	Can't paste OLE object.
2244	An unrecoverable error occurred while reading the file '¦'.
2245	Specified icon is corrupted.
2246	Can't run query; parameter values too large.
2247-2259	Reserved Error
2260	An error occurred while sending data to the object application.
2261	Reserved Error
2262	This value must be a number.
2263	The number is too large.
2264	Not a recognized unit of measurement.
2265	Must specify a unit of measurement.
2266	'¦' isn't a valid setting for RowSourceType property.
2267	Not enough disk space for printing.
2268	Not enough memory to load some library databases.

continues

Table C.1. Continued

Error code	Message
2269	Some library databases couldn't be loaded because too many were specified.
2270	Couldn't compile module in utility or library databases.
2271	[Libraries] section missing from msacc20.ini; Form and Report Wizards won't be available.
2272	"The setting for the Update Retry Interval must be from 0 to 1,000 milliseconds."
2273	The setting for Update Retries must be from 0 to 10.
2274	The database '¦' is already open as a library database.
2275	The string returned by the builder was too long. Truncating result.
2276	The current window is not the window that invoked the builder. Builder failed.
2277	Error in font initialization.
2278	"Can't save changes to this object because you don't have permission to write to the record. Copy the object to the Clipboard if you want to save it, then choose Undo Field."
2279	The value you entered isn't appropriate for the input mask '¦' specified for this field. Press Esc to cancel your changes.
2280	Too many output formats. Some will not be available.
2281	No output formats installed.
2282	Output format not available.
2283	Invalid format specification for '¦'.
2284	Can't write to file.
2285	Can't create file.
2286	Can't close file.
2287	Can't open a mail session.
2288	Can't load the '¦' format.
2289	Can't output module in the requested format.
2290	Too many message recipients. Message not sent.
2291	Too many message attachments. Message not sent.
2292	Message text is too long. Message not sent.
2293	Can't send message.
2294	Can't attach object. Message not sent.
2295	Unknown message recipient(s). Message not sent.

676

Error code	Message
2296	Logon failed. Message not sent.
2297	Can't open mail session.
2298	"Can't start Wizard, builder, or add-in."
2299	Can't open Zoom box. File UTILITY.MDA is missing or has been modified.
2300	Too many control styles.
2301	Not enough system resources.
2302	Can't open file for writing. Check that the file is not currently in use and that you have enough disk space on the destination drive.
2303	Can't output data.
2304	Can't write to file. Make sure that you have enough disk space on your destination drive.
2305	Too many columns in output.
2306	Too many rows in output.
2307	No data to output.
2308	¦1This file already exists.¦2Replace existing file?
2309	Invalid add-in entry for '¦'.
2310	Too many builder entries in the '¦' section.
2311	Not enough memory to run NotInList event procedure.
2312-2319	Reserved Error
2320	Can't display the field in which Total cell is 'Where'. Turn off the Show option for that field.
2321	Can't set criteria unless you've specified a field.
2322	Can't sort on fields added to the QBE grid with the asterisk.
2323	Can't have a Criteria clause on fields added to the QBE grid with the asterisk.
2324	Can't show Totals on fields added to the QBE grid with the asterisk.
2325	A field name in the LinkMasterFields property is too long.
2326	Value field can't specify Group By in the Totals cell. Specify a function.
2327	Column Heading field must specify Group By in the Totals cell.
2328	Can't run update queries for fields added to the QBE grid with the asterisk.
2329	"Must specify one or more Row Heading(s), one Column Heading, and one Value."

continues

677

Table C.1. Continued

Error code	Message
2330	Can't represent join in Design view: '¦'.
2331	Must specify at least one Row Heading as Group By.
2332	Can't match fields added to the QBE grid with the asterisk to a column or expression in an append query.
2333	Must specify destination table for query.
2334	'¦' is an action query and can't be printed.
2335	LinkChildFields and LinkMasterFields property settings must have the same number of fields.
2336	Reserved Error
2337	Value field can't specify a Criteria clause.
2338	Expression is too long for the QBE grid and has been truncated: '¦'.
2339	Can't create a temporary query.
2340	Expression is too long for the QBE grid.
2341	Reserved Error
2342	RunSQL action can only run action query SQL statements.
2343	The new alias is too long. Aliases can't exceed 64 characters.
2344	Invalid Top Value expression. Please enter an integer value or percentage.
2345	Invalid Top Value expression. Please enter a percentage between 1% and 100%.
2346	Invalid Top Value expression. Please enter a number greater than zero.
2347	Invalid database filename.
2348	Can't set alias to a null value.
2349	Invalid Top Value expression. Please enter a smaller number.
2350	"Can't save query of this type as SQL statement, or query contains a syntax error. Please save query as a named query."
2351	Can't represent implicit VALUES clause in QBE grid.
2352-2359	Reserved Error
2360	Missing field name.
2361	Table doesn't have any fields; can't save.
2362	Duplicate field name: '¦'.
2363	Only one Counter field is allowed per table.
2364	Can't open table in Datasheet view.

Error code	Message
2365	Reserved Error
2366	Errors were encountered during save. All changes were saved except the field ordering was not saved successfully.
2367-2369	Reserved Error
2370	Removing or changing the index for this field would require removal of the primary key.
2371	Can't create primary key. Changes weren't saved.
2372	Not a valid field name.
2373	The setting for Field Size must be from 0 to 255.
2374	Can't create an index or primary key on more than 10 fields.
2375	Can't paste beyond end of table.
2376	Can't create primary key; too many fields.
2377	Can't change data type to Counter in a table with data.
2378	This table is read-only. Use a different name in the Save As dialog box to save your changes.
2379	Can't create a primary key on a field of this data type.
2380	Can't create primary key; no fields selected.
2381	Can't create primary key; field doesn't have a name.
2382	Can't switch to Datasheet view and can't return to Design view.
2383	"Couldn't change data type, because there either isn't enough disk space or enough memory."
2384	Can't change one field from the Counter type and add another Counter field at the same time.
2385	Errors were encountered during save. ¦
2386	Errors were encountered during save. The new table was not created.
2387	Can't delete table '¦'. It is participating in one or more relation-ships.
2388	Can't change primary key. This table is the Primary Table in one or more relationships.
2389	Can't delete field '¦'. It is part of one or more relationships.
2390	Can't change the data type or field size of this field. It is part of one or more relationships.
2391	Couldn't append. Field '¦1' does not exist in destination table '¦2'.
2392	Can't set the Unique property of a primary key to No.
2393	Can't set the IgnoreNulls property of a primary key to Yes.

continues

Table C.1. Continued

Error code	Message
2394	Invalid index name.
2395	Can't have indexes without names.
2396	Can't create index or primary key because one or more field names are missing.
2397	Duplicate index name: '¦'.
2398	Changes were made to the primary key. This table is the primary table in one or more relationships. Changes to the primary key won't be saved.
2399	Reserved Error
2400	No room to insert.
2401-2419	Reserved Error
2420	Syntax error in number
2421	Syntax error in date
2422	Syntax error in string
2423	"Invalid use of '.', '!', or '()'."
2424	Unknown name
2425	Unknown function name
2426	Function isn't available in expressions
2427	Object has no value
2428	Invalid arguments used with domain function
2429	In operator requires parentheses: ()
2430	Between operator without And
2431	Syntax error
2432	Syntax error
2433	Syntax error
2434	Syntax error
2435	Extra right parenthesis:)
2436	"Missing),], or ¦"
2437	Invalid use of vertical bars
2438	Syntax error
2439	Wrong number of arguments used with function
2440	IIF function requires parentheses: ()
2441	Reserved Error
2442	Invalid use of parentheses

Error code	Message
2443	Invalid use of Is operator
2444	Reserved Error
2445	Expression too complex
2446	Out of memory during calculation
2447	"Invalid use of '.', '!', or '()'."
2448	Can't set value.
2449	Invalid method in expression.
2450	Invalid reference to form '¦'.
2451	Invalid reference to report '¦'.
2452	Invalid reference to Parent property.
2453	Invalid reference to control '¦'.
2454	Invalid reference to '!¦'.
2455	Invalid reference to property '¦'.
2456	Invalid form number reference.
2457	Invalid report number reference.
2458	Invalid control number reference.
2459	Can't refer to Parent property in Design view.
2460	Can't refer to RecordsetClone property in Design view.
2461	Invalid section reference.
2462	Invalid section number reference.
2463	Invalid group level reference.
2464	Invalid group level number reference.
2465	Invalid reference to field '¦'.
2466	Invalid reference to Dynaset property.
2467	Object referred to in expression no longer exists.
2468	"Invalid argument used with DatePart, DateAdd or DateDiff function."
2469	¦1 in validation rule: '¦2'.
2470	¦ in validation rule.
2471	¦ in query.
2472	¦ in linked master field.
2473	¦1 in '¦2' expression.
2474	No control is active.
2475	No form is active.

continues

Table C.1. Continued

Error code	Message
2476	No report is active.
2477	Invalid subclass '¦' referred to in TypeOf function.
2478	Can't use this method in the current view.
2479	Event procedure '¦' can't be a function.
2480	Numeric reference to Property object is out of range.
2481	Can't set value while in print preview.
2482	Invalid reference to '¦'.
2483	Can't move to previous control when no other control has had the focus.
2484	Reserved Error
2485	Macro '¦' not found.
2486	Can't run this action while in current code context.
2487	Invalid object type.
2488	Action isn't available because current window isn't a form or report window.
2489	Object '¦' isn't open.
2490	Options argument in Quit action isn't valid.
2491	Action isn't valid because the form or report isn't bound to a table or query.
2492	Can't find Macro Name '¦2' in Macro Group '¦1'.
2493	Action requires an Object Name argument.
2494	Action requires a Form Name argument.
2495	Action requires a Table Name argument.
2496	Action requires a Query Name argument.
2497	Action requires a Report Name argument.
2498	Argument type mismatch.
2499	Can't use GoToRecord action on an object in Design view.
2500	RepeatCount argument in RunMacro action can't be less than 0.
2501	Action ¦ was cancelled.
2502	Action requires a Macro Name argument.
2503	Can't use this command with DoCmd.
2504	Action requires at least ¦ argument(s).
2505	Not a valid value for argument '¦'.
2506	Not a valid value for the Transfer Type argument.

Error code	Message
2507	'¦' isn't an installed database type.
2508	Not a valid value for the Spreadsheet Type argument.
2509	Range argument can't be longer than 255 characters.
2510	Specification Name argument can't be longer than 64 characters.
2511	A Specification Name is required for fixed-width import/export.
2512	Can't parse expression: '¦'.
2513	Macro Name argument can't be longer than 64 characters.
2514	Action requires a Control Name argument.
2515	Can't open macro ¦. This macro was saved using a different version of Microsoft Access.
2516	Module '¦' not found.
2517	Procedure '¦' not found.
2518	Action requires a Macro Name argument.
2519	SelectObject action requires an open database.
2520	Action requires a Module or Procedure Name argument.
2521	Procedure '¦' not found in the specified module.
2522	Action requires a File Name argument.
2523	Invalid Show argument.
2524-2539	Reserved Error
2540	File '¦' is in use and can't be deleted.
2541	The contents of the Clipboard have been deleted and can't be pasted.
2542	Can't run macro from command line without specifying a database.
2543	Can't paste an object onto itself. You must specify a different name.
2544	There is no ¦.
2545	You must specify a destination database or a new name in order to copy.
2546	Can't carry out ¦ action because nothing is selected.
2547	File '¦' can't be deleted.
2548	Can't copy '¦' to itself.
2549	Couldn't delete '¦1' after compacting it. Compacted database is named '¦2'
2550	Couldn't delete '¦1' after encrypting it. Encrypted database is named '¦2'
2551	Couldn't delete '¦1' after decrypting it. Decrypted database is named '¦2'

continues

683

Table C.1. Continued

Error code	Message
2552	Couldn't encrypt. Only the owner of a database may encrypt it.
2553	Couldn't decrypt. Only the owner of a database may decrypt it.
2554	"Can't run application, missing command line arguments."
2555	Can't convert a database if the source and destination databases have the same name and path.
2556	Can't deliver an encrypted database.
2557	This database is already in the current database format.
2558	Can't convert this database. You must have 'Modify Design' permissions on all tables.
2559	¦ attached tables could not be refreshed during conversion.
2560-2579	Reserved Error
2580	This report is bound to a table or query that doesn't exist: '¦'.
2581	You must specify a field or expression to sort on.
2582	GroupInterval can be set to zero only when GroupOn is set to Each Value.
2583	The ApplyFilter action can be called only from a macro run from the OnOpen property.
2584	You can't use aggregate functions in a page header or footer.
2585	Can't run this action while processing a form or report event.
2586	The MoveLayout and NextRecord run-time properties can't both be set to FALSE; to ensure that the report advances both have been set back to TRUE.
2587	Syntax error or missing report output function.
2588-2599	Reserved Error
2600	Please verify the new password by entering it in the Verify box and pressing Enter.
2601	You don't have permission to read '¦'.
2602	You don't have permission to modify '¦'.
2603	You don't have permission to execute '¦'.
2604	You can't view this object's permissions.
2605	Can't remove user from group '¦'.
2606	Not a valid Microsoft Access object type.
2607	You don't have permission to cut '¦'.
2608	You don't have permission to copy '¦'.

Error code	Message
2609	You don't have permission to delete '¦'.
2610	You must enter a personal identifier (PID) consisting of at least 4 and no more than 20 characters and digits.
2611	Reserved Error
2612	Not a valid account name.
2613	You don't have permission to rename '¦'.
2614	You don't have permission to read this form.
2615	You don't have permission to change the owner of '¦'.
2616	You can't change permissions for '¦'.
2617	You don't have permission to import or export '¦'.
2618-2645	Reserved Error
2646	Can't create relationship to enforce referential integrity. Existing data in table '¦' violates referential integrity rules.
2647	Table '¦' has no primary key. You can't select it as the related table in a one-to-one relationship.
2648	The relationship has been created as a one-to-one relationship because there is a unique index on the field(s) specified for the related table.
2649	Can't create relationship to enforce referential integrity. The field(s) in the primary table must be the primary key or have a unique index.
2650	Can't create relationship to enforce referential integrity. Matching fields must have the same data type.
2651	"Can't create a relationship between fields with the Memo, OLE Object, or Yes/No data type."
2652-2679	Reserved Error
2680	Maximum number of OLE objects already loaded.
2681-2682	Reserved Error
2683	There is no object in this control.
2684	This field is empty. Use Insert Object to create a new object.
2685	The data in this field is not recognized as an OLE object.
2686	Unable to save the ¦ object.
2687	There was a problem reading the ¦ object.
2688-2689	Reserved Error
2690	A system resource necessary for drawing the ¦ object was not available.
2691	Can't connect with object application.

continues

Table C.1. Continued

Error code	Message
2692-2693	Reserved Error
2694	Clipboard operation failed. It may be in use by another application or you may be low on memory.
2695	Unable to generate a presentation from the converted ¦ object.
2696	Improperly formed OLE information.
2697	There was a problem loading the ¦ object.
2698	There was a problem saving the ¦ object.
2699	A problem occurred while using the object application.
2700	The other application or a .DLL could not be found. Verify that it is properly registered.
2701	The other application is already in use.
2702	The ¦ object does not appear to be correctly registered.
2703	A problem occurred while trying to exchange data with the ¦ object.
2704	This ¦ object has no presentation information.
2705-2706	Reserved Error
2707	A file needed to complete the operation could not be opened.
2708-2710	Reserved Error
2711	An object needed to complete the operation is missing.
2712	Reserved Error
2713	A problem occurred using the ¦ object's name information.
2714	The ¦ object has no supported verbs.
2715	The verb index is out of range for this ¦ object.
2716	Reserved Error
2717	This ¦ object is not initialized or is missing presentation information.
2718	Reserved Error
2719	A problem occurred while operating on the ¦ object.
2720-2722	Reserved Error
2723	This ¦ object does not support the attempted operation.
2724	One or more of the OLE support .DLL's installed on your machine is the incorrect version.
2725	There is a problem with the registration database.
2726	I/O Error reading REG.DAT.
2727	I/O Error writing REG.DAT.

Error code	Message
2728	Operation was cancelled.
2729	The active OLE object is busy. Complete the current operation or press Enter and then try again.
2730	Can't communicate with object application. Please try again later.
2731	An error occurred with the object application. It may not be registered correctly.
2732	A problem occurred accessing the ¦ object's storage.
2733	Object storage cannot be accessed.
2734	The ¦ object cannot be saved at this time.
2735	Write protect error while saving the ¦ object.
2736	That file already exists.
2737	The file could not be found.
2738	Insufficient memory to access ¦ object's storage.
2739	The storage is in use by another user.
2740	The ¦ object's storage is locked by another user.
2741	Out of space while saving the ¦ object.
2742	No more files could be created.
2743	The ¦ object is stored in a format not compatible with the version of OLE on your computer.
2744	The path you specified was not found.
2745	SHARE.EXE must be installed for OLE support to work correctly.
2746	Too many OLE objects on your form.
2747	An error occurred while drawing a ¦ object.
2748	That feature is not available for the ¦ object.
2749	Not enough memory to complete the operation on the ¦ object.
2750	The operation on the ¦ object could not be successfully completed.
2751	Operation aborted.
2752	An internal error occurred passing an argument.
2753	Error during OLE operation.
2754	Error communicating with object application.
2755	Error while driving object application.
2756	Error accessing OLE object's storage.
2757	Error using OLE object.
2758	There was a problem initializing MSAOLE20.DLL.

continues

Table C.1. Continued

Error code	Message
2759	More arguments were supplied than are accepted by the object member.
2760	An internal error occurred while referencing the object member.
2761	An error occurred while referencing the object member.
2762	¦ returned an error while referencing the object member.
2763	¦1 returned the following error: ¦2
2764	The object does not allow the member to be set.
2765	The object cannot convert one of the arguments passed to the member.
2766	The object does not contain a member named ¦.
2767	The object does not support the language in use.
2768	The array index is outside the bounds of the object member.
2769	The object member contains a data type not supported by Access Basic.
2770	The object referenced is not an active OLE object.
2771	Object frame doesn't contain an OLE object.
2772	Can't find OLE object class '¦'.
2773	The class ¦ does not support OLE Automation.
2774	The object does not support OLE Automation.
2775	More arguments are being passed to the object member than are supported by Access Basic.
2776	The object member is not an array.
2777	The required class name was not supplied or was invalid.
2778	Either a class or file name is missing.
2779	No data was returned by the object member.
2780	The class ¦ does not support loading objects from a file.
2781	No object of class ¦1 could be loaded from file ¦2. Check both the class and file name.
2782	The object member does not contain a value.
2783	Invalid setting of Action property.
2784	The SourceDoc property entry is too long.
2785	Invalid SourceDoc or SourceItem properties were set. The source application couldn't open the document.
2786	The OLE object created or in use is not a linked OLE object.
2787	Can't copy unbound OLE object in browse mode.
2788	The ¦ object is not stored as linked object.

Error code	Message
2789	The Action property can be set only in Form view.
2790	Can't create an embedded OLE object in a control that only allows Linked OLE object.
2791	Can't create a Linked OLE object in a control that only allows Embedded OLE object.
2792	Can't save a locked OLE object.
2793	Can't perform the operation specified in the Action property setting because the object frame is either locked or disabled.
2794	The OLE Custom Control does not match its description in the registration database.
2795	The ¦ object contains an event name longer than or results in a procedure name longer than 40 characters.
2796	The ¦ object event contains an unnamed parameter.
2797	OLE 1 objects cannot be presented as icons
2798	Can't perform the OLE_DELETE operation specified in the Action property on an object in a bound object frame.
2799	The object cannot be activated on receiving focus.
2800	The object is locked and any changes you made will be discarded when the form is closed.
2801	The OLE object is not loaded because the unbound OLE control has not been initialized.
2802	An OLE Custom Control may only be placed in an unbound object frame.
2803	You do not have sufficient access rights or license as required to open or create the OLE object.
2804-2999	Reserved Error
3000	Reserved error (¦); there is no message for this error.
3001	Invalid argument.
3002	Couldn't start session.
3003	Couldn't start transaction; too many transactions already nested.
3004	Couldn't find database '¦'.
3005	'¦' isn't a valid database name.
3006	Database '¦' is exclusively locked.
3007	Can't open library database '¦'.
3008	Table '¦' is exclusively locked.
3009	Couldn't lock table '¦'; currently in use.

continues

Table C.1. Continued

Error code	Message
3010	Table '¦' already exists.
3011	Couldn't find object '¦'.
3012	Object '¦' already exists.
3013	Couldn't rename installable ISAM file.
3014	Can't open any more tables.
3015	'¦' isn't an index in this table.
3016	Field won't fit in record.
3017	Field length is too long.
3018	Couldn't find field '¦'.
3019	Operation invalid without a current index.
3020	Update without AddNew or Edit.
3021	No current record.
3022	"Duplicate value in index, primary key, or relationship. Changes were unsuccessful."
3023	AddNew or Edit already used.
3024	Couldn't find file '¦'.
3025	Can't open any more files.
3026	Not enough space on disk.
3027	Can't update. Database or object is read-only.
3028	Can't start Microsoft Access. The system database (typically SYSTEM.MDA) is missing or opened exclusively by another user.
3029	Not a valid account name or password.
3030	'¦' isn't a valid account name.
3031	Not a valid password.
3032	Can't perform this operation.
3033	No permission for '¦'.
3034	Commit or Rollback without BeginTrans.
3035	Reserved Error
3036	Database has reached maximum size.
3037	Can't open any more tables or queries.
3038	Reserved Error
3039	Couldn't create index; too many indexes already defined.
3040	Disk I/O error during read.

Error code	Message
3041	Can't open a database created with a version of Microsoft Access that is newer than this one.
3042	Out of MS-DOS file handles.
3043	Disk or network error.
3044	'¦' isn't a valid path.
3045	Couldn't use '¦'; file already in use.
3046	Couldn't save; currently locked by another user.
3047	Record is too large.
3048	Can't open any more databases.
3049	"Can't open database '¦'. It may not be a Microsoft Access database, or the file may be corrupt."
3050	Couldn't lock file; SHARE.EXE hasn't been loaded.
3051	Couldn't open file '¦'.
3052	MS-DOS file sharing lock count exceeded. You need to increase the number of locks installed with SHARE.EXE.
3053	Too many client tasks.
3054	Too many Memo or OLE object fields.
3055	Not a valid file name.
3056	Couldn't repair this database.
3057	Operation not supported on attached tables.
3058	Index or primary key can't contain a null value.
3059	Operation cancelled by user.
3060	Wrong data type for parameter '¦'.
3061	"¦1 parameters were expected, but only ¦2 were supplied."
3062	Duplicate output alias '¦'.
3063	Duplicate output destination '¦'.
3064	Can't open action query '¦'.
3065	Can't execute a non-action query.
3066	Query must have at least one output field.
3067	Query input must contain at least one table or query.
3068	Not a valid alias name.
3069	Can't have action query '¦' as an input.
3070	Can't bind name '¦'.
3071	Can't evaluate expression.

continues

Table C.1. Continued

Error code	Message
3072	Reserved Error
3073	Operation must use an updatable query.
3074	Can't repeat table name '¦' in FROM clause.
3075	¦1 in query expression '¦2'.
3076	¦ in criteria expression.
3077	¦ in expression.
3078	Couldn't find input table or query '¦'.
3079	Ambiguous field reference '¦'.
3080	Joined table '¦' not listed in FROM clause.
3081	Can't join more than one table with the same name (¦).
3082	JOIN operation '¦' refers to a non-joined table.
3083	Can't use internal report query.
3084	Can't insert into action query.
3085	Undefined function '¦' in expression.
3086	Couldn't delete from specified tables.
3087	Too many expressions in GROUP BY clause.
3088	Too many expressions in ORDER BY clause.
3089	Too many expressions in DISTINCT output.
3090	Resultant table may not have more than one Counter field.
3091	HAVING clause (¦) without grouping or aggregation.
3092	Can't use HAVING clause in TRANSFORM statement.
0000	ORDER BY clause (¦) conflicts with DISTINCT.
3094	ORDER BY clause (¦) conflicts with GROUP BY clause.
3095	Can't have aggregate function in expression (¦).
3096	Can't have aggregate function in WHERE clause (¦).
3097	Can't have aggregate function in ORDER BY clause (¦).
3098	Can't have aggregate function in GROUP BY clause (¦).
3099	Can't have aggregate function in JOIN operation (¦).
3100	Can't set field '¦' in join key to Null.
3101	There is no record in table '¦2' with key matching field(s) '¦1'.
3102	Circular reference caused by '¦'.
3103	Circular reference caused by alias '¦' in query definition's SELECT list.

Error code	Message
3104	Can't specify Fixed Column Heading '¦' in a crosstab query more than once.
3105	Missing destination field name in SELECT INTO statement (¦).
3106	Missing destination field name in UPDATE statement (¦).
3107	Record(s) can't be added; no Insert Data permission on '¦'.
3108	Record(s) can't be edited; no Update Data permission on '¦'.
3109	Record(s) can't be deleted; no Delete Data permission on '¦'.
3110	Couldn't read definitions; no Read Design permission for table or query '¦'.
3111	Couldn't create; no Create permission for table or query '¦'.
3112	Record(s) can't be read; no Read Data permission on '¦'.
3113	Can't update '¦'; field not updatable.
3114	Can't include Memo or OLE object when you select unique values (¦).
3115	Can't have Memo or OLE object in aggregate argument (¦).
3116	Can't have Memo or OLE object in criteria (¦) for aggregate function.
3117	Can't sort on Memo or OLE object (¦).
3118	Can't join on Memo or OLE object (¦).
3119	Can't group on Memo or OLE object (¦).
3120	Can't group on fields selected with '*' (¦).
3121	Can't group on fields selected with '*'.
3122	'¦' not part of aggregate function or grouping.
3123	Can't use '*' in crosstab query.
3124	Can't input from internal report query (¦).
3125	'¦' isn't a valid name.
3126	Invalid bracketing of name '¦'.
3127	INSERT INTO statement contains unknown field name '¦'.
3128	Must specify tables to delete from.
3129	"Invalid SQL statement; expected 'DELETE', 'INSERT', 'PROCEDURE', 'SELECT', or 'UPDATE'."
3130	Syntax error in DELETE statement.
3131	Syntax error in FROM clause.
3132	Syntax error in GROUP BY clause.
3133	Syntax error in HAVING clause.

continues

Table C.1. Continued

Error code	Message
3134	Syntax error in INSERT statement.
3135	Syntax error in JOIN operation.
3136	Syntax error in LEVEL clause.
3137	Missing semicolon (;) at end of SQL statement.
3138	Syntax error in ORDER BY clause.
3139	Syntax error in PARAMETER clause.
3140	Syntax error in PROCEDURE clause.
3141	Syntax error in SELECT statement.
3142	Characters found after end of SQL statement.
3143	Syntax error in TRANSFORM statement.
3144	Syntax error in UPDATE statement.
3145	Syntax error in WHERE clause.
3146	ODBC—call failed.
3147-3150	Reserved Error
3151	ODBC—connection to '¦' failed.
3152-3153	Reserved Error
3154	ODBC—couldn't find DLL '¦'.
3155	ODBC—insert failed on attached table '¦'.
3156	ODBC—delete failed on attached table '¦'.
3157	ODBC—update failed on attached table '¦'.
3158	Couldn't save record; currently locked by another user.
3159	Not a valid bookmark.
3160	Table isn't open.
3161	Couldn't decrypt file.
3162	Null is invalid.
3163	Couldn't insert or paste; data too long for field.
3164	Field can't be updated.
3165	Couldn't open .INF file.
3166	Missing memo file.
3167	Record is deleted.
3168	Invalid .INF file.
3169	Illegal type in expression.

694

Error code	Message
3170	Couldn't find installable ISAM.
3171	Couldn't find net path or user name.
3172	Couldn't open PARADOX.NET.
3173	Couldn't open table 'MSysAccounts' in the system database file (SYSTEM.MDA).
3174	Couldn't open table 'MSysGroups' in the system database file (SYSTEM.MDA).
3175	Date is out of range or is in an invalid format.
3176	Couldn't open file '¦'.
3177	Not a valid table name.
3178	Reserved Error
3179	Encountered unexpected end of file.
3180	Couldn't write to file '¦'.
3181	Invalid range.
3182	Invalid file format.
3183	Not enough space on temporary disk.
3184	Couldn't execute query; couldn't find linked table.
3185	SELECT INTO remote database tried to produce too many fields.
3186	Couldn't save; currently locked by user '¦2' on machine '¦1'.
3187	Couldn't read; currently locked by user '¦2' on machine '¦1'.
3188	Couldn't update; currently locked by another session on this machine.
3189	Table '¦1' is exclusively locked by user '¦3' on machine '¦2'.
3190	Too many fields defined.
3191	Can't define field more than once.
3192	Couldn't find output table '¦'.
3193	(unknown)
3194	(unknown)
3195	(expression)
3196	Couldn't use '¦'; database already in use.
3197	Data has changed; operation stopped.
3198	Couldn't start session. Too many sessions already active.
3199	Couldn't find reference.
3200	"Can't delete or change record. Since related records exist in table '¦', referential integrity rules would be violated."

continues

Table C.1. Continued

Error code	Message
3201	Can't add or change record. Referential integrity rules require a related record in table '¦'.
3202	Couldn't save; currently locked by another user.
3203	Can't specify subquery in expression (¦).
3204	Database already exists.
3205	Too many crosstab column headers (¦).
3206	Can't create a relationship between a field and itself.
3207	Operation not supported on Paradox table with no primary key.
3208	Invalid Deleted entry in [dBASE ISAM] section in msacc20.ini.
3209	Invalid Stats entry in [dBASE ISAM] section in msacc20.ini.
3210	Connection string too long.
3211	Couldn't lock table '¦'; currently in use.
3212	Can't lock table '¦1'; currently in use by user '¦3' on machine '¦2'.
3213	Invalid Date entry in [dBASE ISAM] section in msacc20.ini.
3214	Invalid Mark entry in [dBASE ISAM] section in msacc20.ini.
3215	Too many Btrieve tasks.
3216	Parameter '¦' specified where a table name is required.
3217	Parameter '¦' specified where a database name is required.
3218	Couldn't update; currently locked.
3219	Invalid operation.
3220	Wrong Paradox sort sequence.
3221	Invalid entries in [Btrieve] section in WIN.INI.
3222	Query can't contain a Database parameter.
3223	'¦' isn't a valid parameter name.
3224	Can't read Btrieve data dictionary.
3225	Encountered record locking deadlock while performing Btrieve operation.
3226	Errors encountered while using the Btrieve DLL.
3227	Invalid Century entry in [dBASE ISAM] section in msacc20.ini.
3228	Invalid CollatingSequence entry in [Paradox ISAM] or [dBASE ISAM] section in msacc20.ini.
3229	Btrieve—can't change field.
3230	Out-of-date Paradox lock file.
3231	ODBC—field would be too long; data truncated.

Error code	Message
3232	ODBC—couldn't create table.
3233	Reserved Error
3234	ODBC—remote query timeout expired.
3235	ODBC—data type not supported on server.
3236	Reserved Error
3237	Reserved Error
3238	ODBC—data out of range.
3239	Too many active users.
3240	Btrieve—missing WBTRCALL.DLL.
3241	Btrieve—out of resources.
3242	Invalid reference in SELECT statement.
3243	None of the import field names match fields in the appended table.
3244	Can't import password-protected spreadsheet.
3245	Couldn't parse field names from first row of import table.
3246	Operation not supported in transactions.
3247	ODBC—linked table definition has changed.
3248	Invalid NetworkAccess entry in msacc20.ini.
3249	Invalid PageTimeout entry in msacc20.ini.
3250	Couldn't build key.
3251	Feature not available.
3252	Can't open form whose underlying query contains a user-defined function that attempts to set or get the form's RecordsetClone property.
3253	Reserved Error
3254	ODBC—Can't lock all records.
3255	Reserved Error
3256	Index file not found.
3257	Syntax error in WITH OWNERACCESS OPTION declaration.
3258	Query contains ambiguous outer joins.
3259	Invalid field data type.
3260	Couldn't update; currently locked by user '¦2' on machine '¦1'.
3261	¦
3262	¦
3263	Invalid database object.

continues

Table C.1. Continued

Error code	Message
3264	No fields defined - cannot append table.
3265	Name not found in this collection.
3266	Can't append. Field is part of a TableDefs collection.
3267	Property can be set only when the field is part of a Recordset object's Fields collection.
3268	Can't set this property once the object is part of a collection.
3269	Can't append. Index is part of a TableDefs collection.
3270	Property not found.
3271	Invalid property value.
3272	Object isn't a collection.
3273	Method not applicable for this object.
3274	External table isn't in the expected format.
3275	Unexpected error from external database driver (¦).
3276	Invalid database ID.
3277	Can't have more than 10 fields in an index.
3278	Database engine hasn't been initialized.
3279	Database engine has already been initialized.
3280	Can't delete a field that is part of an index.
3281	Can't delete this index. It is either the current index or is used in a relationship.
3282	Can't define field or index in a table that contains data.
3283	Primary key already exists.
3284	Index already exists.
3285	Invalid index definition.
3286	Format of memo file doesn't match specified external database format.
3287	Can't create index on Memo field or OLE Object field.
3288	Paradox index is not primary.
3289	Syntax error in CONSTRAINT clause.
3290	Syntax error in CREATE TABLE statement.
3291	Syntax error in CREATE INDEX statement.
3292	Syntax error in field definition.
3293	Syntax error in ALTER TABLE statement.
3294	Syntax error in DROP INDEX statement.

Error code	Message
3295	Syntax error in DROP TABLE statement.
3296	Join expression not supported.
3297	"Can't import table or query. No records found, or all records contain errors."
3298	There are several tables with that name. Please specify owner in the format 'owner.table'.
3299	ODBC Specification Conformance Error (¦). This error should be reported to the ODBC driver vendor.
3300	Can't create a relationship.
3301	Can't perform this operation; features in this version of Microsoft Access are not available in databases with older formats.
3302	Can't change a rule while the rules for this table are in use.
3303	Can't delete this field. It's part of one or more relationships.
3304	You must enter a personal identifier (PID) consisting of at least four and no more than 20 characters and digits.
3305	Invalid connection string in pass-through query.
3306	At most one field can be returned from a subquery that doesn't use the EXISTS keyword.
3307	The number of columns in the two selected tables or queries of a union query don't match.
3308	Invalid TOP argument in select query.
3309	Property setting can't be larger than 2 KB.
3310	This property isn't supported for external data sources or for databases created in a previous version of Microsoft Access.
3311	Property specified already exists.
3312	Validation rules and default values can't be placed on system or attached tables.
3313	Can't place this validation expression on this field.
3314	Field '¦' can't contain a null value.
3315	Field '¦' can't be a zero-length string.
3316	¦
3317	One or more values entered is prohibited by the validation rule '¦2' set for '¦1'.
3318	Top not allowed in delete queries.
3319	Syntax error in union query.

continues

699

Table C.1. Continued

Error code	Message
3320	¦ in table-level validation expression.
3321	No database specified in connection string or IN clause.
3322	Crosstab query contains one or more invalid fixed column headings.
3323	Query does not return records.
3324	Execute method must be used on action or data-definition queries.
3325	Pass-through query with ReturnsRecords property set to True did not return any records.
3326	This Recordset is not updatable.
3327	Field '¦' is based on an expression and can't be edited.
3328	Table '¦2' is read-only.
3329	Record in table '¦' was deleted by another user.
3330	Record in table '¦' is locked by another user.
3331	"To make changes to this field, first save the record."
3332	Can't enter value into blank field on 'one' side of outer join.
3333	Records in table '¦' would have no record on the 'one' side.
3334	Can be present only in version 1.0 format.
3335	DeleteOnly called with non-zero cbData.
3336	Btrieve: Invalid IndexDDF option in msacc20.ini.
3337	Invalid DataCodePage option in msacc20.ini.
3338	Btrieve: Xtrieve options aren't correct in msacc20.ini.
3339	Btrieve: Invalid IndexDeleteRenumber option in msacc20.ini.
3340	Query '¦' is corrupt.
3341	Current field must match join key '¦' on 'one' side of outer join.
3342	Invalid Memo or OLE object in subquery '¦'.
3343	Unrecognized database format '¦'.
3344	Unknown or invalid reference '¦1' in validation expression or default value in table '¦2'.
3345	Unknown or invalid field reference '¦'.
3346	Number of query values and destination fields aren't the same.
3347	Can't add record(s); primary key for table '¦' not in recordset.
3348	Can't add record(s); join key of table '¦' not in recordset.
3349	Numeric field overflow.
3350	Object is invalid for operation.

Error code	Message
3351	ORDER BY expression (¦) uses non-output fields.
3352	No destination field name in INSERT statement (¦).
3353	Btrieve: Can't find file FIELD.DDF.
3354	At most one record can be returned by this subquery.
3355	Syntax error in default value.
3356	The database is opened by user '¦2' on machine '¦1'. You can't open this database exclusively.
3357	This query is not a properly formed data- definition query.
3358	Can't open Microsoft Access system database (typically SYSTEM.MDA).
3359	Pass-through query must contain at least one character.
3360	Query is too complex.
3361	Unions not allowed in a subquery.
3362	Single-row update/delete affected more than one row of a remote table. Index specified as unique contains duplicate values.
3363	Record(s) can't be added; no corresponding record on the 'one' side.
3364	Can't use Memo or OLE object field '¦' in SELECT clause of a union query.
3365	Can't set this property for remote objects.
3366	Can't append a relation with no fields defined.
3367	Can't append. Object already in collection.
3368	Relationship must be on the same number of fields with the same data types.
3369	Can't find field in index definition.
3370	Can't modify the design of table '¦'. It's in a read-only database.
3371	Can't find table or constraint.
3372	No such index '¦2' on table '¦1'.
3373	Can't create relationship. Referenced table '¦' doesn't have a primary key.
3374	The specified fields are not uniquely indexed in table '¦'.
3375	Table '¦1' already has an index named '¦2'.
3376	Table '¦' doesn't exist.
3377	No such relationship '¦2' on table '¦1'.
3378	There is already a relationship named '¦' in the current database.
3379	Can't create relationships to enforce referential integrity. Existing data in table '¦2' violates referential integrity rules with related table '¦1'.

continues

Table C.1. Continued

Error code	Message
3380	Field '¦2' already exists in table '¦1'.
3381	There is no field named '¦2' in table '¦1'.
3382	Field '¦' size must be 1 to 255.
3383	Can't delete field '¦'. It's part of one or more relationships.
3384	Can't delete a built-in property.
3385	User defined properties don't support a Null value.
3386	Property '¦' must be set before using this method.
3387	Can't find TEMP directory.
3388	Unknown function '¦2' in validation expression or default value on '¦1'.
3389	Query support unavailable.
3390	Account name already exists.
3391	An error has occurred. Properties were not saved.
3392	There is no primary key in table '¦'.
3393	"Can't perform join, group, or sort. Combined fields are too long."
3394	Can't save property; property is a schema property.
3395	Invalid referential integrity constraint.
3396	"Can't perform cascading operation. Since related records exist in table '¦', referential integrity rules would be violated."
3397	Can't perform cascading operation. There must be a related record in table '¦'.
3398	Can't perform cascading operation. It would result in a null key in table '¦'.
3399	Can't perform cascading operation. It would result in a duplicate key in table '¦'.
3400	Can't perform cascading operation. It would result in two updates on field '¦2' in table '¦1'.
3401	"Can't perform cascading operation. It would cause field '¦' to become null, which is not allowed."
3402	"Can't perform cascading operation. It would cause field '¦' to become a zero-length string, which is not allowed."
3403	Can't perform cascading operation: '¦'
3404	Can't perform cascading operation. The value entered is prohibited by the validation rule '¦2' set for '¦1'.
3405	Error '¦' in validation rule.

Error code	Message
3406	Error '¦' in default value.
3407	"The server's MSysConf table exists, but is in an incorrect format. Contact your system administrator."
3408	Too many FastFind Sessions were invoked.
3409	Invalid field name '¦' in definition of index or relationship.
3410	Can't open this database for update.
3411	Invalid entry. Can't perform cascading operation specified in table '¦1' because value entered is too big for field '¦2'.
3412	¦
3413	Can't perform cascading update on table '¦1' because it is currently in use by user '¦3' on machine '¦2'.
3414	Can't perform cascading update on table '¦' because it is currently in use.
3415	Zero-length string is valid only in a text or Memo field.
3416	¦
3417	Can't have action query as an input.
3418	Can't open '¦'. Another user has the table open using a different network control file or locking style.
3419	Can't open this Paradox 4.x table because ParadoxNetStyle is set to 3.x in msacc20.ini.
3420	Object is no longer valid.
3421	Data type conversion error.
3422	Can't modify table structure. Another user has the table open.
3423	You cannot use ODBC to attach an external Microsoft Access or ISAM database table to your database.
3424	Can't create database; Invalid locale.
3425	This method or property is not currently available on this Recordset.
3426	The action was cancelled by an associated object.
3427	Error in DAO automation.
3428	"The Jet database engine has encountered a problem in your database. To correct the problem, you must repair and compact the database."
3429-7749	Reserved Error
7750	Can't set this property because the control is part of an option group.
7751	Can't retrieve the ObjectPalette property setting of a bound OLE object in Design view.

continues

Table C.1. Continued

Error code	Message
7752	Can't apply filter if all records are locked.
7753	¦
7754	Can't move datasheet column.
7755	Can't start Chart Wizard. Make sure Form Wizards are installed.
7756-7849	Reserved Error
7850	"Can't find Wizard, or there is a syntax error in the Declarations section of an Access Basic module. Check the [Libraries] section of msacc20.ini for required Wizard libraries, and compile all Access Basic modules in the database."
7851	This database already contains a toolbar named '¦'.
7852	'¦' isn't a valid toolbar name.
7853	The default column width must be at least 0.1 inch.
7854	Tables are the only objects that can be exported from version 2.0 to version 1.x databases. No objects can be imported or attached to in version 1.x databases opened in Microsoft Access 2.0.
7855	Can't load import/export functions.
7856	Can't change menu while object application is active.
7857	Can't display system information.
7858	The tab stop width must be an integer from 1 to 30.
7859-7899	Reserved Error
7900	Can't create error table; unable to convert database.
7901	Can't write to error table; unable to convert database.
7902	Errors occurred converting ¦1 validation rules and default values. See error table '¦2' for errors.
7903	Can't insert this field. There are too many fields in the table.
7904	An error has occurred in the Field Builder.
7905	"Can't change field data types. Some data in this table violates the record validation rule. Before any data types can be changed, remove the record validation rule or correct the data."
7906-7949	Reserved Error
7950	Can't refer to RecordsetClone property in Design view.
7951	Invalid reference to RecordsetClone property.
7952-7999	Reserved Error

Converting Old Code

A few of the examples in this book use techniques that have been made obsolete by new features found in Microsoft Access 2.0. There are several good reasons why you might want to continue using the older techniques, such as:

- Most of the older techniques continue to work, so all Access users—not just those that have upgraded to 2.0—can use the examples.

- Most of the older techniques result in smaller, faster, or more efficient code.

- Some newer techniques require additional arguments you might not otherwise know. To use the new **GoToPage** method, for example, you must first identify the forms object to which the method applies. In contrast, you can use the older **GoToPage** macro action without first determining the form.

Throughout this book, the older techniques have been identified so that you can convert them to the newer techniques. You may want to convert them for any of these reasons:

- On your particular system, the newer techniques happen to execute more quickly.

- You develop applications in an Access 2.0-only environment and do not have to worry about backward compatibility.

- You prefer to sacrifice performance in exchange for consistency throughout your applications.

- You are concerned that the older techniques may no longer work in a future version of Microsoft Access.

However, experience suggests there is litle reason to believe the older functions, methods, properties, and macro actions will be removed from the product. Historically, Microsoft has consistently carried older functionality forward into newer versions of its products.

 For more detailed information about converting older techniques, search Help for "converting code."

Index

D

J-K

L

M

O

X–Y–Z

Installing the Disk Files

The disk that accompanies *Access 2 Power Programming* includes the sample HomeFinder application.

To install the disk files, follow these steps:

1. In the Windows Program Manager, choose Run from the File menu.

2. Type **a:install** in the Command Line text box and then choose OK. (If you are installing files from a floppy drive other than A, substitute the correct letter in the command.)

   Note: If you have a CD-ROM drive and the Install program displays an error message, choose Cancel to continue.

3. A welcoming screen appears. Press any key to continue to the Main menu.

4. If desired, select a different destination drive for installing the disk files. Press Enter to continue.

5. If desired, type the name of a different installation directory. Press Enter to begin installing the files. After the files are installed, a completion message appears.

6. Press any key to return to the Windows Program Manager.

Licensing Agreement

By opening this package, you are agreeing to be bound by the following agreement:

This software product is copyrighted, and all rights are reserved by the publisher and author. You are licensed to use this software on a single computer. You may copy and/or modify the software as needed to facilitate your use of it on a single computer. Making copies of the software for any other purpose is a violation of United States copyright laws.

This software is sold *as is* without warranty of any kind, either expressed or implied, including but not limited to the implied warranties of merchantability and fitness for a particular purpose. Neither the publisher nor its dealers or distributors assumes any liability for any alleged or actual damages arising from the use of this program. (Some states do not allow for the exclusion of implied warranties, so the exclusion may not apply to you.)